THE MODERN LAW (

AUSTRALIA AND NEW ZEALAND
The Law Book Company Ltd.
Sydney : Melbourne : Perth

CANADA AND U.S.A.
The Carswell Company Ltd.
Agincourt, Ontario

INDIA
N. M. Tripathi Private Ltd.
Bombay
and
Eastern Law House Private Ltd.
Calcutta and Delhi
M.P.P. House
Bangalore

ISRAEL
Steimatzky's Agency Ltd.
Jerusalem : Tel Aviv : Haifa

MALAYSIA : SINGAPORE : BRUNEI
Malayan Law Journal (Pte) Ltd.
Singapore

PAKISTAN
Pakistan Law House
Karachi

THE MODERN
LAW OF TRUSTS

By

DAVID B. PARKER, LL.B.
*of Gray's Inn, Barrister, Queen Victoria Professor of Law
in the University of Liverpool*

and

ANTHONY R. MELLOWS
T.D., B.D., Ph.D., LL.D.
*Solicitor of the Supreme Court, Professor of the Law of Property
in the University of London*

Fellow of King's College London

FIFTH EDITION

LONDON
SWEET & MAXWELL
1983

First Edition *1966*
Second Edition *1970*
Third Edition *1975*
Fourth Edition *1979*
Fifth Edition *1983*

Published by
Sweet & Maxwell Limited of
11, New Fetter Lane, London.
Computerset by MFK Typesetting Limited,
Saffron Walden, Essex
and printed by
Richard Clay (The Chaucer Press) Limited,
Bungay, Suffolk

British Library Cataloguing in Publication Data

Parker, David B.
    The modern law of trusts.—5th ed.
    1. Trusts and trustees—   England
    I. Title   II. Mellows, Anthony R.
    344.2065'9   KD1480

    ISBN 0-421-30970-9
    ISBN 0-421-30980-6 Pbk

PREFACE

In the preface to the first edition of this book we said that the law of trusts "is a branch of the law which is developing at a rapid pace and which is highly relevant to modern conditions, not merely to a bygone age." Those words remain as true today as they were when they were first written in 1966. The recent developments in this branch of the law have occurred largely through decisions of the courts, partly on traditional issues, but also on points which arise affecting capital taxation in a wide variety of situations. Despite their taxation context, many of these decisions are of much wider significance, going to the fundamental basis of rules in this branch of the law.

Although many of the recent developments have been related to taxation, we hope that legislation relating to non-fiscal aspects of the law of trusts may not be too far distant. In October 1982 the Law Reform Committee issued its Twenty-Third Report, on the powers and duties of trustees. The Committee has made a number of important recommendations, mainly on the appointment of trustees; the law relating to investment; the apportionment rules; delegation; the standard of conduct of trustees; and the charging of remuneration. We have referred to many of these recommendations, but so that the reader will not be confused into thinking that there is a present legislative base for them, we have confined our references to footnotes. We hope that by the time that the next edition of this book is published most of the recommendations will be reflected in legislation, which we can discuss in the main body of the text. Such legislation should remove many of the anomalies and anachronisms which mar this branch of the law.

This edition follows the same order as the last, but we have taken the opportunity to expand into separate chapters the treatment of Income from the Trust Fund, and the Application of Trust Capital. These topics are assuming greater significance in view of their bearing on liability to income and capital taxation. We have also taken the opportunity of rewriting substantially and expanding into a new chapter the material on Trustees' Remuneration and Benefits. The chapter on Exporting Trusts, which has also been rewritten, illustrates the changes which are taking place in this branch of the law. At the time when the previous edition of this book was published, Exchange Control was still in operation in the United Kingdom. Since that time, not only have the taxation rules affecting overseas trusts been substantially altered, but the control has been withdrawn—but, as we write, many new overseas trusts are being established in the hope that they will be outside the scope of any future control should it be reintroduced.

More generally, we have updated the other parts of this book which have been affected by recent developments.

The law is generally stated as at May 1, 1983, although certain developments after that date have been included.

D.B.P.
University of Liverpool

A.R.M.
King's College, London.

June 1983

CONTENTS

TABLE OF CASES

TABLE OF STATUTES

CHAPTER 1

INTRODUCTION

THE TRUST TODAY

EVER since the trust was invented, no lawyer has been able to give a comprehensive service to his client without a thorough grasp of the subject. This is more true today than it ever has been. Throughout its history the trust has been used by lawyers as a device to get round inconvenient rules of law.

In medieval times the "use," which was the forerunner of the trust, was brought into being by A transferring property to B to the use of C. B then became the owner of the property in law, but held the legal estate for the benefit of C. There were several circumstances in which this device was used. Thus before 1540 it was not possible to leave freehold land by will, but if Oswald, an owner, wished to achieve the same result, he could have conveyed the land to Rupert to the use of Oswald during his life, and thereafter to the use of Clarence. Oswald would continue to derive the benefit from his land as long as he lived, and on his death Clarence would automatically become entitled. Taking another case, the Statutes of Mortmain imposed prohibitions on the gift of land to ecclesiastical foundations, in an attempt to prevent land being taken out of circulation more or less permanently, but these statutes could often be overcome by taking advantage of a use. Thus a conveyance of land to Percy to the use of the Franciscan friars of Framlingham would for a time have been effective.[1]

But probably the use was employed most frequently as a device to overcome feudal dues. It was the medieval equivalent of a "tax avoidance scheme." Suppose that Nigel held land as a tenant in knight service, and that Erasmus his son and heir, was aged two. If Nigel died without altering the legal position, the lord of the manor would be entitled to use Nigel's land for his own benefit until Erasmus reached the age of 21.[2] The lord could select a spouse for Erasmus, and if Erasmus could not endure the thought of spending a lifetime locked in the arms of the lord's choice[3] and refused to marry her, the lord could exact a fine.[4] When Erasmus became 21, the lord was entitled to a further half year's profits of the land before transferring it to Erasmus. All these and other feudal incidents would be avoided if on his deathbed Nigel conveyed his land to his

---

[1] Until 15 Ric. II, c. 5.

[2] Magna Carta 1215, cc.4, 5.

[3] The lord could not put forward the most unattractive girl he could find in the hope that the infant would refuse, and so give the lord the right to this fine. For a list of defects in a potential spouse which prevented the lord from putting her forward, see Co.Litt. 80 a, b.

[4] Magna Carta 1215, c. 3.

1

friends to hold to the use of Erasmus. In this way an infant would never be the legal owner, and the lord would be deprived of his rights.

The Statute of Uses 1535 attempted to abolish the advantages of the use, but its effect was short-lived. By the eighteenth century the use had returned under the name of the trust.

In subsequent centuries the use or trust was used to tie up land or wealth for succeeding generations of the family, and to make provision for dependants. It also had other purposes. For example, the common law rule, which was of general application, that a married woman could not hold property in her own right was overcome by vesting that property in trustees to hold upon trust for her. Likewise, unincorporated associations such as clubs, friendly societies and trade unions, which are not themselves legal entities, and so cannot hold property, would not have developed as they have if it had not been possible for property to be held by trustees on their behalf.

The principal uses of the trust today are these:

1. To enable property, particularly land, to be held for persons who cannot themselves hold it. Thus the legal title to land cannot be vested in an infant[5] but there is no objection to land being held upon trust for an infant. Statute has now adopted this principle, to the extent that a purported conveyance of a legal estate to an infant operates as an agreement for a valuable consideration to create a settlement of that land on the infant and in the meantime to hold the land on trust for the infant.[6]

2. To enable a man to make provision for dependants privately. The most obvious examples are the mistress and bastard child. During his lifetime there is no problem, but if a man provides for a mistress or bastard by will the circumstances may well leak out, for when probate has been obtained a will becomes a public document, and is open to public inspection. But a trust deed escapes publicity of this sort.

3. To tie up property so that it can benefit persons in succession. An outright gift may be made to a parent, in the *hope* that on the parent's death that property will go to his child, but there is no guarantee that it will do so. A gift to trustees to hold upon trust for the parent for life with remainder to the child, will ensure[7] that the child derives a benefit. One cannot normally ensure that the person ultimately entitled will receive the very property that is settled, for the trustees will almost always have power to sell that property, and to re-invest the proceeds. But one can virtually ensure that the person ultimately entitled does receive the benefit which is derived from that property.

4. To protect family property from wastrels. A person may feel that an outright gift of money to his widow or son will lead to its being dissipated. A gift of that money to trustees to hold upon trust to pay part of it to the widow or son will probably prevent this. The trustees may be given a

---

[5] Law of Property Act 1925, s. 19.
[6] Settled Land Act 1925, s. 27.
[7] Unless the child agrees to bring the trust to an end prematurely.

discretion as to the amount (if any) which they will pay over at any one time, or property can be given to trustees to hold upon trust for a beneficiary in such a way that it will be preserved if the beneficiary goes bankrupt.[8]

5. To make a gift in the future, in the light of circumstances which have not yet arisen. If, for example, a man has three young daughters, he may by his will set up a trust whereby a sum of money is given to trustees for them to distribute among his daughters, either as they think fit, or having regard to stated factors. They might, for example, in due course give one-quarter each to two of the daughters who married well, and half to the poorer unmarried daughter.

6. To make provision, particularly by will, for causes or non-human objects. By means of a trust one may donate money for the furtherance of education, or to provide a daily saucerful of milk for "my tom-cat Tiddles so long as he shall live."

7. To enable two or more persons to own land. One of the curious features of English land law is that not more than one person may be the absolute and beneficial owner of land, but that if two or more persons wish to own land jointly, they may do so by means of a trust.[9] Since the last war it has become increasingly popular for married couples to have the matrimonial home vested in their joint names, so that at present perhaps half the houses in the country are owned jointly in this way. Thus, technically, about half the houses in the country are held upon trust—though this fact would surprise most of their occupants.[10]

8. To provide pensions for retired employees and their dependants. Again since 1945 pension schemes have enjoyed a marked increase in popularity.[11] These are either non-contributory, in which case the whole of the money is provided by the employer, or contributory, in which case both the employer and the employee pay into the fund. In many cases these funds are held by trustees so that the employee is assured that his pension will in fact be forthcoming, and that in the meantime his employer cannot in any way dispose of the money.

9. To facilitate investment through unit trusts. In their simpler form, trustees purchase holdings in a large number of companies, and then invite members of the public to purchase "units," or shares, in the trust fund. A unit trust may be entirely general, or the majority of its holdings may be in companies operating in a particular sphere, such as shipping. The trustees, or managers of the trust, receive the dividends on the

---

[8] The device known as a protective trust.

[9] Either a "trust for sale," or a "settlement."

[10] This has come to be so much a matter of course that some solicitors are thought now to have given up explaining the provisions of the purchase deeds declaring the trusts, so that the fact that the property is to be held on trust may never even have been mentioned to the purchasers.

[11] Nearly 12 million adult employees were covered by private pension schemes by 1979 [Institute of Actuaries' 6th Private Pensions Survey].

investments from the various companies, and, after payment of their administration expenses, either distribute the remainder of the income among those who have purchased units, or re-invest the income to increase the total value of the fund, and so of the individual units in the fund. The result of investing in a unit trust is that the holder of a unit has a minute stake in a large number of companies, and is therefore able to spread his risk. Further, the fund is sufficiently large for its investments to be supervised on a full-time basis.[12]

10. To minimise the incidence of income tax, capital gains tax and capital transfer tax. There are numerous possibilities in this field, and a high proportion of tax saving schemes involve a trust[13] but one example will suffice. If a person with a high income[14] has an asset which produces an income of £10,000 p.a. he will pay income tax of £7,500[15] on that income. If, however, the asset is held on trust for five members of his family, each of whom is only of modest means,[16] and the income is distributed between them, the total tax payable will be £3,000.[17] Considered as a whole, the family will therefore have derived a net benefit of £4,500.[18]

One of the great advantages of a trust is the flexibility of purpose for which it can be used. Another is that the rules which govern a trust are by and large the same whatever the purpose for which it is employed. The remainder of this book attempts to explain those rules.

I. Definition of a Trust

Difficulty has been found in providing a comprehensive definition of a trust, but various attempts have been made. The following may be considered:

(1) Coke's definition

Lord Coke defined a trust as "a confidence reposed in some other, not issuing out of the land but as a thing collateral thereto, annexed in privity to the estate of the land, and to the person touching the land, for which *cestui que trust* has no remedy but by subpoena in the Chancery."[19] The language may require elucidation. When Coke says it is collateral to land not issuing out of it he means that it differs from a legal interest: a legal interest continues to subsist even on the purchase for value without notice of that interest, whereas an equitable

---

[12] In broad terms, if a unit trust is incorporated, it is known as an investment trust company. Such a company is subject to the provisions of the Companies Acts 1948–81 and not, as in the case of a unit trust, subject to trust law. However, a unit trust is itself subject, in addition to the normal provisions of trust law, to special legislation designed to protect the public against fraud.

[13] Such schemes "involve" trusts, because in the majority of cases they will necessitate trusts being set up, or existing trusts being broken, or a combination of the two.

[14] *i.e.* over £31,500 p.a.

[15] This is the top effective rate of income tax for 1983/84: Finance Act 1983, s.12.

[16] *i.e.* income of less than £14,600 p.a. each.

[17] At the rates for 1983/84.

[18] *i.e.* a reduction of the income tax liability from £7,500 to £3,000.

[19] Co.Litt. 272b.

interest such as trust does not, and it is, for that reason, collateral. When he says it is annexed in privity to the estate he means that the trust will only continue while the estate continues. By annexation in privity to the person it is shown that a purchaser for value of the legal estate without notice of the trust takes free of it.

It has to be said, however, that there are some objections to Coke's formulation. In the first place, what is a "confidence"? This expression does not explain precisely the meaning of "trust." Secondly, the definition imports the idea of a reliance placed by one person in another person. But this may not be universally correct. The *cestui que trust* (or "beneficiary") may be a baby in arms or unborn or ignorant of the trust. The trust in such cases may still be effective but the *cestui que trust* will place no "reliance" in the trustee. Thirdly, it applies only to real property, whereas the subject-matter of a trust may be personal property also. It also ignores the principle of "overreaching" by which equitable interests such as the interest of the beneficiaries under trusts are kept off the title to the legal estate, and are overreached on the sale of the legal estate to a purchaser who accordingly takes free of them. And, finally, it is procedurally out of date: the Court of Chancery no longer exists and all branches of the High Court have jurisdiction in equity.[20] Nevertheless this early definition still deserves a mention: subject to the criticisms that can be made it is as useful as most modern definitions.

(2) Underhill's definition

Sir Arthur Underhill described a trust as "an equitable obligation binding a person (who is called a trustee) to deal with property over which he has control (which is called trust property) for the benefit of persons (who are called beneficiaries or *cestuis que trust*[21]) of whom he may himself be one and any one of whom may enforce the obligation."[22]

As a comprehensive definition of all kinds of trusts it may be objected that it does not in terms cover charitable trusts, and, moreover, does not provide for the so-called "trust of imperfect obligation,"[23] such as a trust 'for the maintenance and support of my dog Fido"; this may well amount to a valid trust but it is of imperfect obligation because Fido cannot enforce it. The editors of Underhill have pointed out that charitable trusts are outside the scope of the book but, in any case, are covered by the definition, because such a trust is for the benefit of persons, *viz.* the public, on whose behalf the Attorney-General may enforce it.[24] And trusts of imperfect obligation are not referred to because they are acknwledged to be "anomalous and exceptional."[25]

---

[20] Supreme Court of Judicature (Consolidation) Act 1925, s.4 (4).

[21] This is the plural: "Cestuis que trustent" is "hopelessly wrong": Sweet (1910) 26 L.Q.R. 196.

[22] Underhill's *Law of Trusts and Trustees* (13th ed.), p. 13. The definition was approved by Cohen J. in *Re Marshall's Will Trusts* [1945] Ch. 217 at p. 219.

[23] See *post*, p. 176.

[24] See *post*, p. 241.

[25] See *post*, p. 178.

(3) **Lewin's definition**

Perhaps the best definition is that adopted in the present edition of Lewin's *Trusts*.[26] It is based on a definition given by Mayo J. in *Re Scott*.[27] According to this formulation, "the word 'trust' refers to the duty or aggregate accumulation of obligations that rest upon a person described as trustee. The responsibilities are in relation to property held by him, or under his control. That property he will be compelled by a court in its equitable jurisdiction to administer in the manner lawfully prescribed by the trust instrument, or where there be no specific provision written or oral, or to the extent that such provision is invalid or lacking, in accordance with equitable principles. As a consequence the administration will be in such a manner that the consequential benefits and advantages accrue, not to the trustee, but to the persons called *cestuis que trust*, or beneficiaries, if there be any; if not, for some purpose which the law will recognise and enforce. A trustee may be a beneficiary, in which case advantages will accrue in his favour to the extent of his beneficial interest."[28]

Trusts "in the higher sense" and trusts "in the lower sense"

It should be clear from the definitions offered that the type of trust with which we are concerned is an equitable obligation which is enforceable in the courts.[29] There is, however, no magic in the word "trust," as Lord O'Hagan once said,[30] and it can mean different things in different contexts. For example, a person may be in a position of trust without being a trustee in the equitable sense, and terms such as "anti-trust" or "trust territories" are not intended as relating to a trust enforceable in a court of equity. By the same token, a trust in the conventional legal sense may be created without using the word "trust."[31] In each case one has to consider whether such a trust was intended.[32]

This basic question of definition arose for decision in *Tito* v. *Waddell* (*No.* 2),[33] a case which Megarry V.-C aptly described as "litigation on the grand scale."[34] The case involved Ocean Island, a small island in the Pacific. It was called Banaba by its inhabitants and they themselves were known as Banabans. The island was formerly part of the Gilbert and Ellice

---

[26] (16th ed.), p.1.

[27] [1948] S.A.S.R. 193 at p. 196.

[28] For a similar and well-known definition see Keeton and Sheridan, *Law of Trusts* (10th ed.), p. 5. For other definitions by text writers, see Halsbury's *Laws of England* (3rd ed.), Vol 38, pp. 809–810; American Law Institute, *Restatement of the Law of Trusts*, p. 6, para.2. For judicial definitions, see *Sturt* v. *Mellish* (1743) 2 Atk. 610 at p. 612, *per* Lord Hardwicke L.C.; *Burgess* v. *Wheate* (1759) 1 Eden 177 at p. 223, *per* Lord Mansfield C.J.: *Re Williams* [1897] 2 Ch. 12, at p. 19 (C.A.), *per* Lindley L.J. As to the meaning of "trust" and "trustee" in T.A. 1925, see *ibid.* s.68(17).

[29] This is the general rule, but one exception is provided by the so-called "trust of imperfect obligation," *e.g.* a trust to maintain a monument or tomb or a particular animal. Such a trust is not enforceable, but nevertheless, anomalously, is valid: see *post,* p. 176.

[30] *Kinloch* v. *Secretary of State for India in Council* (1882) 7 App.Cas. 619 at p. 630.

[31] *Tito* v. *Waddell* (*No.* 2) [1977] Ch. 106 at p. 211 *per* Megarry V.-C.

[32] See *post,* p. 60.

[33] [1977] Ch. 106.

[34] *Ibid.* at p. 123. The report of Megarry V.-C.s judgment runs to 241 pages. The Vice-Chancellor also held a view of the *locus in quo*.

Islands protectorate which subsequently became a colony. At the beginning of this century phosphate was discovered on the island, and royalties for mining the phosphate were paid to the islanders. As time passed the Banabans sought increases in the royalties. Some increases were paid but they were considerably less than what the Banabans claimed. The Banabans continued to make various claims politically and internationally but when they failed, brought these proceedings. They claimed that the rates of royalty payable under certain transactions had been less than the proper rates and accordingly that the Crown as the responsible authority was subject to a trust or fiduciary duty for the benefit of the plaintiffs or their predecessors, and was liable for breach thereof.

The question whether there was a trust or fiduciary duty involved the construction of various agreements and ordinances as well as other documentation. In the result, it was held that there was not. The essential elements of the decision for purpose of definition[35] appear to be as follows:

(1) Although the work "trust" was occasionally used with reference to the Crown or its agents it did not create a trust enforceable in the courts (what Megarry V.-C. described as a "trust in the lower sense" or "true trust") but rather a trust "in the higher sense" by which was meant a governmental obligation which was not enforceable in the courts.[36]

(2) Such a trust "in the higher sense" involved the discharge under the direction of the Crown of the duties and functions belonging to the prerogative and authority of the Crown.[37] There might be many means available of persuading the Crown, for example by international pressure, to honour its governmental obligations, and it might be more than a mere moral obligation, but it was not enforceable by the court.[38]

(3) Although various ordinances imposed statutory duties they did not impose fiduciary obligations. It will be seen later that in some cases a person may be in a fiduciary position even though he is not a trustee in the proper sense of the word (for example, an agent or a partner or a company director) and he will be liable if he is in breach of his fiduciary obligations.[39] The relationship from which the fiduciary obligations arise may be equitable or legal or statutory, but it is required that it be a relationship with enforceable legal consequences.[40] However, as Megarry V.-C. held, "a trust in the higher sense or governmental obligation lacks this characteristic and where the primary obligation itself is one which the courts will not enforce, then . . . it [cannot] of itself give rise to a secondary obligation which is enforceable by the courts."[41]

---

[35] For other aspects of the decision, see *post*, pp. 164, 165, 458.

[36] Adopting the language of Lord Selborne L.C. in *Kinloch* v. *Secretary of State for India in Council, supra* at p. 625.

[37] *Tito* v. *Waddell (No. 2) ibid.* at p. 216.

[38] *Ibid.* at p. 217.

[39] See *post*, pp. 165, 166, 169.

[40] *Ibid.* at p. 224.

[41] *Ibid.* at p. 225.

(4) If a duty is imposed by statute (such as the ordinances in this case) to perform certain functions it does not, as a general rule, impose fiduciary obligations, nor is it to be presumed to impose any. It has to be shown that the statute imposes such obligations.[42]

It may suffice to say that this book is concerned with "trusts in the lower sense" or "true trusts" and with those situations which give rise to enforceable fiduciary obligations.

II. Subject Matter of a Trust

The subject matter of a trust may be real or personal property. Furthermore, the trust may be not only of a legal estate but also of an equitable interest in property. If the legal estate in property is to be conveyed to T1 and T2 as trustees to hold on trust for X, the subject matter of the trust is the legal estate. But X may convey his equitable interest under the trust to Y and Z to hold such interest upon trust for P and Q. The subject matter of the second trust will be the equitable interest: the legal estate will remain vested in T1 and T2.[43]

But the question remains, who owns the actual trust property—the trustee or the beneficiary? This question has not been finally answered,[44] although the Divisional Court in *Schalit* v. *Joseph Nadler Ltd.*[45] held that a beneficiary was not entitled to distrain for rent under a lease granted by the trustee. As the court said: "The right of the *cestui que trust* whose trustee has demised property subject to the trust is not to the rent, but to an account from the trustees of the profits received from the trust."[46] This decision appears to accord with principle.

III. Distinction from Other Legal Concepts

1. *Contract*

The general rule is that a contract is not enforceable by a person who is not a party to the contract, whereas a trust can be enforced by a beneficiary who is not (indeed he rarely is) a party to the instrument creating the trust. The rule of contract is one of general application and seems to have been firmly established by *Midland Silicones Ltd.* v. *Scruttons Ltd.*[47] and *Beswick* v. *Beswick*[48] but

---

[42] *Ibid.* at p. 235; see also *Swain* v. *The Law Society* [1982] 3 W.L.R. 261, H.L. (in exercising a statutory power the Law Society was performing not a private duty but a public duty for breach of which there was no remedy in breach of trust or equitable account); see further *post*, p. 163.   [43] See *Gilbert* v. *Overton* (1804) 2 H. & M. 110.

[44] See Latham (1954) 32 Can. B.R. 520, on the question generally.   [45] [1933] 2 K.B. 79.

[46] *Ibid.* at p. 83. *Cf. Baker* v. *Archer-Shee* [1927] A.C. 844 (where the beneficiary was held to be the real owner of the trust assets for *income tax* purposes).

[47] [1962] A.C. 446. *Cf. New Zealand Shipping Co. Ltd.* v. *A. M. Satterthwaite & Co. Ltd.*; *The Eurymedon* [1975] A.C. 154, P.C., where a stevedore was allowed to claim the benefit of limitation clauses in a bill of lading; *cf.* also *Jackson* v. *Horizon Holidays Ltd.* [1975] 1 W.L.R. 1468, C.A., where it was held that the plaintiff had made a contract for a family holiday, and though only he could sue for damages for breaches of that contract, he could sue for damages not only for his own discomfort and distress but for that suffered by his wife and children by reason of the defendant's breach of contract to provide them with the holiday contracted for; but see *Woodar Investment Development Ltd.* v. *Wimpey Construction U.K. Ltd* [1980] 1 All E.R. 571, H.L. rejecting the opinion of Lord Denning M.R. in *Jackson's* case so far as he suggested that a third party could sue on a contract.   [48] [1968] A.C. 58.

there are some recognised exceptions to it which are founded in statute.[49] They have no particular relevance to the law of trusts.

In addition, however, to the intervention of statute into the general law of privity of contract, the rigidity of the rule itself has also been mitigated in some (though rather small and uncertain) degree by recourse to the concept of the trust and this requires some discussion. For although the rule remains intact that only a person who is a party to a contract can sue upon it, yet if one of the parties expressly or impliedly contracts as *trustee* for a third party the latter is entitled to the benefit of that contract. Therefore, if, in a contract made between A and B, A contracts in this way as trustee for the benefit of C, C will take the benefit. The machinery for enforcement if A is in breach, may take a number of forms. B can recover on behalf of C the damages suffered by C as well as the nominal damages suffered by himself.[50] Alternatively C can sue as *cestui que trust* joining B as co-plaintiff and if B will not join in that capacity he can be joined with A as a co-defendant.[51]

No difficulty will arise if there is an express declaration of trust, or an assignment of the benefit of the contract to trustees. The real difficulty is to know when a trust is to be *implied* and this is shown by the way in which the case-law has developed. One of the earlier cases is *Re Flavell*[52] where articles of partnership provided that an annuity should be paid by the surviving partner to the widow of his co-partner. It was held that this created a trust of the annuity in favour of the widow which was free from the claims of the co-partner's creditors. Again, in *Les Affréteurs Réunis S.A.* v. *Leopold Walford (London) Ltd.*[53] the decision was to a like effect although in this case the position was simplified by an agreement enabling the third party to sue.

The principles at stake were later discussed in *Harmer* v. *Armstrong*,[54] where there was a contract for the sale of copyright in certain periodicals and the plaintiff for whose benefit the contract had been made claimed specific performance of the contract. The Court of Appeal held that the plaintiff as *cestui que trust* of the agreement could himself specifically enforce it. Lawrence L.J. said there were two distinct rules as to neither of which there could be any reasonable doubt: (i) that the law does not recognise any *jus quaesitum tertio* arising by way of *contract*; but (ii) that such a right may be conferred by way of property under a *trust*.[55] These dicta might appear to suggest that it is easy to discover whether or not a trust in favour of a third party has been created. But in fact it is by no means easy, for there are other cases where the court has declined to

---

[49] See *e.g.* Married Women's Property Act 1882, s.11; Marine Insurance Act 1906, s.14(2); L.P.A. 1925, s. 47(1); L.P.A. 1925, s. 56; Occupiers' Liability Act 1957, s. 3; Road Traffic Act 1972, s. 148(4).

[50] See *Gregory and Parker* v. *Williams* (1871) 3 Mer. 582; *Lloyd's* v. *Harper* (1880) 16 Ch.D. 290.

[51] See *Vandepitte* v. *Preferred Accident Insurance Corpn. of New York* [1933] A.C. 70 at p. 79.

[52] (1883) 25 Ch.D. 89.

[53] [1919] A.C. 801.

[54] [1934] Ch. 65.

[55] *Ibid.* at pp. 87–88; *cf.* Romer L.J. at pp. 93–94.

imply the existence of a trust although one might think that if the court had been so disposed the implication could easily have been made. Thus, in *Vandepitte* v. *Preferred Accident Insurance Corpn. of New York*,[56] B had insured his car in British Columbia against third party risks with the defendant and it was agreed that the policy should cover all persons driving with B's consent. B's daughter, while driving the car with his consent, injured the plaintiff and the plaintiff obtained judgment against her in an action of negligence. The judgment was not satisfied. Under the relevant Act in British Columbia a plaintiff, if he failed to recover his damages against a guilty motorist, could avail himself of any rights which the motorist enjoyed against the insurance company. The question, was whether B's daughter was a beneficiary under the policy. She was not a party to the contract of insurance: the result, therefore, depended on the presence or absence of a trust. The Privy Council held that no trust had been proved: the intention to prove a trust must be affirmatively shown and this had not been done.

A similar result occurred in *Re Schebsman*.[57] A company agreed with its employee, in consideration of his retirement, to pay certain sums to him and after his death to his wife and child. He went bankrupt and soon afterwards died. The question was whether the trustee in bankruptcy could "intercept" the money which the employers were willing to pay to the wife and child. The Court of Appeal held that the employee had not entered into the contract as a trustee for his wife and child, so the company were free to perform the terms of the contract and make the required payments. Since the employee would not have been able to intercept the payments, the trustee in bankruptcy could be in no better position. Du Parcq L.J. said that unless an intention to create a trust is clearly to be collected from the language used and the circumstances of the case the court ought not to be "astute" to discover implications of such an intention.[58]

A like reluctance to imply a trust was manifested in *Swain* v. *The Law Society*.[59] This case concerned the master policy which The Law Society had arranged under statutory powers for indemnity insurance and which was compulsory for all practising solicitors. It had been agreed that a proportion of the commission earned by the insurance brokers in arranging the insurance should be paid to The Law Society which would apply it for the benefit of the profession as a whole. Two solicitors were dissatisfied with the scheme and claimed (*inter alia*) that The Law Society was a trustee of the benefit of the master policy contract for the benefit of all individual solicitors and was, therefore, accountable for the proportion of the commission which it received. Reliance was placed on the fact that the policy contract stated that the policy was entered into "on behalf of" solicitors and former solicitors, and these words, it was claimed, imputed an intention to create a trust. The House of

---

[56] [1933] A.C. 70.
[57] [1944] Ch. 83.
[58] *Ibid.* at p. 104.
[59] [1982] 3 W.L.R. 261.

Lords (reversing the Court of Appeal) rejected this argument. It was held that these words clearly did not *express* a trust and they did not necessarily *imply* a trust. As Lord Brightman said,[60] "it would indeed, be surprising if a society of lawyers, who above all might be expected to make their intention clear in a document they compose, should have failed to express the existence of a trust if that was what they intended to create." Moreover, it was unnecessary, as had been argued, to imply a trust to secure the commercial viability of the scheme; this was a statutory indemnity scheme, the policy had statutory authority, and accordingly all persons insured had a direct remedy against the insurers if they declined to perform their obligations.

These cases indicate that it may, in practice, be extremely difficult to provide a test by which one determines whether A is contracting with B as trustee for C.[61] Indeed the view has been expressed that the way in which the court will decide a novel case is almost entirely unpredictable.[62]

The suggestion has also been made, as a reason for this difficulty, that trusteeship is too highly charged with magic to admit of an accurate test. "There is a vast deal of magic in words and among the words most highly charged with magic to be found is the word 'trustee.'"[63] However, whether or not this is the true reason, it would appear from decisions like *Re Schebsman* and *Swain* v. *The Law Society*, that the courts are now reluctant to interpret a contract as creating a trust in the absence of the clearest possible evidence that a trust is intended. It is certainly unwise to place any reliance in the trust concept as providing a loophole in the principle of privity of contract.[64]

It is also noteworthy that no reliance was placed on it in the House of Lords decision in *Beswick* v. *Beswick*[65] where relief was only obtained as a result of the particular facts of that case. The facts were that a nephew was employed by his uncle in his business as a coal merchant. An agreement was made between them whereby the uncle assigned the business to the nephew in return for the latter's promise to pay the uncle £6 10s. 0d. a week for the rest of his life and when he

---

[60] *Ibid.* at p. 276.

[61] In addition to the cases mentioned in the text see *Tomlinson* v. *Gill* (1756) Amb. 330; *Gregory and Parker* v. *Williams* (1817) 3 Mer. 582; *Lloyd's* v. *Harper* (1880) 16 Ch.D. 290; *Royal Exchange Assurance* v. *Hope* [1928] Ch. 179; *Re Gordon* [1940] Ch. 851; *Re Webb* [1941] Ch. 225. In these cases a trust was established. This was also held to be the position in *Fletcher* v. *Fletcher* (1844) 4 Hare 67, *sed quaere*: see *post*, p. 52. See also *Colyear* v. *Lady Mulgrave* (1836) 2 Keen 81; *Re Engelbach's Estate* [1924] 2 Ch. 348; *Re Sinclair's Life Policy* [1938] Ch. 799; *Re Foster (No. 1)* [1938] 3 All E.R. 357. In these cases a trust was *not* established.

[62] Williams (1944) 7 M.L.R. 123.

[63] Corbin (1930) 46 L.Q.R. 20.

[64] See also, generally, in addition to the articles mentioned in notes 62 and 63, Williston (1902) 15 H.L.R. 767; Dowrick (1956) 19 M.L.R. 374; Scamell (1955) 8 Cur.Leg.Pro. 131; Elliott (1956) 20 Conv.(N.S.) 43, 114; Andrews (1959) Conv.(N.S.) 179; Elliott (1960) 76 L.Q.R. 100; Hornby (1962) 79 L.Q.R. 228; Matheson (1966) 29 M.L.R. 397; Lee (1969) 85 L.Q.R. 213; Barton (1975) 91 L.Q.R. 236; Meagher and Lehane (1976) 92 L.Q.R. 427; Friend (1982) Conv. 280.

[65] [1968] A.C. 58. See also *Jackson* v. *Horizon Holidays Ltd.* [1975] 1 W.L.R. 1468, (C.A.) where it was held that the plaintiff was entitled to damages for himself and family by reason of breach of contract. The notion of a trust arising was, however, rejected: see p. 8, n. 47, *ante*; cf. *Woodar Investment Development Ltd.* v. *Wimpey Construction U.K. Ltd.* [1980] 1 All E.R. 571, H.L.

died to pay the uncle's widow an annuity of £5 a week. The uncle died, and after making one payment to the widow, the nephew stopped all payments. The widow sued the nephew both in her personal capacity and as administratrix of her husband's estate. It was held that she had no claim in the former capacity because she was not a party to the contract. But because she was administratrix she could enforce the provisions of the agreement for the benefit of herself in her personal capacity by specific performance. If she had not been the administratrix and the widow of the promisee she would have been without a remedy. The case shows up the unsatisfactory state of the law regarding third party beneficiaries.[66]

A further allied problem arises out of the principle that equity will not assist a volunteer who is not a party to the contract even though it is made under seal. Despite the arguments of academic writers that in such a case an enforceable trust of the benefit of the contract may have been constituted, thereby obviating the application of the equitable principle, the court continues to uphold this principle—not perhaps surprisingly in view of the fact that is was enunciated long ago by Lord Eldon and is supported by a body of case-law in the intervening years.[67]

2. Estates of deceased persons

In a sense the legal personal representative—executor in the case of a will, administrator in the case of intestacy—of a deceased person is a trustee for the creditors and beneficiaries claiming under the deceased; he holds the real and personal estate for their benefit and not his own. Moreover, by virtue of section 69 of the Trustee Act 1925, the provisions of the Act also apply to personal representatives.[68] But it would be an error to equate their legal position, because certain differences still persist, primarily as the result of other statutory enactments. For example, an action by a beneficiary to recover *trust* property or in respect of any breach of trust cannot, in the absence of fraud or retention of the property by the trustee,[69] be brought after the expiration of six years.[70] Personal representatives are subject to a different period of limitation, namely, 12 years for a claim to personal estate,[71] and six years for actions to recover arrears of interest in respect of legacies.[72] On the other hand, the objection of fraud or retention applies to personal representatives as it does to trustees.[73] The authority of personal representatives in handling pure personalty is *several*, whereas that of trustees is *joint*[74] However, over realty (including since 1925, for

---

[66] See (1967) 83 L.Q.R. 465.
[67] This matter is discussed further, *post*, p. 50, in relation to "Completely and Incompletely Constituted Trusts."
[68] See also A.E.A. 1925, ss. 33, 39 and see generally *post*, p. 49.
[69] Limitation Act 1980, s.21(1).
[70] *Ibid.* s. 21(3) and see *post*, p. 457.
[71] *Ibid.* s. 22.
[72] *Ibid.*
[73] *Ibid.* See also *post*, p. 457.
[74] *Jacomb* v. *Harwood* (1751) 2 Ves.Sen. 265; *Attenborough* v. *Solomon* [1913] A.C. 76. For historical reasons, see 1 Spence's *Equitable Jurisdiction* (1846), p. 578.

this purpose, leaseholds)[75] the authority of personal representatives, like that of trustees, is joint.[76] The difference lies in the fact that one of a number of personal representatives can give a valid title to a purchaser or pledgee of pure personalty; one of a number of co-trustees cannot: all must act.

The *functions* of personal representatives are also different from those of trustees. The duty of trustees is to administer a trust on behalf of beneficiaries, some of whom may be minors or unborn, and this may be a long continuing process, since many years may elapse before a trust is brought to an end. On the other hand, the primary duty of personal representatives is to wind up the estate by paying debts and capital transfer tax, and applying the net residue to the persons beneficially entitled to it under the will or intestacy[77] or to trustees, who may be themselves, to hold on trust. Furthermore, whereas a beneficiary has an equitable interest in the trust property as soon as the trust takes effect,[78] a legatee or devisee or person entitled on intestacy has no proprietary interest (legal or equitable) whilst the assets of the estate remain in course of administration. All he has is a right to require the deceased's estate to be duly administered by the personal representatives.[79]

It follows that although a personal representative has, like a trustee, fiduciary duties to perform, those duties are owed to the estate as a whole; it does not, therefore, necessarily follow that the duty of an executor in the course of administering an estate is subject to the trustee's duty of holding the balance evenly between the beneficiaries.[80] In *Re Hayes's Will Trusts*[81] it was accordingly held that where executors exercised a testamentary power of sale in favour of one of the children of the testator at an estate duty valuation, his other children could not attack the valuation on the ground that the executors did not consider the question of holding the balance evenly between the beneficiaries.

Personal representative becoming trustee. It is a question of some complexity to determine the time when, and the circumstances in which, a personal representative may become a trustee in cases where he has been appointed to both offices. It must be emphasised at the outset, however, that a personal representative holds his office as such for all time unless the grant to him is limited or the court revokes it[82]: the question is whether he has exhausted all his duties and functions as such and taken on himself the character of a trustee.

No problem will arise if the technically correct practice is followed in cases where trusts of *land* are designed to continue after completion of the administra-

---

[75] A.E.A. 1925, s. 3(1), 54.

[76] *Ibid.* s.2(2.).

[77] Considered in more detail *post*, p. 248.

[78] At any rate, in the case of a "fixed trust," but not in the case of a "discretionary trust": see *post*, p. 93.

[79] *Commissioner of Stamp Duties (Queensland)* v. *Livingston* [1965] A.C. 694: *Eastbourne Mutual B.S.* v. *Hastings Corporation* [1965] 1 W.L.R. 861; *Lall* v. *Lall* [1965] 1 W.L.R. 1249; *Re Leigh's Will Trusts* [1970] Ch. 277. See further, Mellows, *Law of Succession* (4th ed.), p. 368.

[80] *Re Hayes's Will Trusts* [1971] 1 W.L.R. 758 at p. 764; and see *post*, p. 328, for discussion of *trustees'* duty in this respect.

[81] *Supra.*

[82] See *Attenborough* v. *Solomon* [1913] A.C. 76 and see generally *post*, p. 14.

tion of the estate. This is that the personal representatives vest the property, by a document known as an assent,[83] in favour of themselves as trustees.[84] In such circumstances it is clear that there is a change in character from representation to trusteeship, even though liability *qua* personal representative may still persist. But until recently the practice appeared to be established that an assent on these lines was not essential. Thus, in *Re Ponder*[85] Sargant J. held that a personal representative became a trustee when the estate had been fully administered in the sense that all funeral and testamentary expenses and all debts and liabilities had been discharged and the residue ascertained. This principle was more recently applied in *Re Cockburn's Will Trusts*[86] where Dankwerts J. held that completion of administration sufficed to enable the personal representatives to exercise their statutory powers to appoint new trustees in their place.

But the validity of this general principle has now been rendered distinctly doubtful. Doubts were entertained in the first place by Sir Raymond Evershed M.R. *in Harvell* v. *Foster.*[87] The Master of the Rolls was unable to accept the view that clearing of the estate necessarily and automatically discharged them from their obligations as personal representatives and in particular from the obligation of any bond entered into by them for administration of the estate. But the doubt apparently felt in this case about the validity of the decision in *Re Ponder* was regarded by Danckwerts J. in *Re Cockburn's Will Trusts*[88] as *obiter* and unjustified. No doubt, if a personal representative failed to perform his duties as such he was still under a liability in that capacity and this, according to the judge, was the sole point in issue in *Harvell* v. *Foster*: it did not alter the rule established in *Re Ponder.*[89] However, the real difficulty arises from the decision of Pennycuick J. in *Re King's Will Trusts*,[90] where the question again arose, more directly, for decision. In this case although no assent had been made, a sole surviving executor of a trustee had executed a deed of appointment appointing another person to be a trustee jointly with himself. The judge held that this deed was not an assent in writing within the meaning of section 36(4) of the Administration of Estates Act 1925. This subsection contemplates that, for this purpose, a person may by assent vest an estate in himself in another capacity: but such vesting necessarily implies that he divests himself of the estate in his original capacity, which, it was held, was not the position here. Moreover, the implied vesting declaration contained in section 40 of the Trustee Act 1925[91] (impliedly vesting the property in the new trustees) did not convert the appoint-

---

[83] See *Attenborough* v. *Solomon, ibid.* at p. 83.

[84] As in *Re Bowden* (1890) 45 Ch.D. 444; *Re Swain* [1891] 3 Ch. 233; *Re Timmis* [1902] 1 Ch. 176; *Re Oliver* [1927] 2 Ch. 323 (where property was to be held for persons in succession); and as in *Re Claremont* [1923] 2 K.B. 718 (where the property was to be held on trust for sale).

[85] [1921] 2 Ch. 59, followed in *Re Pitt* (1928) 44 T.L.R. 371.

[86] [1957] Ch. 438.

[87] [1954] 2 Q.B. 367.

[88] [1957] Ch. 438 at p. 440.

[89] *Supra*.

[90] [1964] Ch. 542.

[91] See *post*, p. 263.

ment into an assent within the meaning of the Administration of Estates Act 1925 because section 40 applied only to estates and interests which formed part of the existing trust property and not where they were vested in a person in some other capacity, *e.g.* as personal representative. Pennycuick J. in the course of his judgment rather summarily rejected the rule established in *Re Ponder* which was affirmed by *Re Cockburn's Will Trusts*. He did not specifically refer to either of these cases, and to reject the rule in *Re Ponder* without full consideration may be thought somewhat unfortunate. For the rule itself had been often followed in conveyancing practice, even though an express assent is technically (because it admits of no doubt) more desirable on completion of administration. Further, the case rendered a number of titles technically faulty which may need to be put in order, usually by the execution of further documents such as an assent coupled, if necessary, with a confirmatory conveyance, if a conveyance has already been made on the basis that an assent is not essential.[92]

Re King's Will Trusts was assumed by the Court of Appeal in *Re Edwards's Will Trusts*[93] to have been correctly decided, but was distinguished on the facts. The testator had failed to assent to the vesting of the legal estate in himself, but nevertheless it was held on the facts that, having enjoyed beneficial occupation of the property for nearly 20 years, he had acquired the equitable beneficial interest in the property which accordingly formed part of his estate on death. As Buckley L.J. held, an assent to the vesting of an *equitable* interest need not to be in writing; it may be inferred from conduct. The correctness of *Re King's Will Trusts*, so far as it concerns the devolution of the *legal* estate, remains open to reconsideration by the Court of Appeal.

It should be emphasised that the foregoing has been concerned with trusts of land. If the property is personal property an assent can be implied, so that on completion of administration a personal representative may be taken to have impliedly assented to himself as trustee, thereby effecting the change in character from representation to trusteeship.

3. *Agency*

The relationship between principal and agent has some resemblances to the relationship between trustee and beneficiary. For example, agents are liable to their principals, as are trustees to beneficiaries, for any profits made out of the property or business entrusted to them. In such circumstances their respective positions may coincide.[94] The main difference, from which other consequences follow, is that the relationship between principal and agent is primarily that of creditor and debtor. So a trustee has full title to the property vested in him[95]: an agent has not. Agents act on behalf of the principal and subject to his control: trustees do not.[96] Agency is based on agreement: it is not necessary that there

---

[92] See Walker (1964) 80 L.Q.R. 328; Garner (1964) 28 Conv.(N.S.) 298.
[93] [1982] Ch. 30, C.A.
[94] See *post,* pp. 162, 169.
[95] See *ante,* p. 4.
[96] See *post,* p. 383.

should be—indeed there rarely is—an agreement between trustee and beneficiary.

4. *Equitable Charges*

This distinction is that a charge merely imposes a liability on the property which is subject to it; a trust imposes a fiduciary character on the owner of the property.[97] This has a number of consequences. Thus, if property is held subject to a charge and the chargee satisfies the charge he will hold the property beneficially,[98] whereas a trustee will, on the termination of the trust, hold the property on a resulting trust.[99] Again, a chargee is not accountable for rents and profits during the subsistence of the charge,[1] whereas a trustee is.[2] On the other hand, a basic similarity consists in the fact that both are equitable interests and may, therefore, be overriden on a purchase for value of the legal estate.[3]

5. *Conditions*

A condition may, in certain carefully defined circumstances, operate as a trust.

Property may be given to A on condition that he does something or confers a benefit on somebody. But it is only if that condition can, or must necessarily, be fulfilled or satisfied out of the property that it will take effect as a trust.[4] This will not be its effect if the duty is merely collateral.[5]

6. *Powers*

The distinction between a trust and a power is considered in Chapter 4.[6] It will be seen that the basic distinction, subject however to much elaboration, is that a power (such as a power to appoint funds amongst a class of beneficiaries) is discretionary, whereas a trust is imperative. This subject has been of great importance in recent years.

---

[97] *Cunningham* v. *Foot* (1878) 3 App.Cas. 974 at pp. 992–993, *per* Lord O'Hagan.
[98] *Re Oliver* (1890) 62 L.T. 533.
[99] See *post*, p. 148.
[1] *Re Oliver, supra.*
[2] See *post*,.
[3] *Parker* v. *Judkin* [1931] 1 Ch. 475.
[4] *Att.-Gen.* v. *Wax Chandlers Co.* (1873) L.R. 6 H.L. 1; *Cunningham* v. *Foot* (1878) 3 App.Cas. 974 at p. 995, *per* Lord O'Hagan.
[5] See *Re Brace* [1954] 1 W.L.R. 955 (house devised to a daughter on condition that "she provides a home" for another daughter: no trust arose). *Cf. Re Frame* [1939] Ch. 700 (a condition in a will that a legatee should adopt the testator's daughter did constitute a trust); *Re Niyazi's Will Trusts* [1978] 1 W.L.R. 910 (the words "on condition that" were held apt to create a trust). *Cf. Swain* v. *The Law Society* [1982] 3 W.L.R. 261, H.L.: (the words "on behalf of" did not express or imply a trust) ; see *ante*, p. 10 and *post*, p. 163.
[6] *Post*, p. 67.

CHAPTER 2

CLASSIFICATION OF TRUSTS

I. STATUTORY, EXPRESS, IMPLIED AND CONSTRUCTIVE TRUSTS

TRUSTS may be created (i) by statute—these are *statutory* trusts; (ii) intentionally by act of parties—*express* trusts; (iii) impliedly, *i.e.* arising from the presumed intention of the settlor—*implied* trusts, or (iv) by operation of law—*constructive* trusts.[1]

1. *Statutory Trusts*

A number of trusts have been expressly created or implied by statute. The following examples[2] may be taken:

(a) Section 34 of the Law of Property Act 1925 provides that whenever land is conveyed to persons in undivided shares it will vest in the first four persons named on a statutory trust for sale for all grantees beneficially as tenants in common.

(b) Under section 36 of the Law of Property Act 1925, where land is conveyed to joint tenants, it vests in the first four named as on a statutory trust for sale for all the grantees beneficially as joint tenants.

(c) Under section 33 of the Administration of Estates Act 1925, on the death of a person intestate, his property vests in his personal representatives upon trust for sale and division between the issue of the intestate or other relatives specified in the Act.[3]

2. *Express Trusts*

An express trust is created by express declaration of the settlor. It may be by will, deed, writing not under seal or by parol.[4] Whichever form is used, it is a trust which has been intentionally created by the settlor. A trust will indeed still be regarded as express even if the settlor has, for example, expressed himself ambiguously if the court concludes, upon a true construction of the instrument, that a trust was *intended* by the settlor. Thus words of prayer, entreaty or expectation, known as precatory words, may be held to create an express trust.[5]

---

[1] For a well-known classification, see *Cook* v. *Fountain* (1676) 3 Swanst. 585, *per* Lord Nottingham L.C. *Cf. Soar* v. *Ashwell* [1893] 2 Q.B. 390; *Re Llanover Settled Estates* [1926] Ch. 626.

[2] For further examples see S.L.A. 1925, s. 36; L.P.A. 1925, s. 19.

[3] See *post*, p. 249.

[4] See *post*, p. 23 for cases where writing is necessary.

[5] See *post*, p. 60.

Furthermore, a power to distribute property among a class of persons may possibly be construed as indicating an intention to create an express trust in favour of that class if there is no gift over in default of appointment; the question in each case is one entirely of construction of the relevant instrument.[6]

3. *Implied Trusts*

These are trusts arising from the unexpressed but presumed intention of the settlor. Such trusts are often known as "resulting trusts" because the beneficial interest may "result" to the settlor or his estate. Thus, to take two examples only at this stage: first, where the settlor of an express trust fails to deal effectually with the whole of the beneficial interest the court will imply that so much of the beneficial interest as is undisposed of will be held on trust for the settlor himself; and, secondly, where a purchase is made in another person's name, a similar resulting trust may arise in favour of the person who provided the purchase-money.[7]

4. *Constructive Trusts*

Such a trust has been defined as "a trust which is imposed by equity in order to satisfy the demands of justice and good conscience, without reference to any express or presumed intention of the parties."[8] To give an example, in one case the trustee of leasehold property used his position, on the determination of the lease, to induce the landlord to renew the lease to him. This was held to be an attempt to obtain a personal advantage for himself and was accordingly antagonistic to the beneficiaries' interest; it was an act of bad faith and the trustee was directed to hold the new lease upon the same trusts as he held the old lease.[9]

II. Simple and Special Trusts

1. *Simple Trusts*

A simple trust arises where a trustee is simply a repository of the trust property with no active duties to perform.[10] In such a case, he is known as a bare trustee. So if A gives the legal estate in property to B on trust for C absolutely, the trust is a simple trust. The only duty B has to perform is to transfer the legal estate in the property to C if C so directs.[11]

2. *Special Trusts*

A special trust arises where the trustee is appointed to carry out a purpose designated by the settlor and must exert himself actively in the performance of

---

[6] See *post*, p. 71.   [7] See further *post*, p. 126.
[8] Snell's *Principles of Equity* (28th ed.), p. 192.
[9] *Keech* v. *Sandford* (1726) Sel.Cas.*t.*King 61 and see also generally *post*, p. 162.
[10] *Cf.* Underhill's *Law of Trusts and Trustees* (13th ed.), p. 23.
[11] See *Christie* v. *Ovington* (1875) 1 Ch.D. 279; *Re Cunningham and Frayling* [1891] 2 Ch. 567.

the trust.[11a] He is called an active trustee. Thus if the trust is that, during A's life, A is to collect the rents and profits of the trust property, to pay the cost of repairs and insurance and pay the residue of the rents and profits to B for life and, on B's death, upon trust for C absolutely, the trust is a special one during B's life because the trustee has active duties to perform during that period. On B's death the trust becomes a simple trust and the trustee a bare trustee, because the only duty remaining to the trustee is to transfer the property to C.

Special trusts are subdivided into ministerial and discretionary trusts. The first requires for its performance no more than ordinary business intelligence on the part of the trustees, such as the collection of rents and profits of the trust property. The second requires the exercise of a discretion on the part of the trustees. For example, where money is simply left to trustees to divide among charities such as the Dog's Home, the Cat's Home and the Home for Distressed Gentlewomen at their discretion, the trust is of is nature discretionary. It is similarly discretionary where the trustees have a discretion to determine the amount of income to be paid to each member of a class of beneficiaries.[12] Discretionary trusts are considered in detail in Chapter 4.

III. EXECUTED AND EXECUTORY TRUSTS

A trust is *executed* in its technical meaning when the terms of the trust are specified in the trust instrument or declaration that constitutes it. A trust is *executory* where the instument or declaration requires the execution of a further instrument setting out the detailed terms of the trust. A conventional, if old-fashioned, example is marriage articles from which a formal marriage settlement is later to be prepared.[13]

IV. COMPLETELY AND INCOMPLETELY CONSTITUTED TRUSTS

Both executed and executory trusts are completely constituted. The distinction between them is that, in the former, the settlor has, in the language of the time, been his own conveyancer[14]; in the latter he has not.

A trust which is described as completely constituted is one which is perfectly created. It requires nothing more to be done by the settlor. But if something does remain to be done by him it is imperfect and is described as incompletely constituted. For example, if the settlor intends to vest property in another person as trustee he must, in order to render the trust completely constituted, comply with all the formalities required for a transfer of the property in question.[15]

V. FIXED AND DISCRETIONARY TRUSTS

Discretionary trusts have been mentioned as a form of "special trust." They should also be contrasted with trusts in favour of fixed beneficiaries or classes of

---

[11a] See n.10.   [12] See *post,* p. 67.   [13] For further discussion, see *post* p. 41.
[14] *Egerton* v. *Brownlow* (1853) 4 H.L.C. 1 at p. 210, *per* Lord St. Leonards.
[15] For further discussion, see *post*, p.44.

beneficiaries, called fixed trusts. In the latter, each of the beneficiaries is entitled in equity to a fixed share of the trust property and their rights thereto may be enforced against the trustees. In the case of a discretionary trust, because the trustees have a discretion to exercise in deciding whether the beneficiaries shall receive what, if any, part of the trust property, the beneficiaries have no interest until the discretion is exercised in their favour.[16]

VI. PRIVATE AND CHARITABLE TRUSTS

A private trust aims to benefit either one person or a defined number of pesons. A charitable trust aims, in general, to achieve a purpose which will benefit society or some considerable section of it. Because of their public nature, charitable trusts enjoy a number of privileges not shared by private trusts, for example, in relation to perpetuity and certainty and—most important today—with regard to liability to tax and rates.[17]

VII. A NEW CLASSIFICATION?

The traditional classification of implied, resulting and constructive trusts, which has generally been thought to be workable, has been somewhat disturbed by recent judicial dicta.

In the first place, a subdivision of resulting trusts has been suggested. The suggestion was made by Megarry J. in *Re Vandervell's Trusts (No. 2)*[18] where he made a distinction between a "presumed resulting trust" and an "automatic resulting trust." The first class of case would arise when a purchase is made in another person's name but not on trust; there is then a rebuttable presumption that the other holds the property on a resulting trust for the real purchaser. In such a case there is an implied or presumed intention to that effect which can be rebutted by evidence to the contrary.[19] The second class of case is where a transfer has been made on trusts which leave the whole or part of the beneficial interest undisposed of (for example, because the trusts are ineffective or incomplete). Here the transferee automatically holds on a resulting trust for the transferor to the extent that the beneficial interest is not disposed of. In such a case, according to Megarry J., the resulting trust "does not depend on any intentions or presumptions, but is the automatic consequence of [the transferor's] failure to dispose of what is vested in him."[20] Such is an example of an "automatic resulting trust."

If this formulation is correct, it follows that an "automatic resulting trust" is not, as has been commonly supposed, an example of an implied trust, but stands separate and apart. On the face of it, the distinction between "presumed" and

---

[16] They do, however, have a right to compel the due administration of the trust, and can share in the fund on a premature determination. See *post*, p. 94.

[17] The distinctions are discussed *post*, p. 183.

[18] [1974] Ch. 269, at pp. 294, 295. Megarry J.'s decision was reversed by the Court of Appeal ([1974] Ch. 269), but no comment was made on the judge's formulation.

[19] See *post*, p. 131 for the ways in which it may be rebutted.

[20] *Ibid.* at 294.

"automatic" resulting trusts appears to accord with common sense, but perhaps it should not be accepted too uncritically. A counter-argument could be that, just as an implied or presumed resulting trust is said to be created on purchase in the name of another, so also an intention could be implied on the part of the settlor that the property should result to him in so far as he has failed to dispose of it. The implication of an intention does not appear to be markedly more artificial in the one case than in the other. The point is open to debate. It is doubtful if it has any particular practical, as opposed to theoretical, significance.

Secondly, and (it seems) of greater importance, has been an attempt to bring the concepts of resulting and constructive trusts closer together. Lord Denning M.R. has been largely responsible for this approach. In *Hussey* v. *Palmer*,[21] for example, he claimed that the distinction between resulting and constructive trusts was "more a matter for words than anything else." He went on to say: "The two run together. By whatever name it is described, it is a trust imposed by law whenever justice and good conscience require it. . . . It is an equitable remedy by which the court can enable an aggrieved party to obtain restitution."[22]

In *Hussey* v. *Palmer*,[23] an elderly widow went to live with her daughter and son-in-law. She paid for an extension to be built to the house to form a bedroom for her. Later they quarrelled and the widow went to live elsewhere. It was held that it was against conscience for the son-in-law to retain the benefit of the extension and, according to Lord Denning M.R., it was held on a constructive trust for her.[24]

It may be that, on the facts of a given case, both a resulting trust based on implied intention and a constructive trust based on the activity of equity irrespectively of intention may provide the same solution. But to unite the two concepts in this way may lead to confusion, first because it undermines the traditional basis of resulting trusts, implied intention, which appears still to be applicable in respect of purchase in the name of another,[25] and, more generally, it is not in accordance with long-established authority.

Thirdly, it will be noted that Lord Denning M.R. said in terms in *Hussey* v. *Palmer* that a constructive trust is a *remedy*. On this it may be said that this also is not in accordance with English[26] authority which treats this form of constructive trust as a substantive institution.[27] In *Re Sharpe*,[28] for example, Browne-Wilkinson J. described the imposition of a constructive trust as a remedy as a "novel concept in English law."

[21] [1972] 1 W.L.R. 1286; and see also, for further examples, *post*, p. 142.
[22] At pp. 1289, 1290.   [23] *Ibid.*
[24] Phillimore L.J. agreed but thought that a resulting trust was created. Cairns L.J. dissented on the ground that the payment was made as a loan, and that was inconsistent with a resulting trust. In *Re Sharpe* [1980] 1 W.L.R. 219 at p. 223 Browne-Wilkinson J. was of the same opinion as Cairns L.J. He also considered that the facts of *Hussey* v. *Palmer* were very special: "a clue to the decision may be that, although described in evidence as a loan, the parties did not in fact intend a loan since there was never any discussion of repayment; "and even if it were a loan, "it was something akin to a lien on the property." See also *post*, p. 32.
[25] See *Re Vandervell's Trusts (No. 2)*, *supra*.
[26] As opposed to American: see *post*, p. 160.
[27] See *post*, p. 162.   [28] [1980] 1 W.L.R. 219 at p. 225.

CHAPTER 3

EXPRESS PRIVATE TRUSTS

I. Capacity to Create a Trust

In general, if a person has a power of disposition over a particular type of property, he can create a trust of it. Accordingly, any person over the age of 18[1] may create an express trust of any property which is capable of disposition, unless he is suffering from mental incapacity, and he may also create a trust of certain types of property of which he cannot dispose. If a company grants a pension to a retired director, and includes in the pension agreement a provision that the pension is non-assignable, the retired director may nevertheless be able to create a valid trust of the benefit of that agreement. So far as concerns mental incapacity, the position depends on whether the settlor is incapable of managing his affairs, and a receiver has been appointed under section 101 of the Mental Health Act 1959. Where a receiver has been appointed, any purported trust would be void.[2] The court may, however, either on the application of another person or on its own initiative direct the creation of a trust of a mental patient's property.[3] Further, since January 1, 1970, the court has been able to make a will on behalf of the patient,[4] and it can vary any trust which is made at any time until the patient's death.[5]

Even where there is no receiver, a trust will be set aside if it can be shown that the settlor did not understand the nature of the act in which he was engaged. It seems that the burden of proof will always lie at the outset upon the person seeking to set the trust aside, but where there is a long history of mental illness, this burden will be easily discharged, and the court will then require evidence that the trust was created during a lucid interval.[6] Where the trust was created for valuable consideration, it will not be set aside if the person providing the consideration was unaware of the mental incapacity at the time when the trust was made.[7]

A person under the age of 18 cannot hold land,[8] although he can own an

---

[1] Family Law Reform Act 1969, s.1(1).
[2] There is no authority under the 1959 Act, but see *Re Marshall* [1920] 1 Ch. 284, a decision on the Lunacy Act 1890.
[3] Mental Health Act 1959, s.103(1)(*d*) as amended by the Mental Health (Amendment) Act 1982, Sched 4.
[4] *Ibid.* s. 103(1)(*dd*) as amended by the Mental Health (Amendment) Act 1982, Sched 4.
[5] *Ibid.*
[6] See *Cleare* v. *Cleare* (1869) 1 P. & D. 655; *Chambers and Yatman* v. *Queen's Proctor* (1840) 2 Curt. 415.
[7] *Price* v. *Berrington* (1851) 3 Mac. & G. 486.
[8] Law of Property Act 1925, s.1(6); Family Law Reform Act 1969, s.1.

equitable interest in land. A minor cannot, therefore, create a settlement of a legal estate in land, for this has never been vested in him, but he can create a trust of property which he does hold, including equitable interests. The trust is voidable until shortly after the minor attains the age of 18, and if he does not repudiate it the trust will become fully binding.[9]

It was previously possible for a female minor aged 17 or over to make a binding settlement, but this power no longer exists.[10]

In order to create even a voidable trust, a minor must be old enough to appreciate the nature of his act. If he is too young to appreciate this the act is void, and where property has been transferred, the recipient will hold upon a resulting trust[11] for the infant. Little does the unsuspecting adult who has a sticky bag of sweets pushed into his hand by a toddler appreciate that thereafter he holds them on a resulting trust.[12] The same principle would apply where a person suffering from mental incapacity seeks to create a trust which is void, and transfers property to a trustee. Therefore, although full capacity is required before a fully binding express trust can be created, a resulting trust may arise as a result of a person's involuntary actions.

II. STATUTORY REQUIREMENTS FOR THE CREATION OF AN EXPRESS TRUST

Certain statutory provisions governing the creation of a trust demand consideration because these require writing. When these provisions are inapplicable the trust may be created orally. It may indeed be thought surprising that, as will be seen, a declaration of trust must be evidenced by writing if it relates to a square foot of land, but need not be if it relates to a £ million of cash.

1. *Law of Property Act* 1925, s.53 (1)(b)[13]

This provides that a declaration of trust respecting any land or any interest therein[14] must be manifested and proved by some writing signed by some person who is able to declare such trust, or by his will.[15] It will be observed that a declaration of trust should in effect be merely *evidenced* by writing; it has not necessarily to be created by writing. And the evidence may take the most diverse forms,[16] provided that it contains all the terms of the trust (*i.e.* parties,

---

[9] *Edwards* v. *Carter* [1893] A.C. 360.

[10] The power was conferred by the Infant Settlements Act 1855, but this has been repealed by the Family Law Reform Act 1969, s.11(*a*).

[11] See *post*, p. 148.

[12] Presumably he should sell them and convert them into authorised investments: see *post*, p. 301.

[13] This replaces Statute of Frauds 1677, s.4 (in part), s.7

[14] This includes freehold and leasehold property: L.P.A. 1925, s.205(1)(ix); and also apparently a share in the proceeds of sale of land: *ibid.* s.40.

[15] If made by will and intended only to operate after death, it must comply with the Wills Act 1837, s.9; *post*, p. 29.

[16] *e.g.* the memorandum may be in correspondence(*Forster* v. *Hale* (1798) 3 Ves.Jun. 696); a recital is an instrument (*Re Hoyle* [1893] 1 Ch. 84); an answer to interrogatories (*Hampton* v. *Spencer* (1693) 2 Vern. 288); or a telegram (*McBlain* v. *Cross* (1871) 25 L.T. 804).

property and the way in which the property is to be dealt with[17]). Writing will still be required even if the land is abroad and is unnecessary according to the *lex situs*, because this is a rule of evidence which must be complied with in an English court.[18] It will also be noticed that this provision does not sanction signature by an agent.

Resulting, implied and constructive trusts are exempt from these requirements.[19]

2. *Law of Property Act* 1925, *s.*53(1)(*c*)[20]

It is enacted that a disposition of an equitable interest or trust subsisting at the time of the disposition must be in writing and signed by the person disposing of the same or by his agent lawfully authorised in writing, or by his will. It is therefore required that an assignment of an equitable interest or trust must be *in writing*, not merely evidenced by writing; but the writing need not in all cases be completely detailed and, for example, if the assignee is to hold in a fiduciary capacity, the writing need not comprise particulars of the trust.[21] At the same time, it appears to be unnecessary that the writing be contained in one document; a number of documents may be joined together for the purpose of satisfying the statute, provided that they are sufficiently interconnected.[22] Section 53(1)(*c*), however, does not cover the area of law covered by subsection (1)(*b*) because that deals only with the creation of trusts, not with their disposition. And the provision in section 53(2) which exempts resulting, implied and constructive trusts from the formalities of the section does not appear to apply.[23]

The effect of section 53(1)(*c*) and, in particular, the term "disposition" came under consideration by the House of Lords in *Grey* v. *I.R.C.*[24] In this case the settlor, having made six settlements, *orally* directed the trustees to hold 18,000 £1 shares transferred to them on the trusts of these settlements. The trustees then executed six declarations of trust: they were all in similar form and each recited that the trustees were holders of shares, the settlor's oral direction and their acceptance of the trust reposed in them by that direction. These transactions amounted to an ingenious exercise to avoid payment of stamp duty normally chargeable on transfer of shares[25]; but, as it happened, the six

---

[17] *Forster* v. *Hale, ante.*   [18] *Rochefoucauld* v. *Boustead* [1897] 1 Ch. 196, at p. 207.
[19] L.P.A. 1925, s.53(2), and see *post*, p. 28.
[20] This replaces the Statute of Frauds 1677, s.9. See, generally, Battersby (1979) Conv. 17.
[21] *Re Tyler* [1967] 1 W.L.R. 1269.
[22] *Re Danish Bacon Co.Ltd. Staff Pension Fund Trusts* [1971] 1 W.L.R. 248. This was, *per* Megarry J., a novel question on which there appeared to be no previous direct authority.
[23] *Post*, p. 28.
[24] [1960] A.C. 1.
[25] Stamp duty is a tax which is payable on documents, so that where a transaction is properly effected orally, no duty is payable. A method of avoiding duty was evolved some time ago, whereby the settlor orally makes a declaration of trust, and some time later signs a document merely recording what he has done. As long as these two events are separate—see *Cohen and Moore* v. *I.R.C.* [1933] 2 K.B. 126—as the trust is effected by the oral declaration, no duty is payable. *Grey's* case was an attempt to extend this principle. It really consisted of three stages:

declarations of trust were assessed to *ad valorem* stamp duty, and the exercise failed. It was held that the directions given by the settlor were in fact *dispositions* by him of his equitable interest in the shares within the meaning of the section and, because they were not made in writing as required by the provision, were ineffective; but they became effective on the execution of the late declarations of trust. The word "disposition" had to be given the wide meaning which it bears in normal usage and the declarations of trust were, accordingly, rightly assessed.

It had been persuasively argued that section 53 was merely a consolidation of three sections of the Statute of Frauds 1677, *viz.* sections 3, 7 and 9, and, so treated, the term "disposition" was merely the equivalent of the former words of section 9—"grants and assignments" and these would not cover the transaction concerned. It was, as Lord Radcliffe said, a "nice question" whether a parol declaration of trust was or was not within the mischief of that section. The point had never been decided and perhaps never would be. But that question was only relevant if section 53 was to be treated as a true consolidation of these three sections of the Statute of Frauds and as governed, therefore, by the general principle that a consolidating Act is not to be read as effecting change in the existing law unless the words are too clear to admit of any other construction. The House of Lords held, however, that it was impossible to regard section 53 as a consolidating enactment in this sense. The Law of Property Act was no doubt strictly a consolidating statute but what it consolidated was not merely the Law of Property Act 1922, but also the Law of Property (Amendment) Act 1924. The sections of the Statute of Frauds were untouched by the 1922 Act but were repealed and re-enacted in altered form by the 1924 Act. And, so it was held, there was no direct link between section 53(1)(c) and section 9 of the Statute of Frauds: the link was broken by the changes introduced by the 1924 Act, and it was those changes, not the original statute, that section 53 must be taken as consolidating. If so, it was inadmissible to allow the construction of the word "disposition" to be limited or controlled by any meaning attached to "grant or assignment" in section 9 of the old Act.[26]

However, although section 53(1)(c) was given a wide meaning in one aspect in *Grey* v. *I.R.C.*, it was more narrowly construed in another in *Vandervell* v. *I.R.C.*,[27] which also went to the House of Lords, and in *Re Vandervell's Trusts (No. 2)*[28] which went to the Court of Appeal, although the context of construction was different in each case. The facts of this unfortunate litigation require

---

(a) a transfer by the settlor of the shares to the trustees to hold as nominees on his behalf (because there was no change in the beneficial interest, duty of only 50p was payable);

(b) the oral direction to the trustees (no duty);

(c) subsequent declarations of trust.

Without s.53(1)(c), the oral declaration would have been sufficient to pass the equitable interest, and so no duty would have been payable. But by virtue of the requirement of s.53(1)(c), the disposition had to be in writing, and the disposition was not effective until the declarations of trust were signed. Duty was therefore payable.

[26] [1960] A.C. 1 at 17–18.

[27] [1967] 2 A.C. 291.

[28] [1974] Ch. 269.

fairly detailed examination.[29] Mr. Vandervell had during his lifetime been a very successful businessman. He ran a private products company in which he owned virtually all the shares, and he could declare dividends as and when he pleased. In 1949 he declared trusts in favour of his children, and did this by forming a trustee company and transferring money and shares to the trustee company to be held in trust for his children (the so-called "children's settlement"). In 1958 he decided to found a chair of pharmacology at the Royal College of Surgeons and to endow it by providing £150,000. He then transferred shares in his products company to the College, not however by direct gift, but by requiring the College at the date of transfer to grant to his trustee company an option to re-purchase the shares for £5,000 (a figure much less than market value) at any time within five years. The purpose of this transaction was that when £150,000 had been raised, he or his trustee company would be able to regain the shares which it could use for other purposes. From 1958 to 1961 the products company declared dividends on the shares which were more than sufficient to found the chair at the College. Unfortunately, Mr. Vandervell failed to specify the trusts on which the trustee company was to hold the option. (It appeared that he had not made up his mind whether the option should be held in trust for his children or the employees of his products company.) The Revenue thereupon argued that Mr. Vandervell was liable to surtax on the dividends,[30] the reason being that he had failed to define the trusts on which the option was to be held. Subsequently, in *Vandervell* v. *I.R.C.*[31] the House of Lords, by a majority of three to two, held that as no trusts of the option had been declared, there was a resulting trust in favour of Mr. Vandervell and, therefore, he had been rightly assessed.

This was sufficient to dispose of the case, but the Revenue also argued that in any event section 53(1)(c) was not complied with, with the result that the beneficial interest was never divested from him. The Lords rejected this contention, holding that section 53(1)(c) has no application in cases where the disposition intended to be made was not merely of the equitable interest but also of the legal interest in the property. In other words, section 53(1)(c), in dealing with the disposition of an equitable interest, only applies where the disponer is not also the controller of the legal interest. It is directed to cases where the dealings with the equitable interest are divorced from the legal interest.

The last mentioned point indicates that section 53(1)(c) is thus limited in that sense. However, the actual decision in *Vandervell* v. *I.R.C.* that there was a resulting trust with serious tax consequences led directly to *Re Vandervell's Trusts* (*No.* 2)[32] which involved section 53(1)(c) in another way. To resume the recital of the sequence of events. Thus far, the trusts of the option to

---

[29] The judgment of Lord Denning M.R. in *Re Vandervell's Trusts* (*No.* 2), *supra*, contains an incisive statement of the facts.

[30] Amounting to £250,000; under the Income Tax Act 1952, s.415.

[31] [1967] 2 A.C. 291; applied, as between different parties, in *Re Vandervell's Trusts* (*No.* 2) [1974] Ch. 269, with regard to the period 1958–61; see *infra*.

[32] [1974] Ch. 269.

repurchase had not been specified, and the option itself had not been exercised. In October 1961, however, the trustee company exercised the option. They paid £5,000 from money of the children's settlement to the College. Accordingly, they became legal owners of the shares themselves, no longer merely of the option to re-purchase the shares. But at this stage Mr. Vandervell did not expressly declare the trusts on which the shares of dividends should be held. Only in January 1965 did he execute a deed transferring to the trustee company such interest as he might have in the shares or dividends, expressly declaring that the trustee company was to hold them on the trusts of the children's settlement. He died in 1967.

Re Vandervell's Trusts (*No. 2*) concerned the period between October 1961 and January 1965. The Revenue, on the basis that Mr. Vandervell had not divested himself of his interest in the shares or the option until January 1965, assessed his estate to surtax in respect of the dividends received during this period.[33] The Revenue was not, however, a party to *Re Vandervell's Trusts* (*No. 2*).[34] What had happened was that Mr. Vandervell had made no provision in his will for his children because, as he thought, he had sufficiently provided for them in the children's settlement. The executors of the will on behalf of the beneficiaries of the will claimed that they were entitled to all moneys received by the trustee company as dividends between October 1961 and January 1965 thereby ousting the claims of the children. The executors' appeal against the revenue assessment was stood over pending the action against the trustee company.

It has been mentioned that the moneys for the exercise of the option were provided from the children's settlement. It was also a fact that thereafter all dividends received by the trustee company were paid by them to the children's settlement and treated as part of the funds of that settlement. Furthermore, the solicitors for the trustee company had written a letter to the Revenue stating that the shares would be held on the trusts of the children's settlement. The Revenue admitted that all these dealings, which were done with Mr. Vandervell's approval, showed that Mr. Vandervell and the trustee company *intended* that the shares should be held on trust for the children's settlement, but it was argued that this intention was unavailing, the reasons being as follows: (1) that until October 1961 Mr. Vandervell had an equitable interest under a resulting trust[35]; (2) that he himself never disposed of that interest; and (3) that in any case it was a disposition of an equitable interest which, by virtue of section 53(1)(*c*) of the Law of Property Act 1925, had to be in writing. The Court of Appeal rejected this argument as fallacious and held (*inter alia*)[36] that the dealings with the moneys during this period not only showed an intention to

---

[33] Amounting to £628,229.

[34] The Revenue had failed in their application to be joined in the proceedings: *Re Vandervell's Trusts* [1971] A.C. 912. In the result, paradoxically, the executors had the duty of fighting the Revenue's battle for them, because if they succeeded they would have to meet the surtax assessments.

[35] See *Vandervell* v. *I.R.C.* [1967] 2 A.C. 291, *supra*.

[36] See further, *post*, pp. 46, 58.

create but actually created a trust of the shares in favour of the children's settlement which, because it involved personality, could be created without writing.[37] Section 53(1)(c) was, therefore, irrelevant.

Such was the decision, but some doubts must remain. In the first place, it appears dubious whether a valid trust of the shares was constituted by the events referred to.[38] And, secondly, with regard to section 53(1)(c), it is difficult to infer that he intended to dispose or did dispose of his equitable interest under the resulting trust of the option since he was unaware at the time that he had such an interest, and even if he had disposed of the interest, he did not dispose of it by writing so as to comply with section 53(1)(c).[39]

No doubt, the case could have been appealed, but no appeal was made, unfortunately perhaps for legal theory, but presumably not for the Vandervell trustees.

Summary of Vandervell with reference to section 53(1)(c)

(1) Section 53(1)(c) only applies to the disposition of an equitable interest where the disponer does not also control the legal interest (*Vandervell* v. *I.R.C.*).

(2) An express declaration of trust which brings a resulting trust to an end is not a disposition within section 53(1)(c). (*Re Vandervell's Trusts* (*No.* 2); compare *Grey* v. *I.R.C.*)

3. *Law of Property Act* 1925, s.53(2)

This subsection provides that section 53 as a whole does not apply to the creation or operation of resulting, implied or constructive trusts.[40] It clearly exempts such trusts from section 53(1)(b), but not, it seems, from section 53(1)(c), for "creation" and "operation" do not appear to cover *transfer* of equitable interests. The question arose only indirectly in another decision of the House of Lords, *Oughtred* v. *I.R.C.*,[41] where there was an oral agreement for the transfer of shares owned by a mother to her son and in exchange he was to make her absolute beneficial owner of certain other shares which were settled on trust for his benefit by transferring to her his beneficial reversionary interest in them. A transfer was later executed completing the transaction. But until completion of the transfer it appeared that the son had held the settled shares as a constructive trustee[42] for his mother, and the fundamental question was whether payment of stamp duty on the later transfer had been avoided on the ground that the mother now had an equitable interest in the property. However, the existence of the constructive trust was regarded by the House of Lords

---

[37] The Law of Property Act 1925, s.53(1)(b) applies only to trusts of realty. See *ante*, p. 23.

[38] See *post*, p. 48.

[39] See the summary of the argument by Stephenson L.J. in *Re Vandervell's Trusts* (*No.* 2) [1974] Ch. 269 at pp. 322, 323. The point had not been argued before Megarry J. at first instance.

[40] See *ante*, p. 24.

[41] [1960] A.C. 206; considered in *Re Holt's Settlement* [1969] 1 Ch. 100 (variation of trusts) *post*, p. 424.

[42] A contract to sell may give rise to a constructive trust in favour of the purchaser: see *post*, p. 174.

(though only on a three to two majority) to be immaterial: the essential point was that the transfer in question was the completion of an oral contract (itself ineffective as it stood by reason of section 53(1)(c)) and liable to *ad valorem* stamp duty accordingly. The reasoning behind the decision of the majority was stated by Lord Jenkins in the following passage:

> "The constructive trust in favour of a purchaser which arises on the conclusion of a contract for sale is founded upon the purchaser's right to enforce the contract in proceedings for specific performance. In other words he is treated in equity as entitled by virtue of the contract to the property which the vendor is bound under the contract to convey to him. The interest under the contract is, no doubt, a proprietary interest of a sort which arises, so to speak in anticipation, of the execution of the transfer for which the purchaser is entitled to call. But its existence has never (so far as I know) been held to prevent a subsequent transfer, in performance of the contract, of the property contracted to be sold from constituting for stamp duty purposes a transfer on sale of the property in question. Take the simple case of a contract for the sale of land. In such a case a constructive trust in favour of the purchaser arises on the conclusion of the contract for sale, but (so far as I know) it has never been held on this account that a conveyance subsequently executed in performance of the contract is not stampable *ad valorem* on a transfer on sale."[43]

This was the basis of the decision, so section 53(2) was not directly in issue, but there are dicta by Lords Radcliffe, Cohen and Denning which indicate that this subsection, because of its wording, did not apply to section 53(1)(c).[44]

A case which indicates the application of section 53(2) rather more directly is *Hodgson* v. *Marks*.[45] H, a widow aged 83, owned a house and E was her lodger. She placed her confidence in him and conveyed the house to him; it was then registered in his name. E later transferred the property to M. It was held by the Court of Appeal that E held the property on a resulting trust for H and, further, the statutory formalities required by section 53(1)(b) did not apply.[46]

4. *Law of Property Act* 1925, *s.*55

This section provides (*inter alia*) that nothing in section 53 is to invalidate dispositions by will or affect any interest validly created before the commencement of the Act, or the acquisition of title by adverse possession, or affect the law relating to part performance.

5. *Wills Act* 1837, *s.*9

This section (as substituted by section 17 of the Administration of Justice Act 1982) provides that no will shall be valid unless (a) it is in writing and signed by

---

[43] *Ibid.* at p. 240 and see also *post*, p. 174.
[44] At 228, 230, 233.   [45] [1971] Ch. 892.
[46] It was also held that she was entitled to an "overriding interest" under L.R.A. 1925, s.70(1)(g) which was binding on M.

the testator or by some other person in his presence and by his direction; and (b) it appears that the testator intended by his signature to give effect to the will; and (c) the signature is made or acknowledged by the testator in the presence of two or more witnesses present at the same time; and (d) each witness either, (i) attests and signs the will or (ii) acknowledges his signature in the presence of the testator (but not necessarily in the presence of any other witness), but no form of attestation shall be necessary. A will executed without these formalities is void; and this applies both to an equitable interest as well as to a legal estate disposed of by the will.

6. *Equity will not Allow a Statute to be Used as an Instrument of Fraud*

The court will not allow the statutory provisions mentioned above, any more than they would allow the relevant sections of the Statute of Frauds 1677, to be applied in such a way as to achieve a fraudulent purpose. A basic maxim of equity is that it will not allow a statute to be used as a "cloak" or "engine" for fraud. No doubt an important purpose behind the statutory provisions already mentioned—and indeed this was true of the Statute of Frauds itself—is the prevention of fraud. But it is easy to visualise a situation where an automatic application of the statutes would have the unintended effect of allowing fraud by one party to succeed and in such circumstances the court will intervene for a party's protection under the umbrella of the equitable maxim. Thus in *Bannister* v. *Bannister*,[47] A conveyed a cottage to B. B orally agreed to allow A to occupy it rent free so long as she wished. B attempted to turn A out, but it was held by the Court of Appeal that the agreement must be enforced: it would have been a fraud on the part of B to renounce the agreement with A by reason only of the absence of writing. A was held, in the result, to be a tenant for life within the Settled Land Act 1925 and could not be ousted against her will.

The facts and result were not too dissimilar in *Binions* v. *Evans*,[48] where a somewhat similar, if confusingly worded, agreement, though this time in writing, was unanimously held to give the occupier security from eviction against subsequent purchasers of the property who had purchased subject to the agreement. There was, however, a difference of approach in reaching this result. Lord Denning M.R. was of opinion that the interest taken by the occupier was that of contractual licensee, and when the owner sold the property to the purchaser subject to the licence, the court would impose a constructive trust in favour of the licensee, and such constructive trust would be protected against the purchaser.[49] Megaw and Stephenson L.JJ. held that the effect of the

---

[47] [1948] 2 All E.R. 133; see also *Rochefoucauld* v. *Boustead* [1897] 1 Ch. 196 where the rule was applied to foreign land, and *Davies* v. *Otty* (*No. 2*) (1865) 35 Beav. 208 where property was transferred by a person fearing prosecution for bigamy, on the oral understanding that it would later be retransferred to him. *Bannister* v. *Bannister* was distinguished in *Chandler* v. *Kerley* [1978] 1 W.L.R. 693, C.A. (contractual licence held to arise) (discussed *post*, p. 32) and see *Hardwick* v. *Johnson* [1978] 1 W.L.R. 683, C.A.

[48] [1972] Ch. 359.

[49] Lord Denning M.R. also suggested *obiter* that even if the land had not been purchased expressly "subject to" the contractual licence, a constructive trust would still be imposed if he

agreement was that the occupier was a tenant for life under the Settled Land Act 1925 and since the purchasers took with notice of that agreement they were in the position of constructive trustees and could not turn her out. The reasoning of the Lords Justices appears to be more in accord with *Bannister* v. *Bannister*, although the conveyancing implications of holding that a settlement arose may have been ignored. For example, there is difficulty in deciding what is the "settlement" in these circumstances for the purposes of section 1(1) of the Settled Land Act 1925.[50] Moreover, the tenant for life under the settlement presumably obtains all the statutory powers of a tenant for life, including that of sale—more than would normally have been intended. These points were made by Goff L.J. in *Griffiths* v. *Williams*,[51] but it was unnecessary to decide the question in that case.[52]

The difficulties of this area of the law were emphasised by Dillon J. in *Lyus* v. *Prowsa Developments Ltd.*[53] The plaintiffs agreed to purchase land from the vendor company and paid a deposit. The land was to be transferred to the plaintiffs when a house had been built upon it. However, the company became insolvent before the house was completed. The company's bank held a legal charge over land including the land agreed to be sold, and sold that land to A subject to the plaintiffs' contract. A subsequently agreed to sell to B subject to the contract "so far, if at all, as it might be enforceable" against A. Dillon J. applied both *Bannister* v. *Bannister* and the judgment of Lord Denning M.R. in *Binions* v. *Evans* in holding that both A and B held the land upon a constructive trust in favour of the plaintiffs who accordingly were entitled to an order of specific performance of their contract against B.

It should be observed that in *Binions* v. *Evans*, in Lord Denning M.R.'s view, the court would impose a constructive trust "for the simple reason that it would be inequitable for the plaintiffs to turn the defendant out contrary to the stipulation subject to which they took the premises."[54] It will be seen later that the concept of constructive trust is of some width in English law,[55] for example, if an agent for trustees knowingly receives trust funds and also knows that they are being transferred to him in breach of trust, he will, even in the absence of fraud, hold the funds on a constructive trust. But the question for present purposes is whether "inequitable" conduct which may give rise to a constructive

---

took the land impliedly subject to the licence, *e.g.* where the licensee was in actual occupation of the land: *cf. Hodgson* v. *Marks* [1971] Ch. 892 (referred to *ante*, p. 29); *cf.* also *Chandler* v. *Kerley* (*supra*) (where there was a contractual licence, constructive trusteeship was irrelevant; the matter was regulated by the contract); see *per* Lord Scarman at p. 696; but see *Re Sharpe* [1980] 1 .W.L.R. 219, discussed *post*, p. 32.

[50] A settlement is created when land is "limited in trust for any persons by way of succession."

[51] *Guardian Gazette*, 1130, December 21, 1977 (C.A.); see also *Chandler* v. *Kerley* (*supra*) *per* Lord Scarman at p. 698 to a similar effect; *cf. Dodsworth* v. *Dodsworth* (1973) 228 E.G. 1115, C.A.

[52] The question involved the effect of an equity arising by estoppel. For the analogous conveyancing problems in cases of proprietary estoppel, see *post*, p. 59.

[53] [1982] 1 W.L.R. 1044.

[54] [1972] Ch. 359, at 368.

[55] See *post*, p. 160.

trust but falling short of fraud[56] may render compliance with statutory provisions, such as section 53 of the Law of Property Act 1925, unnecessary. The
problem, it seems, largely hinges around the meaning of "fraud," and for this
purpose it is useful to consider the judgment of Scott L.J. in *Bannister* v.
Bannister.[57] He said:

> "It is . . . clearly a mistake to suppose that the equitable principle on which
> a constructive trust is raised against a person who insists on the absolute
> character of a conveyance to himself for the purpose of defeating a
> beneficial interest which, according to the true bargain, was to belong to
> another, is confined to cases in which the conveyance itself was
> fraudulently obtained. *The fraud which brings the principle into play arises
> as soon as the absolute character of the conveyance is set up for the purpose
> of defeating the beneficial interest*[58] and that is the fraud to cover which the
> Statute of Frauds or the corresponding provisions of the Law of Property
> Act 1925, cannot be called in aid in cases in which no written evidence of
> the bargain is available."

In some cases, however, it may be sufficient to rely on a contractual or other
licence without the need to seek the assistance of equity in setting up a
constructive trust. This was held to be the position in *Chandler* v. *Kerley*,[59]
which involved a contractual licence terminable on reasonable notice to occupy
a house; it was held that the question of duration of occupation was governed by
the contract alone. But in other cases this may not be sufficient; the facts may
require the additional imposition of a constructive trust in order to do justice to
the parties. Accordingly, in *Re Sharpe*[60] an aged aunt lent £17,000 to her
nephew to purchase a house as part of an arrangement whereby the aunt was to
live with her nephew and his wife in it. The nephew had become bankrupt and
his trustee in bankruptcy agreed to sell the property. Browne-Wilkinson J.
held that, as against her nephew, the aunt had an irrevocable licence to occupy
the property until the loan was repaid and, further, that the licence arose under
a constructive trust which bound the trustee in bankruptcy.[61]

7. Secret Trusts

Of some importance in connection with this maxim of equity is the law relating
to secret trusts. When a person dies his will becomes open to public inspection

---

[56] This was not, of course, the position in *Binions* v. *Evans*, because the agreement in that
case was in writing, but the point (and the formulation of Denning M.R.) are relevant to cases
where absence of writing is relied upon to defeat a beneficial interest. See also *Hussey* v.
Palmer [1972] 1 W.L.R. 1286: Denning M.R. held that a person who paid for an extension to
be added to the legal owner's property acquired an equitable interest in it because "justice
and good conscience" so required; *Re Sharpe* [1980] 1 W.L.R. 219 (discussed *post*, p. 59) see
also *ante*, p. 21.

[57] [1948] 2 All E.R. 133 at p. 136.

[58] Our italics.   [59] [1978] 1 W.L.R. 693, C.A.

[60] [1980] 1 W.L.R. 219; see also *ante* p. 59 and, in relation to proprietary estoppel, *post*, p.
21.

[61] Applying *D H N Food Distributors Ltd.* v. *London Borough of Tower Hamlets* [1976] 1
W.L.R. 852; and see *Binions* v. *Evans*, *supra*.

and secret trusts usually arise when a testator wishes to make provision for somebody but does not want the whole world to know about it, sometimes because the provision is for the testator's mistress or illegitimate children. In the usual way the secret trust will arise under the will itself, but this does not exhaust the possibilities, and the same principles will apply to a case where a testator has decided not to make a will,[62] or, alternatively, revoke a will he has already made[63] on the strength of a promise by someone to dispose of property in a specified manner. Usually the disposition is to be made *inter vivos* but a secret trust may also arise where a testator has made a will in favour of a person on the basis that that person will himself later dispose of the property by will elsewhere.[64] The method by which the trustee is to carry out the obligation, whether by making a will in favour of the secret beneficiary or by some form of *inter vivos* disposition, is immaterial.[65]

The original basis of the jurisdiction was that equity would not allow the Wills Act 1837 to be used as an instrument of fraud.[66] But this is clearly not now the sole ground on which such trusts are enforced, because in many cases—as will be seen from some of the decisions discussed in the text—there is no question of fraud. Nevertheless, the prevention of fraud was, and may still be in some cases, a decisive factor and this makes it appropriate to discuss the subject at this stage.[67]

Basis of secret trusts. A secret trust is essentially an equitable obligation communicated to an intended trustee in the testator's lifetime. In enforcing such a trust, one might be inclined to think that equity directly contradicts the terms of section 9 of the Wills Act 1837[67a], but this is not so, because the basis of the doctrine of secret trusts is that the trust operates outside the will: indeed, the Act is not concerned with it at all. As Viscount Sumner said in the leading case of *Blackwell* v. *Blackwell*[68]:

> "For the prevention of fraud equity fastens on the conscience of the legatee a trust which otherwise would be inoperative: in other words, it makes him do what the will has nothing to do with, it lets him take what the will gives him, and then makes him apply it as the Court of Conscience directs, and it does so in order to give effect to the wishes of the testator, which would not otherwise be effectual."

The basis of the doctrine is the existence of a validly executed will which passes the title of property to A and the acceptance by A of an equitable obligation in the testator's lifetime; A is thereupon bound by that obligation. This basic principle is illustrated by *Re Young*.[69] Here one of the intended

---

[62] *Re Gardner* [1920] 2 Ch. 523.
[63] *Tharp* v. *Tharp* [1916] 1 Ch. 142.
[64] *Ottaway* v. *Norman* [1972] Ch. 698.
[65] *Ibid.* at 711.
[66] *Drakeford* v. *Wilks* [1747] 3 Atk. 539; *McCormick* v. *Grogan* (1869) L.R. 4 H.L. at pp. 88–89, 97; *Blackwell* v. *Blackwell* [1929] A.C. 318, at pp. 334–335.
[67] See generally Fleming (1947) 12 Conv. (N.S.) 28; Sheridan (1951) 67 L.Q.R. 314.
[67a] As substituted by A.J.A., 1982, s.17. [68] [1929] A.C. 318, 335.   [69] [1951] Ch. 344.

beneficiaries under a secret trust had witnessed the will and the question was
whether he forfeited his legacy under section 15 of the Wills Act 1837.[70]
Danckwerts J. held there was no forfeiture because the whole theory of the
formation of a secret trust was that the Act had nothing to do with the matter.
The forms required by the Wills Act were to be entirely disregarded because the
beneficiary did not take by virtue of the gift in the will but by virtue of a secret
trust imposed on an apparent beneficiary who did take under the will and who
was bound by the trust.[71] It was also held in *Re Gardner*,[72] for the same reason,
that the interest of a secret beneficiary who predeceases the testator will not
lapse (although the case seems to have been wrongly decided for another
reason, *viz.* that the trust could not take effect until the testator's death and the
secret beneficiary would have no interest until that date). However, it does
appear that if it is the devisee or legatee *who accepts the secret trust* who
precedeases the testator the trust will not take effect. In such circumstances it
seems that the beneficiary will not be able to establish his title because the
devise or bequest on which the trust is based has itself failed.[73]

The subject of secret trusts has to be divided into two parts: (i) fully secret
trusts and (ii) half-secret trusts.

(1) Fully secret trusts

These are trusts which are fully concealed by the testator. They will arise
where on the face of the will the alleged trustee takes absolutely and
beneficially. If property is given by will to X absolutely and a communication is
made to X by the testator during his lifetime that he is to hold the property on
specified trusts, and provided also that X accepts the trust, a fully secret trust
which is enforceable will come into being.[74]

Evidence, oral[75] or written, is admissible to show the terms of a trust—even
in the form of a memorandum made by the trustee after the testator's death[76]—
and if it is satisfactorily established by such evidence, the trust will be enforced.

---

[70] This provides that a witness to a will cannot take a benefit under it.
[71] *Ibid.* at p. 350.   [72] [1923] 1 Ch. 230.
[73] *Re Maddock* [1902] 2 Ch. 220 at p. 231; *cf. Blackwell* v. *Blackwell* [1929] A.C. 318 at p.
328, *per* Lord Buckmaster.
[74] In *Ottaway* v. *Norman* [1972] Ch. 698, 711, Brightman J. stated the essential
requirements of a secret trust as follows: (i) the intention of the testator to subject the primary
donee to an obligation in favour of the secondary donee; (ii) communication of that intention
to the primary donee, and (iii) the acceptance of that obligation by the primary donee either
expressly or by acquiescence. By "primary donee" the judge referred to the person on whom
such a trust was imposed, and by "secondary donee" he referred to the beneficiary under that
trust.
[75] At any rate, if the trust relates to personal property, *sed quaere* if the trust concerns land;
see *post*, p. 41.
[76] *Re Gardner's Will Trusts* [1936] 3 All E.R. 938 (admissible because not against trustees'
personal or proprietary interests). See Civil Evidence Act 1968, s.2, which admits such
evidence in any case. See also *Shenton* v. *Tyler* [1939] Ch. 620 (interrogatories to widow
admissible); *cf.* (1939) 2 M.L.R. 319; (1939) 55 L.Q.R. 330; (1940) 56 L.Q.R. 137. However,
although evidence is admissible, even in the trustee's favour, it may have little weight if it is
uncorroborated or if the donee is not only a trustee but also stands in a professional or
quasi-professional relationship to the testator: see *Re Tyler* [1967] 1 W.L.R. 1269. See *post*, p.
41 for cases where writing may be necessary.

In *McCormick* v. *Grogan*[77] Lord Westbury said[78] that the "clearest and most indisputable evidence" was required to set up a secret trust contrary to the absolute terms of a disposition, words which indicate a very high standard of proof. They were, however, interpreted by Brightman J. in *Ottaway* v. *Norman*[79] to mean merely that "clear evidence" is needed before the court will assume that the testator did not mean what he said but intended that the gift should be held by the beneficiary subject to a secret trust. In this case it was held that the evidence was sufficiently cogent to establish that the alleged trustee was under an obligation to dispose of a bungalow by will in favour of the secret beneficiary. Brightman J. was also of the opinion that the standard of proof to establish a secret trust was "perhaps" analogous to that which the court requires for the rectification of a written instrument. On the other hand, in *Re Snowden*,[80] Megarry V.-C. considered that the standard of proof for rectification was not the appropriate analogy.[81] He thought that, in the absence of fraud[82] or other special circumstances, the standard of proof of a secret trust was merely the ordinary civil standard of proof (namely, balance of probability) to establish an ordinary trust. The testatrix had left her residuary estate to her brother who subsequently died leaving his estate to his only son. There was some evidence that the testatrix had said that the brother would "know what to do" and "would deal with everything" for her, but it was held that although there was some arrangement between the parties it amounted only to a moral obligation which was not intended to be binding and accordingly the brother took the residue free from any secret trust and on his death it passed to his son absolutely.

The doctrine of fully secret trusts has a fairly lengthy history: its basis was established as long ago as the eighteenth century. Thus, in *Drakeford* v. *Wilks*,[83] the testatrix bequeathed a bond to the plaintiff. She was then induced to make a new will by which she bequeathed the bond to X on the strength of a promise by X that on X's death the bond would go to the plaintiff. It was held that the plaintiff could compel the performance of the trust.

The general principles now governing fully secret trusts are clearly established[84], subject only to the possible doubt as to the standard of proof required to establish such trusts which has just been considered.

1. It is essential to show that the testator did in fact communicate the trust during his lifetime to the legatee or devisee and that the latter expressly or impliedly accepted it. If the devisee or legatee only hears of the trust after the testator's death the secret trust will fail and he will take absolutely (assuming

---

[77] (1869) L.R. 4 H.L. 82.

[78] *Ibid.* at pp. 97, 98.

[79] [1972] Ch. 698 at p. 712.

[80] [1979] Ch. 528.

[81] "Strong" evidence is required in a rectification action to contradict the evidence of the instrument: *ibid.*, at p. 535.

[82] See Hodge (1980) Conv. 341.

[83] (1747) 3 Atk. 539.

[84] See also the formulation by Brightman J. in *Ottaway* v. *Norman* [1972] Ch. 698 at p. 711 cited at p. 34, n. 74, *ante*.

that the gift is to him in absolute terms). There is no fraud on his part in this event. There is what appears to be an absolute gift to him; he can, therefore, set up section 9 of the Wills Act 1837,[84a] and say that any later communication (for example, in an unattested document) does not comply with the Act. So in *Wallgrave* v. *Tebbs*[85] the legatees only knew of the trusts after the testator's death, and since they took absolutely on the face of the will, the absolute bequest to them could not be impeached.

2. The communication of the trust and its acceptance may be made either before or after the date of the will provided it is made during the life of the testator. In the well-known case of *Moss* v. *Cooper*,[86] for example, the communication was made after the execution of the will and, moreover, by an agent for the testator, and Wood V.-C. held it to be effectual.

3. If the fully secret trust is *accepted* by the trustee *qua* trustee, but the actual objects are not communicated during the testator's life, the trust will not take effect and the trustee will hold the property for the residuary devisee or legatee or, if there is no gift of residue in the will, in favour of the persons entitled on intestacy. Thus in *Re Boyes*[87] the testator gave his property to X absolutely and appointed him executor. The testator had previously told X that he wished him to hold the property according to directions which he would communicate by letter. X agreed. These directions were not, however, given to the testator, but after his death two unattested documents were found in which the testator stated that he wished a Mrs. Y to have the property. Kay J. decided that X held the property for the testator's next-of-kin, there being no gift of residue in this case.

4. Communication and acceptance of the trust may be effected constructively. In *Re Boyes*[88] Kay J. expressed the view that a trust put in writing and placed in the trustees' hands in a sealed envelope would constitute communication and acceptance at the date of delivery for this purpose. And in *Re Keen*,[89] the Court of Appeal accepted this view: this was a case of a half-secret trust but it would seem that if the rule applies to half-secret trusts it should also apply to fully secret trusts.

5. It is, of course, required that the property the subject of the intended secret trust should be certain: this is a rule which applies generally in the law of trusts.[90] For example, in *Ottaway* v. *Norman*[91] it was contended that the alleged trustee was under an obligation to dispose of "money" in favour of the secret beneficiary.[92] It was held that there was insufficient evidence to establish this obligation and the claim failed. It was, however, also said that if the alleged trustee had the

---

[84a] As substituted by the Administration of Justice Act 1982, s.17.

[85] (1855) 2 K. & J. 313.

[86] (1861) 1 J. & H. 352.

[87] (1884) 26 Ch. D. 531 and see *Re Hawksley's Settlement* [1934] Ch. 384.

[88] *Supra.*

[89] [1937] Ch. 236.

[90] See p. 64, *post.*

[91] [1972] Ch. 698.

[92] For another aspect of the decision where it was held that a secret trust did arise in respect of other property, see p. 35 *ante.*

right to mingle his own money with that derived from the testator, there would be no ascertainable property on which the trust could bite at death.

(2) Half-secret trusts

These arise where the trustee takes as trustee on the face of the will, but the terms of the trust are not in fact specified. If property is, for example, given to X upon trust "for purposes which I have communicated to him" or "for purposes with which he is fully acquainted," a half-secret trust will arise. Here, as in the case of a fully secret trust, certain governing principles can be stated, but one of them raises considerable doubt.

1. It is clearly established that evidence cannot be adduced to contradict the terms of the will. Accordingly, if the will points to a future communication, *e.g.* "to my trustees for purposes which I will communicate to them," evidence cannot be admitted of communications made before the will was executed. Similarly, if the will points to a contemporaneous or past communication, evidence cannot be admitted of a communication after the will was executed. The first and governing rule is that one has to consider the terms of the will to see what communications are admissible, and the other principles applicable to half-secret trusts take effect subject to this.[93] It should, however, be noticed at this stage that it appears, in the present state of the law, that future communications, whether or not the will points to them, are not, in any event, admissible.[94]

2. Where the communication of the trust is made before or at the same time as the execution of the will, evidence is admissible to show the terms of the trust and the trustee is bound by it. A leading case is *Blackwell* v. *Blackwell*.[95] A testator by codicil bequeathed a legacy to five persons upon trust to invest at their discretion and "to apply the income . . . for the purposes indicated by me to them" and to apply capital "to such person or persons indicated by me to them." Before the codicil was executed the objects of the trust were communicated to the five persons. The House of Lords held that evidence of the communication was admissible to show the terms of the trust and the trustees were bound.

3. The principle governing communication made subsequently to the will, yet before the testator's death, is extremely difficult to state. The leading case on this question is *Re Keen*,[96] a decision of the Court of Appeal, but from which unfortunately it is a matter of some difficulty to extract the precise *ratio decidendi*. The facts were that the testator gave a sum of money to his executors "to be held upon trust and disposed of by them among such person, persons or charities as may be notified by me to them or either of them during my lifetime." Shortly before the will the testator had given one of the executors a sealed envelope containing the name of the intended beneficiary and directed that it

---

[93] See *e.g. Re Keen* [1937] Ch. 236; *Re Tyler* [1967] 1 W.L.R. 1269.
[94] *Infra.*
[95] [1929] A.C. 318. See also to a like effect *Re Fleetwood* (1880) 15 Ch.D. 594; *Re Huxtable* [1902] 2 Ch. 793, C.A.
[96] [1937] Ch. 236.

was not to be opened before his death. The view expressed in *Re Boyes*[97] was accepted that the handing over of this sealed envelope was a sufficient communication at the date of delivery. Therefore the communication was made *before* the will. This necessarily meant considering the words used in the will in the light of the first governing rule mentioned above that evidence is not admissible to contradict the terms of the will, so that if a will points to a future communication evidence is inadmissible of a communication before the will is executed and vice versa. The court held that the terms of the will quoted above could only be considered as pointing to a future definition of trusts which had not at the date of the will been established; in other words, the will pointed to a future communication. In fact, as already held, the trusts had been communicated before the will, the handing over of a sealed envelope being a sufficient communication for this purpose. Accordingly, by reason of the terms of the will, evidence of a communication made before the will was executed was not admissible. If this is the only ground of the decision there can be no dispute with it. But Lord Wright M.R. went on to discuss the question on a broader basis and held that, even if the words of the will could be construed as pointing to a past as well as a future communication, they would be equally ineffective. If this statement is to be treated as part of the *ratio decidendi* (and from the general tenor of the judgment it may well be so) it means that communications made after the will but during the testator's lifetime are not in any event admissible to show the terms of the trust, or, stated in other words, you cannot successfully set up a half-secret trust if the terms of the trust are communicated subsequently to the execution of the will.

There are also dicta, although these are clearly *obiter*, in *Blackwell* v. *Blackwell* which are apparently to the same effect. Thus Viscount Sumner said in this case[98]: "The limits, beyond which the rules as to unspecified trusts must not be carried, have often been discussed. A testator cannot reserve to himself a power of making future unwitnessed dispositions by merely naming a trustee and leaving the purposes of the trust to be supplied afterwards. . . . To hold otherwise would indeed be to enable the testator to 'give the go-by' to the requirements of the Wills Act because he did not choose to comply with them."

But there are not only the decision in *Re Keen*[99] and the dicta in *Blackwell* v. *Blackwell*; there is also the earlier case of *Johnson* v. *Ball*.[1] Here a testator gave the proceeds of a policy of assurance to two trustees to "hold the same upon the uses appointed by letter signed by them and myself." No such letter complying with the precise terms of the will at any time existed though there had been other communications before and after the making of the will. It would have been sufficient to hold that the latter communications did not accord with the formalities prescribed by the will and were inadmissible for that reason. But Parker V.-C. was not content to do this. He chose to hold on a more general

---

[97] (1884) 26 Ch.D. 531.
[98] [1929] A.C. 318, 339.
[99] [1937] Ch. 236.
[1] (1851) 5 De G. & Sm. 85.

basis that the communication of the trust was not admissible in evidence because a testator could not by will prospectively create for himself a power to dispose of his property by an instrument not duly executed as a will or codicil. The same principle was adopted in *Re Bateman's Will Trusts*[2] by Pennycuick V.-C., who thought the position to be "really clear."

In view of the foregoing it is no easy task to state the true principles on subsequent communications. There is no doubt that judicial opinion is against their admissibility. But the authors venture to think that this opinion is fallacious.[3] The basis of secret trusts—half-secret as well as fully secret—is that the trusts operate outside the will. The only necessity is that the will be validly made in accordance with the Wills Act; the Act is not concerned with the enforceability of the trust. The essence of the matter is or should be simply (i) a validly executed will which passes to X the title to the property and (ii) the acceptance by X of an obligation in the lifetime of the testator, before or after the execution of the will, but before the testator's death, by which X is equitably bound. A further reason for saying that a subsequent communication should be possible is that such a communication is, as has been seen, effectual in a fully secret trust and it might be thought somewhat inconsistent if this is not possible in a half-secret trust.

It might appear that there has been some confusion in *Re Keen* and the other cases between the equitable doctrine of secret trusts and the probate doctrine of incorporation by reference. This doctrine of probate means that it is possible to incorporate in a will, which has been validly made, a document which is not executed in accordance with the Wills Act. For the doctrine to apply, however, the document must be in existence at the date of the will and must be specifically referred to in the will. These conditions must be satisfied because, if not, that other rule comes into play, that a testator cannot prospectively reserve to himself a power to dispose of his property by an instrument not duly executed as a will or codicil.[4] But this rule is concerned purely with the validity of the will itself and the documents to be incorporated within it; it does not or should not relate to secret trusts which, according to true principle, operate outside the will.[5]

4. Those named as trustees[6]—and they will, of course, be named as such in a half-secret trust—cannot in any event take beneficially. Indeed, they are

---

[2] [1970] 1 W.L.R. 1463.

[3] See also Holdsworth (1937) 53 L.Q.R. 501; Snell (28th ed.), p. 113, Hanbury and Maudsley (11th ed.), p. 261; Keeton and Sheridan (10th ed.), p. 78; *Cf.* the Irish and American law which admits such communications: see Sheridan (1951) 67 L.Q.R. 314 (Irish); *Restatement of Law of Trusts*, p. 43 (American).

[4] See, *e.g. Re Jones* [1942] Ch. 328; *Re Edwards' Will Trusts* [1948] Ch. 440; *Re Schintz's Will Trusts* [1951] Ch. 870.

[5] *Cf.* Matthews (1979) Conv. 360.

[6] If the testator's directions are expressed *not* to create a trust they will of course take beneficially: *Re Falkiner* [1924] 1 Ch. 88; *Re Stirling* [1954] 1 W.L.R. 763. See also *Irvine* v. *Sullivan* (1869) L.R. 8 Eq. 673. On the other hand if the terms of the will do not create a trust but they agree with the testator to hold on trust, the trust will be enforceable: *Re Spencer's Will* (1887) 57 L.T. 519.

prohibited from adducing evidence to this effect. Accordingly, in *Re Rees*[7]; the trustee was named as such on the face of the will and directed to dispose of the estate in accordance with the testator's directions. The Court of Appeal held that he could not adduce evidence to show that he was, in fact, intended to be one of the beneficiaries. It follows that if the half-secret trust fails for any reason the trustees will hold upon trust for the residuary legatee or devisee if there is a gift of residue in the will; if there is no such residuary gift they will hold for those entitled on intestacy.

5. If a testator wishes to carry out his purpose by making a number of secret trusts piecemeal he must take the trustees into his confidence as to every addition to the secret object. Thus, in *Re Colin Cooper*[8] a testator by will bequeathed £5,000 to two trustees "upon trusts already communicated to them." He had in fact communicated the nature of such trusts to them. By a further will he purported to increase the sum to be devoted to the secret trust to £10,000 without informing the trustees. The result was that although the first instalment of £5,000 could be devoted to the secret trusts, the second instalment could not. This case involved a half-secret trust, but it seems clear that the principle of the decision should also apply to a fully secret trust.

(3) Gifts to concurrent owners on fully secret trusts

According to the law as it stands at the present time, it is necessary to make a distinction, which appears to be totally unjustified,[9] between joint tenancies and tenancies in common. It must be stressed that the rules apply only to fully secret trusts.

(a) **Joint tenants.** An antecedent promise merely by one of the joint tenants on the strength of which the will is made, binds both or all joint tenants. The reason is stated to be that no person can claim an interest under a fraud committed by another. But a subsequent promise by one of the joint tenants alone, on the strength of which the will is left unrevoked, binds only the one who promised if the other joint tenant or tenants know nothing of the matter until the testator's death. The reason is stated to be that the gift is not tainted with any fraud in procuring the execution of the will,[10] but this explanation is inadequate: although there may be no fraud in the execution of the will, there may be fraud which induces the testator not to *revoke* his will once made.

(b) **Tenants in common.** An antecedent promise by one of the tenants in common, where the other knows nothing of the matter until after the testator's death, binds only the one who promised. A gift to tenants in common is therefore distinguishable in this respect from a similar gift to joint tenants. Furthermore, a subsequent promise by one of the tenants in common will bind

---

[7] [1950] Ch. 204; followed in *Re Pugh's Will Trusts* [1967] 1 W.L.R. 1262, but distinguished in *Re Tyler* [1967] 1 W.L.R. 1269.

[8] [1939] Ch. 811.

[9] See Perrins (1972) 88 L.Q.R. 225.

[10] See the discussion by Farwell J. in *Re Stead* [1900] 1 Ch. 237 at 241 where the cases in support of these propositions are reviewed.

only him. The reason stated for these rules is that to hold otherwise would enable one beneficiary to deprive the rest of their benefits by setting up a secret trust.[11]

The difference can be seen to lie in an antecedent promise: whether this binds both will depend on whether they are joint tenants or tenants in common. Although reasons have been judicially expressed, they appear to be completely lacking in merit.

(4) Express trust or constructive trust?

Secret trusts have been dealt with here under the heading of express trusts, but the view has been expressed that they—or at least fully secret trusts—are really constructive.[12] The point is of importance because it will determine whether a secret trust of land requires to be evidenced in writing under section 53(1)(b) of the Law of Property Act 1925.[13] Apparently, it will if it is express, but it will not if it is constructive.[14] It seems self-evident that a half-secret trust must be express because the trustees are actually named by the will even though the objects of the trust are not specified, and evidence in writing for such trusts if they relate to land will be required.[15] There is, however, perhaps more to be said for including a fully secret trust among constructive trusts because the existence of the trust is fully concealed. But even here it seems that a trust has *been declared*, albeit in secrecy, and because of that must be express. If so it will also need to be evidenced in writing if it relates to land. But there remains a possibility: it may be open to the court to say, with regard to both fully secret and half-secret trusts, that it will not allow section 53(1)(b) to be used as an instrument of fraud.[16] The argument would be that if a fraudulent purpose[17] would otherwise be effected, the court could impose a constructive trust upon the alleged trustee, and that that trust would be enforceable notwithstanding the absence of writing. This would have the result that what is *ex hypothesi* an (unenforceable) express trust would be transmuted into a constructive trust which could be enforced. There seems to be no objection in principle to such a result.[18]

III. EXECUTED AND EXECUTORY TRUSTS

The basic distinction between such trusts has already been mentioned[19]: we are now concerned with amplifying this distinction and also with distinguishing both

---

[11] See note 2, *ante*.

[12] Nathan and Marshall (7th ed.), p. 431.

[13] See *ante*, p. 23.

[14] L.P.A. 1925, s.53(2), see *ante*, p. 28.

[15] This was the decision in *Re Baillie* (1886) 2 T.L.R. 660; see also Sheridan (1951) 67 L.Q.R. 314.

[16] See *ante*, p. 30.

[17] In the meaning discussed *ante*, p. 32.

[18] It is perhaps fair to point out that in some modern cases such as *Ottaway* v. *Norman* [1972] Ch. 698 (discussed *ante*, p. 35) which involved real property, and where documentary evidence was lacking, the question was not considered.

[19] See *ante*, p. 19.

such trusts from trusts which are completely or incompletely constituted. An executed trust arises when the settlor has defined in the trust instrument precisely what interests are to be taken by the beneficiaries.[20] An executory trust, on the other hand, arises where the instrument or declaration requires the subsequent execution of a further instrument and does not itself define precisely the terms of that instrument.[21]

The practical importance of the distinction between executed and executory trusts lies in the field of construction although since 1925 the position is no longer of as much importance as it used to be.[22] The construction of an executed trust is governed by rules of law, whereas executory trusts are construed more liberally and always with a view to carrying out the settlor's true intention. This may be illustrated by comparing two cases. On the one hand, in *Re Bostock's Settlement*,[23] the settlor had omitted certain words of limitation which, if they had been inserted, would have given the fee simple to the beneficiaries. It was held that, in the absence of such words, the beneficiaries took only a life estate even though it was probably intended that the beneficiaries should take the fee simple. This was a case of an executed trust and in the absence of the necessary technical expressions the limitation was construed according to rules of law. On the other hand, in *Glenorchy* v. *Bosville*[24] the testator devised real property to trustees upon trust to convey the estate, after the marriage of his grand-daughter, to the use of her for life, remainder to the use of her husband for life, remainder to the use of the issue of her body. Under the rule of construction known as the rule in *Shelley's Case*[25] the grand-daughter would have taken an estate tail if this had been an executed trust. But as this was a case of an executory trust the court could look into the true intention of the testator. His intention was clearly to provide for the children of the marriage, and it was held that the trustees should, regardless of the rule in *Shelley's Case*, convey the property to the granddaughter for life, remainder to her first and other sons in tail, remainder to her daughter.

These cases illustrate the practical importance of the distinction between executed and executory trusts in matters of construction. But there is one case where it might be argued that the distinction is not as clear-cut as is often thought. This case is *Re Arden*[26] where it was held, in effect, that the use of an untechnical expression by the creator of an executed trust gave the court a loophole for applying a construction in accordance with the real intentions of the settlor. Here the settlor had used the word "absolutely," and Clauson J. held that the use of this word entitled him to decide that the beneficiaries in whose favour it was used took an equitable fee simple, though if it had been

---

[20] See *Egerton* v. *Brownlow* (1853) 4 H.L.C. 1, at p. 210, *per* Lord St. Leonards.

[21] Nevertheless the directions as to the trusts to be defined must not be too ambiguous; if they are there will be no executory trust: *Re Flavel's Will Trusts* [1969] 1 W.L.R. 444.

[22] See *post*, p. 43.

[23] [1921] 2 Ch. 469.

[24] (1733) Cas.*t*.Talb. 3, see also *Papillon* v. *Voice* (1728) P.Wms. 471.

[25] (1581) 1 Co.Rep. 88b. This case will not apply to instruments taking effect after 1925: see *post*, p. 43.

[26] [1935] Ch. 326.

omitted, it was acknowledged that he would only have taken a life estate. If this decision is correct, and doubts may be entertained as to that, an untechnical expression may be given a technical meaning even in an executed trust, but the lack of such an expression—as in *Re Bostock's Settlement*[27]—has the effect prescribed by law.

1. *Marriage Articles*

One class of executory trusts has been given special treatment. These are executory trusts arising under marriage articles. In such a case the presumption is that the intention of the settlor was to provide for the issue of the marriage, so that despite any technical rule of construction the husband and wife will normally take life interests.[28] And the presumption will apply unless the parties clearly intended to create some other interest. This presumption is a strong one and will only be rebutted by the clearest evidence to the contrary. It was particularly significant in the application of the rule in *Shelley's Case*. In a limitation of land before 1926 for X for life, remainder to the heirs of his body, X would have taken an estate tail by reason of the rule of construction established by this case. But if an executory trust on these lines was contained in marriage articles the court would strive to avoid this construction and give only a life estate. For otherwise he could bar the entail, that is, bar his successors' interest, and thereby convert his interest into a fee simple, thus defeating his issue. But in the case of other executory trusts, which will normally arise under wills, the court, although it will, of course, construe the instrument with a view to ascertaining the settlor's true intention, will consider the whole question of construction on its merits. So, in the ancient case of *Sweetapple* v. *Bindon*[29] a testator gave £300 to trustees upon trust to lay it out in the purchase of land and settle the land to "the only use of M and her children," and if M died without issue "the land to be divided between her brothers and sisters then living." The question of construction, since this was an executory trust under a will, was approached on these lines: there was no overriding necessity to give M a life interest and it was held that M took an estate tail.

2. *Effect of* 1925 *Legislation*

The whole of the foregoing still applies in principle but it—and the cases given in illustration—must now be read subject to the effect of the 1925 legislation. This has done two things in this context: it has, as to instruments taking effect after 1925—(i) abolished the rule in *Shelley's Case*[30] and (ii) removed the necessity for words of limitation for the creation of a fee simple.[31] But the distinction must still be borne in mind because of the continuing necessity for words of limitation for the creation of entailed interests.[32]

---

[27] [1921] Ch. 469.
[28] *Jervoise* v. *Duke of Northumberland* (1820) 1 Jac. & W. 559 at p. 574; *Trevor* v. *Trevor* (1720) 1 P.Wms. 622.
[29] (1706) 2 Vern. 536.
[30] L.P.A. 1925, s.131.   [31] *Ibid.* s.60.   [32] *Ibid.* s.130.

3. *Distinction from Completely and Incompletely Constituted Trusts*

It is important to notice that in the case both of an executed and of an executory trust, the trust itself is completely constituted. This is so because *ex hypothesi* the trust property will be vested in the trustees in both cases. In an executory trust the trustees may have duties to perform with regard to the definition of the trust but the trust itself will be perfectly created. Indeed, the question whether a trust is executed or executory will only arise if this is so.

IV. Completely and Incompletely Constituted Trusts

In this subject the equitable maxims—"Equity will not assist a volunteer" and "Equity will not perfect an imperfect gift" may apply. The question in issue will be whether the beneficiaries can enforce the trust. And in answering the question, the most important point is whether or not the trust has been completely constituted, *i.e.* whether it has been perfectly created. If it has, it will be enforceable by the beneficiaries against the trustees and, moreover, will be binding upon everyone with the exception of a bona fide purchaser of the legal estate for value. A trust which has not been perfectly created cannot operate as a trust; it will only be enforceable as a contract to create a trust, and to be enforceable as such it requires consideration from the beneficiaries. Equity will not assist a volunteer.

There are two questions to consider: (i) When is a trust completely constituted? (ii) If it is not, who is a volunteer? An express trust is completely constituted either by an effective transfer of the trust property to trustees or by an effective declaration of trust. The implications of this principle were clearly brought out in the classic judgment of Turner L.J. in *Milroy* v. *Lord*[33] when he said: "In order to render a voluntary settlement valid and effectual, the settlor must have done everything which according to the nature of the property comprised in the settlement was necessary to be done in order to render the settlement binding upon him. He may, of course, do this by actually transferring the property to the persons for whom he intends to provide and the provision will then be effectual and it will be equally effectual if he transfers the property to a trustee for the purposes of the settlement, or declares that he himself holds it in trust for those purposes; and if the property is personal, the trust may, as I apprehend, be declared either in writing or parol; but, in order to render the settlement binding, one or other of these modes must, as I understand the law of this court, be resorted to, for there is no equity in this court to perfect an imperfect gift."

1. *Transfer of Trust Property*

If the subject matter of the trust is a legal estate or interest the transfer must be effective to vest such estate in the trustees. This has the consequence that the settlor must comply with all the formalities required for a complete transfer of

---

[33] (1862) 4 De G.F. & J. 264, at p. 274, applied and quoted by Upjohn J. in *Re Wale* [1956] 1 W.L.R. 1346.

the property in order that the trustees have a full legal title to it. Thus if land is the subject matter of the trust it should be conveyed by deed[34]; if it is copyright then writing is necessary[35]; if it is a bill of exchange payable to bearer, delivery and indorsement are necessary,[36] and if it is shares in a company the correct form of transfer should be used.[37] And although personal chattels can be transferred by mere delivery, the delivery must be effectual. This last point is illustrated by the decision of the Court of Appeal in *Re Cole*[38] where the facts of the case, concerning an alleged delivery of furniture by husband to wife who were living together in a common establishment, did not unequivocally establish a change in possession or delivery of the furniture and accordingly there was no effected or perfected gift to her. The curt rejected a contention to the effect that a perfect gift of chattels is constituted simply by showing them to the donee and speaking words of gift.

The rules which apply to the complete constitution of a trust apply also where the intention is to make a direct gift to a donee. The gift will fail if anything remains to be done by the donor to divest himself of the legal title: the same formalities must be observed. Equity will not perfect an imperfect gift.

(1) Transfer of shares

A number of modern cases involving the transfer of shares in a company illustrate these propositions. In *Re Fry*,[39] for example, the intending donor, who was domiciled in the United States, had shares in a limited company. He executed transfers of these shares, partly by way of gift to his son and partly to a trust. The company were unable to register the transfers because the consent of the Treasury had not been obtained under the Defence Regulations then operative. The forms required for obtaining this consent were sent to him; he signed them and posted them back to England. But he died before the consent was given. Romer J. held that the trust was not completely constituted and the shares, therefore, formed part of his residuary estate. It appeared that in order to perfect the transaction it would have been necessary for the donor to effect confirmatory transfers after the consent had been given.[40] The principle that emerges from this case is that if something remains to be done by the transferor in order to render the voluntary transfer effective, then it will remain abortive.[41] But if the transferor has done everything which it is necessary for him to do to render it effectual but something has yet to be done by a third party, the transfer will be valid *in equity*. Thus, in *Re Rose*[42] the transferor executed on March 30 transfers of shares in a company to be held on trust. The transfers were

---

[34] L.P.A. 1925, s.52.

[35] Copyright Act 1956, s.5(2).

[36] See *Antrobus* v. *Smith* (1806) 12 Ves. 39; *Jones* v. *Lock* (1865) 1 Ch.App. 25.

[37] *Milroy* v. *Lord* (1862) 4 De G.F. & J. 264; *Re Wale* [1956] 1 W.L.R. 1346, see also, *post*, p. 46. The relevant Act is the Stock Transfer Act 1963, s.1.

[38] [1964] Ch. 175.

[39] [1946] Ch. 312.

[40] *Ibid.* at p. 316.

[41] See also *Letts* v. *I.R.C.* [1951] 1 W.L.R. 201 (direction by father to company to allot shares direct to children).

[42] [1952] Ch. 499, following *Re Rose* [1949] 1 Ch. 78.

registered by the company on June 30. The transferor died more than five years after the execution of the transfers, but within five years of the registration by the company. The transaction would not have attracted estate duty if the gift had been made five years or more before his death. The all-important question in this case, therefore, was whether or not the gift had been perfected at the date of execution of the transfer. The Court of Appeal held there was nothing more the transferor could do to divest himself of the shares in favour of the transferees. The formality of registration was to be performed by a third party, namely the company, and the transferor had nothing to do with that. Accordingly, the transfer was effective in equity. By effectiveness in equity is meant that until the registration is effected by the company the transferor will be a trustee for the transferee: when it is effected the transfer will be effective at law.

The case of *Re Vandervell's Trusts (No. 2)*,[43] however, raises some difficulties in this respect. Lord Denning M.R., as an alternative ground for his decision, was of the opinion[44] that Mr. Vandervell had made a perfect gift to the trustee company of the dividends on the shares "so far as they were handed over or treated by him as belonging to the trustee company for the benefit of the children." In this he purported to follow *Milroy* v. *Lord*.[45] In that case bank shares were not formally transferred to the trustee, and accordingly the transfer was ineffective and the bank shares belonged to the settlor's estate. However, dividends had been paid by the bank to the trustee who paid them to the beneficiary who in turn used them to buy shares in a company. It was held that the settlor should be treated as having made a gift of the dividends to the beneficiary and, therefore, his executors had no claim to the shares which had been purchased with the dividends. One would have thought, however, that the two cases were distinguishable: in *Re Vandervell's Trusts (No. 2)*, Mr. Vandervell was unaware that he retained an equitable interest in the option relating to the shares of his products company.

(2) **Equitable interests**

The foregoing cases are illustrations of the important rule that if the subject-matter of the trust of gift is a legal interest the transferor must do everything that he can do to render it completely constituted. The same principle applies to the transfer of an equitable interest. It is not, of course, necessary for the transferor to procure a conveyance of the legal estate (which is in the trustees): all that is necessary is that he should make a perfect assignment of his interest, which in this case will be universally required by section 53(1)(c) of the Law of Property Act 1925 to be in writing.[46] This assignment will, where a trust is being constituted, be followed by a direction to the trustees to hold it in future upon trust for the assignee.[47] This is as much as the transferor of an equitable interest

---

[43] [1974] Ch. 269. The facts are stated *ante*, p. 26.
[44] *Ibid.* at p. 321.   [45] (1862) 4 De G.F. & J. 264.
[46] See *Kekewich* v. *Manning* (1851) De G.M. & G. 176 (assignment of equitable reversionary interest in shares); *Gilbert* v. *Overton* (1864) 2 H. & M. 110 (assignment of agreement for lease); and see *ante*, p. 24.
[47] See *Grey* v. *I.R.C.* [1960] A.C. 1 (direction to trustees to hold on trust may take effect as an assignment), discussed *ante*, p. 24.

is able to do. But the fact that this at least must be done is shown by the decision of the Court of Appeal in *Re McArdle*.[48] In this case, X and his brothers and sister were entitled under the will of their father to a house after the death of their mother, and X and his wife lived with her in that house. After the wife had effected various improvements to the house, X and his brothers and sister signed a document addressed to her, stating that "in consideration of your carrying out certain alterations and improvements to the property . . . we . . . hereby agree that the executors . . . shall repay to you from the estate when distributed the sum of £488" in settlement of the amount spent on improvement. The court held, in effect, that the document was neither one thing nor the other. If it was contractual it lacked consideration (the consideration being past). If it was an attempted gift it was imperfect, because the donors had not done all that lay in their power to make the gift complete: it was still necessary for them to authorise the executors to pay and until this was done it was ineffectual.

2. *Declaration of Trust*

An effective transfer to trustees is the first means by which a trust may be completely constituted. The second means is by a declaration of trust by the settlor, although, in fact, it is much more common for a settlor to transfer property to trustees than to declare himself to be a trustee. It is not necessary, however, in order to amount to an effective declaration that the settlor should say, in terms, "I hereby declare myself to be a trustee." Any words that clearly express the intention to create a present irrevocable trust are effectual. At the same time, this intention must be satisfactorily shown. This was not the case in *Jones* v. *Lock*,[49] which may also be considered in relation to the question whether a transfer is effective. The facts were that a father put a cheque into the hands of his son saying: "Look you here, I give this to baby; it is for himself." Then he took back the cheque and put it away. He subsequently reiterated his intention of giving the amount of the cheque to his son. Shortly afterwards the father died and the cheque was found among his effects. Lord Cranworth L.C. held that there was neither a gift nor a valid declaration of trust. It was quite impossible to regard the somewhat theatrical exercise enacted by the father as a delivery of the moneys represented by the cheque. To effect a perfect transfer he should have opened a bank account in his son's name or in the name of trustees on his son's behalf. Nor had he made a valid declaration of trust: the inference that he had made himself a trustee could not be deduced from his words and actions. It is also established that even though it is clear that the transferor intended to create a trust *by transfer*, but he happens to use an ineffectual method of transfer, that in itself will not be interpreted as an effectual declaration of trust. Thus, in *Richards* v. *Delbridge*,[50] the deceased owned certain leasehold premises. He indorsed and signed on the lease a

---

[48] [1951] Ch. 669.
[49] (1865) 1 Ch.App. 25.
[50] (1874) L.R. 18 Eq. 11.

memorandum in these words: "This deed and all thereto I give to R from this time forth, with all the stock-in-trade." The Court of Appeal held there was no perfected transfer, for the indorsement, not being under seal, was ineffective to transfer the leasehold interest. Nor could it in the circumstances take effect as a declaration of trust. This case, therefore, plainly establishes the principle that, however clearly there may have been an intention to create a trust by transfer, this will not be construed as a declaration of trust if an ineffectual method of transfer is used. But although this is so, there may be in a particular case be an effective declaration of trust as well as an ineffective transfer. Thus, in *Re Ralli's Will Trusts*[51] Buckley J. held that there was both a covenant to settle property *and* a declaration of trust of that property whilst the covenant remained to be honoured, and that declaration was effectual.

In such cases it is a question of construction of the words used, taking into account the surrounding circumstances, whether they amount to a clear declaration of trust. So, in *Paul* v. *Constance*,[52] acknowledged[53] to be a "borderline" case, the words used by the deceased were, "The money is as much yours as mine," often repeated to the plaintiff, a woman with whom he had lived for a number of years. He was referring to money in a bank account. It was held, distinguishing *Jones* v. *Lock* and *Richards* v. *Delbridge*, that the words, taken with the use of the account, conveyed a present declaration that the plaintiff was entitled to half of the existing balance.

The foregoing appears to be reasonably clear, but the requirements, it seems, were materially relaxed in *Re Vandervell's Trusts (No. 2)*.[54] The Court of Appeal managed to find an effective declaration of trust by the trustee company of shares in favour of a settlement for the benefit of Mr. Vandervell's children from the following facts: (1) the trustee company had used £5,000 from the children's settlement for the purpose of exercising an option to re-purchase the shares; (2) that thereafter all dividends received by the trustee company were paid by them to the children's settlement and treated as part of the funds of that settlement; and (3) that the solicitors for the trustee company had written to the Revenue stating that the shares would be held on the trusts of the settlement. None of these facts, least of all the third, would, however, seem to indicate a present irrevocable declaration of trust[55]; and, in addition, as Stephenson L.J. indicated, there may be difficulties in a limited company (as the trustee company was) declaring a trust by parol or conduct and without a resolution of the board of directors.[56] There also remains the problem arising from a failure to comply with section 53(1)(c) of the Law of Property Act 1925 requiring a disposition in writing of the equitable interest apparently outstanding in Mr. Vandervell to the trustee company to hold on trust.[57]

---

[51] [1964] Ch. 288. See also *Middleton* v. *Pollock* (1876) 2 Ch.D. 194, where effective declarations of trust were made.
[52] [1977] 1 W.L.R. 527.
[53] *Ibid.* at 532 *per* Scarman L.J.
[54] [1974] Ch. 269. The facts are stated in detail at p. 26, *ante*.
[55] The question was not argued before Megarry J. at first instance.
[56] *Ibid.*, at p. 323.
[57] See *ante*, p. 28.

It will be recalled that a declaration of trust must be evidenced in writing if it concerns land.[58]

Volunteers

Effectual transfer or declaration is the method by which a trust is completely constituted. If it is not completely constituted because the methods of creation are ineffectual, then the equitable maxim that equity will not assist a volunteer applies. A trust which is not completely constituted is only enforceable as an agreement to create a trust and this will only be so if consideration is furnished. To put this in another way, if A promises B that he will create a trust but fails to do so, or alternatively, creates it imperfectly, then B can only compel the performance of the trust if he is not a volunteer.[59] A person is not a volunteer if (i) he has given valuable consideration in the common law sense, *e.g.* money or money's worth, or (ii) he is within a marriage consideration. It will be observed that "good consideration" (such as natural love and affection *simpliciter*) is not enough. The notion of "valuable consideration" is self-evident, but marriage as consideration requires further discussion. There are two basic points to notice here. Either the settlement must be made before and in consideration of marriage or, alternatively, if made after marriage, it must be made in pursuance of an ante-nuptial agreement.

The principles are illustrated by the case of *Pullan* v. *Koe*.[60] A wife was given a sum of money which was bound by a covenant executed by herself and her husband in their marriage settlement to settle her after-acquired property. The money was eventually invested in bonds which remained at the husband's bank. When the husband died the bonds came into his executor's hands. There were several children by the marriage and since, therefore, they were within the marriage consideration they could enforce the transfer of the bonds to the trustees of the marriage settlement.

But if the settlement is made after marriage and not in pursuance of an ante-nuptial agreement, it is voluntary. This is so because, although there may be consideration between husband and wife, that consideration would not be their marriage—such being past—but consideration of some other kind to which their children would be strangers.[61]

It now appears to be settled, subject to one qualification,[62] that the only persons within the marriage consideration are the husband, wife and issue[63] of the marriage. For example, in *Re Cook's Settlement Trusts*,[64] C had covenanted in a settlement with his father and trustees not to sell certain property (including valuable paintings) which had been transferred to him by his father, and that if

---

[58] Law of Property Act 1925, s.53(1)(*b*), see p. 23 *ante*.
[59] *Ellison* v. *Ellison* (1802) 6 Ves. 656, at p. 662, *per* Lord Eldon L.C.; see also *Jefferys* v. *Jefferys* (1841) Cr. & Ph. 138.
[60] [1913] 1 Ch. 9.
[61] *Re Cook's Settlement Trusts* [1965] Ch. 902.
[62] See *infra*.
[63] Issue includes children and grandchildren; see *MacDonald* v. *Scott* [1893] A.C. 642 at p. 650.
[64] [1965] Ch. 902.

any such paintings were sold the proceeds of sale should be held by his trustees on trust for C's children. In 1962 C gave to his then wife a painting by Rembrandt. She wanted to sell it. The sons and daughters of his previous marriages contended that the gift to her was ineffective. Buckley J. held they were volunteers and not being parties to the covenant could not enforce it.

But there is, as already indicated, a qualification to this general rule. Even if it is not yet decisive, there is some authority for the proposition that children of an earlier marriage may enforce a covenant where their interests are "interwoven" with those of the children of the marriage in consideration of which the covenant is made. This was suggested in *Att.-Gen.* v. *Jacobs-Smith*[65] and was supported by Buckley J. in *Re Cook's Settlement Trusts.*[66] But this qualification, which in any case is somewhat ambiguous, appears to go only thus far and will not apparently be extended. It was not extended to the children in this last mentioned case because the covenant in question was not made in consideration of marriage.

At any rate, there is no doubt that the next-of-kin of the settlor are volunteers and this will be so whatever the settlor's intention may have been. This is illustrated by *Re Plumptre's Settlement*[67]: the husband and wife, on their marriage, covenanted with their trustees to settle the wife's after-acquired property for the benefit of herself and her husband successively for life, then for the issue of the marriage and then for the wife's next-of-kin. The husband bought certain stock in the wife's name and the wife afterwards sold it and invested the proceeds of sale in other stock. The wife then died without issue, leaving her husband her administrator. It was held that the next-of-kin, because they were volunteers, could not enforce the wife's covenant against her husband as administrator. Nor (it was also held) could the trustees sue for damages for breach of covenant because the claim was statute-barred.

(a) Contracts under seal

The last point emerging from *Re Plumptre's Settlement*[68] has been found to have complicated implications. In the case of a contract under seal, the absence of consideration is not relevant and one might have thought that, if the claim is not statute-barred, the trustees could make use of the usual common law remedy of suing for damages for breach of covenant. But the position is not nearly so straightforward as that. The question under consideration is illustrated by *Re Pryce,*[69] where a covenant in a contract under seal was made to settle after-acquired funds ultimately for the next-of-kin. Eve J. held that the next-of-kin were volunteers who could not enforce the covenant and, furthermore, that the court would not direct the trustees to perform it or indeed to claim damages for breach of covenant, because to do so would give to the next-of-kin by indirect means what they could not obtain by direct procedure. Indeed, the

---

[65] [1895] 2 Q.B. 341, at p. 354, *per* Kay L.J.

[66] *Ante.* See also *Re D'Avigdor-Goldsmid* [1951] Ch. 1038 at p. 1053 (overruled on other grounds [1953] A.C. 347).

[67] [1910] 1 Ch. 609. See also to a like effect *Re D'Angibau* (1880) 15 Ch.D. 228.

[68] *Supra.*

[69] [1917] 1 Ch. 234.

position was taken further by Simonds J. in *Re Kay's Settlement*[70] where he went so far as to direct the trustees not to sue. Unlike the decision in *Re Pryce* where the decision was negative in its effect that the trustee should not sue, in *Re Kay's Settlement* the court made a positive intervention. These cases have since been followed in *Re Cook's Settlement Trusts*.[71] In all of them the trustees simply sought the directions of the court, but it would be highly surprising if the trustees could sue directly (*i.e.* without seeking directions) or if they did that they would be successful.[72]

However, no difficulties will apparently arise if the volunteer is a party to the deed in question and a direct covenantee under it: he will be entitled to damages for breach of the covenant contained in the deed. This was in fact decided in *Cannon* v. *Hartley*[73] where a father had refused to implement a clause in a deed of separation by which he covenanted to settle after-acquired property on his wife and daughter. After the wife's death, the daughter, who had been expressed as a party to the deed, sued for damages for breach of covenant and it was held that she could recover. This case is authority for the proposition that a volunteer, if a party to the deed of covenant to create a trust, is entitled to damages (which are a *common law* remedy for breach of covenant) even though no consideration moves from the covenantee. But the principle seems clear in the present state of the law that neither a trustee on behalf of a volunteer nor the volunteer himself (not being a party to the covenant) can come to a court of equity—even if the contract is made under seal—and ask for relief peculiar to that court. Equity will not order specific performance of voluntary promises, even though under seal—a rule laid down by Lord Eldon many years ago[74]— and this principle perhaps accounts for the decisions in *Re Pryce*[75] and *Re Kay's Settlement*,[75] where the assistance of a court of equity was invoked even though with a view to obtaining a common law remedy.

The judiciary's approach has been strenuously criticised.[76] The argument is that *Re Pryce* and *Re Kay* were wrongly decided,[77] that a trust of the benefit of a

---

[70] [1939] Ch. 329.   [71] [1965] Ch. 902.

[72] Nevertheless the argument has been put forward (see Elliott (1960) 76 L.Q.R. 100 who also argues that the damages would be substantial; see also Hornby (1962) 78 L.Q.R. 228). There is, however, a case for the damages being nominal, the trustees not having themselves suffered damage. Another opinion is that the damages would be substantial but held on a resulting trust for the settlor (Lee (1969) 85 L.Q.R. 213). There is also debate as to whether the trustees "may" (according to Elliott) or "must" (according to Hornby) sue for such damages. If the argument were in essence a valid one, the latter view would seem to be correct, since otherwise the trustees would be in breach of trust.

[73] [1949] Ch. 213.

[74] *Ellison* v. *Ellison* (1802) 6 Ves. 656 at p. 662: " . . . if you want the assistance of the court to constitute you *cestui que trust*, and the instrument is voluntary, you shall not have that assistance. . . . "   [75] *Supra*.

[76] See Elliott (1960) 76 L.Q.R. 100; Hornby (1962) 78 L.Q.R. 228; Barton (1975), 91 L.Q.R. 236; Meagher and Lehane (1976) 92 L.Q.R. 427. *Cf.* Lee (1969) 85 L.Q.R. 213; Friend (1982) Conv. 280, who argue to the opposite effect.

[77] Elliott subjects *Re Pryce* to detailed linguistic analysis. His argument appears to run as follows: The question before the court was whether the trustees were "bound" to enforce the covenant; Eve J. answered the question by holding that they "ought" not to do so; but this was not the answer to the question; the judge should have held that they "need not"; accordingly the decision on "ought not" was *obiter*. See also note 72 *ante*.

contract is in fact capable of being completely constituted; and if it is so constituted it is enforceable by the trustees or the volunteer-beneficiaries.[78] There is no doubt that the benefit of a contract is capable of being the subject-matter of a trust and in some cases this has been held to be the position.[79] For example, in *Fletcher* v. *Fletcher*,[80] an obscure decision which has achieved a certain prominence in modern legal writings, Wigram V.-C. said that there can quite easily be a trust of a covenant the benefit of which effectively belongs to a third party. Here the settlor by a voluntary deed covenanted with trustees that if X and Y (who were his natural sons) or either of them should survive him, his personal representatives should within a period of 12 months pay £60,000 to the trustees to hold on trust for X and Y or whoever of them should attain 21. It was held that this created a trust in favour of X who, as it happened, alone survived the testator and, although the trustees declined to sue for breach of covenant, X was nevertheless held entitled to recover payment from the assets of the settlor.

The facts of this case hardly indicate that a trust was indeed intended, but assuming for the sake of argument that this was the intention,[81] it does not appear to assist the critics of the present state of the law. The reason (as expressed by Buckley J. in *Re Cook's Settlement Trusts*[82]) is this: that in cases like *Re Pryce* and *Re Kay* there was not, as there may have been in *Fletcher* v. *Fletcher*, a debt enforceable at law which was capable of being the subject-matter of a trust[83]; or any other definite property which was then in existence[84] but simply an executory contract to settle property which at that date did not exist and might never come into existence. As Buckley J. said, this involves the law of contract, not the law of trusts. In view of the weight of case law it is not surprising that he re-affirmed the conventional approach. In any case it will be recalled that other modern cases show that very clear words are required to create a trust of the benefit of a contract,[85] and it seems doubtful whether in *Fletcher* v. *Fletcher* the deduction was correctly made, even though the property in question was theoretically capable of being the subject matter of a trust.[86]

This is not to say that the present law is satisfactory. Far from it. But any reform of the law must hinge not merely on the ability of a volunteer who is not a party to the contract to create a trust to sue upon it, but also the whole doctrine of privity of contract which refuses a right of action to a third party.

---

[78] See, particularly, Hornby, *loc. cit.*

[79] See *ante*, p. 9.

[80] (1844) 4 Hare 67.

[81] The trustees were unaware of the alleged trust and wished to refuse it when they learned of it.

[82] [1965] Ch. 902 (the facts are discussed *ante*, p. 49.)

[83] It has been held that future property such as a mere expectancy cannot be the subject-matter of a trust: *Re Ellenborough* [1903] 1 Ch. 697. See also Lee, *loc. cit. cf.* Meagher and Lehane, *loc. cit.*

[84] As in *Re Cavendish Browne Settlement Trusts* [1916] W.N. 341.

[85] See *ante*, p. 10.

[86] Needless to say, perhaps, the debate continues. Meagher and Lehane (*loc. cit.*) have since argued that it is the benefit of the contract that is the subject-matter of the trust, and it is immaterial that the property to which the benefit relates may be after-acquired; and see also Friend (1982) Conv. 280.

(b) **Exceptions to the rule that equity will not assist a volunteer or perfect an imperfect gift**

The general rule is, as seen above, that equity will not assist a volunteer, and to enforce an incompletely constituted trust the plaintiff must have furnished valuable consideration as understood by the common law or brought himself within a marriage consideration. There are, however, a number of important exceptions to the general rule which will now be considered.

(i) *The rule in Strong v. Bird.*[87] The principle established by this case is that the intention to release a debt or make a gift is effected by making the debtor or donee one's executor. A complete gift involves two elements: an intention to make the gift, and the transfer of the legal title to the donee. The principle underlying *Strong v. Bird* is that where there is a continuing intention to make a gift the other requirement for a complete gift is fulfilled when the legal title vests in the executor by operation of law on the death of the donor. The appointment of the intended donee as executor perfects the intention of the donor and completes the gift. The equity of the beneficiaries (if any) under the will is said to be displaced by the donee's prior equity. The facts of *Strong v. Bird* were that the defendant borrowed £1,000 from his stepmother who lived in his house, paying £200 a quarter for board. It was agreed that the debt should be paid off by deduction of £100 from each quarter's payment. Deductions of this amount were made for two quarters, but on the third quarter-day the stepmother generously refused to hold to the agreement any longer and paid the full £200 board due on each quarter-day, and until her death four years later she continued to pay this amount each quarter. The defendant was the sole executor of her will and he proved the will. The next-of-kin then claimed that the defendant still owed the balance of the debt to her estate. It was held that the debt was extinguished because the appointment of the defendant as executor released it: any claim in equity was rebutted by evidence of a continuing intention to release it on the stepmother's part.

The same principle was applied, in *Re James*,[88] and, reluctantly, in *Re Gonin*,[89] to cases where the intended donee had taken out letters of administration to the donor's estate, and, in *Re Ralli's Will Trusts*,[90] to a trustee.

But it is essential to show a *continuing* intention to make an *immediate* gift *inter vivos*. Thus, in *Re Freeland*[91] a testatrix promised to give the plaintiff a motorcar at a future date but never did so. The plaintiff on the testatrix's death became her executrix and claimed that the imperfect gift had thereby been perfected. The Court of Appeal, however, refused to apply the rule in *Strong v. Bird* because the gift had never become absolute. Likewise, in *Re Gonin*,[89] Walton J. held that no such intention had been made out with regard to the gift

---

[87] (1874) 18 Eq. 315. See also *Re Stewart* [1908] 2 Ch. 251.

[88] [1935] Ch. 449.

[89] 1979 Ch. 16. Walton J. expressed the view that *Strong v. Bird* should only benefit an executor personally selected by the testator, not an administrator appointed by operation of law, which made the appointment "pure chance."

[90] [1964] Ch. 288.

[91] [1952] Ch. 110; see also *Re Innes* [1910] 1 Ch. 188.

of a house, but only to the furniture in it. It also appears from *Re Wale*[92] that the same result will follow if the testator, though having once had the intention to give, had forgotten about it and treated the property as his own. It is obvious that the donor in most cases will not be aware of the effect of an appointment of the donee as his personal representative and this was manifested in the somewhat novel circumstances of *Re Ralli's Will Trusts*.[93] Buckley J. there held that the means by which a trustee had acquired a legal title to the fund was irrelevant in deciding whether an imperfect gift had been perfected. This case demonstrates what may be the unexpected consequences of the doctrine itself; the appointment as trustee may have been, as it was in this case, a purely fortuitous event; nevertheless that was not material to the applicability of the doctrine.[94]

(ii) *Donationes mortis causa.* These gifts provide a further exception to the maxim that equity will not perfect an imperfect gift. For an effectual *donatio mortis causa*, however, four things must be present:

(A) The gift must have been made in contemplation of death. Here it is necessary only that the donor contemplated death at the time of the gift. Although the point has never been expressly decided in England[95]; the test would seem to be subjective and not objective. It is the donor's own state of mind, not the actual circumstances, which is material. Moreover, the title of the donee will not be invalidated if the donor dies from some other cause than, for example, the disease from which he is suffering.[96] So, in *Wilkes* v. *Allington*,[97] the donor was suffering from an incurable disease and made the gift knowing that he had not long to live. As things turned out, he lived an even shorter time than he thought, because he died two months later from pneumonia. The gift, however, remained valid.

(B) The gift must have been made under circumstances indicating that the subject matter of the gift is conditional on death. In this respect it is different from a gift *inter vivos* in that that is absolute, whereas a *donatio mortis causa* is necessarily conditional on death. The condition is not usually expressed but an inference to this effect will usually be made from the illness of the donor.[98] This means that the subject matter will revert to the donor if he recovers from his

---

[92] [1956] 1 W.L.R. 1346. See also *Re Eiser's Will Trusts* [1937] 1 All E.R. 244 (donor subsequently took security for the debt given).

[93] [1964] Ch. 288.

[94] See n. 89, *ante.*

[95] It appears that an objective test has been adopted in Canada: see the Canadian cases cited in n. 96, *post*; and see 81 L.Q.R. 21.

[96] It need not, perhaps, necessarily be illness, though it normally is. Nor apparently need the donor be *in extremis*. The contrary suggestion is made in *Thomson* v. *Meechan* [1958] D.L.R. 103, but this seems incorrect. For a similar suggestion, see *Canada Trust Co.* v. *Labrador* [1962] O.R. 151. See also 81 L.Q.R. 21.

[97] [1931] 2 Ch. 104 and see *Mills* v. *Shields* [1948] I.R. 367 (death from suicide); *cf. Re Dudman* [1925] Ch. 553 (contemplation of suicide insufficient) but this last case was decided before the Suicide Act 1961, under which suicide is no longer a crime; it is possibly arguable that such a gift may now be valid.

[98] *Re Lillingston* [1952] 2 All E.R. 184.

illness and also that it can at any time be revoked by the donor during his lifetime.[99]

Express revocation by the donor will essentially take the form of resuming dominion over it,[1] though there is some authority for the proposition that it is sufficient if the donor simply informs the donee of the revocation.[2] But a purported revocation by will is not enough because obviously the will cannot take effect until the death of the testator and at that time the donee will have become unconditionally entitled.[3]

Nevertheless, although conditional in this sense, it must be a *present* gift and not a gift to take effect in the future.[4]

(C) The donor must have delivered the subject matter of the gift to the donee or alternatively the means or part of the means of getting at the subject matter. It is, of course, a precondition, whatever the subject matter may be, that the donor intended to part with dominion[5] and this will be a matter of fact.

No difficulties will normally arise in the case of ordinary chattels. Delivery[6] will be effected either by delivery of the chattel itself or a means of getting at the chattel, *e.g.* the keys of a wardrobe containing it.[7] At the same time it must also be made in such circumstances as to demonstrate that the donor can no longer interfere with the subject matter.[8]

However, some choses in action, *e.g.* a bank account, are incapable of physical delivery[9] and the question will arise whether the donee can compel the personal representatives to complete the gift to him of the chose. The essential condition that must be satisfied is, according to the conventional formulation, that the donor must have delivered to the donee a document which is the essential evidence of his title to the chose in question. This test was applied in *Re Weston*,[10] where a dying man had handed over to his fiancée his Post Office Savings Bank book and this action was held sufficient to constitute an effective *donatio mortis causa* of the savings set out in it. It was in this last case that Byrne J. expressed the opinion that the document in question must contain all the essential terms of the contract. But this view has now been expressly disapproved by the Court of Appeal in *Birch* v. *Treasury Solicitor*.[11] It is easy to visualise circumstances where a strict application of the test would work in-

[99] *Staniland* v. *Willott* (1850) 3 Mac. & G. 664.
[1] *Bunn* v. *Markham* (1816) 7 Taunt. 224 at 231.
[2] *Jones* v. *Selby* (1710) Prec.Ch. 300 at p. 303. Resuming mere *possession* (*e.g.* for safe custody) is not enough: *Re Hawkins* [1924] 2 Ch. 47.
[3] *Jones* v. *Selby, supra.*
[4] *Re Ward* [1946] 2 All E.R. 206.
[5] *Birch* v. *Treasury Solicitor* [1951] Ch. 298.
[6] See *Re Cole* [1964] Ch. 175.
[7] *Re Mustapha* (1891) 8 T.L.R. 160 and see *Re Lillingston* [1952] 2 All E.R. 184.
[8] *Re Craven's Estates* (*No. 1*) [1937] Ch. 423 at 427, delivery of one of two keys is insufficient.
[9] A chose in action *may* be transferable by delivery, *e.g.* bearer bonds. Delivery of the documents will be sufficient to constitute an effective *donatio mortis causa*; see *Re Wasserberg* [1915] 1 Ch. 195. So also will, *e.g.* delivery of a key of a box containing such choses: *Re Wasserberg, supra.*
[10] [1902] 1 Ch. 680.
[11] [1951] Ch. 298.

justice, although it did not do so in *Re Weston*. The correct approach now, in the words of Lord Evershed M.R. in *Birch* v. *Treasury Solicitor*, is that a document should be delivered that would have to be produced in court in an action on the chose to establish the donee's title.

It must, however, be emphasised that a legal title to the chose in action will not be automatically acquired by the donee on delivery in the manner prescribed. The gift of the moneys or other property represented by the document will still be imperfect. But the important point is, in this context, that the donor's personal representative will be compelled to perfect it.[12] And it is therefore in the case of *donationes mortis causa* of choses in action that an exception to the general rule that equity will not perfect an imperfect gift occurs.

(D) The final requirement for an effective *donatio mortis causa* is that the property is capable of being the subject matter of such a gift. It has been seen that there can be a valid *donatio* by delivery if the property can pass by that means, or if it cannot, by handing over an appropriate document. In general it seems that most property is eligible.[13]

(iii) *Proprietary estoppel.* It would not perhaps be worth mentioning estoppel as it is commonly applied because this usually works only defensively so as to prevent a party asserting his rights. As such it does not operate to perfect an imperfect gift or complete an incompletely constituted trust.[14] But it appears to be the position that estoppel can in some cases be used *offensively*, "as a sword" as it is sometimes described, in order that, in this context, the imperfect gift can be perfected, if the donor stands by and watches the donee improve property or do other acts to his detriment on the supposition that there has been or will be an effective gift. The doctrine appears to be of early origin,[15] but it must be emphasised that it is recent cases which have resurrected it and its scope is not decisively determined.

A useful starting-point is *Dillwyn* v. *Llewelyn*[16] where a father put his son into possession of land without a conveyance. It was intended that the son should build a house on the land. The son successfully claimed that the land should be formally conveyed to him. Lord Westbury L.C. said: "If A puts B in possession of a piece of land and tells him 'I give it to you that you may build a house on it,' and B, on the strength of that promise, with the knowledge of A, expends a large sum of money in building a house accordingly, I cannot doubt that the donee acquires a right from the subsequent transaction to call on the

---

[12] *Re Dillon* (1890) 44 Ch. D. 76 at pp. 82–83.

[13] In *Duffield* v. *Elwes* (1827) 1 Bli.(N.S.) 497, Lord Eldon appeared to suggest that land is not capable of being the subject-matter of such a gift. On the other hand, the giving of the donor's cheque is clearly not sufficient to take effect as a D.M.C. because this is not property, but simply a revocable order to the bank to make payment to the payee: *Re Leaper* [1916] 1 Ch. 579.

[14] This is so in a case of so-called promissory estoppel. The latter, unlike proprietary estoppel, is also not permanent in its effect, for the promisor can resile from his position if he gives the promisee notice which provides him with a reasonable opportunity of resuming his former position: see *Re Vandervell* (*No. 2*) [1964] Ch. 269 at 301 *per* Megarry J.

[15] See *Foxcroft* v. *Lester* (1703) 2 Vern. 456.

[16] (1862) 4 De G.F. & J. 517.

donor to perform that contract, and complete the imperfect donation which was made." In other words, the subsequent acts of the donor gave the donee a right which he did not acquire from the original gift.

What estate or interest the donee takes depends on the circumstances of the case. In *Dillwyn* v. *Llewelyn* the donee took the fee simple. This was also the result more recently in *Pascoe* v. *Turner*[17] where the parties had lived together in a house as man and wife and the man had encouraged or acquiesced in the mistress improving the house in the belief that it belonged to her. He was ordered to execute a conveyance of the house to her. But the facts may indicate a lesser estate or some other right. Thus, in *Inwards* v. *Baker*[18] the donee was held entitled to remain in occupation as long as he wished. And in *E.R. Ives Investments Ltd.* v. *High*[19] the defendant was allowed a right of way so long as the plaintiff and his successors in title maintained the foundations of a building on the defendant's land, because the plaintiff's predecessors by licensing the defendant to use the yard in question had encouraged him to build a garage on it and this created an estoppel. Moreover the equitable interest which thus arose was not subject to the rules regarding the registration of land charges.[20]

Such cases were applied in *Crabb* v. *Arun District Council*[21] where there was an agreement "in principle" (not amounting to a contract) that the plaintiff should have a right of access, and relying on it he sold the front portion of his land without reserving a right of way over the back portion. It was held by the Court of Appeal that it was a case of proprietary estoppel entitling him to an easement or licence.[22] He had been encouraged to act to his detriment by the defendant's conduct.[23] Similarly, in *Jones* v. *Jones*,[24] T had led F to believe that a house would be his home for the rest of his life, and F had given up his job and moved on the basis of that expectation. It was held that he could pray in aid the doctrine of estoppel, and both T and his administrator were estopped from turning F out during his life. Again, in *Re Sharpe*,[25] where an aged aunt lent money for the purchase of a house by her nephew so that she could live with him and his wife in it, it was held that an irrevocable licence to occupy the house arose in favour of the aunt until the loan was repaid.

Moreover, the burden of proof is on the plaintiff to show that the defendant has not acted to his detriment or prejudice where the latter relies upon estoppel. So, in *Greasley* v. *Cooke*[26] assurances had been given that the defendant could

---

[17] [1979] 1 W.L.R. 431, C.A.
[18] [1965] 2 Q.B. 29, C.A. See also *Ward* v. *Kirkland* [1967] Ch. 194, where a perpetual easement of drainage was granted.
[19] [1967] 2 Q.B. 289, C.A.
[20] Under the Land Charges Act 1972.
[21] [1976] Ch. 179.
[22] An easement (according to Lord Denning M.R. and Lawton L.J.); an easement or licence (according to Scarman L.J.).
[23] One of the acts to his detriment was the sale of land separate from the land over which the access was to be granted. Normally, the acts involve expenditure in relation to the actual land intended to be disposed of.
[24] [1977] 1 W.L.R. 438, C.A.
[25] [1980] 1 W.L.R. 219 (the facts are stated *ante*, p. 32).
[26] [1980] 1 W.L.R. 1306, C.A.

remain in a house, where not only had she been employed as a maid from 1938 but also had lived with one of the children of the family as man and wife. It was held that these assurances raised an equity in her favour and it was to be presumed that she had acted on the faith of those assurances. The plaintiffs failed to rebut the presumption.[27]

It is, however, essential for a case of proprietary estoppel that a party acted as he did to his detriment in the expectation of acquiring a right to or over somebody else's land. The point arose in *Western Fish Products Ltd.* v. *Penwith District Council.*[28] It was held on the facts that even if the plaintiffs had to their detriment spent money on their land at the encouragement of the Council, they had not done so in the expectation of acquiring any rights over the Council's or any other land and could not therefore rely on proprietary estoppel.[29]

Furthermore, to raise an estoppel of this kind, the conduct of the owner of the property must give rise in some degree to inequitable consequences, and it is conjectural whether this basic principle was correctly applied in *Re Vandervell's Trusts (No. 2)*[30] although it is fair to say that this was not the sole ground on which the Court of Appeal reached its decision.[31] The court was of opinion that if Mr. Vandervell, who had concurred in the dealings with the moneys and shares carried out by the trustee company,[32] had been alive, he would have been estopped from denying the existence of the beneficial interest for the children, and his executors could be in no better position. However, as Megarry J. pointed out at first instance,[33] the company had not been able to show that, when the option was exercised, Mr. Vandervell knew that he was the beneficial owner of it and, therefore, he was not guilty of any unconscionable behaviour, such behaviour being an element in establishing proprietary estoppel.[34] This argument which is based on the necessity for knowledge on the part of the person alleged to be estopped is attractive and would appear to be difficult to avoid, but Oliver J. appeared to reject it in *Taylors Fashions Ltd.* v. *Liverpool Victoria Trustees Co. Ltd.*[35] in holding that knowledge of the true position by the party alleged to be estopped was merely one of the relevant factors in the overall enquiry. The essential question was

---

[27] Lord Denning M.R. said (at p. 1311) that the incurring of expenditure of money or other prejudice was not a necessary element. However, this appears to be far too wide a generalisation. *cf.* Dunn L.J. at p. 1313.

[28] [1981] 2 All E.R. 204, C.A.; see also *Haslemere Estates Ltd.* v. *Baker* [1982] 3 All E.R. 525 (there was no legitimate hope or expectation of obtaining any interest in the land).

[29] It was also held that in any event an estoppel could not be raised to prevent a statutory body exercising its statutory discretion or performing a statutory duty; see also *Rootkin* v. *Kent County Council* [1981] 1 W.L.R. 1186 as to the exercise of a statutory discretion relating to the payment of travelling expenses of a school pupil.

[30] [1974] Ch. 269. The question was not fully argued before Megarry J. (whose decision was reversed) at first instance.

[31] See *ante*, p. 26.

[32] These dealings are referred to *ante*, p. 27.　　　　　　　　　　[33] *Ibid.* at p. 301.

[34] This is assuming that the court relied on proprietary estoppel. If the estoppel relied on was promissory (see *ante*, p. 56), Megarry J. said (at p. 302) that there would appear to be difficulty in establishing such an estoppel where the person making representations did not know his rights: but *cf. Amalgamated Investment & Property Co. Ltd.* v. *Texas Commerce International Bank Ltd.* [1982] Q.B. 84; leave to appeal dismissed, [1982] 1 W.L.R. 1, H.L.

[35] [1982] Q.B. 133n.

whether, in the particular circumstances, it would be unconscionable for a party to be permitted to deny that which, knowingly or unknowingly, he had allowed or encouraged another to assume to his detriment. Accordingly, it was held that the principle could apply where, at the time the expectation was encouraged, both parties (not just the representee) were acting under a mistake of law as to their rights.[36] This case, which emphasises the flexibility of the equitable doctrine did not involve the law of trusts, but if correctly decided must have its effect on it.

So far as the law of trusts is concerned, particularly in a tax case like *Re Rose*,[37] the doctrine could give rise to further difficulty. Thus, one question could be whether a gift or trust perfected by estoppel is to be regarded as being constituted at the making of the gift, or on the happening of the subsequent events which created the estoppel. The latter seems clearly to be the correct approach.[38] In other respects, however, the position is more doubtful. Thus, in *Williams* v. *Staite*,[39] Cumming-Bruce L.J. considered, without finding it necessary to decide the question, that the rights of an equitable licensee for life did not necessarily crystallise when his rights came into existence but when the court came to determine his interest (if any) in the property. Lord Denning M.R. also thought that in an extreme case an equitable licence might be revoked,[40] but the conduct of the licensees, involving excessive user and bad behaviour, was not of a kind to bring the equity established in their favour to an end; their behaviour could be remedied by damages. It may be debatable whether an established equity can be forfeited in this way, but at least it seems clear that, when a person is asserting a right to an equity for the first time, his conduct may be taken into account in deciding whether to implement it, thereby applying the basic maxim that "he who comes to equity must come with clean hands."[41] Indeed, very much must depend on the facts of the case. In some cases, such as *Re Sharpe*[42] where the licensee was not in any way guilty of misconduct, it is essential that the rights must have arisen at the time of the transaction in order that the licensee can have any rights the breach of which can be remedied, in which case the equity must predate any order of the court.[43] The distinction, it seems, is between the pre-existence of an equity and the manner in which the court may choose, in the exercise of its discretion on the facts, to implement it.

It should also be mentioned that the conveyancing implications of proprietary estoppel have not been fully worked out. In *Dodsworth* v. *Dodsworth*[44] the Court of Appeal held that if the equity were implemented by giving the claimant the right to occupy a house for his life, the result would be to create a tenancy for life within the Settled Land Act 1925, with the consequence that he would get

---

[36] See also *Thomas Bates & Son Ltd.* v. *Wyndhams (Lingerie) Ltd.* [1981] 1 W.L.R. 505: estoppel applied where the mistake was a unilateral rather than a common mistake.

[37] [1952] Ch. 499, discussed *ante*, p. 45.

[38] See generally on the subject, Jackson (1965) 81 L.Q.R. 84, 223; Poole (1968) 38 Conv. (N.S.) 96; Sunnucks (1968) 118 New L.J. 769.

[39] [1979] Ch. 291. C.A.   [40] *Ibid*. at p. 297.

[41] Goff L.J. was of this opinion in *Williams* v. *Staite (supra)*, at p. 299.

[42] [1980] 1 W.L.R. 219. The facts are stated *ante* p. 32.

[43] *Ibid*. at p. 225.   [44] (1973) 228 E.G. 1115.

more than it had ever been represented that he should have, because he would get the statutory powers of a tenant for life under the Act. But, as Goff L.J. indicated in *Griffiths* v. *Williams*,[45] the court did not seem to have considered what might be in such circumstances a difficult problem: what was the "settlement" within section 1(1) of the Settled Land Act 1925? It was not easy, he said, where an equity was being set up by these means, to see how that could be within the terms of the section. The question did not, however, arise for decision.[46]

(iv) *Statutory exceptions.* There are also exceptions provided for by statute:

(A) A minor cannot hold a legal estate in land.[47] But a conveyance of such an estate to him will (under section 19(6) of the Law of Property Act 1925 and under section 27(1) of the Settled Land Act 1925) operate as an agreement for valuable consideration by the grantor to execute a settlement in the minor's favour and in the meantime to hold the legal estate in trust for him.

(B) It is not possible to create a proper settlement of the legal estate in land without two documents—a trust instrument and a vesting deed or assent.[48] An instrument other than a vesting deed or assent will not pass the legal estate. However, under section 9 of the Settled Land Act such a document will operate as a trust instrument and, therefore, take effect as an enforceable trust. The trustees may then execute the appropriate vesting deed and indeed they are compelled to do so if the tenant for life under the settlement so requests.

V. CERTAINTY

1. *The Three Certainties of Trust*

In the leading case of *Knight* v. *Knight*[49] Lord Langdale laid down that three certainties are required for the creation of a trust:

(1) The words used must be so couched that, taken as a whole, they may be deemed to be imperative;
(2) The subject matter of the trust must be certain;
(3) The persons or objects intended to be benefited must also be certain.

(1) **Certainty of words**

Equity looks to the intent rather than the form. No particular form of words is required for the creation of a trust: the use of the word "trust" is not essential, though, of course, highly desirable. It is possible, therefore, that words expressing desire, belief, recommendation or hope (known as precatory words) may create a trust. And if an intention to create a trust can be clearly deduced from the expressions used by the settlor, even though these are in precatory form, the court will give effect to that intention.

---

[45] 74 *Guardian Gazette* 1130, December 21, 1977, C.A.
[46] For analogous conveyancing problems in constructive trusts, see *ante*, p. 31.
[47] L.P.A. 1925, s.1(6).
[48] S.L.A. 1925, s.4.
[49] (1840) 3 Beav. 148 at p. 173.

It is in connection with this subject that an important change in outlook has occurred. Before the middle of the nineteenth century, the courts tended to take the view that any expression of desire or hope or the like on the part of the testator was imperative and, therefore, created a binding trust. Indeed, it may be said that in the older cases on precatory trusts one can see an intention attributed to a testator which made for an artificial certainty where no certainty really existed. This practice derived from a rule relating to executors. When the estates of deceased persons were administered by the ecclesiastical courts an executor was permitted to take the residue of the estate (if any) which had been undisposed of by the will. This was obviously unsatisfactory and when the Court of Chancery took over this work it endeavoured to make the executor a *trustee* of the undisposed-of residue. This had the accidental consequence that the rules relating to certainty of words became confused with the equitable practice in respect of executors. Just as the Court of Chancery was anxious to make the executor a trustee of the undisposed-of residue for the next-of-kin so the court would seize on any expression of hope or desire to negative the presumption that the executor was intended to take beneficially. But the court also went so far as to regard in the same light any precatory words as sufficient to create a trust even though the alleged trustee was not an executor and even though there was no undisposed-of residue.

Thus the confusion apparently arose. However, in 1830, the Executors Act was passed providing that the executor should hold any undisposed-of residue for the next-of-kin unless the testator had shown an intention that the executor should take beneficially. The result of the statute was that it was no longer necessary or desirable to create a trust in cases where precatory words were used. And during the nineteenth century the change took place. Words such as "desire," "wish," "have full confidence" and so on received fresh considera- tion.[50] Thus, to take one of many cases, in *Re Adams and Kensington Vestry*,[51] a testator gave all his real and personal estate to his wife "in full confidence that she would do what was right as to the disposal thereof between my children." It was held that under these words the widow took an absolute interest in the property unfettered by any trust in favour of the children. It was also said that some cases had gone very far and unjustifiably imposed upon words a meaning beyond that which they would bear if looked at alone. It is perhaps true to say that by the time this well-known case was decided the wind had already changed direction and beneficiaries were no longer to be made into trustees unless this was clearly intended by the testator.

(a) **The modern test.** The intention of the testator became all-important. The use of precatory words can still create a trust in an appropriate case, but the intention to create it has to be established upon a construction of the instru- ment. The question what is an appropriate case can be peculiarly difficult in

---

[50] Perhaps the earliest case illustrating the new doctrine is *Lambe* v. *Eames* (1871) L.R. 6 Ch. 597 (property to be at disposal of widow "in any way she may think best for the benefit of herself and family").

[51] (1884) 27 Ch.D. 394.

practice. It cannot be considered *in vacuo* and can only be answered by examining carefully the words used in the instrument in question.[52] This fact one might think is self-evident. It was indeed stated as follows by Lindley L.J. in *Re Hamilton*[53]:

> "You must take the will which you have to construe and see what it means, and if you come to the conclusion that no trust was intended you say so, although previous judges have said the contrary on some wills more or less similar to the one you have to construe."

But perhaps some doubts were cast on this impeccable principle by *Re Steele's Will Trusts*[54] for Wynn-Parry J.'s judgment is capable of meaning that if in fact identical words to those before the court had been held to create a trust in a previous case that case should be followed unless it was clearly wrongly decided. Such an approach is rather different from a construction of the instrument on its merits, albeit taking other earlier decisions into account.[55]

(b) **Illustrations of the modern rule.** It would be a difficult—and probably also a fruitless—exercise to consider even a small number of the many cases on this topic. But at the risk of making the subject seem easier than it is, two cases, one on each side of the line, may be considered. On the one hand there is *Re Diggles*[56] where a testatrix gave all her property to her daughter, her heirs and assigns and said "And it is my *desire*[57] that she allows to A.G. an annuity of £25 during her life." The Court of Appeal held that no trust to pay this money had been imposed on the daughter.[58] On the other hand, in *Comiskey* v. *Bowring-Hanbury*,[59] which may also be usefully compared with the decision in *Re Adams and Kensington Vestry*,[60] the testator gave all his property to his wife "absolutely *in full confidence*[61] that she will make such use of it as I would have made myself and that at her death she will devise it to such one or more of my nieces as

---

[52] It is now provided by Administration of Justice Act 1982, s.21, that extrinsic evidence, including evidence of the testator's intention, may be admitted to assist in the interpretation of a will (a) in so far as any part of it is meaningless; (b) in so far as the language used in any part of it is ambiguous on the face of it; (c) in so far as evidence, other than evidence of the testator's intention, shows that the language used in any part of it is ambiguous in the light of the surrounding circumstances. It is also provided (*ibid.* s.20) that the court has jurisdiction to rectify a will if satisfied that it is so expressed that it fails to carry out the testator's intention in consequence of a clerical error or of a failure to understand his instructions.

[53] [1895] 2 Ch. 370 at p. 373. See also *Re Williams* [1897] 2 Ch. 12, at p. 14; *Comiskey* v. *Bowring-Hambury* [1905] A.C. 84 at p. 89.

[54] [1948] Ch. 603, following *Shelley* v. *Shelley* (1868) L.R. 6 Eq. 540.

[55] *Cf.* Langan (1968) 32 Conv. (N.S.) 361.

[56] (1888) 39 Ch.D. 253.

[57] Our italics.

[58] No trust was created in the following cases: *Lambe* v. *Eames, supra; Re Hutchinson and Tenant* (1878) 8 Ch.D. 540 ("have confidence"); *Mussoorie Bank* v. *Raynor* (1882) 7 App.Cas. 321, P.C. ("feeling confident"); *Re Hamilton* [1895] 2 Ch. 370 ("wish"); *Hill* v. *Hill* [1897] 1 Q.B. 483 ("request"); *Re Williams* [1897] 2 Ch. 12 ("fullest trust and confidence"); *Re Connolly* [1910] 1 Ch. 219 ("specially desire"); *Re Johnson* [1939] 2 All E.R. 458 ("request"); *Swain* v. *The Law Society* [1982] 3 W.L.R. 261, H.L. ("on behalf of").

[59] [1905] A.C. 84.

[60] *Supra*; see also *Re Williams, supra*.

[61] Our italics.

she may think fit." The House of Lords held that, on a true construction of the whole will, the words "in full confidence" created a trust. Whatever doubts one may have about the correctness of the actual decision—the significance of the word "absolutely" not being perhaps fully appreciated—it nevertheless, because it is of the highest authority, underlines the rule that in the last analysis the problem should be one of construing the whole instrument.[62]

A modern illustration of some interest, involving the winding-up of a company, is *Re Kayford Ltd.*[63] which involved rather different considerations. The company carried on a mail order business, and the customers paid the full price in advance or paid a deposit. Difficulties arose over supply and delivery of goods, and a separate bank account was opened by the company called a "Customer Trust Deposit Account," with the object that all further moneys paid by customers for goods should be paid into that account and withdrawn only when the goods had been delivered. Its purpose was that if the company had to go into liquidation, the money could be refunded to those who had paid it. The company subsequently went into liquidation, and the question before the court was whether the money in the bank account was held in trust for those who paid, or whether it formed part of the general assets of the company. Megarry J. had no doubt on the facts that a trust was created, the facts showing that the moneys remained in the beneficial ownership of those who sent them until the goods were delivered.[64]

It will therefore be seen that what is meant by "certainty of words" is certainty of intention to create a trust appearing from the words in the instrument.[65] It should be noted, moreover, that the legal effect of the wording is relevant not simply in deciding whether a trust proper has been created, or a mere moral obligation. Other possibilities are that a power of appointment has been created,[66] or if the Crown holds property, it may be administering it in the exercise of its governmental functions without creating a trust,[67] and the mere fact that the word "trust" is used in relation to the Crown is not decisive.[68]

The cases cited in the text involved private trusts. If the intention of the instrument is to create a charitable trust but there is an ambiguity in the wording, it was confirmed by the House of Lords in *I.R.C.* v. *McMullen*[69] that a

---

[62] A trust *was* created in the following cases: *Re Steele's Will Trusts* [1948] Ch. 603, *ante* ("request"); *Re Endacott* [1960] Ch. 232 ("for the purpose of").

[63] [1975] 1 W.L.R. 279.

[64] Megarry J. made it clear that the general rule was that if money is sent to a company for goods which are not delivered, the sender is merely a creditor of the company unless a trust has been created. In this case, however, there was a trust whereupon "the obligations in respect of the money are transformed from contract to property, from debt to trust": *ibid.* at p. 282. The judge also indicated that a trust of this kind might not be effective in favour of trade creditors, but in this case the court was only concerned with members of the public.

[65] The question whether a trust or a power has been created is considered *post*, p. 71.

[66] See *post*, p. 71.

[67] As a "trust in the higher sense": see *Tito* v. *Waddell (No. 2)* [1977] Ch. 106 at p. 216; see *ante*, p. 7.

[68] *Ibid.* at p. 212. The Crown *can* be a trustee but only if it deliberately chooses to do so: *Civilian War Claimants Association Ltd.* v. *The King* [1932] A.C. 14, at p. 27; *Nissan* v. *Att.-Gen.* [1970]. A.C. 179 at p. 223; *Tito* v. *Waddell (No. 2) supra* at p. 212.

[69] [1981] A.C. 1. The facts are stated *post*, p. 213.

"benignant" construction should be given if possible.[70] It was not, however, necessary to resort to such a construction in that case.

(2) Certainty of subject matter

This also is an essential ingredient for the effectual creation of a trust. One aspect of the rule is illustrated in *Curtis* v. *Rippon*.[71] There the testator left all his property to his wife "trusting that she should, in fear of God, and in love of the children committed to her care, make such use of it as should be for her own and their spiritual and temporal good, remembering always, according to circumstances, the Church of God and the poor." The beneficial interest was, therefore, to be taken by an ascertained beneficiary, subject to the right of others to unascertained portions of it. The rights of the latter were held to fail and the ascertained beneficiary took the entirety.

The situation illustrated by *Curtis* v. *Rippon* must be distinguished from two other possibilities: (i) that *all* the beneficial interests are unascertained, as would happen, for example, in a case where a number of houses are left on trust but the settlor fails to make it clear which and how many of the houses are to be taken by each of the beneficiaries; and (ii) that the *trust property itself* is unascertained as it would be, for example, if a settlor gives "the bulk" of my property[72] to be held on trust. In (i) the entirety of beneficial interest having failed it should apparently be held on a resulting trust for the settlor, though, as will be seen, this will not necessarily happen. In (ii) the whole transaction will fail from the start.[73]

Another illustration, from the many cases on certainty of subject matter, is to be found in *Re Kolb's Will Trusts*[74] as applied to the construction of an investment clause in a will where the testator referred to, among other things, investment in "blue-chip" securities. This term is often used to denote shares in large public companies thought to be entirely safe, but it is not a term of art and it lacks precision. Cross J. held that the term depended essentially on the standard applied by the testator and should not be regarded as an objective quality of the investment. If the testator had made his trustees the judges of the standard to be applied, then all would have been well, but as he did not, that part of the clause in which the term was contained was void for uncertainty.

This decision may be contrasted with *Re Golay's Will Trusts*.[75] Here the testator by will directed the trustees to let T "enjoy one of my flats during her lifetime and to receive a reasonable income from my other properties." The question was what was meant by "reasonable." Ungoed-Thomas J., in upholding the gift, held that the yardstick of "reasonable income" indicated by the testator was not what he or some other specified person *subjectively* considered to be reasonable, but what he identified *objectively* as "reasonable income," and the court could, therefore, quantify that income. This seems a dubious

---

[70] *Ibid.* at p. 14.
[71] (1820) 5 Madd. 434. See also *Sprange* v. *Barnard* (1789) 2 Bro.C.C. 585.
[72] *Palmer* v. *Simmonds* (1854) 2 Drew. 221; *cf. Bromley* v. *Tryon* [1952] A.C. 265.
[73] See *post*, p. 65 for "Effect of Uncertainty."
[74] [1962] Ch. 531.
[75] [1965] 1 W.L.R. 969.

decision; it is also difficult to reconcile it with the reasoning of Cross J. in *Re Kolb's Will Trusts*,[76] which is preferred.[77]

(3) Certainty of objects

This question will be discussed in some detail in Chapter 4.[78] It will be seen that the test of certainty is that the objects should be certain or capable of being rendered certain: that the test was restrictively interpreted in *I.R.C.* v. *Broadway Cottages Trust*[79] to require that the trustees should at any time be able to make a full list of the beneficiaries and if the class was unascertainable at any time, the trust would fail for uncertainty; and that, with regard to trust powers in favour of a discretionary class of objects, this test was discarded by the House of Lords in *McPhail* v. *Doulton*,[80] and a new test formulated. This test is identical to that used for powers, *viz.* whether it can be said of any given person whether or not he is a member of the class. Some outstanding difficulties, however, appear to remain.[81]

It should, however, be observed that there is an important exception to the rule that the objects be certain. This is in the case of charitable trusts where, provided that a paramount general intention of charity is manifested, certainty in the charitable objects is not essential to validity.[82] In such a case a *cy-près* scheme may be made enabling the funds to be devoted to definite charitable purposes.

2. *Effect of Uncertainty*

(1) Words

If an intention to create a trust cannot be derived from the words used in the instrument, but at most a mere moral obligation, the donee will take the property beneficially,[83] but not if it is construed as a power of appointment.[84]

(2) Subject matter

1. If the actual trust property is uncertain the transaction will fail *in limine*. In such circumstances there is nothing certain on which the trust can fasten.[85]

2. If it is the beneficial interest to be taken by the beneficiaries that is uncertain, the property should apparently be held on a resulting trust for the settlor or (if he is dead) for the residuary legatee or devisee under his will, or if there is no gift of residue, on trust for the persons entitled to his estate on

---

[76] *Supra.*
[77] See also *Re Steel* [1979] Ch. 218 (residue to be divided between legatees who had only received "small amounts"; held (by Megarry V.-C.) to be valid as being mere words of explanation explaining the testator's motives: residue divided between all legatees equally whatever the size of their legacies).
[78] See *post*, p. 75.
[79] [1955] Ch. 20; see also *Re Sayer* [1957] Ch. 423.
[80] [1971] A.C. 424.
[81] *Post*, p. 79.
[82] *Post*, p. 184.
[83] See cases cited at note 58, *ante*, p. 62.
[84] See *post*, p. 75.
[85] *Palmer* v. *Simmonds* (1854) 2 Drew. 221; *cf. Bromley* v. *Tryon* [1952] A.C. 265.

intestacy. In such a case, assuming that there is certainty of words, clearly a trust will have been *intended* and its failure on grounds of uncertainty of the beneficial interest will not enable the trustees to take beneficially.[86] But there is some authority for the proposition that the court may apply the maxim "equality is equity" and divide the entirety of the beneficial interest equally between the beneficiaries.[87] The best-known mode of application of the maxim is to be found in cases involving joint banking accounts held by husband and wife where after dissolution of the marriage it is found impracticable to divide the fund meticulously between them.[88] However convenient and "equitable" it may be, it is somewhat difficult to justify in principle the application of the maxim in a case involving uncertainty of the actual beneficial interest taken by trust objects and the position remains doubtful.

3. If the beneficial interest is clearly vested in a beneficiary but he is directed to apply unascertained parts of it to given objects he will take the whole beneficially and the direction, being uncertain, will be disregarded.[89]

(3) Objects

On the assumption that there is sufficient certainty of words to create a trust, but the objects are uncertain, the property will be held on a resulting trust for the settlor or his estate.[90]

---

[86] See *Briggs* v. *Penny* (1851) 3 Mac. & G. 546 at p. 557, *per* Lord Truro L.C.; *Boyce* v. *Boyce* (1849) 16 Sim. 476.

[87] See *Doyley* v. *Att.-Gen.* (1735) 2 Eq.Cas.Abr. 194.

[88] See, *e.g. Jones* v. *Maynard* [1951] Ch. 572; *Rimmer* v. *Rimmer* [1953] 1 Q.B. 63.

[89] *Curtis* v. *Rippon, supra.*

[90] See *ante*, p. 65, *post*, p. 75.

CHAPTER 4

DISCRETIONARY TRUSTS AND POWERS

I. THE CREATION OF DISCRETIONARY TRUSTS AND POWERS

1. *Generally*

ALMOST all trusts involve the exercise of a power or discretion by the trustees. In many cases this does not affect beneficial entitlement. So, depending on the circumstances of the particular trust, trustees will often have powers which include those to vary the investments of the trust[1]; to grant a lease of property which is subject to the trust[2]; to settle claims[3]; to apply income for the support of an infant beneficiary or to accumulate it[4]; to apply to the court for guidance as to the execution of the trust[5]; and to insure trust property.[6] Trustees or any other person designated in the trust instrument for this purpose may have other powers, such as those to remove trustees and to appoint new ones.[7] Indeed it is of the fundamental nature of a trust that a trustee is not a puppet at the end of a wire pulled by the settlor or the beneficiaries,[8] but is a person who is to exercise an independent judgment over a wide field.

The trustees' discretion need not, however, be limited to the administrative and other matters just indicated, but can extend to beneficial entitlement. Trustees can be given a power to select which of a group of persons shall receive any benefit at all from the trust. Alternatively, while the trust instrument may provide that each member of a class of beneficiaries is to receive some benefit, the trustees may be given the power to determine how much each beneficiary will receive. Further, the trustees may have the power to decide whether to distribute income, or to accumulate it.[9] This chapter is generally concerned with considerations affecting the exercise of powers or discretions as to beneficial entitlements, but most of the principles will apply to the other powers and discretions which trustees are given.

---

[1] See *post*, p. 302.
[2] Law of Property Act 1925, s.28; Settled Land Act 1925, s.41.
[3] Trustee Act 1925, s.15.
[4] See *post*, p. 346.   [5] See *post*, p. 276.
[6] Trustee Act 1925, s.19. The position is surprising. Trustees are under no duty to insure (*Re McEacharn* (1911) 103 L.T. 900) and the statutory power is only to insure for a sum up to three-quarters of the value of the property. Express powers of insuring usually allow the cover to be effected in the full reinstatement value.
[7] See *post*, p. 243.
[8] It is in this respect that the position of a trustee differs from that of a nominee, who is often under an express or implied contractual obligation to comply in all respects with the beneficiary's directions.
[9] See *post*, p. 346.

2. *Reasons for Creating Discretionary Trusts and Powers*

Some of the reasons for creating trusts with discretionary provisions as to beneficial entitlement have already been mentioned.[10] A settlor or testator often wishes to make a present disposition but to confer a benefit at some time in the future according to circumstances. It may be that a person who is creating a trust for his children or grandchildren wishes the amount, if any, which each receives to depend on their conduct; their financial need; or their success. A much larger payment may be justified to a beneficiary who is an undergraduate or who is training for entry into a profession or vocation than his brother who is already well established in business. Or it may be that a person wishes to devote funds to charitable causes, but to allow the particular recipient to be selected according to the social or other need which seems most pressing at the time.

Apart from this, there are two general considerations. First, there is no suggestion that where there is a discretionary trust the objects *must* be treated unequally. So the father who creates a trust for his children leaves the trustees free to treat them all alike unless some special circumstance occurs. Secondly, the settlor is likely to be able to exercise *de facto* control over the exercise of the discretion. He has no legal rights as settlor[11] but he may have appointed himself to be one of the trustees. Even if he did not do so, he himself will usually have appointed the trustees, and they are likely to listen to his views. A discretionary trust is in practice often used as a method of divesting oneself of the ownership of property while still being able in practice to control its ultimate devolution.

3. *Taxation Considerations*

At the present time, tax reasons are often the most important for the creation of discretionary trusts. Both income tax and capital transfer tax are so-called "progressive" taxes. This means that income tax is imposed on the "slices" of a person's income, and capital transfer tax is imposed on the "slices" of a person's capital value transferred, at a progressively increasing rate. In the case of income tax, each person is entitled to receive the first slice of his income free of tax.[12] The next slice of £14,600 is taxable at the basic rate of 30 per cent.[13] Thereafter, higher rates apply to the slices covering the next £21,400[14] until all income over £36,000 is taxable at 60 per cent. or 75 per cent., according to whether it is earned or unearned.[15]

---

[10] *Ante,* p. 3.

[11] Generally, once a trust is created, the function of a settlor as such is fulfilled. Occasionally, however, in the case of the variation of a trust, his wishes will be taken into account: see *post,* p. 417.

[12] The amount of this "slice" is calculated by means of personal allowances, which vary according to the personal circumstances of the individual. For the year 1983/84 a married man is entitled to a personal allowance of £2,795 and a single person to an allowance of £1,785. Additional allowances are available for dependent children; for a housekeeper in certain circumstances; for widows with children; for dependent relatives; and to cover various other circumstances. The amounts of these allowances are often altered annually.

[13] This is the rate for 1983/84; F.A. 1983, s.12.   [14] *Ibid.*

[15] In general, unearned income in excess of £7,100 p.a. is taxed at an additional rate of 15 per cent.

In the case of capital transfer tax, the first £58,000 of value transferred by a person in each 10 year of his lifetime[16] is not subject to capital transfer tax.[17] Between £58,000 and £80,000 the rate is 15 per cent. or 30 per cent., according to the time when the transfer is made,[18] and thereafter the rates increase until transfers over £2,636,000 are taxable at 75 per cent.[19]

In tax planning a discretionary trust has three main advantages. First, the terms of the trust instrument usually allow the trustees to decide whether to distribute or withhold income. They can, therefore, distribute income to a beneficiary in a year when his total income is low, so that his total liability to tax is kept down, and withhold income when the beneficiary's total income is high. Secondly, the trust instrument usually allows the trustees to accumulate income, so that it becomes converted into capital.[20] Thirdly, a discretionary trust allows income and capital to be spread among members of a family, rather than being bunched in the hands of one member. Take a simple example. Suppose that Andrew, Basil and Colin are brothers. Suppose also that Andrew's top rate of income tax is 75 per cent., Basil's top rate is 50 per cent., and Colin's top rate is 30 per cent. In principle,[21] if Andrew receives £1,000 of investment income,[22] he would pay £750 of income tax on it, and be left with £250 in his pocket. If, however, the investment income arises in a discretionary trust, and in that year £250 is paid to Basil and £750 to Colin, Basil will pay £125 in tax and Colin will pay £225 in tax. The family as a whole, therefore, now only pays £350 in tax, a reduction of £400.

As a result of the widespread use of discretionary trusts in order to preserve income and capital for the benefit of the family, discretionary trusts in general have come under increasing fiscal attack. The income arising to a discretionary trust is in general taxed at 15 per cent. above the rate applicable to a trust with fixed beneficial interests[23]; and a charge to capital transfer tax is imposed on every tenth anniversary of the creation of the trust.[24] While, however, there is this attack on ordinary discretionary trusts, the legislature has given privileged treatment to a special type of discretionary trust, known as an accumulation and maintenance settlement. This is a trust for the benefit of one or more children[25] who will become entitled to the trust property[26] upon reaching an age not exceeding 25, but where, until that age, the trustees either accumulate the income or apply it for the maintenance, education or benefit of the children.

---

[16] *i.e.* from March 26, 1974, when capital transfer tax came into force. There are various exemptions covering small amounts of value transferred in each year.

[17] F.A. 1982, s.91.

[18] The lower rate applies to transfers made by a person at least three years before his death.

[19] F.A. 1982, s.91.

[20] See *post*, p. 351.

[21] This example is only given to illustrate the principle. The result is modified by a number of provisions of the income tax legislation.

[22] Over £7,100: F.A. 1983, s.12.

[23] F.A. 1973, s.16.

[24] F.A. 1982, s.107.

[25] Usually the children or grandchildren of the settlor; F.A. 1982, s.114.

[26] Or to an immediate vested interest in the income of the trust property: para. 15(1)(*a*).

Discretionary trusts have a particular advantage for the purposes of capital transfer tax. If there is a fixed interest trust, when a life interest[27] comes to an end, the settled property is aggregated with the beneficiary's personal assets in order to determine the rate at which tax is payable. In the case of discretionary trusts, however, there is no such aggregation.

Man goes to considerable lengths to preserve his wealth, and the device of a discretionary trust remains a very popular way of so doing. In face of the possibility of a transfer tax regime governing discretionary trusts, as well as the possible re-imposition of exchange control[28] there is an increasing use of discretionary trusts formed in other jurisdictions whose trust law is either based on English trust law,[29] or whose trust law has been specifically adapted to embrace the English concept of a trust.[30]

II. THE BASIC TOOLS: TRUSTS AND POWERS

1. *Generally*

Where it is left to the trustees or others to decide whether a person shall receive a benefit from the trust at all, or the extent of that benefit, the trustees' discretion will be one of two broad types, depending on whether they are under an obligation to exercise it. If they are under an obligation to exercise it, it is known as a trust power, or a power in the nature of a trust. Where they are not under such an obligation, it is known as a mere power, or sometimes, as a power collateral.[31] It is, however, necessary to keep separate the two questions which arise in the process:

(a) must the trustees consider whether the power should be exercised; and
(b) the power should be exercised, how should it be exercised|?

Trustees are under a fundamental obligation to do the best they can for the beneficiaries as a whole, and it seems that they are under an obligation to consider from time to time whether *any* power should be exercised. This clearly does not apply to powers which in the circumstances of the particular trust cannot be exercised. So, while trustees are given a statutory power of leasing,[32] this will not have to be considered if there is no property capable of being let. Apart from this the trustees must consider whether to exercise all powers, and this is so whether they are mere powers or trust powers. The distinction between the two is, however, relevant at the second stage. Having considered whether to

---

[27] Known for the purposes of capital transfer tax as an "interest in possessions."
[28] See *post*, p. 427.
[29] *e.g.* the Channel Islands, the Isle of Man, Bermuda, the Bahamas, the Cayman Islands, and a number of other Caribbean tax havens.
[30] *e.g.* Liechtenstein. For a person domiciled and resident in some part of the U.K., the creation of a non-resident settlement involves a number of problems: see *post*, p. 429.
[31] See *Vestey v. I.R.C. (No.* 2) [1979] Ch. 198 at p. 206 (affirmed on other grounds: *Vestey v. I.R.C. (Nos.* 1 *and* 2) [1979] A.C. 1148) *per* Walton J. and *Re Hay's Settlement Trusts* [1982] 1 W.L.R. 202 at p. 210, *per* Megarry V.-C. as to the nature of a mere power.
[32] Law of Property Act 1925, s.28; Settled Land Act 1925, s.41.

exercise it, trustees can decide not to exercise a mere power. They must, however, exercise a trust power, and the question is then how that power should be exercised.

2. *The Distinction*

It is now proposed to consider the distinction between trust powers and mere powers more closely. While powers are most frequently found as provisions in trust instruments, they can exist outside a trust, and it is therefore necessary to consider a power as a separate concept. A power can be said to be the right to exercise, in respect of property belonging to another, one or more of the rights which are the normal incidents of ownership. Some differences are immediately apparent. For example, a trust is necessarily equitable: a power may or may not be. Thus a power of attorney to convey the legal estate is legal. So is a power of sale of the legal estate exercisable by a mortgagee. On the other hand a power affecting beneficial entitlement is now necessarily equitable.[33] But, as has been said, the primary basis of the distinction is that a trust is imperative; a power is not. The distinction is shown by contrasting a trust for sale and a power of sale. If land is given by will to trustees on *trust* for sale, then, because there is a binding obligation to sell, the land will be converted, in the eye of the law (even if not in fact converted), into money as soon as the will takes effect, *i.e.* on the testator's death. This is still the position even if a power to postpone sale is contained in the trust instrument and the power of postponement is exercised: the duty to convert is nevertheless regarded as an imperative one. The same considerations apply to a deed *inter vivos*, in which case the land will be treated as money as soon as the deed is executed. On the other hand, if there is merely a *power* of sale, whether in a will or deed, the land will only be converted into money when the power itself is exercised, and the person in whom the power is vested will not be compelled to exercise it.

The question whether or not a trust or a power has been created is essentially one of the construction of the instrument. The distinction may be a fine one in any individual case, because the trust instrument may give what on the face of it appears to be a mere power, but which is in fact a trust power. Although trust powers appear as powers they are construed and take effect as trusts.

The question, therefore, is, when is a power a trust power? The question is ultimately decided, as will be seen, by extracting, from the actual words used, the real intention of the settlor. But although it is, in the last analysis, a question of construction, certain preliminary general principles are clear:

(A) A *general* power of appointment is incapable of its nature of being a trust power. A general power confers on the donee of the power a power to appoint amongst whomsoever he pleases, including the donee himself. Since the donee can appoint to himself beneficially, the court cannot compel an appointment elsewhere. A special power of appointment (*i.e.* a power to appoint among designated persons or classes of persons) is, however, capable of taking effect as

---

[33] L.P.A. 1925, s.1(7).

a trust power. So also, it seems, is a hybrid or intermediate power, *i.e.* a power "betwixt and between,"[34] neither strictly general nor special, such as a power to appoint to anybody other than the donee himself.[35]

(B) If there is a gift over in default of appointment (*i.e.* if there is an alternative gift in the event of the donee of the power failing to exercise it), the "power" cannot be a trust power. A gift over is incompatible with the imperative duties of a trust and operates as a denial of its existence. For example, in *Re Mills*,[36] a power was given to appoint among children and remoter issue who in the opinion of the donee of the power should evidence a desire to maintain the family fortune. There then followed a gift elsewhere in default of appointment. The Court of Appeal held that because there was a gift over, the power did not operate as a trust.

However, a residuary gift (*i.e.* a gift of that part of the testator's property which has not been specifically devised or bequeathed) is not a gift over for this purpose, so the presence of a residuary gift will not of necessity deprive the power of the character of a trust. Accordingly, in *Re Brierley*[37] a testator gave his wife a life interest in £50,000. He also gave her the power to bequeath or appoint amongst such of her relatives or next-of-kin as she thought proper. She was also given the residue of her husband's estate absolutely. The wife released and thereby purported to extinguish the power of appointment and claimed the whole £50,000 as her own beneficially under the gift of residue. The court held that this was not possible: a gift of residue was totally different from a gift over of *specific* property which is the subject of the power of appointment.

The gift over must also be *in default of appointment*, in order to prevent a trust power being deduced. If, therefore, the gift over is to take effect in the event of failure of the appointees or their not attaining a specific age, the power is still capable of being a trust power.[38]

(C) If there is no gift over in default of appointment, there may or may not be a trust power. It is entirely a question of construction whether or not it is: it depends on the real intention of the settlor extracted from the words used in the instrument,[38a] as the following cases show. For example, on one side of the line, in *Burrough* v. *Philcox*,[39] the testator directed that after certain contingencies had been fulfilled, property was to be held in trust for his two children for life, with remainder to their issue, and declared that if they should both die without issue, the survivor should have power to dispose by will of the property among his nephews, nieces and children as he should think fit. The testator's children in fact died without issue and without any appointment

---

[34] *Re Gestetner Settlement* [1953] Ch. 672 at p. 685.
[35] As in *Re Park* [1932] 1 Ch. 580. See also *Re Jones* [1945] Ch. 105 (power to appoint to anybody being a person and not a corporation); *Blausten* v. *I.R.C.* [1972] Ch. 256; *Re Manisty's Settlement* [1974] Ch. 17; *Re Hay's Settlement Trusts* [1982] 1 W.L.R. 202. In such cases there may be a power to introduce members to a class of beneficiaries, with certain exceptions: see *post*, p. 79.
[36] [1930] 1 Ch. 654.
[37] (1894) 43 W.R. 36.
[38] *Re Llewellyn's Settlement* [1921] 2 Ch. 281.
[38a] Extrinsic evidence, including that of the testator's intention, may be admitted in certain cases: see A.J.A. 1982, s.21; and see *ante*, p. 62, n. 52.
[39] (1840) 5 Myl. & Cr. 72.

having been made by the survivor. It was held that a *trust* was created in favour of the testator's nephews and nieces and their children: the trust was simply subject to a power of selection vested in the surviving child. Lord Cottenham stated the principle in these words: "Where there appears a general intention in favour of a class, and a particular intention in favour of individuals of a class to be selected by another person, and the particular intention fails from that selection not having been made, the court will carry into effect the general intention in favour of the class."[40] And, assuming the power is not exercised, if it is in favour of his relations generally and a *trust* is deduced in their favour, the trust takes effect in favour of the settlor's statutory next-of-kin.[41]

Burrough v. *Philcox* was a case where there was no gift over in default of appointment. But it must be emphasised that it does not necessarily follow from the absence of a gift over that the implication of a trust is automatically to be made. It is evident from other decisions that a trust will not be implied unless there is, upon a true construction, an indication in the instrument of a clear intention to benefit the designated person or class or in any event with only a mere power of selection conferred. Thus, in *Re Weekes' Settlement*,[42] there was a gift to the testatrix's husband for life in certain real property, with "power to dispose of all such property by will amongst our children." There was no gift over in default of appointment, and the power of appointment was not exercised in favour of the children. Romer J. held that the power gave to the husband a mere power, not one coupled with a trust, and accordingly there was no gift to the children by implication. The judge pointed out that there was no gift to such of the class as the husband might appoint—as there was, in effect, in *Burrough* v. *Philcox*[43]—but merely a bare power to appoint amongst a class. Similarly, in *Re Combe*[44] a life interest in property was given to the son of the testator and, after his death, the property was to be held "in trust for such person or persons as my said son shall appoint but . . . such appointment must be confined to any relation of mine of the whole blood." Again there was no gift over in default of appointment. It was held that the words quoted created a mere power and not a trust. There was nothing in the words of the will, according to Tomlin J., for importing into it something that was not there. The principle of both these cases was applied in the more recent decision in *Re Perowne*.[45] Here the testatrix gave all her estate to her husband for life and also added these words: "Knowing that he will make arrangements for the disposal of my estate, according to my wishes, for the benefit of my family." The husband did in fact make an appointment but this was void; and the question arose whether, since the power had not been effectively exercised, a trust in favour of the family or a mere power to appoint in their favour had been

---

[40] *Ibid.* at p. 92.
[41] *Re Scarisbrick's Will Trusts* [1951] Ch. 622, C.A.; *Re Baden's Deed Trusts* (*No. 2*) [1973] Ch. 9 at p. 30, *per* Stamp L.J.
[42] [1897] 1 Ch. 289.
[43] *Supra.*
[44] [1925] Ch. 210.
[45] [1951] Ch. 785.

created. Harman J. refused to spell a trust out of the words used and held they gave a mere power to distribute among the large and indefinite class in question.

One can see from these cases that the question is one of construction, whether or not the settlor has shown an intention to benefit the objects of the power. And the absence of a gift over in default of appointment is an argument, and no more, that that was the settlor's intention: it does not raise a necessary inference that a trust was intended. And because it is a question of construction the solution of the problem may depend on "a few words" and "mere straws in the wind."[46]

That this is inescapable in matters of construction is demonstrated by the leading case of *McPhail* v. *Doulton*.[47] The deed in question in this case provided that the trustees should apply the net income in making payments at their absolute discretion "to or for the benefit of any of the officers and employees or ex-officers or ex-employees of the company or to any relatives or dependants of any such persons in such amounts or on such conditions (if any) as they think fit." One question was whether the clause prescribed a trust or a power. At first instance Goff J.[48] held that it created a power; the Court of Appeal[49] by a majority held likewise; but the House of Lords[50] unanimously held that it was a trust power and accordingly took effect as a trust: the clearly expressed scheme of the deed pointed to a mandatory construction. But bearing in mind, no doubt, the differing judicial opinions expressed in the various stages of the case, Lord Wilberforce said[51]:

"It is striking how narrow and in a sense artificial is the distinction, in cases such as the present, between trusts, or as the particular type of trust is called, trust powers, and powers. It is only necessary to read the learned judgments in the Court of Appeal to see that what to one mind may appear as a power of distribution coupled with a trust to dispose of the undistributed surplus, by accumulation or otherwise, may to another appear as a trust for distribution coupled with a power to withhold a portion and accumulate or otherwise dispose of it. A layman and, I suspect, also a logician would find it hard to understand what difference there is."

In the Court of Appeal in *McPhail* v. *Doulton*,[52] the majority held that in cases where the considerations were evenly balanced in arriving at one or other construction, the court was at liberty to lean towards the construction which might effectuate rather than frustrate the settlor's intentions.[53] In other words, the court could take account of the legal consequences of any given interpreta-

[46] *Re Baden's Deed Trusts* [1969] 2 Ch. 388 at p. 398, *per* Harman L.J. For a formulation of rules for construction, see *Re Leek* [1967] Ch. 1061 at p. 1073, *per* Buckley J.
[47] [1971] A.C. 424.
[48] [1967] 1 W.L.R. 1457.
[49] [1969] 2 Ch. 126. Russell L.J. dissented.
[50] [1971] A.C. 424.   [51] *Ibid.* at p. 448.
[52] [1969] 2 Ch. 126 (*sub nom. Re Baden's Deed Trusts.*)
[53] On the principle of *ut res magis valeat quam pereat*.

tion, more particularly that if, according to the rules of certainty which were then thought to apply, one construed the instrument as a trust it might fail, but if one construed it as a power it might prevail, then the court would lean in favour of a power. This approach did not fall to be considered in the House of Lords in *McPhail* v. *Doulton*,[54] because it was there held that the same test of certainty applies to trusts (or at any rate trust powers) as to powers. But the point could still possibly be significant because trusts and powers were not assimilated for other purposes.

3. *The Requirement of Certainty*[55]

The distinction between trusts and powers used to be of prime importance in connection with the requirements of certainty of objects. The general rule for private trusts is that the objects must be certain or capable of being rendered certain but this rule was restrictively interpreted to mean that the whole range of eligible beneficiaries must be capable of ascertainment. In short, the trustees had to be able to make a list of beneficiaries and if they could not, the trust would fail for uncertainty. The test for powers was different. It was, and is, simply necessary to be able to say with certainty of any individual whether he is or is not a member of the class of beneficiaries. However, the House of Lords, by a majority, in *McPhail* v. *Doulton*[56] has, it seems, revolutionised the test of certainty for trusts. It has largely equated the test for trusts (or at any rate trust powers) with that for powers. Lord Wilberforce, with whom Lord Reid and Viscount Dilhorne agreed, described the old distinction as "unfortunate and wrong."[57] But although *McPhail* v. *Doulton* has clearly had a decisive impact on this area of the law it has not apparently solved all problems, and it seems useful to consider the recent background to the decision.

Certainty for powers. The modern shape of the rule derives from *Re Gestetner Settlement*,[58] where Harman J., as he later regretted,[59] established the distinction between discretionary powers and discretionary trusts. In this case capital was held in trust for such member or members of a specified class as the trustees might think fit. The specified class comprised certain named individuals; any person living or thereafter born who was a descendant of the settlor's father or uncle; any spouse, widow or widower of any such person; five charitable bodies; any former employee of the settlor or his wife or widow or widower of such employee; any director or employee of a named company. Harman J. said that if the trustees had been under a *duty* to distribute (*i.e.* they held on trust to do so) "there was much to be said for the view that [they] should be able to review

---

[54] [1971] A.C. 424.

[55] See Harris (1971) 87 L.Q.R. 31; Hopkins [1971] C.L.J. 68; Emery (1982) L.Q.R. 551.

[56] [1971] A.C. 424.

[57] *Ibid.* at p. 456. Lords Hodson and Guest dissented on this question: they preferred to retain the old test of certainty for trusts.

[58] [1953] Ch. 672.

[59] See *Re Baden's Deed Trusts* [1969] 2 Ch. 388 at p. 397.

the whole field in order to exercise [their] judgment properly."[60] But it was held that there was no *duty* on the trustees to appoint among members of the specified class: they merely had the obligation to consider the merits of such persons of the specified class as were known to them and, if they thought fit, to give them something.[61] It was therefore a power and not a trust power. The material question, however, was whether the class was sufficiently certain. The test for deciding this question was held to be whether it could be ascertained with certainty of any given "postulant" that he was, or was not, entitled to receive the settlor's bounty. It was accordingly unnecessary in a power of this kind to establish that the objects themselves were all capable of ascertainment. It was simply necessary that one could say of any given person, John Doe or Richard Roe, that he was an object of the power. The trustees did not have "to worry their heads to survey the world from China to Peru"[62] to find out who was within the designated class. There was no difficulty in *Re Gestetner* in ascertaining whether any given postulant was a member of the class. In this case, therefore, the power in question was held to be valid.

But, since that case was decided, the question precisely how Harman J.'s test should be applied or whether it should be modified attracted detailed scrutiny in subsequent cases. Essentially the question was whether the *Gestetner* test should be applied strictly so that if one did not know whether a given individual was within the power, it would fail even though other classes were clearly within it. Or, alternatively, whether an even more diluted test than this (itself relaxed compared with that for trusts) should be adopted with the result that difficulty in saying whether a person was or was not within the category should not be fatal, provided that *somebody* was clearly within it. The *Gestetner* test was supported by a preponderance of authority.[63] Only on isolated occasions was the other test used, notably by Lord Denning M.R.[64]

---

[60] *Re Gestetner Settlement* [1953] Ch. 672 at p. 685.

[61] The nature of a mere power was forumlated in similar terms by Walton J. in *Vestey* v. *I.R.C.* (*No.* 2) [1979] Ch. 198 (affirmed *Vestey* v. *I.R.C.* (*Nos.* 1 *and* 2 [1979] A.C. 1148) and by Megarry V.-C. in *Re Hay's Settlement Trusts* [1982] 1 W.L.R. 202 at p. 210.

[62] *Re Gestetner Settlement, supra* at pp. 688, 689: an expression incorrectly attributed by Harman J. to Alexander Pope: see *per* Harman J. in *Re Baden's Deed Trusts* [1969] 2 Ch. 388, at p. 397. In fact, the words are those of Samuel Johnson.

[63] *Re Coates* [1955] Ch. 495 (for any friends his wife might feel he had forgotten); *Re Sayer Trust* [1957] Ch. 423 (power in favour of employees, ex-employees, widow, children and "dependants") (in these cases the power was held valid). See also *I.R.C.* v. *Broadway Cottages Trust* [1955] Ch. 20, C.A. at pp. 32, 33, *per* Jenkins L.J. (where, however, a trust, not a power, was held to arise); *Re Gresham's Settlement* [1956] 1 W.L.R. 573; *Re Allan* [1958] 1 W.L.R. 220; *Re Hain's Settlement* [1961] 1 W.L.R. 440, at p. 445, *per* Evershed M.R.

[64] In *Re Gulbenkian's Settlement Trusts* [1968] 1 Ch. 126 at p. 134, and see also *per* Winn L.J. at p. 138. For similar formulations, see *Re Gibbard* [1967] 1 W.L.R. 42 ("old friends"), at pp. 47, 48, *per* Plowman J.; and *Re Leek* [1967] Ch. 1061 (persons having a "moral claim"), at p. 1073, *per* Buckley J.; affirmed on different grounds [1969] 1 Ch. 563.

Semble, however, that this test applies where there are merely individual gifts with a condition precedent or description attached: *Re Allen* [1953] Ch. 810, C.A., applied in *Re Barlow's Will Trusts* [1979] 1 W.L.R. 278 (direction to trustees to allow "family" and "friends" to purchase pictures: valid); see *post*, p. 82; see also *Re Tuck's Settlement Trusts* [1978] Ch. 49, C.A. (condition of marriage to a woman of Jewish blood and faith: valid).

The position remained uncertain until the decision of the House of Lords in *Re Gulbenkian's Settlement*.[65] This case involved the construction of a clause in a work of precedents used by the profession. It was to the effect that a special power of appointment could be exercised for the maintenance and personal support of all or any one or more of the following: the husband, wife, children or remoter issue of any persons in whose house or apartments or in whose company or under whose care and control or by whom the husband might from time to time be employed or residing as the trustee should in its absolute discretion think fit. The clause had been considered before in *Re Gresham's Settlement*,[66] where it was held by Harman J. that the provisions were void for uncertainty because there might be a number of persons of whom it could not be postulated that they were (or were not) within the dragnet of this unusually constructed clause. The case was distinguished from *Re Gestetner* because there, although one did not know all the persons who were within the specified class, one could say whether *any given person* was within the class or not, but in *Re Gresham* even this could not be done.

However, the House of Lords in *Re Gulbenkian* overruled this case and held that the clause was sufficiently certain to be valid within the *Gestetner* test. Lord Upjohn, in affirming the latter test, was unable to accept the relaxed test put forward by Lord Denning in the Court of Appeal.[67] It was generally agreed and may be taken as established[68] that the requirements for certainty will be satisfied if it can be said of "any given postulant" that he is or is not a member of the class of beneficiaries.

Certainty for trusts. It was, therefore, in the case of discretionary powers that a difference of approach with regard to certainty of objects was apparent. The rule relating to trusts that the objects must all be ascertainable was a much more stringent one than that required for powers of this nature. It has already been observed that Harman J. in *Re Gestetner*[69] indicated—though not by way of decision as the point did not arise—that there was a distinction in this matter between trusts and powers. The distinction was, however, definitely established by the Court of Appeal in *I.R.C.* v. *Broadway Cottages Trust*[70] which was, unlike *Re Gestetner*, a case of a *trust*. In this case the trustees held the funds upon trust to apply the income for the benefit of all or any of a class of beneficiaries as the trustees might think fit. It was held, upon a true construction of the instrument, that this created a trust in favour of the specified class and was void for uncertainty on the ground that the class was unascertainable at any given time; the whole range of objects eligible for selection must be ascertained or capable of ascertainment. The basis of the decision was that the court, if

---

[65] [1970] A.C. 508; applied in *Re Denley's Trust Deed* [1968] Ch. 373.

[66] [1956] 1 W.L.R. 573, followed in *Re Allan* [1958] 1 W.L.R. 220; the same clause was in question.

[67] Lord Donovan reserved his opinion on this point.

[68] See also *McPhail* v. *Doulton* [1971] A.C. 424.

[69] [1953] Ch. 672.

[70] [1955] Ch. 20: see also *Re Ogden* [1933] Ch. 678; *Re Sayer* [1957] Ch. 423; *Re Eden* [1957] 1 W.L.R. 788.

called upon to the execute the trust, could only do so on the basis of equal division, and there could not be equal division unless all the members of the class were known. Moreover, a valid power could not be spelt out of an invalid trust, so it could not be argued that the objects were sufficiently certain on that basis.[71]

This case was overruled by *McPhail* v. *Doulton*[72] and much of the learning which had developed appears to have become redundant. But even before this decision the unnecessary complexity of this branch of the law was judicially recognised. In the Court of Appeal in the same case Harman L.J. felt a "sense of frustration" at the emptiness of the question and that the distinction was "absurd and embarrassing."[73] There was also doubt about the precise application of the *Broadway* test to an admitted trust, for suggestions had been made that a "probability" of complete ascertainment was sufficient[74] and that "common sense" should come into the matter.[75] The time had therefore arrived for the rules of certainty for trusts and powers to be equated. The case for rigid rules for trusts is admittedly a persuasive one and had been stated earlier by Lord Upjohn: the imperative nature of trusts should entail the consequence that *all* the objects should be known.[76] But, as Lord Wilberforce indicated in *McPhail* v. *Doulton*, the law should take account of practicalities, particularly the narrow distinction between trusts of this kind (trust powers) and mere powers. The theory specifically postulated in *I.R.C.* v. *Broadway Cottages Trust* that the court can only execute a trust by ordering equal distribution in which every beneficiary shares was rejected as inappropriate: "equal division among all may, probably would, produce a result beneficial to none."[77]

Continuing distinctions. The fact that the test for validity has been assimilated does not, however, mean that trust powers and powers themselves have been assimilated. There remains the basic distinction that in the case of a power the court will not normally compel its exercise and will only interfere where the trustees exceed their power or possibly if they exercise it capriciously. On the other hand, in the case of a trust power, if the trustees do not exercise it, the court will do so, and in a manner thought most appropriate to carry out the settlor's intentions.[78] Moreover, because of this distinction, "a wider and

---

[71] *I.R.C.* v. *Broadway Cottages Trust, ibid.* at p. 36 (*per* Jenkins L.J.). See *post*, p. 180. See also generally, Fleming (1948) 13 Conv. (N.S.) 20; (1953) 69 L.Q.R. 309; Marshall (1957) 35 Can.B.Rev. 1060.

[72] [1971] A.C. 424.

[73] *Sub nom. Re Baden's Deed Trusts* [1969] 2 Ch. 388. For other judicial criticism, see *Re Hain's Settlement* [1961] 1 W.L.R. 440 at p. 445, *per* Evershed M.R.; *Re Leek* [1969] 1 Ch. 563 at p. 583, *per* Sachs L.J.

[74] *Re Saxone Shoe Co. Ltd's Trust Deed* [1962] 1 W.L.R. 943 (Cross J.). This approach was supported by Evershed M.R. in *Re Hain's Settlement* [1961] 1 W.L.R. 440, where he declined to take account of certain odd-job men who might be the beneficiaries of the trust and who might be difficult to identify.

[75] *Re Hain's Settlement* [1961] 1 W.L.R. 440 at p. 447, *per* Evershed M.R.

[76] *Re Gulbenkian's Settlements* [1970] A.C. 508. The point was re-stated by Lord Hodson (dissenting) in *McPhail* v. *Doulton* [1971] A.C. 424 at p. 442.

[77] [1971] A.C. 424 at p. 451, *per* Lord Wilberforce.

[78] See further *post*, p. 93.

more comprehensive range of inquiry" as to the range of objects is called for in the case of trust powers than in the case of powers.[79]

Outstanding problems. (1) It is clear that *McPhail* v. *Doulton* by applying the "given postulant" test to trusts has reaffirmed that this is the appropriate test for powers. In other respects there may be room for debate. Thus one question may be, does the decision only apply to the type of trust in question in *McPhail* v. *Doulton*? The trust involved in this case was a trust power in favour of a discretionary class; it accordingly took effect as a discretionary trust. The particular problem is whether the test applies to trusts in favour of fixed beneficiaries (sometimes called "fixed trusts") as opposed to discretionary beneficiaries. One view is that the rule should not be thus extended,[80] but there seems to be no reason in principle why it should not be. Just as an order for distribution (not necessarily, as has been seen, on the basis of equal division) can be made by the court in the case of a discretionary trust, so also, one would have thought, it could be made in the case of a fixed trust where one or more of the beneficiaries are not ascertainable. Our reading of Lord Wilberforce's speech is that the new test applies to *all* trusts. Furthermore, it would be regrettable if this were not so, because a trust power and a discretionary trust are *trusts*, although having close affinities with powers.[81]

(2) A further problem still not wholly resolved relates to the question of certainty itself. In *Re Gulbenkian's Settlements*[82] Lord Upjohn posed the distinction between linguistic or semantic uncertainty which, if the court cannot resolve it, renders the gift void, and mere evidential difficulty, such as the existence or whereabouts of members of the class, which the court can deal with on an application for directions. This distinction was adopted in *McPhail* v. *Doulton*[83] by Lord Wilberforce who also added a third class, *viz.* where "the meaning of the words used is clear but the definition of beneficiaries is so hopelessly wide as not to form 'anything like a class' so that the trust is administratively unworkable" (one example being "all the residents of Greater London").

Difficulties are not normally likely to arise with regard to whether a case falls within the third situation instanced by Lord Wilberforce, at any rate in the case of a special power. As to hybrid or intermediate powers, the position is not, however, so clear-cut. Such powers, particularly if they contain a power to admit new members to a class, are apparently becoming increasingly popular: it has been said they "arm the trustees with a weapon which will enable them to consider all developments and all future mishaps and disasters."[84] For example,

---

[79] *Ibid.* at p. 457.

[80] See Hanbury and Maudsley, *Modern Equity* (11th ed.), p. 211.

[81] The question is probably more academic than real. It would, for example, arise in the case of a trust for objects such as those in *McPhail* v. *Doulton* but with provision for distribution to the objects in equal or other definite shares. It is hardly likely that such a provision would be found in a professionally drawn instrument.

[82] [1970] A.C. 508 at p. 524.

[83] [1971] A.C. 424 at p. 457.

[84] *Re Manisty's Settlement* [1974] Ch. 17 at p. 27.

in *Blausten* v. *I.R.C.*[85] the trustees had power to introduce to the class of beneficiaries any person other than the settlor. The argument that the power was void for uncertainty was rejected on the ground that although the trustees had this admittedly wide power it could only be exercised with the written consent of the settlor and hence only during his lifetime. Therefore, it could not be said that the settlor had failed to set "metes and bounds" to the beneficial interests which he intended to create or permit to be created under the settlement. This reasoning is, however, difficult to reconcile with the decision of Templeman J. in *Re Manisty's Settlement*.[86] In this case the trustees had the power to add beneficiaries and to benefit the persons so added, and the power was exercisable in favour of anyone in the world except the settlor, his wife and other persons. It was not a general power in favour of anyone, nor a special power exercisable in favour of a class, but a hybrid or intermediate power exercisable in favour of anyone, with certain exceptions. It was held that the power did not fail for uncertainty even though (unlike *Re Blausten*) there were no expressed restrictions on its operation by the trustees.

The problem of reconciliation of the two last-mentioned cases was considered in *Re Hay's Settlement Trusts*,[87] again involving a hybrid or intermediate power. Megarry V.-C. gave detailed consideration to the view of Buckley L.J. in *Blausten* v. *I.R.C.* that the power in that case was saved from invalidity only by the requirement for the consent of the settlor, because otherwise the class of persons who had possible claims was too wide and this would make it impossible for the trustees to perform their duty of considering from time to time whether to exercise the power. In *Re Hay's Settlement Trusts*, however, Megarry V.-C. was of the opinion that mere numbers should not inhibit the trustees in exercising a power and accordingly a particularly wide intermediate power in that case was valid.

Even more fundamental problems could still emerge from the distinction between linguistic (often called conceptual) uncertainty and evidential difficulty. In *Re Baden's Deed Trusts (No. 2)*,[88] the sequel to *McPhail* v. *Doulton*,[89] the Court of Appeal was faced with the problem of deciding whether the trust in question was in fact valid, applying the new test of certainty laid down by the House of Lords. In the result it was unanimously held to be valid, but controversy centred around the meaning of the words "or was not" in the test (whether one can say with certainty whether any given individual was *or was not* a member of the class), Sachs and Megaw L.JJ. held that, when considering whether a candidate was or was not a member of a class, if he could not establish that he *was* a member, then he must be held to be *not* a member. It was sufficient if it could be said with certainty that a substantial number of objects

---

[85] [1972] Ch. 256.
[86] [1974] Ch. 17; see also *post*, p. 89.
[87] [1982] 1 W.L.R. 202.
[88] [1973] Ch. 9.
[89] The case was remitted by the House of Lords to the Chancery Division to decide whether upon the test of certainty now enuciated the trust was valid. Brightman J. held ([1972] Ch. 607) that it was valid. An appeal was made to the C.A.

were within the class, even though it could not be proved that a substantial number of other persons were not within it. This reasoning might be thought to be inadequate.[90] Indeed, Stamp L.J. was of opinion that one had to say *affirmatively* whether a given individual was within the class or whether he was outside it. How then were these respective interpretations of the test applied to "relatives" in the clause in question? Sachs and Megaw L.JJ. held that upon the widest meaning attributable to the word, *i.e.* descendants of a common ancestor, there was no conceptual uncertainty attaching to the word, and moreover no evidential difficulty in ascertaining whether a candidate was a relative. Stamp L.J. applying his own interpretation of the test, held that if the word was given this wide meaning the trust would fail for uncertainty, because one could not say with certainty whether any given individual did *not* fall into this category but he managed to decide that the trust was valid on the basis that "relatives" meant the "next-of-kin," in which event there would be no conceptual or evidential difficulty.[91]

There are undoubtedly serious difficulties in determining the precise effect of this decision so far as conceptual uncertainty is concerned. In *Re Hay's Settlement Trusts*,[92] a case involving a hybrid or intermediate power, Megarry V.-C, after a close examination of the decision, suggested that what is needed is an "appreciation of the width of the field, and this whether a selection is to be made from a dozen or, instead, from thousands or millions. . . . Only when the trustee has applied his mind to the 'size of the problem' should he then consider in individual cases whether, in relation to other possible claimants, a particular grant is appropriate." It may perhaps, however, be argued that merely to have an appreciation of the "field" or the "problem" is not enough: the "given postulant" test of certainty of objects appeared to be formulated more narrowly in *McPhail* v. *Doulton*.

This case was, of course, a complex case and it must not be thought that problems of this kind will often arise. More straightforward illustrations are to be found in earlier cases where it was plain that there was, and would still be, conceptual uncertainty in the objects of the trust. Thus, in *Re Astor's Settlement Trusts*,[93] which concerned the *Observer* newspaper, a settlement provided for income to be applied to a number of non-charitable purposes including the "maintenance of good understanding, sympathy and co-operation between nations" and "the preservation of the independence and integrity of newspapers" and other such purposes for the protection of newspapers. Roxburgh J. held the trusts to be void because (*inter alia*) they included objects such as those above which were void for uncertainty. The purposes must be stated in

---

[90] It is also arguably a reversion to the test adumbrated by Lord Denning M.R. in *Re Gulbenkian's Settlement Trusts* [1968] 1 Ch. 126, and since rejected: *semble*, however, that the latter test applies where there are merely individual gifts with a condition precedent or description attached: *Re Allen* [1953] Ch. 810, C.A.; *Re Barlow's Will Trusts* [1979] 1 W.L.R. 278; *Re Tuck's Settlement Trusts* [1978] Ch. 49, C.A.; see *post*, p. 82.

[91] All members of the C.A. were in agreement that the word "dependants" introduced no conceptual uncertainty whichever interpretation of the test was applied.

[92] [1982] 1 W.L.R. 202 at p. 210.

[93] [1952] Ch. 534. See also *post*, p. 177.

phrases which embody definite concepts and, moreover, the means by which the trustees are to attain them must be prescribed with a sufficient degree of certainty. Similarly, in *Re Endacott*[94] it was held by the Court of Appeal that a trust which was in essence for "useful" purposes failed because it was not clear what was meant by "utility." Such cases would be decided in the same way today.

(3) It has been explained that in *Re Gulbenkian's Settlement*[95] the House of Lords rejected the view of Lord Denning M.R. in the Court of Appeal[96] that a power was sufficiently certain if some person or persons were clearly within it even though it was difficult to say whether other persons were or were not within it. Nevertheless Lord Denning's test may still apply in certain special cases. It appears in effect to have been applied in *Re Barlow's Will Trusts*[97] where a testatrix left a valuable collection of paintings and directed her executor to sell some of the collection subject to the proviso that any members of her family or any *friends* of hers who might wish to do so might purchase any of the paintings at prices which were in fact considerably below market value. Browne-Wilkinson J. held that the direction to allow friends of the testatrix to purchase paintings did not require all members of the class of beneficiaries to be established before it took effect because any uncertainty as to some of the persons intended to benefit did not affect the quantum of the gift to those who undoubtedly qualified. Accordingly, the direction would be valid if it was possible to say that one or more claimants qualified even if it was difficult to say that others qualified.[98] The circumstances of the case, involving individual gifts with a condition precedent attached, were different from the circumstances in *Re Gulbenkian* and *McPhail* v. *Doulton* where it was necessary to determine the objects of the power and trust power respectively for purposes of direct beneficial entitlement.[99]

III. POWERS OF APPOINTMENT, AND OTHER POWERS AND DISCRETIONS

Having considered the distinction in concept between a trust and a power, it is now possible to consider certain aspects of the distinction in its practical application. The types of device which may be encountered are:

(a) powers of appointment;
(b) others powers and discretions; and
(c) discretionary trusts.

---

[94] [1960] Ch. 232.

[95] [1970] A.C. 508.

[96] [1968] 1 Ch. 126.

[97] [1979] 1 W.L.R. 278, applying *Re Allen* [1953] Ch. 810, C.A.; See also *Re Tuck's Settlement Trusts* [1978] Ch. 49., C.A. (condition of marriage to a woman of Jewish blood and faith: valid).

[98] Whether a person qualified depended on whether (1) the relationship with the testatrix was of long standing; (2) the relationship was social as opposed to business or professional; and (3) they met frequently when circumstances permitted: *ibid.* at p. 282.

[99] *Cf.* McKay (1980) Conv. 263.

The distinction between powers of appointment and other powers is dealt with here, and discretionary trusts are dealt with later.[1]

In some cases, the classification is not straightforward. For example, in *Bond v. Pickford*[2] the trustees were given power to "apply capital for the benefit of any one or more of the beneficiaries...by...allocating or appropriating to such beneficiary such sum or sums out of or investments forming part of the capital of the trust fund" as they thought fit. Nourse J. held that this power of "allocation or appropriation" was akin to a limited special power of appointment.

Where there exists a power to decide which of the members of a group shall derive benefit from a fund, that power may be a power of appointment; or it may be another type of power, usually called a discretion. This distinction has nothing to do with that between trust powers and mere powers, and, in principle, both powers of appointment and discretions may be either trust powers or mere powers. Nevertheless, there are three important differences between powers of appointment and discretions:

(a) With regard to income a power of appointment governs, strictly, money to arise or to become payable in the future, whereas a discretion deals with funds which are already in hand. The analogy is that of the railway where each wagon represents a payment. The exercise of a power of appointment in favour of a beneficiary is like setting the points towards a particular track. In itself, that does not cause a wagon to pass down the track, but when the trains come then so long as the points remain set in that direction (or while the appointment remains unrevoked), all trains (or income) will go to that destination (or beneficiary) automatically, and without any further action, or decision, being taken. The exercise of a discretion on the other hand is like the operation of a marshalling yard, where the wagons are already under the control of the marshaller, and he has to make a separate decision in respect of each wagon, by deciding to which of the several tracks it will go.

This distinction is particularly important in respect of income. If income is subject to a power of appointment, then, once the appointment is made, all income will go to the appointee without any further decision being necessary. In the case of a discretion, however, a separate decision must be taken at each stage. This was shown clearly in *Wilson v. Turner*.[3] In that case the trustees had a power to pay or apply income arising from the trusts to or for the maintenance of an infant beneficiary.[4] They did not make a conscious decision, but merely handed over the income to the infant's father, and the Court of Appeal held that the money should be repaid to the trust fund. If, however, the trustees had from time to time actively considered the merits of the case, and had consciously decided to apply the income for the maintenance of the infant, their decision would have been valid.[5]

---

[1] *Post*, p. 83.   [2] [1982] STC 403; (*The Times*, C.A., May 24, 1983).
[3] (1883) 22 Ch.D. 521.   [4] As to the statutory power of maintenance, see *post*, p. 354.
[5] A further example of the same principle is *Re Greenwood* ((1911) 105 L.T. 509), considered *post*, p. 273.

The distinction as it applies to income is of crucial importance in respect of capital transfer tax. It will be seen[6] that the charge to capital transfer tax on settled property depends on whether or not a beneficiary has an interest in possession in that property. Where there is an appointment of income in favour of a beneficiary, that beneficiary has an interest in possession, even if the appointment is revocable. A beneficiary who is only entitled to income on the exercise of the trustees' discretion does not have an interest in possession.

(b) The second difference between a power of appointment and a discretion is in relation to formalities. Although in principle no formality is necessary for the exercise of a power of appointment, in practice some formality is almost always prescribed in the instrument by which the power is conferred. Where this is so, considerable importance is placed on the formal requisites. So, if a power of appointment is to be exercised by deed, it cannot be exercised by will,[7] and a power to be exercised by will cannot be exercised by any instrument which is not a will.[8] If, however, the donor not only specifies the type of instrument by which the power is to be exercised, such as deed or will, but specifies particular formalities to be observed in the execution of that instrument, such as requiring six witnesses, these stipulations may be modified by two statutory provisions. The first provides that in the case of a power to be exercised by deed, the exercise will be formally valid if the deed is executed in the presence of at least two witnesses,[9] and in the case of a will it will be formally valid if it complies with the provisions of the Wills Acts.[10]

As a further exception to the general principle that formal requirements must be strictly observed, just as equity will in certain cases perfect an imperfect gift[11] so in somewhat similar cases equity will perfect an imperfect exercise of a power. These will be, broadly, where the donee of the power intended to exercise it, and the exercise was to satisfy a moral obligation.[12]

By contrast, no formality is required for the exercise of a discretion, for the discretion is exercised at the moment when those exercising it reach their decision.[13] In general, therefore, the exercise of a power of appointment requires a physical act, while the exercise of a discretion is a metaphysical act.

Questions of formality are not to be confused, however, with any requirement to obtain the consent of any person. The exercise both of a power of appointment and of a discretion can be made subject to consents being obtained, and any purported exercise without those consents will be ineffective.

(c) The third difference between powers of appointment and discretions

---

[6] See *post*, p. 298.

[7] *Lord Darlington* v. *Pulteney* (1797) 3 Ves.Jr. 384; *Lady Cavan* v. *Doe* (1795) 6 Bro.P.C. 175; *Re Phillips* (1884) 41 Ch.D. 417.

[8] *Reid* v. *Shergold* (1805) 10 Ves.Jr. 370; *Re Evered* [1910] 2 Ch. 147.

[9] Law of Property Act 1925, s.159.

[10] *i.e.* Wills Act 1837, s.10; Wills Act 1963, s.2.

[11] See *ante*, p. 53.

[12] *Chapman* v. *Gibson* (1791) 3 Bro.C.C. 229; *Garth* v. *Townsend* (1869) L.R. 7 Eq. 220; *Kennard* v. *Kennard* (1872) L.R. 8 Ch.App. 227.

[13] It would in theory be possible for the donor of the power to prescribe some formal requirement, but it is most unlikely that this would be done.

relates to revocability. When a discretion is exercised, its effect is to confer upon the beneficiary a right to a sum which is in hand. The beneficiary has the right to demand payment, and payment is in fact usually made to him promptly. It is then too late for the person exercising his discretion to seek to change his mind, and to recall the money.[14] On the other hand, because a power of appointment looks towards the future, it can be expressed to be revocable, and, subject to the terms of the instrument by which it was conferred, the appointment can be revoked and a new appointment made without limit.[15]

It will be appreciated that a discretion and a revocable power of appointment can both be used to achieve the same general effect. For example, suppose there is a fund of income which for the year 1985 is to go to Charles; for 1986 to go to Douglas; and for 1987 to go to Edward. If there is a revocable power of appointment, at the beginning of 1985 the income can be appointed to Charles; at the beginning of 1986 the appointment can be revoked, and a new appointment made in favour of Douglas; and at the beginning of 1987 the appointment can again be revoked and a new appointment made in favour of Edward. On the other hand if the matter is dealt with by discretion, a decision can be made at or after the end of 1985 in favour of Charles; at or after the end of 1986 in favour of Douglas; and at or after the end of 1987 in favour of Edward. The result so far as the beneficiaries are concerned is the same in both cases. If under the trust instrument the trustees can take either course of action, they will usually be influenced by the taxation implications.

IV. Factors Affecting the Exercise of Powers and Discretions

1. *Delegation*

There is some uncertainty as to the extent to which trustees or others can delegate their powers and discretions. The basic position is that matters involving a decision on a matter of policy, or importance, which would include whether a person is to benefit, and, if so, to what extent, cannot be delegated,[16] but that ancillary decisions taken in order to give effect to the trustees' decision can be delegated.[17] So, if the trustees in the exercise of their discretion decide to give a beneficiary £5, they could leave it to their solicitor to decide whether to pay that sum by cheque or in cash.

The instrument by which a power is conferred can expressly authorise delegation of its exercise, and, occasionally, by express provision statutory

---

[14] Again in theory it would be possible for the donor of the power to provide that the trustees could change their mind before the sum was actually paid over to the beneficiary, but it is also most unlikely that this would be done.

[15] There appears to be a presumption that an appointment is to be irrevocable, and that this will apply until it can be shown that there is an express or implied intention that it shall be revocable.

[16] *Re May* [1926] 1 Ch. 136; *Re Mewburn* [1934] Ch. 112; *Re Wills' Will Trusts* [1959] Ch. 1.

[17] *Att.-Gen.* v. *Scott* (1750) 1 Ves.Sen. 413; *Re Hetling and Merton's Contract* [1893] 3 Ch. 269.

powers can be delegated.[18] Where there is no express authority, it seems that delegation can only be made effectively where there is an implied power to this effect in the instrument creating the power. So far as beneficial entitlements are concerned, the question most often arises where there is a power to appoint a fund among a group, and in making the appointment, the appointor seeks to appoint the fund not absolutely, but on certain trusts. Unless there is an express or implied power in the trust instrument, the appointor cannot appoint the fund upon discretionary trusts, because in so doing he is delegating to others, namely the trustees of the new trust, the power of deciding what the beneficiary shall in fact receive.[19] Similarly, if an appointment is made on protective trusts[20] the fixed interest part of the appointment is valid, even though the discretionary trusts which would arise on the determination of the life interest are void.[21] On the other hand, where, under the terms of the power, an appointment is validly made upon trust for a life tenant, with remainders over, it is implied that the appointor can include a provision for advancement.[22]

The extent to which trustees can delegate their powers of management and administration, and to appoint agents, is considered in later chapters.[23]

2. *Improper Exercise of Powers and Discretions*

Certain principles have been evolved governing the exercise of powers and discretions. These are:

(a) As well as complying with any formal requirement,[24] a power or discretion is only validly exercised by a positive mental act, and not by allowing a situation to arise merely by inaction. The decision in *Wilson* v. *Turner*[25] has already been mentioned,[26] and the position is considered further in a later chapter.[27]

(b) Unless they choose to do so, the trustees cannot be compelled to give reasons for their decisions. This is also considered later.[28]

(c) Where the power has been exercised honestly, the court will support it, even if it would itself have reached a contrary decision.[29]

---

[18] An example of statutory authority to delegate is that conferred by s.29 of the Law of Property Act 1925, enabling trustees for sale to delegate their powers of management; and see also *post*, pp. 271, 282.

[19] *Re Morris' Settlement* [1951] 2 All E.R. 528.

[20] See *post*, p. 120.

[21] *Re Boulton's Settlement Trusts* [1928] Ch. 703; *Re Morris' Settlement, supra; Re Hunter* [1963] Ch. 372.

[22] *Re Wills' Will Trusts* [1959] Ch. 1; *Pilkington* v. *I.R.C.* [1964] A.C. 612.

[23] *Post*, pp. 271, 282.

[24] *Ante*, p. 84.

[25] (1883) 22 Ch.D. 521.

[26] *Ante*, p. 83.

[27] *Post*, p. 273.

[28] *Post*, p. 275.

[29] See *e.g. R.* v. *Archbishop of Canterbury and Bishop of London* [1903] 1 K.B. 289. See also *Re Hastings-Bass* [1975] Ch. 25, C.A., where the exercise of a discretion by trustees was held valid even though made under a mistake of law; and see *post*, p. 377.

(d) Where the power has not been exercised honestly, it will be invalid. In this case there is said to be a "fraud on the power." The word "fraud" in equity denotes only improper motive and the expression "fraud on a power" is used both in connection with the exercise of a power, and the exercise of a discretion. In this discussion the word power includes discretion. Various attempts have been made to categorise the circumstances in which there is a fraud on the power,[30] but the most common situations are where a power is exercised in favour of an object where there is a prior agreement with him that he will apply the funds in whole or in part in favour of a non-object[31]; and where, even without such a prior agreement, the power is exercised with the intention of benefiting someone outside the scope of the power.[32] From the cases four points emerge:

(i) The fact that a power is exercised in such a way as to defeat the intention of the donor does not automatically make the exercise void.[33] This is comparable to the fact that beneficiaries may in some cases join together to bring a trust to an end even although the settlor intended that it should continue.[34] Once a power is conferred, or a trust created, the donor or settlor ceases to have any control as such, although the donor of a power could provide at the time of creation of the power that his consent should be obtained to its exercise.

(ii) In each case it is necessary to identify who would be entitled in default of the exercise of the power. The persons to take in default may be specified in the trust instrument, or there may be a resulting trust in their favour. These are the persons who lose by an improper exercise of the power, and, if they agree to it, knowing all relevant facts, the exercise is valid.[35]

(iii) The essential feature which makes the exercise of a power improper is the intention of the person exercising it. If it is exercised with the intention of benefiting some non-object of the power, whether it be the appointor or someone else, the exercise is void. If it is not done with this intention, but the exercise does in fact benefit a non-object, it is valid. Take the situation where a father has a power to appoint in favour of his child. In general, such an appointment is valid[36] but if it is exercised when the child is very ill, with the intention that the appointor will benefit by taking the child's estate on its death, the exercise is invalid[37]; and this is strictly the position even if the child subsequently recovers. If as part of a tax-saving scheme it is desired to bring the trust to an end by exercising the power, and the appointment is made with the intention of benefiting the object, the appointment is valid even although the appointment brings some incidental benefit on the appointor or others.[38]

---

[30] See *Vatcher* v. *Paull* [1915] A.C. 372.

[31] *Ibid.*

[32] *Portland* v. *Topham* (1867) 11 H.L.Cas. 32; *Vatcher* v. *Paull, supra.*

[33] *Lee* v. *Ferrie* (1839) 1 B. 483.

[34] See *post*, p. 94.

[35] *Re Turner's Settled Estates* (1884) 28 Ch.D. 205; *Re Greaves* [1954] Ch. 434.

[36] *Henty* v. *Wrey* (1882) 21 Ch.D. 332.

[37] *Lord Hinchinbroke* v. *Seymour* (1789) 1 Bro.C.C. 395.

[38] *Re Merton* [1953] 1 W.L.R. 1096; *Re Robertson's Will Trusts* [1960] 1 W.L.R. 1050.

(iv) Where a power is to be exercised in favour of an object of it, but there is the hope that the recipient will benefit a non-object, the validity of the exercise will depend upon whether the person in whose favour the power was exercised had legal and moral freedom of action.[39] Suppose that a power is exercisable in favour of a person who makes it known that if the power is in fact exercised in his favour he will give part of the fund to his parents, who are not objects. If the intention of the appointment is to benefit the parents, the exercise is invalid under the previous paragraph. If the object of the power is under great pressure to benefit the parents, the exercise is also invalid.[40] If, however, the object of the power has genuine freedom of action, but wishes to give his parents a benefit, the exercise of the power is good.[41]

3. Effects of Invalid Exercise of a Power or Discretion

In principle, where the exercise of a power is improper, it is totally invalid.[42] This can work harshly on the objects. If the appointor reaches an agreement with an object that the appointor will appoint to the object £1,000, provided the object pays £500 to a non-object, then, in principle, the whole appointment is invalid, and the object receives nothing. Accordingly, in an attempt to help objects, in some cases the court will try to sever the improper element in the appointment from the remainder.[43] Clearly, if there is no intent to benefit the object of the power at all, the exercise is entirely invalid.[44] If, however, there is an intent to benefit the object to some extent, and the improper element is in the form of a condition attached to the appointment, the court will delete the condition to leave the object free to take unconditionally.[45]

V. SOME PROVISIONS OF DISCRETIONARY TRUSTS

The expression "discretionary trust" is used in two senses. The first is in the sense of a discretion of the nature considered previously, where there is an obligation to exercise it. But more commonly, it is used to denote the total provisions of the trust instrument, which will probably contain a combination of powers of appointment, discretionary and other powers, both of the nature of mere powers and of trust powers. Two aspects of the provisions commonly found will now be considered.

1. Time for Exercise

Trustees must exercise any discretion within a reasonable time. What is reasonable depends on the facts of each case. In Re Gulbenkian's Settlement Trusts

---

[39] Birley v. Birley (1858) 25 B. 299.
[40] Re Crawshay [1948] Ch. 123; Re Dick [1953] Ch. 343.
[41] Re Marsden's Trusts (1859) 4 Drew. 594.
[42] Daubeney v. Cockburn (1816) 1 Mer. 626.
[43] Topham v. Duke of Portland (1858) 1 D.J. & S. 517.
[44] Re Cohen [1911] 1 Ch. 37.
[45] Hay v. Watkins (1850) 3 Dr. & War. 339.

(*No.* 2)[46] trustees learned in April 1957 of a decision[47] which cast doubt on the validity of a provision as to the accumulation of income. They therefore retained the income without accumulating it. The doubt was not resolved until the decision of the House of Lords in *Re Gulbenkians' Settlement Trusts* (*No.* 1)[48] in October 1968. Plowman J. held that their retention of the income was not unreasonable in the circumstances and they could still exercise their discretion in respect of the income which had accrued since 1957. It therefore follows that if the circumstances are reasonable, trustees can retain income for some time, as income, and then accumulate it.

If the trustees do not exercise their discretion within a reasonable time, the result depends on whether their discretion was permissive or obligatory. If the discretion was permissive, that is, while the trustees were under a duty to consider whether to exercise their discretion, they were not under a duty to exercise it, the discretion is lost if it is not exercised within a reasonable time.[49] If, however, the trustees were under an obligation to exercise their discretion, the discretion is not extinguished by lapse of time. Accordingly, the trustees can exercise it much later, and, if they do not do so, the court will direct them to do so.[50]

2. Modifying the Class of Beneficiaries

There has been a general trend towards making trusts more and more flexible, so that the discretionary trust has become much more popular than the trust with fixed interests. Two recent developments have been to include powers to alter the class of beneficiaries, or even to revoke all the trusts and declare new ones. The latter provision is considered elsewhere but it is now established that the former is valid. In principle it seems that there is no objection either to giving trustees power to add persons to a class; or to declare a very wide class, and merely give the trustees power to exclude particular persons, usually as a result of new legislation. The practice was approved in *Re Manisty's Settlement*.[51] In that case there was a discretionary trust for the benefit of the children and remoter issue of the settlor. The settlement conferred upon the trustees power to bring other persons into the class, and they purported to exercise this power by bringing in the settlor's mother, and any person who should be a widow of the settlor. Templeman J. held that such a power could be validly conferred on trustees, and that their exercise of it was therefore valid.[52]

---

[46] [1970] Ch. 408.

[47] *Re Gresham's Settlement* [1956] 1 W.L.R. 573, subsequently overruled.

[48] [1970] A.C. 508; and see *ante*, p. 77.

[49] *Re Gourju's Will Trusts* [1943] Ch. 24; *Re Wise* [1896] 1 Ch. 281; *Re Allen-Meyrick's Will Trusts* [1966] 1 W.L.R. 499.

[50] *Re Locker's Settlement Trusts* [1978] 1 All E.R. 216; see *post*, p. 273, 352.

[51] [1974] Ch. 17; and see *Blausten* v. *I.R.C.* [1982] Ch. 256 and *Re Hay's Settlement Trusts* [1982] 1 W.L.R. 202, discussed *ante*, p. 80.

[52] The decision is in line with the approval of a power of delegation by resettlement in *Pilkington* v. *I.R.C.* [1964] A.C. 612, discussed *post*, p. 375.

VI. RELEASE OF POWERS

1. *Reasons*

Trustees are sometimes asked to release powers. This may be as a result of changes in fiscal legislation. For example, before April 1973, all income of a trust was taxable in the hands of the trustees at the same rate. With effect from April 6, 1973, however, an additional charge to tax was imposed on income which can be accumulated.[53] If, therefore, there is a trust under which trustees have a power to accumulate, but subject thereto to pay to a named person, they might be asked to release their power to accumulate so that the named beneficiary would be entitled to the whole of the income, and the increased charge to tax would not apply. More likely, however, trustees may be asked to release powers in order to create indefeasible interests. Suppose that trustees hold a fund upon trust for such of Michael, Norman and Oliver as they should appoint, and in default of appointment for those three equally. As long as the power of appointment is exercisable, none of the beneficiaries can be sure that they will receive any benefit, for the power may be exercised in favour of the others. Thus, if say, Michael wishes to raise money by selling or mortgaging his interest, he may ask the trustees to release the power, in order to give him a fixed interest which he can then deal with. Other reasons for releasing powers may arise, as in *Re Wills' Trust Deeds*[54] where there was a power to appoint between charitable and non-charitable objects, and it was desired to release the latter power, in order to convert the trust into one which was entirely charitable.

Two questions arise: can a power be properly released, and the extent to which any release is effective.

2. *Propriety of Release*

It has been shown in connection with fraud on powers that the primary objects of the power are considered to be those entitled in default. Accordingly, it has been held that the doctrine of fraud on a power does not apply to the release of a power, for the release benefits those entitled in default.[55] The same principle applies where a power of appointment which has been exercised is revoked.[56] But it seems that the decisions have applied to mere powers and not to trust powers.[57] If there is no gift over in default of appointment, and in any case where the power is a trust power, the same reasoning does not apply, and it seems that no release will be proper if it is not expressly authorised by the trust instrument.

In *Re Wills' Trust Deeds*[58] the circumstances in which a power could be

---

[53] Finance Act 1973, s.16; see *ante*, p. 68.
[54] [1964] Ch. 219.
[55] *Re Somes* [1896] 1 Ch. 250.
[56] *Re Greaves* [1954] Ch. 434.
[57] *Shirley* v. *Fisher* (1882) 47 L.T. 109; *Re Jones' Settlement* [1915] 1 Ch. 373; *Re Graves* [1954] Ch. 434.
[58] [1964] Ch. 219.

effectively released were considered, and Buckley J. formulated the following general propositions on the subject.[59]

(i) If a power is granted to appoint among a class of objects and in default of appointment there is a *trust*, express or implied, in favour of members of that class, the donee cannot defeat the interest of the members of the class by releasing the power, or, which comes to the same thing, by refusing to appoint.

(ii) A power of the kind just mentioned cannot be released, for the donee is under a duty to exercise it, notwithstanding the fact that the court may not be able to compel him personally to perform that duty.

(iii) Where a power is conferred on trustees *virtute officii* in relation to their trust property they cannot release it or bind themselves not to exercise it.

(iv) The same is true if the power is conferred on persons who are trustees of a settlement but is conferred on them by name and not by reference to their office if on the facts they were selected as donees of the power because they were trustees.

(v) Where a power is conferred on someone who is not a trustee of property to which the power relates or if he be a trustee is not conferred on him in that capacity, then in the absence of a trust in favour of the object of the power in default of appointment the donee is not under any duty recognised by the court to exercise the power such as to disable him from releasing it.

The first of these propositions is self-evident, as the judge said, and so also is the fifth. But the second appears to be highly debatable as it is stated: the fact would appear to be that if the donee of a power is not under a duty to exercise it, he can surely release it, even though the release would be ineffectual in view of the trust in default of appointment.

The third and fourth propositions are of great interest. They suggest that if a power is conferred on persons *qua* trustees, the principle which governs the relationship of trustees to a trust should also govern their relationship to the exercise of a power conferred on them in their fiduciary capacity. In other words, it would appear that the capacity in which the donee of the power holds (*i.e.* whether or not he holds in a fiduciary capacity) must be taken into account. But although it seems on the face of it a desirable conclusion, it does have the consequence that the distinction between trusts and powers of appointment in matters of release has become rather blurred. The point is of practical importance, for many trusts of the discretionary kind today involve a mélange, as it were, of trusts and powers: the appointment of trustees and the vesting of powers of appointment in them.[60] These two propositions are, however, to be read subject to the rider later introduced by the Court of Appeal in *Muir* v. *I.R.C.*[61] that even if a power is conferred on trustees *virtute officii* they can still release it if the instrument authorises them to do so. In this case it was held that

---

[59] *Ibid*, pp. 236, 237. In cases of doubt whether a release should be effected it seems possible to apply to the court for directions: see *Re Allen-Meyrick's Will Trusts* [1966] 1 W.L.R. 499; or, alternatively, in cases where a variation of trusts is sought, an application to the court on the question may be made under the Variation of Trusts Act 1958, see *post*, p. 413.

[60] See *ante*, p. 68.   [61] [1966] 1 W.L.R. 1269.

the wording of the relevant clause enabled them to do this. In effect this was the position also in *Blausten* v. *I.R.C.*[62] where the Court of Appeal came to the conclusion that a resettlement of the trust fund upon trusts identical with the existing trusts, but excluding a particular power in the trustees, was a good exercise of the power of appointment. The immediate effect of the appointment was simply to exclude the wife of the settlor from the objects of the discretionary trusts of income and that was held to be within the terms of the power of appointment.

3. *Effectiveness of Release*

In *Re Wills' Trust Deeds* it was held that the power of appointment in question was not coupled with a duty or trust and was capable of being released accordingly. But the judge also raised a fresh point—on which there appeared to be no prior direct authority—in holding that, although the present trustees, by releasing the power, precluded themselves from exercising it, that would not prevent their successors in title from exercising it. "A power granted to successive holders of an office," he said, "is unlike trust property, the entire ownership of which is vested in the trustees for the time being of the settlement and devolves on each change of trustee by succession. Where a power is granted to successive holders of an office all that is vested in the incumbent for the time being of the office is the capacity to exercise the power while he holds that office."[63]

4. *Failure to Exercise Power*

Until such time, if at all, as the power is effectively released, it remains with the trustees and they alone must exercise it. In *Re Allen-Meyrick's Will Trusts*[64] the trustees of a will held the trust fund upon trust to pay so much of the income as they thought fit to the husband of the testatrix and, subject to the exercise of their discretion in his favour, upon trust for her god-daughters. The husband was an undischarged bankrupt and the trustees had in the exercise of their discretion paid the rent of the house in which he lived, but apart from this they could not agree on whether to make a further payment to him. They asked the court to accept a surrender of their discretion, but Buckley J. refused. It is open to trustees of any trust to seek the directions of the court in any particular circumstances, and the court was prepared to give directions as to what should be done with the income which had accrued, but it would not accept a surrender of the trustees' discretion for the future. This seems to have been largely for procedural reasons, because, had the court accepted that surrender, there would have been no ready way in which it could be informed of the actual circumstaces of the beneficiaries each time a decision had to be made. It is, however, possible that although this would not have been welcomed by the

---

[62] [1972] Ch. 256.
[63] [1964] Ch. 219 at p. 238.
[64] [1966] 1 W.L.R. 499.

court, the trustees could have sought the directions of the court on a new application each year or so.

VII. THE POSITION OF BENEFICIARIES

1. *The Beneficiaries Themselves*

What is the position of the object of a power, whether it be a mere power or a trust power, pending its exercise? There are two aspects:

(1) **As an individual object**

As one of several objects of a power, a person can require the trustees to consider exercising the power in his favour, or in favour of any other object.[65] Accordingly, if the object can show that the trustees have refused to consider him, following his request, he can apply to the court for an order to remove them.[66]

The object of a power may also apply to the court if, although giving his own position due consideration, they act capriciously in other respects. In *Re Manisty's Settlement*[67] Templeman J. said[68] that the trustees would act capriciously if they acted "for reasons which I apprehend could be said to be irrational, perverse, or irrelevant to any sensible expectation of the settlor; for example, if they chose a beneficiary by height or complexion or by the irrelevant fact that he was a resident of Greater London."

In other respects the object of a power is in a curious position. On the one hand it seems clear that trustees are not obliged to inform him that he is an object of the power.[69] On the other hand, if he knows that he is an object it seems that he is entitled to apply to the court if there is any improper administration of the trust, and, in order to see whether this is so, to obtain the same information as a beneficiary having a fixed interest.[70] This is, therefore, a reason for keeping the class of objects narrow.

This is, however, subject to any contrary provision in the trust instrument. Thus, some modern discretionary trust deeds authorise the trustees to exercise their discretion in favour of some objects without even considering the other objects.

(2) **As one of a group of objects**

There is one respect in which the object has a more direct interest in the trust fund.

It will be seen later that where a beneficiary is of full age and *sui juris*, and he is alone entitled to the trust fund, he may bring the trust to an end.[71] Somewhat

---

[65] *Re Gestetner* [1953] Ch. 672, *per* Harman J., p. 688; *Re Manisty's Settlement* [1973] 2 All E.R. 1203, *per* Templeman J., at p. 1210.

[66] *Re Manisty's Settlement, supra.*

[67] [1973] 2 All E.R. 1203.

[68] *Ibid.* at p. 1210.

[69] *Re Manisty's Settlement, supra*, p. 1209.

[70] See *post*, pp. 274, 385.

[71] See *post*, p. 386.

similarly, where all the objects of a discretionary trust combine then they may together deal with the beneficial interest. This was shown by *Re Smith*.[72] In that case the sole trustee held a fund, broadly, upon a discretionary trust as to income and capital for Lilian and after her death for her children. Lilian and her three children, who between them were the only persons who took benefit under the trust, together assigned all their interest under the will to an insurance company. The assignee was held entitled to demand the whole of the income. Romer J. said that in such a case "you treat all the people put together as though they formed one person, for whose benefit the trustees were directed to apply the whole of a particular fund."[73]

(3) Release of interest

Just as a man cannot be forced to accept a gift[74] so a man cannot be forced to remain an object of a power or discretionary trust, and he can, if he so wishes, release his rights under the trust. In that event, the trust is administered as if his name did not appear among the class of the discretionary beneficiaries.[75]

Position of Assignees and Trustees in Bankruptcy

An assignee or trustee in bankruptcy is, in principle, in the same position as the discretionary beneficiary himself. So, in *Re Coleman*[76] the Court of Appeal held that where the discretionary beneficiary had assigned his beneficial interest the trustees were compelled to pay to the assignee the amount which they allotted to the beneficiary. On this point *Re Smith*,[77] which was mentioned above, is similar. In principle, the position of a trustee in bankruptcy is the same, but this is subject to the general rule of bankruptcy that a bankrupt is entitled to retain sufficient funds for his support, the trustee in bankruptcy being entitled only to the balance. This rule was applied by Vaughan Williams J. in *Re Ashby*.[78] In that case a discretionary beneficiary became bankrupt, and the trustees continued to make payments to him. The beneficiary was entitled to retain what was necessary for his mere support, and his trustee in bankruptcy was able to claim the excess.

The terms of the trust instrument may require payment to be made to the beneficiary personally, but on the other hand the trustees may be entitled either to pay to the beneficiary or to make payments for his benefit. In *Re Bullock*[79] which was concerned with a discretionary trust of the latter type, Kekewich J. held that when a discretionary beneficiary became bankrupt, the trustees could continue to pay income for his benefit. The scope of this decision is in doubt, and it has been suggested that the power is restricted so that the trustees can

---

[72] [1928] Ch. 915.
[73] See also *Re Nelson* [1928] Ch. 920n.
[74] *Thompson* v. *Leach* (1690) 2 Vent. 198; *Re Stratton's Deed of Disclaimer* [1958] 2 Ch. 42.
[75] *Re Gulbenkian's Settlement Trusts (No. 2)* [1970] Ch. 408.
[76] (1889) 39 Ch.D. 443.
[77] *Ante.*
[78] [1892] 1 Q.B. 872.
[79] (1891) 64 L.T. 736.

only pay to the bankrupt for his necessaries. This, however, is probably not correct. It seems that so far as the trustees are concerned they may continue to apply funds for the benefit of the beneficiary in the same way as they could have done before the bankruptcy. If as a result assets come into the hands of the beneficiary which are not required for his necessaries, as where the trustees apply the money in providing a luxurious holiday for the beneficiary, it seems that the trustee in bankruptcy is powerless to interfere. Of course, the trustees must exercise their discretion in good faith, and must make the decision to benefit the beneficiary and not to spite the trustee in bankruptcy.

CHAPTER 5

LEGALITY OF A TRUST

I. GENERALLY

IT is an elementary principle that a trust which is *wholly* illegal or contrary to public policy will not be enforced. The court indeed will not only prevent the illegal trust taking effect but will generally go so far as to refuse its assistance to the settlor in recovering the property. "Those who violate the law," said Lord Truro L.C., "must not apply to the law for protection."[1] The principle will not, however, be stretched to its uttermost limit. A settlor is entitled to recover the property where the illegal purpose is merely *contemplated*; in these circumstances there is what is described as a *locus poenitentiae*.[2]

The consequences of a *partially* unlawful trust may be rather different. Strictly, it appears that if part of the trust funds is to be devoted in the first instance to an unlawful purpose and the remainder to a lawful purpose, but the first part cannot be ascertained, the whole trust will fail, for it would be impossible to ascertain the residue.[3]

But there must be a true impossibility of ascertainment and it does appear that the court will, if it is practicable, strive to ascertain it and uphold the remainder of the gift.[4] Indeed there is some—admittedly indecisive—authority[5] for the proposition that the whole of the property will go to the lawful purpose if that is charitable and that the trust for the illegal purpose will be completely disregarded; but in view of the confused state of the case-law it is by no means certain that this truly represents the law, however convenient it may be.

The law relating to bankruptcy and perpetuity is of the utmost importance in any discussion of the legality of a trust, and these subjects are dealt with later in the chapter. But it is beyond the scope of this book to deal exhaustively with the many other classes of illegality and the like which will vitiate a trust as they will vitiate any other transaction. Only a few examples will be briefly considered to indicate in what circumstances a trust will be rendered bad on this basis.

---

[1] *Benyon* v. *Nettlefold* (1850) 3 Mac. & G. 94 at 102. And see *Ayerst* v. *Jenkins* (1873) L.R. 16 Eq. 275, *cf. Phillips* v. *Probyn* [1899] 1 Ch. 811.
[2] *Symes* v. *Hughes* (1870) L.R. 9 Eq. 475.
[3] See *Chapman* v. *Brown* (1801) 6 Ves. 404.
[4] See *Mitford* v. *Reynolds* (1842) 1 Ph. 185.
[5] See *Fisk* v. *Att.-Gen.* (1867) L.R. 4 Eq. 521; *Hunter* v. *Bullock* (1872) L.R. 14 Eq. 45; *Dawson* v. *Small* (1874) L.R. 18 Eq. 114; *Re Williams* (1877) 5 Ch.D. 735; *Re Birkett* (1878) 9 Ch.D. 576 (all trusts for maintenance of tombs with surplus for a charitable purpose); see also *Re Rogerson* [1901] 1 Ch. 715.

(1) **Restraints on alienation**

A restraint on alienation of property given to a beneficiary absolutely is contrary to public policy and void.[6]

(2) **Illegitimate children**

In certain circumstances trusts coming into force before 1970, whether by deed[7] or will,[8] in favour of illegitimate children yet to be born were void on the ground that they promoted immorality, and so were contrary to public policy. The test of public policy was whether or not future immorality was promoted. However, this does not apply in the case of an *inter vivos* gift made, or a will of a person dying, after 1969.[9]

(3) **Restraint of marriage**

If a condition, or a gift over to take effect upon such condition, is contained in a settlement, and it tends to restrain marriage altogether, the condition and gift over are void.[10] But this rule does not apply to a gift over in the event of a second marriage.[11] Nor does it apply to a *partial* restraint operating against designated persons only.[12]

On the other hand, a limitation of property *until* marriage—as opposed to a limitation to a person *on condition* that he does not marry—is perfectly good.[13] The question whether or not a limitation of this sort will be valid will depend on whether it is construed as creating a determinable interest or an interest upon condition. The distinction is perhaps an unnecessarily fine one, but it is well established.

The same difficulties, curiously enough, do not attach to a *condition* requiring *consent* to marriage. It is, of course, easy to see that if consent is withheld it will effectively bar marriage. But despite the apparent illogicality, it seems to be clearly established that the condition will be valid.[14]

(4) **Trusts separating parent and child**

If a trust is designed to separate a parent (even if he or she has been divorced[15]) from his or her child, that, too, will be void as contrary to public policy.[16] Yet again a trust will fail if it tends to interfere with parental duties: such duties should be discharged solely with a view to the moral and spiritual welfare of the child and without being influenced by mercenary considerations.[17]

---

[6] See *e.g. Floyer* v. *Bankes* (1869) L.R. 8 Eq. 115.

[7] *Blodwell* v. *Edwards* (1596) Cro.Eliz. 509; and see *Occleston* v. *Fullalove* (1874) 9 Ch.App. 147, *per* Mellish L.J.

[8] *Metham* v. *Duke of Devonshire* (1718) 1 P.Wms. 529.

[9] Family Law Reform Act 1969, s. 15(7).

[10] *Lloyd* v. *Lloyd* (1852) 2 Sim. (N.S.) 255.

[11] *Allen* v. *Jackson* (1842) 1 Ch.D. 399, C.A.

[12] *Jenner* v. *Turner* (1880) 16 Ch.D. 188.

[13] *Re Lovell* [1920] 1 Ch. 122.

[14] *Re Whiting's Settlement* [1905] 1 Ch. 96.

[15] *Re Piper* [1946] 2 All E.R. 503.

[16] *Re Boulter* [1922] 1 Ch. 75; *Re Sandbrook* [1912] 2 Ch. 471.

[17] *Re Borwick* [1933] Ch. 657.

(5) **Name and arms clauses**

A number of decisions were overruled by the Court of Appeal in *Re Neeld*[18] to produce the unexceptionable principle that a name and arms clause (which many people would regard as harmless if anachronistic), requiring a husband to whom a woman may be married to change his name on marriage, is neither contrary to public policy nor uncertain.

II. PERPETUITIES AND ACCUMULATIONS

Since medieval times, English law has been subject to the tension between two conflicting influences. Land and other property owners have desired to tie up their property indefinitely, usually for the benefit of their family or for some institution or cause, while the courts and the legislature have always felt that it is in the interest of the nation as a whole that wealth should circulate freely and that property should not be made inalienable. The result has been a compromise. Property may be tied up indefinitely for a purpose which the law wishes to advance, namely, a charity.[19] Otherwise property may be tied up but only for a comparatively short period. The rule which governs this is known as the rule against perpetuity.

1. *Perpetuities*

This rule has two aspects. First, that relating to vesting. In its basic form, it provides that property must vest in the recipient within the period of a life or lives in being at the time when the gift is made, and 21 years thereafter (with allowance being made where appropriate for the period of gestation).[20] The second aspect is that property must not be limited in such a way that it is inalienable in the hands of the recipient.

The rule has, however, been bedevilled by an excess of zeal on the part of the judges. Starting from the basis that property *must* vest within the perpetuity period, the judges have striven to find some possibility, no matter how remote, whereby it might not vest within that period. If they were able to envisage any such possibility, the gift was bad. In so doing, common sense went out of the window, and Alice walked in the front door. The almost unbelievable nonsense which ensued is illustrated by *Re Dawson*.[21] There a testator gave property to trustees to hold upon trust for his daughter for life, with remainder to such of her children as should attain the age of 21, with a provision that if any of her children should die under the age of 21, but should themselves leave issue, such issue on attaining the age of 21 would take the share of their parent. When the will came into operation, the testator's daughter was aged over 60, and all her children were over 21. Nevertheless, the court managed to hold this gift to be bad. With blithe disregard to the principles of biology, it was held that the

---

[18] [1962] Ch. 643.
[19] See *post*, p. 183
[20] *Cadell* v. *Palmer* (1833) 1 Cl. & Fin. 372; *Re Wilmer's Trusts* [1903] 2 Ch. 411.
[21] (1888) 39 Ch.D. 155

daughter was still capable of giving birth to a child, A. A might himself have died before reaching the age of 21, but leaving a child B. A was not alive at the death of the testator, so that the life in being was the testator's daughter. B would not have attained his vested interest within 21 years from the death of the daughter. As it was possible for the property not to vest within the perpetuity period, the whole gift failed. Again in *Re Gaite*[22] the judicial reasoning solemnly proceeded on the basis that a girl aged less than five could give birth to a child. In the apt expression of Morris and Leach[23] the judicial world would seem to be populated by fertile octogenarians, precocious toddlers, etc.

To overcome some of the traps, and generally to restore some semblance of sanity, Parliament has intervened on two occasions. Small amendments were made by the Law of Property Act 1925 and large scale alterations were made by the Perpetuities and Accumulations Act 1964. With only few exceptions[24] the latter Act applies only to instruments coming into effect after July 15, 1964[25] so that it is necessary to understand both the old rules and those prescribed by the 1964 Act.

The rule may be stated as follows:

Where a future gift is made, it must be seen from the instrument by which it is created that if it will vest at all, then it must vest within the period prescribed by law; but in the case of post-1964 instruments, if it appears that the gift might or might not vest within the prescribed period, the gift is treated as if it does not offend against the rule until such time, if at all, as it becomes clear that it cannot vest within that period.

The elements of this definition must now be examined and expanded.

(1) Rule is directed to vesting

The rule requires that a gift must vest within the perpetuity period. The aspect of the rule now being considered—as contrasted with the rule against inalienability which is considered later[26]—has no application to the length of time for which property may be enjoyed. Accordingly, if an outright gift is made to a limited company so that the gift vests immediately, the company may hold the property for over a thousand years without the rule having any operation.[27]

It is, therefore, essential to know what is meant by "vesting." A future gift may be either vested or contingent. A gift is vested if:

(a) the person or persons entitled to the gift are in existence and are ascertained;

(b) the size of the beneficiaries' interests are ascertained[28]; and

(c) any conditions attached to the gift are satisfied.

---

[22] [1949] 1 All E.R. 459.

[23] *The Rule Against Perpetuities* (2nd ed.), p.89.

[24] See s. 8(2)

[25] The date of the Royal Assent (s. 15(5)).

[26] *Post,* p. 106.

[27] See, however, *post,* p. 107.

[28] *Pearks* v. *Moseley* (1880) 5 App.Cas. 714. This requirement for vesting applies only to the rule against perpetuities.

If, therefore, property is left upon trust for Romeo for life, with remainder to Juliet, the interest of Juliet is vested even if Romeo is still alive. Juliet's interest is vested because she herself is alive and is an ascertained person; the extent of her interest, namely, in the whole fund, is ascertained; and no conditions have to be satisfied before she becomes entitled. On the other hand, if the gift was to Romeo for life, with remainder to Juliet provided she has danced on the moon, her gift does not become vested until that condition is fulfilled.

A vested interest, therefore, may or may not carry the right to present enjoyment.[29] To show this distinction, vested interests are classified as being:

(a) vested in possession, where the interest does carry the right to present possession or enjoyment; and
(b) vested in interest, where the interest only carries the right to future possession or enjoyment.

The relevance of this for the purposes of the perpetuity rule is that the rule is satisfied if the gift is only vested in interest. Thus, it was held in *Re Hargreaves*[30] that a gift to A for life, with remainder to any woman who may become his widow for life, with remainder to his children who attain the age of 21, was good. It is true that the person who might become A's wife need not be alive at the date of the settlement, but at the end of the perpetuity period (21 years after the death of A) it will be possible to say that his widow (if any) and his children who have attained 21 are between them the absolute owners of the property.

(2) Scope of rule

The general principle is that the rule applies to all future gifts. In particular, for the purposes of the law of trusts, it applies to future gifts arising under an *inter vivos* settlement or trust, and to trusts created by will. To this general principle there are three exceptions:

(a) a gift to charity is exempt from the rule if the prior interests are also given to charity. This is considered in further detail at page 184;
(b) rights of redemption under mortgages are not within the rule, so that a mortgagor's right to redeem can be exercisable outside the perpetuity period.[31] Likewise certain provisions of leases, such as options to renew[32] and options to purchase the reversion[33] are not within the rule; and
(c) future personal obligations are not within the rule. An example would be a covenant to pay mining royalties.[34]

(3) The perpetuity period

The maximum period for which vesting may be postponed is either:

---

[29] It is a question of construction whether an interest is contingent or is vested liable to be divested: *Brotherton* v. *I.R.C.* [1978] 1 .W.L.R. 610.
[30] (1889) 43 Ch.D. 401.
[31] *Knightsbridge Estates Trust Ltd.* v. *Byrne* [1939] Ch. 441.
[32] *Woodall* v. *Clifton* [1905] 2 Ch. 257 at 265, 268.
[33] Perpetuities and Accumulations Act 1964, s. 9(1).
[34] *Witham* v. *Vane* (1883) Challis R.P. 440.

(a) the period of a life or lives in being, and a further period of 21 years; or
(b) where there is no life in being, a period of 21 years; or
(c) in the case of post-1964 gifts, a period not exceeding 80 years which is specified in the instrument creating the gift as the perpetuity period.

In certain circumstances, the statutory period may be shorter than the common law period, but the use of the statutory period has the advantage of simplicity and certainty.

One of the more difficult questions affecting perpetuities is to identify the life or lives in being. It is clear that the life or lives chosen need take no benefit. Thus, it is common to use a "royal lives clause," that is, a clause which selects the lives of the descendants of His late Majesty King George V in being at the date of the gift.[35] In principle, there is no limit to the number of lives which may be selected, provided they can be identified. In *Re Moore*[36] the settlor specified as the lives in being all persons then living, but the gift was void on the ground that it was impossible to identify the survivor. Because it is so difficult as to be virtually impossible to identify the living descendants of any monarch before King George V, it is considered unsafe when using a royal lives clause to specify the descendants of any previous sovereign.[37]

In the royal lives and similar clauses, it is apparent from the words of the instrument that they are intended as the lives in being for the purposes of the rule. In other cases it may be far more difficult to decide whether a person is to be taken as a life in being. The principle may be stated that every person who is living at the date of the gift and is mentioned in it or is implied by it, is a life in being. Thus, a gift by a testator to "my grandchildren" presupposes the existence of his children, and if they are in fact alive, they will be taken as lives in being for the purposes of the rule.

A child *en ventre sa mère* is treated as a child who is alive if this is necessary to save a gift. Accordingly, if Susan is pregnant, a gift to the children of the child *en ventre* will be valid, for that child will by implication be regarded as a life in being.[38] Similarly, the perpetuity period itself may be extended where there is a pregnancy. If, therefore, a period of 80 years is prescribed, and at the end of that time a woman is pregnant with a child who would, if alive, take, subject to being born alive that child will in fact take.[39]

There is a dictum in the Irish decision, *Re Kelly*[40] that the life chosen must be that of a human and not of an animal—one would have thought an obvious if amusing proposition. It appears that only an Irish court has seen fit to pronounce formally upon it.

In the case of post-1964 instruments where advantage is not taken of specifying a period of not more than 80 years, section 3(4) of the 1964 Act prescribes

---

[35] *Re Leverhulme* [1943] 2 All E.R. 274.
[36] [1901] 1 Ch. 936.
[37] See doubts cast on the validity of using the lives of descendants of Queen Victoria in *Re Moore, supra.*
[38] *Long* v. *Blackall* (1797) 7 T.R. 100.
[39] See *Cadell* v. *Palmer* (1833) 1 Cl. & F. 372, especially at pp. 421, 422.
[40] [1932] I.R. 255 at 260, 261.

rules for identifying the lives in being. The Act provides that such of the following who are alive and ascertainable at the date of the gift, and no other person, shall constitute the lives in being:

(a) the person who made the disposition. This clearly has no relevance to will trusts;

(b) in the case of a contingent gift to an individual or individuals, any person who may in time satisfy the conditions; or his parent or grandparent;

(c) in the case of a class gift, any member or potential member of the class; or his parent or grandparent;

(d) any person who is given any power, option, or other right in connection with the gift; and

(e) where the interest is to arise only if the prior interest of some person determines, that person having the prior interest.

There are further provisions which apply where there is a special power of appointment.[41]

The lives of persons in categories (b), (c) and (d) are disregarded if the number of those persons is so large as to render it impossible to ascertain the date of death of the survivor.

(4) "Possibilities not probabilities"

The general principle is that any possibility of the gift not vesting within the perpetuity period makes the gift void. This can be expressed by saying that the rule is concerned with "possibilities not probabilities," subject to the "wait and see" rule considered below.[42] Illustrations of this are provided by the decisions in *Re Dawson* and *Re Gaite* which were mentioned above, but the advances in biological knowledge now enable the court, when considering gifts to which the 1964 Act applies, to make certain presumptions.[43] These are that a male cannot have a child at an age less than 14, and that a female can have a child between the ages of 12 and 55, but not outside that age-span.

(5) "Wait and see"

As regards pre-1964 gifts, one has to construe the instrument creating the gift at the date when it comes into operation. So that if a gift is made to A for life, with remainder to his eldest son to go to Canada, and at the date when the gift comes into force A has no children, the gift to the eldest son would be void for remoteness: the life in being is A, and his eldest son *may* not go to Canada within 21 years from A's death. Under the rules, relating to pre-1964 gifts, one may not wait and see whether in fact A does have a son who goes to Canada within 21 years from A's death.

Section 3 of the 1964 Act, however, provides that in some cases the court may "wait and see" if a particular gift will offend against the rule. The first and most important case is that where a gift may or may not become vested within the

---

[41] See *post* p. 105.
[42] See *post*, para. (5).
[43] 1964 Act, s. 2.

perpetuity period—and this means either the common law period or the statutory period of up to 80 years—the gift is to be treated as if it does not offend against the rule until it can be definitely shown that the gift *must* vest, if at all, after the end of the period. Thus, if an instrument coming into operation after July 15, 1964, contains a gift to A (a bachelor) for life, with remainder to his eldest son to go to Canada, and if A leaves a son, one may wait and see whether he does, in fact, go to Canada within 21 years of A's death. If he does, the gift is valid.

(6) Age-reducing provisions

Section 163(1) of the Law of Property Act 1925 provides that where the vesting of property is made to depend on the attainment by the beneficiary of an age greater than 21, and that by virtue of that condition the gift would be void for remoteness, the age of 21 is to be substituted for the age stated in the instrument. The section applies only when the gift would have been void for remoteness.

As regards instruments coming into operation after July 15, 1964, section 4 of the 1964 Act replaces section 163. By this section there is not substituted the age of 21, but the age nearest to the age which would have prevented the disposition from being void. Under the 1964 Act, therefore, the instrument is altered only to the extent necessary to save the disposition from offending against the rule.

Before applying section 4 of the 1964 Act, it is necessary to apply the "wait and see" rule. Suppose, therefore, that there is a gift to the children of William at the age of 30. Suppose also that William has a child who is aged four when the testator dies. As William is a life in being, it is necessary to wait until his death and see the position then. If by then the child has reached the age of 10, the gift must vest within the period. If, however, the child's age is then five, the vesting age will be reduced to 25, so that the vesting takes place within 21 years from the death of William.

A similar provision of the 1964 Act, which has no equivalent in the 1925 Act, enables gifts to children to be saved in other situations. Suppose there is a gift to such of the children of Andrew who should be living at the date of death of the survivor of Andrew and his wife. This gift is void at common law, because Andrew might subsequently marry a woman who was not born at the date of the gift. Accordingly, Andrew, and not his wife, would be the life in being, and as his wife might survive him for more than 21 years, the interest of the children might vest outside the perpetuity period. Again the "wait and see" rule is applied. If this does not save the gift, then by virtue of section 5 of the Act the gift vests immediately before the end of the perpetuity period. Accordingly, the gift would vest 21 years from the death of Andrew.

(7) Class gifts

Special provisions relate to "class gifts." For this purpose, a class is a number of persons who "come within a certain category or description defined by a general or collective formula, and who, if they take at all, are to take one divisible subject in certain proportionate shares."[44] As regards gifts in pre-1964 instruments, for the gift to be valid every member of the class must have fulfilled any necessary conditions within the perpetuity period: if any member has not fulfilled the conditions, the whole gift is void.[45]

Where the 1964 Act applies, however, many class gifts will in any case be saved by the wait and see provisions. But where these do not assist, the gift may still be saved by section 4(4). Under this subsection, if some members of the class have fulfilled the condition, but others have not, the class closes at the end of the perpetuity period to the exclusion of the others. Suppose, then, that there is a gift to A for life with remainder to such of his children as shall marry, and at the date of the gift A has no children. A would be the life in being and one may use the wait and see provisions to ascertain whether at the end of the perpetuity period—21 years after the death of A if no period is specified—A has had any children. If at that time there are three children of A, and two have married, the class will then close, to the exclusion of the unmarried child, and the two married children will between them take the whole of the property comprised in the gift.

(8) Dependent limitations

The rule of common law is that where a gift follows and is dependent upon prior limitations which are void, that gift is also void.[46] In order to apply the rule, however, it was necessary to distinguish between a gift which merely followed a prior void gift, and a gift which both followed and was dependent upon that prior void gift.[47] In practice it is difficult to decide whether a gift is dependent in this sense[48] and, in broad terms, a gift must have its own independent date of vesting if it is not to be regarded as dependent.[49]

(9) Powers of appointment

(a) **Classification of powers.** The classification of powers has been discussed earlier.[50] Whether for the purpose of the perpetuity rule hybrid powers should be classified at common law as general or special is doubtful, but it is suggested that the rules prescribed by the 1964 Act for post-1964 instruments should be followed for common law purposes. In any event, by virtue of section 7 of the 1964 Act a general power is a power exercisable by one person only, which can be exercised by the donee of the power to transfer property to himself without the consent of any other person.[51] A power may be general even if it is

---

[44] *Per* Lord Selborne L.C. in *Pearks* v. *Moseley* (1880) 5 App.Cas. 714 at p. 723.

[45] *Pearks* v. *Moseley* (1880) 5 App.Cas. 714; *Re Hooper's Settlement Trust* [1948] Ch. 586. The effect has been alleviated to some extent by the class closing rules: see the so-called Rule in *Andrews* v. *Partington* (1791) 3 Bro.C.C. 401; for recent illustrations of the working of the Rule, see *Re Chapman's Settlement Trusts* [1977] 1 W.L.R. 1163, C.A.; *Re Clifford's Settlement Trusts* [1981] Ch. 63.

[46] *Re Hubbard* [1963] Ch. 275; *Re Buckton* [1964] Ch. 497; *cf. Re Robinson* [1963] 1 W.L.R. 628.

[47] *Re Coleman* [1936] Ch. 528.

[48] *Re Backhouse* [1921] 2 Ch. 51.

[49] *Re Coleman, ante.*   [50] *Ante*, p. 71.

[51] Except where consent is required as to the mode of exercise of the power.

exercisable by will only, and not *inter vivos*.[52] For the purposes of the perpetuity rule it follows that dependent on its terms a hybrid power may be either general or special. If there is a power to appoint to anyone except Sanders, this will be a general power unless the donee of the power is Sanders himself.

(b) **Validity of powers.** There are two questions to be considered:

(a) is the power itself valid?
(b) is the appointment under the power valid?

(a) *Validity of power*

(i) **Special powers.** A special power is void if it is capable of being exercised outside the perpetuity period.[53] However, for post-1964 instruments, the wait and see rule may be applied, to see whether it is in fact fully exercised within the period. Where it is exercised within the period, but only partially, the power is only void to the extent that it was not exercised within the period.[54]

(ii) **General powers.** Because the donee of the power may appoint to himself, property subject to a general power is regarded for most purposes as property belonging to the donee. Therefore, so far as the validity of the power is concerned, it is necessary only that the power should be acquired within the perpetuity period: it is not necessary for it to be exercised within that period.[55] However, where the general power is *exercisable by will*, the same rule applies as for special powers.[56]

(b) *Validity of appointments*

(i) **Special powers.** Because the disposition of property subject to a special power is restricted, the perpetuity period commences with the date when the power is created, not when it is exercised. In principle, therefore, it is necessary at common law to consider the position as at the date of creation of the power; assume that the appointment is then made; and then see whether the gift vests within the perpetuity period. Even at common law, however, it is permissible to take into account the circumstances prevailing at the time when the power is exercised. If, therefore, by the terms of the appointment the gift could vest outside the perpetuity period, but when related to the circumstances existing at the time of the appointment it is seen that the vesting must occur within the period, if at all, the appointment is valid. This may be shown by an example. Suppose Charles by will gives property to Desmond for life, and that he also gives Desmond a power to appoint that property to his children. Suppose also that Desmond has a son Fergus who is born after the death of Charles. When Fergus reaches the age of 10, Desmond appoints the property to Fergus "as and when he attains the age of 30." Looking at the situation at the date of creation of

---

[52] This is also the position at common law—*Rous* v. *Jackson* (1885) 29 Ch.D. 521.
[53] *Re Abbot* [1893] 1 Ch. 54.
[54] 1964 Act, s. 3(3).
[55] *Re Fane* [1913] 1 Ch. 404.
[56] *Woolaston* v. *King* (1868) L.R. 8 Eq. 165.

the power, on the death of Charles, the gift and appointment are read together as if they provided: "to Desmond for life, with remainder to Fergus as and when he attains the age of 30." As Fergus is not then alive, it is clear that Fergus may take after 21 years from the death of Desmond, and the gift would prima facie be void. However, the modified wait and see rule is applied so that in the light of the circumstances existing when the power was exercised, it is seen that the gift must vest within 20 years of the death of Desmond, with the result that the appointment is valid.

The general wait and see provisions of the 1964 Act apply to powers which are both created and exercised after that date.[57]

(ii) **General powers.** The perpetuity period runs from the date of exercise of the power, and not from the date of its creation. The rules in respect of property comprised in a general power are the same as for property comprised in an absolute gift. However, if a power is general in its terms, but is only exercisable by more than one donee, it is treated as a special power.[58]

(10) General effect of the Act

The 1964 Act, which, it is repeated, applies only to gifts coming into force after July 15, 1964,[59] therefore contains provisions which in the long term are welcome[60] but which in the short term create a duality.

If a limitation in a trust instrument infringes the perpetuity rule, that interest will be held upon a resulting trust[61] for the settlor. Where the void limitation is contained in a will, that property will fall into residue, or will be distributed as on intestacy.

2. *Inalienability*

(1) Generally

The corollary to the rule that a gift must vest, if at all, within the perpetuity period is the principle that property must not be rendered inalienable.[62] The reason for this principle is to keep land and other property freely marketable and in circulation among members of the community. A gift is alienable if there is some provision which prevents the property being disposed of. This provision may be either a term of the gift itself,[63] or, in the case of a gift to a club or association, a rule of that club or association.[64]

To this general principle there are two exceptions. First, by analogy with the perpetuity rule, it seems that property may validly be made inalienable during

---

[57] 1964 Act, s. 15(5).

[58] *Re the Earl of Coventry's Indentures* [1974] Ch. 77.

[59] With the minor exception of s. 7.

[60] Except s. 10, they represent the recommendations of the Law Reform Committee, Cmnd. 18 (November 1956).

[61] See *post*, p. 148.

[62] *Carne v. Long* (1860) 2 De G.F. & J. 75 at p. 80.

[63] *Re Patten* [1929] 2 Ch. 276.

[64] *Rickard v. Robson* (1862) 31 Beav. 244; *Re Nottage* [1895] 2 Ch. 649; *Re Drummond* [1914] 2 Ch. 90.

the lifetime or times of persons in being at the time of the gift, and for 21 years thereafter.[65] Secondly, property may be made inalienable in the hands of a charity.[66]

A gift to a body corporate, which is not a charity, will in general not offend against the rule against inalienability. Even though the company may, if it so wishes, retain the property indefinitely for the benefit of its shareholders, if the gift is absolute, it will not be under any obligation to retain it. If, however, a condition is imposed on the gift prohibiting the company from disposing of it, the gift does offend against the rule and is void.[67]

In principle, the position is the same where there is a gift to an unincorporated association.[68] The possible circumstances in which a gift is made were classified by Cross J. in *Neville Estates Ltd.* v. *Madden*[69] as follows:

(*a*) The gift may be made to the members of the association at the date of the gift. If they are tenants in common they can take their share. If they are joint tenants, any member can sever his share and then claim it, whether or not he remains a member. There is in this situation nothing to offend against the rule against inalienability.[70]

(*b*) The gift may be to members of the association at the date of the gift, *qua* members, and not *qua* joint tenants. Where the members take in their capacity as members of the association, they take subject to their mutual contractual rights and liabilities, and these preclude a member from claiming his share unless all the other members of the association agree. A gift of this nature does not offend against the rule because it does not prevent all the members of the association from joining together to distribute the property of the association between them.[71]

(*c*) The gift may be made upon condition that it should be held in trust for, or applied for, the purposes of the association. In this event the gift is void.[72]

In many cases the category into which a particular gift falls will depend on a nice question of construction. Thus, where there is a gift "for the general purposes of the association," these words may seek to impose a perpetual trust; or they may be disregarded by the court, as having virtually no meaning, to enable the gift to be regarded as absolute.[73]

---

[65] *Carne* v. *Long* (1860) 2 De G.F. & J. 75; *Re Dean* (1889) 41 Ch.D. 552 at p. 557.

[66] *Chamberlayne* v. *Brockett* (1872) 8 Ch.App. 206 at 211.

[67] A further reason for it being void is that no person could enforce the trust: *Morice* v. *Bishop of Durham* (1805) 10 Ves. 521 at p. 539; *Bowman* v. *Secular Society Ltd.* [1917] A.C. 406 at p. 441; *Re Wood* [1949] Ch. 498.

[68] For discussion of the general characteristics of an unincorporated association, see *Conservative and Unionist Central Office* v. *Burrell* [1982] 1 W.L.R. 522, C.A.

[69] [1962] Ch. 832 at p. 849.

[70] *Re Smith* [1914] 1 Ch. 937.

[71] *Cocks* v. *Manners* (1871) L.R. 12 Eq. 571; *Re Drummond* [1914] 2 Ch. 90; *Re Ray's Will Trusts* [1936] Ch. 520.

[72] *Re Macaulay's Estate* [1943] Ch. 435.

[73] See Viscount Simonds in *Leahy* v. *Att.-Gen. for New South Wales* [1959] A.C. 457 at pp. 478, 479.

In other cases the general circumstances of the gift may indicate its nature. Thus in *Leahy* v. *Att.-Gen. for New South Wales*[74] a testator gave an area of grazing land to his trustees for such order of nuns as they should select. The Privy Council decided that the testator intended the order to be selected to take the property upon a perpetual trust, and that the individual members of the order were not to take beneficially. This decision was reached on the terms of the gift, which referred to an order as such, and not to the members of the order; and to the fact that as the members of the order might be spread throughout the world it was difficult to regard the testator as having intended to make an immediate beneficial gift to them. The Privy Council also took into account the fact that the subject-matter of the gift, grazing land, made it unlikely that the members of the order were to take beneficially.

On the other hand, in *Re Lipinski's Will Trusts*,[75] where there was an absolute gift to an unincorporated non-charitable association with a super-added direction that the funds were to be used solely in constructing and improving certain "new" buildings, the gift was held to fall within the second category of Cross J.'s formulation in *Neville Estates Ltd.* v. *Madden*.[76] Oliver J. was clearly influenced by the fact that the trustees and the beneficiaries were the same persons. As he said, "where the donee association is itself the beneficiary of the prescribed purpose, there seems to me the strongest argument in common sense for saying that the gift should be construed as an absolute one within the second category—the more so where, if the purpose is carried out, the members can, by appropriate act, vest the resulting property in themselves."[77] Moreover, the reference by the testator to "new" buildings did not import any idea of continuity so as to infringe the rule against perpetuities.

For the gift to be valid as being within either the first or the second of the categories specified by Cross J., the association must be in existence at the date when the gift takes effect. In *Re Recher's Will Trusts*[78] the court was concerned with the will of a testatrix dated May 23, 1957, under which she gave her residuary estate to a named anti-vivisection society.[79] In January 1957, however, that society had amalgamated with another, and subsequently the combined society became incorporated. The company claimed the residue. Brightman J. held that if the society named by the testatrix had continued its separate existence, the gift of residue would have been a valid legacy to the members of the association beneficially, as an accretion to the funds of the society subject to the contract the members had *inter se* as set out in the rules of the society.[80] However, as the effect of the amalgamation of the society had

---

[74] [1959] A.C. 457.

[75] [1976] Ch. 235.

[76] *Supra.*

[77] *Ibid.* at p. 246.

[78] *Re Recher's Will Trusts, National Westminster Bank Ltd.* v. *National Anti-Vivisection Society Ltd.* [1972] Ch. 526; [1971] 3 All E.R. 401.

[79] This was not a charitable body: see, *post*, p. 209.

[80] The judge therefore followed the decision in *Neville Estates Ltd.* v. *Madden, supra,* and refused to follow the Australian decision in *Bacon* v. *Pianta* [1966] A.L.R. 1044.

been to dissolve it, and to terminate the contract between its members, the gift by the will failed. A gift to the members of one society could not be treated as a gift to the members of another society.

It should be emphasised that it is a necessary characteristic of any gift within the second category of Cross J.'s formulation that the members of the association can by an appropriate majority (if the rules so provide) or acting unanimously if they do not, alter the rules so as to provide that the funds or part of them should be applied for some new purpose or even distributed amongst the members for their own benefit.[81] Thus, in *Re Grant's Will Trusts*[82] Vinelott J. held that a bequest for the benefit of a local constituency labour party could not take effect as a gift within the second category because the members of the party could not alter the rules so as to apply it to other purposes.

In certain circumstances there may be no intention to confer a beneficial interest upon members of the association. In *Re Edis's Trusts*[83] there was a declaration of trust to hold a drill hall and premises at St. Pancras for a volunteer unit which became the 21st Special Air Service Regiment (The Artists' Rifles) of the Territorial Army. In 1967 the then units of the Territorial Army were disbanded, and new units were raised to form the Territorial and Army Volunteer Reserve.[84] The question arose whether, upon the disbandment of this unit in 1967, the premises were held upon trust for the officers and men of that unit. Goulding J. held that they were not in the same position as the members of an unincorporated association as the essential link between them was not one of contract, but their common military service to the Sovereign. The principles enunciated in *Neville Estates Ltd.* v. *Madden*[85] did not, therefore, apply and the premises were held to belong to the Crown.[86]

(2) **Purpose trusts**

One of the aspects of this subject which is of particular importance to the law of trusts is in relation to "purpose" trusts, that is, trusts for non-charitable purposes which the settlor wishes to further, such as the maintenance of his tomb. This is discussed later[87] but it may be noted here that these gifts, although not charitable, may be valid within certain limits. A similar period of a life or lives in being, plus 21 years, was evolved by analogy to limit the time for which, prima facie, these trusts could exist.[88] Section 15(4) of the 1964 Act, however, provides that a donor of property for purpose trusts will not be able to import a period of up to 80 years for the duration of the trust by analogy with the

---

[81] *Per* Vinelott J. in *Re Grant's Will Trusts* [1980] 1 W.L.R. 360 at p. 374.

[82] *Supra.*

[83] *Re Edis's Trusts, Campbell-Smith* v. *Davies* [1972] 1 W.L.R. 1135; [1972] 2 All E.R. 769.

[84] The traditions of this famous and brave unit were continued in 1967 with the formation of the 21st Special Air Service Regiment (Artists) (Volunteers), within the Territorial and Army Volunteer Reserve.

[85] [1962] Ch. 832; *ante*, p. 107.

[86] The premises vested in the Crown under the provisions of the Military Land Act 1892, and not as *bona vacantia.*

[87] *Post*, p. 176.

[88] But possible ways of circumventing this are mentioned *post*, p. 181.

provision of section 1, and in this respect the pre-1964 position remains unaltered.[89]

As will be explained later[90] a gift to charity is not void even if it is made inalienable, and a gift over from one charity to another charity is not void although the vesting in the second charity may take place at any time in the future.[91] The normal perpetuity provisions apply, however, in the case of a gift from a non-charity to a charity or from a charity to a non-charity.

3. *Accumulations*

Another result of the policy of the law that property and wealth generally should be free to circulate has been the statutory control of accumulations. This resulted from the decision in *Thellusson* v. *Woodford*[92] where Thellusson directed that the income from his property should be accumulated for the perpetuity period, which in his case was somewhat over 70 years.

Parliament intervened and passed the Thellusson Act in 1800 to restrict accumulations to a fairly short period, and the position is now governed by sections 164 to 166 of the Law of Property Act 1925, as amended by section 13 of the Perpetuities and Accumulations Act 1964.[93]

Section 164 of the Law of Property Act 1925 lays down the general rule that income may not be accumulated for longer than any one of the following periods:

(*a*) the life of the settlor (this is the period adopted in the case of gifts *inter vivos* where no other period is specified);

(*b*) 21 years from the death of the testator or settlor (this is the period adopted in the case of gifts by will where no other period is specified);

(*c*) the duration of the minority or minorities of any persons living at the death of the testator or settlor (this period begins from the death of the settlor or testator);

(*d*) the duration of the minority or minorities of any persons entitled under the settlement (in this case the beneficiary need not be alive at the death of the testator or settlor and the accumulation period wil commence at the birth of that beneficiary).

The 1964 Act added, in respect of instruments coming into operation after July 15, 1964,

(*e*) the period of 21 years from the date of making the disposition; and

(*f*) the duration of the minority or minorities of any persons in being at the date of making an *inter vivos* disposition.

---

[89] The provision appears to be clearly to this effect, but *cf.* Hanbury and Maudsley (11th ed.), p. 439, in which the opposite is argued.

[90] *Post*, p. 183.

[91] *Re Tyler* [1891] 3 Ch. 252; and see *post*, p. 181.

[92] (1798) 4 Ves.Jun. 227.

[93] As further amended by Family Law Reform Act 1969, Sched. 3, para. 7.

A direction to accumulate for a period longer than one of the foregoing makes the whole gift void if the accumulation is directed for longer than the perpetuity period, but if the accumulation is not directed for longer than the perpetuity period, the direction is invalid only as to the excess over the authorised period.[94]

Section 165 expressly declares to be valid the case where income is directed to be accumulated for one of the authorised periods, and at the end of that period, the income has to be accumulated under the general law, or under some other statutory provision. As will be noted in due course[95] where by virtue of section 31 of the Trustee Act 1925 money is held upon trust for an infant, such of the income from that money as is not applied for the infant's benefit is to be accumulated until he reaches the age of majority. Thus, suppose T gives property to A for life, with remainder to A's eldest son, and there is a direction to accumulate for a period of 21 years from the death of T. In the event of A's eldest son being a minor at the death of A, accumulations will arise under the gift for the first 21 years, and thereafter until the eldest son attains his majority by virtue of section 31 of the Trustee Act 1925.[96]

There are certain exceptions from the general restrictions on accumulations, and in these cases any period of accumulation may be specified. These cases are:

(*a*) accumulations for the payment of the debts of any person;

(*b*) accumulations for the purpose of raising portions[97] for children or issue of the settlor, or any person entitled under the settlement; and

(*c*) accumulations of the produce of timber or wood.[98]

III. Safeguarding Property from Creditors

For almost as long as the trust has been invented, it has repeatedly been used in an attempt to achieve protection from their creditors by those who contemplate the actual or potential threat of financial ruin. If a man effectively transfers his property to another upon trust for his wife, or other friend or relative, and goes bankrupt, on general principles that man's trustee in bankruptcy will not be able to claim the property subject to the trust. Thus it is and has been common for a man to give his property upon trust for his wife, with the intention that should bankruptcy occur, as the property is in his wife's name, it cannot be taken away, yet he will nevertheless be able to enjoy it. Alternatively, a man may wish to give his property upon trust for his wife or to some other close relative or friend in the hope that they will derive the benefit from it rather than his creditors. Not surprisingly statutory restrictions have long been placed on the use of the trust for this purpose, and it is with these that this section is concerned but nevertheless the basic principle remains true that where the statutory provisions do not

---

[94] *Re Jefferies* [1936] 2 All E.R. 626.
[95] Chap. 18, section 2, *post.*
[96] And see *Re Maber* [1928] Ch. 88.
[97] *Re Bourne* (1946) 115 L.J.Ch. 152.
[98] L.P.A., s. 164(2).

operate the trust may be an effective means of preventing creditors from laying their hands upon a person's property.[99]

The statutory provisions themselves are found in two Acts. First, section 172 of the Law of Property Act 1925 enables, within certain limits, dispositions of property made with intent to defraud creditors to be upset. This provision re-enacts with certain modifications the Elizabethan Act against Fraudulent Deeds and Alienations 1571[1] and applies whether or not the person who made the disposition is bankrupt. Secondly, section 42 of the Bankruptcy Act 1914 enables various dispositions to be set aside where the person who made them has become bankrupt. To some extent these provisions overlap, and if an attempt is being made to upset a disposition, both should be considered. Both provisions refer to dispositions, and dispositions by way of trust are within their scope, but they are not confined to trusts.

1. *Bankruptcy Act* 1914, *s.*42(1)

Section 42(1) of the Bankruptcy Act 1914 provides that a voluntary settlement may be set aside—

(*a*) if the settlor becomes bankrupt within two years from the date of the settlement; or

(*b*) if the settlor becomes bankrupt after two years but within 10 years from the date of the settlement, unless the persons who claim the benefit of the settlement can prove

    (i) that at the date of the settlement the settlor was able to pay all his debts without taking into account the property settled; and

    (ii) that the settlor's interest passed to the trustee of the settlement when it was executed.

Paragraph (*a*) applies even if the bankrupt was able to pay all his debts at the time of the settlement.

For the purpose of this subsection, and of the other provisions of section 42 to be considered later, the word "settlement" is widely construed. It is defined to include "any conveyance or transfer of property"[2] and an illustration of its width was contained in the recent decision of *Re A Debtor, ex p. The Official Receiver* v. *Morrison.*[3] In January 1961 a house was purchased in the name of a wife, although the husband arranged the whole of the purchase price, paying down part from his own resources on the purchase of the property, and raising the remainder on mortgage. The husband became bankrupt in December 1961. Stamp J., declaring that this arrangement was within the term "settlement" under section 42, commented[4]: "In construing the section, I must have regard to the fact that it is clearly a section framed to prevent properties from being put

---

[99] *Post* p. 120.
[1] 13 Eliz. 1, c. 5.
[2] s. 42(4).
[3] [1965] 1 W.L.R. 1498.
[4] *Ibid.* at p. 1502.

into the hands of relatives to the disadvantage of creditors. . . . I cannot hold that section 42 may be defeated by the conveyancing machinery adopted for carrying out a transaction which would otherwise be within it." For there to be a "settlement," however, there must be an intention that the property shall be retained or preserved for the benefit of the donee, in such form that it can be traced,[5] and it must be intended, in the case of a gift, that it should not be spent at once.[6]

The operation of the section is limited to *voluntary* settlements and does not apply to settlements made before and in consideration of marriage or made in good faith and for valuable consideration or made on or for the wife or children of the settlor of property which has accrued to the settlor after marriage in right of his wife. The meaning of this provision was considered in *Re Densham*,[7] where a wife had made contributions to the purchase of a house which was vested in her husband who had subsequently become bankrupt. It was held that the property was not purchased in consideration of marriage, nor was the purchase made in favour of the wife as a purchaser in good faith and for valuable consideration, in the latter case because her contributions did no more than entitle her to an aliquot share in the house; consideration in the ordinary commercial sense was required. A similar result occurred in *Re Windle*[8] where the bankrupt transferred the matrimonial home to his wife in consideration of her expressly covenanting with the mortgagees to discharge all liabilities under the mortgage. It was held that the covenant of indemnity in respect of a house where the equity of redemption was of value was not a sufficient *quid pro quo* to constitute valuable consideration for the purposes of the section. On the other hand, in *Re Abbott*[9] the expression "purchaser for valuable consideration" was held to be wide enough to cover a spouse whose claim to a property adjustment order under section 24 of the Matrimonial Causes Act 1973 had been compromised: a compromise of a bona fide claim constituted the claimant a purchaser for valuable consideration of what the purchaser received under the compromise even though no interest in property was transferred by the purchaser and the consideration provided was not measurable in money.

Section 42(1) declares that the settlement is "void," but this has been construed as meaning "voidable,"[10] with the result that where a bona fide purchaser for value acquires a beneficial interest under the settlement, and does not have notice of the relevant act of bankruptcy, his title is good.[11]

It is important to note that the intention of the settlor is irrelevant. Provided the settlement comes within the conditions mentioned above, it may be upset although the settlor did not make the settlement for the purpose of defrauding creditors.

---

[5] *Re Plummer* [1900] 2 Q.B. 790.
[6] *Re Player* (1885) 15 Q.B.D. 682.
[7] [1975] 1 W.L.R. 1519.
[8] [1975] 1 W.L.R. 1628.
[9] [1982] 3 W.L.R. 86.
[10] *e.g. Re Brail* [1893] 2 Q.B. 381.
[11] *Re Carter & Kenderdine's Contract* [1897] 1 Ch. 776.

2. *Bankruptcy Act* 1914, *s*.42(2), (3)

Subsection (2) of section 42 deals with the situation where in a marriage settlement a person covenants to pay money for the benefit of his spouse or children, or to settle upon his spouse or children future acquired property in which he had no interest[12] at the date of his marriage.

A covenant of this nature, being one for valuable consideration, would normally bind a trustee in bankruptcy, but special provision is necessary to prevent abuse. For example, if a man upon marriage executed a marriage settlement under which he covenanted to pay £500,000 to his wife, although he was in fact quite poor, and took no action on the covenant before he became bankrupt, upon his bankruptcy the wife would have a claim under the covenant which would be likely to deprive the creditors of any chance of recovering their debts. Section 42(2) therefore provides:

(*a*) that such a covenant is void against the settlor's creditors upon bankruptcy unless the money was paid or the property was transferred under the covenant before the settlor committed the relevant act of bankruptcy; and

(*b*) that in respect of unsatisfied covenants, the wife or children may prove in the bankruptcy, but their claim is postponed to other creditors for valuable consideration.[13]

Even if covenants of this nature given in consideration of marriage are not declared void against the creditors under the provision just mentioned, transactions made in pursuance of them may still be rendered void against the trustee in bankruptcy by section 42(3). By this subsection, in order that the transfer of property of payment of money may be effective, the person to whom it was transferred must prove one of the following:

(*a*) that the transfer or payment was made more than two years before the commencement of the bankruptcy; or

(*b*) that at the time it was made the settlor was able to pay all his debts in full without resorting to that property or money; or

(*c*) that the covenant related to property or money expected to be received by way of *inter vivos* gift from, or upon the death of, a particular named person, and that the settlor in fact transferred the property or money within three months from the date when it came under his control.

As in the case of section 42(1), subsections 42(2) and (3) will apply even if there was no intention whatever to defraud creditors.

3. *Law of Property Act* 1925, *s*.172

The general principle of section 172, as stated in subsection (1), is that every conveyance of property which was made with intent to defraud creditors is

---

[12] The interest may be vested or contingent; in possession or in reversion: *Re Andrews Trusts* [1878] 7 Ch.D. 635; *Bulteel* v. *Manley* [1917] 1 Ch. 251.

[13] *Re Cumming & West* [1929] 1 Ch. 534; *Re Howes* [1934] Ch. 49.

voidable at the instance of any person thereby prejudiced.[14] The definition of "conveyance" in section 205 is wide enough to cover any type of disposition of property, except a will, and "property" includes both real and personal property. The scope of the section is, therefore, very wide. No time limit is imposed, and it is not necessary for bankruptcy proceedings to be taken. It is, however, necessary to prove an intent to defraud creditors.

Sometimes this will present no difficulties. In *Reese River Co.* v. *Atwell*,[15] for example, a director of a company was sued by that company. He knew the company's circumstances as well as his own, and thought that judgment would be obtained against him by the company. He therefore assigned all his property to his daughter, but the court had no hesitation in finding that his intention was fraudulent.

There is, however, considerable dispute whether the court will declare there to be an intention to defraud creditors from the surrounding circumstances, even if this cannot be proved positively. There is no doubt that from the settlor's conduct and the surrounding circumstances the court may raise a rebuttable presumption of intent to defraud: the question is whether in any circumstances an irrebuttable presumption will be made. *Freeman* v. *Pope*[16] concerned the transfer by a clergyman of his major asset to his goddaughter when he was under pressure from his creditors. It was agreed that the clergyman in fact had no intent to defraud, but in upsetting the disposition the court appears to have declared that as a matter of law the clergyman must have had the necessary intention to fulfil the requirement of the statute. Lord Hatherley L.C. said: "If a person owing debts makes a settlement which subtracts from the property which is the proper fund for the payment of his debts an amount without which the debts cannot be paid, then, since it is the necessary consequence of the settlement (supposing it effectual) that some creditors must remain unpaid, it would be the duty of the judge to direct the jury that they *must*[17] infer the intent of the settlor to have been to defeat or delay his creditors, and that the case is within the statute." In view of this dictum[18] it was not surprising that in the subsequent case of *Re Wise*[19] counsel argued that if the necessary consequence of the settlement was to defeat the settlor's creditors, then as a matter of law the court was bound to find present the intent necessary to fulfil the section, whatever the settlor's actual intention in fact was. Paying less than accustomed

---

[14] See *Cadogan* v. *Cadogan* [1977] 1 W.L.R. 1041, C.A., where it was held to be "arguable" that the protection of the section was available to any person prejudiced by a conveyance with intent to defraud creditors although that person could not properly be described as a creditor: since the husband had transferred the matrimonial home to a child of the marriage and had subsequently died and since his wife was accordingly deprived of her right to apply for financial relief under the Inheritance (Family Provision) Act, as amended, it was "arguable" that she was a person prejudiced within the meaning of the section. The decision was made in rejecting an application to strike out part of the statement of claim, thereby allowing the matter to be argued, if necessary, at a later date.

[15] (1869) L.R. 7 Eq. 347; see also *Twyne's Case* (1601) 3 Coke 80.

[16] (1870) L.R. 5 Ch. 538.

[17] Emphasis supplied.

[18] See also the judgment of Gifford L.J.

[19] (1886) 17 Q.B.D. 290.

deference to his predecessors, Lord Esher M.R. observed with refreshing frankness: "In support of that proposition dicta of great and eminent judges were cited. I will venture to say as strongly as I can that to my mind that proposition is monstrous." He continued that if "circumstances make you believe that the man did not intend to do that which you are asked to find that he did intend, to say that, because that was the necessary result of what he did, you must find, contrary to the other evidence, that he did actually intend to do it, is to ask one to find that to be a fact which one really believes to be untrue in fact." The facts of *Re Wise* involved a sailor who sailed between two ports, in both of which, following nautical tradition, he had a girl. He agreed to marry his girl at Portsmouth. He then set sail for Hong Kong, and in May 1881 married his girl in Hong Kong. In August 1881 the English girl took proceedings for breach of promise in the English court, and at the same time the sailor learned that he had been left a legacy of £500. He at once made a settlement of his money on his wife and issue in Hong Kong. The English girl obtained judgment against the sailor in 1882 for, as chance would have it, £500, but, the sailor having no money of his own, the victory was Pyrrhic. Bent on satisfaction, however, the English girl then commenced proceedings to upset the settlement, in the hope that there would then be sufficient money to satisfy the judgment. The sailor gave evidence that in making his settlement, he was not influenced by the breach of promise proceedings, which he did not take seriously, and which he thought would come to nothing. Perhaps luckily he was able to convince the court of this. The court, therefore, held that as at the time when the settlement was made the sailor had no intention to defraud his creditors, the settlement could not be upset. The English girl's victory in the breach action remained Pyrrhic.

Attempts have been made to reconcile *Freeman* v. *Pope* with *Re Wise*. It has been suggested[20] that, because at the date of the settlement the sailor was not indebted, the inevitable result of the settlement in *Re Wise* was not at its date to defeat creditors, and that *Freeman* v. *Pope* can apply where the settlement at its date does lead inevitably to such a result. But this is unsatisfactory. Such a technical reconciliation may be possible, but in the later decision of *Godfrey* v. *Poole*[21] the Privy Council approved a dictum of Kindersley V.-C.[22] that "the court is to decide in each particular case whether on all the circumstances it can come to the conclusion that the intention of the settlor in making the settlement was to defeat, hinder or delay his creditors."

There are two other aspects of the requirement of intent to defraud. In the first place, "defraud" is a wide concept. It is not confined to defeating entirely the creditors' claims but extends to delaying payment to creditors even if payment is ultimately made.[23] Secondly, it is sufficient if there is intention to defraud *any* creditors: the creditors actually defrauded need not be those who were in the contemplation of the settlor. Thus in *Re Butterworth*[24] a man had for

[20] Underhill (13th ed.), p. 216.
[21] (1888) 13 App.Cas. 497.
[22] In *Thompson* v. *Webster* (1859) 4 Drew. 628 at p. 632.
[23] *Thompson* v. *Webster* (1859) 4 Drew. 628.
[24] (1882) 19 Ch.D. 588.

many years successfully carried on the business of a baker. He then proposed to purchase a grocery business, but realising the risks of *that* business he settled most of his property on his wife and children. He subsequently bought the business but, when it lost money, sold it, obtaining the same amount that he paid for it. He was then left with his baker's business which about three years later failed. It was held that as the settlement was made with the intention of putting the property out of the reach of some creditors, it could be upset, albeit at the instance of other creditors.

Further difficulties have been encountered under section 172 by virtue of subsection (3), which declares that the section "does not extend to any estate or interest in property conveyed for valuable consideration and in good faith, or upon good consideration and in good faith to any person not having, at the time of the conveyance, notice of the intent to defraud creditors."

Section 172 can, therefore, apply to settlements made for valuable consideration where the beneficiary does not take in good faith, or takes with knowledge of the intent to defraud. It seems that the object of some unromantic folk in getting married is to defraud creditors. In *Colombine v. Penhall*[25] a man in perilous financial circumstances married his mistress, and by ante-nuptial settlement transferred his property upon trust for his wife and children. Within two months of the marriage he had been made bankrupt. It was held that the wife was aware that the marriage was part of a scheme to deprive the creditors of the bankrupt's property, with the result that although she had given valuable consideration, she was not acting in good faith, thus enabling the settlement to be set aside. It is not sufficient to show that the wife knew that the husband was heavily indebted: before the settlement may be set aside, it must be shown that the wife's prime motive was to participate in the fraud upon creditors. Such was the wife's motive in *Colombine v. Penhall*.

The provision in the Act of Elizabeth which section 172(3) replaced was confined to settlements made for valuable consideration, but section 172(3) itself extends also to settlements made "upon good consideration and in good faith." Thus post-nuptial settlements made in consideration of natural love and affection for a spouse and children, which were previously treated as purely voluntary, are, after 1925, equated with settlements made for value.

This statement, which seems to be the only explanation of the insertion of the words "upon good consideration and in good faith," needs however to be read subject to *Re Eichholz*.[26] Eichholz was a solicitor who had large continental connections, as a result of which he received instructions to invest foreign funds in English securities. Very large sums were remitted to him for this purpose, but he misappropriated much of the money to enable him to live a life in some respects of remarkable extravagance. For him a visit to the opera might involve flying over to Milan for the evening. By the time he married his second wife in 1955 he was heavily insolvent, but his wife never knew of this. A month or so after his marriage, he purchased a house for £15,000 in the name of his wife, and

---

[25] (1853) 1 Sm. & Giff. 228.
[26] [1959] Ch. 708.

after his death in 1957 and the consequent discovery of his defalcations, an attempt was made to upset the transaction. Harman J. found that at all times the wife acted in good faith, and he also found that there was not an ante-nuptial agreement, so that there was no valuable consideration. There was, however, one would have thought, good consideration. But inexplicably—unless he was determined to recover something for the creditors—Harman J. did not even discuss this. He managed to conclude that because there was no valuable consideration, there was no consideration at all, and because there was no consideration section 172(3) could not apply. It seems impossible to reconcile this decision with principle.

A recent decision in which section 172 was considered was *Lloyds Bank Ltd.* v. *Marcan*.[27] In that case a man who had mortgaged his house and certain other property to the bank was sued for possession of the property by the bank. After the bank commenced the proceedings, but before they were determined, the man granted a lease of the house to his wife at a rack-rent. He knew that the bank attributed value to the property with vacant possession, but did not know that upon sale the bank could get a higher price for the property with vacant possession than subject to the lease. At first instance, Pennycuick V.-C. held[28] that the lease was granted "with intent to defraud" because the man intended to deprive the bank of timely recourse to the property charged. The Court of Appeal affirmed the decision. Although the lease was granted at a rack-rent, it was granted to weaken the bank's position, and that was "sharp practice."[29] It seems, therefore, that a disposition will be treated as fraudulent if, although it was for full value, it was made with the deliberate intention of hindering creditors.

4. *Generally*

It may be useful to contrast, by way of summary, section 42 of the Bankruptcy Act 1914 with section 172 of the Law of Property Act 1925.

Bankruptcy Act, s.42	*Law of Property Act, s.172*
1. Only applies if bankruptcy proceedings taken	Applies whether or not bankruptcy proceedings taken
2. Can only apply if disposition within 10 years of bankruptcy	No time limit
3. The need to prove intention	Must show intention to defraud.

The combined effect of these provisions has been in most circumstances to prevent a trust set up with the intention to defraud creditors from achieving its purpose, although a trust not set up with this object, or one which has been in existence for a considerable time, may in fact be successful. Further, a protective trust[30] may be effective to defeat creditors where the beneficiary is not the

---

[27] [1973] 1 W.L.R. 1387; [1973] 3 All E.R. 754, C.A.
[28] [1973] 1 W.L.R. 339; [1973] 2 All E.R. 359.
[29] [1973] 1 W.L.R. at p. 1392; [1973] 3 All E.R. at p. 759 (Russell L.J.).
[30] *Post,* p. 120.

settlor. In particular, a trust set up by a person is not an effective safeguard of that person's property against the risks of business. At the time when this was becoming fixed Jessel M.R. said: "A man is not entitled to go into a hazardous business and, immediately before doing so, settle all his property voluntarily, the object being this: 'If I succeed in business, I make a fortune for myself. If I fail, I leave my creditors unpaid.'" But it is ironic that at this time the companies legislation was being introduced into our legal system, under which one may legitimately say[31]: "If I succeed in business, I make a fortune for myself. If I fail, I leave my creditors unpaid."

---

[31] This is subject to the Companies Act 1948, s. 31 (as substituted by C.A. 1980, Sched. 3) which provides that if a company carries on business without having at least two members and does so for more than six months, a person who is a member of the company and knows that it is carrying on business with only one member shall be liable (jointly and severally with company) for the payment of the debts of the company contracted during that period. It is also subject to the C.A. 1948, s. 202 which provides that the directors of a company will be personally liable for its debts if its constitution so provides.

CHAPTER 6

PROTECTIVE TRUSTS

IT has been seen that a trust which contravenes the policy of the bankruptcy laws will be invalid,[1] but there are indirect means available by which this result can be avoided. It is, however, essential to make two points clear at the outset:

(i) that a *proviso* or *condition* contained in a trust of property in favour of a *third party* that it is not to be subject to the claims of creditors will be void[2]; and

(ii) that a trust set up by a person in favour of *himself until* bankruptcy, with remainders over may also be ineffective.[3] If he goes bankrupt the property will generally vest in his trustee in bankruptcy. But the fact that this will not always be the position is illustrated by *Re Detmold*[4] A husband had settled his own property on trust for himself for life or until alienation, either voluntary or involuntary by process of law in favour of a particular creditor, and then over to his wife and children. North J. held that the gift over in favour of the wife and children was valid and effective on an involuntary alienation. It operated in any event other than the settlor's bankruptcy, which took place afterwards. In other words, if a person goes bankrupt after the gift over has taken effect, as in *Re Detmold*, the trustee in bankruptcy can take nothing. It will be seen, therefore, that the provision for determination will be effective in the happening of events other than the bankruptcy of the settlor.

But it is true to say that if a settlor wishes to achieve his purpose in protecting the estate against a spendthrift or reckless beneficiary and thereby guard against alienation or bankruptcy he must use more sophisticated machinery. Essentially this will take the form of the creation of a determinable interest in favour of a third party coupled, if necessary, with protective and discretionary trusts.

I. DETERMINABLE INTERESTS

It may be thought somewhat surprising that, although a settlor cannot settle property on a beneficiary subject to a condition or proviso that it will not be

---

[1] See *ante*, p. 111.

[2] *Younghusband* v. *Gisborne* (1844) 1 Coll.C.C. 400, affirmed. (1846) 15 L.J. Ch. 355; *Re Sanderson's Trust* (1857) 3 Kay & J. 497.

[3] *Re Burroughs-Fowler* [1916] 2 Ch. 251.

[4] (1889) 40 Ch.D. 585; and see *Re Johnson Johnson* [1904] 1 K.B. 134.

available to his creditors on bankruptcy, he can grant a determinable interest in favour of that beneficiary (if this is not the settlor himself) *until* bankruptcy, which will be perfectly effective.[5] The distinction between a conditional and determinable interest is *au fond* a logical one, however outmoded. A *condition* of its nature cuts down an interest already granted; provision for a *determining* event merely delimits the interest to be granted. The existence of this distinction makes it essential for a draftsman to be careful not to create a conditional interest by accident and, thereby, defeat the intentions of the settlor.

II. Protective Trusts[6]

These trusts provide a highly effective means of restraining spendthrift beneficiaries. They combine a determinable life interest with a discretionary trust. The beneficiary's life interest will normally be made determinable on alienation or bankruptcy and will be followed in such an event by a discretionary trust in favour of the former life tenant and/or members of his family.

(1) **Trustee Act 1925, s.33**

It was formerly the practice to set out protective trusts *in extenso*. But with a view to shortening the length of settlements, section 33 of the Trustee Act 1925 provides that a mere reference to "protective trusts" will bring into play the protective trusts set forth in that section.

This section provides that where *income*, including an annuity or other periodical payment, is directed to be held on protective trusts for the benefit of any person for his life or any less period[7] (such person being described in the section as "the principal beneficiary") then during that period the income is held on the following trusts, although this must be without prejudice to any prior interests:

(1) Upon trust for the principal beneficiary during the trust period *or* until he does or attempts to do any act or thing, or any event happens (other than an advance under any statutory or express power) whereby, if the income were payable during the trust period to the principal beneficiary absolutely during that period, he would be deprived of the right to receive the same or any part thereof;

(2) If the trust fails or determines during the trust period, then for the residue of that period, the income is to be held upon trust to be applied as the trustees in their absolute discretion (without being liable to account for the exercise of such discretion) think fit, for the maintenance or support or otherwise for the benefit of all or any of the following persons:

(*a*) The principal beneficiary and his or her wife or husband, if any, and his or her children or more remote issue,[8] if any, *or*

---

[5] *Billson* v. *Crofts* (1873) L.R. 15 Eq. 314; *Re Aylwin's Trusts* (1873) L.R. 16 Eq. 585.

[6] See Sheridan (1957) 21 Conv.(N.S.) 110.

[7] For an illustration of protective trusts designed to last until remarriage and the effect of a nullity decree on the second marriage: see *D'Altroy's Will Trusts* [1968] 1 W.L.R. 120; and see Matrimonial Causes Act 1973, ss. 11, 12, 16.

[8] Including illegitimate children and issue: Family Law Reform Act 1969, s. 15(3).

(*b*) the principal beneficiary and the persons who would, if he were dead, be entitled to the trust property or the income where there is no wife or husband or issue in existence.[9]

The section does not apply to trusts coming into operation before the commencement of the Act, and, moreover, it is subject to any variations which may be made in the trust instrument.[10] It is also provided that nothing in the section operates to validate any trust which, if contained in the trust instrument, would be liable to be set aside.[11]

(2) "On protective trusts"

The purpose of the section is to avoid the necessity to set out the trusts expressly in the trust instrument. But protective trusts can, and often still are, expressly created, and in any case there is, as has been seen, provision for modification of the statutory provisions[12] to suit the circumstances of the individual trust. Furthermore, whether the statutory form is used or its essence is set out in terms, its effect is only to engraft trusts on the life interest. Accordingly, it was held by Vaisey J. in *Re Allsopp's Marriage Settlement*[13] that if the life intererst is extinguished, as it was in that case by an order of the Divorce Court, the engrafted protective trusts, being incapable of any separate existence, are also extinguished.

(3) Determining events

The question what events will be sufficient to cause a forfeiture of a protected life interest (as the interest of the principal beneficiary is described) and bring the discretionary trusts into operation has been considered in a large number of cases. The point will be of importance not only where the trusts contained in section 33 are employed but also where there is an express protective trust. Many of the cases to be considered involved express protective trusts, but it is thought that the principles laid down have an equal application to the statutory trusts.

It is self-evident that bankruptcy of or alienation by the principal beneficiary will bring about a forfeiture of the protected life interest. But it is not perhaps so obvious (but it was nevertheless so held by Luxmoore L.J. in *Re Walker*[14]) that this will still be the case if the bankruptcy has already occurred when the trust comes into operation. In other cases the determining events have taken the most diverse forms as the following illustrations show.

In *Re Balfour's Settlement,*[15] for example, various sums had been advanced by the trustees to the principal beneficiary. They then asserted their right to

---

[9] s. 33(1).

[10] s. 33(2).

[11] s. 33(3). Accordingly, a settlement made on the settlor himself until bankruptcy and then on discretionary trusts may be ineffective: *Re Burroughs-Fowler* [1916] 2 Ch. 251. See *ante*, p. 120.

[12] See note 10, *ante*.

[13] [1959] Ch. 81.

[14] [1939] Ch. 974.

[15] [1938] Ch. 928.

retain the income of the fund in order to make good the breach of trust. The principal beneficiary then went bankrupt. Farwell J. held that since the trustees had asserted their right to the income before the date of bankruptcy the discretionary trusts had come into operation and, therefore, nothing passed to the trustee in bankruptcy. Again, in *Re Baring's Settlement Trusts*,[16] the principal beneficiary had failed to bring her children within the jurisdiction and a writ of sequestration was thereupon issued empowering the sequestrators to take possession of all her real and personal estate until she did so. The sequestrators also gave the trustees notice not to pay further money to her and required that income be paid to them. Morton J. held that since the trusts were designed to confer continuous enjoyment of the income on the principal beneficiary, the sequestration was effective to determine her life interest. Yet again, in *Re Dennis' Settlement Trusts*,[17] Farwell J. held that the execution of a deed of variation of protective trusts contained in the principal deed—the variation providing for payment of part of the income to another person—brought the forfeiture clause into operation.

But there are also many other cases where the events in question were held *not* to determine the protected life interest. Again, they take a diversity of forms. Not surprisingly, for example, in *Re Tancred's Settlement*,[18] Buckley J. held that an appointment of the trustees as his attorneys to receive the income of the settled funds did not cause the beneficiary's life interest to be forfeited. The same result occurred in *Re Oppenheim's Will Trusts*[19] on the effect of the appointment of a receiver to a principal beneficiary who had been certified as a person of unsound mind. It was similarly held by the Court of Appeal in *Re Westby's Settlement*[20] that a statutory charge, *viz.* the expenses of a receiver in such circumstances, was not the kind of charge intended to be aimed at by forfeiture clauses. All these cases tend to show, in Farwell J.'s words, that "we must bear in mind that the courts do not construe gifts on forfeitures so as to extend their limits beyond the fair meaning of the words unless they are actually driven to it. Forfeitures are not regarded with favour."[21]

The effect of an order of the court on a forfeiture clause has also come into question. Thus in *Re Mair*[22] Farwell J. held that an order of the court under section 57 of the Trustee Act 1925,[23] giving power to trustees to raise capital moneys for the benefit of life tenants, would not cause a forfeiture of protected

---

[16] [1940] Ch. 737.
[17] [1942] Ch. 283.
[18] [1903] 1 Ch. 715.
[19] [1950] Ch. 633.
[20] [1950] Ch. 296.
[21] *Re Greenwood* [1901] 1 Ch. 887, 891 (assignment of income accrued due in the hands of trustees: no forfeiture). See also *Re Longman* [1955] 1 W.L.R. 197 (authority given by beneficiary for payment of debts out of a future dividend: dividend never declared: no forfeiture). For other cases involving the application of the Trading with the Enemy Act 1939, see *Re Gourju's Will Trusts* [1943] Ch. 24; *Re Hall* [1944] Ch. 46; *Re Wittke* [1944] 1 All E.R. 383; *Re Furness* [1944] 1 All E.R. 575; *Re Harris* [1945] Ch. 316; *Re Pozot's Settlement Trusts* [1952] Ch. 427.
[22] [1935] Ch. 562.
[23] See *post*, p. 410.

life interests because the section is an overriding one, the provisions of which are deemed to be read into every settlement. But this decision should be compared with that of Eve J. in *Re Salting*[24] where the result was that if the scheme sanctioned by the court under section 57 involved an agreement by the life tenant to pay premiums on insurance policies with a promise that if they are not duly paid the trustees are to pay them out of income, the failure by the life tenant to pay will create a forfeiture. In such a case it is plain that it will be his act or omission which creates it and not the exercise by the court of its overriding power.

The principles established by the last two decisions are clear enough. But otherwise the position is by no means straightforward. Especial difficulty arises from other cases involving an order of the Divorce Court varying protective trusts. The Court of Appeal in *General Accident, Fire and Life Assurance Corporation Ltd.* v. *Inland Revenue Commissioners*[25] were in no doubt that an order of the Divorce Court to pay an annual sum of money to the wife during her life did not bring about a forfeiture of the husband's protected life interest under section 33 and, accordingly, the discretionary trusts under this section did not arise. This was so because the court order overrode the settlement trusts, was an event to which both life tenant and trustee had to bow and, moreover, was not such an event as was contemplated by the section, this being intended as a protection to spendthrift or improvident or weak life tenants.[26] But if the principle adumbrated by the Court of Appeal is to be applied generally, it is by no means easy to reconcile the earlier decision of Danckwerts J. in *Re Richardson's Will Trusts*[27] where an order had been made by the Divorce Court for payment of an annual sum for the wife of the protected life tenant to be charged on his life interest, and it was also ordered that a deed be settled to give effect to the charge. It was held that because the order was not complied with by the execution of a deed, its effect was to create an equitable charge on the interest; this involved forfeiture of that interest; and the discretionary trusts under section 33 came into operation. In some ways no doubt this was a convenient result because the life tenant had later been adjudicated bankrupt; and the antecedent forfeiture meant that the income escaped the hands of his trustee in bankruptcy. However, it would seem a rather curious result if a failure to comply with an order of the court to settle the deed of variation will result in a forfeiture of such an interest, but compliance with such an order will not.

It is considered that the policy behind the decision of the Court of Appeal in *General Accident, Fire and Life Assurance Corporation Ltd.* v. *I.R.C.*[28] is undoubtedly desirable: it is only doubted whether the principle applied is the correct one. The effect of an order of the Family Division—whether or not it is to be implemented by a deed—is to deprive the life tenant of some or all of his income; and this would surely be caught by the terms of section 33 and,

---

[24] [1932] 2 Ch. 57.
[25] [1963] 1 W.L.R. 1207.
[26] *Ibid.* at p. 1218, *per* Donovan L.J.
[27] [1958] Ch. 504
[28] *Supra.*

probably, by most express protective trusts. On the other hand different considerations may apply to an order of the court under section 57 of the Trustee Act 1925 because that section is to be read into every settlement.

(4) Advances

Section 33 expressly exempts advances under any express or statutory[29] power from causing a forfeiture and bringing the discretionary trusts into play.[30] The question, however, that may be asked is whether the *absence* of exempting words such as these in an *express* protective trust will of necessity mean that the protected life interest will determine if an advancement is made.

The authorities are only in slight disarray, and the general consensus of judicial opinion is that an advancement made under an express or statutory power will not bring about a forfeiture. In *Re Hodgson*[31] Neville J. held that an advance under an express power did not have this result. The reasoning which appealed to the judge was that the forfeiture clause "should be read as though there had been inserted at the end of the clause 'But this provision is not to affect any steps taken by the husband to enable the advances by the trustees hereinafter provided for to take effect,'" And in *Re Shaw's Settlement*[32] Harman J. came to the same conclusion on similar facts. Finally, in *Re Rees*,[33] Upjohn J. held that the same applied to a statutory power of advancement under section 32 of the Trustee Act 1925. Only in *Re Stimpson's Trusts*,[34] where there was again no express advancement clause and reliance was put on the statutory power, was it held that a life tenant forfeited his interest on consenting to an advancement under section 32. There is a factual distinction between the last two cases. It is that in *Re Stimpson* the will was *made* in 1906 (although it did not come into effect until 1929) and the draftsman obviously could not have had in mind the section (section 32) of an Act to be enacted nearly 20 years later, whereas in *Re Rees* the will was made in 1935 and the draftsman must be taken to have been well aware of the section.

It is therefore, a possibility (admittedly a remote one) that if a case like *Re Stimpson* came before the court today, *i.e.* where a will made before 1926 contains no express advancement clause but the life tenant after 1925 consents to an advancement under the statutory power, then it would be decided in the same way. Although the validity of the decision has been doubted[35] it appears to apply the correct principle. For the statutory power can be ousted by a contrary intention[36] and the fact that the will is made before 1926 may be such a contrary intention for this purpose.

---

[29] Under T.A. 1925, s. 32, *post* p. 367.
[30] s. 33(1)
[31] [1913] 1 Ch. 34, at p. 40.
[32] [1951] Ch. 833.
[33] [1954] Ch. 202.
[34] [1931] 2 Ch. 77.
[35] See *per* Upjohn J. in *Re Rees* [1954] Ch. 202 at p. 209.
[36] T.A. 1925, s. 69.

CHAPTER 7

IMPLIED OR RESULTING TRUSTS

IN all the following cases, with the exception of "mutual wills," the beneficial interest "results" to the settlor or his estate, and for this reason such trusts are often described as "resulting trusts." But they are traditionally described as *implied* trusts because they arise or are presumed to arise from the *implied* intention of the settlor.

It is possible to argue that this basis is at times unreal. For example, in *Vandervell* v. *I.R.C.*[1] it could be said that it was far from Mr. Vandervell's intention that he should retain a beneficial interest in an option to re-purchase shares which he had ineffectually disposed of, and yet it was held that the option was to be held on a resulting trust for him. It is therefore noteworthy that Megarry J., in *Re Vandervell's Trusts (No. 2)*,[2] made a distinction between an "automatic" and a "presumed" resulting trust. In the former, as in *Vandervell* v. *I.R.C.,* the resulting trust does not depend upon any intention or presumption but is an automatic consequence of a settlor's failure to dispose of what is vested in him. If, however, a purchase of property is made in another person's name, this is a case of a "presumed" resulting trust, for there can fairly be said to be a presumption or intention that the property is to be held on a resulting trust for the true purchaser. The question to what extent this should be treated as an appropriate redefinition has already been discussed.[3]

I. PURCHASE IN ANOTHER'S NAME

This is one of the most important and common forms of resulting trust. The rule is that where real[4] or personal[5] property is vested in a purchaser jointly with others or in another or other persons alone, a resulting trust will be presumed in favour of the person who is proved to have paid the purchase-money[6]; the beneficial interest in the property "results" to the true purchaser. The general principle of such trusts was established as long ago as 1788 in *Dyer* v *Dyer*[7] by Eyre C.B., and may nowadays be relevant in deciding on the destination of the

---

[1] [1967] 2 A.C. 291, applied in *Re Vandervell's Trusts (No. 2)* [1974] Ch. 269, as between different parties, for the period under consideration in *Vandervell* v. *I.R.C.*; see *ante*, p. 25.

[2] *Supra.*

[3] *Ante*, p. 20.

[4] *Dyer* v. *Dyer* (1788) 2 Cox Eq. 92.

[5] *Re Scottish Equitable Life Assurance Society* [1902] Ch. 282, in respect of personal property.

[6] *Supra.*

[7] (1788) 2 Cox Eq. 92 at p. 93.

matrimonial home on breakdown of marriage—a topic discussed separately later in this chapter.[8]

There may be other variations on this theme. Thus if the purchase-money is paid partly by the person in whose favour the property is vested and partly by another, and if they advance it in equal shares, they will prima facie take jointly. But if the payment is made in *unequal* shares then a trust will result to each of them in proportion to the amount of his payment.[9]

But the principle will not be applied arbitrarily. It is essential that a *purchase* be made. Thus, if the payment is made at the request of and by way of loan to a person in whose name the property is vested, there will be no resulting trust, because in such circumstances the lender did not advance the purchase-money as purchaser but merely as lender.[10] And in any case there will be no resulting trust if it would be contrary to the law or to public policy to allow the presumption to arise. So, in an early case it was decided that if a person purchased an estate in the name of another so as to give him a vote at a parliamentary election the other will take beneficially even if there was no intention to give it to him.[11]

It has already been stated that this kind of resulting trust is based upon presumed intention. Accordingly, where no such intention can be implied, the trust will not arise. So, in *Savage* v. *Dunningham*[12] it was held that, where there was an informal flat-sharing arrangement under which contributions were made to the rent, there would not be a resulting trust in favour of the others when one of the flat-sharers purchased the flat. Plowman J. held that an income payment such as rent did not indicate an intention in respect of the subsequent acquisition of the capital asset. The facts were different in *Dewar* v. *Dewar*.[13] In this case the plaintiff and the defendant, who were brothers, and their mother, bought a house, the plaintiff and the mother each providing £500, and the defendant raising £3,250 on mortgage. The house was conveyed to the defendant. Goff J. held that the plaintiff's £500 was not a loan; the presumption of a resulting trust applied; and, therefore, he was entitled to an aliquot share in the house. The mother's £500 was held on the facts to be a gift and there was no resulting trust in her favour.

Rebuttable nature of the presumption

The presumption which thus arises on a purchase in the name of another is also rebuttable by parol or other evidence that the purchaser intended to benefit

---

[8] *Post*, p. 136.

[9] *Wray* v. *Steele* (1814) 2 V. & B. 388.

[10] *Aveling* v. *Knipe* (1815) 19 Ves. 441. The opinion of Phillimore L.J. in *Hussey* v. *Palmer* [1972] 1 W.L.R. 1286 at p. 1291, which appears to be to the opposite effect, would seem to be erroneous. Different considerations apply where money is lent for a particular purpose which fails. In such a case the money is held on a resulting trust for the lender: see *Barclays Bank Ltd.* v. *Quistclose Investments Ltd.* [1970] A.C. 567; and see *post*, p. 149.

[11] *Groves* v. *Groves* (1829) 3 Y. & J. 163 at p. 175 and see *Gascoigne* v. *Gascoigne* [1918] 1 K.B. 223; *Re Emery's Investment Trusts* [1959] Ch. 410; *Chettiar* v. *Chettiar* (*No.* 2) [1962] A.C. 294.

[12] [1974] Ch. 181.

[13] [1975] 1 W.L.R. 1532.

the other. Further, in certain circumstances there is a presumption the other way, namely, that there is no resulting trust. This applies where the person in whom the property is vested is the lawful wife or child of the purchaser or was a person to whom he stood *in loco parentis*. In these cases, the donor is presumed to have intended to "advance" the donee. It should also be remembered in this connection that section 53(1)(*b*) of the Law of Property Act 1925 (that a declaration of trust as to land must be manifested and proved by writing) does not apply to implied, resulting or constructive trusts. This means that oral evidence is admissible to show what was the true nature of the transaction.[14]

1. *Intention to Benefit*

This is entirely a matter of evidence. And if it can be shown that there was an intention to benefit the donee no resulting trust can arise. Thus in *Standing* v. *Bowring*[15] the plaintiff transferred £6,000 Consols into the joint names of herself and her godson. She did this with the express intention that the godson, in the event of his surviving her, should have them but that she herself should retain the dividends during her life. She had been told that her act was irrevocable. The Court of Appeal held that the presumption of a resulting trust had been rebutted. There was ample evidence that at the time of the transfer and for some time previously the plaintiff intended to confer a benefit by the transfer on her godson. Similarly, in *Dewar* v *Dewar*[15a] the presumption of a resulting trust in favour of a mother who had made a contribution to the purchase of property in her son's name was rebutted by evidence of her intention to make a gift.

(1) **Joint banking accounts**

An intention to benefit has been presumed in cases where a bank balance has been transferred into joint names.[16] It may well be thought, however, that if the donor maintained the right to use the substance of the gift during his lifetime, the gift of the balance of the account to the other would be in the nature of a testamentary provision and, not being made in accordance with the Wills Act 1837,[17] would be ineffective. This argument indeed appealed to Romer J. in *Young* v. *Sealey*[18] but he declined to apply it because of the disturbing effect it would have on existing titles. The point is still open for adjudication by the Court of Appeal.

(2) **Joint banking accounts of husband and wife**

A variant upon the foregoing will arise in cases where husband and wife have maintained a joint bank account into which their mutual resources have been

---

[14] L.P.A. 1925, s. 53(2).
[15] (1885) 31 Ch.D. 282.
[15a] [1975] 1 W.L.R. 1532.
[16] See *Marshal* v. *Crutwell* (1875) L.R. 20 Eq. 328 at p. 330, *per* Jessel M.R. In that case the presumption of advancement was rebutted on the ground that the joint account was opened for convenience. However, in *Re Figgis* [1969] 1 Ch. 123 it was held that the presumption was not rebutted by the available evidence: the "convenience" principle did not apply.
[17] s. 9 (as substituted by Administration of Justice Act 1982, s.17   [18] [1949] Ch. 278.

pooled. It will be difficult, and in many cases impossible, to dissect the balance by ascertaining how much was paid in by each. It has, therefore been held that, in the event of dissolution of the marriage, each will be entitled to one-half. And the same will apply to investments which have been made by the husband in his own name out of moneys belonging to such a joint banking account.[19] But it should be noted that if such investments were made in the name of the wife the ordinary presumption of advancement may apply and, if so, she would prima facie take them beneficially.[20]

2. *Presumption of Advancement*

This is the second case in which the presumption of a resulting trust does not operate. It only applies, however, where the real purchaser is the husband or father of or person standing *in loco parentis* to the nominal purchaser. In these cases the presumption is that the transferor intended to advance the transferee, in fact to give the property to him or her, and there is no resulting trust. And once the presumption has arisen and is not rebutted it will not be upset by any subsequent event. This can be illustrated by the old case of *Crabb* v. *Crabb*,[21] where a father transferred stock from his own name into the name of the son and a broker. He also told the broker to carry the dividends to the son's account. The father by a codicil made subsequently then bequeathed the stock to another. It was held, however, that the son took absolutely.

(a) **Wife.** It will be seen later in this chapter[22] that the presumption of advancement by a husband in favour of his wife may now have a limited application, particularly where the marriage has broken down. In so far, however, as the presumption may still be operative, it is immaterial that the marriage is later dissolved or indeed if a decree of nullity is made where the marriage is regarded as voidable.[23] However, if the marriage is void *ab initio* it appears that the presumption of advancement does not apply because the marriage is treated as never having had any existence at all.[24] The essential point is that the wife should be the lawful wife of the transferor. So the presumption does not apply in favour of the transferor's mistress.[25]

Nor does it apply if the wife purchases property in her husband's name: a

---

[19] *Jones* v. *Maynard* [1951] Ch. 572; *Rimmer* v. *Rimmer* [1953] 1 Q.B. 63; *cf. Re Cohen* [1953] Ch. 88 where a bundle of notes found hidden in the matrimonial home after the death of both spouses, who died within a few months of each other, was held to be the property of the wife to whom the residue belonged.

[20] See *infra*.

[21] (1834) 1 Myl. & K. 511.

[22] *Post*, p. 140.

[23] *Dunbar* v. *Dunbar* [1909] 2 Ch. 639. A nullity decree in respect of a *voidable* marriage now has a prospective, not a retrospective effect; accordingly the marriage is to be treated as if it had existed until the decree: Matrimonial Causes Act 1973, s. 16. For the grounds on which a marriage is regarded as void or voidable, see *ibid*. ss. 11, 12.

[24] See *Re Ames' Settlement* [1946] Ch. 217. See also *Re D'Altroy's Will Trusts* [1968] 1 W.L.R. 120.

[25] *Soar* v. *Foster* (1858) 4 K. & J. 152.

resulting trust will prima facie arise.[26] It used to be the position that a resulting trust would only be deduced in this event if the property was purchased with the wife's *capital*, not where it was purchased with income. But in *Mercier* v. *Mercier*[27] the Court of Appeal held that there was no fundamental distinction between capital and income except in degree, although Romer L.J. made it clear that the fact could be of importance when he said[28]: "No doubt in certain cases, in considering whether a gift was intended, the fact of the money having been income received by him with her consent may be material in respect of the weight of evidence but there is no other distinction, so far as I am aware, between capital and income." It is indisputable that the effect of this decision was to upset the previous law, and the fact that income has been applied will only be material evidentially in deciding whether or not there was an intention to benefit the husband and thereby rebut the presumption of a resulting trust in favour of the wife.

(b) **Child.** The reference here is to a legitimate child. The rule is that if a *father* purchases property in the name of his child the presumption of advancement applies.[29] But if a mother does the same thing it appears—according to the last case on the point—that it will not apply.[30] But the position is by no means clear-cut and the case law is in some degree conflicting. In the first place, in *Re De Visme*[31] it was held that the presumption of advancement would not arise because a married woman was under no obligation to maintain her children. Secondly, in *Sayre* v. *Hughes,*[32] Stuart V.-C. appeared to hold that the mere motive of benefit on the mother's part was the most material thing. This is a wide conception and, if accepted, could work an advancement in favour of the child. And, finally, in *Bennet* v. *Bennet*[33] Jessel M.R. held essentially that the presumption of advancement applied only to the father but this was so, not because—as was held, in effect, in *Re De Visme*—the mother was under no liability to maintain her children, but because the father alone was under a *moral* obligation to make provision for his child; the mother was under no such obligation. The National Assistance Act 1948[34] imposed a *statutory* duty on the mother to care for her children. But this statutory duty will not affect the position if Jessel M.R. was right in postulating the test of a moral obligation.

The position revealed is unsatisfactory. It is particularly difficult to see why a mother, especially if she has money, is not under the same moral obligation as the father is said to be.[35] It should, however, be borne in mind that the

---

[26] Although if the property is part of the matrimonial assets the court may apply the maxim that equality is equity: see, *e.g. Jones* v. *Maynard* [1951] Ch. 572; *Rimmer* v. *Rimmer* [1953] 1 Q.B. 63; and see *ante*, p. 128, *post*, p. 144.

[27] [1903] 2 Ch. 98.

[28] *Ibid.* at p. 101.

[29] *Dyer* v. *Dyer* (1788) 2 Cox Eq. 92.

[30] *Bennet* v. *Bennet* (1879) 10 Ch.D. 474.

[31] (1863) 2 De G.J. & S. 17.

[32] (1868) L.R. 5 Eq. 376.

[33] *Supra.*   [34] ss. 42(1), 64(1).

[35] In *Loades-Carter* v. *Loades-Carter, The Times,* January 14, 1966, Lord Denning M.R. thought, *obiter*, that the presumption of advancement would apply to a gift by a mother.

presumption of a resulting trust in favour of the mother, if it does in fact follow, can be rebutted in the usual way by showing an intention on her part to benefit the child,[36] and it is quite probable that this will not be difficult to achieve.

(c) **Persons in loco parentis.** This expression applies to a person standing in the position of a parent, *i.e.* in the situation of a person described as the lawful father of the child. A person *in loco parentis* is, according to Jessel M.R. in *Bennet* v. *Bennet,*[37] a person taking upon himself the duty of a father of a child to make provision for that child. For example, an uncle or grandfather may, in the particular circumstances of the case, put himself *in loco parentis* to a child, *e.g.* after the death of his father.[38] Again, a father of an illegitimate child may, in the circumstances, be *in loco parentis* to that child.[39] Yet, a person if he is to be *in loco parentis* must place himself in the situation of the father: for example, simply to pay an illegitimate child's school fees would not be enough in itself to raise the presumption.[40]

Rebuttable nature of the presumption

However, just as the presumption of a resulting trust may be rebutted, so also may the presumption of advancement be rebutted; and it may be done in the same way by evidence of actual intention.

(a) **Admissibility of evidence in rebuttal.** The important question is *how* it can be rebutted, *i.e.* what sort of evidence is admissible for this purpose. The leading case on admissibility is *Shephard* v. *Cartwright.*[41] In this case the deceased had been a successful businessman. He had at various times formed a number of private companies. These had succeeded so well that he had amalgamated them into a public company. At varying times he had shares in this company allotted to his three children. There was no evidence that any share certificates had been issued. In any case, the father continued to deal in these shares: at various times he sold them and received the proceeds of sale. Subsequently, he placed to the credit of the children in separate deposit accounts the exact amount of the cash consideration for the shares he had sold. Later still he obtained the children's signature to documents (as to the contents of which the children were ignorant) authorising him to withdraw money from these accounts and, indeed, without their knowledge, he drew on them; by the end of 1936 the accounts were exhausted. The deceased died in 1949. His children brought an action against the father's executors claiming an account of money due to them. They were met with the defence, which succeeded in the Court of Appeal, that the presumption of advancement was rebutted by the control continually exercised by the father over the shares. The House of Lords, however, held (reversing the Court of Appeal) that the shares registered in the

---

[36] See *Beecher* v. *Major* (1865) 2 Drew. & Sm. 431.
[37] (1879) 10 Ch.D. 474 at p. 477.
[38] *Ebrand* v. *Dancer* (1680) 2 Ch.Cas. 26 (grandchild whose father was dead); *Currant* v. *Jago* (1844) 1 Coll.C.C. 261 (nephew of wife maintained by her husband).
[39] *Beckford* v. *Beckford* (1774) Lofft 490.
[40] *Tucker* v. *Burrow* (1865) 2 Hem. & M. 515.
[41] [1955] A.C. 431.

name of the children were an advancement and that presumption had not been rebutted. The law on the admissibility of evidence in rebuttal was made quite explicit by Viscount Simonds. He adopted[42] a passage from Snell's *Principles of Equity*[43]:

> "The acts and declarations of the parties before or at the time of the purchase, or so immediately after it as to constitute a part of the trans-action, are admissible in evidence either for or against the party who did the act or made the declaration; subsequent acts and declarations are only admissible as evidence against the party who made them, and not in his favour."

There are numerous cases of high authority,[44] as Viscount Simonds said, on which this passage is founded. Therefore, the applicable law—after having been somewhat disturbed by the Court of Appeal, which appeared to hold that subsequent acts were admissible in favour of the parties who did them—is no longer in doubt. There is not, perhaps, too much difficulty in stating these principles in the abstract. They will mean (i) that a father's declaration at the date of the transaction will be admissible in his favour to rebut the presumption, but if made after that date will not be admissible in his favour but only against him by the son in order to support the presumption,[45] and (ii) that subsequent acts and declarations by the son will be admissible against him by the father to rebut the presumption.[46] But in practice difficulties may well be found in applying these general rules. Thus one question in particular may be whether a subsequent act is part of the same transaction as the original purchase or transfer and this may make for problems. For there is no universal criterion by which a link can, for this purpose, be found between one event and another but it is essential that one be able to find a link.[47] In *Shephard* v. *Cartwright* itself Viscount Simonds pointed out that the events which happened after the allot-ment of shares to the children did not form part of the original transaction, *viz.* the allotment. Those events were independent of that transaction and, so far from flowing inevitably from it, they would never have happened but for the phenomenal success of the testator's business.

A second practical problem is whether, and if so what, subsequent acts and declarations will rebut the presumption. An early case which shows that there may be difficulty in rebutting the presumption on this basis is *Lord Grey* v. *Lady Grey*[48] where Lord Finch L.C., in considering the fact that the son permitted his father to receive the profits of the property, said that fact was insufficient to rebut the presumption because it was an "act of reverence and good man-

---

[42] *Ibid.* at p. 445.

[43] (28th ed). at p. 185.

[44] See, *e.g.* the cases cited in notes 45 and 46, *infra*.

[45] *Stock* v. *McAvoy* (1872) L.R. 15 Eq. 55; *Redington* v. *Redington* (1794) 3 Ridg.P.R. 106 at p. 177; *Sidmouth* v. *Sidmouth* (1840) 2 Beav. 447.

[46] *Scawin* v. *Scawin* (1841) 1 Y. & C.C.C. 65.

[47] [1955] A.C. 431 at pp. 448–449, *per* Viscount Simonds.

[48] (1677) 2 Swans. 594.

ners."[49] But there are, of course, circumstances which will go to rebut it. Thus, it was held in *Warren* v. *Gurney*[50] that if a father retained the title deeds, although that was not itself conclusive, it was of great significance when coupled with contemporaneous declarations by the father. Moreover, the fact that the son is the father's solicitor is another circumstance which assists in rebutting it.[51]

Yet, as Viscount Simonds said in *Shephard* v *Cartwright*,[52] any such evidence of subsequent acts is regarded jealously. A question which arose in this case was whether, if the events which happened after the allotments could not be admitted as part of the original transaction, they could nevertheless be admitted as an admission against interest. It is, however, an indispe&'$e condition of such conduct being admissible that it should be performed with knowledge of the material facts. But the undisputed fact in *Shephard* v *Cartwright* itself was that the children, under their father's guidance, did what they were told without inquiry or knowledge, and this fact precluded the admission in evidence of their conduct as constituting an admission against their own interest and if it were admitted would deprive it of all probative value.

(b) **Illegal and fraudulent conduct.** There is a further restriction on the ability to adduce evidence in rebuttal. This is that the transferor cannot rebut the presumption by evidence that he made the transfer for a fraudulent or illegal purpose and intended to retain the beneficial interest. Accordingly, in *Gascoigne* v. *Gascoigne*[53] a husband put money into his wife's name but it was held that he could not adduce evidence to show that he did so for the purpose of defeating his creditors. The point was given an interesting application in the Privy Council decision in *Chettiar* v. *Chettiar* (*No. 2*).[54] Certain regulations governed the holding of rubber plantations in Malaya. The material regulations differentiated between holdings of more than 100 acres on the one hand and less than that number on the other. If more were held the permissible production was controlled by an assessment committee. The father owned 99 acres and then acquired a further 40. In order to avoid having to disclose to the authorities that he held more than 100 acres he transferred the 40 acres into the name of his son. He had no intention of giving them. He now claimed that the son held the land in trust for him. The Judicial Committee in an opinion delivered by Lord Denning held that to make out his claim he had to rebut the presumption of advancement. In so doing, he necessarily had to disclose his own illegality in making the transfer, namely, his deceit of the public administration. The court was bound to take notice of the illegality: it would not therefore lend its aid to the father and would let the legal estate lie where it fell.

---

[49] *Ibid.* at p. 600.
[50] [1944] 2 All E.R. 472.
[51] *Garrett* v. *Wilkinson* (1848) 2 De G. & Sm. 244.
[52] [1955] A.C. 431 at p. 449.
[53] [1918] 1 K.B. 223 and see *Re Emery's Investment Trusts* [1959] Ch. 410 (avoiding payment of taxes).
[54] [1962] A.C. 294.

The principle of such cases was applied in *Tinker* v. *Tinker*[55] to a case where the husband's intention in putting property into his wife's name was apparently *honest*. The husband in this case was, as Lord Denning M.R. said, on the horns of a dilemma. He could not say that the house was his own, and at one and the same time, say that it was his wife's. As against his wife he wanted to say that it belonged to *him*. As against his creditors, that it belonged to *her*. That, however, was not possible. Either it was conveyed to her for her own use absolutely; or it was conveyed to her as trustee for her husband. It had to be one or the other. The presumption was that it was conveyed to her for her own use, and the husband did not rebut the presumption by saying that he only did it to defeat his creditors.

II. JOINT PURCHASES AND VESTING

It has already been seen that where property has been purchased in the name of another it will prima facie result to the person or persons (who may include the nominal purchaser) in proportion to the money actually contributed by each. The situation now being considered arises where the money is contributed by two or more persons and the property is vested in them all. And the question is, to what shares are the purchasers beneficially entitled? The answer will depend essentially on whether the money has been contributed in *equal* or *unequal* shares. If the purchase is made in unequal shares and the conveyance is made to A and B jointly, then on A's death B will become legally entitled to the whole of the property, but he will hold A's share on trust for A's estate. The reason for this is that, in many cases, equity leans against a joint tenancy with its attendant consequence that the survivor is entitled to the entirety, *i.e.* the right of survivorship. Inequality in contributions to the purchase price is considered to be incompatible with this right and equity accordingly imposes a trust on the survivor.

But if the moneys are contributed in equal shares, no such considerations will come into play; the purchasers will prima facie be deemed, if the property is conveyed to them jointly, to have purchased with a view to the right of survivorship.[56] But this will not apply to partners; here, even in the event of equality of contributions, the right of survivorship will not arise because in a commercial enterprise such as a partnership an intention to this effect cannot be attributed to them.[57]

---

[55] [1970] P. 136. *Gascoigne* v. *Gascoigne* and *Tinker* v. *Tinker* were distinguished in *Griffiths* v. *Griffiths* [1973] 1 W.L.R. 1454 where a husband's false reprresentation as to ownership formed no part of the legal proceedings between him and his wife (varied by the C.A. on other grounds [1974] 1 All E.R. 932). *Cf.* also *Heseltine* v. *Heseltine* [1972] 1 W.L.R. 342 (where there was no ulterior or improper purpose in making the transfer to the husband, but it was held that property was held on a resulting trust for the wife).

[56] *Lake* v. *Gibson* (1729) 1 Eq.Cas.Abr. 290; *Lake* v. *Craddock* (1732) 3 P.Wms. 158.

[57] *Lake* v. *Gibson, supra.*

III. JOINT MORTGAGES

The position in a case of joint mortgages should be contrasted with that of joint purchases. If two persons advance money on mortgage and take a mortgage in their own favour jointly the survivor is deemed—and this is so whether or not the money is advanced in equal shares—to hold the deceased mortgagee's share as a trustee for the deceased's estate. The reason is stated to be that a mortgage is a commercial undertaking and therefore there cannot be an intention that an interest in it should survive.[58]

IV. VOLUNTARY CONVEYANCE OR TRANSFER

This situation envisages a direct gift without consideration, and to answer the question whether the presumption of a resulting trust applies it is necessary to consider realty and personalty separately.

1. *Realty*

Before 1926, where a conveyance was intended to be voluntary, it would usually be expressed to be made for the use or benefit of the grantee, for in the absence of words such as these, the grantor would have had a resulting trust of the equitable interest, and the legal estate would have been carried back to the grantor by virtue of the Statute of Uses 1535. The Statute of Uses was repealed by the Law of Property Act 1925, and as a consequential provision, section 60(3) of that Act provides that in a voluntary conveyance of land (including leaseholds) a resulting trust for the grantor shall not be implied *merely* by reason that the property is not expressed to be conveyed for the use or benefit of the grantee. There appears to be nothing in section 60(3) which prevents a resulting trust from being implied for other reasons, particularly by the operation of general equitable principles, and to prevent such a resulting trust express words are almost invariably inserted in a voluntary conveyance to rebut the equitable presumption.[59]

2. *Personalty (excluding leaseholds)*

It appears that a transferee of personalty on a voluntary transfer will prima facie hold the property upon a resulting trust for the transferor.[60] Thus, in *Re Vinogradoff*,[61] War Loan was transferred into the joint names of the transferor and her granddaughter who was then four years old, but to whom she was not *in loco parentis*. A resulting trust was held by Farwell J. to arise. The counter-presumption of advancement will, of course, arise if the transferor is the husband or father of, or *in loco parentis* to, the transferee.

---

[58] *Morley* v. *Bird* (1798) 3 Ves. 628.
[59] Some writers are of a different opinion: see, *e.g.* Hanbury and Maudsley (11th ed.), p. 319; but *cf.* Underhill (12th ed.), p. 219, (but see 13th ed., p. 282). It may be relevant that in *Hodgradoff* v. *Marks* [1971] Ch. 892, Russell L.J. said that the question was "debatable."
[60] See also *Fowkes* v. *Pascoe* (1875) 10 Ch.App. 343 at pp. 345–348.
[61] [1935] W.N. 68.

V. Ownership of the Matrimonial Home

1. *The Problem*

It is appropriate to consider separately trusts affecting the matrimonial home for this is the type of resulting or implied trust which has given rise to the greatest difficulty during the last 25 years. In part the difficulty has been due to a marked conflict among the judges as to the basic approach to the problem: is the ownership of the matrimonial home to be decided on the one hand by the strict application of traditional property rights, or on the other hand is it to be decided on wider grounds of social justice? If the former, are all the traditional rules to be applied, or only some? If the latter, and the decision is to be made on the grounds of social justice, can the courts nevertheless establish limits so that some certainty is left in the law?

Consider a common situation. A husband purchases a house for £14,000 to form the matrimonial home, and the conveyance is taken in his name alone. He pays £3,000 in cash, and his wife provides £1,000. The balance of the purchase price, £10,000, is provided by a mortgage. The husband pays the mortgage instalments. His wife continues to work, and uses her earnings towards the family's food and routine living expenses. They do various jobs in the house and garden, as a result of which its value is increased by £2,000. Seven years later the house is sold for £18,000. By that time the mortgage debt has been reduced to £9,000. Who is entitled to the balance?

Some of the possibilities are:

(a) The husband is entitled to all, because the property is in his name;
(b) the husband and wife share equally, because they have both contributed;
(c) the husband is repaid £3,000; the wife is repaid £1,000, the balance is divided equally;
(d) the wife is regarded as making a loan of £1,000 to the husband. She is therefore entitled to the return of that, and the husband takes the balance;
(e) the wife is entitled to her contribution, and also to the value of her work. On this basis, the wife is given £2,000 and the husband takes the balance.

The approach to the problem is now governed by a combination of rapidly developing equitable principles and statutory intervention.[62] The result is that it may be necessary to consider three questions:

(a) What are the proprietary rights of the parties?
(b) Are those proprietary rights to be adjusted?
(c) How is effect to be given to these rights?

The first of these questions may be regulated by the Married Women's Property Act 1882, and the second and third by the Matrimonial Causes Act 1973.

---

[62] Particularly the Married Women's Property Act 1882, the Matrimonial Proceedings and Property Act 1970, and the Matrimonial Causes Act 1973.

Section 17 of the Act of 1882 provides, so far as is relevant for present purposes, as follows:

"In any question between husband and wife as to the title to or possession of property, either party . . . may apply by summons or otherwise in a summary way to any judge of the High Court of Justice . . . and the judge . . . may make such order with respect to the property in dispute . . . as he thinks fit."

The section appears to confer an unrestricted discretion on the judge, and as a general rule of statutory interpretation, where a limitation is to be placed on the discretion of the court, this is usually made explicit. Some judges had held that the section was sufficiently wide to override existing property rights, and enable them to dispose of the property in a manner which was considered just and equitable in the whole circumstances of the case.[63] Others disagreed,[64] holding that the section was merely procedural, and this view was affirmed by the House of Lords in *Pettitt* v. *Pettitt*.[65] In the result the question of ownership can only be decided under the section by conventional principles of equity. The procedure under the section is available, but only on the same basis, to a former spouse for three years from the date of dissolution or annulment,[66] and to a person engaged to be married provided that the proceedings are brought within three years of the termination of the agreement to marry.[67]

Secondly, however, the proprietary rights of the parties may be actually modified by the court under section 24 of the Matrimonial Causes Act 1973. Where there are proceedings for divorce, nullity or judicial separation, this section empowers the court to order either spouse to transfer or settle property for the benefit of the other or for the benefit of the children; or to vary an agreement or arrangement between the spouses with regard to property.[68] By section 25 of the Act the court is directed to exercise its power[69] so "as to place the parties, so far as it is practicable and, having regard to their conduct, just to do so, in the financial position in which they would have been if the marriage had not broken down and each had properly discharged his or her financial obligations and responsibilities towards the other." This involves considering three questions[70]:

(i) What would the financial position of the parties have been if the marriage had not broken down?

---

[63] See *Wilson* v. *Wilson* [1963] 1 W.L.R. 601; *Hine* v. *Hine* [1962] 1 W.L.R. 1124.

[64] *National Provincial Bank Ltd.* v. *Ainsworth* [1965] A.C. 1175; *Bedson* v. *Bedson* [1963] 2 Q.B. 666.

[65] [1970] A.C. 777.

[66] Matrimonial Proceedings and Property Act 1970, s. 39.

[67] Law Reform (Miscellaneous Provisions) Act 1970, s. 2(2).

[68] Referred to in the Act as a "nuptial settlement." The expression includes a house in which both parties have a beneficial interest.

[69] And also its powers to make orders for periodical payments under s. 23 of the Act.

[70] *Per* Bagnall J. in *Harnett* v. *Harnett* [1973] 2 All E.R. 593 at p. 596; affirmed [1974] 1 W.L.R. 219, C.A.

(ii) How far is it practicable to place the parties in that financial position?

(iii) How far is it just to do so.

The first two questions are essentially factual; the third involves the exercise by the court of its discretionary jurisdiction related to the facts of the case.[71] Because of this discretion, which is wide-ranging, it is unnecessry, and inappropriate, for an application to be made to determine the strict proprietary rights of the parties in the first instance.[72]

Section 17 of the Married Womens Property Act 1882 has, therefore, clearly declined in importance. Where there are matrimonial proceedings, application should be made under the Matrimonial Causes Act 1973 for a property adjustment order. Such an order may incidentally involve the modification or variation of a trust,[73] but this is effected by virtue of the court's wide discretionary power and does not generally involve the application of general trust law. The same considerations apply where the court has to decide how effect is to be given to the rights of the parties, such as whether or not the matrimonial home should be sold.[74] Such matters, involving as they do the exercise of a discretion, are not considered further in this chapter.[75] But in some cases it may still be necessary to determine the strict proprietary interests of the spouses and section 17 of the 1882 Act may still be relevant: for example, where there are no proceedings for divorce, nullity or judicial separation, or where one of the spouses has remarried after divorce without an application having been made under the 1973 Act.[76] In such cases the ascertainment of proprietary rights must be made under section 17 of the 1882 Act, *i.e.* determined by equitable principles relating to trusts. Further, in cases where the parties are not married,[77] neither the 1882 Act nor the 1973 Act can apply, and the matter can only be determined by equitable principles.[78] It is with these situations that the law of trusts has a part to play.

---

[71] *e.g.* whether or not the matrimonial home should be sold: see *Rawlings* v. *Rawlings* [1964] P. 398; *Halden* v. *Halden* [1966] 1 W.L.R. 1481; *Re Hardy's Trust* [1970] 114 S.J. 864; *Jackson* v. *Jackson* [1971] 1 W.L.R. 1539; *Williams* v. *Williams* [1976] Ch. 278, C.A. According to the last mentioned case, on breakdown of marriage, the question should be dealt with under the court's discretionary jurisdiction. The court has jurisdiction to determine not only the rights and interests of husband and wife in property but also those third parties who had intervened in the application to claim an interest in the property: *Tebbutt* v. *Haynes* [1981] 2 All E.R. 238, C.A. See also *Hanlon* v. *Hanlon* [1978] 1 W.L.R. 592, C.A.; *cf.* L.P.A. 1925, s.30 where the parties are not married: n.78, *infra*. See also Matrimonial Homes and Property Act 1981, s.7.

[72] *Wachtel* v. *Wachtel* [1973] Fam. 70, at p. 92, C.A.; *Kowalczuk* v. *Kowalczuk* [1973] 1 W.L.R. 930 at p. 934, C.A. *Hunter* v. *Hunter* [1973] 1 W.L.R. 958 at p. 961 (C.A.); *Griffiths* v. *Griffiths* [1974] 1 W.L.R. 1350 at p. 1358, C.A.

[73] See *post*, p. 411.

[74] See the cases cited in note 71, *ante*, and the bankruptcy case cited in note 78, *post*.

[75] These matters are dealt with in some detail in the books on Family Law: see, *e.g.* Cretney, *Family Law* (2nd ed.), Chap. 6.

[76] *Suttill* v. *Graham* [1977] 1 W.L.R. 819, C.A.

[77] It is assumed that they have not been engaged to be married: see *ante*, p. 137.

[78] Likewise, where one of the spouses has died and the survivor claims a beneficial interest (see *Re Cummins* [1972] Ch. 62, C.A., *Re Nicholson* [1974] 1 W.L.R. 476); and where a spouse becomes bankrupt and the other claims an interest against the trustee in bankruptcy (see *Re Solomon* [1967] Ch. 573; *Re Turner* [1974] 1 W.L.R. 556; *Re Densham* [1975] 1

2. *Ascertaining the Proprietary Rights*

(1) **Express agreement**

The parties may have reached an express agreement as to the beneficial ownership of the property, and where this is so, the general principle is that that agreement will prevail. Most of the cases in this field would not have been necessary if there had been such an agreement, and the problems have been such that it is desirable[79] for a solicitor acting for a husband or a married or indeed an unmarried couple purchasing a house to recommend in the strongest terms that a subsidary agreement should be prepared determining the beneficial interests in the property, and in particular providing for the disposal of the proceeds of sale. In the usual case, an express statement that the spouses are purchasing as beneficial joint tenants can easily be inserted in the purchase deed.[80]

Such an agreement will be effective, subject to the following limitations:

(a) an agreement made during the subsistence of a happy marriage as to what is to happen in the event of separation or divorce is generally void for public policy.[81] Accordingly, any such agreement must relate to the disposal of the property in any circumstances and not merely in the event of separation or divorce.

(b) an agreement, once made, can be altered by a subsequent agreement, either express or by implication, but the courts will be slow to find in any case that the legal situation which prevailed at the time when the property was purchased has been subsequently altered.[82]

(c) any agreement will amount to an ante-nuptial or post-nuptial settlement according to whether the property was purchased before or after the date of the marriage, and so is capable of variation by the court under the Matrimonial Causes Act 1973.

As a result of the reluctance of the courts to hold that the original agreement or intention has been altered, it will usually be difficult for one spouse to

---

W.L.R. 1519; *Re Windle* [1975] 1 W.L.R. 1628; *Re Bailey* [1977] 1 W.L.R. 278); *Re Holliday* [1981] 2 W.L.R. 996, C.A.); or whether property (*e.g.* the family house) should be sold under L.P.A. 1925, s. 30: the Court in deciding whether to order a sale, takes account of the underlying purpose of the trust for sale (*e.g.* whether a house was purchased as a home for the family and whether that purpose still subsists): see *Re Buchanan-Wollaston's Conveyance* [1939] Ch. 738; *Jones* v. *Challenger* [1961] 1 Q.B. 176, C.A.; *Rawlings* v. *Rawlings* [1964] P. 398, C.A.; *Re Evers's Trust* [1980] 1 W.L.R. 1327, C.A.; *Dennis* v. *McDonald* [1982] Fam. 63, C.A.; *Bernard* v. *Josephs* [1982] 2 W.L.R. 1052, C.A.

[79] Although such an agreement is very desirable, it is still rare for it to be concluded where the property is conveyed to one of the spouses alone. Its desirability was emphasised by Griffiths L.J. in *Bernard* v. *Josephs* [1982] 2 W.L.R. 1052, C.A. at p. 1062.

[80] This should be conclusive in the absence of fraud or mistake, so that the spouses should take half each: see *Pettitt* v. *Pettitt* [1970] A.C. 777, *per* Lord Upjohn at p. 813; followed in *Re John's Assignment Trusts* [1970] 1 W.L.R. 955; *Leake* v. *Bruzzi* [1974] 1 W.L.R. 1529. *Cf. Burgess* v. *Rawnsley* [1975] Ch. 429 (as to when the purpose of the purchase fails): see *post*, p. 153.

[81] *Cartwright* v. *Cartwright* (1853) 3 De G.M. 982.

[82] *Pettitt* v. *Pettitt* [1970] A.C. 777; [1969] 2 All E.R. 385, H.L. See also *Cowcher* v. *Cowcher* [1972] 1 W.L.R. 425; [1972] 1 All E.R. 943, *per* Bagnall J. at p. 432 and p. 950.

establish a proprietary interest in the property where the other acquired it before marriage. So, in *Kowalczuk* v. *Kowalczuk*[83] the husband bought a house in 1955, before he met his future wife, whom he married in 1957. The parties both contributed to the common living expenses, including some of the mortgage payments, although these were minimal. The Court of Appeal held that the wife had no beneficial interest in the property on this ground.[84]

(2) **Implying or imputing an intention**[85]

Until recently, it was thought that the traditional rules of resulting trusts and advancement applied in this field as in any other. Thus, if the husband provided the purchase price, and the house was purchased in joint names, the husband would be presumed to have made to her an advancement of a half share, whereas if the wife provided the purchase price, and the house was in joint names, the husband and wife would hold the legal estate upon a resulting trust for the wife alone. The position has now been stated by Lord Diplock in *Pettitt* v. *Pettitt*[86] as follows[87]:

> "A presumption of fact is no more than a consensus of judicial opinion disclosed by reported cases as to the most likely inference of fact to be drawn in the absence of any evidence to the contrary; for example, presumptions of legitimacy, of death or survival, and the like. But the most likely inference as to a person's intention in the transactions of his everyday life depends on the social environment in which he lives and the common habits of thought of those who live in it. The consensus of judical opinion which gave rise to the presumptions of 'advancement' and 'resulting trust' in transactions between husband and wife is to be found in cases relating to the propertied classes of the nineteenth century and the first quarter of the twentieth century among whom marriage settlements were common, and it was unusual for the wife to contribute her earnings to the family income. It was not until after World War II that the courts were required to consider the proprietary rights in family assets of a different social class. The advent of legal aid, the wider employment of married women in industry, commerce and the professions, and the emergence of a property-owning, particularly a real-property-mortgaged-to-a-building-society-owning democracy has compelled the courts to direct their attention to this during the last 20 years. It would, in my view, be an abuse of the legal technique for ascertaining or imputing intention to apply to transactions between the post-war generation of married couples 'presumptions' which are based on inferences of fact which an earlier generation of judges drew

---

[83] [1973] 1 W.L.R. 930.

[84] The result would have been different if the wife had made a substantial direct contribution to the mortgage payments: *per* Lord Denning M.R. at p. 933. The case was remitted for further inquiry whether the wife had made a substantial contribution by carrying out improvements, as to which see *post*, p. 145.

[85] See, generally, Zuckerman (1978) 94 L.Q.R. 26.

[86] [1970] A.C. 777.

[87] *Ibid.* at p. 783.

as to the most likely intentions of earlier generations of spouses belonging to the propertied classes of a different social era."

Notwithstanding these remarks of Lord Diplock, the doctrine of advancement can still have some application in these cases, particularly where for some reason, such as death, one or both of the parties are unable to give evidence. Where both parties are available to give evidence the court much prefers to hear them and to form its own view of their intention. Where this is done the presumption will rarely have any effect.[88]

Most of the difficulties in this area of the law have concerned the circumstances in which an intention can be implied on the part of the spouses as to their beneficial entitlement to the property. A modern starting point is the decision of the House of Lords in *Pettitt* v *Pettitt*,[89] where a cottage had been purchased by a wife from her own funds, and was conveyed into her name alone. The husband made various improvements to the property by carrying out internal decorations and modifications, and by improving the garden. He valued that work at £723, and claimed that when the property was sold, the value of the property had been increased by £1,000. The House of Lords, overruling a similar decision to the contrary in the Court of Appeal[90] held that he had acquired no rights as a result of his work. Secondly, in *Gissing* v *Gissing*[91] the property was in the sole name of the husband, and there was no express agreement as to how the property should be held. The wife spent a small sum on improving the lawn[92] and paid certain living expenses from her earnings. However, these were not paid in order to assist the husband in meeting the mortgage payments, and the House of Lords held that the wife had no beneficial interest in the property.

In both cases, therefore, the claims of the spouses were not substantiated, but the House of Lords discussed the general principles to be applied in determining the proprietary interests. Unfortunately, there was a difference of emphasis. In *Pettitt* v. *Pettitt*, Lord Reid[93] and Lord Diplock[94] appeared to be of opinion that the function of the court under section 17 of the Married Womens Property Act 1882, under which the claim had been brought, was to decide what the spouses would, as a reasonable husband and wife, have agreed as to their respective beneficial interests, had they directed their minds to the question. The other members of the court appeared to take the view that the beneficial interests must be those which arise under a resulting trust based on the proportions in which the purchase money was actually provided or under an agreement or

---

[88] *Ibid.* at p. 793; in *Falconer* v. *Falconer* [1970] 1 W.L.R. 1333 Lord Denning M.R. described it as outmoded and refused to apply it in favour of a wife who had left her husband and taken a lover.

[89] [1970] A.C. 777.

[90] In *Appleton* v. *Appleton* [1965] 1 W.L.R. 25.

[91] [1971] A.C. 886; [1970] 2 All E.R. 780.

[92] As to the circumstances in which a beneficial interest is acquired or enhanced through improvements, see *post*, p. 145.

[93] *Supra* at p. 795.

[94] *Supra* at p. 823.

common intention expressed or to be inferred from all the relevant facts.[95] In *Gissing* v. *Gissing*, Lord Reid repeated his original opinion, but otherwise the case seemed to establish that the beneficial interest in property must either (i) coincide with the legal estate, or (ii) arise under a resulting trust from the actual provision of the purchase price, or (iii) arise from a common agreement or common intention either express or to be inferred from the facts.[96] Thus, it seems to be implicit in the majority consensus in both cases, although not clearly beyond doubt, that the court cannot ascribe to the parties intentions which they never had and, further, that those intentions have to be ascertained at the date of the purchase and not subsequently.[97]

It would appear that the differences of approach or emphasis in these cases were subsequently exploited by the Court of Appeal, in which Lord Denning M.R. played a major role, to achieve a rather different result from that which was intended. In particular, controversy has surrounded the question of what contributions may be taken into account, and whether those contributions may be direct or indirect. It has, however, now been held in a line of decisions of the Court of Appeal[98] that the inference of a trust will be readily drawn where each has made a substantial financial contribution to the purchase price or the mortgage instalments, not only directly, as where the contributions were stated to be such, but also indirectly, where both parties, for example, went out to work and one paid for the housekeeping and the other the mortgage instalments. What shares they are to be given depends on their respective contributions.

The difficulty lies in inferring a link between the purchase of the property and the subsequent indirect contributions, whatever form the latter may take. According to the majority consensus in *Pettitt* v. *Pettitt* and *Gissing* v. *Gissing,* a link must be found because the common intention of the parties as to beneficial entitlement has to be inferred at the date of the purchase.[99] But Lord Denning M.R. did not concern himself with such niceties. In *Hazell* v. *Hazell*,[1] for example, he claimed that the wife could get a share by reason simply of her contributions, even though there was no agreement, express or implied. One would have thought, however, that the requirement of a "common intention" referred to by the House of Lords would import an express or implied agreement as to beneficial entitlement. Indeed, in the same case, it was even held that such indirect contributions need not be "referable" to the acquisition of the

---

[95] See *per* Lord Morris of Borth-y-Gest, *supra* at p. 804, *per* Lord Hodson at p. 807; *per* Lord Upjohn at p. 818.

[96] This analysis is borrowed from Bagnall J.'s judgment in *Cowcher* v. *Cowcher* [1972] 1 W.L.R. 425 at p. 433.

[97] See *per* Lord Morris of Borth-y-Gest, *supra* at p. 898, but *cf.* Lord Pearson at p. 902 and Lord Diplock at p. 906.

[98] See, *e.g. Falconer* v. *Falconer* [1970] 1 W.L.R. 1333; *Heseltine* v. *Heseltine* [1971] 1 W.L.R. 342; *Hargrave* v. *Newton* [1971] 1 W.L.R. 1611; *Re Cummins* [1972] Ch. 62; *Hazell* v. *Hazell* [1972] 1 W.L.R. 301; *Cooke* v. *Head* [1972] 1 W.L.R. 518; *Eves* v. *Eves* [1975] 1 W.L.R. 1338.

[99] See also to the same effect *Re Nicholson* [1974] 1 W.L.R. 476 at p. 480, *per* Pennycuick V.-C.; *Eves* v. *Eves* [1975] 1 W.L.R. 1338 at p. 1345, *per* Brightman J.

[1] [1972] 1 W.L.R. 301.

property; nor was it necessary to show that the husband could not have bought it without them: it was sufficient if they relieved the husband of expenditure which he would otherwise have had to bear.

In view of this judicial activity, the question has to be asked: what type of trust arises and in essence whether it is a resulting trust or a constructive trust? Lord Denning M.R. has spoken of "imputing" a trust in these circumstances,[2] and there seems to be no doubt that, as he said in terms in *Eves* v. *Eves*,[3] and hinted at as much in *Hazell* v. *Hazell*, that the type of trust which is here "imputed" is a constructive trust, *i.e.* imposed by law in the interest of conscience, not based (as a resulting trust is traditionally supposed to be based) on implied intention.[4] Such a solution, although removing the necessity of finding a link between the original purchase and the subsequent contributions, does, however, run counter to the requirement of a common intention referred to by the House of Lords in *Pettitt* v. *Pettitt* and *Gissing* v. *Gissing*, and which is only compatible with a resulting trust.

Indeed, other members of the Court of Appeal have on occasion found greater difficulty in adopting this approach. Thus, in *Eves* v. *Eves*,[5] Brightman J., although agreeing in the result with Lord Denning M.R., found that it was an implied part of the bargain between the parties that the plaintiff should contribute her labour towards the repair of a house in which she was also to have a beneficial interest, thereby finding a link between the original purchase and her subsequent indirect contribution.[6] This argument may, however, be somewhat artificial in some cases, and in *Bernard* v. *Josephs*[7] Griffiths L.J. put the point more robustly. He said[8]:

> "In the absence of any special circumstances . . . the time at which the beneficial interest crystallised is the time of acquisition, but to ascertain this [the judge] must look at all the evidence including all the contributions made by the parties. As a general rule the only relevant contributions will be those up to the date of the separation but it does not necessarily follow that what happens after the separation will in every case be irrelevant. In my opinion the judge should examine all the evidence placed before him and not regard the date of separation as the cut-off point. The task imposed upon the judge is so difficult that every scrap of evidence may be of value, and should be available to him."

In *Bernard* v. *Josephs* a house was conveyed to an unmarried couple in their joint names but with no declaration of trust as to their beneficial interests. They

---

[2] See, *e.g. Heseltine* v. *Heseltine* [1971] 1 W.L.R. 342 at p. 345; *Hargrave* v. *Newton* [1971] 1 W.L.R. 1611 at 1613; *Hazell* v. *Hazell* [1972] 1 W.L.R. 301 at p. 305; *Eves* v. *Eves* [1975] 1 W.L.R. 1338 at p. 1342.

[3] [1975] 1 W.L.R. 1338.

[4] See also *Re Densham* [1975] 1 W.L.R. 1519 where Goff J. imposed a constructive trust in respect of matrimonial property in favour of the wife.

[5] *Supra* (for the facts see *post*, p. 148).

[6] Browne L.J. agreed with Brightman J.

[7] [1982] 2 W.L.R. 1052, C.A.

[8] *Ibid.* at p. 1063.

lived in the house together but subsequently separated, and later the man married another woman and took her to live with him in the house. The woman with whom he had previously lived successfully applied for an order for sale of the property[9] and for a declaration that she was entitled to a half-share of the net proceeds of sale. The order of sale was not to be enforced if the man paid the woman the sum of £6,000 within four months.

The House of Lords has not had an opportunity as yet of ruling on these developments. But it would seem unlikely that the long line of Court of Appeal decisions will now be disturbed. It would also probably be undesirable in view of the practice which is now established.

It should perhaps be mentioned that in *Cowcher* v. *Cowcher*[10] Bagnall J. essayed an elaborate distinction between two classes of common agreement or intention, one a "money consensus," the other, an "interest consensus," the first being where the parties agree that they should be treated as having subscribed in particular shares other than those in which they had in fact subscribed, and the latter, where they agree to take certain interests. Further, according to Bagnall J., a "money consensus" is consistent with and operates as a resulting trust, but an "interest consensus" is an express trust and fails unless evidenced in writing under section 53(1)(*b*) of the Law of Property Act 1925,[11] or contained in an agreement of which the court will order specific performance. Quite apart from the activity of the Court of Appeal, however, this analysis is difficult to reconcile with the realities of house purchase, and in *Re Densham*[12] Goff J. disagreed with it. As he said[13]: "in the vast majority of cases, parties do not direct their minds to treating the money payments as notionally other than they are. What they think about, if they think at all, is ownership."

(3) Quantifying the beneficial interests

Where the parties have imputed to them an intention that each should have a beneficial interest in the property, it is then necessary to ascertain the extent of that interest. The provisions of the purchase deed may show that the beneficial interests are equal. In other cases, the respective beneficial interests of the parties depend on the proportions in which they each contributed to the purchase price or deposit, and in which they each contributed to any mortgage repayments. In *Cowcher* v. *Cowcher*[14] the house was purchased in 1962 for £12,000, of which the wife provided £4,000 and the husband, by mortgage, £8,000. By the time of the hearing of the case in 1971, the house was worth £18,000, or subject to planning permission being obtained for development, £42,000. The property was purchased in the name of the husband alone. Husband and wife both contributed to the common living expenses, including

---

[9] Under L.P.A., 1925, s.30: see *ante* p. 139; *cf. Brikierst* v. *Jones* [1981] 125 S. J. 323, C.A.
[10] [1972] 1 W.L.R. 425.
[11] See *ante*, p. 23.
[12] [1975] 1 W.L.R. 1519.
[13] *Ibid.* at p. 1525. In *Kowalczuk* v. *Kowalczuk* [1973] 1 W.L.R. 930; Lord Denning M.R. said (at p. 933) that "Bagnall J. might have expressed himself differently if he had seen the report in *Hazell* v. *Hazell*."
[14] [1972] 1 W.L.R. 425; [1972] 1 All E.R. 943.

the mortgage payments. Bagnall J. held that the basic inference was that the wife was to have a one-third equitable interest and the husband two-thirds. There was no evidence to show that the parties intended to contribute and to own the property equally, and the basic inference prevailed.[15] But an exact mathematical calculation will often be impossible. In *Hargrave* v. *Newton*[16] the house was bought in the name of the husband alone with the aid of a mortgage for the full purchase price. Both husband and wife contributed to the living expenses and mortgage payments, although the wife's contributions were less than her husband's. On the other hand, she found in a wood some money which had been stolen in the Great Train Robbery, and received a reward for handing it in, part of which was also used for the living expenses. The Court of Appeal did not attempt to make an exact calculation but held the parties to be equally entitled. Similarly, in *Bernard* v*Josephs*,[17] where the parties were not married to each other, the Court of Appeal held that the circumstances, including the respective contributions of the parties, showed that a house which they had owned and occupied was to be held for them in equal shares.[18]

(4) Improvements to property

(a) **General principles.** There are two general principles of property law which relate to improvements made by one person on the land of another:

(i) in general, where a person carries out work on the land of another without agreement with the owner, and without the request of the other, that person acquires no rights in the property[19]; but

(ii) if the owner, having knowledge of the work being carried out, acquiesces in it, the courts may in exceptional circumstances presume from that that the person carrying out the improvements was to have rights in the property on the basis of proprietary estoppel. The presumed agreement must be, however, that property rights are to be acquired in the property, and not merely that the property should be improved for some other purpose. The scope of the rule is, therefore, very restricted.[20]

These rules apply to property owned by spouses; but their effect has to be considered in the light of the rule, previously mentioned, that the courts are concerned with the intention of the parties at the time when the property was

---

[15] In *Kowalczuk* v. *Kowalczuk* [1973] 1 W.L.R. 930 although Lord Denning M.R. said at p. 933 that Bagnall J. in *Cowcher* v. *Cowcher* "might have expressed himself differently," this probably does not imply criticism of the result of the case. See also *ante*, p. 144.

[16] [1971] 1 W.L.R. 1611, C.A.; [1971] 3 All E.R. 866.

[17] [1982] 2 W.L.R. 1052; see *ante*, p. 143, *post*, p. 148.

[18] For other examples of quantification of the beneficial interests see the cases cited at p. 142, n. 98, *ante*.

[19] See *ante*, p. 56.

[20] See, *e.g.* Lord Reid in *Pettitt* v. *Pettitt* [1970] A.C. 777. It is possibly arguable that the requirements may be in process of relaxation; see the discussion of the modern case law, *ante*, p. 57. It is perhaps surprising that little has been heard of the use of a constructive trust to provide relief in this particular context; but see *Hussey* v. *Palmer* [1972] 1 W.L.R. 1286 and *post*, p. 162.

acquired; and very clear evidence will be required to show that that intention has been altered by mutual agreement. The rules also have to be considered subject to the provisions of the Matrimonial Causes Act 1973 which is mentioned above.[21]

In general, therefore, improvements made to a house by one or both spouses will be regarded as improvements made for their common enjoyment, and not with a view to existing property rights being altered.

Thus, in *Pettitt* v. *Pettitt* the House of Lords held that the husband had acquired no rights as a result of his work. As Lord Diplock said[22]:

> "If the husband likes to occupy his leisure by laying a new lawn in the garden or building a fitted wardrobe in the bedroom while the wife does the shopping, cooks the family dinner or baths the children, I, for my part, find it impossible to impute to them as reasonable husband and wife any common intention that these domestic activities or any of them are to have any effect on the existing proprietary rights in the family home on which they are undertaken. It is only in the bitterness engendered by the break-up of the marriage that so bizarre a notion would enter their heads."

In exceptional circumstances, however, the parties may reach an agreement that property rights are to be acquired. Such a case was *Jansen* v. *Jansen*.[23] In that case the husband had still managed to remain a student at the age of 31. His wife was a psychiatric social worker who had been married previously. From her own resources the wife purchased, in her own name alone, a large house suitable for conversion. By agreement with his wife, the husband gave up his studies, and devoted his time to the conversion of the property, although there was no agreement as to the disposal of the profits of the conversion. Upon the sale of the property, the husband was held to have an interest in the property, which was assessed at £1,000.

(b) **Statutory provision.** As between husband and wife[24] the situation exemplified in *Pettitt* v. *Pettitt*[25] has been modified by section 37 of the Matrimonial Proceedings and Property Act 1970.[26] This section applies where a spouse makes a *substantial* contribution in money or money's worth to the improvement of any real or personal property in which either or both of them has a beneficial interest. The section provides that as a result of that contribution, the contributing spouse acquires a share or a larger share, in the property

---

[21] *Ante*, p. 138.

[22] [1970] A.C. 777 at p. 826.

[23] [1965] P. 478; [1965] 3 All E.R. 363.

[24] Applying also as between engaged couples provided that the proceedings are brought within three years of the termination of the agreement to marry: Law Reform (Miscellaneous Provisions) Act 1970, s. 2(1).

[25] Although this case antedated the Act of 1970, it would probably have been decided in the same way after the Act, because the improvements would not appear to have been sufficiently "substantial," but more in the nature of minor "do-it-yourself" jobs.

[26] It is considered that the section did effect a change in the law, and was not merely declaratory, notwithstanding the contrary view expressed by Lord Denning M.R. in *Davis* v. *Vale* [1971] 2 All E.R. 1021 at p. 1025.

to an extent which seems to the court to be just. The operation of this section was one of the points which was considered in *Harnett* v. *Harnett*.[27] The husband was a builder. He built the first matrimonial home of the parties himself with building material costing a total of over £2,000. The wife claimed an interest in the property as a result of section 37, on two grounds. First, she purchased materials for £100. Secondly, she claimed that she physically helped with the building work, drove the builder's van, and dealt with contractors. Bagnall J. rejected her contentions. In the first place, he thought that her contribution was not "substantial."[28] In the second place he stated[29] that "the contributions must be identifiable with the relevant improvement as well as substantial." What the wife had done in this case was not identifiable.[30] Unless the initial construction is genuinely the joint work of both parties it seems that for the contribution to be identifiable, there must be some separate physical feature, such as a garage or an extension to the room, or a central heating installation. The Act does not specify how the share of the contributing party is to be calculated, but the starting points must be the value of the improvement when carried out, and the increase in the value of the property as a whole.[31]

(5) Unmarried "Spouses"[32]

The relevance of these principles, so far as they concern beneficial entitlement, where the parties are not married was considered by the Court of Appeal in *Cooke* v. *Head*.[33] A married man met a young woman in 1962 and she subsequently became his mistress. In 1964 they decided to acquire land and build a bungalow on it, in the hope that the man would obtain a divorce and that they could establish a matrimonial home in it. In 1966, just before the construction was complete, the parties separated. The conveyance was taken in the name of the man alone, and, when it was being sold, the mistress claimed a share. She did not contribute to the deposit, but both contributed towards the mortgage payments, and the actual building work. With regard to the latter, the mistress "did quite an unusual amount of work for a woman. She used a sledgehammer to demolish some old buildings. She filled the wheelbarrow with rubble and hardcore and wheeled it up the bank. She worked the cement mixer, which was out of order and difficult to work. She did painting, and so forth."[34] The Court of Appeal held that the trust imposed on a legal owner in the case of a husband and wife who by their joint efforts acquired property to be used for their joint benefit applied to a man and his mistress where they intended setting up home together, so that in this case the man held upon trust for himself and his mistress. The extent of the beneficial interest of the mistress was to be deter-

---

[27] [1973] 2 All E.R. 593 (at first instance); *cf. Re Nicholson* [1974] 1 W.L.R. 476.

[28] The judge accepted the husband's contention that the wife only helped with the work occasionally "as any wife would" (p. 604).

[29] At p. 603.

[30] The decision was affirmed by the Court of Appeal on other grounds: [1974] 1 W.L.R. 219.

[31] *Re Nicholson* [1974] 1 W.L.R. 476; see *Griffiths* v. *Griffiths* [1974] 1 All E.R. 932 as to the form of the court order.

[32] See, generally, Richards (1976) 40 Conv. (N.S.) 351.

[33] [1972] 2 All E.R. 38, C.A.   [34] *Per* Lord Denning M.R. at p. 40.

mined in the same way as in the case of husband and wife, and in the circumstances it was held that the mistress had a one-third beneficial interest.

Another energetic unmarried lady made a claim to a share in a house in *Eves* v. *Eves*.[35] She also had wielded a sledgehammer and did other work[36] in putting a dirty and dilapidated house in order. Lord Denning M.R. held that her lover held on a constructive trust for her; Brightman J.[37] that it could be inferred from the condition of the house and the work that she did to it that it was part of the bargain that she should contribute her labour in return for a beneficial interest in it. In the result, she was held to be entitled to a quarter of the beneficial interest.[38]

More recently, in *Bernard* v. *Josephs*,[39] again involving an unmarried couple, the Court of Appeal confirmed that the same legal principles are to be applied, whether the dispute is between married or unmarried couples, in determining the beneficial interests of the parties. Indeed, Lord Denning M.R. thought that disputes about the homes of unmarried as well as married couples should be dealt with in the Family Division rather than the Chancery Division.[40] But Griffiths L.J., with whom Kerr L.J. agreed, sounded "a note of caution."[41] He emphasised that there are many reasons why a man and a woman may decide to live together without marrying, and one of them is that each values his independence and does not wish to make the commitment of marriage; in such a case it would be misleading to make the same assumptions and to draw the same inferences from their behaviour as in the case of a married couple. "The judge must look most carefully at the nature of the relationship, and only if satisfied that it was intended to involve the same degree of commitment as marriage will it be legitimate to regard them as no different from a married couple."

If these principles are to be applied in this way to married and unmarried couples, logically they should also apply to other persons who have made contributions to the acquisition or enhancement of property.[42]

VI. Failure of the Trust or Beneficial Interest

1. *Trust Failing*

Where the trusts fail there is a resulting trust of the trust property for the settlor or his estate. Thus in *Re Ames' Settlement*,[43] the funds of a marriage settlement

---

[35] [1975] 1 W.L.R. 1338, C.A.

[36] According to Lord Denning M.R. "much more than many wives would do": *ibid.* at p. 1340.

[37] With whom Browne L.J. agreed.

[38] *Cf. Richards* v. *Dove* [1974] 1 All E.R. 888, where the mistress had made a loan to her lover and had paid for and cooked the food they ate. Walton J. held that she had acquired no beneficial interest in the house. In *Eves* v. *Eves, supra*, Lord Denning M.R. said that *Richards* v. *Dove* was not of general application.

[39] [1982] 2 W.L.R. 1052; see *ante*, p. 143 for the facts.

[40] *Ibid.* at p. 1060.

[41] *Ibid.* at p. 1061.

[42] They were applied in *Hussey* v. *Palmer* [1972] 1 W.L.R. 1286 to a mother-in-law who paid for an extension to be built to the house.

[43] [1946] Ch. 217.

were held on a resulting trust for the settlor's estate after the marriage had been declared void on a decree of nullity made by a Kenyan court. The settlement of which the marriage had been the consideration completely failed because the legal effect of the decree was that the parties not only were no longer married but never had been.[44] And likewise if property is given to a person on trust and not beneficially, but no effective trusts are ever established, the property will be held on a resulting trust for the grantor.[45]

The same applies if a loan is made for a particular purpose which fails: the money is held on a resulting trust for the lender. So, in *Barclays Bank Ltd.* v. *Quistclose Investments Ltd.*,[46] which concerned the collapse of Rolls Razor Ltd., an arrangement had been made whereby Quistclose agreed to lend money to the company but only for the purpose of paying a dividend on the company's shares. Before the dividend was paid the company went into liquidation, and it could not then be paid. It was held that Quistclose was entitled to the repayment of the money on the basis of a resulting trust, the purpose for which it was lent having failed. The money had been paid into an account at the company's bank. It was further held that the bank had notice of the resulting trust and could not retain it against Quistclose so as to reduce the company's overdraft; the bank was a constructive trustee.

2. *Beneficial Interest Unexhausted*

The same principle will be applied where the beneficial interest is not wholly disposed of but not, as will be seen, in all cases. A modern illustration is *Re Gillingham Bus Disaster Fund*.[47] In 1951 24 cadets were killed when a motor-vehicle ran into them. The mayors of several boroughs in the area wrote a letter to the *Daily Telegraph* to the following effect: "The Mayors have decided to promote a Royal Marine Cadet Memorial Fund to be devoted . . . to defraying funeral expenses, caring for the boys who may be disabled and then to such worthy cause or causes in memory of the boys who lost their lives as the Mayors may determine." This appeal resulted in subscriptions amounting to nearly £9,000 contributed partly by known persons but mainly anonymously as a result of street collections and the like. The trustees spent about £2,500 and then took out a summons to decide what to do with the surplus. Harman J. held that because the trust failed as a charity, the surplus should be held on a resulting trust for the donors, even though many of them were in fact anonymous. This

---

[44] In this case the marriage was voidable, but the effect of the nullity decree was that the marriage was void *ab initio*. Since the Nullity of Marriage Act 1971, s. 5 (now Matrimonial Causes Act 1973, s. 16), this will no longer be the position in England, for it is thereby provided that a nullity decree in respect of a voidable marriage has a prospective, not a retrospective, effect. If however, the marriage were "void" the marriage is treated as never having taken place at all. For a list of the grounds on which a marriage will be void or voidable, see Matrimonial Causes Act 1973, ss. 11, 12.

[45] *Re Vandervell's Trusts (No. 2)* [1974] Ch. 269.

[46] [1970] A.C. 567.

[47] [1958] Ch. 300 (affirmed on points not affecting the decision [1959] Ch. 62, C.A.: see also *post*, p. 221; Atiyah (1958) 74 L.Q.R. 190. For charitable gifts the position is otherwise; see Charities Act 1960, s.14, and see *post*, p. 232.

followed naturally from the principle that where money was held upon trust and the trust declared did not exhaust the fund it would revert to the donor or settlor upon a resulting trust. The reasoning behind this principle, as applied to the facts, was that a donor did not part with the money out and out, but only *sub modo* to the intent that his wishes as declared by the declaration of trust should be carried into effect. It is important to observe, as Harman J. observed, that this doctrine did not rest on any evidence of the state of mind of the donor for no doubt in the vast majority of cases such as this he would not expect to get his money back in any case. A resulting trust would still arise even where the expectation was cheated on fruition for some unknown reason: it might well be, as it was here, an inference of law based on after-knowledge of the event.

The basis of *Re Gillingham* must be emphasised, *viz.* that there was no intention on the part of the donors to part with their money out and out when they contributed it. More particularly, such an intention should no more be attributed to the anonymous contributor who had made his gift in a street collection than it should to a contributor who was identifiable. As Harman J. said,[48] "I see no reason myself to suppose that the small giver who is anonymous has any wider intention than the large giver who is named. They all give for the one object. If they can be found by inquiry the resulting trust can be executed in their favour. If they cannot I do not see how the money could then . . . change its destination and become *bona vacantia.*"[49]

This last remark indicates the problem, for if it can be shown that the donor made his gift out and out with no intention of reclaiming it whatever the fate of the appeal might be, the money will belong to the Crown as *bona vacantia.* There is also no doubt that with regard to, for example, the proceeds of collecting boxes, the latter solution would be more practicable because it would be likely to be a fruitless exercise to try to establish, by way of a resulting trust, who in fact contributed their pennies to the collection; and in the result the money would have to be paid into court.[50] The question, however, is whether Harman J.'s decision on the question is correct as a matter of law. And in *Re West Sussex Constabulary's Widows, Children and Benevolent (1930) Fund Trusts*[51] Goff J. declined to follow *Re Gillingham,* at any rate with regard to the proceeds of collecting boxes. It was held that persons who put money into collecting boxes should be taken to have intended to part with the money out and out absolutely in all circumstances. Therefore, the Crown was entitled to it as *bona vacantia* on later failure of the trusts. There are admittedly dicta in favour of this view,[52] but they are not very weighty. They are all concerned with

---

[48] [1958] Ch. 300 at p. 314.

[49] In similar circumstances a resulting trust was held to arise in *Re Hobourn Aero Components Ltd.'s Air Raid Distress Fund* [1946] Ch. 86, but in that case there was no argument for *bona vacantia. Cf. Re Hillier's Trusts* [1954] 1 W.L.R. 9, where Upjohn J. held in these circumstances for *bona vacantia* (affirmed [1954] 1 W.L.R. 700; in C.A. Denning L.J. approved Upjohn J.'s formulation).

[50] Under T.A. 1925, s. 63.   [51] [1971] Ch. 1.

[52] *Re Hillier's Trusts* [1954] 1 W.L.R. 700 at p. 715, *per* Denning L.J.; *Re Welsh Hospital (Netley) Fund* [1921] 1 Ch. 655 at pp. 659, 660, *per* P.O. Lawrence J.; *Re North Devon and Somerset Relief Fund Trusts* [1953] 1 W.L.R. 260 at pp. 1266, 1267, *per* Wynn-Parry J.

the question whether the fact that contributions were made by unidentifiable donors to an appeal for *charitable* purposes indicated an intention to make the gifts outright, so that funds could be applied *cy-pres, i.e.* to other analogous charitable purposes.[53] The question is accordingly not settled by *Re West Sussex,* and indeed one is inclined to conclude that to make a distinction between the intention of unidentified donors in such circumstances and that of identified donors is an artificial exercise, although no doubt the consequence of a resulting trust is highly inconvenient.

It will have been observed that thus far we have been concerned with the destination of funds collected by collecting boxes. Goff J. in *Re West Sussex* made a distinction (Harman J. did not in *Re Gillingham*) between such moneys, on the one hand, and the proceeds of entertainments, raffles and sweepstakes, on the other hand. With regard to the latter activities, he held that it was not appropriate to apply the doctrine of resulting trusts for two reasons: (i) the relationship was one of contract, not of trust (a contributor paid his money as the price of what was offered and that he received), and (ii) there was no direct contribution to the fund at all: it was only the profit, if any, which was ultimately received. The distinction between contract and trust appears to be a sound one in respect of these sources of collection. It had in fact been held earlier, and on a more straightforward set of facts, in *Cunnack* v. *Edwards,*[54] that the personal representatives of members of a society founded to provide funds for the widows of the members could not claim a share when the purposes of the society came to an end. The members, in making their contributions to the society, had received all that they had contracted for in the form of pensions for the widows; they had parted with the money out and out; and the Crown took the surplus as *bona vacantia.*

Cunnack v. *Edwards* shows that, in considering whether a trust or a contract has been created, the court may have to determine, as a matter of construction, the intention of the parties. The point was made again in *Universe Tankers Inc. of Monrovia* v *International Transport Workers Federation.*[54a] Shipowners had contributed money to the Federations' welfare fund which had been set up to provide welfare, social and recreational facilities in ports around the world for seafarers of all nations. They contributed the money in order to enable their ship to sail. They later sought to argue (*inter alia*) that they were entitled to recover their contributions to the welfare fund on the ground that it was impressed with a trust which was void because the fund was set up for non-charitable purposes[54b] and, accordingly, the money was held on a resulting trust for them. The House of Lords held, however, as a matter of

---

[53] See *post*, p. 233.

[54] [1891] 2 Ch. 699. The same result occurred in *Re West Sussex* in respect of *members' contributions*. The discussion in the text is concerned with that part of the decision relating to funds derived from outside sources. *cf. Re Bucks Constabulary Widows' and Orphans' Fund Friendly Society (No.* 2) [1979] 1 W.L.R. 936 (surplus assets to he held for members at the date of dissolution to the exclusion of the Crown's claim thereto as *bona vacantia*; but this was provided for by the Friendly Societies Act 1896, s.49(1): the society was registered under that Act).

[54a] [1982] 2 W.L.R. 803   [54b] See *Post*, p. 176.

construction, in the light of the surrounding circumstances, that the welfare fund was set up by way of contract rather than by way of trust.

Incomplete trust

A resulting trust solution will also generally follow where the instrument is silent as to the way in which the beneficial interest is to be applied. Thus if property is given to X upon trust to pay the income to Y for life and the instrument makes no provision for the destination of the property on Y's death, X will prima facie hold the property on a resulting trust for the settlor or his estate (as in *Re Cochrane*[55] where apparently, as a result of the draftsman's blunder a proviso was left out of the instrument, so that the funds were not effectively disposed of), for in such a situation there is no doubt that since X is nominated as trustee he cannot take beneficially, and moreover, he cannot adduce evidence to that effect.[56] Yet it must be emphasised that this is a prima facie implication and it may, as a matter of construction of the instrument, be overridden. The court may be still able to construe the instrument in such a way that X takes beneficially subject to the fulfilment of the trust in favour of Y. So, in *Re Foord*[57] property was given by will to the testator's sister absolutely on trust to pay his wife an annuity. The income was more than sufficient to meet the annuity; and, upon a true construction of the will, the sister was held entitled to the balance. A similar conclusion was arrived at in *Re Andrew's Trust*[58] where a fund had been subscribed for the education of the children of a distressed clergyman and "not for equal division between them." Kekewich J. held that after completion of the education the children were entitled to the balance equally: there was no resulting trust. However, it may be somewhat difficult to reconcile this decision with *Re The Trusts of the Abbott Fund*[59] where a fund had been subscribed for the maintenance of two distressed ladies and Stirling J. held that on the death of the survivor the balance was held on a resulting trust for the donors. Kekewich J. justified his decision in *Re Andrew's Trust* on the ground that education was merely the motive of the gift and the subscribers parted with the money out and out when they gave it. The distinction between these two cases is a very fine one. It is, nevertheless, a question of construction in every case, and it is possible that both *Re Andrew* and *Re Abbott* may have been right on their particular facts. The point was made in *Re Osoba*,[60] where gifts had been made to the mother, wife, and daughter of the testator for various purposes which had failed or become exhausted. The Court of Appeal held, on a construction of the will, that these created trusts for the benefit of the beneficiaries and the respective purposes were to be disregarded as no more than expressions of the testator's motives in making the gifts.

---

[55] [1955] Ch. 309.
[56] *Re Rees' Will Trusts* [1949] Ch. 541.
[57] [1922] 2 Ch. 519.   [58] [1905] 2 Ch. 48.
[59] [1900] 2 Ch. 326. In *Re West Sussex Constabulary's Widows, Children and Benevolent (1930) Fund Trusts* [1971] Ch. 1, it was held that *Re Abbott* was indistinguishable with regard to funds derived from donations and legacies from *identified* persons. For discussion of other aspects of *Re West Sussex*, see *ante*, p. 150.
[60] [1979] 1 W.L.R. 247, C.A.

Failure of a common purpose

In most cases the parties have the same purpose, but this is not necessarily so. The question is, where two or more persons acquire property each for a separate purpose and only one of those purposes (uncommunicated to the other persons) fails, whether a resulting trust arises. It appears that it does not. The question was considered in *Burgess* v. *Rawnsley*.[61] Mr. H and Mrs. R, an elderly widowed couple, met and became friendly.[62] He was the tenant of a house in which he lived in the downstairs flat, the upstairs flat being vacant. Subsequently, they agreed to purchase the house, each of them providing half of the purchase price, and it was conveyed to them as joint tenants. Mr. H. bought the house as a matrimonial home in contemplation of marriage, but Mrs. R said that she intended to live in the upstairs flat and that Mr. H had never mentioned marriage to her. In fact they did not marry and Mrs. R never moved into the house. Later, she orally agreed to sell her share in the house to him, but later refused to sell. Mr. H then died, and his daughter, as administratrix of his estate, claimed that there was a resulting trust of his share in favour of his estate or, alternatively, that the joint tenancy had been severed by the oral agreement to sell. Mrs. R claimed that the house was hers by survivorship. The Court of Appeal unanimously held that the joint tenancy had been severed, and that was sufficient to dispose of the case; but there was a difference of opinion in deciding whether there was also a resulting trust. Browne L.J. and Sir John Pennycuick held that, since Mr. H alone had entered into the conveyance in contemplation of marriage and he had not communicated that purpose to Mrs. R, there was no common purpose which had failed so as to give rise to a resulting trust. Lord Denning M.R. considered, however, that where parties contemplate different objects which both fail, the position is the same as where their common object fails, and there is a resulting trust proportionate to their payments. The view of the majority seems to be the more logical.

Termination

It has been seen that a resulting trust comes into existence whenever there is a gap in the beneficial ownership. Accordingly, as was held *Re Vandervell's Trusts (No. 2)*,[63] when that gap is filled by someone becoming beneficially entitled, or where a trust is expressly declared, the resulting trust comes to an end.[64]

3. *Bona Vacantia*

It has been seen[65] that in some circumstances funds will be applied as *bona vacantia* rather than upon a resulting trust. It is also useful to consider under this head the case where a beneficiary is entitled to property but he later dies

---

[61] [1975] Ch. 429.

[62] Apparently despite the fact that, according to her evidence, "he looked like a tramp" and "had been picking up fag-ends."

[63] [1974] Ch. 269. The facts are stated *ante*, p. 25.

[64] *Ibid.* at p. 320. *Seq quaere*, whether the equitable interest under the resulting trust should be disposed of by writing under L.P.A. 1925, s.53(1)(c): see *ante*, p. 28.

[65] See *ante*, p. 150.

intestate in whole or part. It was formerly necessary to distinguish between two classes of case: (i) where the property is vested in *trustees*; and (ii) where it is vested in *executors*.

(1) **Trustees**

If, for example, property is vested in trustees upon trust absolutely for a beneficiary who is living when the interest takes effect and the beneficiary then dies intestate and leaves nobody in whom his interest can vest, there cannot be a resulting trust because the beneficial interest will have effectively vested in the beneficiary. It is clearly established that if the property is personalty the rule was and is that the interest in such circumstances belongs to the Crown as *bona vacantia*: it has no owner and must devolve accordingly.

But if the property is realty the position was at one time different. The law used to be that the trustee took it beneficially. This was so because the Chancery Court did not apply the law of escheat to interests in realty. The law was changed first by the Intestates Estates Act 1884[66] and then by the Administration of Estates Act 1925 so that now, if a person dies after 1925, his real estate, like his personal estate, will go as *bona vacantia* to the Crown.[67]

(2) **Executors**

So far as vesting in an executor is concerned, the position at law at one time was that, if a testator died without disposing of the residue, the executor was entitled to it if the residue was personal estate or to the extent to which it consisted of personalty. And equity followed the rule at law unless it was shown, upon a true construction of the will, that the testator intended to exclude the executor from taking a benefit. If such an intention could be shown he would, of course, hold as trustee for the next-of-kin.[68]

The law was changed by statute, namely, the Executors Act 1830, which laid down that an executor should hold as trustee for the next-of-kin unless it could be shown from the will that he was intended to take beneficially. This in effect shifted the burden of proof. But he still, pausing at this date, remained entitled beneficially if there were no next-of-kin. This last loophole was closed, although not until the Administration of Estates Act 1925, when it was provided that, even in the absence of persons entitled on intestacy, the executor will hold as *bona vacantia*, and this rule will only be overridden if the will clearly shows that he is to take beneficially.[69]

VII. MUTUAL WILLS

This is another case where an implied,[70] though not a resulting, trust will arise. If two testators desire to make provision for each other, they may, if they

---

[66] ss. 4 and 7.

[67] A.E.A. 1925, ss. 45, 46.

[68] See *ante*, p. 60: "Certainty of words."

[69] ss. 46, 49.

[70] The view is sometimes taken that these give rise to a *constructive* trust: see *Re Cleaver* [1981] 1 W.L.R. 939 (Nourse J., applying the Australian case of *Birmingham* v. *Renfrew*

choose, make separate wills in substantially identical terms in the other's favour with remainder to the same ultimate beneficiary; and these are known as "mutual wills."[71] A great deal of the advantage of such wills would be lost if a testator remained free to revoke his will. At the same time it has to be remembered that every will is revocable by a testator until his death. But this rule of testamentary law will not prevent the possibility of a *trust* arising by implication in favour of a beneficiary. What is required if an implied trust is thus to arise is that there should be an agreement between the parties to create irrevocable interests in favour of ascertainable beneficiaries. The revocable nature of the wills under which the interest arises is fully recognised by the Probate Court, but equity will protect and enforce the interests created by the agreement despite revocation of the will by a testator after the death of the other without having revoked his will.[72]

(1) **Evidence of agreement**

There must, however, be evidence of an *agreement* to create irrevocable interests. If there is no such evidence, an implied trust will not come into being. Equity will not protect a beneficiary under mutual wills merely because they have been made in identical or almost identical terms. Accordingly, in *Re Oldham*[73] each testator bequeathed an absolute interest to the other, with identical alternatives in the event of lapse, but there was no clear agreement on the facts to create mutual wills and a trust could not therefore be established. The fact that absolute interests were conferred was apparently regarded as an additional argument militating against the implication of such an agreement. But in itself it was not—or should not be—decisive. If there had been clear evidence of an agreement, the result should have been different, notwithstanding the fact that absolute interests were conferred upon the survivor.[74]

The requisite evidence of the agreement may be expressly contained in the wills themselves or be deduced from them or from circumstances outside them, and if it is sufficiently precise it will be enforced by the courts.[75] A well-known illustration is *Re Hagger*,[76] where a husband and wife who had always treated their savings as their common property made a joint will. It provided that on the death of whichever testator died first the whole of the property should pass to

---

(1936) C. L.R. 666, 690, said (at p. 947) that cases of mutual wills were only one example of a wider category of cases, for example, secret trusts, in which a court of equity would intervene to impose a constructive trust); see also Nathan and Marshall (7th ed., p. 45). *Sed quaere*: it may be argued that the trusts are implied from the circumstances, but if a testator acts in breach of trust, he becomes a constructive trustee (see *ante*, p. 41 in relation to secret trusts). Moreover, the question of classification in this case does not appear to have any practical significance and it therefore seems unnecessary to disturb the traditional classification of them which is to treat them as *implied* trusts.

[71] Or, alternatively, they may make a *joint* mutual will which has the same effect.

[72] See Theobald (13th ed.), § § 98, 99; Williams and Mortimer, Chap. 55. See also *Dufour* v. *Pereira* (1769) 1 Dickens 419 for an early formulation of the general principle.

[73] [1925] Ch. 75; see also *Gray* v. *Perpetual Trustee Co. Ltd.* [1928] A.C. 391, P.C.; *Vine* v. *Joyce, The Times*, October 24, 1963; *Re Cleaver* [1981] 1 W.L.R. 939.

[74] *Re Cleaver, supra*, (absolute interests were given to the survivor, but enforceable mutual wills were held to arise): see further, *post*, p. 156.

[75] See *Birmingham* v. *Renfrew* (1936) C.L.R. 666.   [76] [1930] 2 Ch. 190.

the trustee upon trust for the survivor for life and thereafter upon trust for sale and division among nine persons. Moreover, they expressly agreed that neither of them should alter or revoke the will without the consent of the other. In 1904 the wife died. This meant that so much of the will as concerned her estate came into operation, *i.e.* her share of the combined resources became subject to the trusts of the will. In 1924 the husband died. In 1921, however, he had made another will, and in this he directed that everything of which he was capable of disposing should be held by trustees upon trust for certain other persons. The question, therefore, was whether the 1921 will affected the husband's share of the common property. Clauson J. held that it did not: the contract not to revoke contained in the joint will operated on the wife's death to render the husband a *trustee* of his property to hold it on trust and apply it in the manner prescribed by the joint will.

Another, more recent, example is *Re Cleaver*[77] where the testator and testatrix married when he was aged 78 and she was aged 74. He had three children; she had none. They each had assets of their own and kept their finances separate. They made wills in similar terms by which the residue of his or her estate was left to the survivor of them and in default of survival to the testator's children in equal shares. The testator later decided that one of his children (a daughter) should receive only a life interest in his residuary estate, because he did not wish her husband to benefit from it. In 1974, they therefore made further wills similar to the earlier ones, except that the daughter's interest was cut down to a life interest in one third of the residuary estate. The testator then died, and the testatrix became absolutely entitled to his estate. In May 1975 the testatrix made a will in substantially identical terms to her 1974 will. In November 1975 she made a new will leaving her residuary estate to the testator's three children in equal shares. Finally she made a will leaving the residuary estate to the daughter and her husband absolutely in equal shares and left nothing to the testator's two other children. Nourse J. held that the evidence was sufficiently clear, at the time the 1974 wills were executed, to establish an enforceable agreement to dispose of property in a similar way. Accordingly, her executors were bound to administer and distribute the estate in accordance with her 1974 will.

(2) **Ambit of trust**

It is a question of construction what particular property is bound by the trusts. In *Re Hagger*, for example, the trust was held to bind the whole of the interest owned by each party, so that the survivor could not disregard the trusts even in respect of his own property.[78] But it should be compared on this point with *Re Green*.[79] Here there were separate mutual wills made by husband and wife.

---

[77] [1981] 1 W.L.R. 939.
[78] See also *Szabo* v. *Boros* (1966) 60 D.L.R. (2d) 186, where it was held that if mutual wills are made disposing of property in a manner inconsistent with the continuation of a joint tenancy held by the testators in that property, then the joint tenancy is treated as severed so that the survivor cannot claim the property absolutely by survivorship.
[79] [1951] Ch. 148.

They recited that it was agreed that the survivor of them (i) was to have all their property, and (ii) he was to leave half of it to certain persons. The husband survived; he remarried; he made a second will. It was held that his second will could only operate on one-half of the property because the other half was at his death subject to a trust for the named persons. In consequence, the trust bound—and this was a necessary result of the construction of the wills—merely a fraction of the estate.

Two problems demand consideration. If the trust is expressed to bind the whole of the property of each party, can the survivor deal with his own property *inter vivos*? The answer, strictly speaking, however inconvenient, should be, No. If the property is trust property, he will be liable for breach of trust if he purports to deal with that property contrary to the trust, and it should make no difference whether the dealing takes the form of attempted revocation or attempted disposition *inter vivos*.[80] A second question is whether property acquired by the survivor before his death would be caught by a trust which is expressed to bind the whole of the property of the testator. The answer would seem to be, Yes: if the trust extended to the whole of the property of each party, it should catch after-acquired property (whether after the death of the first to die or before), as well as property already acquired at the execution of the will: but there is no direct authority on the point.[81]

It may be, however, that some assistance in answering these questions can be found in *Ottaway* v. *Norman*,[82] although the case itself was concerned with secret trusts. Brightman J. said[83]:

> "I am content to assume for present purposes but without so deciding that if property is given to the primary donee on the understanding that the primary donee will dispose by will of such assets, if any, as he may have at his command at his death in favour of the secondary donee, a valid trust is created in favour of the secondary donee which is in suspense during the lifetime of the primary donee, but attaches to the estate of the primary donee at the moment of the latter's death."

Ottaway v. *Norman*, it is repeated, was a case on secret trusts, but the reasoning of Brightman J. could be applied to a mutual will situation, and might possibly be a guide to future developments in this branch of the law.

(3) Commencement of trust

A trust can only arise, if at all, on the death of the first testator to die. It can only arise at that date and not before because only then would it be *inequitable* to allow the surviving testator to benefit under the other's will and at the same time revoke his own will in breach of his agreement. Only then will he become a trustee. It follows that, before the death of the first to die, the agreement

---

[80] See Mitchell (1951) 14 M.L.R. 136; Burgess (1970) 34 Conv. (N.S.) 230; see also *Birmingham* v. *Renfrew* (*Supra*); *Re Cleaver* [1981] 1 W.L.R. 939.
[81] See Mitchell (1951) 14 M.L.R. 136; Burgess (1970) 34 Conv.(N.S.) 230.
[82] [1972] Ch. 698; discussed *ante*, pp. 35, 36.
[83] *Ibid.* at p. 713.

(whether express or implied) not to revoke is entirely contractual: it does not partake of the trust relationship at all. It is a contract made in pursuance of mutual promises. And it can, accordingly, at that stage be revoked by mutual agreement or indeed by unilateral breach (*i.e.* by one testator revoking in breach of contract without the concurrence of the other).[84]

Revocation by mutual agreement creates no problems. If the contract is broken unilaterally, the estate of the testator who revokes in breach of contract will be liable in damages, and that is as far as the remedy goes. However, the damages are difficult to quantify if one party is in unilateral breach; the other has lost only the potential right to an unascertained amount.

A question of some nicety that bears on the effect of unilateral breach is the marriage or remarriage of one of the testators. Marriage (or remarriage), subject to certain exceptions, automatically revokes a will.[85] Can damages be obtained for revocation in such circumstances? The question seems essentially to be whether the revocation must be intentional: revocation by marriage takes effect by operation of law. One might be inclined to the conclusion that there should be no distinction between revocation by act of parties and revocation by operation of law and that both should attract damages for breach of contract. But it was held by the Court of Appeal in *Re Marsland*[86] that a covenant "not to revoke" a will, the covenant being contained in a deed of separation between husband and wife, applied only to acts of intentional revocation and not where, as in marriage, the revocation followed as a matter of law, whether the testator wished it or not. If this principle were applied to mutual wills—and there seems no reason why it is not applicable—it would clearly oust the contractual remedy. But it appears reasonably clear that marriage, after the death of the first testator to die, would not be effectual to upset a *trust* which by then would have come into being. A purported revocation, however achieved, should have no effect on an equitable obligation which has already been created.[87]

---

[84] See *Stone* v. *Hoskins* [1905] P. 194.

[85] Wills Act 1837, s.18 (as substituted by Administration of Justice Act 1982, s.18(1)). Marriage includes a voidable marriage: *Re Roberts* [1978] 1 W.L.R. 653, C.A.: see *ante*, p. 129). Exceptions are provided by Wills Act 1837, s.18 (as substituted) : (i) a disposition in a will in exercise of a power of appointment shall take effect notwithstanding the testator's subsequent marriage unless the property so appointed would in default of appointment pass to his personal representatives. (ii) where it appears from the will that at the time it was made the testator was expecting to be married to a particular person and that he intended that a disposition in the will should not be revoked by the marriage the will shall not be revoked by his marriage to that person; (iii) where it appears from the will that at the time it was made the testator was expecting to be married to a particular person and that he intended a disposition in the will should not be revoked by his marriage to that person, the disposition shall take effect notwithstanding the marriage, and any other disposition in the will shall also take effect unless it appears from the will that the testator intended the disposition to be revoked by the marriage. For the effect of dissolution or annulment of marriage on wills, see Wills Act 1837, s.18A (as inserted by Administration of Justice Act 1982, s.18(2)).

[86] [1939] Ch. 820, C.A.

[87] See *Re Green* [1951] Ch. 148.

(4) **Disclaimer of benefit**

At one time it appeared to be established in some of the early cases, such as *Dufour* v *Pereira*,[88] that the intervention of the Court of Equity was based solely on the ground that the survivor had taken the benefit of the agreement. This generally accords with the actual position: it would be inequitable, if not fraudulent, if, after the death of the first to die, the survivor, having taken the benefit of the former's estate, could resile from the agreement. But a further problem that requires consideration is whether, if the survivor disclaims the benefit of the agreement (*i.e.* the benefit under the will of the deceased testator), he is thereby released from the agreement. Again, the question has not been directly decided. However, Clauson J. in *Re Hagger*[89] expressed the view *obiter* that the trust which had arisen would still continue. This seems to be the correct solution. The fact that one of the beneficiaries under the trust disclaims his beneficial interest should have no effect on the continuing subsistence of the trust. If this is so, the notion that a benefit must, of necessity, be taken by the survivor is today erroneous.

---

[88] (1769) 1 Dickens 419.
[89] [1930] 2 Ch. 190 at p. 195; Mitchell, *loc. cit.* at p. 138.

CHAPTER 8

CONSTRUCTIVE TRUSTS

A CONSTRUCTIVE trust does not arise from the express or implied intention of the parties. Rather the reverse: the possibility of his becoming a trustee is usually very far from a man's thoughts. It has been seen that the fundamental basis of an *implied* trust is that it is supposed to be derived from the implied intention of the settlor. However, a constructive trust is normally[1] regarded as a relationship created by equity in the interest of conscience. It has nothing to do with the express or implied intention of the parties.

It appears in English law that, although the demarcation lines cannot be precisely drawn, there are certain general categories in which relief may be available under this head although these may be capable of extension. In fact they have been much extended in recent times.[2] On the other hand the law of the United States of America appears to give a relatively precise meaning to a constructive trust, although wider in its effect.[3] Thus, the American Restatement of Restitution states the principle as follows: "Where a person holding title to property is subject to an equitable duty to convey it to another on the ground that he would be unjustly enriched if he were permitted to retain it, a constructive trust arises."[4] But it is not possible to treat this as a valid generalisation on the law of constructive trusts in this country. Indeed in this country unjust enrichment or other personal advantage is not a *sine qua non*. Thus in *Nelson* v. *Larholt*[5] the defendant was not financially better off by drawing cheques without authority, but he was held liable to refund to the estate because (*inter alia*) he was a constructive trustee. Nevertheless, the concept of unjust enrichment has some value, as Edmund Davies L.J. explained in *Carl Zeiss Stiftung* v. *Herbert Smith & Co.*,[6] in providing an example of the "want of probity" (as he described it) which tends to underlie this branch of the law. At the same time he suggested that perhaps the boundaries of constructive trusts have been left deliberately vague so as not to restrict the court by technicalities in deciding what the justice of a particular case may demand. And, more recently, in *English* v. *Dedham Vale Properties Ltd.*,[7] Slade J. said that the

---

[1] *cf.* the attitude of Lord Denning M.R. in *Hussey* v. *Palmer* [1972] 1 W.L.R. 1286; see *ante*, p. 21.

[2] *Infra.*

[3] See *post*, p. 162.

[4] At para. 160.

[5] [1948] 1 K.B. 339.

[6] [1969] 2 Ch. 276.

[7] [1978] 1 W.L.R. 93.

categories of fiduciary relationships which give rise to a constructive trusteeship should not be regarded as "falling into a limited number of strait-jackets or as being necessarily closed" and that they are "no more than formulae for equitable relief."

The concept of constructive trusteeship is, therefore, an elusive one,[8] but perhaps the following general points can be made:

(1) It has already been seen that the constructive trust has been made use of in a diverse number of situations. For example, it may arise if a party relies on non-compliance by the other party with a statutory formality (such as s.53 of the Law of Property Act 1925) in order to achieve a fraudulent purpose[9]; he may be saddled with constructive trusteeship. It may be relevant in cases concerned with beneficial entitlement to property on breakdown of marriage or termination of cohabitation where property has been acquired and the parties have contributed to its acquisition.[10] Further, there appears to be a correlation with proprietary estoppel; this, like constructive trusteeship, requiring a degree of inequitable conduct on the part of the person to be estopped.[11] Furthermore, there are problems, of limited practical importance, in classifying secret trusts[12] and trusts under mutual wills[13] as express, implied or constructive.

(2) It will be seen later that constructive trusteeship may be material in cases where a trustee or person in a fiduciary position is in breach of his duty to avoid conflict of interest in the practical administration of the trust.[14] To take some examples: the duty of trustees to act without remuneration or other profit[15]; the duty of trustees who are appointed directors of a company, the shares of which are the subject matter of the trust, to account in certain circumstances to the beneficiaries for their directors' fees[16]; the rule that a purchase of trust property by the trustee can be avoided by the beneficiaries,[17] and likewise that the purchase of a beneficial interest in trust property by the trustee may in certain cases be avoided.[18] These are general rules, though there may be exceptions to them. They are related in practical terms to the doctrine of constructive trusts.

(3) Formerly, it was thought not only that only a limited number of situations would give rise to a constructive trust, but that if it did arise, then the trust would be a substantive institution, rather like an express or resulting trust. In view of the judicial activity already referred to,[19] it may well be that a constructive trust is to be treated in certain cases as going much further: to take effect as a *remedy*,

---

[8] See generally, Oakley, *Constructive Trusts*; for articles, see Scott (1955) 71 L.Q.R. 39; Maudsley (1959) 75 L.Q.R. 236 and (1977) 28 N.I.L.Q. 123; Oakley (1973) 26 C.L.P. 17.

[9] *Ante*, p. 30.

[10] *Ante*, p. 140.

[11] *Ante*, p. 56.

[12] *Ante*, p. 41.

[13] *Ante*, p. 154.

[14] See generally, Chaps. 21, 22.

[15] *Post*, p. 390.

[16] *Post*, p. 398.

[17] *Post*, p. 404.

[18] *Post*, p. 405.

[19] *Ante*, p. 140.

rather like an injunction. In *Hussey* v. *Palmer,*[20] for example, Lord Denning M.R. said so plainly. Admittedly, the Americans treat it as a remedy,[21] but this has not traditionally been so in English law (indeed, Browne-Wilkinson J. in *Re Sharpe*[22] recently described the notion of a constructive trust taking effect as a remedy as a "novel" concept); and the problems that such a ready, if not automatic, invocation of the doctrine, may create may be far from academic. To take two examples:

(a) There may be conveyancing difficulties from the point of view of a purchaser of property who may have no knowledge or means of knowledge that it is subject to a constructive trust[23];

(b) If such a trust arises, the beneficiary under the trust takes priority over the general creditors of the trustee if the trustee is insolvent.[24] Further, he is entitled to trace trust money into property acquired by the trustee[25] with the help of the trust money even though it is mixed with money of his own[26]; again a practical matter if the trustee is insolvent.

In short, it would be generally desirable to know reasonably precisely when a constructive trust can arise, but the law is in a state of flux; more so than usual. It is proposed in the chapter to deal with certain types of constructive trusts which are traditionally considered to be substantive institutions.

I. Constructive Trusts of Profits made by a Person in a Fiduciary Position

If a person manages property and is in a fiduciary position he is prohibited from obtaining any personal benefit by availing himself of his position in the absence of authorisation from the beneficiary. And if he does obtain an advantage he is a constructive trustee of any benefits for the persons beneficially entitled to the property in question. The basis of the rule is that a trustee or person holding a fiduciary position should not place himself in a position where his duty and interest conflict.[27]

The principle is illustrated by the leading case of *Keech* v. *Sandford.*[28] Here an express trustee was a trustee of the lease of a market for an infant. On the expiration of the lease the trustee applied for a renewal. The lessor would not renew because the infant, by reason of his contractual incapacity, could not

---

[20] [1972] 1 W.L.R. 1286, C.A.; and see *ante*, p. 21. Lord Denning M.R. also went so far as to say that a resulting trust and constructive trust amounted to the same thing. See also the cases cited in the field of matrimonial and quasi-matrimonial property: *ante*, p. 140.

[21] See the American Restatement of Restitution, § 160, cited *supra*.

[22] [1980] 1 W.L.R. 219.

[23] See also the conveyancing problems referred to *ante*, p. 31.

[24] See *ante* p. 111.

[25] The tracing remedy may also operate against an innocent volunteer who acquires property with the aid of the trust money: see *post*.

[26] See *post*.

[27] See further illustrations of the principle in Chap. 22.

[28] (1726) Sel.Cas.Ch. 61. See also *Re Knowles' Will Trusts* [1948] 1 All E.R. 866 where the trustee acquired a renewal of the lease.

enter into the usual convenants. The trustee thereupon took a lease for his own benefit. It was held that the trustee must still hold it on trust for the infant.

This principle, sometimes known as the doctrine in *Keech* v. *Sandford*, extends beyond the strict trust relationship: it will be noticed that in that particular case the lessee was an express trustee. Thus, it has been held to apply to agents,[29] tenants for life,[30] partners,[31] mortgagors,[32] mortgagees,[33] joint tenants,[34] tenants in common[35] and also to an employee in a confidential capacity.[36] The same applies to the purchase by a lessee in a fiduciary position of a reversion on a lease.[37] Similarly, a purchaser may be a constructive trustee for the person beneficially entitled if he knew, when the transfer of the property was made to him, that it was trust property.[38] Likewise, a person cannot claim title to land by adverse possession if he acquires the property in consequence of his title as trustee.[39] To what extent the relationship in any given case gives rise to a presumption which a person cannot rebut (and is thereby *ipso facto* disabled from claiming a benefit) is debatable. It seems, however, that in most cases the presumption is irrebuttable.[40] It will, of course, be appreciated that if the beneficiary, being *sui juris*, assents to such a person taking a benefit, then the presumption will not arise at all. Likewise it will not arise where there is no fiduciary or quasi-fiduciary relationship. Thus, in *Re Biss*,[41] a shopkeeper, who was holding under a yearly tenancy, died intestate. He left a widow and three children. The widow was appointed administratrix of his estate, and she carried on the business with the help of one of the sons. She then applied for a new lease and she was refused. The son then applied and he was accepted. The Court of Appeal held that the son was entitled to keep the lease for himself beneficially. He was not in a fiduciary position to other persons entitled on intestacy and had not abused his position in the business.

Similarly, in *Swain* v. *The Law Society*[42] the House of Lords held that The Law Society was neither in a fiduciary relationship to members of the solicitors'

---

[29] *Boardman* v. *Phipps* [1967] 2 A.C. 46 (discussed *post*, p. 165); *English* v. *Dedham Vale Properties Ltd.* [1978] 1 All E.R. 382 (discussed *post*, p. 164).

[30] *James* v. *Dean* (1808) 15 Ves. 236.

[31] *Featherstonhaugh* v. *Fenwick* (1819) 17 Ves. 298.

[32] *Leigh* v. *Burnett* (1865) 29 Ch.D. 231.

[33] *Rushworth's Case* (1676) Freem.Ch. 13.   [34] *Palmer* v. *Young* (1684) 1 Vern. 276.

[35] *Kennedy* v. *De Trafford* [1897] A.C. 180.

[36] *Industrial Development Consultants Ltd.* v. *Cooley* [1972] 1 W.L.R. 443.

[37] The rule at one time was that this was the case only where the lease was renewable by agreement or custom (*Phillips* v. *Phillips* (1885) 29 Ch.D. 673), but not otherwise (*Bevan* v. *Webb* [1905] 1 Ch. 620). This distinction now appears to be irrelevant (see *Protheroe* v. *Protheroe* [1968] 1 W.L.R. 519, (discussed *post*, p. 402), where the C.A. took no account of it).

[38] *Peffer* v. *Rigg* [1977] 1 W.L.R. 285. In that case a purchaser for a nominal consideration knew that the vendor held the property on trust for himself and another in equal shares. She accordingly took the property on a constructive trust which was a new trust imposed by equity and distinct from the express trust which bound the vendor. See also *Barclays Bank Ltd.* v. *Quistclose Investments Ltd.* [1970] A.C. 567: *ante*, p. 149.

[39] *Re Edwards's Will Trusts* [1982] Ch. 30, C.A.; See *ante*, p. 15.

[40] The only exceptions in the situations listed in the text are those of mortgagors, mortgagees and partners, where, it seems, the presumption can be rebutted.

[41] [1903] 2 Ch. 40.   [42] [1982] 3 W.L.R. 261; see also *ante*, p. 10.

profession nor had it acted contrary to the requirements of justice and good conscience in receiving a proportion of the commission payable to the insurance brokers who had arranged a policy for indemnity insurance of all solicitors. It had not, therefore, become a constructive trustee for the benefit of individual solicitors for the proportion of the commission it received and was not liable to account to the solicitors for that commission. Lord Brightman said[43] that it would be "extravagant to claim that The Law Society is acting in an unconscionable manner because it has turned its unique bargaining position to account and obtained a sum of money (which would otherwise have enhanced the profits of the brokers) and applied such money for the benefit of the profession as a whole."

But all cases turn on their own facts. For example, in *English* v. *Dedham Vale Properties Ltd.*,[44] Slade J. held that a fiduciary relationship had arisen. In this case, during negotiations for a contract for the purchase of property, the purchasers, in the name of and purportedly as agents for the vendors, made an application for planning permission, but without the vendors' consent or authority. If the vendors had been aware of the application, it would have influenced them in deciding whether to conclude the contract. It was held that a fiduciary relationship arose between the parties, and as the purchasers had failed to disclose what they had done as self-appointed agents for the vendors, they were liable to account to the vendors for the profits which had accrued to them as the result of the subsequent grant of the planning permission.

It is, however, clear that, before a fiduciary obligation can arise, there must be property which can be impressed with the fiduciary obligation. This basic proposition may possibly have an oblique application. If, for example, copyright is held in trust for a beneficiary, the trustee must avoid any conflict of interest in dealing with the copyright or the beneficiary's interest in it,[45] but if he is merely a trustee of the royalties as they fall due, he has no such fiduciary obligation in relation to the copyright itself. As Megarry V.-C. said in *Tito* v. *Waddell (No. 2)*,[46] "a trust of a tree may impose a fiduciary duty in relation to the fruit of that tree, but it would be remarkable if a trust of the gathered fruit of the tree were to impose a fiduciary duty in relation to the tree itself." Likewise, if a person is a trustee of A's land and then in a transaction relating to B's land (of which he is not a trustee) obtains an increase in payment in respect of A's land, he is not thereby impressed with a fiduciary obligation to B[47]; this was held to be the position in respect of royalty payments for mining phosphate in *Tito* v. *Waddell (No.2)*.

It will also be recalled[48] that a statutory duty does not normally impose fiduciary obligations. It has to be shown positively that such obligations were

---

[43] *Ibid.* at p. 278.
[44] [1978] 1 W.L.R. 93.
[45] See *post* p. 403.
[46] [1977] Ch. 106 at p. 227; see also *ante*, p. 6.
[47] *Ibid.* at p. 227.
[48] See *ante* p. 8.

intended to be created by the statute,[49] and, furthermore, the Crown will only become a trustee if it deliberately chooses to do so.[50]

A particularly wide principle was propounded by Asquith L.J. in *Reading* v. *Att.-Gen.*[51] when he said that a fiduciary relationship arose "whenever the plaintiff entrusts to the defendant a job to be performed."[52] In that case a Crown servant (an Army sergeant stationed in Egypt) was held to be accountable to the the the Crown for bribes which he had taken in misusing his position of responsibility under the Crown. The case was, however, distinguished in *Tito* v. *Waddell (No.* 2),[53] where it was argued that this principle applied to a situation where the function of fixing a royalty was imposed by statute and assumed by the Crown, and this put the Crown into a fiduciary position. Megarry V.-C. rejected this argument on the ground that the imposition of a statutory duty did not, as a general rule, impose fiduciary obligations; it had to be shown that it did. Furthermore, *Reading* v. *Att.-Gen.* was a case in which the Crown servant was held to be accountable to the Crown, whereas in *Tito* v. *Waddell* it was contended that the Crown was accountable to a third party by reason of a statutory duty imposed on a resident commissioner, and that involved different considerations.[54] It seems plain, in the present state of the law, that the use of the concept of "a job to be performed" so as to give rise to fiduciary obligations has to be restricted.[55]

"Knowledge" as Trust Property

One of the most important cases in recent times on these general principles is the decision of the House of Lords in *Boardman* v. *Phipps*[56] which is particularly noteworthy for the principle which emerged that "knowledge" can be trust property. In this case part of the trust shareholding was in a private company, L Ltd. One of the defendants was a beneficiary under the trust and the other acted as solicitor to the trust. The defendants were dissatisfied with the manner in which the business was conducted and they acquired all the shares in L Ltd. other than those owned by the trust and thereby made a substantial profit. The plaintiff, who was also beneficially entitled, claimed that neither of the defendants was entitled to keep the shares he had acquired and also was bound to account for the profit on those shares. And this contention was accepted, by a bare majority, by the House of Lords. The conclusion was essentially arrived at for two reasons. First, on the facts, the two defendants were throughout in the position of agents for the trustees (whether they so regarded themselves or not) for the purpose of using the trust shareholding to acquire knowledge of the

---

[49] *Tito* v. *Waddell (No.* 2), *supra* at p. 235; and see *Swain* v. *The Law Society* [1982] 3 W.L.R. 261, H.L; see *ante*, p. 163.
[50] *Ibid.* at p. 212.
[51] [1949] 2 K.B. 232; affirmed [1951] A.C. 507.
[52] *Ibid.* at p. 236.
[53] [1977] Ch. 106.
[54] *Ibid.* at p. 230.
[55] See also *Swain* v. *The Law Society [1982] 3 W.L.R. 261, H.L.*
[56] *[1967] 2 A.C. 46, and see post*, p. 394.

affairs of L Ltd. The knowledge they had thus acquired was trust property. The acts of both of them were within the scope of agents for the trustees. Secondly, it was admitted that if there had been disclosure to and authority from the plaintiff the position would have been different. But it was held on the facts that although there had been correspondence and an interview there had not been sufficiently full information offered to the plaintiff to enable him adequately to appraise the situation. This was a matter which required careful explanation and possibly expert advice. Neither of these was forthcoming in this case.

Lord Hodson stated the principle involved as follows[57]:

> "The proposition of law involved in this case is that no person standing in a fiduciary position, when a demand is made upon him by the person to whom he stands in the fiduciary relationship to account for profits acquired by him by reason of his fiduciary position and by reason of the opportunity and the knowledge, or either, resulting from it, is entitled to defeat the claim upon any ground save that he made profits with the knowledge and assent of the other person."[58]

It was admitted by the House of Lords that not all knowledge is property or indeed trust property. For example, it would be difficult to establish that the Public Trustee or other corporate trustees, who handle a great many trusts, would be liable to account if they made use of knowledge acquired in one trust for their own advantage or of other trusts. But in *Boardman* v. *Phipps* the confidential information which had been acquired and which was capable of being and was turned to account was properly regarded as being the property of the trust. Lord Upjohn, who dissented, took the view that information was not property in any normal sense: the position was simply that equity would restrain its transmission to another if it was in breach of some confidential relationship which, in his view, did not exist in this case.

Finally, it should be added that the fact that the trustee was unwilling (as here) or unable to take part in the purchase of shares was irrelevant, according to the majority.[59]

Directors

Directors of companies as constructive trustees call for separate treatment. In *Belmont Finance Corpn. Ltd.* v. *Williams Furniture Ltd. (No. 2)*[60] Buckley L.J. stated the law as follows[61]:

> "A limited company of course is not a trustee of its own funds: it is their beneficial owner; but in consequence of the fiduciary character of their

[57] [1967] 2 A.C. 46 at p. 105.
[58] See also *English* v. *Dedham Vale Properties Ltd.* [1978] 1 W.L.R. 93 for the circumstances in which a "self-appointed" agent may be accountable; see *ante*, p. 164.
[59] It was very relevant to Lord Upjohn, dissenting. But assuming that knowledge can amount to trust property, the majority view is supported by *Keech* v. *Sandford* itself.
[60] [1980] 1 All E.R. 393, C.A.
[61] *Ibid.* at p. 405.

duties the directors of a limited company are treated as if they were trustees of those funds of the company which are in their hands or under their control, and if they misapply them they commit a breach of trust. . . . So, if directors of a company in breach of their fiduciary duties misapply the funds of their company so that they come into the hands of some stranger to the trust who receives them with knowledge (actual or constructive) of the breach, he cannot conscientiously retain those funds against the company unless he has some better equity. He becomes a constructive trustee for the company of the misapplied funds."

In *Regal (Hastings) Ltd.* v. *Gulliver*[62] Lord Russell of Killowen put the position somewhat differently, he said[63]: "Directors of a limited company are the creatures of statute. In some respects they resemble trustees: in others they do not. In some respects they resemble agents: in others they do not. In some respects they resemble managing partners: in others they do not." Nevertheless it was established in this case that the rule laid down in *Keech* v. *Sandford* applied to directors on the facts and they were, therefore, accountable for profits made by them through acting on exclusive knowledge acquired by them when acting as directors. The directors had taken up shares and made a profit. It was originally intended that the company should buy the shares but it did not have the money to do so. Likewise in *Belmont Finance Corpn. Ltd.* v. *Williams Furniture Ltd.* (*No.* 2)[64] a company was held liable as a constructive trustee because it had through its directors known of the misapplication of funds and had received them in such a way as to become accountable for them. It was also held for similar reasons in *Industrial Development Consultants Ltd.* v. *Cooley*[65] that a person who deliberately put his personal interest as a potential contracting party into direct conflict with his pre-existing and continuing duty as managing director of a company, was accountable to the company for the benefit of a contract which he had purportedly entered into in his personal capacity.

This general rule has been applied by case law in other connections. Directors cannot take advantage of their position to enter into beneficial contracts with the company,[66] nor can they buy property and then resell it to the company at a profit.[67] They will also be liable in breach of trust if, being in control of a credit at a company's bank account, they fraudulently apply it for other than the company's purposes.[68] Promoters of a company (who are in an analogous position to directors) are also in a fiduciary relationship towards the company:

---

[62] [1942] 1 All E.R. 378, H.L.; applied in *Boardman* v. *Phipps* [1967] 2 A.C. 46.
[63] *Ibid.* at p. 387.
[64] [1972] 1 W.L.R. 433; *cf. Queensland Mines Ltd.* v. *Hudson* (1978) 18 A.L.R. 1 (P.C.): managing director resigned to develop mining licences personally but did so with the full knowledge of the board of directors and therefore was not accountable to the company; and see *Thomas Marshall (Exports) Ltd.* v. *Guinle* [1979] Ch. 227.
[65] [1980] 1 All E.R. 393, C.A.
[66] *Great Luxembourg Ry. Co.* v. *Magnay* (1858) 25 Beav. 586; *Aberdeen Ry. Co.* v. *Blaikie* (1854) 1 Macq. H.L. 461.
[67] This is subject to Article 84, Table A, of the Companies Act 1948.
[68] *Selangor United Rubber Estates Ltd.* v. *Cradock* (*No.* 3) [1968] 1 W.L.R. 1555.

they cannot, therefore, be allowed to retain a secret commission received from the vendors of property which a company has been formed for the purpose of purchasing.[69] Again, directors cannot receive commission from other parties when the property of the company is sold.[70] And if they act in disregard of their duties as directors on the directions of a stranger to the company (as in *Selangor United Rubber Estates Ltd.* v. *Cradock* (*No. 3*)[71] which concerned the fraudulent use of the company's money for the purpose of purchasing its own shares) they will be fixed with the stranger's knowledge and liable accordingly. Even if they are voices without mind, they will be given the mind of the person who manipulates them.[72] In addition, statutory duties are imposed in certain circumstances.[73] Indeed, it is true to say generally that, in the absence of authorisation from the company, they cannot act for their own advantage with any of the property or shares of the company.

Limits of the principle

It has already been stated that the principle that a trustee or person in the position of a trustee should not profit from the trust is part of the wider principle that a trustee should not place himself in a position where his interest and duty conflict. So far as directors are concerned this was formulated in terms by Lord Cranworth L.C. in *Aberdeen Railway Co.* v. *Blaikie*[74] when he said:

"And it is a rule of universal application, that no one having such duties to discharge, shall be allowed to enter into engagements in which he has, or can have, a personal interest conflicting, or which may possibly conflict, with the interest of those whom he is bound to protect. So strictly is this principle adhered to, that no question is allowed to be raised as to the fairness or unfairness of a contract entered into."

But it is important to emphasise that this is a rule for the protection of the person to whom the duty is owed, which such person may relax if he thinks fit. Such a duty was not established in *Boulting* v. *Association of Cinematograph, Television and Allied Technicians.*[75] The Boulting brothers had been managing directors of a film production company. They had contracts of service with this

---

[69] *Hitchens* v. *Congreve* (1828) cited 1 Russ. & Myl. 150; *Fawcett* v. *Whitehouse* (1829) 1 Russ. & Myl. 132.
[70] *Aberdeen Ry. Co.* v. *Blaikie* (1854) 1 Macq. H.L. 461 at p. 471.
[71] [1968] 1 W.L.R. 1555.
[72] *Selangor United Rubber Estates Ltd.* v. *Cradock* (*No. 3*) [1968] 1 W.L.R. 1555 at pp. 1613, 1614. *cf.* n. 3 and 4, *infra.*
[73] *e.g.* the duty of directors to notify the company of their interest (and that of their spouses and children) in shares in, and debentures of, the company or associated companies: Companies Act 1967, ss. 27, 28, 31, as amended by C.A. 1976, s. 24, C.A. 1981, Sched. 3. The company has to keep a register of directors' shareholdings, etc. : C.A. 1967, s. 29; and to notify the stock exchange of acquisition of its shares by directors: C.A. 1967, s. 25. Dealings by directors, their spouses and children in options to buy or sell quoted shares in, or quoted debentures of, the company or associated companies are penalised: C.A. 1967, s. 30. Certain loans to directors may be prohibited: C.A. 1980, ss. 49–53. For prohibition of substantial property transactions involving directors see C.A. 1980, s. 48.
[74] *Supra.*
[75] [1963] 2 Q.B. 606.

company which involved their production and direction of films, writing of scripts and the like. In 1941 they became members of the defendant union. In course of time great difficulty and friction arose between the plaintiffs and the defendants, as to who should be employed as assistant director, or as editor or in other capacities. And in due course the plaintiffs sought a declaration (*inter alia*) that they were ineligible for membership of the union while producing and directing films as managing directors. They argued that there was a conflict of duty and interest here. But the argument was rejected by the majority of the Court of Appeal. The court asked: To whom did the plaintiffs in this case owe a duty? The answer was that they owed it to the *company* of which they were directors. And the rule, therefore, did not entitle the plaintiffs, as distinct from the company, to have the plaintiffs' contract of membership with the union set aside or declared void or illegal, even if it would or might lead to a conflict of interests.[76]

More generally, it should be noted that directors owe their fiduciary duties only to the company, not to the shareholders.[77] Moreover, their duties of care are not as onerous as those of trustees[78]; and unlike trust property, the assets of the company are not vested in them, but in the company.[79] The legal position of directors and trustees cannot, therefore, be fully equated.

II. STRANGER INTERMEDDLING WITH TRUST PROPERTY

The rule is that if a stranger knowingly receives trust property and also knows that it is transferred to him in breach of trust he holds it upon a constructive trust for the beneficiaries. The knowledge may be actual or constructive,[80] but the fact that this must be present is all important.[81] This is a rule of general application but it is also, for example, specifically insisted on in section 13 of the Partnership Act 1890. This provides in effect that a *partner* of a trustee who has improperly applied trust property in the partnership is not liable for breach of trust unless he has notice of the breach committed by the other partner.

But receipt of trust property is not essential for liability as a constructive trustee on the basis of "intermeddling." A person will still become a construc-

---

[76] Lord Denning M.R. dissented on the ground that if directors are compelled to become members of a union on the terms that they are to obey the instructions of the union in the company's affairs, the tendency is so harmful that a rule to that effect is unlawful; and this will apply unless some provision is made so as to ensure that they are not required to act disloyally to those whose interests they are bound to protect.

[77] *Percival* v. *Wright* [1902] 2 Ch. 421. However, in exceptional circumstances, where the directors hold themselves out to the shareholders as their agents, they will owe a duty to the shareholders themselves: *Allen* v. *Hyatt* (1914) 30 T.L.R. 444.

[78] *Re City Equitable Fire Insurance Co. Ltd.* [1925] Ch. 407; and see *post*, p. 445.

[79] The assets of a company are also not vested in the liquidator on the winding-up of a company; nevertheless, the powers of dealing with the company's assets are exercisable by the liquidator for the benefit of the persons entitled to share in the proceeds of realisation, and the company as a legal person is not entitled to any part of the proceeds: *Ayerst* v. *C. & K. (Construction)* [1976] A.C. 167.

[80] See *Belmont Finance Corpn. Ltd.* v. *Williams Furniture Ltd. (No. 2)* [1980] 1 All E.R. 393, C.A.; and see *post*, p. 173.

[81] *Lee* v. *Sankey* (1872) L.R. 15 Eq. 204 at p. 211; *Soar* v. *Ashwell* [1893] 2 Q.B. 390 at p. 396; *Re Diplock* [1948] Ch. 465, at pp. 478, 524, 539, and see *post*, p. 465.

tive trustee *if he knowingly enables a fraudulent purpose to be effected*, but again, knowledge, actual or constructive,[82] is necessary.[83]

In such cases, however, the constructive trust may arise at different times, for it appears to be the position that where the defendant has received trust property he will become a trustee before the acts or omissions complained of, but where he has participated in a fraud it is the very act or omission which gives rise to liability which causes the constructive trusteeship.[84] In the one case it arises automatically; in the other, only on the occurrence of the conduct complained of.[85]

The case law on the principles stated above is instructive. Thus in *Barnes* v. *Addy*,[86] for example, trust funds were settled as to one moiety for A's wife and children and as to the other for B's wife and children. A was the surviving trustee of the settlement and he chose to appoint B as sole trustee of the second moiety, retaining the other in his own name. A's solicitor advised strongly against the execution of the deed appointing B as sole trustee although he reluctantly prepared it all the same. B's solicitor had also warned B's wife of the risks of a sole trustee. As it happened, B later misapplied the funds and it was sought (*inter alia*) to make A's solicitor responsible for the loss. It was held, however, not surprisingly on these facts, that he was not liable. As Lord Selborne L.C. said[87]: "Strangers are not to be made constructive trustees merely because they act as the agents of trustees in transactions within their legal powers, transactions perhaps of which a court of equity may disapprove, *unless those agents receive and become chargeable with some part of the trust property, or unless they assist with knowledge in a dishonest and fraudulent*[88] *design on the part of the trustee.*"[89] It is clear that the pre-conditions for he solicitor's liability as constructive trustee were not satisfied in this case. The principle stated by Lord Selborne has been followed in later decisions. In *Barnes* v. *Addy* the solicitors never actually took possession of the trust

---

[82] See the cases cited in note 83, *infra*, but *cf. Belmont Finance Corpn. Ltd.* v. *Williams Furniture Ltd.* [1979] Ch. 250, C.A. at 267, 268 where Buckley L.J. considered, but did not decide, that actual knowledge or a reckless failure to make inquiries was required.

[83] See *Selangor United Rubber Estates Ltd.* v. *Cradock (No. 3)* [1968] 1 W.L.R. 1555 at p. 1590; *Karak Rubber Co. Ltd.* v. *Burden (No. 2)* [1972] 1 W.L.R. 602 at p. 634; and see *post*, p. 173.

[84] See *Competitive Insurance Co. Ltd.* v. *Davies Investments Ltd.* [1975] 1 W.L.R. 1240, at p. 1247, *per* Goff J., applying *Selangor United Rubber Estates Ltd.* v. *Cradock (No. 3)* [1968] 1 W.L.R. 1555 at p. 1579, *per* Ungoed-Thomas J.; *Rowlandson* v. *National Westminster Bank Ltd.* [1978] 1 W.L.R. 798. See also *Carl Zeiss Stiftung* v. *Herbert Smith & Co.* [1969] 2 Ch. 276, discussed *post*, p. 172; *Belmont Finance Corpn.* v. *Williams Furniture Ltd.*, *supra*.

[85] This approach could offend the purists who might well argue that a constructive trust treated as a substantive institution should only arise when the alleged trustee is in possession of the property, and that where he is not, he should merely be under a duty to account. However, the modern cases, *e.g.* those cited in n. 84, make no such distinction; and see also *Boardman* v. *Phipps* [1967] 2 A.C. 46, where the terms "constructive trusteeship" and "accountability" are used interchangeably: see *ante*, p. 165.

[86] (1874) 9 Ch.App. 244.

[87] *Ibid.* at p. 251.

[88] "Dishonest" and "fraudulent" have the same meaning: *Belmont Finance Corpn.* v. *Williams Furniture Ltd.* [1979] Ch. 250 at p. 274.

[89] Our italics.

property, but the basis of the case was applied by the Court of Appeal in *Mara* v. *Browne*[90] to a case where the agents for the trustees did actually receive it. Here the beneficiaries sought to make two solicitors who carried on business in partnership liable for breach of trust. The alleged breaches of trust were in respect of advances of trust money on certain mortgages suggested by one of the solicitors, but which were alleged to be speculative and risky and an unjustified investment. Before the moneys were advanced they came into the hands of this solicitor and were paid to him into his own bank account. He then made the advances to the various mortgagors, basing himself on the authority of persons purporting to act as trustees of the settled funds. It was established on the facts that the investment amounted to a breach of trust, but the court exonerated the solicitors from liability on the ground that they never became constructive trustees. The basis of the decision is not as explicit as it might be,[91] but it was taken by Bennett J. in *Williams-Ashman* v. *Price and Williams*[92] to establish the principle that "an agent in possession of money which he knows to be trust money, so long as he acts honestly, is not accountable to the beneficiaries interested in the trust money unless he intermeddles in the trust by doing acts characteristic of a trustee and outside the duties of an agent." In *Williams-Ashman's* case, which involved investment of trust money made by a solicitor and a managing clerk in breach of trust, it was held that as they acted purely as agents on behalf of and with the authority of the principal they never came under any duty to the beneficiaries interested in the trust fund, and, again, were held not liable.

Similar considerations were in issue in *Re Bell's Indenture*.[93] A solicitor assisted in the misappropriation of trust funds by trustees and it was admitted that he was a constructive trustee, but it was argued that his partner was also liable as a constructive trustee on the basis of joint and several liability because where, as was the case here, the money had been paid into the firm's client account and paid out for a purpose which the other partner knew to be a breach of trust, all the partners were liable (*inter alia*) as constructive trustees. Vinelott J. held, however, that although a solicitor had the implied authority of his partner to receive trust money, he did not have implied authority to constitute himself a constructive trustee of trust money; and where the solicitor did constitute himself a constructive trustee, his partner was not liable for any misapplication if he had taken no part in and was ignorant of the transaction in question. Moreover, it made no difference whether the money was paid into a client account or a personal account. Accordingly, the partner's estate was held not liable.

It would seem hardly necessary to state that mere knowledge of a claim asserted by a party to legal proceedings is totally insufficient to render an agent (such as a solicitor acting for the other side) liable as a constructive trustee for

---

[90] [1896] 1 Ch. 199; *Re Barney* [1892] 2 Ch. 265.
[91] In *Re Bell's Indenture* [1980] 1 W.L.R. 1217, Vinelott J. (at p. 1230) described Lord Herschell's judgment in *Mara* v. *Browne* as "elliptical."
[92] [1980] 1 W.L.R. 1217; [1942] Ch. 219, at p. 228.
[93] [1942] Ch. 219 at p. 228; [1980] 1 W.L.R. 1217.

dealing with property derived from his principal and in accordance with his instructions—unless the agent knew that the other party's claim was well founded and that the principal had no authority to give him instructions. But the point was established in *Carl Zeiss Stiftung* v. *Herbert Smith & Co.*,[94] where the Court of Appeal rejected an application to make the solicitors liable in a case where unsolved questions of fact and difficult questions of German and English law were concerned. Danckwerts L.J. largely relied on lack of knowledge: it could not be assumed that the claims were well founded. "Claims" he said, "are not the same as facts."[95] Sachs L.J. held that, whatever the nature of the knowledge or notice required, cognisance of "a doubtful equity" was not enough.[96] He also held that the solicitors were under no duty to inquire into the facts, and also that they were liable only to their own principal, not directly to their principal's *cestui que trust*.[97] Edmund Davies L.J. considered that a "want of probity" was necessary to secure liability.[98]

The above decisions should be contrasted with the earlier decision of Stirling J. in *Blyth* v. *Fladgate*.[99] In this case a firm of solicitors were made liable because they dealt with trust moneys in breach of trust and without instructions from or authority of any principal. The sequence of events shows the reasons for making them liable. Whilst there was only one trustee of a marriage settlement, the trust funds were invested in Exchequer bills which had been deposited with the solicitors' bank and were in fact thus deposited on the death of the sole trustee. Later, before new trustees were appointed, the bills were sold by the solicitors and the proceeds of sale placed to their credit at their bank. This money was then paid by the solicitors to a mortgagor who executed a mortgage in favour of persons who were, as it happened, only subsequently appointed trustees. The advance on mortgage was in fact improper and it is not surprising that the solicitors were held liable. The facts of the case were clearly different from those in the cases previously cited and dictated a different result.[1] Moreover, there is no distinction between the liability of an express trustee who has misappropriated trust money and the liability of a person liable as a constructive trustee. The liability of both of them is to replace the trust money.[2]

The meaning of the word "knowledge" (which a party must have before liability as constructive trustee can be imposed on him) was discussed by

---

[94] [1969] 2 Ch. 276, distinguished in *Karak Rubber Co. Ltd.* v. *Burden (No. 2)* [1972] 1 W.L.R. 602, but applied in *Competitive Insurance Co. Ltd.* v. *Davies Investments Ltd.* [1975] 1 W.L.R. 1240.

[95] [1969] 2 Ch. 276 at p. 293.

[96] At p. 296.

[97] At p. 297.

[98] At p. 301.

[99] [1891] 1 Ch. 337. See also *Lee* v. *Sankey* (1873) L.R. 15 Eq. 204, where the solicitors took it upon themselves to pay trust money in their hands to one only of the trustees; they were held liable.

[1] *Blyth* v. *Fladgate* was specifically distinguished in *Re Bell's Indenture* [1980] 1 W.L.R. 1217 (see *ante*, p. 171). In the former case the firm became trustees because there were no trustees at the time when the trust moneys were received by them and they could not, therefore, be considered agents of trustees: *ibid.* at p. 1228.

[2] *Re Bell's Indenture, supra* at p. 1236.

Ungoed-Thomas J. in *Selangor United Rubber Estates Ltd.* v. *Cradock (No.* 3).[3] On this point he held that in a case of fraud or dishonesty "knowledge" was knowledge of circumstances which would indicate to an "honest, reasonable man" that a dishonest and fraudulent design, *i.e.* conduct which was morally reprehensible,[4] was being committed or would put him on inquiry whether it was being committed. Accordingly, according to this formulation, *actual* knowledge is not essential. In *Karak Rubber Co. Ltd.* v. *Burden (No.* 2), Brightman J. put the point as follows: "A person may have knowledge of an existing fact because in an objective sense he is actually aware of that fact. In an appropriate context a court of law may attribute knowledge of an existing fact to that person because in a subjective sense he has knowledge of circumstances which would lead a postulated man to the conclusion that the fact exists or which would put a postulated man upon inquiry as to whether the fact exists." In that case it was held that a bank acting for one of the parties in a fraudulent misapplication of the company's funds in the purchase of its own shares was liable as constructive trustee: it had sufficient notice, in the sense described, of the fraudulent conduct. However, although in these cases, both of first instance, constructive knowledge of the fraud was regarded as sufficient to secure liability, the question has yet to be finally decided. In *Belmont Finance Corpn. Ltd.* v. *Williams Furniture Ltd.*[5] Buckley L.J. considered, although he did not decide, that actual knowledge of the fraud or reckless failure to make inquiries was required.

The cases just cited were concerned with fraud or dishonesty and did not deal specifically with the degree of knowledge required in cases where fraud or dishonesty is absent, yet where conceivably constructive trusteeship can be imposed on a third party by reason of his receipt of trust property and becoming chargeable with it. In this situation, however, it appears to be established that constructive knowledge is sufficient to secure liability as a constructive trustee. This was the effect of the decision of the Court of Appeal in *Belmont Finance Corpn. Ltd.* v. *Williams Furniture Ltd. (No.* 2).[6]

So far the discussion has been concerned with cases where an intermeddling stranger has been rendered liable as a constructive trustee, first, by reason of his receipt of trust property and chargeability and, secondly, by reason of his

---

[3] [1968] 1 W.L.R. 1555 at p. 1590; *Karak Rubber Co. Ltd.* v. *Burden (No.* 2) [1972] 1 W.L.R. 602 at p. 634; *Rowlandson* v. *National Westminster Bank Ltd.* [1978] 1 W.L.R. 798; cf. *Carl Zeiss Stiftung* v. *Herbert Smith & Co.* [1969] 2 Ch. 276; *Competitive Insurance Co. Ltd.* v. *Competitive Insurance Co. Ltd.* v. *Davies Investments Ltd.* [1975] 1 W.L.R. 1240; *Belmont Finance Corpn. Ltd.* v. *Williams Furniture Ltd.* [1979] Ch. 250, C.A.

[4] An arguably nebulous formulation which was disapproved by Goff L.J. in *Belmont Finance Corpn. Ltd.* v. *Williams Furniture Ltd., supra,* p. 274: dishonesty is required, and particulars of knowledge of dishonesty must be pleaded. Dishonesty was not established in *Belmont Finance Corpn. Ltd.* v. *Williams Furniture Ltd. (No.* 2) (1980) 1 All E.R. 393, C.A., because the party concerned had acted genuinely and, therefore, the company could not be said to have participated in a dishonest and fraudulent design.

[5] [1979] Ch. 250, C.A. at pp. 267, 268.

[6] [1980] 1 All E.R. 393 (applied in *International Sales and Agencies Ltd.* v. *Marcus* [1982] 3 All E.R. 551). The facts are stated *ante,* p. 167; see in particular the statement of principle by Buckley L.J. (*ibid.* at p. 405) cited *ante,* p. 166.

participation in fraud. There is a third possibility to be added: where fraud is not asserted, yet constructive trusteeship is alleged, not automatically by "receipt and chargeability," but simply because of the acts or omissions of the stranger. This possibility was considered in *Competitive Insurance Co. Ltd.* v. *Davies Investments Ltd.*,[7] where the essential question was whether the liquidator of a company had constructive notice of an alleged constructive trust affecting shares of the company and whether he was to be made personally liable even though he was honest in his failure to recognise the trust. Goff J., in holding him not liable, applied the reasoning in *Carl Zeiss Stiftung* v. *Herbert Smith & Co.*[8] He held that the alleged constructive trust gave rise merely to a "doubtful equity" or that there was no "lack of probity" in his conduct. It should be said that the two cases are factually distinguishable. In *Carl Zeiss* the solicitors received payment of the alleged trust moneys from someone else, the alleged trustee; in *Competitive Insurance* the liquidator received nothing but himself caused the alleged trust funds to be paid away to persons other than the claimant *cestui que trust*. And, secondly, in *Carl Zeiss*, the solicitors did not know the relevant facts, but merely general facts about the claim, whereas in *Competitive Insurance* it was alleged that the liquidator did know or because of his means of knowledge must be taken as knowing the facts.[9] Nevertheless, the principles propounded in *Carl Zeiss* were, as Goff J. acknowledged, very useful in deciding what knowledge on the liquidator's part was required and, in any event, in what circumstances he would be held liable.

In the result, it appears in the present state of the law that in order to establish liability on a stranger by reason simply of his conduct, but where he has not received the trust property or become chargeable with it nor participated in fraud or dishonesty, little short of actual knowledge on his part will suffice.

III. Vendor of Land as Constructive Trustee

The effect of a binding contract for the sale of land is to render the vendor a constructive trustee of the land.[10] The basis of the trusteeship is that the purchaser is entitled to call for specific performance of the contract and therefore takes an equitable interest in the property. It follows that the contract in question must be specifically enforceable. The trusteeship is, however, of a somewhat novel kind because the vendor also retains until completion a beneficial interest in the property and this means that he can occupy the land and enjoy the rents and profits until that date. At the same time he must, because he is a trustee, manage and maintain the property with all the care required of any other trustee.

Some divergencies of opinion have appeared in the cases as to the nature of the trusteeship and in particular as to the time at which the vendor becomes a

---

[7] [1975] 1 W.L.R. 1240.

[8] [1969] 2 Ch. 276; see *ante*, p. 172.

[9] The distinctions were made by Goff J. in these terms in *Competitive Insurance Co. Ltd.* v. *Davies Investments Ltd., supra.*

[10] See also *Oughtred* v. *I.R.C.* [1960] A.C. 206; *ante*, p. 28.

trustee. Thus, in *Lysaght* v. *Edwards*,[11] Jessel M.R. said it had been settled for two centuries that the vendor is a constructive trustee for the purchaser from the time the contract is made. In a second case, *Rayner* v. *Preston*,[12] no less than three different views were expressed by each of the Lords Justices of Appeal. Cotton L.J. said that there was merely what he described as a "qualified" trust relationship.[13] Brett L.J. thought there was no trust relationship at all.[14] And James L.J. expressed the opinion that there was, on completion of the contract, a true trust relationship relating back to the time of making the contract.[15]

The opinion of James L.J. is more closely in accord with the principle that equity looks on that as done which ought to be done: the contract should, therefore, have an immediate effect. It has also been applied by Farwell J. in *Rideout* v. *Fowler*[16] and represents the practice today.

IV. Mortgagee as a Constructive Trustee

It is important to notice at the outset that a mortgagee is *not* a trustee of his power of sale of the mortgaged property. The power is his beneficially and, provided that he exercises it in good faith, the court will not interfere in any sale, however disadvantageous it may be, that he makes.[17] At the same time he *is* a trustee of any surplus proceeds of sale for subsequent mortgagees and also for the mortgagor[18]; and if he pays the money to his solicitor the latter also ranks as trustee.[19] However, the mortgagee will become entitled to any surplus beneficially if the rights of the mortgagor or subsequent mortgagees become barred by lapse of time.[20]

---

[11] (1876) 2 Ch.D. 499 at p. 507.
[12] (1881) 18 Ch.D. 1.
[13] *Ibid.* at p. 6.
[14] *Ibid.* at p. 13.
[15] *Ibid.* at p. 10.
[16] [1904] 2 Ch. 93.
[17] *Warner* v. *Jacob* (1882) 20 Ch.D. 220; *Waring* v. *London and Manchester Assurance Co. Ltd.* [1935] Ch. 310; *Cuckmere Brick Co. Ltd.* v. *Mutual Finance Ltd.* [1971] Ch. 949; there is, however, a duty to take reasonable care to obtain a proper price. *cf.* Building Societies Act 1962, s.36, which requires a building society in exercising the power of sale to take reasonable care to ensure that the property is sold at the best price which can reasonably be obtained.
[18] L.P.A. 1925, s.105.
[19] *Re Bull* (1886) 34 Ch.D. 462.
[20] *Re Moat House Farm, Thurlby* [1948] Ch. 191.

CHAPTER 9

TRUSTS OF IMPERFECT OBLIGATION

THESE are trusts of a hybrid nature.[1] A trust must, as a general rule, be enforceable by the beneficiary. A trust requires a *cestui que trust*.[2] But although a trust "of imperfect obligation" will not be enforced, yet the court will not forbid its performance if the trustees desire to perform it. They, therefore, constitute an anomalous class of trust, but it is clearly established by the authorities that they may in certain, though very carefully defined, circumstances be valid. They are strikingly illustrated by what may be called the "monument" and "animal" cases.[3]

I. "MONUMENT" CASES

A trust for erection of a particular monument or for the maintenance of a particular grave is not charitable, but it has been held that it may be valid as a trust of imperfect obligation. Thus in *Musset* v. *Bingle*[4] a somewhat bizarre gift for the erection of a monument to the testator's widow's first husband was upheld on this basis. Similarly in *Re Hooper*[5] a gift to trustees for the upkeep of graves and monuments "so long as they can legally do so" was held to be valid for 21 years. In these cases, and others deciding the same principle, it was made clear that the trustees could not be compelled to erect the monument or keep up the grave, but if they decided to do so they would not be prevented, provided that the trusts were kept within the perpetuity period. At the same time, if the trustees are unwilling to perform the trust or if there is a surplus after the purpose has been carried out, they will hold the property or the surplus on a resulting trust for the settlor's estate. It will also "result" on the determination of the period stipulated in the instrument for the duration of the trust or of the perpetuity period, as the case may be.

---

[1] See generally Morris and Leach, *The Rule against Perpetuities* (2nd ed.), pp. 306 *et seq.*

[2] *Re Wood* [1949] Ch. 498 at p. 499, *per* Harman J. (gift to B.B.C. programme *The Week's Good Cause* invalid); see also *Morice* v. *Bishop of Durham* (1804) 9 Ves. 399 at p. 405, *per* Grant M.R.: "There must be somebody in whose favour the court can decree performance."

[3] It is argued by Morris and Leach, *op. cit.* that trusts for masses for the dead and trusts for unincorporated associations should also take effect on the same basis. The former may, however, be charitable (see *post*, p. 208) and the latter should, it seems, be treated as a form of express private trust (see *ante* p. 107).

[4] [1876] W.N. 171.

[5] [1932] 1 Ch. 38, following *Pirbright* v. *Salwey* [1896] W.N. 86 (as gift of consols for application "so long as law permitted," to keep up burial inclosure: valid for 21 years).

II. "ANIMALS"

Gifts for the maintenance of animals generally are charitable.[6] But gifts for the maintenance of a *particular* animal or particular animals are not: they can only take effect, if at all, as trusts of imperfect obligation. Thus in *Pettingall* v. *Pettingall*,[7] the testator bequeathed £50 a year to the executor to provide for his favourite black mare. It was held he could perform the testator's wishes and might keep the surplus for his own purposes. But it was also indicated that if the executor failed to look after the mare the beneficiaries could apply to the court to reconsider the arrangement, but subject to that the trust was to last during the animal's life.

There is also the case of *Re Dean*,[8] where there was a bequest of an annual sum for the maintenance of the testator's horses and hounds for a period of 50 years, if any of the horses and hounds should so long live. This was held valid: the trustees were clearly at liberty to carry out the terms of the gift, although the beneficiaries being dumb, could not compel them to do so. *Re Dean* is an explicit authority—not all the early cases in this area of the law are particularly explicit—that a trust of imperfect obligation for the upkeep of a given animal may be valid notwithstanding the fact that by its nature it is not enforceable by the beneficiary.

Somewhat the same solution, though probably by unjustified extension, was reached in *Re Thompson*[9] where a legacy of £1,000 to be applied by the legatee towards the promotion of foxhunting was held valid. Until this case was decided trusts of imperfect obligation were concerned with the maintenance of particular animals, monuments and tombs. Whether it can be safely followed today is doubtful in view of the recent case law which will now be considered.

III. THE MODERN RULE

The first in a line of important decisions which reconsidered the whole question of trusts of imperfect obligation is *Re Astor's Settlement Trusts*[10] (the *Observer* trust case), which has already been considered on the question of certainty of objects and where it was held, but only as a secondary ground for decision, that the objects of the trusts were too uncertain: this was clearly correct because they were not defined in terms of concepts capable of clear ascertainment. The question first suggested itself: if the objects had been certain would the arrangement have been valid *qua* trust of imperfect obligation? Roxburgh J. reached the conclusion—and this was the primary ground of his decision—that the general principle was that gifts on trust must have a *cestui que trust* and said the cases of horses and dogs, graves and monuments provided an exception. These cases he suggested (following Underhill's view[11]) should be regarded as conces-

---

[6] See *post* p. 208.
[7] (1842) 11 L.J.Ch. 176.
[8] (1889) 41 Ch.D. 552.
[9] [1934] Ch. 342.
[10] [1952] Ch. 534.
[11] (13th ed.), p. 117.

sions to human weakness or sentiment, but they could not be used to justify a proposition that a court of equity would recognise as an equitable obligation a direction to apply funds in furtherance of enumerated non-charitable purposes in a manner no court could control.[12]

The views of Roxburgh J. were applied in another decision of first instance, *Re Shaw*,[13] where the main question was whether George Bernard Shaw's testamentary trusts of residue for 21 years for experimentation in the reform of the English alphabet of 26 letters were valid charitable trusts. In the event they were held not to be so. The question then arose whether they could be valid, in effect, as trusts of imperfect obligation. Harman J. held that, since they lacked a *cestui que trust*, they were invalid.

The compass of these trusts had, one would have thought, been firmly confined by a decision of the Court of Appeal. This is *Re Endacott*[14] where the testator had given his residuary estate to the North Tawton Parish Council "for the purpose of providing some useful memorial to myself." The court held that this trust did not fall within the "anomalous" class of trusts of imperfect obligation. It was of too wide and uncertain nature to qualify. Harman L.J. affirmed the views on this class of trust expressed by Roxburgh J. in *Re Astor's Settlement Trusts*. He said[15]: "I applaud the orthodox sentiments expressed by Roxburgh J. and I think as I think he does, that though one knows there have been decisions which are not satisfactorily classified but are merely occasions when Homer has nodded, yet the cases stand by themselves and ought not to be increased in number nor indeed followed except where the one is exactly like the other." And he added that he could not think that a case of this kind, the case of providing outside a church an unspecified and unidentified memorial, was the kind of instance which should be added to these "troublesome, anomalous and aberrant" cases.

It will also be recalled[16] that, in a number of cases involving trusts for unincorporated associations, it was held that where the subject matter of the gift was to be held in trust for the purposes of the association as a quasi-corporate entity it would tend to a perpetuity and would be void on that ground. Such cases are primarily concerned with perpetuity and it has been thought appropriate to consider them under that head. But in one of the leading cases, *Leahy v. Att.-Gen. for New South Wales*,[17] although the actual decision was that the gift was void for perpetuity, Viscount Simonds seemed clearly to be of the opinion that such a purpose trust would in any event (apart from perpetuity) be void because there was no *cestui que trust* to enforce it. He said[18]: "If the words 'for the general purposes of the association' were held to import a trust, the question would have to be asked, what is the trust and who are the benefici-

---

[12] [1952] Ch. 534 at p. 547.
[13] [1957] 1 W.L.R. 729.
[14] [1960] Ch. 232.
[15] *Ibid.* at pp. 250–251.
[16] See *ante*, p. 107.
[17] [1959] A.C. 457.
[18] *Ibid.* at p. 478.

aries? A gift can be made to persons (including a corporation) but it cannot be made to a purpose or to an object; so also a trust may be created for the benefit of persons as *cestuis que trust* but not for a purpose or object unless the purpose or object be charitable. For a purpose or object cannot sue but, if it be charitable, the Attorney-General can sue to enforce it."[19]

Cases such as *Re Astor's Settlement Trusts* and *Re Shaw* in particular raised the problem whether the categories of trusts of imperfect obligation could be extended to other non-charitable purposes provided, of course, that they were stated in terms embodying certainty. The answer, in view of what was said in *Re Endacott* as well as *Leahy* v. *Att.-Gen. for New South Wales,* seems to be, No. The reasoning, *viz.* the lack of a *cestui que trust* to enforce them, thereby putting the execution of the trust outside the control of the court, appears to be unimpeachable. And yet it might still be said that the position is not entirely satisfactory. In the present state of the law, you can give your money to human beings, whether good or bad. You can give it to charity. You can even set up trusts for your dogs and cats. But it seems *as a general rule* that you cannot give it for a social experiment falling outside the confines of the law of charity if it is defined in terms of purposes and however certain those purposes may be.[20]

We say "as a general rule" because, according to the decision of Goff J. in *Re Denley's Trust Deed,*[21] there may in certain circumstances be a way out of these difficulties. For he held that this rule was confined to purpose trusts which were "abstract or impersonal"; but that a trust, even though expressed as a purpose, which directly or indirectly was for the benefit of an individual or individuals was valid, provided that the individuals were ascertainable and the trust was not otherwise void for uncertainty. Here the expressed purpose of the trust was the maintenance of a sports ground primarily for the benefit of employees of a company, and secondarily for the benefit of such other persons as the trustees allowed to use it. No question of perpetuity was involved. The judge held that it was valid on the basis that this was an express private trust in favour of ascertainable beneficiaries who *ex hypothesi* could enforce it. But whether this approach is correct, however commendable as an attempt to "liberalise" the law, seems doubtful. The reason is that if a provision is framed as a *purpose* which, as a matter of construction, plainly seemed to be the position in *Re Denley,* even though it is for the benefit of individuals, it is the purpose which is the dominant factor and if it is non-charitable it should fail unless it falls within the recognised exceptions.

Nevertheless, the case was followed in *Re Lipinski's Will Trusts*[22] where the testator left his residuary estate to trustees for an unincorporated recreational

---

[19] In *Re Lipinski's Will Trusts* [1976] Ch. 235, Oliver J. argued (at p. 246) that this was not intended as an exhaustive statement or to do more than indicate the broad division of trusts into those where there are ascertainable beneficiaries (whether for particular purposes or not) and trusts where there are none.

[20] Marshall (1953) 6 C.L.P. 151. See also, generally, on the subject Kiralfy (1950) 14 Conv. (N.S.) 374; Sheridan (1953) 17 Conv. (N.S.) 46.

[21] [1969] 1 Ch. 373.

[22] [1976] Ch. 235.

association (which was not charitable) to be used for constructing and improving buildings for the association. Oliver J. held that this was a valid purpose trust, the main reason being that the beneficiaries (the members of the association) were ascertainable and could enforce the purpose. As a matter of construction, *Re Lipinski* may be a stronger case than *Re Denley* because, as it was held, the gift was to an unincorporated association and was also upheld on that basis[23]; this was not the case in *Re Denley*.

These cases, both of first instance, indicate that this type of purpose trust may be treated as a valid express private trust for the benefit of ascertainable beneficiaries, albeit for a particular purpose. But whether or not these cases were correctly decided, it is important to emphasise that a valid power cannot be deduced from what is intended to be a trust, and this will apply to a trust of imperfect obligation, as it applies to other trusts.[24] You cannot treat a trust as a power if a trust is intended.[25]

From a practical point of view it is not advisable to endeavour to provide expressly for a non-charitable purpose trust, otherwise than for animals, tombs and monuments, in the hope that it may be declared valid for other reasons. The simplest solution is to form a company, the objects of which need not be charitable, and make gifts by will or *inter vivos* to the company.[26]

IV. PERPETUITY

With regard to those trusts of imperfect obligation which will still be held valid the question whether they should be confined within the perpetuity period requires consideration.[27] This question has not always been fully discussed in the cases, but it now seems to be established that these trusts are not exempt from this requirement. In some of the animal cases the matter has been passed over.[28] In some, words such as "as far as the law allows" have been used, in which case a 21 year period has been limited for the duration of the trust.[29] Or, alternatively, judicial notice may be taken of the expected life of the animal in question, being less than the 21-year period.[30] In a large number of cases, animals will live for a time much shorter than this period, and it would seem convenient and not at all improper that if a period is not stipulated in the trust instrument, the contemplated duration of the life of the animal in question should be taken and if it falls short of the 21-year period, the trust should not

---

[23] It was held that it was valid as a gift in favour of an unincorporated association with a superadded discretion: see *ante*, p. 108.

[24] *I.R.C.* v. *Broadway Cottages Trust* [1955] Ch. 20 at p. 36; *Re Endacott, supra* at p. 246, and see *ante*, pp. 78, 178. This principle is not affected by *McPhail* v. *Doulton* [1971] A.C. 424 (*ante*, p. 78).

[25] *cf.* Morris and Leach, *op. cit.*, pp. 319 *et seq.*

[26] The Goodman Committee on Charity and Law and Voluntary Organisations (see p. 183, *post*) has now recommended that trusts for non-charitable purposes should be valid.

[27] *cf.* Morris and Leach, pp. 321 *et seq.*

[28] See *Re Dean* (1889) 41 Ch.D. 552; *Pettingall* v. *Pettingall* (1842) 11 L.J.Ch. 176.

[29] See *Pirbright* v. *Salwey* [1896] W.N. 86; *Re Hooper* [1932] 1 Ch. 38.

[30] *Re Haines, The Times*, November 7, 1952 (life of cat approximately 16 years); but this may be wrong: see Morris and Leach, *op cit.* p. 323, and *cf. Re Kelly* [1932] I.R. 255 at pp. 260–261.

fail. But the correct (and safest) approach is to limit the duration of the trust to the perpetuity period not exceeding a life or lives in being and/or 21 years.[31] It should be noted that if a life is taken for this purpose it must be a human life,[32] for otherwise it would be open to an eccentric settlor to tie up property indefinitely by settling it on trusts limited to the lives of tortoises or other animals noted for their longevity.

But although it may be possible for the court to take judicial notice of the expected life of your dog Fido, this cannot be done of your grandfather's tomb, and it will accordingly be essential to limit the duration of trusts for tombs and monuments to the perpetuity period (although an expression such as "as far as the law allows" will make the trust good for 21 years), unless it can be upheld on the basis now to be discussed.[32a]

V. Maintenance of Tombs by Trusts of Perpetual Duration

It has just been mentioned that a trust for the maintenance of a tomb may be valid as a trust of imperfect obligation of its duration is limited to the perpetuity period. But it may be possible for a testator to ensure that a trust of perpetual duration for this purpose is valid. But the ways in which it may be achieved are, as will be seen, somewhat complex and heavy-handed.

(1) A gift for the maintenance of the whole of the churchyard containing the tomb in question is a valid charitable gift,[33] and if the gift is made in this way the maintenance of the tomb for ever will be successfully achieved.

(2) A gift to one charity with a gift over to another if the tomb is not kept in repair may also be successful. But it is most important to ensure that no actual trust is imposed on the first charity to keep up the tomb, and a comparison of two cases may be instructive in underlining this rule. Thus in *Re Tyler*[34] a sum of stock was given to the trustees of the London Missionary Society with a gift over to the Blue Coat School if the Society failed to keep the tomb in repair. Since both the donees were charitable bodies the perpetuity rule did not apply to them,[35] but the question still remained whether the *condition* in question (*i.e.* for the maintenance of the tomb) contravened the rule. It was held by the Court of Appeal that since the testator had not actually required the Society to maintain the tomb, the condition was valid. On the other hand, in *Re Dalziel*,[36] the testator gave to the governors of St. Bartholomew's Hospital the sum of £20,000 "upon and subject to the conditon" that they should use income so far as necessary for the upkeep of a certain mausoleum, and if they failed to carry

---

[31] Perpetuities and Accumulations Act 1964, s.15(4); and see *ante* p. 109.

[32] *Re Kelly* [1932] I.R. 255.

[32a] It may also be possible to take advantage of s.1 of the Parish Councils and Burial Authorities (Miscellaneous Provisions) Act 1970 which authorises local authorities and burial authorities to make an agreement to maintain graves, etc., for a period not exceeding 99 years. The text is concerned with the use of trust machinery for this purpose.

[33] *Re Pardoe* [1906] 2 Ch. 184.

[34] [1891] 3 Ch. 252.

[35] See *post* p. 183.

[36] [1943] Ch. 277.

out this purpose there was a gift over to such other charities as the trustees might select on the same conditions. In this case, the condition, on its true construction, amounted to a positive direction that the income was to be applied in the first instance to the maintenance of the mausoleum: it did not—as conversely was the case in *Re Tyler*—simply impose a moral obligation and, accordingly, Cohen J. held that the trust failed.

(3) A third method, which in any case was a highly controversial one and is now apparently no longer available, was to rely on the decision in *Re Chardon*.[37] The facts were that the testator gave to his trustees £200 for investment and to pay income to a cemetery company "during such period as they shall continue to maintain and keep the graves of my great grandfather and . . . Priscilla Navone in good order and condition." He further provided that if the graves were not maintained, the income was to go into residue. Romer J. held this gift to be valid. Very great difficulty has been found with the meaning of this case, but perhaps the best view is, though this does not emerge clearly from the judgment, that it could be justified at the time it was decided on the ground that a determinable interest such as that given to the cemetery company, which may determine at any time in the future, was not subject to the perpetuity rule. The case was followed by Wynn-Parry J. on virtually identical facts in *Re Chambers Will Trusts*[38] but distinguished by the same judge in *Re Wightwick's Will Trusts*.[39] In the latter case, it was distinguished on the ground that there the gift constituted a *trust* of income for an indefinite period for a non-charitable purpose and was, therefore, void as tending to a perpetuity, whereas there was no actual trust in *Re Chardon*. *Re Wightwick* showed that there may have been yet another facet of the case—*viz.* whether or not there is a trust—which had to be taken into account. In view of the uncertain state of the law, even before the passing of the Perpetuities and Accumulations Act 1964, he was a brave man who relied on *Re Chardon*.[40] But the Act appears to have rendered this discussion academic. It provides that a determinable interest is now to be subject to the perpetuity rule,[41] *i.e.* it must be limited to lives in being and/or 21 years.

---

[37] [1928] Ch. 464.
[38] [1950] Ch. 267.
[39] [1950] Ch. 260.
[40] See generally Hart (1937) 53 L.Q.R. 24; Albery (1938) 54 L.Q.R. 258.
[41] Perpetuities and Accumulations Act 1964, s. 12.

CHAPTER 10

CHARITABLE TRUSTS

I. CHARITIES ACT 1960

The law and practice of charitable trusts was radically reformed by the Charities Act 1960.[1] This Act achieved the arduous task of renovating the appalling mass of statute law relating to charitable trusts. It cleared a great deal of dead wood from the Statute Book, especially that body of statutes known as the Charitable Trusts Acts 1853–1939. What was not obsolete was extracted from them and conveniently contained in the new statute. It is true to say that this Act contains the whole of the statute law relating to charitable trusts from the sixteenth century to the present day, and also adds new provisions in keeping with modern circumstances, although, as will be seen, it is primarily with the statute law that the Act is concerned, and not with the legal nature of charity. It implemented, wholly or in part, many of the recommendations of the Nathan Committee on such trusts which published its report in 1952.[2] The Act came into force on January 1, 1961. Its effect and scope, where of general interest, is considered in the succeeding pages.

It is possible that further changes in the law may not be too far distant. The Goodman Committee[3] which reported in 1976 made a number of recommendations for reform, but none have so far been implemented.

II. DISTINCTIONS FROM PRIVATE TRUSTS

A charitable trust is aimed to benefit society at large or an appreciable part of it. A private trust is aimed to benefit defined persons or defined classes of persons. In general, charitable trusts are subject to the same rules as private trusts, but because of their public nature they enjoy a number of advantages which are not shared by private trusts.

(1) Perpetuity[4]

Charitable trusts are not subject to that aspect of the perpetuity rule commonly called the rule against inalienability. The objects of the charity may last

---

[1] For accounts of the Act, see Nathan, *Charities Act 1960*; Maurice, *Charities Act 1960*. And see *post*, pp. 233, *et seq.*

[2] Cmd. 9538. (Its full title is the "Committee on the Law and Practice relating to Charitable Trusts.")

[3] This was an independent committee on Charity Law and Voluntary Organisations set up by the National Council of Social Service under the chairmanship of Lord Goodman. It is herein referred to as "the Goodman Committee." The Expenditure Committee of the House of Commons (10th Report Session 1974–75) (herein referred to as "the Expenditure Committee"), has also made recommendations on charity law and administration.

[4] See *ante*, p. 98.

for ever, but a gift for such purpose will still be valid.[5] But they are, generally, subject to the perpetuity rule in the sense that the interest must vest in the charity within the perpetuity period. Thus, in *Re Lord Stratheden and Campbell*[6] an annuity of £100 was bequeathed for provision "for the Central London Rangers on the appointment of the next lieutenant-colonel." Since the next lieutenant-colonel might not be appointed within the perpetuity period, the limitation transgressed the rule and the gift was held by Romer J. to be invalid. However, even here there is an exception: provided that the trust in favour of one charity takes effect within the period, a gift over from that charity to another on the happening of an event which may be too remote will still be valid.[7] But this exception will not apply to a *gift over* to a charity after a gift to a non-charity[8]; in such a case the normal rules as to vesting in the second charity within the perpetuity period must be observed. It is as if for this purpose the law regards "charity" as a unity—thus a gift from one charity to another charity is from or to this "unity" so that there is no scope for the operation of the perpetuity rule, while a gift from or to this unity is subject to it in the usual way.

(2) **Certainty**

A charity will not fail for uncertainty of objects provided that the settlor clearly intended the fund to go exclusively to charity.[9] If this is satisfied the trust will not fail if he omits to specify the objects with particularity. In such circumstances a *cy-près* scheme[10] will be made to render the objects more precise. Again, for this purpose, it seems that the law regards charity as a unity, so that once the gift to this unity is established, it cannot fail.

(3) **Construction**

In construing instruments the intention of which is to set up a charitable trust but where there is an ambiguity, a "benignant" construction should be given if possible.[11] This was confirmed by the House of Lords in *I.R.C.* v. *McMullen*.[12] It was not, however, necessary to resort to such a construction in that case.

(4) **Taxation**

For taxation purposes, the distinction between a charitable trust and a private trust is seen both in the special taxation privileges which are afforded to a charitable trust, and to the taxation inducements which are offered to individuals for them to confer benefits on charitable trusts.

---

[5] *Chamberlayne* v. *Brockett* (1872) L.R. 8 Ch.App. 206.

[6] [1894] 3 Ch. 265. Applying *Chamberlayne* v. *Brockett* (1872) L.R. 8 Ch.App. 206. It is now possible to take advantage of the "wait and see" rule introduced by the Perpetuities and Accumulations Act 1964, s. 3, in respect of instruments taking effect after the commencement of the Act.

[7] *Re Tyler* [1891] 3 Ch. 252; *cf. Re Dalziel* [1943] Ch. 277; these cases are discussed at p. 181, *ante.*

[8] *Re Bowen* [1893] 2 Ch. 491 at p. 494; *Re Peel's Release* [1921] 2 Ch. 218; *Re Wightwick's Will Trusts* [1950] Ch. 260; *Re Spensley's Will Trusts* [1954] Ch. 233.

[9] See *Moggridge* v. *Thackwell* (1803) 7 Ves. 36, affirmed (1807) 13 Ves. 416.

[10] See *post*, p. 223.

[11] See *ante*, p. 60 in relation to construction of private trusts.

[12] [1981] A.C. 1 at p. 16. The facts are stated *post*, p. 213.

(a) *Income tax and corporation tax*. With regard to income tax, it is necessary to distinguish between the *investment* income and the *trading* income of the charity. Its investment income is exempt from income tax provided that it is applied for charitable purposes only.[13] If the charity carries on trade, its profits from the trade are exempt from income tax only if they are applied solely for its purpose and *either* (a) if the purpose or one of the primary purposes of the charity is to carry on that particular trade, *or* (b) if the work in connection with the trade is mainly carried out by the beneficiaries of the charity.[14] Where the charity is incorporated, the same principles as for income tax apply to corporation tax.[15]

The question whether a body is established for charitable purposes is a question of law to be decided in accordance with the usual principles, but the question whether or to what extent income is applied to charitable purposes is one of fact.[16] However, in *I.R.C.* v. *Helen Slater Charitable Trust Ltd.*[17] the Court of Appeal held that one charity "applies" its income for charitable purposes if it pays that income to another charity, albeit that the terms of the instrument governing the second charity are almost identical to those of the instrument governing the first charity.

(b) *Deeds of covenant*.[18] If a person executes a deed of convenant by which he covenants to pay a part of his income to a charity for a period capable of exceeding three years that part of his income is treated as the income of the charity for the purposes of the basic rate of income tax.[19] In practice, the covenantor deducts income tax at the basic rate from his payment, and the charity is entitled to claim a refund of the tax.[20] Furthermore, on the first £5,000 of gross income which an individual pays under covenant to a charity, the individual obtains income tax relief at his top rate of income tax, including the investment income surcharge.[21] For 1983/84 the top rate of income tax which an individual can pay is 75 per cent.[22] Accordingly, where an individual is liable to income tax at this rate, the net cost, after income tax, to him of paying £5,000 p.a. to charity is £1,250.

The same general principles apply to the case of a company which enters into a deed of covenant. It may deduct the gross amount of the payments from its profits before these are assessed for corporation tax, provided that it deducts income tax at the basic rate from the gross amount before making the payment to the charity and accounts to the Revenue for the tax so deducted.[23]

[13] Income and Corporation Taxes Act 1970, s. 360.
[14] *Ibid.*
[15] *Ibid.* s. 360(4).
[16] See *Williams' Trustees* v. *I.R.C.* [1947] A.C. 447.
[17] [1981] 3 All E.R. 98, C.A.
[18] The Goodman Committee estimate that deeds of covenant in favour of charities are executed at the rate of almost 400,000 a year and produce payments totalling some £60m. gross.
[19] I.C.T.A. 1970, s. 434(1A), added by F.A. 1980, s. 55(1).
[20] I.C.T.A. 1970, s. 52.
[21] I.C.T.A. 1970, s. 457(1A), added by F.A. 1980, s. 56(2).
[22] F.A. 1983, s.12.
[23] *Ibid.* s.53.

(c) *Capital gains tax*. A capital gain accruing to a charity will not attract capital gains tax provided that it is both applicable and is in fact applied to the charitable purposes.[24] If the charity is incorporated, then it is entitled to exemption from corporation tax on its capital gains on the same basis.[25]

There is also a substantial inducement to make gifts *to* a charity. Normally, when a person makes a gift, capital gains tax is payable by him on, broadly, the difference between the value of the asset at the time of the gift, and its value at the time of acquisition.[26] However, no capital gains tax is payable where the disposal is to a charity.[27]

(d) *Capital transfer tax*. It has been seen that estate duty has been effectively replaced by capital transfer tax[28] which operates not only on death, but also in respect of lifetime gifts. Compared with other private persons or bodies, charities enjoy important privileges with regard to capital transfer tax:

(i)   gifts made to charities, whether by will or *inter vivos*, are wholly exempt from the tax[29];

(ii) gifts made to nationally important institutions, such as the National Gallery, the British Museum or the National Trust, are wholly exempt from the tax, whether the gift takes effect on death or *inter vivos*[30];

(iii) gifts made to a charity by way of a payment from a discretionary trust are entitled to unlimited exemption[31];

(iv) the Treasury is empowered to exempt, for example, a gift of land of outstanding scenic or historical or scientific interest; gifts of buildings of outstanding historical or architectural or aesthetic interest; property given as a source of income for the upkeep of such land or buildings; and pictures, books, manuscripts, works of art, etc., of national or historic or scientific interest.[32]

It is, however, important to emphasise that, as a general rule, the exemptions apply only to gifts to charities which are immediate and absolute.[33] To this general rule there is the qualification that if the donor wishes a charity to benefit only after the death of himself and his spouse, he can leave a life interest in the property to the spouse, and on the latter's death, to the charity absolutely. Capital transfer tax is not payable on the death either of the donor or his spouse.[34]

---

[24] Capital Gains Tax Act 1979, s. 145.
[25] I.C.T.A. 1970, s. 265(2). Capital gains tax applies only to capital gains made by individuals. Capital gains made by corporations are subject to corporation tax.
[26] C.G.T.A. 1979, s. 1.
[27] C.G.T.A. 1979, s. 146.
[28] As a result of the F.A. 1975 as subsequently amended; see *post*, p. 298.
[29] F.A. 1975, s.26(3); Sched. 6, para. 10(1).
[30] *Ibid*. Sched. 6, para. 12.
[31] F.A. 1982, s. 119.
[32] F.A. 1975, Sched. 6, para. 13 as amended by F.A. 1976, s. 76.
[33] *Ibid*. Sched. 6, para. 15(3).
[34] *Ibid*. Sched. 6, para. 1(1).

In addition to taking advantage of these immunities which are peculiar to charity, a donor may also take advantage of two other exemptions which apply generally, namely, (i) that gifts to a total value of £3,000 in any one year are exempt,[35] and (ii) that gifts made as part of the donor's normal expenditure out of income are exempt if the donor is left with sufficient income to maintain his usual standard of living.[36]

There is, therefore, considerable encouragement to make gifts to charity. Moreover, from the charity's point of view, any capital distributions made by it are also exempt.[37]

(e) *Stamp duty.*[38] Charities are exempt from stamp duty in relation to any conveyance, transfer or letting made or agreed to be made to them.[39]

(f) *Development land tax.* Charities are exempt from development land tax.[40]

(g) *Value added tax.* Although there is no general exemption for charities from value added tax, certain medical charities are, in effect, exempt from the tax,[41] and supplies to such charities are also exempt.[42]

(h) *Rating.* The general law of rating is governed by the General Rate Act 1967, section 40 of which provides for the rating relief (both mandatory and discretionary) given to charities.

Mandatory relief to the extent of 50 per cent.[43] of the rates which would otherwise be chargeable is available in respect of land (i) occupied by or used by trustees for a charity and (ii) wholly or mainly used for charitable purposes.[44] With regard to occupation, it is in most cases clear that the charity or the trustees of the charity are in occupation. More difficult questions may arise where the charity has provided a house or accommodation for servants or staff and whether mandatory relief can be claimed in respect of it. The test appears to be whether the occupation of the servant is required with a view to the more efficient performance of his duties so as to constitute occupation by the charity.[45] Secondly, with regard to the requirement that the land be wholly or mainly used for charitable purposes, it appears to be required that the charity's use of the property be wholly "ancillary to" or "directly facilitates" the carrying out of its main charitable purposes.[46] The meaning of these expressions was

---

[35] *Ibid.* Sched. 6, para. 2(1); F.A. 1981, s. 94.
[36] *Ibid.* Sched. 6, para. 5(1). A deed of covenant in favour of charity would normally indicate that such gifts were part of the donor's normal expenditure.
[37] By virtue of F.A. 1982, s. 102(1)(*a*).
[38] See *post*, p. 289.
[39] F.A. 1982, s. 129.
[40] Development Land Tax Act 1976, s. 24, substituted by F.A. 1980, ss. 24 and 25.
[41] F.A. 1972, Sched. 4, Group 16, as substituted by the VAT (Handicapped Persons and Charities) Order 1981, item 4.
[42] *Ibid.* item 5.
[43] Special mandatory relief in the form of total exemption from rates is available in respect of places of public religious worship and buildings ancillary thereto: General Rate Act 1967, s.39; and see *Broxtowe Borough Council* v. *Birch* [1983] 1 All E.R. 641, C.A., for the meaning of "public religious worship."
[44] General Rate Act 1967, s. 40(1).
[45] *Glasgow Corporation* v. *Johnstone* [1965] A.C. 609; *Northern Ireland Valuation Court* v. *Fermanagh Protestant Board of Education* [1969] 1 W.L.R. 1708.
[46] *Glasgow Corporation* v. *Johnstone, supra* at p. 622, *per* Lord Reid.

considered by the House of Lords in *Oxfam* v. *Birmingham City District Council*,[47] where Oxfam claimed relief from rates in respect of gift shops which it used for the sale of articles, mostly clothing, which had been donated to it, the profits being applied to Oxfam's objects. It was held that the charity gift shops did not "directly facilitate" the main object of the charity, and rating relief could not be claimed. There was a distinction, said Lord Cross of Chelsea,[48] between user for the purpose of getting in, raising or earning money for the charity, as opposed to user for purposes directly related to the achievement of the objects of the charity. The charity gift shops simply raised money for Oxfam and were accordingly excluded from relief.[49]

In addition to this relief, which is obtainable as of right, the rating authority has a discretion to reduce further, or remit entirely, the rates payable by a charity.[50]

III. Definition of a Charity

What is a charity?[51] For the reasons implicit in the distinctions already made between charitable and private trusts, it is essential to know when a trust is charitable and when it is not. The answer to this question is to be found, if at all, almost entirely in the case law. But the answer—in borderline cases, at any rate—may be difficult to find. In fact the whole subject has been condemned in the words of one writer as the "wilderness of legal charity."[52] There is a vast number of cases, and they certainly do not present an orderly picture.

In borderline cases, it may still be necessary to go back to a statute of Elizabeth I (43 Eliz. I, c. 4, 1601) commonly called the Charitable Uses Act 1601, in the preamble of which certain objects are listed. These are as follows:

> "The relief of aged, impotent and poor people; the maintenance of sick and maimed soldiers and mariners, schools of learning, free schools and schools in universities; the repair of bridges, ports, havens, causeways, churches, sea-banks and highways; the education and preferment of orphans; the relief, stock or maintenance for houses of correction; the marriage of poor maids; the supportation, aid and help of young tradesmen, handicraftsmen and persons decayed; the relief or redemption of prisoners or captives; and the aid or ease of any poor inhabitants concerning payment of fifteens, setting out of soldiers and other taxes."

The statute itself was repealed by the Mortmain and Charitable Uses Act 1888, but in effect the preamble remained alive.[53] Admittedly, the purposes listed in this ancient statute have never been treated as sacrosanct. In many

---

[47] [1976] A.C. 126; *cf. Aldous* v. *Southwark London B.C.* [1968] 1 W.L.R. 1671.
[48] *Ibid.* at p. 146.
[49] The Rating (Charity Shops) Act 1976 remedied the effect of this decision with regard to charity shops so as to make them eligible for relief, but otherwise the decision remains intact.
[50] General Rate Act 1967, s. 40(5).
[51] See, for general surveys, Brunyate (1945) 61 L.Q.R. 268; Cross (1956) 72 L.Q.R. 187.
[52] Bentwich (1936) 49 L.Q.R. 520.
[53] *Infra.*

cases they have been extended by the addition of a multitude of analogous objects, analogy upon analogy, and in some cases the analogies are perhaps rather far-fetched. In others, the decision has been based on a more general question whether the purpose is or is not within the "spirit and intendment" or the "equity" or the "mischief" of the statute—with analogy used only as a "handmaid."[54] Even so, one can still find a number of cases based on a detailed examination of the words of the statute in recent years.[55]

The living preamble. It was commonly thought that section 13(2) of the Mortmain and Charitable Uses Act 1888, although this repealed the Statute of Elizabeth I, had expressly preserved the preamble; and when this subsection was itself repealed by the Charities Act 1960[56] the preamble was thereby destroyed. However, if one considers section 13(2) it seems to fall short of providing that in *all* cases the court must continue to refer to the preamble; it refers specifically only to enactments and documents in which a reference to charity is made, and these do not prima facie include the reported judgments of superior courts. But the main point is that even if section 13(2) had been omitted altogether from the 1888 Act, the court would still have been bound to decide a case with the preamble in mind, because the practice of the courts had developed into a rule of law. And this rule of law—having, as it were, an independent existence irrespective of statute—could not be extinguished without an express statutory provision to that effect. Indeed the Charities Act 1960 made it reasonably clear that no change in the law was intended. The Act repeals section 13(2) but in substitution provides that a reference in any enactment or document to a charity within the preamble should be construed as a reference to charity in the meaning it bears as a legal term according to the law of England and Wales.[57] Thus the Charities Act itself seems to make it clear that the law of England and Wales, based on the preamble over a period of 380 years, should remain intact. In other words the repeal of section 13(2) with the substitution of new provisions does not affect the edifice of law built on the foundations of the preamble.[58]

This approach, based on a construction of the relevant statutory provisions, seems reasonably conclusive on its own. The relevance of the preamble has, however, also been affirmed by recent authoritative judicial decisions. Thus in *Scottish Burial Reform and Cremation Society* v. *Glasgow City Corporation*,[59] where cremation was held to be a charitable purpose, the House of Lords acknowledged that this was undoubtedly the accepted test, though, as Lord

---

[54] *Incorporated Council of Law Reporting for England and Wales* v. *Att.-Gen.* [1972] Ch. 73 at p. 88 *per* Russell L.J.
[55] See for recent examples, *Re Cole* [1958] Ch. 877, C.A.; *Re Sahal's Will Trusts* [1958] 1 W.L.R. 1243.
[56] s. 38(1).
[57] s.38(4). See also the definition of "charity" in s.45(1) and "charitable purposes" in s.46(1). For the purposes of s.45(1) the charity must be subject to control by the High Court in the exercise of the court's jurisdiction with respect to charities: see *Construction Training Board* v. *Att.-Gen.* [1973] Ch. 173; and see *post*, p. 235.
[58] See *Tudor on Charities*, (6th ed.), pp. 5 *et seq.*
[59] [1968] A.C. 138.

Upjohn said, "in only a very wide and broad sense,"[60] meaning, as Lord
Wilberforce put it, "that what must be regarded is not the wording of the
preamble, but the effect of decisions given by the courts as to its scope, decisions
which have endeavoured to keep the law as to charities moving according as
new social needs arise or old ones become obsolete or satisfied."[61] Likewise, in
Incorporated Council of Law Reporting for England and Wales v. Att.-Gen.,[62]
the Court of Appeal, in affirming the charitable status of the Council, specifically held that the publication or dissemination of law reports was a purpose
beneficial to the community, being within the spirit and intendment of the
preamble to the Statute of Elizabeth.

In short, it is still technically necessary today to decide whether a case falls
within "the letter or the spirit and intendment" of the preamble. In practice, in
most cases, it will be sufficient to refer to the relevant prior case law to dispose of
the problem whether a particular trust is charitable or not. Only in a novel case
may the court be compelled to refer back to the basic principles or indeed the
letter of the preamble.

Reform. The preamble was not, of course, a *definition* of charity. It was
simply a catalogue of purposes which in 1601 were regarded as charitable.
Indeed at no time has there been a statutory definition, except for the limited
one provided for in section 1 of the Recreational Charities Act 1958.[63]
Suggestions were made before the Charities Act 1960 was passed that there
ought to be a definition of charity in the Act.[64] But these suggestions were
resisted because it was thought to be almost impossible to provide a foolproof
definition applicable to all the cases that might arise.[65] If it had been provided it
might have proved an erratic or insufficient yardstick. The question is debatable. Many laymen and some lawyers find it extraordinary that the question
whether a trust is charitable—with all the fiscal and other privileges enjoyed by
legal charity—should depend at the present day on a statutory provision of the
early seventeenth century and the welter of case law which has grown up
around it.

The point has been judicially recognised. For example, Lord Upjohn once
said that the preamble had been "stretched almost to breaking-point."[66] The
difficulties are undoubtedly exacerbated by the immunity from taxation which
all English charities enjoy. In the words of Lord Cross of Chelsea in *Dingle* v.

---

[60] *Ibid.* at p. 151.
[61] *Ibid.* at p. 154.
[62] [1972] Ch. 73.
[63] See *post*, p. 209.
[64] See *e.g.* Nathan Report.
[65] "There is no limit to the number and diversity of the ways in which man will seek to
benefit his fellow men"; *I.R.C.* v. *Baddeley* [1955] A.C. 572 at p. 583, *per* Viscount Simonds.
[66] *Scottish Burial Reform and Cremation Society* v. *Glasgow City Corporation* [1968] A.C.
138 at p. 153, *cf. Incorporated Council of Law Reporting for England and Wales* v. *Att.-Gen.*
[1972] Ch. 73 at p. 94 *per* Sachs L.J.: "I appreciate the wisdom of the legislature in refraining
from providing a detailed definition of charitable purposes in the 1960 Act. . . . Any statutory
definition might well produce a fresh spate of litigation and provide a set of undesirable
artificial distinctions."

Turner,[67] validity and fiscal immunity march hand in hand. He suggested that one possible solution would be to separate them and say that only some charities should enjoy fiscal privileges. No doubt this would cause a great deal of contention, but might prove to be a practical proposition. Perhaps the membership of this country of the European Economic Community—as well as the growing number of transnational charities—may impel us to embark on a statutory rationalisation of the law.[68]

The problems of definition should not, however, be underestimated and it may be noteworthy that the Goodman Committee was unable to devise one, but instead recommended that the categories of charity should be re-stated in simple and modern language replacing that of the Act of 1601 and extending these to include objects now considered to be within the scope of charity (so-called "guide-lines").[69] The case law would not be irrelevant but the court would have more freedom to reconsider it in the light of the new categorisation. On the other hand, the Expenditure Committee has recommended that a statutory definition of charity is needed. They do not, however, provide one; they simply emphasise that all charities should be required to satisfy the test of benefit to the community.[70] On this it may be observed that one of the difficulties in this area of the law is to define what is, and what is not, for the "public benefit."[71]

Legislation embodying the Goodman Committee's "guide-lines" would be helpful in modernising the law.

IV. CLASSIFICATION OF CHARITABLE TRUSTS

A leading case in which a classification of charitable trusts was made and on which many succeeding cases have been based is *Commissioners for Special Purposes of Income Tax* v. *Pemsel*.[72] Here Lord Macnaghten classified the trusts which have been held to be charitable under four heads:

(1) Trusts for the relief of poverty;
(2) Trusts for the advancement of education;
(3) Trusts for the advancement of religion;
(4) Trusts for other purposes beneficial to the community not falling under any of the other three heads.[73]

---

[67] [1972] A.C. 601 at p. 624; a case involving the relief of poverty, discussed *post*, p. 196.

[68] See Official Report of Debates of the Council of Europe, 1972, Vol. 3, p. 598; Doc. 3052, 1972, of the Council of Europe, Vol. 11. See also *Trusts and Foundations in Europe* (ed. Neuhoff and Pavel); Pomey, *Traité des Fondations D'Utilité Publique*; Boúúaert, *Tax Problems of Cultural Foundations and of Patronage in the European Community*.

[69] At p. 16. These "guide-lines" are set out in Appendix 1 to the Report (p. 123).

[70] At p. xiii.

[71] See *post*, p. 192.

[72] [1891] A.C. 531 at p. 583. *cf.* the classification in the American *Restatement of Trusts* which specifically refers also to two other purposes: (1) promotion of health and (2) governmental and municipal purposes (Vol. II, p. 1140).

[73] The classification was based on the argument of Sir Samuel Romilly in *Morice* v. *Bishop of Durham* (1805) 10 Ves. 522 at p. 532.

This is the nearest that one can get to a definition in English law. The first three heads do not, generally, present too much difficulty. A case falling within any of those heads will prima facie be assumed to be charitable as being for the benefit of the community, unless the contrary is shown. The fourth head presents, as will be seen, greater difficulty but it seems that the courts prefer the vague and undefined approach based on the "equity" or the "mischief" of the preamble, rather than the stepping-stones approach based on analogy, in determining the question whether a trust falling under this head is charitable.[74]

Before each head is considered, it is necessary to emphasise the requirement, which applies generally, that a charitable trust must have a public character.[75]

1. *Public Element in Charity*

It does not follow from the requirement of a public character that *all* public trusts are charitable. What it means is that a trust is incapable of being charitable in the legal sense unless it is for the benefit of the public, or some section of the public, with the exception only of trusts for the relief of poverty[76]—and whether or not the test is satisfied is decided by the court on the evidence[77] and not on the opinion of the settlor. A number of illustrations, from the many cases on the topic, may be taken. Thus in *Re Compton*[78] a trust for the education of the descendants of three named persons was held not to be a valid charitable trust, because the beneficiaries were defined by reference to a personal relationship and it, therefore, lacked the quality of a public trust. The trust was indeed a family trust and not one for the benefit of a section of the public. Again, in *Re Hobourn Air Raid Distress Fund*[79] an emergency fund which had been built up during the last war had been used partly for comforts for ex-employees serving in the Forces, and later for employees who had suffered distress from air-raids. It was held that because of the absence of a public element no charitable trust had been created and the surplus funds, over which the application had been made to the court, should be returned to the contributors.

But perhaps the most important illustration is to be found in *Oppenheim* v. *Tobacco Securities Trust Co. Ltd.*,[80] where *Re Compton*[81] was applied. Here, trustees were directed under a settlement to apply moneys in providing for the education of children of employees or ex-employees of British American Tobacco or any of its subsidiary or allied companies. The employees numbered

---

[74] The H.L. preferred it in *Scottish Burial Reform and Cremation Society* v. *Glasgow City Corporation* [1968] A.C. 138 and the C.A. preferred it in *Incorporated Council of Law Reporting for England and Wales* v. *Att.-Gen* [1972] Ch. 73.

[75] Another requirement to be satisfied is that the trust be exclusively charitable: see *post*, p. 217.

[76] See *post*, p. 195.

[77] *Re Hummeltenberg* [1923] 1 Ch. 237; *National Anti-Vivisection Society* v. *I.R.C.* [1948] A.C. 31; *Re Wootton* [1968] 1 W.L.R. 681.

[78] [1945] Ch. 123.

[79] [1946] Ch. 194.

[80] [1951] A.C. 297; applied, *I.R.C.* v. *Educational Grants Association Ltd.* [1967] Ch. 993, C.A. (up to 85 per cent. of income of educational trust paid to children of employees of Metal Box Ltd.: income tax not recoverable because income not applied for charitable purposes only).

[81] *Supra.*

over 110,000. The House of Lords held (Lord MacDermott dissenting) that, although the group of persons indicated was numerous, the nexus between them was employment by a particular employer and it therefore followed that the trust did not satisfy the test of public benefit which was required to establish it as charitable. It was argued that the court should take into account the number of employees, but this was rejected by the majority. As Lord Normand said,[82] if there is no public element to be found in the bare nexus of common employment all attempts to build up the public element out of circumstances which had no necessary relation with it but were adventitious, accidental or variable must be unavailing where the settlor has chosen to define the selected class solely by the attribute of common employment. Putting this more generally, an aggregate of individuals ascertained by reference to some personal tie (*e.g.* blood or contract), such as the relations of a particular individual, the members of a particular family, the members of a particular association, does not amount to the public or a section thereof for the purpose of the general rule and will not, accordingly, rank as legally charitable.[83]

It has been said that Lord MacDermott dissented in *Oppenheim's* case. He said[84] that he saw "much difficulty in dividing the qualities or attributes, which may serve to bind human beings into classes, into two mutually exclusive groups, the one involving individual status and purely personal, the other disregarding such status and quite impersonal. As a task this seems to me no less baffling and elusive than the problem to which it is directed, namely, the determination of what is and what is not a section of the public for the purposes of this branch of the law." More recently, in *Dingle* v. *Turner*[85] Lord Cross of Chelsea was of the same opinion. Moreover, he felt that whether or not the potential beneficiaries of a trust could fairly be said to constitute a section of the public was "a question of degree" and depended on the purpose of the trust. This sort of formulation, however, seems to be no more helpful, perhaps less helpful, in the present state of the law than the old formulation based on the distinction between personal and impersonal relationship.

However, if the trust is construed so as to grant a mere preference to a limited class, such as employees or relations, the trust will succeed as a charity. It succeeded, for example, in *Re Koettgen's Will Trusts*,[86] where a trust was established for the furtherance of the commercial education of British-born persons, with a direction that preference be given to employees of a particular firm. The essential question is whether or not it is a mere expression of preference. If it goes beyond that and amounts to a positive obligation the trust will not be regarded as charitable because the obligation will vitiate the public character of the trust. And it is certainly possible to argue on this basis, as it has

---

[82] *Ibid.* at pp. 310–311.
[83] *Re Scarisbrick* [1951] Ch. 622 at p. 649, *per* Jenkins L.J. See also *Re Compton* [1945] Ch. 123.
[84] [1951] A.C. 297 at p. 317.
[85] [1972] A.C. 601 at p. 621.
[86] [1954] Ch. 252.

been argued,[87] that *Re Koettgen's Will Trusts* was wrongly decided. Its validity was indeed doubted by Lord Radcliffe in *Caffoor* v. *Commission of Income Tax, Colombo*,[88] where it was held by the Privy Council that the trust in question was a family trust and not of a public character for charitable purposes. The doubts were repeated by Walton J. in *Re Martin*[89] where a trust to establish a home for old people, with a right for either or both of the testator's daughters to reside there, was held not to be charitable. In essence the question will always be reduced to one of construction.[90]

Overseas charities. A number of major charities carry on part of their activities in foreign countries, and the question which is still not finally settled is whether or how the requirement of public benefit is satisfied in such a case. The essential question is what is meant by the public or a section thereof. The Charity Commissioners appear to have no doubt that the advancement of religion, the advancement of education and the relief of poverty (the first three heads mentioned in *Pemsel's* case[91]) are charitable purposes in whatever part of the world they are carried out; but, with regard to the fourth head of that classification, *i.e.* for other purposes beneficial to the community, such purposes will only be charitable if of benefit to the community of the United Kingdom.[92] The Commissioners concede that benefit to the United Kingdom, when derived from charities carried out overseas, need not be material or direct; accordingly, charities with general humanitarian objects (*e.g.* cancer research) can benefit the community of the United Kingdom even if carried on in foreign countries; but where the purposes are for the local provision of public works or development projects such as roads and irrigation, these will only be charitable "if they are a reasonably direct means to the end of relieving poverty in observable cases."

Such are the views of the Charity Commissioners. There is ample authority of long standing that overseas charities falling within the first three heads of Lord Macnaghten's classification will be charitable[93]; there is little authority, and that conflicting, as to the fourth head. In *Camille and Henry Dreyfus Foundation Inc.* v. *I.R.C.*,[94] Lord Evershed M.R. expressed the opinion, *obiter*, that there should be a benefit to the United Kingdom, whereas in *Re Jacobs*[95] it was held by Foster J. that a gift for the planting of a grove of trees in Israel was a valid

---

[87] See, *e.g.*, *I.R.C.* v. *Educational Grants Association* [1967] Ch. 123.

[88] [1961] A.C. 584 at p. 604. *cf. Re George Drexler Ofrex Foundation Trustees* v. *I.R.C.* [1966] Ch. 675.

[89] *The Times*, November 16, 1977.

[90] For other aspects of "public benefit," particularly in relation to trusts for the advancement of religion and for other purposes beneficial to the community, see *post*, pp. 207, 208.

[91] [1891] A.C. 531 at p. 583.

[92] Report of the Charity Commissioners for England and Wales for 1963, p. 24.

[93] See, *e.g. New* v. *Bonaker* (1867) L.R. 4 Eq. 655 (education); *Re Norman* [1947] Ch. 349 (religion); *Re Robinson* [1931] Ch. 122 (relief of disabled foreign soldiers: to be equated for this purpose with relief of poverty); *Re Niyazi's Will Trusts* [1978] 1 W.L.R. 910 (relief of poverty in Cyprus).

[94] [1954] Ch. 672 at p. 684.

[95] (1970) 114 S.J. 515.

charitable gift.[96] The latter decision is plainly in conflict with the views of the Charity Commissioners, but is not necessarily wrong. It is not easy to distinguish the fourth head of charity from the other preceding heads in this context. Why, for example, should a missionary trust be charitable but not a trust for public works which will raise standards of living? It should be added that a case like *Keren Kayemeth Le Jisroel Ltd.* v. *I.R.C.*,[97] which might seem to support the Commissioners' opinion,[98] is not directly in point. In this case a company had been formed with the main object of purchasing land in Palestine, Syria and other parts of Turkey in Asia, and the peninsula of Sinai, for the purpose of settling Jews in such lands. The House of Lords held that the company's objects were not charitable within Lord Macnaghten's fourth head. The reason, however, for so holding was that the court could not identify the community either as the community of all Jews throughout the world or as the community of the Jews in the regions prescribed for the settlement. It was on the ground of lack of "identifiability" and not on grounds of overseas benefit that the case was decided.[99]

The Goodman Committee has recommended that no distinction should be drawn between charitable activity by English charities at home or abroad; any object which is charitable at home should also be considered as charitable when carried out abroad.[1]

A separate question concerns the status of foreign charities. These cannot acquire charitable status here, for the simple reason that the law of charity in the foreign country may be different from ours.[2]

2. *The Poverty Exception*

The principle that a trust should have a public element is not of absolutely universal application. There is, as indicated above, one important exception to it. This is that trusts for the relief of poverty have been held to be charitable even though they are not for the benefit of the public or a section of it. The exception may arise where the personal tie is one of blood or contract. In the case of

---

[96] As promoting agriculture: see *I.R.C.* v. *Yorkshire Agricultural Society* [1928] 1 K.B. 61, applied in *Brisbane City Council* v. *Att.-Gen. for Queensland* [1979] A.C. 411, P.C. (show-ground); and see *Re Hadden* [1932] 1 Ch. 133.

[97] [1932] A.C. 650.

[98] The Commissioners do not, however, cite any authorities for their views.

[99] See also *Williams' Trustees* v. *I.R.C.* [1947] A.C. 447, which involved an institute for the moral, social and spiritual welfare of Welsh people in London. Lord Simonds held that the difficulty of finding the community of Welsh people was not less than the difficulty of finding the community of Jews in *Keren Kayemeth Le Jisroel* v. *I.R.C.*

[1] The Goodman Committee, however, states that if the overseas activities of the charity are contrary to the public interest of the U.K., there should be a procedure whereby the Foreign Office could make an order requiring the charity to stop that activity (p. 36).

[2] The Goodman Committee has recommended (p. 37) that the law governing foreign charities should remain as it is, but consideration should be given to allowing such charities to register in this country if certain conditions (*e.g.* satisfying the Charity Commissioners that the objects are charitable in English law and filing accounts here) are satisfied and mutual arrangements can be made by international convention. See also the works cited at p. 191 n.68 *ante*.

blood, there are the so-called "poor relations" cases. The case of contract may be exemplified by a trust for the relief of poverty amongst employees of a particular firm or company.

This particular exception cannot be accounted for by reference to any principle,[3] but it was established by authorities of long standing which were binding on the Court of Appeal, and were reaffirmed by the House of Lords in *Dingle* v. *Turner*.[4] In that case there was a trust to apply income in paying pensions to poor employees of a company. It was held that the trust was charitable.

The class of persons within the expression "poor relations" is self-evident[5]: but cases such as *Dingle* v. *Turner* and *Gibson* v. *South American Stores (Gath & Chaves) Ltd.*[6] where a gift to employees of a particular company to whom a poverty qualification was attached was upheld as a valid charitable gift illustrate the contractual tie. And the principle was applied in *Re Young*[7] to members of a club and in *Spiller* v. *Maude*[8] to members of a society. It was argued in *Dingle* v. *Turner* that the tests postulated in *Re Compton*[9] and *Oppenheim* v. *Tobacco Securities Trust Ltd.*[10] ought, in principle, to apply to all charitable trusts and that the "poor relations" cases, the "poor members" cases and the "poor employees" cases were all anomalous and should be overruled; or if it were not practicable to overrule the "poor relations" cases because of their antiquity the same could not be said of the "poor employees" cases which dated only from 1900.[11] But it was held that the "poor members" and "poor employees" decisions were a natural development of the "poor relations" cases and to draw a distinction between them would be quite illogical; and, moreover, although not as old as poor relations trusts, poor employees trusts had been recognised for many years, and there would be a large number of such trusts in operation today.[12] The exception will not, however, be extended to other classes of trusts.[13]

It was also decided by the Court of Appeal in *Re Scarisbrick*[14]—and this did not appear to have been expressly decided before—that the exception was not restricted to perpetual or continuing trusts (to which it will normally apply) but even covered a trust for immediate distribution. Here a gift for poor members of

---

[3] It has been tentatively suggested that "the relief of poverty is of so altruistic a character that the public benefit may necessarily be inferred" : see *Re Scarisbrick* [1951] Ch. 622 at p. 639, *per* Evershed M.R. But this is not the basis of the case law and in any event seems highly debatable. In *Dingle* v. *Turner* [1972] A.C. 601 it was assumed that the law was anomalous.

[4] [1972] A.C. 601.

[5] See, *e.g. Isaac* v. *Defriez* (1754) Amb. 595; *White* v. *White* (1802) 7 Ves. 423; *Att.-Gen.* v. *Price* (1810) 17 Ves. 371; *Re Scarisbrick* [1951] Ch. 622; *Re Cohen* [1973] 1 W.L.R. 415.

[6] [1950] Ch. 177. See also *Re Coulthurst* [1951] Ch. 661 (officers and ex-officers of bank).

[7] [1955] 1 W.L.R. 1269.

[8] (1881) 32 Ch.D. 158n.

[9] [1945] Ch. 123.

[10] [1951] A.C. 297.

[11] *Re Gosling* [1900] 2 W.R. 300.

[12] The Goodman Committee consider that "poor relations" and "poor employees" trusts are not justifiable and should no longer qualify as charitable (p. 17).

[13] *Re Compton, supra* (education); *Oppenheim* v. *Tobacco Securities Trust Ltd., supra* (education); *Davies* v. *Perpetual Trustee Co.* [1959] A.C. 439 (religion).

[14] [1951] Ch. 622.

the class of relations of three children of the testatrix was upheld as a valid charitable trust, although the distribution of the property had to be made within the perpetuity period.

3. *Limits to Public Benefit*

It is important to notice that although the general rule is (subject to trusts for the relief of poverty) that every charitable trust should have a public element, it is not essential that everybody should be able to avail himself of its benefits. As Viscount Simonds said in *Inland Revenue Commissioners* v. *Baddeley*,[15] there is a distinction "between a form of relief extended to the whole community, yet by its very nature advantageous only to the few and a form of relief accorded to a selected few out of a larger number equally willing and able to take advantage of it." Thus, to illustrate the first class cited by Viscount Simonds—which will create a valid charitable trust—a gift for the benefit of New South Wales soldiers returning after the 1914–18 war was held by the Privy Council in *Verge* v. *Somerville*[16] to be valid; so also will a trust for the erection of a sea wall even though this is perhaps of benefit primarily to persons whose houses front the sea.

In illustration of Viscount Simonds' second class—which will fail as a charity—a gift to Presbyterians who could claim a particular descent failed for this reason in the Privy Council decision in *Davies* v. *Perpetual Trustee Co.*[17] A trust in favour of the Methodists in West Ham and Leyton in *I.R.C.* v. *Baddeley*[17a] also failed.

4. *Lord Macnaghten's Classification*

(1) **Trusts for the relief of poverty**

The Act of 1601 included among its objects the relief of "the aged, impotent and poor." But although the word "and" was used it became well-settled that the expression should be read disjunctively.[18] This rule was confirmed in *Re Robinson*[19] where there was a gift to the old over 65 years of a certain district: and in *Re Lewis*,[20] where there was a gift for 20 blind children of another district. Both gifts were upheld. The question was most recently considered in *Joseph Rowntree Memorial Trust Housing Association Ltd* v *Att.-Gen.*[20a] where Peter Gibson J., although confirming the disjunctive reading, added a significant rider, which did not appear from the cases previously cited, namely, that in order to be charitable, the gift to the beneficiaries (the aged or the impotent) had to have as its purpose the relief of a need attributable to their

---

[15] [1955] A.C. 572 at p. 592. The case is considered *post*, p. 209.

[16] [1924] A.C. 496.

[17] [1959] A.C. 439.

[17a] See n. 15.

[18] *Re Fraser* (1883) 22 Ch.D. 827; *Re Elliott* (1910) 102 L.T. 528; *Re Glyn* (1950) 66 T.L.R. (Pt. 2) 510; *Re Cottam* [1955] 1 W.L.R. 1299; and see also the cases cited in the text.

[19] [1951] Ch. 198.

[20] [1955] Ch. 104.

[20a] [1983] 2 W.L.R. 284.

condition. It is hoped that this approach will finally scotch the theory that a trust for the relief of "aged peers" or "impotent millionaires" will be charitable.[20b] A gift of money to such persons would not relieve a need of theirs as aged or impotent persons. In the case itself, a charitable housing association wished to build small self-contained dwellings for sale to elderly people on long leases in consideration of a capital payment. It was held that since the provision of special accommodation relieved a particular need of the elderly, whether poor or not, attributable to their aged condition, the proposed housing schemes were charitable. Peter Gibson J., in reaching this conclusion, applied the reasoning of Lord Wilberforce in *Re Resch's Will Trusts*,[20c] which concerned a private hospital which charged substantial fees but was not run for the profit of individuals. A gift to the hospital was held to be charitable.

The next question is, what is meant by the words "aged," "impotent" and "poor" in this context? First, what is meant by "poverty"? It is clear that the degree of poverty need not be acute. It is unnecessary to show destitution. Accordingly gifts for such objects as "ladies of limited means"[21] or "decayed actors"[22] and similar purposes are well recognised as being charitable. All that seems to be required is that the individuals in question be in straitened circumstances and unable to maintain a modest standard of living.[23] But it is essential that all the objects fall within the designation "poor" if a trust for the relief of poverty is to be upheld. If someone who is not poor is able to benefit, the gift will fail as a gift for the relief of poverty. Thus, in *Re Gwyon*[24] a fund was directed to be set aside to provide "knickers" (by which was meant a type of short trouser) for the boys of Farnham. The garments were unusual not only in their name but also because there were to be embroidered on the waistband the words "Gwyon's Present." Successful applicants were to be entitled to a new pair of knickers each year provided that on the subsequent application the legend "Gwyon's Present" was still decipherable on the old ones. Whatever may have been the testator's intention none of these conditions *necessarily* imported poverty, and the trust failed as a charity. Moreover it was held in *Re Sanders' Will Trusts*[25] that a gift for the "working classes" was not a gift for the relief of poverty because this expression did not necessarily indicate poor persons. It is possible, as Harman J. said—and indeed it has been so held[26]— that if the gift had been made to members of the "working classes" who were aged or widows, then the object of relieving poverty might be implied. But in *Re Sanders*, as Harman J. made plain, there was nothing of this kind. The members

---

[20b] (1955) 71 L.Q.R. 16 (R.E.M.)

[20c] [1969] 1 A.C. 514, P.C.; and see *Re Neal* (1966) 110 Sol. Jo. 549

[21] *Re Gardom* [1914] 1 Ch. 662.

[22] *Spiller* v. *Maude* (1881) 32 Ch.D. 158n.

[23] See *Re Mary Clark Homes* [1904] 2 K.B. 645; *Re Gardom* [1914] 1 Ch. 662; *Shaw* v. *Halifax Corporation* [1915] 2 K.B. 170; *Re Clarke* [1923] 2 Ch. 407; *Re De Carteret* [1933] Ch. 103. See also Cross (1956) 72 L.Q.R. 182 at p. 206.

[24] [1930] 1 Ch. 225.

[25] [1954] Ch. 265 (appeal settled, *The Times*, July 22, 1954).

[26] *Re Glyn* (1950) 66 T.L.R. (Pt. 2) 510; see also *Re Cottam* [1955] 1 W.L.R. 1299 (provision of flats for aged).

of the working class were not old persons, they were not widows, they were simply men working in the docks and their families. It was, therefore, impossible to infer any element of poverty. This case was, however, distinguished in *Re Niyazi's Will Trusts*[27] where a trust for a working men's hostel in Famagusta, Cyprus, providing modest accommodation for persons of the lower income group, was upheld as charitable, although, in the words of Megarry V.-C., the case was "desperately near the border-line."[28]

There is also no decisive definition of the terms "aged" or "impotent." It has been held that people who are not under the age of 50 are aged.[29] But in view of the advance in medical science this now seems very doubtful. If the settlor wishes to specify an age he may be taking a risk today if the age is lower than 60. The word "impotent" has been generously construed, although never precisely defined. It includes permanent disability,[30] the seriously ill or wounded,[31] and also covers the prevention of cruelty to children.[32]

It is, of course, essential to establish that in the case of relief of poverty there is a trust for the relief of poverty in the proper sense of that expression. The point is that a trust for poor persons may take effect as a private rather than a charitable trust. The distinction is—and this is a matter of construction—whether the gift is for the relief of poverty amongst a particular description of poor people *or* is merely a gift to particular poor persons, the relief of poverty among them being the motive of the gift. In the former case the trust is charitable, in the latter it is private.[33]

Housing Associations. A related question involves housing associations, which provide housing for the "aged, impotent and poor" and which enjoy charitable status because they are within the preamble to the Act of 1601. But it is common to find associations feeling the need to adopt a particular policy of tenant selection, for example, selecting tenants who earn less than the average wage, so as to preserve charitable status. Such a policy may be inconvenient and indeed fail if one or more of the residents are not in fact poor.[34] The Goodman Committee recommended[35] that housing trusts should be charitable even though the trustees take account of the housing need, not merely of the income of the tenant, provided that, to avoid abuse, the association is registered with the Housing Corporation under the Housing Acts and registered with the

---

[27] [1978] 1 W.L.R. 910.

[28] *Ibid.* at p. 915.

[29] *Re Wall* (1889) 42 Ch.D. 510. See also *Re Payling's Will Trusts* [1969] 1 W.L.R. 1595; *Re Armitage* [1972] Ch. 438.

[30] *Re Fraser* (1883) 22 Ch.D. 827; *Re Lewis* [1955] Ch. 104.

[31] *Re Hillier* [1944] 1 All E.R. 486.

[32] *C.I.R.* v. *Pemsel* [1891] A.C. 531 at p. 572; *cf. Re Cole* [1958] Ch. 477; *Re Sahal's Will Trusts* [1958] 1 W.L.R. 1243 and see *post.*

[33] *Re Scarisbrick* [1951] Ch. 622, 650, 651 (*per* Jenkins L.J.); *Dingle* v. *Turner* [1972] A.C. 601 at p. 617 (*per* Lord Cross of Chelsea); *Re Cohen* [1973] 1 W.L.R. 415 at p. 423 (*per* Templeman J.).

[34] *Over-Seventies Housing Association* v. *Westminster London Borough Council* (1974) 230 E.G. 1593.

[35] At p. 32.

Charity Commission. Such difficulties now appear to have been alleviated in some degree by the decision in *Joseph Rowntree Memorial Trust Housing Association Ltd.* v *Att.-Gen.*[35a] It was held that it was not essential that a charitable gift be made solely by way of bounty and, accordingly, the beneficiaries could be required to contribute to its cost. The fact that the housing schemes concerned made provision for special housing for the elderly on a contractual basis did not therefore prevent the schemes from being charitable. It was also held that the possibility that a beneficiary might profit by an increase in value of the property on a subsequent sale by him did not alter the fact that the trusts were charitable.

(2) Trusts for the advancement of education

The general rule is conventionally stated to be that there must be an intention that learning should be imparted, not simply that it should be accumulated. This may now be a somewhat misleading yardstick, because the tendency in many of the cases is to widen the field of "education" in this context. But the conventional meaning appears to have been adopted by Harman J. in *Re Shaw*.[36] Here George Bernard Shaw by his will directed his trustees to use his residuary estate for a number of designated purposes. These included (i) inquiries into how much time per individual scribe would be saved by substituting for the established English alphabet one containing at least 40 letters; (ii) to inquire how many persons were speaking and writing English in the usual form at any moment in the world; (iii) to ascertain the time and labour wasted by the lack of at least 14 unequivocal syllables and estimate the loss of income in British and American currency; and (iv) to employ a phonetic expert to transliterate the testator's play *Androcles and the Lion* into the proposed English alphabet. It was held that the trusts were not charitable for they merely tended to an increase of public knowledge in the advantages of the proposed alternative alphabet: the research and propaganda enjoined by the testator merely tended to the increase of public knowledge in a particular respect, namely, the saving of time and money by the use of the proposed alphabet. There was "no element of teaching or education" combined with this. It was also argued that the trusts were charitable as being in some way beneficial to the community (within the fourth head of Lord Macnaghten's classification). This argument was also rejected because it was highly controversial whether the proposals were in fact beneficial.

The question of the ambit of "education" was given fresh consideration by Wilberforce J. in *Re Hopkins' Will Trusts*.[37] The testatrix had given part of her residuary estate to the "Francis Bacon Society" to be applied towards finding the "Bacon-Shakespeare" manuscripts. One of the main objects of the society

---

[35a] [1983] 2 W.L.R. 284. The facts are stated *ante*, p. 198.
[36] [1957] 1 W.L.R. 729; appeal dismissed by consent on terms that a sum of money should be devoted to these inquiries: [1958] 1 All E.R. 245n.
[37] [1965] Ch. 669. See also *Re Shakespeare Memorial Trust* [1923] 2 Ch. 398 (erection and endowment of a Shakespeare Memorial National Theatre with the object of performing Shakespeare's plays, reviving English classical drama and stimulating the art of acting: good charitable trust).

was "to encourage the general study of the evidence of Francis Bacon's authorship of plays commonly ascribed to Shakespeare." The terms of the will were, therefore, held to mean that the money was to be used to search for manuscripts of plays commonly ascribed to Shakespeare but believed by the testatrix and the society to have been written by Bacon. The judge held that the purposes of search or research for original manuscripts of England's greatest dramatist were within the law's conception of a charitable purpose on two grounds, (i) as being for education and (ii) as being for other purposes beneficial to the community within the fourth head of Lord Macnaghten's classification, because it was a gift for the improvement of this country's literary heritage. He had something to say about Harman J.'s dictum in *Re Shaw* that if the object was merely the increase of knowledge that in itself was not a charitable object unless combined with teaching or education. Wilberforce J. was unwilling to treat these words as meaning that the promotion of academic research was not a charitable purpose unless the researchers were engaged in teaching or education in the conventional sense. Many people would agree with the judge's conclusion that the term "education" should be used in a wide sense, certainly as extending beyond teaching.[38] Wilberforce J. also performed the valuable service of spelling out the requirements that must be satisfied by "research" in order to be charitable, though even this formulation was not expressed to be exhaustive: (i) it must be of educational value to the researcher, or (ii) it must be so directed as to lead to something which will pass into the store of educational material, or (iii) so to improve the sum of communicable knowledge in an area which education may cover, education in this last context extending to the formation of literary taste and appreciation.[39]

This decision might be said to be part of a trend which has broadened the field of "education," from which *Re Shaw* is arguably an aberration. Among many cases which demonstrate how widely the idea of education has been considered,[40] one might instance *Re Dupree's Deed Trusts*[41] where a trust for the encouragement of chess playing among the boys and youths of Portsmouth was upheld as charitable. Again, in *Re Delius*[42] the wife of the composer Delius gave her residuary estate for the advancement of her husband's musical work by means of gramophone recordings, publication of his works and financing of public performances of his work. It was held that the purpose of the trust was to spread the knowledge and appreciation of Delius's work throughout the world and constituted an effective educational charity. It seems rather curious that it

---

[38] *Ibid.* at p. 680.

[39] At p. 680. The Goodman Committee has recommended that "research" should be a charitable object in its own right.

[40] See also *Re Mellody* [1918] 1 Ch. 228 (annual school treat); *Re Cranstoun* [1932] 1 Ch. 537 (preservation of ancient buildings); *Re Spence* [1938] Ch. 96 (collection of arms and antiques); *Re Webber* [1954] 1 W.L.R. 1500 (Boy Scouts); *Re Levien* [1955] 1 W.L.R. 964 (raising musical standards); *Re Koettgen's Will Trusts* [1954] Ch. 252 (commercial education); *Royal Choral Society* v. *I.R.C.* (1943) 112 L.J.K.B. 648 (choral society); *Re Royce* [1940] Ch. 514 (church choir).

[41] [1945] Ch. 16.

[42] [1957] Ch. 299.

was found necessary to point out that the fact that pleasure was an incident of that appreciation or that the effect of the trust was to enhance the reputation of Delius did not prevent this result. More conventionally, the promotion of "art" has also been held to be charitable.[43] But perhaps one of the most striking, if not startling, cases in which education was given an extremely and perhaps unjustifiably wide connotation was *Re Shaw's Will Trusts*[44] where the testatrix, who was the wife of George Bernard Shaw and (it is necessary to add) herself of Irish origin bequeathed the residue of her estate upon trusts (*inter alia*) for the teaching, promotion and encouragement in Ireland of self-control, elocution, oratory, deportment, the arts of personal contact, of social intercourse and the other arts of public and private life. It was held that these somewhat eccentric trusts were wholly educational in character and constituted valid charitable trusts. Much less controversial was *Re South Place Ethical Society*[45] where it was held that the cultivation of a rational religious sentiment was for the advancement of education because a rational sentiment could only be cultivated by educational methods.

As one might expect, trusts for the establishment and support of professorships and lectureships are educational in character[46] but it should also be noticed that satellite purposes such as increasing the stipends of university teachers and fellows of colleges will also be upheld.[47] The same principles apply to schools,[48] colleges and universities,[49] and learned societies and institutions.[50]

It was also held in *Incorporated Council of Law Reporting for England and Wales* v. *Att.-Gen.*[51] that the Council was an educational charity[52]: the preparation of law reports was for the advancement of education because their purpose was to record accurately the development and application of judge-made law and thereby disseminate knowledge of that law. The law, it was held by the Court of Appeal, was properly to be regarded as a science and, therefore, books

---

[43] *Re The Town and Country Planning Act* 1947, *Crystal Palace* v. *Minister of Town and Country Planning* [1951] Ch. 132. But "artistic" is too vague to be charitable: see *Associated Artists Ltd.* v. *I.R.C.* [1956] 1 W.L.R. 752. With regard to "the arts" the Goodman Committee has recommended that their promotion should be a proper charitable object in its own right, not merely as a sub-branch of education.

[44] [1952] Ch. 163.

[45] [1980] 1 W.L.R. 1565. For other aspects of the case see *post*, pp. 205, 209, 222.

[46] *Att.-Gen.* v. *Margaret and Regius Professors at Cambridge* (1682) 1 Vern. 55.

[47] *Case of Christ's College, Cambridge* (1751) 1 W.B.1. 90.

[48] See *The Abbey Malvern Wells Ltd.* v. *Ministry of Local Government and Planning* [1951] Ch. 728, where a girls' school was carried on by a private company, but under a trust deed all dividends were applied for school purposes. The school was held charitable. Danckwerts J. said (at p. 737) that all schools of learning are treated as charitable unless they exist purely as profit-making ventures. *cf. Re Girls Public Day School Trust Ltd.* [1951] Ch. 400 where the school in question was not charitable because shareholders were beneficially interested. See also *post*, pp. 203, 209.

[49] *Case of Christ's College, Cambridge* (1751) 1 W.B.1. 90.

[50] *e.g.* the Royal College of Surgeons: see *Royal College of Surgeons* v. *National Provincial Bank Ltd.* [1952] A.C. 631.

[51] [1972] Ch. 73.

[52] Russell L.J. dissented, so far as the educational aspect was concerned, but all members of the C.A. agreed that it was also charitable as being for the benefit of the community within the fourth head of Lord Macnaghten's classification: see *post*, p. 208.

which were produced for the purpose of enabling it to be studied were published for the advancement of education. It was also held that the fact that the reports were used by the legal profession for the purpose of earning fees did not make the purposes non-charitable. It may be observed that, albeit the Council was carrying on a business, its profits could only be applied in pursuit of the Council's objects. If the profits could have enured for the benefit of the individual members it would not have achieved charitable status.[53]

Another case, which may be thought to have given an equally robust interpretation to educational charity, is *London Hospital Medical College* v. *I.R.C.*,[54] which involved the students' union of the London Hospital. The union was under the control of the medical college, an educational charity, and its objects were to "promote social, cultural and athletic activities amongst the members and to add to the comfort and enjoyment of the students." The question was whether the predominant object of the union was the furtherance of the purposes of the medical college as a school of learning (in which case it was charitable); or whether its objects were the private and personal benefit of those students who were members of the union (in which case it would not be).[55] Brightman J. held that it had no *raison d'être* except to further the educational purposes of the medical college and it was accordingly charitable. What it did and was intended to do, said the judge, was to assist the teaching of medicine by providing those physical, cultural and social outlets which were needed, or at any rate highly desirable, if the art of teaching was to be efficiently performed at the College.[56]

But although, generally speaking, education has been regarded as a conception of some width for the purposes of charity, there are limits beyond which the courts will not go. There is, in the end, a question of degree to be determined, and one might argue that the alphabet trust in *Re Shaw* fell on the wrong side of the line. But a case where the trusts were clearly out of order was *Re Pinion*[57] and this was the decision of the Court of Appeal reversing Wilberforce J. A testator gave his studio and pictures, one of which he attributed to Lely and some of which were painted by himself, his antique furniture, silver, china and other things to be offered to the National Trust to be kept intact in the studio and maintained as a collection. If the National Trust declined the trust, as in fact it did, he authorised the appointment of trustees to carry out the trust. It was acknowledged that a gift to found a public museum may be assumed to be charitable if no-one questions it. But if the utility of the gift was brought in question, as it was here, it was essential to know something of the quality of the

---

[53] *cf.* the cases cited in n. 48, *ante.*

[54] [1976] 1 W.L.R. 613; *cf. Re Bushnell* [1975] 1 W.L.R. 1596 in which a trust for the advancement of "socialised medicine" was held not to be educational: discussed *post,* p. 216. In certain cases trusts for sport may be upheld as educational trusts: see *post,* p. 212.

[55] This was the result in *I.R.C.* v. *City of Glasgow Police Athletic Association* [1953] A.C. 380, discussed *post,* p. 212.

[56] *Ibid.* at pp. 623, 624. It was apparently thought relevant that the London Hospital is on a site adjoining the Whitechapel and Commercial Roads in the East End of London; this was described as a "somewhat remote part of London": *ibid.* at p. 621.

[57] [1965] Ch. 85.

exhibits and for this purpose expert evidence was admissible to assist the court in judging the educational value of the gift.[58] The evidence was to the effect that the collection was of low quality—the Lely was bogus and the testator's own paintings were bad. Among the furniture there were some genuine English and Continental pieces of the seventeenth and eighteenth centuries which might be acceptable as a gift to a minor provincial museum. But, according to the terms of the will, everything had to be exhibited together, and the good things would be stifled by the large number of absolutely valueless pictures and objects. Harman L.J. could conceive of no useful purpose in "foisting on the public this mass of junk."[59] The trust had neither public utility nor educational value and, therefore, failed as a charity.

It is, one would have thought, an elementary proposition that if an institution is devoted to educational purposes (or indeed any other specific charitable purposes) its funds can only be applied to those purposes. Nevertheless the question arose for decision in *Baldry* v. *Feintuck*.[60] In this case the University of Sussex Students Union, which was conceded in argument[61] to be an educational charity, voted to authorise payments to "War on Want," a charitable (but non-educational) organisation and to a campaign of protest against the Government's policy of ending the supply of free milk to schoolchildren, this being political and therefore non-charitable.[62] Brightman J. held that the moneys could not be applied for such purposes.

One of the current controversial questions in the field of education, which requires a mention, concerns the charitable status of independent schools[63]; there is no doubt that many are registered charities. The Expenditure Committee has recommended that in order to be charitable, schools should, "manifestly devote the education they provide towards meeting a range of clear educational needs throughout the whole community,"[64] thereby indicating that many independent schools should lose their charitable status. The Goodman Committee consider, however, that any decision to curtail independent education is a political one; that any such policy should be implemented by political decision; and while independent education continues to exist it should, as a general proposition, remain within the ambit of charity.[65]

(3) Trusts for the advancement of religion

As in the criminal law, so in equity there is a large measure of toleration. Indeed a high degree of toleration was recognised over a hundred years ago in *Thornton* v. *Howe*[66] where Sir John Romilly M.R. recognised as charitable a

[58] For another example of expert evidence being admitted, see *Gilmour* v. *Coats* [1949] A.C. 426 and see *post*, p. 207.
[59] [1965] Ch. 85 at p. 107.
[60] [1972] 1 W.L.R. 552.
[61] See *per* Brightman J. in *London Hospital Medical College* v. *I.R.C.* [1976] 1 W.L.R. 613 at p. 624.
[62] See *post*, p. 215.   [63] See *ante*, p. 202.   [64] *Loc. cit.* at p. xvi.
[65] Making the point that the present system makes a very considerable contribution to the field of education, p. 25.
[66] (1862) 31 Beav. 14.

trust for the publication of the work of Joanna Southcott even though he evidently thought her doctrines to be ridiculous. It would also appear from this case that the advancement of all religions which are "not subversive of all morality"[67] will be held to be charitable. As it happens, there is not a great deal of authority on non-Christian religions,[68] but there seems no reason why all of them should not be recognised. Yet there may be limits to the court's liberality, for the court appears in this context to have taken account only of monotheistic religion. Thus in *Yeap Cheah Neo* v. *Ong Cheng Neo*[69] the Privy Council held that a trust requiring ancestor worship was not charitable. This case is not, however, decisive, and it could be distinguished on the ground that the religious observances enjoined were not for the public benefit, merely for the alleged advantage of the deceased and his family. It would appear that the time has come to recognise formally the major religions of the world, whatever their forms, although in certain cases a line has to be drawn. Increasingly today "fringe" religious organisations have come into being. Some are so fanciful or freakish that public benefit can justly be said to be lacking, and charitable status should not be accorded to them.[70]

Clearly, however, a gift for rationalist purposes—designed to demonstrate that religious belief is erroneous—would not fall within the ambit of a trust for the advancement of religion.[71] Likewise, gifts for ethical or moral societies not founded on belief in a deity are not for the advancement of religion. Nevertheless, they may be held to be charitable on other grounds. The question arose in *Re South Place Ethical Society*[72] which was established for the study and dissemination of "ethical principles" and the cultivation of a rational religious sentiment, but eschewing all supernatural belief. "Ethical principles" were described by Dillon J. as belief in the excellence of truth, love and beauty, but not belief in anything supernatural. It was held that the Society was not founded for the advancement of religion because, in the words of the judge, "religion . . . is concerned with man's relations with God, and ethics are concerned with man's relations with man."[73] The objects of the Society were, however, upheld as charitable on other grounds, first, they were for the mental

---

[67] *Ibid.* at p. 20. This principle was applied by Plowman J. in *Re Watson* [1973] 1 W.L.R. 1472 in upholding a trust for the publication and distribution of religious writings of no intrinsic merit but which displayed a religious tendency, and by Walton J. in *Holmes* v. *Att.-Gen.* (1981) Ch. Com. Rep. 10 in upholding a trust for the Exclusive Brethren. The correctness of Romilly M.R.'s statement of principle in *Thornton* v. *Howe*, however, still remains open to review by the court. See also *Bowman* v. *Secular Society Ltd.* [1917] A.C. 406.

[68] But see *Straus* v. *Goldsmid* (1837) 8 Sim. 614 (trust for practice of Jewish religion valid); *Neville Estate Ltd.* v. *Madden* [1962] Ch. 832 (trust for Catford synagogue valid).

[69] (1875) L.R. 381. See also *Re Hummeltenberg* [1923] 1 Ch. 237 (gift to college for training spiritualistic mediums); *Re Price* [1943] Ch. 422 (gift to the "Anthroposophical Society"). Neither case fell within trusts for the advancement of religion, and could only be considered under the fourth head of Lord Macnaghten's classification. The former was held invalid; the latter valid.

[70] The Goodman Committee consider that religious organisations detrimental to the moral welfare of the community should be excluded (p. 23).

[71] *Bowman* v. *Secular Society Ltd.* [1917] A.C. 406.   [72] [1981] 1 W.L.R. 1565.

[73] *Ibid.* at p. 571. It was noted (at p. 573) that Buddhism was accepted as a religion although there was no belief in a god, but that question was not explored further.

and moral improvement of man and were, therefore, beneficial to the community within the fourth head of Lord Macnaghten's classification,[74] and secondly, they were for the advancement of education.[75]

Quite apart from gifts for the advancement of a religion or a religious sect as such, a number of satellite purposes have been recognised as charitable under this head, notably gifts for mission work. Thus in *Re Moon's Will Trusts*[76] a bequest for "mission work" was made. The expression was held on the evidence to connote "Christian mission work" and that was held to be charitable. Similarly, trusts for the maintenance and repair of a church, a stained glass window[77] or vault[78] within the church have been held to be charitable; and the same will apply to the churchyard and burial ground even if restricted to a particular religious sect[79] and also to the graves in it, provided that the maintenance of *all* the graves is the object for the gift.[80] Indeed cremation has also been held to be a charitable purpose.[81]

It is essential that the purpose of a trust should be exclusively charitable, and this rule applies generally in the law, subject to the Charitable Trusts (Validation) Act 1954.[82] In this context, therefore, the purpose of the trust should be exclusively religious. A draftsman may easily say quite unwittingly far too much—even by a word or two—in the trust instrument. The cases on the question whether a trust is exclusively religious are difficult and present several fine distinctions. Normally, a gift will be made to a person holding a religious office, such as a bishop, and the additional words that may permissibly be used to create a valid charitable trust appear to fall into two groups:

(1) They may give an absolute discretion to the donee. In *Re Garrard*,[83] a gift was made "to the vicar and churchwardens of Kingston to be applied by them in such manner as they shall in their sole discretion think fit." Similarly, in *Re Rumball*[84] a gift was made "to the bishop for the time being of the Windward Islands to be applied by him as he thinks fit in his diocese." In both cases, as in several others,[85] where an absolute discretion was conferred, the gift was

---

[74] See *post*, p. 209.

[75] See *ante*, p. 202. The Goodman Committee recommended that ethical and moral societies not founded on belief in a deity should be recognised as charitable on the basis that they promote the moral improvement of the community.

[76] [1948] 1 All E.R. 300.

[77] *Re King* [1923] 1 Ch. 243. See also *Re Royce* [1940] Ch. 514.

[78] *Hoare* v. *Osborne* (1886) L.R. 1 Eq. 585.

[79] *Re Manser* [1905] 1 Ch. 68 (Society of Friends).

[80] *Re Pardoe* [1906] 2 Ch. 184; in this case a gift for a peal of bells on the anniversary of the restoration of the monarchy also held to be charitable: *sed quaere, cf.* Brunyate (1946) 61 L.Q.R. 268, 274; *Re Eighmie* [1935] Ch. 524 (keeping in repair burial ground *and* monument to testator's late husband) and see *ante*, p. 176).

[81] *Scottish Burial Reform and Cremation Society Ltd.* v. *Glasgow Corporation* [1968] A.C. 138.   [82] See *post*, p. 219.   [83] [1907] 1 Ch. 382.

[84] [1956] Ch. 105. The judgment of Jenkins L.J. is a notable exposition of the law.

[85] See *Re Simson* [1946] Ch. 299 (to the Vicar of St.Luke's, Ramsgate, to be used for work in the parish: valid); *cf. Farley* v. *Westminster Bank* [1939] A.C. 430, *infra* ("for parish work" : bad): *Re Flinn* [1948] Ch. 241 (to the Archbishop of Westminster Cathedral to be used by him "for such purposes as he shall in his absolute discretion think fit" : valid). See also *Re Norman* [1947] Ch. 349 (to the editors of a missionary periodical who were also trustees of a missionary church, to be applied "for such objects as they may think fit" : valid).

upheld as charitable. The reason was that the gift was made to a person by his official name whose official status required charitable duties to be performed. Accordingly, the gift was assumed to be made for the charitable purposes inherent in that official status. This principle which arises *virtute officii* applies not merely to religious persons but to the holders of other offices.

(2) The words confine the object of the gift within the ambit of the donee's religious function. For example, in *Re Eastes*[86] there was a gift "to the vicar and churchwardens, to be used by them for any purpose *in connection with the Church*[87] which they shall select." This gift was upheld. But if the testator goes on to invite the donee to take into account the *social* as well as the religious functions of his office, the gift will fail. Here the settlor may unconsciously say too much. This principle—though it may be no more than apparent—is illustrated by the leading case of *Dunne* v. *Byrne*[88] where a gift was made to the Roman Catholic Archbishop of Brisbane and his successors to be used as they *may judge most conducive to the good religion in the diocese.* The italicised words were held by the Privy Council to be too wide and the gift failed. Perhaps the most notorious words to induce fatality are "parish work": a gift failed for this reason in the well-known decision of the House of Lords in *Farley* v. *Westminster Bank.*[89]

What has been said so far represents an attempt at rationalising some of the case law. But the reader should be warned that these cases are difficult and depend on a close reading of the gift or trust. And at times to recognise the distinction between any two cases decided differently requires hair-splitting which seems excessive.[90]

Public benefit.[91] Like other charitable trusts—with the exception of trusts for the relief of poverty—a religious trust must be for the benefit of the public. It is no doubt a difficult task to assess public benefit in a religious trust. Nevertheless the test has to be satisfied. Thus, in the controversial decision in *Gilmour* v. *Coats*,[92] the trust fund was to be applied to the purposes of a Carmelite convent. The convent comprised an association of strictly cloistered and purely contemplative nuns who did not engage in any activities for the benefit of people

---

[86] [1948] Ch. 257. See also *Re Bain* [1930] 1 Ch. 224 (to a vicar "for such objects connected with the church as he shall think fit"); *Re Norton's Will Trusts* [1948] 2 All E.R. 842 ("for the benefit of the parish" : *cf. Farley* v. *Westminster Bank, supra*).

[87] Our italics.   [88] [1912] A.C. 407.

[89] [1939] A.C. 430. The words "parochial institutions or purposes" were also fatal in *Re Stratton* [1931] 1 Ch. 197.

[90] See cases cited in nn. 85 and 86, *supra*.

[91] See Newark (1946) 62 L.Q.R. 234.

[92] [1949] A.C. 426. Likewise see *Cocks* v. *Manners* (1871) L.R. 12 Eq. 574 (enclosed Roman Catholic convent); *Hoare* v. *Hoare* (1886) 56 L.T. 147 (private chapel): *Re Joy* (1889) 60 L.T. 175 (to suppress cruelty to animals by prayer); *Re Warre's Will Trusts* [1953] 1 W.L.R. 725 (retreat house; but this case seems to have been wrongly decided: retreatants do mix in the world: they go into retreat only for a few days' contemplation and prayer). *cf. Neville Estates Ltd.* v. *Madden* [1962] Ch. 832 discussed in the text. *cf.* also *Re Banfield* [1968] 1 W.L.R. 846, where the gift was to a religious community ("Pilsdon Community House") and Goff J. held this to be a charitable trust because of its primarily religious character and also because it was for the general public benefit in providing a temporary home of rest for those who need it.

outside the convent. The House of Lords held that (i) the benefit of intercessory prayer could not be proved in law and (ii) the element of edification was too vague and intangible. One might think that far too stringent a test of public benefit was applied in this case.[93] However, whether this is so or not, it is distinguishable from a case like *Neville Estates Ltd.* v. *Madden.*[94] This involved Catford synagogue which was not open to the public as of right, and Cross J. held that a trust in favour of the synagogue was charitable. The distinction is that the enclosed nuns lived apart from the world, whereas the members of the synagogue lived in the world, and a public benefit accrued as a result of their attendance at a place of religious worship.

Rather different considerations have been applied to trusts for masses for the dead.[95] Luxmoore J. in *Re Caus*[96] held that a gift for such purposes was charitable. There was no provision in the testator's will in this case that the masses should be said in public; and the judge did not distinguish between masses said in public and those said in private. Indeed he seemed to indicate that a gift for masses was in all cases charitable. In view of *Gilmour* v. *Coats* this seems to be wrong. A gift for masses in public clearly promotes public worship and is valid, but not a gift for masses in private for that is not for a public purpose and should, therefore, not be charitable.

(4) Trusts for other purposes beneficial to the community

This is the residuary class in Lord Macnaghten's classification in *Pemsel's* case. It has been seen that the modern trend appears to be to look to the "equity" or the "mischief" of the preamble to the Statute of Elizabeth I, in order to decide whether a given purpose falls within it, rather than rely on the approach based upon analogy.[97] The class certainly presents a most variegated collection of decisions and the following does not profess to be an exhaustive account, but merely illustrations of a number of the purposes allowed admission into this class.[98]

(a) **Animals.** It is clearly established that a trust for the protection of animals generally is a valid charitable trust.[99] This is so, as it has been held, because it benefits humanity by promoting morality and curbing an inborn tendency to cruelty[1]—a somewhat surprising process of reasoning even in an animal-loving

---

[93] The Goodman Committee has suggested that contemplative communities do not normally have proper charitable objects, but a value judgment has to be made in each case.

[94] [1962] Ch. 832; and see *Holmes* v. *Att.-Gen.* (1981) Ch. Com. Rep. 10 (Exclusive Brethren).

[95] It is established that a gift for masses is not void as being for superstitious uses: *Bourne* v. *Kean* [1919] A.C. 815. The question remains however whether it is charitable.

[96] [1934] Ch. 162; but see *Gilmour* v. *Coats, supra,* at pp. 447, 454, 460 which indicates that *Re Caus* may not be followed in the future.

[97] See, *e.g. Scottish Burial Reform and Cremation Society* v. *Glasgow City Corporation* [1968] A.C. 138; *Incorporated Council of Law Reporting for England and Wales* v. *Att.-Gen.* [1972] Ch. 73; and see *ante,* p. 202.

[98] For a detailed treatment, see *Tudor on Charities* (6th ed.), pp. 68 *et seq.*

[99] *Re Wedgwood* [1915] 1 Ch. 113 (secret trust for protection and benefit of animals).

[1] *Re Wedgwood, ibid.* at p. 117, *per* Lord Cozens-Hardy M.R.; *Re Moss* [1949] 1 All E.R. 415 at pp. 497–498, *per* Romer J. (cats and kittens); *cf.* earlier cases *e.g. London University* v. *Yarrow* (1857) 1 De G. & J. 72 (animal hospital) and *Re Douglas* (1887) 35 Ch.D. 472 (Home for Lost Dogs): the court emphasised public utility but this is not the modern trend; *cf.* also "Trusts of imperfect obligation," *ante,* p. 177.

country. But, however surprising, it indicates that the reason for the recognition of these trusts is that they promote the moral or spiritual welfare of the community whereas the basis of most other examples of Lord Macnaghten's fourth head is "public utility."[2]

A second proposition, which arises from the decision of a particular case, *Re Grove-Grady*,[3] is that if the settlor establishes a trust to provide a sanctuary for all kinds of animals from human molestation with no safeguards against the destruction of the weaker animals by the stronger, the trust is not charitable. As Lord Hanworth M.R. pointed out[4] the one characteristic of the trust was that the sanctuary was to be free from molestation by man, while all the fauna within it were to be free to molest and harry one another. And such a purpose did not afford any advantage to animals or any protection from cruelty to animals; nor did it afford any elevating lesson to mankind.[5]

Thirdly, there is the principle established by the House of Lords in *National Anti-Vivisection Society* v. *I.R.C.*[6] that a trust to abolish vivisection is not charitable. It was so held in this case for two reasons, (i) the advantages accruing from the abolition of vivisection did not equal those derived from its retention and (ii) anti-vivisection could not be achieved except by legislation and (so it was said) the law could not stultify itself by holding that it was for the public benefit that the law itself should be changed.[7]

Finally, it should be noticed that although prima facie an animal hospital is a charity[8] it will not be so if it is carried on for private profit as a profession, occupation or trade.[9]

(b) **Recreational Trusts.** The Recreational Charities Act 1958, which came into force on March 3, 1958, regulates recreational trusts. The Act was passed because of the highly inconvenient decision of the House of Lords in *I.R.C.* v. *Baddeley*[10] which concerned certain trusts "for the promotion of the moral, social and physical well-being of persons resident in West Ham and Leyton who for the time being are members or likely to become members of the Methodist Church . . . by the provision of facilities for moral, social and physical training and recreation." It was decided, by a majority, that the trusts failed because

---

[2] For other examples of "moral or spiritual improvement" see *Re Price* [1943] Ch. 422 (gift to the "Anthroposophical Society"); *Re South Place Ethical Society* [1980] 1 W.L.R. 1565 (society for the study and dissemination of "ethical principles" and the cultivation of a rational religious sentiment: see *ante*, p. 205).

[3] [1929] 1 Ch. 557, compromised on appeal *sub nom. Att.-Gen.* v. *Plowden* [1931] W.N. 89.

[4] *Ibid.* at pp. 573–574.

[5] The main reason for citing this case is to emphasise the importance of careful drafting of the trust instrument, so that the "public benefit" requirement is satisfied. There is no doubt that a competently drawn trust for the preservation of wild life, taking due account of public benefit, will be charitable.

[6] [1948] A.C. 31, reversing *Re Foveaux* [1895] 2 Ch. 501. See also *Re Jenkins's Will Trusts* [1966] Ch. 249 (gift to the British Union for the Abolition of Vivisection).

[7] Adopting *Tyssen on Charitable Bequests* (1st ed., 1898), p. 176. See also *Bowman* v. *Secular Society Ltd.* [1917] A.C. 406 at p. 442 (*per* Lord Parker) (political purposes); and see *post*, p. 215.

[8] *London University* v. *Yarrow* (1857) 1 De G. & J. 72.   [10] [1955] A.C. 572.

[9] See *Re Satterthwaite's Will Trusts* [1966] 1 W.L.R. 277 at p. 284, *per* Russell L.J.

they were expressed in language so vague as to permit the property to be used for purposes which the law did not recognise as charitable and also because they did not satisfy the necessary test of public benefit. This case produced a situation where legislation of some kind was essential because as a result of the decision it appeared that there might be grave doubts as to the charitable status of many organisations and trusts, including women's institutes, boys' clubs, miners' welfare trusts and village halls which, it had been assumed, had enjoyed charitable status for a very long time. The legislation that very promptly followed was the Act of 1958. It provides that it shall be and shall be deemed always to have been charitable to provide, or assist in providing, facilities for recreation or other leisure-time occupations if the facilities are provided in the interest of social welfare.[11] This is subject to the overriding proviso that the trust will not be charitable unless it is for the public benefit.[12] Furthermore the requirement that facilities must be provided in the interest of social welfare is not satisfied unless:

  (a) it is provided with the object of improving the conditions of life for the persons for whom the facilities are primarily intended,[13] *and*
  (b) either (i) those persons have need of such facilities by reason of their youth, age, infirmity or disablement, poverty or social and economic circumstances[14] or (ii) the facilities are to be available to the members or female members of the public at large.[15]

The composition of this part of the Act seems to be somewhat curious. It will be noted in particular that ingredient (ii) is alternative to ingredient (i) and this will mean that a trust must satisfy one or other of them. Accordingly, it appears that a recreational trust in favour of a limited class of the public will be within the Act if the beneficiaries are youthful, aged, infirm, disabled, or their "social and economic circumstances" are such that they have need of the facilities provided. But if the beneficiaries do not fall into these prescribed classes, the facilities must be available to the whole of the public, and a trust in favour of a limited class would fail. There may well be a case for thus confining the objectives of the Act. But it is perhaps unfortunate that the position is not formulated with more precision.

The effect of these provisions (in particular the terms "social welfare" and "conditions of life") was considered by the Court of Appeal in *I.R.C.* v. *McMullen*[16] which concerned the Football Association Youth Trust. It was held (*inter alia*) by the majority that the recreational facilities provided were primarily intended for pupils in schools and universities but they were not provided

---

[11] s.1(1). The expression "social welfare" is used in the General Rate Act 1967, s.40(5), see *ante*, p. 187.
[12] s. 1(1) proviso.
[13] s.1(2)(*a*).
[14] s.1(2)(*b*)(i).
[15] s. 1(2)(*b*)(ii).
[16] [1979] 1 W.L.R. 130; for another aspect of the decision and the facts, see *post*, p. 213. See also Warburton (1980) Conv. 173.

with the object of improving the conditions of life of such pupils: they were provided for those of them who were persuaded to, or did, play football or some other game or sport irrespective of their conditions of life. Therefore, the trusts did not fall within the Act. Bridge L.J. dissented on the ground that the provision of recreational facilities for pupils unquestionably improved the pupils' conditions of life and met a social need of youth. This decision was reversed by the House of Lords on other grounds,[17] so the question of the effect of the Act did not fall to be considered. As a matter of statutory interpretation, however, the opinion of Bridge L.J. appears to be highly persuasive.

Subject to the facilities being provided in the interests of social welfare, the Act is specifically applied, in particular, to the "provision of facilities at village halls, community centres and women's institutes and to the provision and maintenance of grounds and buildings to be used for purposes of recreation or leisure-time occupation and extends to the provision of facilities for those purposes by the organising of any activity."[18] But these are simply well-known examples of recreational charity and this provision will not affect the generality of the statutory powers.

Miners' welfare trusts are specially provided for[19]: such trusts as were declared before December 17, 1957,[20] are validated retrospectively though there are certain savings as to past transactions.[21] Indeed this provision appears to be entirely retrospective so that all *new* miners' trusts must fall within the statutory provisions discussed at the outset.[22]

The Act leaves untouched the existing law as to the meaning of charity.[23] It would also seem to leave untouched the other point—that the trusts must be for the public benefit—which came under consideration in *Baddeley's* case. It appeared, certainly in the opinion of Viscount Simonds,[24] that the membership, actual or potential, of the Methodist Church, at least in a defined area, did not amount to a class sufficient to satisfy the test of public benefit, although Lord Reid, who dissented, took a different view.[25] If the opinion of Viscount Simonds is adopted, trusts such as these would still fail. It was that part of the decision that the trusts were too uncertain which aroused apprehension among the women's institutes and other bodies and which the statute was designed to cure. This limited objective may have been successfully achieved, even though the material provisions are somewhat clumsily and ambiguously expressed. It was thought at the time that it would be difficult to apply and probably create more difficulties than it solved,[26] but only occasionally in the reported cases has it arisen for consideration.[27]

---

[17] [1981] A.C. 1; see *post*, p. 213.   [18] s. 1(3).   [19] s. 2.

[20] This was the day of the first reading of the Bill in the House of Lords.

[21] s. 3(2)(3)(4)(5).

[22] *i.e.* s. 1.   [23] s. 3(1).   [24] *Supra*, at pp. 589–593.

[25] *Supra*, at p. 606. Lord Somervell of Harrow seemed to agree with Lord Simonds; Lord Porter and Tucker expressed no opinion on the point.

[26] See Maurice (1959) 23 Conv.(N.S.) 15.

[27] See, *e.g. Wynn* v. *Skegness U.D.C.* [1967] 1 W.L.R. 52 where a seaside holiday home for Derbyshire miners was assumed to fall within the 1958 Act as a recreational charity; *I.R.C.* v. *McMullen* [1979] 1 W.L.R. 130 C.A, reversed on other grounds [1981] A.C. 1, H.L.; discussed *ante*, p. 210, and *post*, p. 213.

(c) **National and local defence.** All trusts which promote the armed forces of the Crown are charitable[28] and this rule will apply even if the means to the end are indirect.[29] Likewise a trust for the Mercantile Marine, though not strictly part of the armed forces of the Crown, is charitable.[30] A more general purpose of promoting the defence of the United Kingdom from the attack of hostile aircraft has also been upheld.[31]

The same applies to more mundane, but equally important, domestic protection. Thus in *Re Wokingham Fire Brigade Trusts*,[32] Danckwerts J. held that the provision and maintenance of a public fire brigade was a charitable purpose because it was designed to prevent damage to property and loss of life. The promotion of the efficiency of the police is also self-evidently charitable. This was stated in *I.R.C.* v. *City of Glasgow Police Athletic Association*,[33] but in that case the question was whether the association itself was charitable and it was held not to be so because it was simply a sports club for the benefit of the members.

(d) **Trusts for sport.** It appears to be settled that a gift for the promotion of any given sport *simpliciter* is not charitable. Accordingly, in *Re Nottage*,[34] where a trust was established to provide annually a cup for the most successful yacht of the season, the testator stating that his object was to encourage the sport of yacht racing, the Court of Appeal held that that was a gift for the encouragement of a mere sport which, though it might be beneficial to the public, was not charitable.[35] But it should be pointed out that trusts for this purpose, if drawn so as to fall within the Recreational Charities Act 1958,[36] will now be effective. In any case, the provision of prizes for sport in a school was held in *Re Mariette*[37] to be valid as advancing that part of the education of students which had to do with their bodily and physical development. And the same result occurred in *Re Gray*,[38] where there was a gift for the promotion of a sport in an army regiment and it was held to be charitable because it increased the army's efficiency; but the validity of this last decision was doubted in *I.R.C.* v. *City of Glasgow Police Athletic Association*.[39] The doubts appear to be

---

[28] *Re Stratheden and Campbell* [1894] 3 Ch. 265 (benefit of volunteer corps); *Re Stephens* (1892) 8 T.L.R. 792 (for teaching shooting); *Re Barker* (1909) 25 T.L.R. 753 (for prizes to be competed for by cadets).

[29] *Re Good* [1905] 2 Ch. 60 (providing a library for officers' mess and providing plate for mess); *Re Donald* [1909] 2 Ch. 410 (for the mess of regiment and poor of regiment); *Re Gray* [1925] Ch. 362 (regimental fund for promotion of sport).

[30] *Re Corbyn* [1941] Ch. 400.

[31] *Re Driffill* [1950] Ch. 92.

[32] [1951] Ch. 373.

[33] [1953] A.C. 380 at 391.

[34] [1895] 2 Ch. 649.

[35] See also to the same effect *Re Clifford* (1911) 106 L.T. 14 (angling); *Re Patten* [1929] 2 Ch. 276, 289, 290 (cricket); *Re King* [1931] W.N. 232 (general sport); *I.R.C.* v. *City of Glasgow Police Athletic Association* [1953] A.C. 380 (athletic sports and general pastimes: discussed *supra.*)

[36] See *infra.*

[37] [1915] 2 Ch. 284. See also *Re Dupree's Deed Trusts* [1945] Ch. 16 (chess: discussed at p. 201, *ante*).

[38] [1925] Ch. 362.

[39] [1953] A.C. 380 at pp. 391, 401.

unfounded because the army's efficiency is indeed promoted if soldiers are physically fit.[40]

It is clear that the trust instrument has to be construed to decide whether a particular charitable purpose is in fact promoted by the prescribed sporting activity. In *I.R.C.* v. *McMullen*,[41] for example, the legal effect of the Football Association Youth Trust had to be decided. Its object was to organise or provide or assist in the oganisation and provision of facilities which would enable and encourage students at schools and universities to play Association Football or other games and sports and thereby to assist in ensuring that due attention was given to the physical education and development of such pupils as well as the occupation of their minds and, with a view to furthering this object, to providing such facilities as playing fields, equipment, etc. The House of Lords held (unanimously reversing Walton J. and the Court of Appeal) that the purpose of the deed was not merely to organise the playing of Association Football in schools and universities, but also to promote the physical education and development of students as an addition to their formal education and, therefore, it created a valid charitable trust for the advancement of education,[42] the sporting activities contributing to a balanced education. Lord Hailsham of St. Marylebone L.C.[43] was at pains to reject any idea which would cramp the education of the young within the school or university campus, limit it to formal instruction or render it devoid of pleasure in the exercise of skill.[44] The principle in *Re Mariette*[45] was held to apply.

(e) **Locality trusts.** A gift to a locality, such as a town or village, will be charitable even if no charitable purposes are specified.[46] A scheme[47] will be made so that the funds can be devoted to such purposes within the locality as are charitable. It has also been decided that the same principle applies to a gift to "my country, England."[48] That such trusts should be valid as charities seems curious[49] but is now established beyond all possible doubt.[50] But it is most

---

[40] The Goodman Committee has recommended that the encouragement of sport and recreation should be recognised as an independent charitable object, provided that the necessary element of benefit to the community is present, and in so far as the Recreational Charities Act 1958 (see *ante*, p. 209) does not make this clear, then it should be amended.

[41] [1981] A.C. 1.

[42] For consideration of the Recreational Charities Act 1958, see *ante*, p. 210.

[43] A former Secretary of State for Education and Science.

[44] *Ibid.* at p. 18.

[45] *Supra.*

[46] See *Goodman* v. *Saltash Corpn.* (1882) 7 App.Cas. 633; *Re Allen* [1905] 2 Ch. 400; *Re Norton's Will Trusts* [1948] 2 All E.R. 842.

[47] See *post*, p. 223.

[48] *Re Smith* [1932] 1 Ch. 153. See also *Nightingale* v. *Goulbourne* (1847) 5 Hare 484 (gift to "the Queen's Chancellor of the Exchequer for the time being" to be used by him for the benefit of "my beloved country, Great Britain": valid. The case can also be justified on the ground that it was made *virtute officii*, see *ante*, p. 207).

[49] See *Tudor on Charities* (6th ed.), pp. 202 *et seq.* And see *Williams' Trustees* v. *I.R.C.* [1947] A.C. 447 at p. 459, *per* Lord Simonds.

[50] The Goodman Committee considered that local and denominational charities should be permitted to continue and be encouraged, and the same general principles should apply to analogous trusts for ethnic or national groups. With regard to the latter, there is a limited exception in favour of charities in the Race Relations Act 1976: it is provided (s. 34) that any

important, if a locality trust is to be upheld, to ensure that either exclusively charitable purposes within the locality be specified in the trust instrument, or, alternatively, that no purposes whatsoever be specified. If the settlor uses words which demonstrate in terms that the subject-matter of the gift may be used for non-charitable purposes it will fail. It failed, for example, in *Houston* v. *Burns*,[51] where the trust was for "public, benevolent or charitable purposes" in a Scottish parish. If, therefore, the purposes are not charitable *per se*, the localisation of them will not of itself make them charitable.[52]

(f) **Institutional and other charities.** A trust which is designed for a village hall, community centre, or other similar institutional purposes if drawn so as to fall within the Recreational Charities Act 1958[53] will create a valid charitable trust. Trusts for hospitals and other kindred purposes have been upheld as charitable as a matter of general law.[54]

Children's homes. The refinements all too evident in the law of charity were brought to the fore in the controversial and unfortunate decision of the Court of Appeal in *Re Cole*,[55] where the majority held that a gift for "the general benefit and general welfare" of children for the time being in a children's home maintained by a local authority was not charitable. Romer L.J. in particular based his decision to this effect on a close reading of the preamble to the Charitable Uses Act 1601 and concluded that the conceivable provision of benefits, and these could include such new-fangled devices as television sets, for the children in question (who might be juvenile delinquents) were not within the express terms of the preamble or within its spirit and intendment. The decision was followed by Danckwerts J. in *Re Sahal's Will Trusts*[56] on similar facts. But the dissenting view of Lord Evershed M.R. in *Re Cole* seems the

---

discrimination necessary to comply with the terms of the governing instrument of a charity which is established to confer a benefit on persons of a particular racial group shall not be unlawful, but it specifically excludes from the exception any provision which restricts the benefits by reference to race or colour. Accordingly, a school for the education of Pakistanis or Spaniards could lawfully be confined to such persons, but any provision *excepting* persons on racial grounds would be in breach of the Act. There is also an exception in favour of charity under the Sex Discrimination Act 1975. It is provided (s. 43) that where the trusts contain a provision for conferring benefits on one sex only, anything done by the charity trustees to comply with that provision is not unlawful. This safeguards the position of single sex charities, like the Y.M.C.A., Y.W.C.A., Boy Scouts and Girl Guides, and many small parochial charities restricted to one sex (such as elderly widows). See further, the Reports of the Charity Commissioners for 1975 and 1976.

[51] [1918] A.C. 337; see also *Att.-Gen.* v. *National Provincial and Union Bank of England* [1924] A.C. 262 (patriotic purposes in the British Empire). And see *Re Strakosch* [1949] Ch. 529. The matter is discussed generally at p. 217, *post.*

[52] *Williams' Trustees* v. *I.R.C., supra*, at pp. 459–460, *per* Lord Simonds. This case involved an Institute of Welshmen in London which was not charitable because they were not an identifiable section of the community.

[53] See *ante*, p. 209.

[54] See, *e.g. Re Dean's Will Trusts* [1950] 1 All E.R. 882; *Re White Will Trusts* [1951] 1 All E.R. 528; *Re Smith's Will Trusts* [1962] 2 All E.R. 563; *Re Adams* [1967] 1 W.L.R. 162; *Le Cras* v. *Perpetual Trustee Co.* [1967] 1 All E.R. 915, P.C.; *Re Resch's Will Trusts* [1969] A.C. 514, P.C.

[55] [1958] Ch. 877.

[56] [1958] 1 W.L.R. 1243.

more commendable, by reason of its wider outlook: "that the inference to be drawn from the preamble is that the care and upbringing of children who for any reason have not got the advantage or opportunity of being looked after and brought up by responsible and competent persons, or who could by these or other reasons, properly be regarded as defenceless or 'deprived' are matters which prima facie qualify as charitable purposes."[57]

(g) **Political trusts.** In *Bowman* v. *Secular Society Ltd.*[58] Lord Parker of Waddington stated the general position as follows:

> "A trust for the attainment of political objects has always been held invalid, not because it is illegal, for everyone is at liberty to advocate or promote by any lawful means a change in the law, but because the court has no means of judging whether a proposed change in the law will or will not be for the public benefit, and therefore cannot say that a gift to secure the change is a charitable gift."

This basic principle, as has been seen,[59] was applied by the House of Lords in *National Anti-Vivisection Society* v. *I.R.C.*[60] in rejecting as charitable a trust to abolish vivisection as it would involve legislation to change the law, and it was reaffirmed more recently by Slade J. in *McGovern* v. *Att.-Gen.*[61] which concerned the legal status of Amnesty International. The general object of this unincorporated non-profit making body was expressed to be to secure throughout the world the observance of the provisions of the Universal Declaration of Human Rights in regard to various categories of persons referred to in its constitution as "prisoners of conscience," namely, persons who were imprisoned, detained or restricted because of their political, religious or conscientiously held beliefs or their ethnic origin, sex, colour or language. There were also various specific objects of the association the legal effect of which required to be considered: (1) the release of prisoners of conscience: this was held to be for political purposes and, therefore, not charitable because it involved putting pressure on foreign governments to change their policies; (2) the abolition of torture or inhumane treatment or punishment: this was not charitable because it would involve legislation requiring the abolition of corporal or capital punishment; and (3) providing research into the observance of human rights and the dissemination of that research: this would, if it had stood alone, have been charitable; but it did not stand alone: the trusts were required to be exclusively charitable and they were not. Accordingly, they all failed. This decision is an important illustration of the principle that, although a trust for the relief of human suffering or distress may well be capable of being of a charitable nature, it will not qualify if the main object is to secure an alteration in the law or government policy not only of the United Kingdom but also of a foreign

---

[57] [1958] Ch. 877 at p. 892.
[58] [1917] A.C. 406.
[59] See *ante*, p. 209.
[60] [1948] A.C. 31.
[61] [1982] 2 W.L.R. 222.

country. It is, therefore, established that a trust to advance a political purpose will fail as a charity. Such trusts are often disguised as educational trusts, but such educational character as they may have will not enable them to succeed as charities if the primary object is political.[62] This was in effect the position in *McGovern* v. *Att.-Gen.* The trusts also failed for this reason in *Bonar Law Memorial Trust* v. *I.R.C.*[63] and in *Re Hopkinson*,[64] Conservative and Labour Party trusts respectively.

These last two mentioned cases were applied in *Re Bushnell*,[65] where the testator had directed a fund to be used "for the advancement and propagation of the teaching of socialised medicine," with directions on how the managers of the fund should carry out and foster this purpose. Goulding J. held that the trust could not be supported as an educational trust: the directions with regard to the principles of "socialised medicine" dominated the whole of the trust. It was also held that the trust was not beneficial to the community (within the fourth head of Lord Macnaghten's classification in *Pemsel's* case) since validity or otherwise had to be tested at the date of the testator's death (in this case in 1941), and at that date the court could not have decided the question because it involved considering the desirability or otherwise of legislation to bring a state health service into being, which would be a political matter. The fact that a state health service was subsequently introduced was irrelevant; the trust had to stand or fall by the character of the objects at the date of the testator's death.

It should be stressed that the mere existence of some political motive is not necessarily fatal to a good charitable trust. The question is whether its leading purpose is political (*e.g.* promoting legislation to change the law), in which case it fails, or whether the purpose is subsidiary. The point was made by Lord Normand in *I.R.C.* v. *National Anti-Vivisection Society*[66] In that case the primary purpose of the Society was political—as were the objects of Amnesty International in *McGovern* v. *Att.-Gen.* It is by no means easy to distinguish the earlier decision of Stirling J. in *Re Scowcroft*,[67] where it was held that a gift for the maintenance of a village club and reading-room "to be used for the furtherance of Conservative principles and religious and mental improvement, and to be kept free from intoxicants and dancing" was good. But it may perhaps be distinguishable on the ground on which the case was apparently decided, that all the purposes prescribed were to be carried out simultaneously, and the political purpose was not, therefore, predominant.

A recent development in charity law and administration is, as the Charity Commissioners have pointed out,[68] the increasing desire of charities for "involvement" in the causes with which their work is connected, for example, housing and other services for the under-privileged in society. *McGovern* v.

---

[62] See *Bowman* v. *Secular Society Ltd.* [1917] A.C. 406.
[63] (1933) 49 T.L.R. 220.
[64] [1949] 1 All E.R. 346.
[65] [1975] 1 W.L.R. 1596.
[66] [1948] A.C. 31 at p. 76, and see *ante*, p. 209.
[67] [1898] 2 Ch. 638.
[68] Report of the Charity Commissioners for England and Wales for 1969, p. 5; see also Report for 1981, p. 19.

Att.-Gen. is an example of the problem in the international arena, but many charities operating in this country also feel that merely to relieve distress in particular cases is not enough. They wish to go further: to draw the attention of the public as forcefully as they can to the need for action to remedy certain social conditions. And the result has been that pressure groups, action groups and lobbies have come into being. The problem is whether such activities are of such a "political" nature as to vitiate the charitable status of the organisation in question. The Charity Commissioners in their Report for 1981 suggested fairly detailed guidelines for charity trustees in these circumstances. These include[69] the following : (i) a charity should undertake only those activities which can reasonably be said to be directed to achieving its purposes and which are within the powers conferred by its governing instrument; (ii) the governing instrument should not include powers to exert political pressure except in a way that is merely ancillary to a charitable purpose; (iii) the powers and purposes of a charity should not include power to bring pressure to bear on the Government to adopt, alter or maintain a particular line of action; (iv) the charity should spend its money on the promotion of public general legislation only if in doing so it is exercising a power which is ancillary to and in furtherance of its charitable purposes; (v) if the objects include the advancement of education, care should be taken not to overstep the boundary between education and propaganda; (vi) if the objects include research, the charity must aim for objectivity and balance; and (vii) charities whether operating in this country or overseas, must avoid (a) seeking to influence or remedy those causes of poverty which lie in the social, economic and political structures of countries or communities,[70] (b) bringing pressure to bear on a government to procure a change in policies or administrative practices and (c) seeking to eliminate social, economic, political or other injustice.

(h) **Trusts for the environment.** Trusts for the protection of the environment and the conservation of the national heritage have become increasingly active. Such trusts are analogous to the public works referred to in the preamble to the Act of 1601.[71] They often appear to be involved in the area of politics, but provided that the political activity carried on by the trustees is ancillary to and not the main object of the trust they would appear to be unobjectionable.[72]

V. THE EXCLUSIVE NATURE OF CHARITY

It is essential, subject to the Charitable Trusts (Validation) Act 1954, where it applies, that the trustees be bound to devote the funds to charitable purposes,

---

[69] For further details, see the Report for 1981 pp. 19–22. Guidelines had been suggested earlier : see the Report for 1969.

[70] See the Report for 1981 (pp. 22–23) for the Commissioners' criticism of the "political" activities of War on Want.

[71] The preamble refers to the repair of bridges, ports, havens, causeways, sea banks and highways.

[72] See *ante*, p. 215. The Goodman Committee (p. 34) has recommended that environmental trusts should continue to enjoy charitable status and that their scope should be widened (*e.g.* so as to deal with the method of development of the environment).

even if these are expressed not specifically, but in a general way. For example, the settlor may join the word "charitable" with another adjective, such as "benevolent," "patriotic," "philanthropic." It might be thought that if the word "and" is used, *e.g.* "for charitable *and* benevolent purposes," the gift would succeed because it could only be applied to such benevolent purposes as are charitable. It might also be thought that if the word "or" is used, *e.g.* "for charitable *or* benevolent purposes," the gift would fail because the property could be applied to "benevolent" purposes which are not charitable. What is thought in the case of "and" and "or" may well turn out to be correct, but one cannot only rely on this being so. It is entirely a question of construction: the word "and" may have been used disjunctively and the word "or" conjunctively.[73] There is a great deal of authority on "and/or."[74] Two leading cases, both of the House of Lords, may be mentioned briefly to emphasise the rule that a trust fund must be capable of being devoted exclusively to charitable purposes, and in which the word "or" was given its normal disjunctive meaning. In *Houston* v. *Burns*[75] the gift was made for "public benevolent or charitable" purposes in a Scottish parish. The gift failed as not being charitable because the words were wide enough to justify the trustees in disposing of the fund to non-charitable purposes. But the case which brought home the effect of this rule with a vengeance was *Chichester Diocesan Fund and Board of Finance (Inc.)* v. *Simpson*.[76] The words used were "charitable or benevolent" and the same result as in *Houston* v. *Burns* occurred. Here the trustees had paid the money, which was considerable, to various charities, not anticipating litigation by the next-of-kin, which in fact occurred. Their case to recover the money from the charities themselves also went to the House of Lords in the leading case of *Re Diplock*.[77]

1. *Apportionment*

It should be remembered, however, that a settlor may direct an apportionment of the funds between charitable and non-charitable purposes. This class of gift will not fail, even if the trustees fail to make the apportionment, because the court will in the last resort apportion the funds equally between the objects. Therefore, if the non-charitable purposes are void, *e.g.* for uncertainty, only that part of the funds devoted to them will fail.[78]

---

[73] See *e.g. Re Sutton* (1885) 28 Ch.D. 464; *Re Best* [1904] 2 Ch. 354.

[74] See, in addition to the cases mentioned in the text, *Morice* v. *Bishop of Durham* (1805) 10 Ves. 522; *Hunter* v. *Att.-Gen.* [1899] A.C. 309; *Blair* v. *Duncan* [1902] A.C. 37; *Re Davidson* [1909] 1 Ch. 567; *Re Da Costa* [1912] 1 Ch. 337; *Att.-Gen. for New Zealand* v. *Brown* [1917] A.C. 393; *Re Chapman* [1922] 2 Ch. 479; *Re Davis* [1923] 1 Ch. 225; *Att.-Gen.* v. *National Provincial and Union Bank of England Ltd.* [1924] A.C. 262; *Att.-Gen. for New Zealand* v. *New Zealand Insurance Co.* [1936] 3 All E.R. 888; *Re Atkinson's Will Trusts* [1978] 1 W.L.R. 586 (evidence inadmissible to show that by "worthy" the testator meant 'charitable").

[75] [1918] A.C. 337.   [76] [1944] A.C. 341.

[77] [1948] Ch. 465 (affirmed *sub nom. Ministry of Health* v. *Simpson* [1951] A.C. 251); *post*, p. 465.

[78] *Salusbury* v. *Denton* (1857) 3 K. & J. 529; *Re Clarke* [1923] 2 Ch. 407.

(2) *Incidental Non-Charitable Purposes*

It is also important to notice that the fact that a non-charitable purpose is incidental or ancillary to the achievement of a purpose which is, in fact, charitable will not destroy the gift. Thus, in *Royal College of Surgeons* v. *National Provincial Bank Ltd.*[79] the House of Lords held that the College was in law a charity, since its object, as recited in the Charter, was "the due promotion and encouragement of the study and practice of surgery," the professional protection of its members provided for in its by-laws being merely ancillary to that object. Likewise, in *Incorporated Council of Law Reporting for England and Wales* v. *Att.-Gen.*,[80] it was held that the fact that legal practitioners used law reports in order to earn their professional fees did not have the result that the objects of the Council were not charitable. The same result occurred in *Re Coxen*[81] where a sum of money was given by the testator to the Court of Aldermen of the City for an annual dinner at their meeting on the business of managing a trust in favour of orthopaedic hospitals which the testator had also set up. The dinner was held by Jenkins J. to be purely ancillary to the primary charitable trust and for its better administration. And in *London Hospital Medical College* v. *I.R.C.*[82] it was held that if the students' union existed to further the educational purposes of the College,[83] then it was immaterial that the union also provided a personal benefit for the individual students who were elected members of the union and chose to make use of its facilities.[84]

3. *Subsidiary Purposes*

Incidental purposes such as those just mentioned must be carefully distinguished from purposes which are *subsidiary* but not merely incidental. A well-known illustration is *Oxford Group* v. *Inland Revenue Commissioners*[85] where the Court of Appeal held that one of the objects set out in the Group's memorandum of association, *i.e.* to support "any charitable or benevolent" associations, actually conferred powers which were so wide that they could not be regarded as charitable; they were not merely ancillary to the main objects, admittedly charitable and also set out elsewhere in the memorandum. The Group did not, therefore, constitute a charity.

4. *Charitable Trusts (Validation) Act* 1954

It was as a result of the decision in *Oxford Group* v. *Inland Revenue Commissioners* that the Nathan Committee in its report recommended some

---

[79] [1952] A.C. 631.
[80] [1972] Ch. 73.
[81] [1948] Ch. 747.
[82] [1976] 1 W.L.R. 613.
[83] This was held to be the position: see *ante*, p. 203.
[84] See also, to a similar effect, *Neville Estates Ltd.* v. *Madden* [1962] Ch. 852, in which it was held that the social activities of a synagogue were merely ancillary to the strictly religious activities of the synagogue: see also *ante*, p. 208.
[85] [1949] 2 All E.R. 537. See also *Ellis* v. *I.R.C.* (1949) 31 Tax Cas. 178.

amendment of the law because the decision was thought to affect a large number of charities.[86] But they did not go so far as to recommend its complete reversal. The legislative result was the Charitable Trusts (Validation) Act 1954,[87] a brief, but, as it has been found, exceptionally difficult, statute to interpret.

First, the Act defines, in section 1(1), as an "imperfect trust provision" any provision declaring the objects and so describing them that consistently with the terms of the provision the property *could* be used exclusively for charitable purposes but could nevertheless be used for purposes which are not charitable. Secondly, the instrument in which the "imperfect trust provision" is contained must take effect before December 16, 1952[88] (the date of the publication of the Nathan Report). Thirdly, the Act is to apply under section 2(1), to any disposition or covenant to make such a disposition where, apart from the Act, the disposition or covenant is invalid[89] under the law of England and Wales, but would be valid if the objects were exclusively charitable. Fourthly, it will not apply if the property or income from it has been paid or distributed on the basis that the imperfect trust provision was void.[90] Finally, and this emphasises the limited applicability of the Act, the imperfect trust provision takes effect (i) as to the period before the Act came into force on July 30, 1954, as if the whole of the declared objects were charitable, and (ii) as to the period after the Act came into force as if the provision required the property to be applied for the declared objects only so far as they are charitable.[91]

Very real difficulty, as already indicated, has been found in the interpretation of these provisions: indeed one Lord Justice of Appeal confessed that he was "floored" by them on two occasions.[92] Especial difficulty has been found in reconciling section 1(1) and section 2(1), which are mentioned above. The definition of an imperfect trust provision is limited to a provision declaring the objects for which the property is held and "objects" is synonymous is section 1(1) with purposes. When one comes to section 2(1) the question is what to make of it. The argument is—and it seems most forcible—that the definition in section 1(1) would include certain gifts which are already valid by the law of England, *e.g.* a gift to certain named purposes for a period limited to the perpetuity period, some of the purposes being charitable and some not (*e.g.* "for my dog Fido")—and which would otherwise be valid. Section 2(1)—according to this line of argument—then took this class of bequest outside the mischief of the Act into which section 1 had put it. One can only agree that it is

---

[86] 1952 Cmd. 8710, Chap. 12.

[87] *cf.* the Conveyancing Act 1919–1954 (N.S.W.), discussed in *Leahy* v. *Att.-Gen. for New South Wales* [1959] A.C. 457.

[88] s. 1(2).

[89] *e.g.* for perpetuity, uncertainty or other similar reason: *Vernon* v. *I.R.C.* [1956] 1 W.L.R. 1169.

[90] s. 2(2).

[91] s. 1(2)(*a*)(*b*).

[92] *Re Harpur's Will Trusts* [1962] Ch. 78 at p. 95, *per* Harman L.J. See also *Re Gillingham Bus Disaster Fund* [1958] 1 Ch. 300 (Harman J.).

"an odd state of things if Acts of Parliament are passed in such a form that it is necessary to amend the effect of the first section by putting in a second."[93]

Apart from this problem other difficulties have arisen. A leading case on one of these is *Re Gillingham Bus Disaster Fund*,[94] some features of which have had a somewhat mixed reception in later cases of first instance. One question was whether the appeal contained in the *Daily Telegraph* was validated by the Act. This appeal was launched by the mayors of several boroughs, after a number of cadets had been killed and injured in a road accident, "to promote a Royal Marine Cadet Memorial Fund to be devoted . . . to defraying funeral expenses, caring for the boys who may be disabled and then to such worthy cause or causes in memory of the boys who lost their lives as the Mayors may determine." A majority of the Court of Appeal held that an imperfect trust provision was not validated unless the contributions to the fund were *dispositions* to which the Act applied, *viz.* dispositions creating more than one interest in the same property.[95] A contribution was admittedly a disposition but, in view of the terms of the appeal, it did not create *separate* interests in the same property, one for funeral expenses, the second for the care of the disabled and the third for worthy causes, and accordingly it was held not to be validated by the Act.[96]

This is also what Harman J. held at first instance and this view would seem to be correct.[97] But he also held *obiter* that section 1(1) of the Act should be construed as applying only to trusts framed in such terms that the objects referred to included some *express* reference to charitable purposes as well as including other non-charitable purposes. It did not apply to purposes stated in a general way (*e.g.* for public purposes) which could embrace charitable purposes but contained no expressed reference to charity or any charitable purpose. As has already been shown, the Court of Appeal by a majority decided the point on a ground which rendered this question irrelevant and, although they expressed some sympathy with the view of Harman J., they abstained from expressing any opinion on it. Ormerod L.J. who dissented and to whose decision alone the point was relevant, decided that section 1(1) should not be construed in the restricted manner favoured by Harman J. but in accordance with its language which he considered to be unambiguous.

In these circumstances Buckley J. in *Re Wykes' Will Trusts*[98] felt himself free to adopt the view on this point favoured by Ormerod L.J. and declared that a trust for "benevolent or welfare" purposes was an imperfect trust provision to which the Act applied. This last decision was considered by Cross J. in *Re Mead's Trust Deed*.[99] He said that a benevolent or welfare fund "is closely akin to a trust for the relief of poverty."[1] It was there held that a trust to provide a

---

[93] *Re Harpur's Will Trusts, supra* at p. 96, *per* Harman L.J.
[94] [1959] Ch. 62.
[95] s. 2(3).
[96] *cf. Re Chitty's Will Trusts* [1970] Ch. 254.
[97] Although dissented from by Ormerod L.J. [1959] Ch. 62.
[98] [1961] Ch. 229.
[99] [1961] 1 W.L.R. 1244.
[1] *Ibid.* at p. 1251.

convalescent home for members of a trade union and a home for poor retired members was validated by the Act and as from the date of the Act the property should be held for those members of the union who were poor persons and, in the case of the home for the aged, for poor retired members. *Re Wykes' Will Trusts* was further considered, again by Cross J., in *Re Saxone Shoe Co. Ltd.'s Trust Deed*[2] and assumed to have been correctly decided, but it was held on the facts that this particular trust was essentially a discretionary private trust and was not, therefore, validated. However, the judge set certain clear limits to the doctrine enunciated by Buckley J. in *Re Wykes*. He said: "In such a phrase as 'welfare purposes' there is at least some flavour of charity which may justify one in saying that the testator was seeking to benefit the public through the relief of a limited class. Here there is nothing of that kind, and if such a trust as this is validated by the Act, I do not see why one should stop short of turning any such invalid private trust into a trust for the relief of such beneficiaries as may from time to time be poor."[3] Nevertheless this problem—which is essentially one of construction of the Act—remains open: it has not been directly adjudicated upon by the Court of Appeal. There seems, however, to be no overriding reason why the restricted application favoured by Harman J. should be adopted: all that seems to be essential is that the expression used has a charitable connotation. Indeed, in *Re South Place Ethical Society*[4] Dillon J. held that the words "for such purposes either religious or civil" as the trustees might appoint constituted an imperfect trust provision within the meaning of the Act; they were to be construed as "such purposes, either religious or civil, being charitable" and the provision was accordingly validated.

The vexed question of the effect of the Act also arose for decision on another matter in *Re Harpur's Will Trusts*.[5] The Court of Appeal had to consider the question whether a trust to divide a trust fund "between such institutions and associations having for their main objects the assistance and care of soldiers, sailors, airmen and other members of H.M. Forces who have been wounded or incapacitated during the recent world war," as the trustees thought fit, had been validated by the Act. It was held that this provision was not within the scope of section 1(1) because that was limited to provisions declaring the objects and so describing them as to enable effect to be given to them by an application to purposes which are exclusively charitable. This has the somewhat surprising result that a gift to institutions, where their *objects* are not described in the instrument, will not be comprehended within the subsection.

It will have been observed that the Act can only apply to instruments taking effect before December 16, 1952. But since the validity of a provision may also arise for consideration on the determination of a life or other limited interest which is still in being, the Act cannot be regarded as merely of academic interest.[6] As time passes, however, its importance will diminish.

---

[2] [1962] 1 W.L.R. 943.
[3] *Ibid.* at pp. 958–959.   [4] [1980] 1 W.L.R. 1565.   [5] [1962] Ch. 78.
[6] If a person has a future interest in property the subject of the provision, he may challenge its validity within one year of the interest vesting in possession: s. 3; *Re Chitty's Will Trusts* [1970] Ch. 254.

VI. CY-PRÈS DOCTRINE

It is possible that a settlor may select a particular object of charity and that object may fail, or be or become impossible or impracticable[7] to carry out, or may have become illegal,[8] or may not exhaust the whole fund. The question is, what happens to the trust in circumstances such as these? The answer is that it will not necessarily fail. It is here that the *cy-près* doctrine[9] may apply and, if so, the funds will be applied to objects as near as possible to the settlor's intention.

1. *Conditions for Application of the Doctrine*

There are two conditions to be satisfied, the first involving the requirement of a "general charitable intention," and the second, the doctrine of "impossibility" and the effect on it of section 13 of the Charities Act 1960.

(a) General charitable intention

The settlor must, in general, have shown a *general charitable intention*. But it must be emphasised that this requirement does not apply universally. It will only apply where the original trust has failed *ab initio*. The absence of a general charitable intention will not be fatal to those trusts which have taken effect but have failed later: in such a case (and also in the case of unidentified donors which is considered later)[10] the funds will be applicable *cy-près*. Once money has been effectively and absolutely dedicated to charity, whether in pursuance of a general or a particular charitable intent, the testator's next-of-kin or residuary legatees are for ever excluded.[11] It was indeed held by the Court of Appeal in *Re Wright*[12] that this will hold good even if the failure occurs during the subsistence of a prior life interest and before the charity is entitled in possession to the funds. This will mean that the material date for the purpose of deciding whether the *cy-près* doctrine is applicable is the date when the trust came into effect (*e.g.* in a will, on the death of the testator). If it has failed then, the question whether a general charitable intention for purposes of *cy-près* has been shown becomes material.

However, it is essential for this purpose that an absolute gift be made. The question is one of construction of the instrument whether (1) an absolute and perpetual gift has been made to charity with a gift over which fails for remoteness or some other reason, but the original gift remains; or (2) whether the gift is

---

[7] See cases cited in text, *post*, and also *Att.-Gen.* v. *City of London* (1790) 3 Bro.C.C. 171 (promotion of Christianity among the infidels of Virginia); *Ironmongers Co.* v. *Att.-Gen.* (1844) 10 Cl. & F. 908 (redemption of British slaves in Turkey or Barbary).

[8] *e.g.* exceeding the rules of accumulation: *Re Monk* [1927] 2 Ch. 197; *Re Bradwell* [1952] Ch. 575 (income settled on trusts exceeding accumulation periods).

[9] For a full survey of the subject, see Sheridan and Delaney, *The Cy-près Doctrine; Tudor on Charities* (6th ed.), pp. 219 *et seq.*

[10] See *post*, p. 232.

[11] *Re Wright* [1954] Ch. 347 at p. 363, *per* Romer L.J. See also *Re Wokingham Fire Brigade* [1951] Ch. 373.

[12] *Ante*; see also to the same effect *Re Moon's Will Trusts* [1948] 1 All E.R. 300.

to charity for a limited period in which case the undisposed-of interest results to the grantor.[13]

(1) Gifts to charitable purposes

In cases of initial failure the question whether or not a general charitable intention has been shown is entirely one of construction of the instrument. One has to consider, as in all matters of construction, its whole scope and intent. The essential question that has to be decided on such construction, is whether the paramount object of the settlor was to benefit a particular object *simpliciter*, or whether it was to effect a particular mode of charity independently of the given object even though an object is specifically indicated.[14]

Subject to the warning that the cases present by no means a consistent picture, one may perhaps divide the authorities into two classes:

(i) One has a class of case where in form the gift is made for a particular charitable purpose but it is possible, taking the instrument as a whole, to say that, notwithstanding the form of the gift, the paramount intention is to give the property in the first instance for a general charitable purpose rather than a specified purpose: one engrafts, as it were, on to the general gift a direction as to the intention of the settlor relating to the manner in which the general gift is to be carried into effect. In this sort of case, even though it may be impossible to carry out the specified directions, the gift for the general charitable purpose will remain perfectly good, and the court or the Charity Commission will direct a scheme as to how it is to be carried out—a *cy-près* scheme.

(ii) The second class of case will arise, where on the true construction of the instrument the gift is not only in form but also in substance one for a particular purpose only, and if, for example, it proves impossible to carry out that particular purpose, the whole gift will fail: there is no room here for the application of *cy-près*.[15]

The question into which class the gift falls often raises serious problems of construction. The way in which the court sets about its task may be illustrated by the following cases. Thus in *Biscoe* v. *Jackson*[16] money was to be applied towards the establishment of a soup kitchen in Shoreditch and a cottage hospital there. It was not in fact possible to apply the fund in the manner indicated. The Court of Appeal held that there was a sufficient general intention of charity for the benefit of the poor of Shoreditch to entitle the court to execute the trust *cy-près*. It was decided in this case, in effect, that the direction to establish a soup kitchen and cottage hospital was only one means of benefiting the poor of Shoreditch whom there was a *general* intention of benefiting. Another rather

---

[13] See *Re Cooper's Conveyance Trusts* [1956] 1 W.L.R. 1096 at p. 1102 (*per* Upjohn J.). *cf. Re Peel's Release* [1921] Ch. 218; *Re Bawden's Settlement* [1954] 1 W.L.R. 33n. The rule in *Lassence* v. *Tierney* (1849) 1 Mac. & G. (gift to donee with superadded directions which do not exhaust the funds: donee may take absolutely) also applies to charitable gifts: *Re Monk* [1927] 2 Ch. 197 at p. 211.

[14] See *Re Taylor* (1888) 58 L.T. 538, 543.

[15] The substance of this formulation is borrowed from *Re Wilson* [1913] 1 Ch. 314 at p. 320. For another formulation, see *per* Buckley J. in *Re Lysaght* [1966] Ch. 191 at pp. 201, 202.

[16] (1887) 35 Ch.D. 460.

more difficult example is *Re Lysaght*.[17] Here the testatrix gave a fund to the Royal College of Surgeons, for the establishment of studentships. She provided (*inter alia*) that Jews and Roman Catholics should be excluded from them. Buckley J. held (1) that this discriminatory provision did not form an essential part of the testatrix's intention; (2) that her paramount intention was that the College should be the trustee of the fund; and (3) that the impracticability of giving effect to this inessential part of her intention (because of the College's refusal to accept subject to it) would not be allowed to defeat her paramount intention. Accordingly a scheme was directed by which the offending provision was deleted. Although the principle behind the decision is clear, it is not, however, easy, as a matter of construction of the will, to accept the Judge's conclusion that such discrimination was not part of the testatrix's paramount intention.

Another illustration, probably more straightforward from the point of view of construction, is *Re Woodhams*,[18] where the testator gave the residue of his estate to two colleges of music to found scholarships which were to be restricted to boys who were orphans from named children's homes. The colleges refused to accept on these conditions (partly because of the decrease in the number of orphans and partly because of the adequacy of public grants for education), but would accept if the restrictions were deleted. Vinelott J. held that the testator chose orphans from these homes as those most likely to need assistance, but it was not an essential part of the scheme that the scholarships should be so restricted and accordingly that the trusts could be modified without frustrating his intention.

A case on the other side of the line which affords a contrast with such cases is *Re Good*,[19] where there was a trust to provide rest homes in Hull. There was a detailed scheme of the types of home to be provided, the types of inmates to be admitted and the management powers of the trustees. The scheme was in fact impracticable, because the funds were insufficient. It was held by Wynn-Parry J. that the language of the will and in particular the detailed instructions were inconsistent with the implication of a general charitable intention and, therefore, the *cy-près* doctrine did not apply. Likewise, in *Re Spence*,[20] Megarry V.-C. held, on a construction of the will, that a gift to a specified old folk's home was one for a specific charitable purpose which, although possible when the will was made, had become impossible. It was not a gift to the old people of a particular district. Accordingly there was no general charitable intention and the gift failed.

---

[17] [1966] Ch. 191, applying *Re Robinson* [1923] 2 Ch. 332 (requirement of wearing a black gown in church held impracticable).

[18] [1981] 1 W.L.R. 493.

[19] [1950] 2 All E.R. 653. See also to the same effect *Re Packe* [1918] 1 Ch. 437 (holiday home for clergymen of Church of England and their wives); *Re White's Trusts* (1886) 33 Ch.D. 449 (almshouses); *Re Wilson* [1913] 1 Ch. 314 (school); *Re Harwood* [1936] Ch. 285; *cf. Re Finger's Will Trusts* [1972] Ch. 286.

[20] [1979] Ch. 483; another gift in the same will to a Blind Home was held to be identifiable with a home for the blind of a different name and address and was valid.

(2) **Gift to charitable institutions**[21]

The above illustrations generally concerned trusts for charitable *purposes*, rather than trusts for charitable *institutions*. It appears to be necessary to deal with the latter separately since the circumstances of the institution may vary considerably. It will also be seen that the existence of a general charitable intention is not necessarily decisive of the matter.[22]

(i) *Non-existent institutions*

It appears to be relatively easy to infer a general charitable intention where the charity named by the testator has never existed. In *Re Harwood*,[23] for example, it was held that a gift to a "peace society" which had never existed indicated a general charitable intention so that the fund could be applied *cy-près* to other exisiting similar organisations. This construction may, however, be rebutted by the circumstances of the gift. Thus, Harman J. held in *Re Goldschmidt*[24] that the presence in the will of a residuary gift in favour of other charitable purposes into which lapsed funds would fall was a factor against deducing a general charitable intention.

(ii) *Institutions ceasing to exist*

Real difficulty is encountered in reconciling some of the cases in this category; much may depend on the wording of the gift and the circumstances of the institution. The main question, however, is whether the institution has ceased to exist, or whether it has merely changed its form so that the original charity may be identified in its new form.

In *Re Rymer*[25] there was a gift by will to the Rector for the time being of St. Thomas' Seminary for the education of priests in the diocese of Westminster for the purposes of such seminary. The seminary ceased to exist in the testator's lifetime. It was held that the gift had been made to a particular institution and it lapsed. Although the case could have been treated as a *purpose* trust, *viz.* for the purpose of training priests (it was not in fact), presumably it would still have failed because a particular, rather than a general, charitable intention was shown. In some cases, however, the gift may be construed as one for the *purposes* of the institution. If so, the gift will not necessarily lapse if the institution ceases to exist. Thus, in *Re Roberts*,[26] there was a gift residue for division among six named charitable institutions including the Sheffield Boys Working Home. The home was not in existence at the testator's death: it had been sold. Wilberforce J. held that the bequest in favour of the home was validly given on charitable trusts because (*inter alia*), although the bequest was a gift for the purposes of the institution, it was not so correlated with the

---

[21] *cf.* the discussion by Hutton (1969) 32 M.L.R. 283.

[22] *cf.* Megarry V.-C. in *Re Spence* [1978] [1979] Ch. 483 at p. 491 that the distinction is between particularity and generality; but this is not exhaustive: see *infra*.

[23] [1936] Ch. 285. See also *Re Davis* [1902] 1 Ch. 876 ("Homes for the Homeless"). See also *Re Satterthwaite's W.T.* [1966] 1 W.L.R. 277, C.A.

[24] [1957] 1 W.L.R. 524 (gift to "Fund for Relief of Distressed German Jews" and no fund of that name existed: failed).

[25] [1895] 1 Ch. 19. See, for a similar result, *Re Goldney* (1946) 115 L.J.Ch. 337.

[26] [1963] 1 W.L.R. 406.

physical entity of the institution that the charity ended when the trusts of the Home ceased to exist. The funds of the Home remained subject to charitable trusts. A scheme was therefore appropriate and the gift was applicable in accordance with that scheme.

The question is not, however, merely one of deducing a continuation of the charitable purposes in this way; it appears that there is an additional requirement to be satisfied, namely, that on the closing down of the institution there are still funds (or endowments) available for carrying out its work. This requirement was insisted on by Plowman J. in *Re Slatter's Will Trusts*[27] where the gift had been made to a hospital which had closed down and it was held that its work was not transferred elsewhere because the need for it had gone and because it had no funds available for carrying out that work.

(iii) *Amalgamated, absorbed or re-organised institutions*

The point made by *Re Slatter's Will Trusts* is also generally relevant in cases where an institution has been amalgamated with, or absorbed in, other institutions, or otherwise re-organised. Such changes may be effected in various ways, most commonly by a scheme made by the court or the Charity Commissioners. Thus, in *Re Faraker*,[28] a scheme had been made by the Commissioners consolidating the endowments of a number of charities with the general purpose of relief of the poor of Rotherhithe. A gift was then made to one of these charities ("Hannah Bayley's Charity") whose object originally was rather more limited. It was held that the gift did not lapse. The principle derived from this case is that an endowed charity cannot be destroyed by alterations made by scheme of the court or the Charity Commissioners and any subsequent accretion to its funds takes effect on the trusts as altered. The case was subsequently applied in similar circumstances in *Re Lucas*.[29]

Alterations to the constitution or objects of the institution in this way may have been made not only by scheme, but by statute,[30] or (improperly) under the terms of the trust deed without the sanction of the court or the Charity Commissioners.[31] Subsequent gifts to an endowed institution will not lapse. Informal changes are sometimes made by trustees (even more improperly) without reference to the terms of the trust deed. The essence of the matter in the case of informal changes of this kind is that just as the court or the Charity Commissioners cannot destroy an endowed charity, neither can the trustees or the governing body destroy it, again with the result that gifts to the original institution will not lapse.[32]

---

[27] [1964] Ch. 512.

[28] [1912] 2 Ch. 488, C.A.

[29] [1948] Ch. 424, C.A.; distinguished in *Re Spence* [1979] Ch. 483.

[30] Many of the cases involved re-organisation of hospitals nationalised and re-organised under the National Health Services Act 1946: see *e.g. Re Morgan's Will Trusts* [1950] Ch. 137; *Re Glass* [1950] Ch. 643n.; *Re Hutchinson's Will Trusts* [1953] Ch. 387.

[31] See *Re Bagshawe* [1954] 1 W.L.R. 238, where a scheme was made simply in accordance with the trust machinery, not by an outside body.

[32] See, to this effect, *Re Watt* [1932] Ch. 243n.; *Re Withall* [1932] Ch. 236; see also *Re Hutchinson's Will Trusts* [1953] Ch. 387. A scheme is necessary or at any rate desirable where an informal change has been effected: see *Re Roberts* [1963] 1 W.L.R. 406.

There is, however, a complicating factor, for if an institution has power to dissolve itself and it formally does so, it appears that a subsequent gift to the institution *will* lapse unless a general charitable intention is shown on the part of the donor. This is the effect of *Re Stemson's Will Trusts*[33] where Plowman J. held that a gift to an incorporated institution lapsed when it had previously been dissolved and its funds had been disposed of in accordance with its constitution. In the result, therefore, it appears that a charity which no one has power to terminate retains its existence despite such vicissitudes as schemes, amalgamations or changes of name, so long as is it has funds. But if the charity is founded, not as a perpetual charity, but as one liable to termination and its constitution provides for disposal of its funds in that event, then if the organisation ceases to exist, and if a gift is subsequently made to the charity, it lapses in the absence of a general charitable intention.[34]

(iv) *Distinction between incorporated and unincorporated institutions*

If the law were not already sufficiently involved, it appears that a distinction must also be drawn between bodies which are incorporated and those which are unincorporated. This distinction was made by Buckley J. in *Re Vernon's Will Trusts*[35] and applied by Goff J. in *Re Finger's Will Trusts*.[36] The reasoning is that in the case of an unincorporated body the gift is *per se* a purpose trust; provided, therefore, that the work is still being carried on, it will be given effect to by a scheme notwithstanding the disappearance of the donee during the lifetime of the testator *unless* there is something positive to show that the continued existence of the donee is essential to the gift. In the case of a corporation, however, the position is different, as there *has to be* something positive in the will to create a purpose trust at all,[37] on the ground that a gift to a corporate body take effect prima facie as a gift to that body beneficially.[38]

On analysis, the distinction may be thought to be debatable, for it is arguable that if a gift or trust is made in favour of an incorporated body, it is not for that body *simpliciter*, but for its purposes: companies have objects. *Re Finger's Will Trusts*[39] illustrates the difficulties. There were gifts by will both to an unincorporated association, the National Radium Commission, and to an incorporated body, the National Council for Maternity and Child Welfare. Both had been dissolved before the testator's death. The gift to the Commission was held to be a purpose trust for the work of the Commission which was not dependent on its continuing existence, and the fund could be applied under a scheme.[40] The gift to the Council, however, failed because the testator could not be taken as intending that the gift could be applied for its purposes. Goff J. managed to avoid this apparently anomalous result by holding that, although the gift to the

---

[33] [1970] Ch. 16.
[34] *Ibid.* at p. 26.
[35] [1972] Ch. 300 (note).
[36] [1972] Ch. 286.
[37] *Ibid.* at p. 295.
[38] See *Re Stemson's Will Trusts* [1970] Ch. 16.
[39] *Supra.*
[40] See also *ante*, p. 227 in respect of re-organisations of charitable institutions.

Council failed, the share of the fund applicable to the Council could be applied *cy-près* because the will as a whole showed a general charitable intention.[41]

(v) *Institutions ceasing to exist after the gift takes effect*

The illustrations above concern cases where the institution has ceased to exist or been otherwise reorganised before the gift takes effect. If the charity ceases to exist after the testator's death it is clear, as was held by the Court of Appeal in *Re Slevin*[42] that it is unnecessary to show a general charitable intention for the gift to be upheld. The subject matter of the gift will have already vested in the recipient and since it has ceased to exist it will devolve on the Crown with the rest of the institution's property. The Crown will in practice allow it to be disposed of in favour of charity.

(3) **Gifts to a mixture of charitable and non-charitable purposes or institutions**

The fact that one finds one gift for a non-charitable purpose among a number of gifts for charitable purposes does not enable one to infer that the testator intended the non-charitable gift to take effect as a charitable gift when in terms it is not charitable. And this is so even though the non-charitable gift may have a close relation to the purposes for which the charitable gifts were made. This was held to be the position in *Re Jenkins's Will Trusts*[43] where a gift had been made to an association for anti-vivisection (non-charitable) coupled with charitable purposes (preventing cruelty to animals). As Buckley J. said, in rejecting an application for a *cy-près* scheme: "If you meet seven men with black hair and one with red hair you are not entitled to say that there are eight men with black hair."[44]

It has been argued[45] that the previous case of *Re Satterthwaite's Will Trusts*[46] is inconsistent with this decision. In this case a human-hating testatrix gave money to the "London Animal Hospital." No hospital of this name could be identified, but because of other gifts in favour of established animal charities, the gift was held by the Court of Appeal to be applicable *cy-près*. The case is, however, probably distinguishable on the ground that a gift to an (admittedly unidentified) animal hospital had a sufficient charitable "flavour" about it to justify this result.

(b) **"Impossibility" and Charities Act 1960, s.13**

The second condition for the application of the *cy-près* doctrine used to be that it was or had become "impossible"[47] to carry out the settlor's intention; or alternatively that a surplus remained after fulfilment of the purpose[48]; indeed,

---

[41] See also *Re Stemson's Will Trusts* [1970] Ch. 16, *supra.*

[42] [1891] 2 Ch. 236.

[43] [1966] Ch. 249.

[44] *Ibid.* at p. 256.

[45] See *Pettit* (4th ed.), p. 231.

[46] [1966] 1 W.L.R. 277.

[47] See cases cited in text, *infra,* and also *Att.-Gen.* v. *City of London* (1790) 3 Bro.C.C. 171 (the promotion of Christianity among the infidels of Virginia); *Re Ironmongers Co.* v. *Att.-Gen.* (1844) 10 Cl. & F. 908 (redemption of British slaves in Turkey and Barbary).

[48] *Re King* [1923] 1 Ch. 243; *Re North Devon and West Somerset Relief Fund* [1953] 1 W.L.R. 1260; *Re Raine* [1956] Ch. 417.

so it has been held,[49] the same applies to any surplus which is directed to be accumulated in excess of the statutory rules for accumulation.

We are here concerned with the meaning of "impossibility." One could not—and indeed still cannot—simply disregard the wishes of a settlor because one does not like them or because one thinks the moneys could be applied to a more beneficial purpose. Nevertheless the word "impossible" was in general widely construed. Thus in *Re Dominion Students Hall Trust*[50] the charity in question was restricted to Dominion students of European origin, yet the objects were stated to be promotion of community of interest in the Empire. An application was made to the court to delete the words "of European origin." Evershed J. held that the retention of these words amounted to a "colour bar" which would defeat the object of the charity: the word "impossible" should be construed widely and covered the case.

In view of the dilution of the term "impossible" it was clearly desirable to provide a new test to replace it. Section 13 of the Charities Act 1960 now provides a comprehensive treatment of the subject. It is sufficient if the matter can be brought under one of the following heads:

(A) Where the original purposes[51] in whole or in part, (i) have been as far as may be fulfilled, or (ii) cannot be carried out, or not according to the directions given and to the spirit of the gift.[52] This expression "spirit of the gift" appears in four of the five paragraphs. It is not a new phrase, but is apparently borrowed from the Education (Scotland) Act 1946.[53] Although doubts about its meaning have been expressed,[54] it should not create any real difficulties. It has been said that "it is equivalent in meaning to the basic intention underlying the gift, as ascertained from its terms in the light of the admissible evidence."[55] The working of paragraph (A) is illustrated by the decision in *Re Lepton's Charity*.[56] This case concerned the gift by will in 1715 of land to be held on trust to pay out of the rents a sum of £3 a year to the minister of a chapel and the net overplus to the poor and aged of the town. The evidence was to the effect that at the date of the will the total income was £5 a year. The land had now been sold and was represented by investments yielding £791 a year. Pennycuick V.-C. held that the basic intention was plainly defeated when, in the conditions of England today, the minister took a derisory £3 out of the total of £791, and made an order by way of scheme to provide for the payment to the minister to be raised from £3 to £100 per annum.

---

[49] *e.g. Re Monk* [1927] 2 Ch. 197; *Re Bradwell* [1952] Ch. 575.

[50] [1947] Ch. 183.

[51] The words "original purposes" appear in all five paragraphs. They are applicable to the trusts of the disposition as a whole, and not severally in relation to its respective parts: *Re Lepton's Charity* [1972] Ch. 276 at p. 285.

[52] s. 13(1)(*a*).

[53] s. 116(2).

[54] Viscount Simonds, 221 H.O.L. Official Report 601 (March 1, 1960).

[55] *Re Lepton's Charity* [1972] 276 at p. 285 (*per* Pennycuick V.-C.). See also *Re Lysaght* [1966] Ch. 191; discussed *ante*, p. 225.

[56] See also *post*, p. 232.

(B) Where the original purposes provide a use for part only of the property.[57] This would be illustrated by the facts of *Re North Devon and West Somerset Relief Fund*[58] where a surplus remained out of funds subscribed for the relief of the flood disaster at Lynmouth.

(C) Where the property given and other property applicable for similar purposes can be more effectively used in conjunction, and to that end can suitably, regard being had to the spirit of the gift, be made applicable for common purposes.[59] Strictly speaking, this is not a *cy-près* scheme and it was never necessary to show "impossibility" to effect a consolidation of a number of charities.[60]

(D) Where the original purposes were laid down by reference to an area which was then, but has since ceased to be, a unit for some other purpose, or by reference to a class of persons or to an area which has for any reason since ceased to be suitable, regard being had to the spirit of the gift, or to be practical in administering the gift.[61] Common examples of the application of this paragraph would arise where the original area of the charity, because of changes in local government boundaries or the class of beneficiaries, is hard to identify or where the area or class of beneficiaries has dwindled or is otherwise provided for, the result being that no public benefit is substantially conferred by fulfilment of the original purposes.

(E) Where the original purposes, in whole or in part have, since they were laid down—

(i) been adequately provided for by other means;
(ii) ceased as being useless or harmful to the community, or, for other reasons, to be in law charitable; or
(iii) ceased in any other way to provide a suitable and effective method of using the property given, regard being had to the spirit of the gift.[62]

The jurisdiction created by this paragraph (in particular sub-paragraphs (i) and (iii)) affords the most important relaxation of the old *cy-près* rule and will probably be of the most practical use in enabling funds to be utilised for the maximum benefit of the public. Sub-paragraph (i) may be illustrated by a *cy-près* application where the original benefits of the charity are now provided for by the statutory services of public or local authorities. This would apply, for example, to a charity for the upkeep of a road or bridge[63]: if the original purpose is kept on foot its only real purpose would be to relieve the rates or exchequer and it is now possible to apply the funds *cy-près*. Sub-paragraph (ii) will not often arise; indeed, there does not appear to be a reported case where a valid charitable trust has ceased to be charitable. But the principle may now, since the

---

[57] s. 13(1)(*b*).
[58] [1953] 1 W.L.R. 1260; see also *Re King* [1923] 1 Ch. 243; *Re Raine* [1956] Ch. 417.
[59] s. 13(1)(*c*).
[60] See *Re Faraker* [1912] 2 Ch. 488.
[61] s. 13(1)(*d*).
[62] s. 13(1)(*e*).
[63] See Charitable Uses Act 1601, *ante*, p. 188.

passing of the Act, possibly be applied more often than may be thought. This is because an institution registered by the Charity Commissioners is conclusively presumed to be a charity while on the register for all purposes other than rectification of the register.[64] This sub-paragraph will therefore arise for application if a charity is *removed*[65] from the register on the ground that its purposes are not in fact, or (less likely to happen) are no longer charitable. It is sub-paragraph (iii), however, which provides the widest relaxation of all. But although the words are very general it does not have a completely unlimited effect. It is still necessary to take into account the spirit of the gift and this will prevent a *cy-près* scheme being made simply because the original purpose selected by the donor would be less effective than some other application. It is still essential to establish that the mode of application which the donor selected has *ceased* to be suitable or effective.[66] In *Re Lepton's Charity*[67] it was held that the court had jurisdiction under this sub-paragraph (as well as under the wider terms of paragraph (A): "Where the original purposes, in whole or in part . . . cannot be carried out, or not according to the directions given and to the spirit of the gift")[68] to direct an application of the property *cy-près*.

The provisions mentioned above, contained in section 13 of the Charities Act, alter the law only so far as it previously required a failure of the original purposes of a charity before a *cy-près* application could be ordered.[69] This will mean therefore that it is still necessary that a *general charitable intention*, on the lines already discussed, should be manifested, subject to the modifications provided for in respect of unidentified donors.[70]

The jurisdiction to make a scheme is exercisable by the court, or almost invariably in practice, by the Charity Commissioners.[71]

2. Unidentified Donors

Section 14 of the Charities Act 1960 introduced reforms which were long overdue. It provides that property given for *specific* charitable purposes which fail are to be applicable *cy-près* as though it had been given for charitable purposes generally, provided that it belongs (a) to donors who, after such advertisements and inquiries as are reasonable,[72] cannot be identified or found *or* (b) to a donor who has executed a written disclaimer of his right to have the property returned.[73] It is further provided that, for these purposes, property is

---

[64] s. 5(1).

[65] s. 5(2).

[66] The Goodman Committee has recommended (p. 95) that the *cy-près* doctrine should be amended or clarified to make it clear in appropriate cases that a fundamental change in the objects of the charity can be allowed.

[67] [1972] Ch. 276.

[68] See *ante*, p. 230. Pennycuick V.-C. was of opinion that this sub-paragraph was no more than "a final writing out at large" of paragraph [A]: *ibid.* at p. 285.

[69] s. 13(2).

[70] *Infra.*

[71] *Post*, p. 233.

[72] See Trustee Act 1925, s.27, and see *post*, p. 281 and see *Re Henry Wood National Memorial Trust (Practice Note)* [1966] 1 W.L.R. 1601, on advertisements required.

[73] s. 14(1).

to be conclusively presumed, without the necessity for advertisements or inquiries, to belong to donors who cannot be identified if it consists of (a) the proceeds of cash collections made by means of collecting boxes or other means not adapted for distinguishing one gift from another *or* (b) the proceeds of any lottery, competition, entertainment, sale or other such money-raising activity, although, as regards the latter, allowance must be made for prizes or articles for sale to enable the activity to be undertaken[74] and the donors of such prizes or articles will be entitled to their return or their proceeds of sale.[75] The other provisions cover cases other than those already mentioned. These are that the court may, by order, direct that property be treated (without advertisement or inquiry) as belonging to donors who cannot be identified whenever it appears to the court *either* (a) that it would be unreasonable, having regard to the amounts likely to be returned to the donor, to incur expense with a view to returning the property, *or* (b) it would be unreasonable, having regard to the nature, circumstances and amount of the gifts, and to the lapse of time since they were made, for the donors to expect the property to be returned.[76] Finally, the section is retrospective: it therefore applies to property given for charitable purposes before the commencement of the Act.[77]

These provisions reversed the previous law. Formerly the law was that unless one could show a *general* charitable intention in the usual way the trustees were bound to refund the money and if the donors could not be found the money had to be paid into court to await the usually remote possibility that they would reclaim it. This was indeed the result in *Re Ulverston*[78] where an appeal was launched for the building of a new hospital and insufficient funds were given for the purpose. The Court of Appeal held that a *specific*, not a general, charitable intention had been manifested and the funds were therefore to be held on a resulting trust for the contributors. As has been seen, the Act reverses the previous law by the simple expedient of providing that donors in the circumstances indicated—but only in those circumstances—shall be *deemed* to have a general charitable intention.[79] Moreover, the fact that the section is retrospective enables money lodged in court, before the commencement of the Act, now to be applied *cy-près*.

VII. ADMINISTRATION OF CHARITIES

1. *Central Authorities*

As a result of the Education Act 1973, there is now only one central authority exercising jurisdiction over those charities which are not exempt from jurisdic-

[74] s. 14(2).
[75] s. 14(6).
[76] s. 14(3).
[77] s. 14(7).
[78] [1956] Ch. 622.
[79] The fact that contributions are from anonymous sources may, however, still be relevant in cases where the trust is *not* charitable: see *ante*, p. 150.

tion,[80] *viz.* the Charity Commissioners for England and Wales.[81] Formerly, the Secretary of State for Education and Science and the Secretary of State for Wales had concurrent jurisdiction with the Charity Commissioners and exercised it in relation to charities of an educational nature.[82] The reason for conferring the exercise of functions under the Charities Act exclusively upon the Commissioners is that these functions are primarily judicial and not, therefore, appropriately exercised by Ministers of the Crown. As to the constitution of the Commission it is provided that there are to be a Chief Charity Commissioner and two other Commissioners,[83] and two at least of them must be barristers or solicitors.[84] They are appointed by the Home Secretary[85] but are quite independent of him in day-to-day administration[86]: they cannot even be compelled to follow any general guidance he may care to give.[87]

2. Official Custodian for Charities

Before the Charities Act there were two officers, one the Official Trustee of Charity Lands and the other the Official Trustee of Charitable Funds. They existed so that the legal title of charity lands and funds respectively could be vested in them. There seemed to be no good reason why there should be two such offices[88] and the Act combines them into one under the title above.[89] There are advantages in vesting property in the Official Custodian as custodian trustee. First, it may render the title more simple and, secondly, and more important, it renders it unnecessary to appoint new trustees on deaths or retirements, thereby saving the expense of new appointments. He is an officer of the Charity Commissioners and ranks as a corporation sole, having perpetual

---

[80] s. 1(1)(*a*); Charities Act 1960, s. 1 and Sched. 1. S. 1(1)(*a*) came into force on February 4, 1974.

[81] C.A. 1960, s. 2(1), now repealed by Education Act 1973, s. 1(1)(*a*). The Goodman Committee has recommended (p. 120) that in addition an independent Charities Board should be created with a chairman and members independent of the Charity Commission. Its members would come from a wide background and from different parts of the country. Its function would include being consulted by the Charity Commissioners and to advise them on matters of policy and administration.

[82] s. 2(1).

[83] Sched. 1 para. 1(1).

[84] Sched. 1, para. 1(2). The Expenditure Committee has recommended (p. 30) that a fourth Commissioner should be appointed aided by a special "task-force" of experts drawn from the voluntary organisations and social services with supporting staff to carry out local reviews of charities and to act in an investigatory role when required.

[85] *Ibid.* para. 1(3).

[86] s. 1(3)(4).

[87] *Ibid.* The Expenditure Committee has recommended (p. 31) that the Home Secretary should answer questions on charities and on the Charity Commissioners (such questions are at the present time referred to the Commissioners who reply in writing), and that the Home Secretary should have more flexibility where amendments to the law are required and wider powers to make orders and statutory instruments affecting the Commissioners and their work, subject to affirmative resolution of the House of Commons. The Goodman Committee, however, consider (p. 122) that the Commissioners should have the same degree of self-regulation as many other public bodies.

[88] See Nathan Report, para. 228.

[89] s. 3(1). See also s. 17 for vesting property in the Official Custodian.

succession and an official seal. Because he is simply a custodian trustee, the actual management and control of the charity remains in the charity trustees.

3. *Registration*

Sections 4 and 5 of the Charities Act[90] provide for a central register of charities. Before the Act was passed it was an alarming fact that neither the actual number of charities nor the amount of money devoted to charitable purposes had ever been known with any sort of precision. In course of time, however, the registration provisions of the Act, which were long overdue, will cure this palpable defect of charity administration. There is now a positive duty on charity trustees to apply for registration.[91] And all charities are registrable[92] unless they are expressly relieved from the requirement.[93] One example of the latter is to be found in the so-called "exempt charities": these are not subject to any of the supervisory powers of the Commissioners because satisfactory arrangements have already been made for carrying out the objects of such trusts and safeguarding the trust property. Examples of exempt charities are certain universities and colleges, the Church Commissioners, industrial and provident societies and friendly societies.[94] Some charities are also entitled to relief from registration in addition to the "exempt charities" so called. These are charities without any permanent endowment (*i.e.* property which must be retained as capital), without property bringing in an income of more than £15 a year and without land which it uses and occupies.[95] Furthermore, any charity excepted by order or regulation is not required to be registered[96]; a number of regulations to this effect covering, for example, voluntary schools,[97] boy scouts and girl guides[98] have been made. A further exemption[99] operates in favour of registered places of worship.[1]

---

[90] These provisions were almost entirely new in their effect. Although a statutory obligation to register was imposed by the Charitable Donations Act 1812, this was not observed in practice.

[91] On December 31, 1981, the total number of charities on the register was 139,289: Report of the Charity Commissioners for England and Wales for 1981.

[92] It is necessary that, in order to be a charity, the organisation in question be subject to control by the High Court in the exercise of the court's jurisdiction with respect to charities. If that jurisdiction is wholly ousted by statute in relation to the organisation, then the organisation is not a charity and cannot be registered: see *Construction Training Board* v. *Att.-Gen.* [1973] Ch. 173, C.A. (where, however, the Board was held to be a charity because the provisions of the Industrial Training Act 1964 did not oust the jurisdiction of the court; the court still had control over the Board's functions).

[93] s. 4.   [94] See Charities Act 1960, s. 4(4)(*a*), Sched. 2.

[95] s. 4(4)(*c*). The Goodman Committee has recommenced (p. 75) that this exemption should be removed.

[96] s. 4(4)(*b*).

[97] The Charities (Exception of Voluntary Schools from Registration) Regulations 1960 (S.I. 1960 No. 2366).

[98] The Charities (Exception of Certain Charities for Boy Scouts and Girl Guides for Registration) Regulations 1961 (No. 1044).

[99] The Goodman Committee has recommended (p. 75) that the Home Secretary should re-examine regularly the validity of exemptions and exceptions.

[1] Charities Act 1960, s. 4(4)(9); and for definition of "Registered Place of Worship," see Places of Worship Registration Act 1855, s. 9.

Registration raises a conclusive presumption that the institution is a charity at any time while it is on the register.[2] This accordingly removes a great deal of uncertainty about the status of certain institutions. But provision is necessarily made for a person who is or may be affected by the registration of an institution or trust as a charity to object to its entry on the register or apply for its removal on the ground that it is not in fact a charity, which is a question of general law.[3] This is intended for people, especially next-of-kin, whose interests will be affected by the answer to the question whether the institutions or trusts should be classified accordingly. An appeal against any decision of the Commissioners may be brought in the High Court.[4] The Commissioners also themselves have the positive duty to remove from the register any institution which no longer appears to them to be a charity and also to remove any charity because it ceases to exist or does not operate.[5]

The register itself is in a convenient form, namely, a card index on which appear particulars of the trusts, the annual income of the trusts and references to any land to which the trusts relate.

4. Co-ordination of Charitable Activities

Sections 10 to 12 of the Act, which were entirely new, have as their aim the foundation of a basis for co-operation between charity and the statutory welfare services. They authorise local authorities to review the working of local charities and arrange for co-ordination of the work of those charities with that of the statutory services.[6] But no obligation is put on a charity to co-operate. It requires mutual agreement between the local authority and the charity.[7] It may lead, as must be hoped, to rationalisation of charitable activities over the country as a whole, but it is fair to say that few reviews have so far been put in hand.[8] Moreover, the review powers relate only to

---

[2] s. 5(1).

[3] s. 5(2).

[4] s. 5(3)(4). The Goodman Committee has recommended that appeals from administrative decisions of the Charity Commissioners should be made to an appellate tribunal; that there should be a right of appeal to the court from the decision of that tribunal on a point of law; and that legal aid should be available for appeals on points of law.

[5] ss. 11, 12. The Goodman Committee has recommended (p.69) that the Charity Commissioners should have power to require such information as they think fit about the proposed activities of the charity with power to refuse registration if it appears appropriate or, alternatively, to grant registration subject to review after three years. A charitable company incorporated under the Companies Acts may also be wound up on an application made by the Attorney-General under C.A. 1960, s. 30(1) : see *Liverpool and District Hospital for Diseases of the Heart* v. *Att.-Gen.* [1981] Ch. 193.

[6] ss. 10, 11, 12.

[7] s. 12(2).

[8] The Goodman Committee has recommended (p. 82) that the review process should be proceeded with as speedily as possible, and that responsibility should be taken from the local authorities and given to the Charity Commissioners. It is also recommended that "neighbourhood trusts," catering for not too large an area, should be set up whenever practicable so as to retain the local character of te trusts. The Expenditure Committee recommended (p. 21) compulsory powers of "municipalisation" of local charities: this is rejected by the Goodman Committee.

local charities. There are no powers to ensure reviews or co-ordination of national charities.[9]

5. *Scheme-Making and Other Powers*

Section 18 of the Act empowers the Commissioners to exercise a jurisdiction concurrent with that of the High Court to make schemes relating to the administration of the charity, or orders for the appointment and removal of trustees and with regard to the vesting or transfer of property.[10] Although the court has a scheme-making power, it should be emphasised that in practice the vast majority of such schemes will be made by the Commissioners.[11] A scheme will obviously take a wide diversity of forms: it may, for example, take the drastic form of rewriting the original user trusts or management trusts of the charity or both. Appointments and removals of trustees will not normally require a scheme: they will be made simply by order of the Commissioners. And the same will apply to vesting the property in the Official Custodian.[12]

In the usual way jurisdiction can only be exercised by the Commissioners on an application made by the charity or on a reference by the court.[13] But they may also, if satisfied that the charity trustees ought, in the interest of the charity, to apply for a scheme but have unreasonably refused or neglected to do so, themselves apply to the Home Secretary for him to refer the case to them with a view to a scheme and, if the Home Secretary does so, they can proceed to make a scheme accordingly.[14]

Power is also specifically given to the Commissioners to act for the protection of charities where there has been misconduct or mismanagement, or the property of the charity should be protected and properly applied.[15] In these circumstances they are empowered (*inter alia*) to remove or appoint trustees or prevent the operation of any banking account.[16]

A number of miscellaneous powers are also conferred on the Commissioners. Most important perhaps of all is the power to make an order, where it appears that the proposed action is in the interests of the charity, authorising dealings or other action to be made or taken, whether or not it is within the administrative powers of the trustees.[17] This power, which is primarily administrative, is akin to the powers conferred by section 57 of the Trustee Act 1925[18] and section 64 of the Settled Land Act 1925.[19] It may, for example,

---

[9] The Goodman Committee has recommended (p.99) that co-operation between national charities should be developed and encouraged by persuasion, not by legal means, and that the Charity Commissioners should initiate a review or reviews to determine how this can be done.

[10] s. 18(1).

[11] s. 18(1)(4).

[12] s. 3(8).

[13] s. 18(4). The Goodman Committee has recommended that the formalities of scheme-making be relaxed in relation to small local charities, especially if the funds are transferred to "Neighbourhood Trusts" (*i.e.* trusts catering for not too large an area) (p.94).

[14] s. 18(6).

[15] s. 20(1).

[16] s. 20(1). For the procedure on appeal against removal (see s. 20(7)), see *Jones* v. *Att.-Gen.* [1974] Ch. 148.

[17] s. 23(1).   [18] *Post*, pp. 277, 410.   [19] *Post*, p. 411.

authorise any given transaction, compromise or application of property or may, more specifically, authorise a charity to use common premises, or employ a common staff or otherwise combine, for any administrative purposes, with any other charity—though the latter are purely examples and do not limit the generality of the statutory power.[20]

Other powers include that of advising charity trustees if the latter apply for advice[21]—a most convenient facility in practice—and powers to preserve charity documents.[22]

6. *Investment*

The powers and duties of trustees of a charity, with regard to investment of trust funds, are governed, in general, in the same manner as in the case of non-charitable trusts, by the terms of the trust instrument (if any) and by the general law of trusts relating to investments.[23]

The Trustee Investments Act 1961[24] enables trustees, subject to a number of safeguards, to invest a proportion, not exceeding one-half of the trust fund, in a wide range of investments including stocks and shares in public companies. But in order to make effective use of the provisions of this Act a substantial fund is necessary so that risk can be spread and management expenses assimilated without difficulty. However, many charities have extremely small trust funds[25] and if special provision had not been made, a large number would not have been able to get effectual benefits from the Act. It was, therefore, desirable to make general provision, by way of common investment schemes, for the joint administration of a number of charitable trust funds for the purposes of investment. Common investment schemes had been made before, but only in particular cases, by statute[26] and the court,[27] and the Charity Commissioners have always had the power to make schemes of a similar nature; but no *general* provisions for the establishment of common investment funds were available until the passing of the Charities Act 1960.

---

[20] s. 23(2).

[21] s. 24.

[22] s. 25.

[23] *Post*, p. 301; and see also *Soldiers', Sailors' and Airmen's Families Association* v. *Att.-Gen.* [1968] 1 W.L.R. 313, where it was held that a corporation incorporated by royal charter cannot by the making of rules, confer upon itself powers wider than those conferred upon it by the general law or the royal charter.

[24] *Post*, p. 310.

[25] According to the Nathan Report (para. 554) at least 35,000 have a gross annual income of less than £25. As to charities which have been *registered* it appears that well over half of the charities have a yearly income of less than £100, while approximately 23 per cent. have a yearly income of less than £5. At the other end of the scale about 6 per cent. of charities enjoy an income in excess of £5,000 per annum: Report of the Charity Commissioners for England and Wales for 1970, p. 8.

[26] See Universities and Colleges (Trusts) Act 1943 which enabled the universities of Oxford and Cambridge and the colleges in those universities, and also Winchester College, to make schemes providing for funds to be administered as a single fund. (See *Re Freeston's Charity* [1978] 1 W.L.R. 741, C.A.). Private Acts have established common investment schemes for other universities; see *e.g.* Liverpool University Act 1931; Birmingham University Act 1948.

[27] See *e.g. Re Royal Society's Charitable Trusts* [1956] Ch. 87; *Re University of London Charitable Trusts* [1964] Ch. 282.

Section 22 of the Act enables the court and the Commissioners to make schemes, known as "common investment schemes," for the establishment of common investment funds, providing (a) for property transferred to the fund by or on behalf of a charity participating in the scheme to be invested under the control of trustees appointed to manage the fund; and (b) for the participating charities to be entitled (subject to the provisions of the scheme) to the capital and income of the fund in shares determined by reference to the amount or value of the property transferred to it by or on behalf of each of them and to the value of the fund at the time of the transfers.[28]

It is expressly provided that the court or the Commissioners may make a common investment scheme on the application of two or more charities.[29] In *Re University of London Charitable Trusts*[30] Wilberforce J. held that this provision enabled an application to be made by the trustees of any two or more charitable trusts, notwithstanding the fact that, as in this case, the trustees of such trusts are the same.

Initially, a scheme was made by the Commissioners, known as the Charities Official Investment Fund, in which all charities may participate[31] and in 1976 two further schemes were made.[32]

7. *Dealings with Charity Property*

Here an important reform was effected by section 29 of the Charities Act 1960. It abolished the old restrictions on dealings in charity property, fraught as they were with excessive complexity. It was necessary in the past to decide for this purpose whether a charity was, in the language employed, a plain or an endowed or a mixed charity. But these distinctions—and their attendant difficulties—can now be forgotten except where a past transaction appears on the title to property and requires investigation.[33] It is now relatively simple to decide whether consent under section 29 is necessary to sell or otherwise dispose of charity land.[34] The question to consider is, what is the class of land in the ownership of the charity? It may be of three kinds: (i) part of the permanent endowment. By "permanent endowment" is meant property held subject to a restriction which prevents its being spent in the same way as income.[35] It is necessary for this purpose, therefore, that a distinction be made in the trust instrument between the expenditure of capital and the expenditure of income;

[28] s. 22(1).
[29] s. 22(2).
[30] [1964] Ch. 282.
[31] It was made on December 4, 1962.
[32] Charinco Charities Narrower-Range Common Investment Fund, and Charibond Charities Narrower-Range Common Investment Fund: see the Report of the Charity Commissioners for 1976.
[33] See *Tudor on Charities* (6th ed.), p. 361.
[34] However, by virtue of Charities Act, 1960, s.28(1) the court can only make an order under s.29 in proceedings which are brought by the charity or by the charity trustees or "by any person interested in the charity." See *Haslemere Estates Ltd.* v. *Baker* [1982] 3 All E.R. 525 (the plaintiffs in that case were not so "interested.") See further *post*, p. 241. as to s.28(1).
[35] s. 45(3).

(ii) it may be "functional land," *i.e.* land which may or may not be part of the permanent endowment but is or has been in the use and occupation of the charity[36]; or (iii) it may be neither of these, but may have been bought as an investment with funds expendable without distinction between capital and income. In cases (i) and (ii) the sanction of the court or the Commissioners is required. In case (iii) it is not[37]; in this case, which is probably the least common of all, a sale would not indicate a radical change in the character of the charity as would a sale under heads (i) and (ii), and for this reason, presumably, no consent is required.

In any case consent is unnecessary in the case of exempt charities; and charities excepted by order or regulation also escape these requirements.[38]

8. *Ex Gratia Payments*

The court and the Attorney-General have the power to authorise charity trustees to make *ex gratia* payments out of funds held on charitable trusts,[39] for example, in pursuance of a moral obligation in favour of relatives of the deceased. This jurisdiction is not, however, exercised lightly: it is necessary to show that if the charity were an individual, it would be morally wrong of him not to make the payment.[40]

9. *Appointment of Charity Trustees*[41]

Generally the rules which apply to private trusts govern appointment of charity trustees.[42] A major general exception is that the restriction on the number of trustees imposed by section 34 of the Trustee Act 1925,[43] does not apply. But there were and still are certain other specific provisions. Under the Trustees Appointment Acts 1850, 1869 and 1890, a convenient mode of appointment was provided. The Acts related to land held on religious or educational trusts where the method of appointment was not prescribed in the trust instrument or had lapsed. All that was required was that the appointment should be made under the hand and seal of the chairman of a meeting of the charity at which the appointment could be made: it was simply to be executed in the presence of the meeting and attested by two witnesses. This was a "conclusive" act of appointment and also operated to vest the property in the new trustees together with the continuing trustees. The Acts were repealed by the Charities Act 1960,[44]

---

[36] s. 29(2).

[37] *Ibid.*

[38] s. 29(4).

[39] *Re Snowden* [1970] Ch. 700.

[40] *Ibid.* at p. 710.

[41] The Goodman Committee has recommended (p. 77) (1) that all charities should normally have a provision for rotation of trustees other than *ex officio* trustees; (2) that there should be an age limit of 70 for trustees other than *ex officio* trustees; (3) that charity executives should not be trustees as a general rule. These recommendations are welcome: too many charities appear to provide employment (albeit often unpaid) for the very aged members of the community. For the powers of a receiver and manager appointed for a charity, see *Att.-Gen.* v. *Schonfeld* [1980] 1 W.L.R. 1182.

[42] See *post*, p. 243.   [43] See *post*, p. 257.   [44] s. 35(6).

but nevertheless the provisions were preserved in relation to land acquired before January 1, 1961.

Apart from this the Charities Act also provides that new trustees may be appointed at a meeting, if a memorandum of the appointment is signed at the meeting by the person presiding or in some other manner prescribed by the meeting, and attested by two witnesses: that is then "sufficient" evidence of the appointment.[45] This provision applies to all charities (unlike the Trustees Appointment Acts), but on the other hand it can be made use of only when the trusts permit it; and (most important) it is only "sufficient" (as opposed to "conclusive") evidence of appointment, thus enabling its sufficiency to be checked on investigation of title by a purchaser.

10. *Mortmain*

The law of mortmain was belatedly repealed by the Charities Act 1960.[46] This law, going back as far as Magna Carta, prevented corporations holding land without a licence from the Crown. Its purpose was to prevent land being tied up in the dead hand (mortmain) of such artificial persons, and it was aimed particularly at religious houses. It had as its underlying purpose the protection of the feudal revenues of the Crown and the mesne lords. The law was extended to gifts to charity by the Charitable Uses Act 1735. This Act, as well as the old law, was re-enacted by the Mortmain and Charitable Uses Act 1888. One of the principal provisions relating to charity in this Act was to require enrolment of every assurance of land in the Central Office of the Supreme Court. It was later replaced by section 29(4) of the Settled Land Act 1925, which required, in place of this, recording with the Commissioners. This subsection, in turn, was repealed and replaced, so far as educational charities were concerned, by section 87(2) of the Education Act 1944, which required assurances of land to be recorded with the Minister of Education.

The registration provisions of the Act have rendered recording unnecessary. But since the whole of the law of mortmain has been abolished, it is not only the field of charity that is affected but the law generally. Moreover, the repeal is retrospective so that the title to property will not be defeated by failure to comply with the Mortmain Acts in the past.[47]

11. *Enforcement of Charitable Trusts*[48]

The Crown has the function of enforcing charitable trusts as *parens patriae*, and the Attorney-General, on behalf of the Crown, will be joined as a party to any proceedings involving charity. However, proceedings may be taken with reference to a charity, not only by the Attorney-General, but also by the charity, by any of the charity trustees, or by any persons interested in the

---

[45] s. 35(1).
[46] s. 38; Sched. 7, Pt. II.
[47] *i.e.* before July 29, 1960; s. 38(2).
[48] For personal liability of charity trustees, see Hawkins (1979) 75 L.Q.R. 99.

charity, or, if it is a local charity, by any two or more inhabitants of the area of the charity,[49] but not where there is a bona fide dispute as to the existence of a charity; if there is such a dispute the Attorney-General should bring the action.[50] All such persons, other than the Attorney-General, must first obtain an order from the Charity Commissioners or the court authorising the institution of proceedings.[51]

[49] Charities Act 1960, s. 28(1).
[50] *Re Belling* [1967] Ch. 425; *Hauxwell* v. *Barton-upon-Humber U.D.C.* [1974] Ch. 432, and see also *Childs* v. *Att.-Gen.* [1973] 1 W.L.R. 497.
[51] *Ibid.* s. 28(2).

CHAPTER 11

THE APPOINTMENT, RETIREMENT AND REMOVAL OF TRUSTEES

THE appointment and retirement of trustees is a matter of prime concern for everyone connected with the trust. Once the trust has been set up the settlor, unless he has specially reserved powers to himself, has handed to his trustees complete control over the property made subject to the trust. The interest of the beneficiaries will only be adequately protected if the trustees are scrupulously honest; prepared to give adequate time to the administration of the trust; have enough common sense and business acumen to do well with the trust property; and are able to treat fairly beneficiaries with possibly conflicting interests, such as tenant for life and remainderman.[1] As far as the trustee himself is concerned, his appointment is not to be considered lightly. Unless there is a provision in the trust instrument to the contrary[2] he will have to devote his time to the administration of the trust entirely without payment or other benefit. He may receive not gratitude from the beneficiaries for his efforts but bitterness,[3] and if he is not very careful and makes a mistake, he may be liable to make good any loss out of his own pocket.[4]

1. TYPES OF TRUSTEE

1. *Ordinary Trustees*

In general, any individual, limited company or other corporation may be appointed a trustee,[5] and a limited company may act as a trustee jointly with an individual.[6] Except in the case of infants[7] there is no statutory prohibition upon the appointment of any person as a trustee, but there are, however, some persons who, while they have the legal capacity to be trustees, may nevertheless

---

[1] The conflict of interest between tenant for life and remainderman is explained in connection with investments, *post,* p. 301, *et seq.*

[2] *Post,* p. 390 *et seq.*

[3] In *Re Londonderry* [1964] Ch. 594, a discretionary beneficiary who, and whose family had received a total of £165,000 showed the reverse of gratitude to the trustees.

[4] *Post,* p. 443.

[5] See *ante,* p. 22.

[6] The Bodies Corporate (Joint Tenancy) Act 1899. See *Re Thompson's Settlement Trusts* [1905] 1 Ch. 229.

[7] *Post,* p. 244.

be so undesirable as trustees that the court will remove them if appointed. A person may in this sense be undesirable either because of a defect in his character involving financial irresponsibility, as manifested by some circumstances leading to bankruptcy[8]; or by conviction of crimes involving dishonesty[9]; or because by being appointed a trustee he would be placed in a position where his interest as a beneficiary under the trust would conflict with his duty as a trustee. It appears however, that there has been a change in attitude with regard to the appointment of a beneficiary as a trustee. In *Forster* v. *Abraham*,[10] in 1874, where the court upheld the appointment of a life tenant as a trustee, the general undesirability of making such appointments was stressed. By contrast, one of the fundamental bases of the Settled Land Act 1925[11] is to make the beneficiary who is a tenant for life also a trustee: Parliament has given the lie to the old notions. While the appointment of a beneficiary as a *sole* trustee may well be undesirable, the appointment of a beneficiary as one of two or more trustees will often be advantageous, because the beneficiary will be induced to do the best he can for the trust by his financial interest in the property as well as his duty as a trustee.

Infants are in a curious position. It is clear than an infant may *be* a trustee. Thus in *Re Vinogradoff*[12] a woman transferred a holding of War Stock into the joint names of herself and her granddaughter, Laura, aged four. There was no presumption of advancement[13] and the court decided that Laura held that stock as a trustee on a resulting trust.[14] But although an infant may be a trustee, he cannot be expressly appointed to be a trustee. Section 20 of the Law of Property Act 1925 declares void the appointment of an infant as a trustee. If, therefore, an infant is to be a trustee, he will have to become a trustee otherwise than by express appointment.

The general principle is that an ordinary trustee is not entitled to remuneration for his services. This is considered in detail later.[15]

2. *Judicial Trustees*

A judicial trustee is a person or corporation appointed by the court to act as a trustee where it is desired that the administration of the trust shall be subject to close supervision by the court. The appointment is made under the provisions of the Judicial Trustees Act 1896, and is not to be confused with the appointment of a private trustee by the court. The appointment of a judicial trustee is generally made on the application of an existing trustee or beneficiary, but the

---

[8] *Re Barker's Trusts* (1875) 1 Ch.D. 43.
[9] *Coombe* v. *Brookes* (1871) L.R. 12 Eq. 61; *Re Forster* (1886) 55 L.T. 479; *Re Henderson* [1940] Ch. 764; and see *post*, p. 255.
[10] (1874) L.R. 17 Eq. 351.
[11] See s.16.
[12] [1935] W.N. 68.
[13] The woman did not stand *in loco parentis* to Laura.
[14] *Ante*, p. 126.
[15] *Post*, p. 390.

appointment can also be made at the instance of a person who is intending to create a trust.[16]

The characteristic features of being a judicial trustee are that the beneficiaries are protected in the event of his defalcation because he is usually required to give security to the court for the proper performance of his duties.[17] He is subject to close supervision by the court, and special provisions govern the auditing of his accounts.[18] In return, a judicial trustee becomes an officer of the court, so that he is able to obtain the directions of the court informally at any time.

In practice it is rare for a judicial trustee to be appointed otherwise than where there is complex litigation,[19] where there has been gross mismanagement of a trust in the past, or where there is a problem of extraordinary complexity or difficulty involved in its administration.[20]

A judicial trustee may always charge for his services[21] and is paid from the trust funds.

3. *Trust Corporations*

(1) **Definition**

It has been shown[22] that, in principle, any company as well as any individual can be appointed a trustee, but a company which is appointed a trustee is not necessarily a trust corporation. This term is applied to a body corporate, such as a bank or insurance company, which undertakes the business of acting as a trustee, and which fulfils certain conditions.[23] The basic conditions are[24]:

1. Its constitution must authorise it to undertake the business of acting as a trustee, and of acting as a personal representative.
2. It must have an issued capital of not less than £250,000, of which not less than £100,000 must have been paid up in cash.
3. The company must either:
    (a) be incorporated in the United Kingdom or

---

[16] Judicial Trustees Act 1896, s.1(1).

[17] Judicial Trustees Act 1896, s.4(1); Judicial Trustee Rules 1897, r. 9.

[18] Judicial Trustees Act 1896, ss.1(6), 4(1); Administration of Justice Act 1982, s.57; *Re Ridsdel, Ridsdel* v. *Rawlinson* [1947] Ch. 597.

[19] See *Re Diplock, Diplock* v. *Wintle* [1948] Ch. 465; affirmed *sub nom. Minister of Health* v. *Simpson* [1951] A.C. 251.

[20] *Re Chisholm* (1898) 43 S.J. 43.

[21] Judicial Trustees Act, ss.1(5), 4(1); Judicial Trustee Rules 1897, r. 17.

[22] *Ante*, p. 243.

[23] The path to the definition is tortuous:
    (a) certain bodies are entitled to act as custodian trustee (see *post*, p. 248) by virtue of the Public Trustee Rules 1912, as amended.
    (b) The Public Trustee Rules 1912, were made under the power conferred by the Public Trustee Act 1906.
    (c) s.68(18) of the T.A. 1925, provides that the definition of a "trust corporation" for the purposes of the Act includes any corporation entitled to act as a custodian trustee under the rules made under the P.T.A. 1906.

[24] The Public Trustee (Custodian Trustee) Rules 1975 (S.I. 1975 No. 1189). The rules were made to implement the EEC Council Directive 73/183/EEC.

(b) be incorporated in any other EEC country.
4. The company must have a place of business in the United Kingdom, wherever it is incorporated.

The second condition, which was intended to afford a considerable measure of protection to beneficiaries, is now totally inadequate to do so. The value of assets in any one trust may exceed by several times the amount of the minimum required paid up capital. Furthermore, the test is as to the amount of the issued share capital of the company, and not as to its asset value. Thus, if a company had issued shares to the extent of £250,000, it would still be eligible to be a trust corporation even if it had by improvidence lost all its shareholders' funds.

In addition to commercial companies which carry on the business of acting as trustees, a number of other bodies also rank as trust corporations. They are given this status so that they can take advantage of the privileges given to trust corporations.[25] The following persons and bodies are included in the definition of trust corporation:

(a) Any body corporate which is appointed by the court to be a trustee in any particular case.[26]
(b) Certain bodies which are incorporated to act as trustees of charitable trusts.[27]
(c) Certain public officers, such as the Public Trustee,[28] the Treasury Solicitor, and the Official Solicitor.[29]
(d) Major local authorities,[30] and certain public authorities, such as the Gas Council and Regional Hospital Boards.[31]

(2) Ability to act

A trust corporation can act in the administration of any trust[32] unless the trust instrument forbids its employment.

(3) Privileges

The general principle is that where statutory provisions require an act to be done by two private trustees, that act can be done by a sole trustee where that trustee is a trust corporation. It follows that the main privileges of a trust corporation are as follows:

1. A trust corporation can by itself give a good receipt for capital money under a trust for sale[33] or a settlement.[34]

---

[25] *Post.*
[26] T.A. 1925, s.68(18).
[27] The incorporation must be by Special Act, or Royal Charter, or under the Charitable Trustees Incorporation Act 1872: Public Trustee Rules 1912, r. 30 (c) (d), as substituted.
[28] Trustee Act 1925, s.68(18).
[29] Law of Property (Amendment) Act 1926, s.3(1).
[30] The Public Trustee Rules 1912, r. 30 (g); Local Government Act 1972, s.241.
[31] The Public Trustee Rules 1912, r. 30 (e) (f).
[32] *Re Cherry's Trusts, Robinson* v. *Wesleyan Methodist Chapel Purposes Trustees* [1914] 1 Ch. 83.
[33] T.A. 1925, s.14(2).
[34] Settled Land Act 1925, ss.94, 95.

2. A trust corporation can by itself exercise various powers of management, such as the apportionment of blended funds; accepting compositions; and effecting compromises.[35]

3. Where a private trustee acts jointly with a trust corporation and the private trustee wishes to delegate the performance of his duties, he may delegate them to the trust corporation.[36] He cannot, however, delegate his powers to his co-trustee if the co-trustee is a private trustee.

4. A private trustee may be discharged without a fresh trustee being appointed in his place where a trust corporation will be left to perform the trusts.[37]

As a result of these provisions, it is common to find a trust corporation acting as the sole trustee of a trust, although it can act jointly with a private trustee.

(4) Remuneration

A trust corporation is generally in the same position as a private trustee[38]; and is only entitled to remuneration where there is a provision to that effect in the trust instrument. In practice, therefore, a commercial body which is a trust corporation will not agree to act until arrangements are made for its remuneration. Where, however, the court appoints a trust corporation to be a trustee, it may fix its remuneration.[39]

4. *The Public Trustee*

The Public Trustee is a corporation sole and was established by the Public Trustee Act 1906. His main function is to administer private trusts, particularly small trusts, although he may also be appointed a judicial[40] or custodian trustee,[41] and be appointed to administer the property of a convict.[42] He may not act as the trustee of a religious or charitable trust[43] and may only carry on a business owned by a trust for the purpose of winding it up.[44] Although the Public Trustee is a public officer, he can only act in the administration of any trust if he has been appointed to do so in the same way as a private individual. Also, he may refuse to accept any trust for any reason other than the smallness of the trust property. He may act either alone or jointly with other trustees.

As he is a corporation sole, the Public Trustee never dies. This means that where he is the sole trustee, it is never necessary for there to be an appointment

---

[35] T.A. 1925, s.19.
[36] T.A. 1925, s.25(1) (2), substituted by the Powers of Attorney Act 1971. See *post*, p. 287.
[37] *Post*, p. 260.
[38] See *post*, p. 390.
[39] T.A. 1925, s.42.
[40] *Ante*, p. 244.
[41] *Post*, p. 248.
[42] P.T.A. 1906, s.5.
[43] *Re Hampton* (1918) 88 L.J.Ch. 103.
[44] Public Trustee Rules 1912, r. 7(1) and (2).

of new trustees. A further advantage is that if he acts improperly, and loss occurs, the State makes good that loss.[45]

The Public Trustee may always charge for his services,[46] his fees being calculated not on the amount of work done, but on the value of the property administered. This provision is particularly important where persons are trustees of a trust instrument which contains no charging clause. They themselves cannot derive any benefit from the trust, and may find it difficult to persuade private trustees to accept office in their stead, but they can hand over to the Public Trustee.

5. *Custodian Trustees*

The function of a custodian trustee, who may be the Public Trustee or any other trust corporation, is to hold the trust property, leaving the administration of the trust in the hands of managing trustees. A custodian trustee is usually appointed so that once the trust property is vested in his name, it will not be necessary to have any further appointment of new trustees, and so that he may have custody of the trust deeds and securities.

A custodian trustee may always charge for the services which he performs in that capacity.[47]

II. The Appointment of Trustees

1. *Persons who can Appoint*

It is necessary to distinguish the occasions on which trustees are appointed, and the manner in which they are appointed. Trustees may be appointed:
  (a) on the creation of a new trust; and
  (b) during the continuance of an existing trust, whether in substitution for a trustee who is retiring or who has died, or in addition to the existing trustees.

In both cases, almost always the appointment is made by deed without the court becoming involved in any way, but in exceptional cases, when there is no one else able to do so, the court will make the appointment itself. Thus one must consider appointments made outside the court, and appointments made by the court itself.

(1) The creation of a new trust

When he creates a trust *inter vivos*, the settlor will usually appoint the first trustees of the settlement himself. If he wishes to appoint people other than himself to be the trustees, he will include a clause appointing them in the original settlement or trust deed. On the other hand, he may wish to appoint himself. He may make a declaration of trust—that is, he may declare that from

[45] P.T.A. 1906, s.7.
[46] P.T.A. 1906, s.9, as amended by the Public Trustee (Fees) Act 1957.
[47] P.T.A. 1906, s.2; see, *post*, p. 395.

the time of that declaration he will hold specified property on certain trusts—and he will then be the only trustee of the trust. Or he may appoint himself and another to be the first trustees. But as soon as the trust has come into existence, the settlor has lost his right *qua settlor* to appoint the trustees of the settlement. He may in the trust instrument have given someone the power to nominate future trustees, and he may have nominated himself[48] but if he makes any future appointment under that power, he will do so because he is the person named in the trust instrument, and not because he was the settlor.

Occasionally, there will be no trustees of a new trust. The trustees named in the settlement may be dead, or may refuse to act. Or the settlor may have forgotten to name any. If the trust instrument nominates someone to appoint new trustees, that power can be used: otherwise the appointment will be made by the court.[49] In doing so, the court will give effect to the equitable maxim that "the court will not allow a trust to fail for want of a trustee."

In practice trusts arise most frequently on death. Where the deceased left a will, he may have expressly set up a trust by his will, or a trust may arise by operation of law. Thus, if he left a legacy to a child, the money cannot actually be paid to that child until he reaches the age of eighteen, because an infant cannot give a good receipt for capital money. Until then the money will have to be held upon trust for the child. If the deceased died intestate, the devolution of his property is governed by the Administration of Estates Act 1925, as varied by subsequent statutes and statutory instruments[50] the last being The Family Provision (Intestate Succession) Order 1981. In some circumstances, the intestate's property will have to be held on statutory trusts. For example, if the deceased was worth £60,000 and left a wife and son, the wife will be entitled to £40,000. The remaining £20,000 is divided into two parts: one part goes to the son, and the other part is held upon trust for the wife for life, with remainder after her death for the son.[51]

It is possible where the trust is created by will to designate different persons as trustees from the executors, but normally the same persons are both executors and trustees. In particular, where there is no appointment of a different person as a trustee, the executor may automatically become the trustee. Whether he will in fact do so depends on the function which the person is discharging at the point in time being considered. The rules which govern the time at which an executor becomes a trustee are not considered here,[52] but it is sufficient to say that the functions of an executor (or, in the case of an intestacy, an administrator) are:

(a) in the case of an executor, obtaining probate of the deceased's will, or

---

[48] *Post*, p. 251.
[49] *Dodkin* v. *Brunt* (1868) L.R. 6 Eq. 580.
[50] *i.e.* the Intestates Estates Act 1952; the Family Provision Act 1966; and the Inheritance (Provision for Family and Dependants) Act 1975.
[51] The wife would in addition receive the personal chattels of the deceased.
[52] See further Mellows, *The Law of Succession* (4th ed.), p. 275.

in the case of an administrator, obtaining letters of administration of his estate;

(b) getting in the deceased's property, and the debts due to him;

(c) paying any capital transfer tax, and the deceased's debts;

(d) paying the legacies;

(e) agreeing the distribution account with the beneficiaries; and

(f) distributing all the property which can be immediately distributed, *i.e.* all the property remaining after the payment of debts and legacies, other than that which is governed by a trust, or which is not payable at once to a beneficiary because he is under eighteen.

When all this has been done, in general, the executor or administrator ceases to be a personal representative and if there is still any of the deceased's property in his name, thenceforth he holds it as a trustee, not as a personal representative. In the case of land, however, an executor or administrator will continue to hold the property as personal representative until he assents to its vesting in himself as trustee.[53] In this case, therefore, the test is not one of function, but whether there has been the formal act of making an assent.

(2) Appointment of a new trustee

Whether the trust was set up *inter vivos* or arose on death, the rules relating to the appointment of new trustees are the same. The trust instrument may make provision for the appointment of new trustees, and if reliance is placed on that power, its terms must be strictly followed. If the trust instrument does not make provision there is a statutory power contained in section 36(1) of the Trustee Act 1925, and if there is conflict between the provisions of the trust instrument and the statutory power, the statutory power prevails. Under the statutory power, the following persons, and in the following order, have the right to appoint new trustees. Only if there is no person in one group, or if they refuse to appoint, can the appointment be made by a person in the subsequent group. These groups are:

Statutory power:

(a) the person or persons nominated in the trust instrument;

(b) the existing trustees;

(c) the personal representatives of the last or only surviving trustee.

Other powers

(d) the beneficiaries in certain limited cases;

(e) the court.

This order is strictly followed. Thus, in *Re Higginbottom*[54] the existing trustee had the power to appoint new trustees, and her right to do so was held to prevail against the wishes of a large majority of the beneficiaries who sought to appoint

---

[53] *Re King's Will Trusts* [1964] Ch. 542; see *ante*, p. 14.
[54] [1892] 3 Ch. 132.

others.[55] Further, where an appointment is made in good faith by the person entitled, the court will not interfere with the appointment even if it would prefer someone else to be appointed.[56]

Where two or more persons have the power of appointing new trustees, they must exercise the power jointly unless there is a provision in the trust instrument to the contrary. If they cannot agree who the new trustee shall be, they are treated as refusing to exercise their power, so that the power becomes exercisable by the persons in the next category. So in *Re Sheppard's Settlement Trusts*[57] the trust instrument gave the power of appointing trustees to two persons. When they could not agree on the appointee, it was held that the power could be exercised by the continuing trustees. The position is the same if the person having the power to appoint cannot be found,[58] or is incapable of making the appointment.[59]

(a) **Persons nominated in the trust instrument.** As was mentioned above,[60] if a settlor wishes himself to make an appointment of trustees of an existing trust, he must have given himself this power in the trust instrument. Otherwise, he has no power to appoint. In many cases, of course, the settlor will give some other person the power to appoint new trustees.

Where a person is nominated in the trust instrument[61] he is usually given the power to appoint new trustees in all circumstances, but if he is only given power to do so in limited circumstances, that power is strictly construed. In *Re Wheeler,*[62] for example, a person was nominated to appoint a new trustee in the place of any trustee being "incapable" of acting. One trustee became bankrupt, and so became "unfit" to act,[63] but not "incapable" of acting. It was held that the nominated person did not have a power to appoint in those circumstances because the condition was not fulfilled.[64] Further, where a power to appoint is given jointly to two or more persons, it can only be exercised by those persons. Unless, therefore, there is evidence of a contrary intention, the power will not be exercisable at all where one of the donees of the power dies, or becomes incapable of making the appointment.[65]

Where a beneficiary is nominated in the trust instrument as having power to appoint new trustees, the power of appointment is generally treated as being

---

[55] See also *Re Brockbank* [1948] Ch. 206; *post,* p. 252.

[56] *Re Gadd, Eastwood* v. *Clark* (1883) 23 Ch.D. 134, C.A.; *Re Norris, Allen* v. *Norris* (1884) 27 Ch.D. 333; *Re Sales, Sales* v. *Sales* (1911) 55 S.J. 838.

[57] [1888] W.N. 234.

[58] *Craddock* v. *Witham* [1895] W.N. 75.

[59] *Re Blake* [1887] W.N. 75.

[60] *Ante,* p. 249.

[61] See *Re Walker and Hughes* (1883) 24 Ch.D. 698 and *Re Sheppard's Settlement Trusts* [1888] W.N. 234.

[62] [1896] 1 Ch. 315 (a case on s.10(1), Trustee Act 1893, re-enacted in s.36(1), Trustee Act 1925).

[63] As to the distinction, see *post,* pp. 255, 256.

[64] See also *Turner* v. *Maule* (1850) 15 Jur. 761; *Re Watts' Settlement* (1851) 9 Hare 106; *Re May's Will Trusts* [1941] Ch. 109.

[65] *Re Harding, Harding* v. *Paterson* [1923] 1 Ch. 182.

detached from the beneficial interest. Thus, if the beneficiary disposes of his interest then, unless there is a provision in the trust instrument to the contrary, he will still be entitled to appoint new trustees.[66]

An illogical difference exists in respect of the appointment of a new trustee between the position where an existing trustee is retiring, and where an additional trustee is to be appointed without the retirement of an existing trustee. If he is acting solely under the statutory power,[67] a person who is nominated in the trust instrument to appoint new trustees may appoint himself to be a trustee in the place of a retiring trustee but not as an additional trustee. This results from a difference of wording in the Trustee Act. Section 36(1), which applies where a new trustee is being appointed in the place of an outgoing trustee, gives the power to the nominated person to "appoint one or more other persons (whether or not being the persons exercising the power) to be a trustee," while section 36(6), which confers the power to appoint additional trustees, gives the nominated person a power to appoint "*another* person or other persons to be the trustee.*" This difference was doubtless unintentional on the part of Parliament.

(b) **The existing trustees, and the personal representatives of the last surviving trustee.** The right of the existing trustees, or if there are none, the personal representatives of the last surviving trustee,[68] to appoint new trustees is one which takes precedence over any wishes of the beneficiaries. In *Re Brockbank*[69] where there was a dispute between the existing trustees and the beneficiaries as to whom should be appointed a new trustee, it was held that as long as the trustees wished to make an appointment, they could do so irrespectively of the wishes of the beneficiaries. The appointment of new trustees was a function which Parliament has entrusted to the continuing trustees, and as long as they were willing to exercise it, the beneficiaries could not interfere.

Rather surprisingly, section 36(8) enacts that the provisions of section 36 which relate to a continuing trustee include a refusing or retiring trustee if he is willing to act in exercising the powers of the section. The result of this is that if a trustee refuses to act as a trustee, or wishes to retire, he must be allowed to join in the appointment of a new trustee if he wishes to do so. But for the purposes of this provision, the expression "refusing or retiring trustee" is narrowly construed. In *Re Stoneham's Settlement Trusts*[70] a new trustee was appointed in the place of another trustee who had remained out of the United Kingdom for longer than twelve months. On his return, the displaced trustee applied to the court to upset the appointment on the ground that he had not participated in it, but Danckwerts J. held that a trustee who is removed compulsorily from the

---

[66] *Hardaker* v. *Moorhouse* (1884) 26 Ch.D. 417.

[67] *Re Power's Settlement Trust* [1951] Ch. 1074. The Law Reform Committee recommend that the person having power to appoint trustees should be able to appoint himself.

[68] *Re Shafto's Trusts* (1885) 29 Ch.D. 247.

[69] [1948] Ch. 206.

[70] [1953] Ch. 59.

trust is not a "refusing or retiring" trustee but a "removed" trustee, so that his participation is not necessary.

Where there are no existing trustees, the appointment can be made by the personal representative of the last surviving trustee. In this respect it is necessary to distinguish the power of appointment itself on the one hand and the method of proving entitlement to exercise that power on the other hand. An executor has the power of appointing new trustees as soon as the last trustee dies. Accordingly, it is not necessary for the executor to obtain a grant of probate before exercising the power.[71] However, a personal representative can only prove his entitlement to exercise the power by producing a grant of probate or letters of administration.

It is the general practice of the English court only to recognise grants of probate or letters of administration which have been issued in the United Kingdom or, if issued by a court overseas, have been re-sealed by a court in the United Kingdom. The point arose in *Re Crowhurst Park*.[72] In that case, the deceased was the sole trustee of various tenancies of land in England. His widow obtained a grant of probate of his will in Jersey, but she did not obtain a grant in the United Kingdom. The widow executed a deed by which, in her capacity as the personal representative of the deceased, she purported to appoint herself as the new trustee of that trust. It was held that while she was entitled to exercise the power of appointment, she could only prove that entitlement by a grant of probate or letters of administration granted in the United Kingdom. Accordingly, the widow could not take action in respect of the tenancies until she obtained a United Kingdom grant.

Although personal representatives of the last surviving trustee may appoint new trustees, this is a mere power, and they cannot be compelled to do so.[73] They are, however, given statutory encouragement to exercise their power. Thus, even if they intend to renounce their office as personal representatives, they are still entitled to appoint new trustees before they renounce.[74] Without the express statutory provision, the exercise of the power would be sufficient to show an acceptance of the office of personal representative.

The appointment of trustees, whether by a surviving or continuing trustee, or by personal representatives of the last surviving trustee, must be made *inter vivos*, and cannot be made by will.[75]

(c) **Beneficiaries.** Where there is no person nominated in the trust instrument, no existing trustees, and no personal representatives of the last surviving trustee in existence and willing to make an appointment, the beneficiaries may probably do so if they are all *sui juris* and between them absolutely entitled to the whole of the beneficial interest, but in this situation it is preferable to obtain an

---

[71] *Re Parker's Trusts* [1894] 1 Ch. 707; *Re Crowhurst Park, Sims-Hilditch* v. *Simmons* [1974] 1 All E.R. 991, at 1001.
[72] [1974] 1 All E.R. 991.
[73] *Re Knight's Will* (1883) 26 Ch.D. 82, C.A.
[74] T.A. 1925, s.36(5).
[75] See *Re Parker's Trust* [1894] 1 Ch. 707.

order of the court appointing the new trustees.[76] As is explained later,[77] where the beneficiaries are unable to make the appointment the court will do so.

2. When a New Trustee may be Appointed

Section 36 of the Trustee Act 1925 makes provision for the appointment of new trustees in two types of case:

(1) in the place of an outgoing trustee; and
(2) as an additional trustee, where all existing trustees are remaining.

(1) In place of outgoing trustee

Section 36(1) provides that in certain specified circumstances, the person nominated for the purpose in the trust instrument, or, if there is no such person, the surviving trustees or trustee, or the personal representatives of the last surviving trustee, in that order, may appoint by writing[78] one or more persons to be trustees in the place of an outgoing trustee. The section applies in the case of any outgoing trustee, whether or not he was the original trustee of the trust, and whether or not he was appointed by the court. Section 36(1) applies:

(a) where a trustee is dead;
(b) where he remains out of the United Kingdom for more than twelve months;
(c) where he desires to be discharged;
(d) where he refuses to act;
(e) where he is unfit to act;
(f) where he is incapable of acting;
(g) where he is an infant; and
(h) by virtue of section 36(3), in the case of a corporation which is a trustee, where that corporation is dissolved.

These provisions require elaboration, but it may be noted at once that these events only give rise to a power to appoint a new trustee: they do not impose a duty to appoint.

(a) **Trustee dead.** This includes the position where a person nominated as a trustee dies without ever having taken up his office. This would be the case, for example, where a person who is nominated as the trustee of a will trust dies before the death of the testator.

(b) **Remaining out of the United Kingdom.** The residence abroad must be a continuous residence and a break for even a very short time, such as a week, will prevent this provision operating.[79] The motive for the residence is irrelevant,[80]

---

[76] *Re Brockbank, ante.*
[77] *Post*, p. 258.
[78] The statute only requires the appointment to be in writing and not by deed. It is desirable to make the appointment by deed in most cases, so that s.40, Trustee Act 1925, may operate; *post*, p. 263.
[79] *Re Walker, Summers* v. *Barrow* [1910] 1 Ch. 259.
[80] *Re Stoneham* [1953] Ch. 59.

so that even if the trustee has been imprisoned abroad, he can still be removed from his trusteeship.

In some circumstances the trust instrument modifies the statutory provision, and seeks to achieve the same broad effect by different wording. Where this is done, the provision must be carefully construed, but the courts lean towards an interpretation that the period abroad must have an element of permanence. This was satisfied in *Re Earl of Stamford*[81] where the power arose if a trustee should "be abroad," and a trustee lived in France, making only occasional visits to England.[82]

The provision can now be totally inappropriate where a foreign trust is to be established, or where an English trust is to be "exported."[83] In such cases, it is prudent to provide expressly that a trustee shall not be capable of being replaced merely because he is resident abroad.

(c) **Desiring to be discharged.** This statutory provision is wide enough to include the position where the trustee desires to be discharged from only part of the trust.[84] This might occur where part of a trust fund is set aside to provide a life interest for a beneficiary and the trustee wishes to retire as a trustee of the main fund, while remaining a trustee of the appropriated fund.

(d) **Refusal to act.** Logically, this provision should apply only to a person who has accepted the trusteeship, and refuses to act after accepting office. Until that time, it is difficult to see how he could be a "trustee." However, there is old authority on the precursor of the section to the effect that it also includes a trustee who disclaims.[85]

(e) **Unfit to act.** There is little authority as to the meaning of "unfitness" for the purposes of this provision, but it seems clear that "unfitness" here refers not to medical infirmity but to defects of character. In the absence of authority, it is only possible to deduce the meaning of the expression from some of the circumstances in which the court will remove trustees.[86] These cases include conviction of a crime involving dishonesty[87] and in certain circumstances bankruptcy. In the case of bankruptcy the court will generally remove a trustee who has become bankrupt,[88] particularly if the beneficiaries request this to be done, if only on the ground that a person who has lost all his own money ought not to be in charge of other people's money. But as an exception to this, the

---

[81] [1896] 1 Ch. 288.
[82] See also *Re Moravian Society* (1858) 26 Beav. 101.
[83] See *post*, Chap. 21.
[84] If this statutory power is excluded, a trustee cannot be discharged from part only of the fund without the intervention of the court: *Savile* v. *Couper* (1887) 36 Ch.D. 520; *Re Moss's Trusts* (1888) 37 Ch.D. 513.
[85] *Noble* v. *Meymott* (1841) 14 Beav. 471; *Re Hadley, ex p. Hadley,* (1851) 5 De G. & Sm. 67; *Viscountess D'Adhemar* v. *Bertrand* (1865) 35 Beav. 19; *Re Birchall, Birchall* v. *Ashton* (1889) 40 Ch.D. 436.
[86] *Post*, p. 262.
[87] *Turner* v. *Maule* (1850) 15 Jur. 761; *Re Wheeler and De Rochow* [1896] 1 Ch. 315; *Re Sichel's Settlements, Sichel* v. *Sichel* [1916] 1 Ch. 358.
[88] *Re Barker's Trusts* (1875) 1 Ch.D. 43.

court refused to remove a trustee whose bankruptcy was due to misfortune and who was entirely free of moral blame.[89]

(f) **Incapable of acting.** Incapacity refers to physical or mental incapacity to attend, or to attend properly, to the administration of the trust.[90] Special provisions affect mental incapacity where the trustee also has a beneficial interest in the property if he is a person whose mental illness makes him subject to the provisions of the Mental Health Act 1959. In this case, no appointment of a new trustee in his place may be made without the consent of the authority having jurisdiction over him under the Mental Health Act 1959.[91]

A person is also incapable of acting if there is any legislation in force which expressly prohibits persons in specified circumstances from holding property or acting as trustees. Such a prohibition has applied to enemy aliens in time of war.[92]

(g) **Trustee a minor.** As has been seen,[93] a minor cannot validly be expressly appointed a trustee, and the provisions will only apply where the minor is a trustee under a resulting or constructive trust.

(2) Additional trustees: existing trustees remaining

The statutory power of appointing additional trustees is contained in section 36(6). The person nominated in the trust instrument for the purpose of appointing new trustees, or the existing trustee or trustees, in that order, may appoint by writing an additional trustee or additional trustees of the trust where there are not more than three existing trustees. Although more than one additional trustee may be appointed at the same time, the total number of trustees must not be increased beyond four, and this restriction applies to all trusts, and is not confined to trusts affecting land.[94] Additional trustees cannot be appointed under this section if any existing trustee is a trust corporation.[94a]

(3) Trustees of separate property

The person who has the power of appointing new trustees may appoint a separate set of trustees for any part of the trust property which is held on trusts distinct from the remainder of the trust property.[95] If, therefore, trustees hold three quarters of the trust fund upon trust for Andrew and his family, and one quarter for Bernard and his family, separate trustees can be appointed of the quarter held for Bernard. While, however, the appointment is valid for all

---

[89] *Re Bridgman* (1860) 1 Drew. & Sm. 164.

[90] *Re Moravian Society* (1858) 26 Beav. 101; *Re Watt's Settlement* (1872) L.R. 7 Ch. 223; *Turner* v. *Maule* (1850) 15 Jur. 761; *Re East* (1873) 8 Ch.App. 735; *Re Lemann's Trusts* (1883) 22 Ch.D. 633; *Re Blake* [1887] W.N. 173, C.A.; *Re Weston's Trusts* [1898] W.N. 151.

[91] Mental Health Act 1959, ss.149(1), 153 and Sched. VII, replacing T.A. 1925, s.36(9).

[92] *Re Sichel's Settlements, Sichel* v. *Sichel, ante.*

[93] *Ante*, p. 244.

[94] See next section.

[94a] The Law Reform Committee recommend the abolition of this rule.

[95] T.A. 1925, s.37(1) (*b*).

purposes connected with the administration of the trust, for certain tax purposes, the original trustees will continue to be regarded as trustees.[96]

3. *Restrictions on the Numbers of Trustees*

The general principle is that any number of persons may be trustees, and the determining factor is not a legal one, but the practical one of having enough trustees to be able to take advantage of various skills and experience, but not too many to make the working of the trust unwieldly.

Nevertheless, there are certain restrictions on the numbers of trustees:

(a) The maximum number of trustees of a settlement of land or of land held upon trust for sale is four, and if more than four persons are named, the first four named who are able and willing to act are the trustees (Trustee Act 1925, s.34). This limitation does not apply in the case of land held upon trust for charitable, ecclesiastical or public purposes.[97]

(b) There need only be one trustee to *hold* land, but unless that trustee is a trust corporation two or more trustees are needed to give a valid receipt for capital money,[98] so that two or more trustees are in fact needed to *sell* land.

(c) Where under a will or on intestacy property is to be held for an infant, and no trustees are appointed by any will, the personal representatives of the deceased may appoint trustees to hold that property on trust for the infant, but the number of those trustees must not exceed four.[99] This applies whatever the nature of the property.

(d) Where an additional trustee is being appointed under the statutory power referred to above and all the existing trustees are remaining, the number of trustees must not be increased to more than four in any case.

(e) Where a trustee wishes to retire, but it is not proposed to appoint a new trustee in his place, he can only do so if, *inter alia*, at least two trustees will remain (Trustee Act 1925, s.39).[1]

In any case a minimum of two trustees is usually *desirable,* in order to give the beneficiaries adequate protection. One of the basic safeguards for beneficiaries is that property must usually be under the control of at least two persons, so that it is very much more difficult for one to misappropriate the money.

4. *Assumption of Office by Conduct*

Acceptance of the office of trustee of an *inter vivos* trust is usually signified by the trustee executing the trust deed. But in any case, where a trustee does any

---

[96] *Roome* v. *Edwards* [1981] 3 All E.R. 736, H.L.
[97] T.A. 1925, s.34(3). The Law Reform Committee recommend that, unless the trust instrument otherwise provides, there should never be more than four trustees of a private trust.
[98] T.A. 1925, s.14(2).
[99] Administration of Estates Act 1925, s.42.
[1] *Post*, p. 260.

act in carrying out the trust, he will be presumed from his conduct to have accepted the office. Any act, even though slight, in carrying out the terms of the trust is sufficient.[2]

5. *Appointment by the Court*

Whenever it is desirable that a new trustee should be appointed, and it is "inexpedient, difficult or impracticable so to do without the assistance of the court" the court may appoint a new trustee either as an additional trustee, or in substitution for an existing trustee.[3] The court will not, in the absence of exceptional circumstances, exercise its power if advantage can be taken of a provision in the trust instrument or of the statutory power.[4] Further, there appears to be no reported decision in which the court has appointed a trustee against the wishes of a person who has the power to appoint and who is prepared to exercise it in good faith. This is so even if the court would prefer to see someone else appointed.[5] Where the court proposes to appoint a new trustee in substitution for an existing trustee, it may do so even against the wishes of the existing trustee.[6]

In practice this power is used mainly (a) where there is doubt whether the statutory power can be exercised, *e.g.* if a trustee is in fact "unfit" to act; (b) where there is no person capable of making an appointment, and (c) where it is desired to increase the number of trustees and the statutory power under section 36 does not apply.

Occasionally an application is made to the court for the appointment of a new trustee, because if a new trustee is appointed by the court it cannot afterwards be alleged that the trustee was appointed in circumstances which were improper or in order to facilitate a breach of trust.[7] The court will, therefore, only exercise its power where it is clearly in the interest of the beneficiaries for it to make the appointment. An example of a case where the court refused to exercise its power is *Re Weston's Settlement*[8] which is discussed in a later chapter.[9]

The court has a discretion as to whom it will appoint as a trustee, but the principles upon which this discretion will be exercised are:

(a) If the settlor has expressly or by clear implication made known his wishes,

---

[2] *Lord Montfort* v. *Lord Cadogan* (1816) 19 Ves. 635; *James* v. *Frearson* (1842) 1 Y. & C.C.C. 370. Thus a person designated a trustee should expressly renounce if he does not wish to act.

[3] Trustee Act 1925, s.41. See also *Re Hodson's Settlement* (1851) 9 Hare 118; *Finlay* v. *Howard* (1842) 2 Dru. & War. 490.

[4] *Re Gibbon* (1882) 45 L.T. 756; 30 W.R. 287.

[5] *Re Higginbottom* [1892] 3 Ch. 132; *ante*, p. 250; *Re Brockbank, Ward* v. *Bates* [1948] Ch. 206, *ante*, p. 252.

[6] *Re Henderson* [1940] Ch. 764.

[7] See *post*, p. 443.

[8] [1969] 1 Ch. 223, C.A.

[9] *Post*, p. 439.

the court will have regard to his wishes. This is particularly so if the settlor has indicated whom he does *not* wish to be appointed.

(b) A trustee will not be appointed to promote the interest of some of the beneficiaries in opposition to the interest of other beneficiaries.[10] The attitude of the courts has, however, changed over the last century or so in two important respects. First, it used to be that the court would not appoint a beneficiary to be a trustee.[11] The reason was the fear that the trustee-beneficiary would be tempted to act more in his own interest than that of the other beneficiaries. However, more recently, following the statutory examples,[12] it has been realised that in some circumstances a person who has a beneficial interest may put a greater effort and enthusiasm into the administration of the trust than someone else, and that the appointment of such a person as a trustee may be appropriate, particularly where there is also an independent trustee. The second respect in which the attitude of the courts has changed is with regard to professional advisers. In the middle of the nineteenth century the courts would almost never appoint the family solicitor to be a trustee,[13] but with perhaps greater confidence in the integrity of professional advisers, and realisation of the advantage which detailed knowledge of the family circumstances brings, such persons may now be appointed, particularly where this is desired by the beneficiaries.

(c) The court will have regard to whether the proposed appointment will promote the execution of the trust, or whether it will impede it.[14]

An interesting situation arises where the existing trustees make it known that they will refuse to act with the person whom the court proposes to appoint. On the one hand the court's dignity is involved. In *Re Tempest*[15] Turner L.J. said: "I think it would be going too far to say that the court ought, on that ground alone, to refuse to appoint the proposed trustee: for this would, as suggested in the argument, be to give the continuing or surviving trustee a veto upon the appointment of the new trustee. In such a case I think it must be the duty of the court to inquire and ascertain whether the objection of the surviving or continuing trustee is well founded or not, and to act or refuse to act upon it accordingly."[16] On the other hand, the basic object of the court's power is to promote the interests of the beneficiaries, and these are not protected if there is serious friction between the trustees. Indeed, on this ground alone the court will sometimes remove a trustee.[17]

---

[10] *Re Parsons, Barnsdale and Smallman v. Parsons* [1940] Ch. 973.
[11] *e.g. Re Harrop's Trusts* (1883) 24 Ch.D. 717; *Re Knowles' Settled Estates* (1884) 27 Ch.D. 707.
[12] *Ante*, p. 244.
[13] *Re Kemp's Settled Estates* (1883) 24 Ch.D. 485, C.A.; *Re Earl of Stamford, Payne v. Stamford* [1896] 1 Ch. 288; *Re Spencer's Settled Estates* [1903] 1 Ch. 75.
[14] *Re Tempest* (1866) 1 Ch.App. 485.
[15] (1866) 1 Ch.App. 485.
[16] (1866) L.R. 1 Ch. 485, 490.
[17] *Re Henderson, ante.*

Unless, presumably, a trustee has been guilty of serious malpractice, so that his removal is a matter of urgency, the court is reluctant to appoint new trustees in the place of existing trustees if to do so would place the existing trustees in a worse financial position. In *Re Pauling's Settlement (No.* 2),[18] it was sought to remove trustees against whom an action had been brought for breach of trust.[19] But this was resisted because they might have been able to have impounded the beneficiaries' interests[20] if they were successful in an appeal in the other action. Wilberforce J. held that even if they were removed they could still exercise their right to impound. As it happened the court refused to appoint new trustees in the place of the existing trustees, because, *inter alia*, to have done so would have deprived them of security for the costs which would be payable to them if the appeal were successful.

III. RETIREMENT

1. *Circumstances in Which Trustees May Retire*

A trustee may retire from his office in any of four ways:

(a) by taking advantage of any power in the trust instrument;
(b) by taking advantage of the powers in the Trustee Act 1925, namely,
   (i) section 36, where a new trustee is being appointed in his place; or
   (ii) section 39, where no new trustee is being appointed;
(c) by obtaining the consent of all beneficiaries, who must be *sui juris* and between them absolutely entitled to the whole beneficial interest;
(d) by obtaining the consent of the court.

If there is provision in the trust instrument for a trustee to retire, then a trustee can take advantage of this power, even though it is wider than the statutory power. But the statutory power in sections 36 and 39 of the Trustee Act 1925 is so wide that specific provisions are not now normally included in trust instruments. Retirement when coupled with the appointment of a new trustee has already been considered, but by section 39 a trustee can retire even where no new trustee is being appointed in his place. Under this section, a trustee may retire if

(a) after his retirement there will remain a minimum of two trustees or a trust corporation; and
(b) he obtains the consent to his retirement of the remaining trustees; and
(c) he obtains the consent of anyone named in the trust instrument as having the power to appoint new trustees; and
(d) the retirement is by deed.

---

[18] [1963] Ch. 576.
[19] This is the case discussed at pp. 371 and 463.
[20] As to the circumstances in which a beneficiary's interest can be impounded, see *post*, p. 464.

None of these conditions applies, however, if one of the remaining trustees is the Public Trustee.[21] The requirement that two trustees or a trust corporation shall remain applies to all trusts: it has no connection with the requirement for two trustees or a trust corporation to give a receipt for land subject to a trust.[22]

Provided the conditions of section 39 are fulfilled, the retirement will be effective, but if the trustee has retired in order to procure or facilitate a breach of trust, he may nevertheless remain liable for such breach.[23]

As a last resort, if none of these cases applies, a trustee may apply to the court to be discharged as a trustee. The court will usually discharge the trustee if there is at least one other trustee who continues or some suitable new trustee can be found, but the trustee who wishes to retire will usually be ordered to pay the costs of the application unless he can show that the circumstances have materially altered since he accepted the trusteeship.[24]

There is one important difference between the scope of section 36 and that of section 39. As has been seen,[25] under section 36 a trustee can retire from part only of the trusts, but under section 39 the trustee can retire only from the whole of the trusts.

2. *Release of Retiring Trustees*

When trustees retire they sometimes request a formal release of any liability arising from the trusteeship. If trustees retire in favour of new trustees, they are not entitled to such a release, but it seems that if they retire upon the winding up of the trust they are entitled.[26] Such a release is only effective to the extent that the beneficiaries are in possession of all relevant facts.

IV. REMOVAL OF TRUSTEES

A trustee may be removed from his office:

(1) under a power contained in the trust instrument;
(2) under the statutory power contained in section 36 of the Trustee Act; or
(3) by the court.

Powers of removing trustees contained in the trust instrument are strictly construed, so that if it is desired to take advantage of any such power, it must be clear that the circumstances envisaged by such power obtain.[27] The power of

---

[21] P.T.A. 1906, s.6.

[22] *Ante*, p. 257.

[23] *Post*, p. 443.

[24] The court has expressed its disapproval of applications being made to the court for the appointment of a new trustee where advantage could be taken of the statutory power, and doubtless it would be equally disapproving if applications were made to it for retirement when advantage could be taken of the statutory power.

[25] *Supra*.

[26] *Tiger* v. *Barclays Bank Ltd.* [1951] 2 K.B. 556.

[27] *London and County Banking Co.* v. *Goddard* [1897] 1 Ch. 642.

removal of trustees under section 36, when a new trustee is being appointed, has been dealt with above. The circumstances are, it will be recalled,

(a) where the trustee remains out of the United Kingdom for more than 12 months consecutively;
(b) where he refuses to act;
(c) where he is unfit to act;
(d) where he is incapable of acting.[28]

Removal by the court presents some difficulty. The court's primary concern is to protect and enhance the interests of the beneficiaries. So that where the trustee is convicted of dishonesty, or by becoming bankrupt or otherwise[29] shows that he is not fit to be in charge of other people's property, the court will remove him.[30] Nevertheless, removal by the court does involve, at least to the outside world, some moral stigma, and difficulties arise where an application is made to remove a trustee, not because he has done anything wrong, but because he cannot agree with or get on with his co-trustees.

The position was considered by the Privy Council in *Letterstedt* v. *Broers*.[31] Lord Blackburn observed: "In exercising so delicate a jurisdiction as that of removing trustees, their Lordships do not venture to lay down any general rule beyond the very broad principle . . . that their main guide must be the welfare of the beneficiaries. Probably it is not possible to lay down any more definite rule in a matter so essentially dependent on details often of great nicety. . . . "[32] Mere friction between trustee and beneficiary is not an adequate ground, but if there is a permanent condition of hostility between one trustee and the other trustees, the court probably would remove him. In *Re Wrightson*[33] Warrington J. said: "You must find something which induces the court to think either that the trust property will not be safe or that the trust will not be properly executed in the interests of the beneficiaries." A permanent condition of hostility between trustees would probably be a sufficient deterrent to efficient administration of the trust for the court to exercise its powers.

It is difficult to appeal successfully against an order by an inferior court ordering the removal of a trustee. Thus, in *Re Edwards Will Trusts*,[34] where Megarry V.-C., had removed a trustee without giving any reasons for so doing, the Court of Appeal refused to interfere with his decisions.

V. DELEGATION OF TRUSTEESHIP

In limited circumstances, a person can delegate his powers as trustee without ceasing to be a trustee. These are considered later.[35]

---

[28] *Re Lemann's Trust* (1883) 22 Ch.D. 633.
[29] *Ibid.*; *Re Phelps' Settlement Trust* (1885) 55 L.J.Ch. 465 (intellectual decay).
[30] See the cases discussed *ante*, p. 255.
[31] (1884) 9 App.Cas. 371. And see *Earl of Portsmouth* v. *Fellows* (1820) 5 Madd. 450.
[32] (1884) 9 App.Cas. 371, at p. 382.
[33] [1908] 1 Ch. 789, at p. 803.
[34] [1981] 2 All E.R. 941, C.A.
[35] *Post*, p. 282.

VI. Vesting of Property on Change of Trustee

One of the first acts that a person should do on his appointment as a trustee is to secure that the trust property is put in the names of himself and his co-trustees. As soon as he is appointed he becomes responsible with his co-trustees for what happens to the trust property, and if he negligently allows property to remain in the names of others and loss occurs, he may be liable to make good the loss to the beneficiaries out of his own pocket.[36]

The property may be placed in the name of the new trustee, jointly with the continuing trustees, by the mode of transfer appropriate to the type of property.[37] The appropriate mode of transfer in respect of the major types of property is:

(a)	freehold land, where title not registered by H.M. Land Registry	Conveyance
(b)	leasehold land, where title not registered by H.M. Land Registry	Assignment
(c)	freehold or leasehold land, where title is registered by H.M. Land Registry	Transfer, and registration of transfer at Land Registry
(d)	stocks and shares	Transfer, and registration of transfer by company or authority concerned
(e)	debts, and other choses in action	Assignment (plus notice to debtor, etc., to secure priority)
(f)	negotiable instruments payable to bearer	Delivery and indorsement
(g)	personal chattels	Either assignment or manual delivery

These formalities can sometimes be avoided, however, by virtue of section 40 of the Trustee Act 1925, when a person is appointed a new trustee, or retires from trusteeship, and the appointment or retirement, as the case may be, is effected by deed. This section provides that unless the deed provides to the contrary, it automatically vests the trust property in the new or remaining trustees as joint tenants. The section applies to all types of trust property except:

(1) mortgages of land, when a formal transfer of mortgage is required;

(2) leasehold land, where the lease provides that before any assignment the permission of the landlord must be obtained, and the landlord's permission has not been obtained before the deed of appointment or retirement has been executed. The reason for this exception is to prevent an unwitting breach of covenant under the lease, so giving rise to a possible claim for forfeiture;

---

[36] See *post*, p. 443.

[37] The use of the appropriate mode of transfer is also discussed in connection with whether a trust is completely constituted; *ante*, p. 44.

(3) stocks and shares, where a formal transfer has to be registered by the company;

(4) land registered by H.M. Land Registry, where, although no transfer is necessary,[38] the deed of appointment or retirement has to be registered so that the proprietorship register is brought up to date.

The first three exceptions arise by virtue of subsection (4) of section 40, and the fourth by section 47 of the Land Registration Act 1925.

Section 40 only applies where there is an appointment of a new trustee of an existing trust. It does not apply where property is held by a personal representative,[39] because, in this case, there is not an existing trust.

VII. Protection of Purchasers

A useful provision for the protection of purchasers is contained in section 38 of the Trustee Act 1925. It will be remembered that under section 36, some of the grounds for the removal of a trustee and the appointment of a new one are that the trustee has remained out of the United Kingdom for more than 12 months, that he refuses to act, or that he is unfit to act. Some of these grounds can give rise to dispute. Thus a displaced trustee might argue that he was not, in fact, unfit to act, so that his purported removal was ineffective. In the absence of a provision to the contrary, in the event of the purported removal being ineffective, a purchaser would not get a good title if he bought from the new trustees. However, section 38 provides that a statement in a deed of appointment that a trustee

(1) has remained out of the United Kingdom for more than 12 months; or
(2) refuses to act; or
(3) is incapable of acting; or
(4) is unfit to act

"shall, in favour of a purchaser of a legal estate, be conclusive evidence of the matter stated." Because it is "conclusive" a purchaser need not look behind the statement.[40] Further, in favour of a purchaser an appointment of trustees which depends on such a statement being true is valid, and any express or implied vesting declaration is also valid.[41]

Section 38 only applies, however, in the case of land, and no protection is conferred by the inclusion of such a statement in other circumstances.

Although the section gives protection to purchasers, it does not affect the position of a person who has not in fact ceased to be a trustee. If,

---

[38] Although a transfer is not essential, for practical purposes it is desirable, as if a transfer is not executed, H.M. Land Registry may insist on retaining the deed of appointment or retirement, or on being supplied with a certified copy of it.

[39] See *ante*, p. 12.

[40] Contrast the position where enactments provide only for "sufficient" evidence. See, *e.g.* Administration of Estates Act 1925, s.36(7), and *Re Duce and Boots Cash Chemists (Southern), Ltd.'s Contract* [1937] Ch. 642.

[41] T.A. 1925, s.38(2).

therefore, a person is purportedly removed as a trustee on the ground that he is unfit to act, and another person is purportedly appointed in his stead, the person purportedly removed could apply to the court for a declaration that he continues to be a trustee. Even if such a declaration is made, however, it would not prejudice a purchaser of land who had relied on the statement in the instrument of appointment.

CHAPTER 12

ACTION ON APPOINTMENT AS TRUSTEE

I. DISCLOSURE PRIOR TO APPOINTMENT

IT will be seen in Chapter 22 that a trustee should not, except with the express consent of the person setting up the trust, or of all the beneficiaries, put himself in a position in which his own interests might conflict with his duties of impartiality as a trustee. As a result of this rule, it has been decided that if a person is asked to become a trustee, before being appointed he ought to disclose any circumstances unknown to the persons appointing him which might bring his interest and duty into conflict. In *Peyton* v. *Robinson*,[1] for example, a beneficiary under a trust was indebted to the trustee personally, but this fact was not known to the settlor. The terms of the trust instrument gave the trustee a discretion to make payments to this beneficiary. In exercise of this discretion, the trustee made payments, but it was held that he could not accept repayment of his debt from the amount paid to the beneficiary. The trustee was placed in a position where his interest, to pay trust money to the beneficiary with a view to being repaid his debt, conflicted with his duty, to exercise his discretion entirely without thought for his own personal advantage.

II. FOLLOWING APPOINTMENT

When a person accepts a trusteeship, he should do four things, and if he fails to do any he may make himself liable for an action for breach of trust. These things are:

(a) acquaint himself with the terms of the trust;
(b) inspect the trust instrument and any other trust deeds;
(c) procure that all the property subject to the trust is vested in the joint names of himself and his co-trustees, and that all title deeds are placed under their joint control; and
(d) in the case of an appointment as a new trustee of an existing trust, to investigate any suspicious circumstances which indicate a prior breach of trust, and to take action to recoup the trust fund if any breach has in fact taken place.

---

[1] (1823) 1 L.J. (o.s) Ch. 191.

(a) **The terms of the trust**

The terms of the trust instrument must be known and understood because, as is explained elsewhere,[2] if a trustee pays money to a wrong beneficiary, or pays the right beneficiary too little money, or departs in any other way without authority from the terms of the trust instrument, he thereby commits a breach of trust, however honestly he may act. In certain circumstances he may apply to the court for relief from liability,[3] but even if the court grants total or partial relief, a breach of trust has still been committed.

(b) **Inspection of trust instrument**

The second duty on appointment, to inspect the trust instrument, is to ascertain whether any notices have previously been given to the trustees of dealings by beneficiaries with their interests in the trust fund. A beneficiary who has an interest under a trust may usually sell, mortgage, give away or in some other manner deal with his interest in the trust fund, just as he may deal with any other property. As far as the trustees are concerned, this disposition is complete when the assignee gives notice of the disposition to the trustees.[4] Once such notice has been given, the trustees must pay to the assignee the trust money to which the beneficiary named in the trust instrument would otherwise be entitled. If a memorandum of the transaction is endorsed on the trust instrument, this is sufficient to give the persons who are the trustees for the time being notice of the dealing by the beneficiary with his equitable interest.[5]

Furthermore, if a beneficiary should attempt to assign or charge his interest more than once, the assignee or chargee who is the first to give notice of the dealing to the trustees takes priority.[6] If, therefore, a newly appointed trustee finds on inspection of the trust instrument more than one notice of assignment, he must ascertain carefully the order in which such notices were received.

(c) **Trust property under joint control**

Thirdly, the trustee must ensure that all the trust property is placed in the joint names of the trustees. By virtue of section 40 of the Trustee Act 1925, which has already been considered,[7] where the trustee is appointed by deed, the trust property may automatically vest in him, but he must ensure that property not covered by this automatic vesting provision is put into his name. A trustee who leaves the trust fund in the sole name, or under the sole control, of his co-trustee or co-trustees will usually be liable if it is lost.[8] Difficulties sometimes arise in connection with "bearer" securities. These are securities issued by companies similar to ordinary securities, but different from them in that they are not registered in the owner's name. The issuing company pays dividends to whomsoever produces to the company when the dividend is payable the bearer

---

[2] *Post*, p. 443.
[3] Under Trustee Act 1925, s.61, discussed *post*, p. 460.
[4] By virtue of the rule in *Dearle* v. *Hall* (1828) 3 Russ. 1.
[5] LPA 1925, s.137.
[6] *Dearle* v. *Hall* (1828) 3 Russ. 1.
[7] See *Ante*, p. 263.
[8] *Lewis* v. *Nobbs* (1878) 8 Ch.D. 591.

certificate, or coupons attached to it. By definition bearer securities cannot be placed in the names of the trustees. Section 7 of the Trustee Act 1925, however, provides that bearer securities shall be deposited by the trustees for safe custody and collection of income with a bank, and that the trustees are not responsible for any loss which may result from such deposit. Provided the bank holds the securities to the order of *all* trustees, they are absolutely protected. But in *Lewis* v. *Nobbs*,[9] where one trustee allowed bearer securities to remain in the hands of his co-trustee, who misappropriated them, it was held that the trustee was guilty of breach of trust in allowing the securities to remain under the control of the other so that they could be so misappropriated. Similarly, all title deeds to trust property should be deposited with a bank or agent to be held to the order of all trustees.[10]

(d) Previous breaches of trust

The last duty on appointment as a trustee of an existing trust is with regard to previous breaches of trust. A new trustee is not expected to act like a bloodhound straining to sniff out some breach of trust; in the absence of suspicious circumstances he may assume that the previous trustees have properly discharged their duties.[11] But the new trustee must inquire into any circumstances which might suggest that a breach of trust has been committed, for if, through not inquiring into such circumstances, the trust fund suffers, the new trustee may be liable. He is liable not because he participated in the original breach of trust, but because he himself has committed a breach of trust in not inquiring.[12] The most obvious circumstances which would put a new trustee on inquiry is if the trust fund is materially less when he is appointed than it has been at some previous time. There may be many bona fide explanations of this, but the new trustee must inquire, and, if appropriate, take action.

---

[9] (1878) 8 Ch.D. 591.
[10] See also *Underwood* v. *Stevens* (1816) 1 Mer. 712; *post*, p. 446; *Thomas Guaranty Ltd* v. *Campbell, The Times,* 18 May, 1983.
[11] *Re Straham, ex. p. Greaves* (1856) 8 De G.M. & G. 291.
[12] *Harvey* v. *Olliver* (1887) 57 L.T. 239.

CHAPTER 13

THE ADMINISTRATION OF A TRUST

THIS chapter is concerned with the general obligations of the trustees with regard to the trust property, and various specific powers which they are given to facilitate its administration.

I. THE TRUSTEES' STANDARD OF CARE

In the management of a trust, one of the most frequent decisions which trustees are likely to take is in respect of investments, and their duties in this respect are dealt with fully in Chapter 16. It is, however, proposed to deal here with the standard of care which trustees are bound to exercise over the whole field of administration of a trust. In a series of cases[1] the rule has been laid down that unpaid trustees are bound to use only such due diligence and care in the management of the trust as an ordinary prudent man of business would use in the management of his own affairs. There is no doubt about the rule, but its application to particular circumstances can cause great difficulty. No doubt this is due, at least in part, to the fact, as Lord Blackburn pointed out in *Speight* v. *Gaunt*,[2] that judges and lawyers who see brought before them the cases in which losses have been incurred, and do not see the infinitely more numerous cases in which expense and trouble and inconvenience are avoided, are apt to think men of business rash.

Each case will of course be decided on its own facts, but several decisions can be quoted. Thus, with regard to debts payable to the trust, trustees should obtain payment with all reasonable speed, and if payment is not made within a reasonable time, proceedings should be instituted,[3] for this is the manner in which an ordinary prudent man of business would deal with debts due to him. But in *Ward* v. *Ward*[4] the House of Lords held that a trustee exercised his discretion reasonably in not suing immediately a beneficiary who was also a debtor to the trust, for had proceedings been taken, that beneficiary would have been ruined, and his children, who were also beneficiaries, placed in difficult circumstances.

---

[1] *Brice* v. *Stokes* (1805) 11 Ves. 319; *Massey* v. *Banner* (1820) 1 Jac. & W. 241; *Bullock* v. *Bullock* (1886) 56 L.J.Ch. 221; *Speight* v. *Gaunt* (1883) 9 App.Cas. 1.

[2] (1883) 9 App.Cas. 1.

[3] *Re Brogden, Billing* v. *Brogden* (1888) 38 Ch.D. 546; *Millar's Trustees* v. *Polson* (1897) 34 Sc.L.R. 798; *Fenwick* v. *Greenwell* (1847) 10 Beav. 412; *Grove* v. *Price* (1858) 26 Beav. 103.

[4] (1843) 2 H.L.Cas. 777.

Where trustees hold shares in a private company, they must exercise reasonable care to obtain information about the affairs of the company, and where a trustee is also a director, he may be held liable in an action by a beneficiary as a result of his conduct of the management of the company. In *Re Lucking's Will Trusts*[5] a trustee was a director of a private company, in which the trust held a majority shareholding. The trustee-director allowed another director to overdraw heavily from the company until he was eventually dismissed. This overdrawing was largely possible because the other director sent blank cheques to the trustee-director, which he signed and returned. In due course the dismissed director was adjudicated bankrupt, owing the company about £16,000. The trustee-director was held liable for the reduction in the value of the trust shares as a result of that defalcation.[6]

A trustee does well to bear in mind continually that at some time in the future a disgruntled benficiary might seek to question his actions. Thus, where, for example, trustees wish to sell or lease property, they should usually ascertain the true value of the property by employing a valuer, and sell or lease with regard to his figures.[7] In so doing they both comply with the test of the ordinary prudent man of business, and also give themselves protection against subsequent accusations by the beneficiaries that the property was dealt with at too low a figure.[8]

Many of the clearest examples of trustees acting but not complying with the standard of the ordinary prudent man of business are cases of failure to take action. Therefore, if a trustee allows rent to get in arrear, he may be ordered to make good the loss[9] and a trustee will also be liable if he fails to register any transaction which needs to be registered, such as a transfer of registered land, or of shares, and by so doing enables someone else to obtain priority.[10]

Occasionally, however, the rule that a trustee must act like an ordinary prudent man of business conflicts with another rule, that a trustee must do the best he can for the beneficiaries. Suppose, for example, that trustees wish to sell a house and receive an offer for £20,000. Suppose they then receive an offer for £22,000. The trustees are under an obligation to consider the second offer, even if, had they been dealing with their own property, they would not have entertained it, if only for considerations of ordinary commercial morality. They still retain their discretion, and if there is some reason which genuinely leads them to conclude that the first offer should be accepted, for example, if the sale to the first proposed purchaser would be completed materially earlier, they may conclude that the first offer should be accepted. But their discretion must be exercised generally in the interests of the beneficiaries[11] and, in the example given, they ought to accept the second offer unless there was some good reason for accepting the first.

[5] [1968] 1 W.L.R. 866.
[6] See also *Re Miller's Deed Trusts*, L.S. Gaz., May 3, 1978.
[7] *Oliver* v. *Court* (1820) 8 Pr. 127.
[8] *Grove* v. *Search* (1906) 22 T.L.R. 290.
[9] *Tebbs* v. *Carpenter* (1816) 1 Madd. 290.
[10] *Macnamara* v. *Carey* (1867) Ir.R. 1 Eq. 9.
[11] *Buttle* v. *Saunders* [1950] 2 All E.R. 193.

The courts appear to recognise that the ordinary prudent man of business does not make a wise decision on every occasion. A trustee is not, therefore, liable merely because he makes an error of judgment. In *Buxton* v. *Buxton*[12] a trustee was directed to sell bonds with all reasonable speed. He decided to delay sale, but the bonds fell in price. It was held that he was not liable to make good the loss. He had actively exercised his discretion, and acted in complete good faith, and was not made liable merely because his decision, as events turned out, was wrong.

What has been said so far applies to the unpaid trustee. Where the trustee is a paid trustee, a higher standard of diligence is required. As Harman J. said in *Re Waterman's Will Trusts*[13] "I do not forget that a paid trustee is expected to exercise a higher standard of diligence and knowledge than an unpaid trustee." The test for the paid trustee may probably be stated to be that he must exercise the degree of diligence and show the degree of knowledge that a specialist in trust administration could be expected to show.

II. JOINT ACTS

Except in rare circumstances, any act or decision to be effective must be the act or decision of all the trustees. There is no question here of a decision of the majority binding all the trustees.[14] The settlor or testator has reposed his trust in all the trustees: the liabilities and responsibilities are those of all the trustees. The acts or decisions in the administration of the trust must therefore be those of all the trustees. It may often happen that one trustee who is more enthusiastic in his duties than his co-trustee will come to be spoken of as the "acting trustee," whose decisions are merely endorsed by the co-trustee. But in this context "acting trustee" is not a concept recognised by law. The trustees must each exercise their discretion, and each is equally liable.[15]

Should a dispute arise, a trustee may be justified in concurring in an action of his co-trustee with which he is not in favour, either because he considers his co-trustee to be more experienced in, or to be more knowledgeable of, the type of transaction in hand,[16] or to prevent a complete deadlock in the administration of the trust. Whether he would be reasonable in deferring to his co-trustee, or whether he should have stood firm and if necessary made an application to the court, will depend on the circumstances of the particular case.

To this general rule that all the trustees must act jointly there are certain exceptions. In the first place, the trust instrument can of course authorise individual action. Secondly, one trustee alone often has power to give a receipt for income, either rent or dividends from shares. The latter is a necessary provision, because the articles of association of most companies provide that

---

[12] (1835) 1 Myl. & Cr. 80.
[13] *Re Waterman's Will Trusts, Lloyds Bank Ltd.* v. *Sutton* [1952] 2 All E.R. 1054. See also *Re Pauling* [1964] Ch. 303.
[14] *Boardman* v. *Phipps* [1967] 2 A.C. 46.
[15] *Munch* v. *Cockerell* (1840) 5 Myl. & Cr. 178.
[16] *Re Schneider* (1906) 22 T.L.R.

dividends are paid to the first-named registered holder of those shares. And, thirdly, just as some acts can be delegated to an agent, so most of those acts can be delegated by all the trustees to one of their number. Lastly, in the case of trustees of a private trust, a majority of trustees can pay money into court[17] even if the minority objects.

Although it is not an exception to the theoretical principle, if a provision to this effect is contained in a trust instrument it is possible to achieve the practical result that not all the trustees need agree on a certain course of action. The method of doing this is to impose a primary duty on the trustees to do an act, but to give them a secondary power not to do it, or to do some other act if they all agree. This method was adopted by the Law of Property Act 1925 in the case of land which is held upon trust for sale,[18] so that trustees are under a primary duty to sell the land, but they have a secondary power to postpone sale. To postpone sale, however, all trustees must agree to exercise their power, with the result that if one only wishes to sell, they all have to give effect to the duty to sell.[19] This is a statutory example, but the principle applies equally to provisions of trust instruments to a similar effect.

In some circumstances, the decision of the majority of trustees of a charity can bind them all.[20]

III. THE TRUSTEES' DISCRETION

It is inherent in a trustee's position that he must exercise his discretion,[21] and must do so in a wide variety of circumstances. The trustee may, of course, only exercise his discretion within the limits prescribed by law, or by the trust instrument, so that if trustees are given a discretion to do certain acts with the consent of some person, they must ensure that that consent is obtained. In *Re Massingberd's Settlement*[22] trustees were given power to vary investments with the consent of the tenant for life. They sold Consols, which were an authorised security, and with consent invested in an unauthorised mortgage. Subsequently they realised that unauthorised mortgage, and reinvested in an authorised mortgage, but without the consent of the tenant for life. As this consent had not been obtained, it was held that they had committed a breach of trust, and were liable to purchase for the trust the same number of Consols as had originally been held, credit being given for the investment which they had made in the authorised security.

Assuming that all such limits on the trustees' discretion are observed, it is of paramount importance that the trustees should exercise their discretion as an

---

[17] T.A. 1925, s.63.

[18] Law of Property Act 1925, s.25.

[19] *Re Mayo* [1943] Ch. 302; but, exceptionally, the court will not compel a sale, where it is contrary to contractual provisions, or involves sharp dealing; *Re Buchanan-Wollaston's Conveyance* [1939] Ch. 738; or where it would defeat the purpose for which the trust was set up: *Jones* v. *Challenger* [1961] 1 Q.B. 176. See also *Rawlings* v. *Rawlings* [1964] P. 378.

[20] *Re Whiteley* [1910] 1 Ch. 600.

[21] Generally with regard to the trustee's discretion, see, *ante*, Chap. 4.

[22] *Re Massingbred's Settlement, Clark* v. *Trelawney* (1890) 63 L.T. 296.

active mental process, and not allow a situation to result merely through inaction. The decision in *Wilson* v. *Turner*[23] is illustrative.[24] In that case the trustees had a power to pay or apply income arising from the trusts to or for the maintenance of an infant beneficiary. They did not make a conscious decision, but merely handed over the income to the infant's father, and the Court of Appeal held that the money should be repaid to the trust fund. If, however, the trustees had actively considered the merits of the case, and had consciously decided to apply the income for the maintenance of the infant, their decision would have been valid. A further case is *Re Greenwood*.[25] Section 15 of the Trustee Act 1925 gives trustees a power to compound liabilities, and, provided they act in good faith, they are protected against loss. In *Re Greenwood*, however, Eve J. said that this section only protects trustees if they have actively exercised their discretion, and if loss results merely through inaction on the part of the trustees they would not be protected. The test is not therefore the result of the trustees' action, or inaction, but their own mental process.[26]

Where, however, the trustees do consciously exercise their discretion, they derive a large measure of support from the courts. Trustees are not obliged to give reasons for their decisions, and if they do not do so, the court will not interfere with their decision unless they acted dishonestly. The court will not interfere even if it would itself have come to a different decision. In *Re Beloved Wilkes Charity*[27] Lord Truro said: "It is to the discretion of the trustees that the execution of the trust is confided, that discretion being exercised with an entire absence of indirect motive, with honesty of intention, and with a fair consideration of the subject. The duty of supervision on the part of this court will thus be confined to the question of the honesty, integrity and fairness with which the deliberation has been conducted, and will not be extended to the accuracy of the conclusion arrived at." It has been established that trustees need not give reasons for their decisions[28] but if they do state reasons for their decisions, the court will examine those reasons to see if the trustees have acted in error.[29]

What is the position of trustees who, having a discretion, fail to exercise it? The answer depends on whether the discretion arises under a power which is merely permissive, or whether it is obligatory. If the power is permissive only, that is, the trustees are not under any obligation to exercise it, it will lapse after a reasonable period, and cannot be revived.[30] If, however, the discretion is obligatory, it will not lapse, but will be enforced. In *Re Locker's Settlement*

---

[23] (1883) 22 Ch. D. 521.

[24] See also *ante*, p. 86.

[25] (1911) 105 L.T. 509.

[26] T.A., 1925, s.15 does not make it necessary for all the beneficiaries to consent before the trustees accept the compromise: *Re Earl of Stafford* [1978] 3 W.L.R. 223.

[27] (1851) 3 Mac. & G. 440.

[28] *R.* v. *Archbishop of Canterbury and Bishop of London* [1903] 1 K.B. 289; and see *post*, p. 274.

[29] *Ibid.*

[30] *Re Allen-Mayrick's Will Trusts, Mangnall* v. *Allen-Mayrick* [1966] 1 W.L.R. 499; *Re Gulbenkian's Settlement Trusts (No.2)*; *Stephens* v. *Maun* [1970] Ch. 408.

Trusts[31] the trustees of a discretionary trust held income upon a positive obligation to distribute the income among such beneficiaries as they should determine. They failed to distribute income which arose during a period of three years, but some years later wished to do so. They applied to the court for a declaration whether the discretion was still exercisable. It was held that it was still exercisable, as the discretion was of an obligatory nature.

IV. Duty to Account and Give Information

A trustee must be prepared at all times to give a beneficiary information as to the state of the trust property, and to dealings with it. This obligation involves

(a) keeping financial accounts; and
(b) providing information, within certain limits, as to action taken in the administration of a trust.[32]

A trustee must therefore, maintain accurate accounts of the trust property. He must allow a beneficiary, or his solicitor, to inspect those accounts, and the vouchers supporting them, and he must be prepared to give full information as to the amount of the trust fund. He is not obliged to supply copies of the accounts, or statements of account, to the beneficiaries, unless the beneficiaries themselves pay for them. In one case[33] it was held that a trustee who was illiterate, and so could not keep accounts, was justified in employing an agent to keep the accounts. Under the modern law, trustees, whether illiterate or not, will be entitled to employ agents for this purpose.[34]

Where trust money is invested, the trustees must on request supply a beneficiary with details of the investments, and even produce to the beneficiary the stock or share certificates, or other deeds and documents, representing that investment. Where, however, a beneficiary requires information as to his position under a trust, and this information cannot be supplied by the trustees without incurring expense, the trustees can pass on the expense to the beneficiary. Trustees who do not keep proper accounts may be ordered to do so by the court, and may be forced to bear personally the costs of the application to the court.[35] As the trustees might at any time be called upon to give information as to the administration of a trust, it is advisable for them to keep in addition to the trust accounts a trust diary. This is a type of minute book in which decisions taken in the administration of a trust are recorded. In view of the fact that a beneficiary is usually entitled to access to the trust diary and, as has just been said, if trustees give reasons for their decisions, the court will inquire into the accuracy of their decision, but not otherwise, trustees may choose to record their decision but not their reasons.

---

[31] [1978] 1 All E.R. 216.
[32] *Tiger* v. *Barclays Bank Ltd.* [1952] W.N. 38; [1952] 1 All E.R. 85.
[33] *Wroe* v. *Seed* (1863) 4 Giff. 425.
[34] *Post*, p. 282.
[35] See (1936) 52 L.Q.R. 365.

DUTY TO ACCOUNT AND GIVE INFORMATION

In the same way that a beneficiary is entitled to inspect deeds and documents representing trust investments, he is entitled to inspect most other documents relating to the trust. This is because, just as the beneficiaries are the equitable owners of the trust property, they are the equitable owners of the documents which have arisen in the course of the trust administration, and often at the expense of the trust. In *O'Rourke* v. *Darbishire*,[36] for example, Lord Wrenbury observed: "a beneficiary has a right of access to the documents which he desires to inspect upon what has been called in the judgments in this case a proprietary right. The beneficiary is entitled to see all trust documents, because they are trust documents, and because he is a beneficiary. They are, in this sense, his own."

In the case of *Re Marquess of Londonderry's Settlement*[37] there was a conflict between the rule just considered, that a beneficiary is entitled to inspect trust documents, and the rule that trustees are not obliged to give reasons for their decisions. In this case the trustees of the settlement were to distribute the trust fund in such proportions as they thought fit among certain named persons. One of these considered that she had received too little[38] and, in order to launch an attack upon the trustees, sought to inspect numerous trust documents which would probably have indicated the reasons which led the trustees to make the distributions that they had made. The disgruntled beneficiary claimed that she had a right to inspect the documents: the trustees claimed that she had not, as they were not to be compelled to give reasons for their decisions, and if the court ordered that the beneficiary was able to see the documents which she wished to see, the rule which enabled the trustees to keep their reasons to themselves would be defeated. The Court of Appeal held, in effect, that the rule enabling a beneficiary to inspect trust documents did not extend to documents which gave reasons for the trustees' decisions, and the court even went so far as to order that if a document was basically in the category of those which the beneficiary is entitled to see, but also contains details of the trustees' reasons, those passages should be covered up when the document is produced to a beneficiary.

The decision is certainly welcome, but the reasons for it are far from clear. This was a case where the court had sympathy with the trustees' contention that if the beneficiary were given access to documents which gave their reasons for dealing with the trust property it would result in family strife. One suspects that here the Court of Appeal decided what answer they wanted to reach, and then strove to find reasons to support it. Harman L.J. considered, but did not decide, whether the documents were "trust documents" at all, with the implication that if they were not, then the beneficiary would not have a right of access to them. He could not make up his mind about this, but said: "I would hold that, even if documents of this type ought properly to be described as trust documents, they are protected for the special reason which protects the trustees' deliberations on

---

[36] [1920] A.C. 581.
[37] [1964] Ch. 594.
[38] She and her family had in fact received £165,000. The total amount of the trust fund is not recorded.

a discretionary matter from disclosure. If necessary, I hold that this principle overrides the ordinary rule."[39] Danckwerts L.J. based his decision firmly on the practical ground that if the trustees' reasons were not protected from disclosure, it would be impossible for them to do their job. The third member of the Court of Appeal, Salmon L.J., also toyed with the idea of declaring that the documents were not trust documents but he had to admit defeat: "The category of trust documents has never been comprehensively defined. Nor could it be—certainly not by me." There are, then, several possible reasons to explain the rule, but the rule itself is now established that beneficiaries do not have a right of access to documents which the trustees intend to be private, and which record the reasons for their decisions.

Re Marquess of Londonderry's Settlement was concerned with a direct application by a beneficiary to inspect trust documents. It was made clear by the Court of Appeal that the decision did not govern the position of disclosure of documents in pending proceedings brought upon some other ground. If, for example, a beneficiary brings proceedings against the trustees for breach of trust, perhaps involving improper motive on the part of the trustees, it may well be that by way of discovery the beneficiary will be entitled to see all the trustees' documents, including those which give reasons for decisions. There is, however, no direct authority on the point.

V. DIRECTIONS OF THE COURT

Where trustees are in doubt as to the manner in which they should act, they may apply to the court on a summons for its directions. If the trustees place before the court all the relevant facts, and subsequently act in accordance with the court's directions, the principle is that they will be absolutely protected. In *Re Londonderry*,[40] for example, the trustees applied to the court for its directions, and Plowman J. decided at first instance that the documents ought to have been disclosed. The trustees appealed, successfully as it turned out, but the Court of Appeal nearly refused to hear the appeal. Harman L.J. observed: "This appeal, as it seems to me, is an irregularity. Trustees seeking the protection of the court are protected by the court's order and it is not for them to appeal."[41] There is little doubt that if the trustees had acted under the (erroneous) decision of Plowman J. they would have been protected. But if, as they did, they considered the decision wrong, and adverse to the interests of the beneficiaries, why should they not appeal? It is particularly ironic that this statement[42] on the part of Harman L.J., which tends to reflect a narrow outlook all too often encountered in the Chancery Division, should be made in a case where, because the trustees did appeal, the law was patently improved—for all trustees. Fortunately Salmon L.J. took a different view: "However, in my view the trustees were fully justified in bringing this appeal. Indeed it was their duty to

---

[39] [1964] Ch. 594, at p. 598.
[40] [1964] Ch. 594.
[41] [1964] Ch. 594, at p. 597.
[42] See also (1965) 29 Conv. (N.S.) 81.

bring it since they believed, rightly, that an appeal was essential for the protection of the general body of beneficiaries." It is remarkable, not that Salmon L.J. made this statement, but that he had to make it.

Unfortunately, Salmon L.J. introduced a further difficulty. One might have thought that the rule should have been that if trustees apply to the court, and are given a decision which is wrong, then they *may* appeal. According to Salmon L.J. they *must* appeal: they have a duty to do so. One day it may fall to be decided how far trustees are protected if they act in accordance with the decision of the court, but believe that decision to be wrong.

A further example of an application to the court by the trustees was *Barker* v. *Peile*,[43] where several actions had arisen out of uncertainty as to who were proper beneficiaries, and the trustee wished to be relieved of the liability and annoyance of being a trustee. Special circumstances must, however, exist, before the court will release a trustee from his obligations in this way.

Trustees may also make an application to the court for the construction of words in a will or settlement where the meaning is uncertain.

A useful power in connection with administration which the court has is contained in section 57 of the Trustee Act 1925. This section is considered in detail later,[44] but for present purposes it may be noted that under it where the trustees wish to effect any sale, letting, charge, or any other disposition of trust property, or wish to purchase property or make an investment with trust money, and there is no power to do so in the trust instrument or under the general law, the court may sanction that transaction. The court has jurisdiction to impose any conditions it thinks fit when approving such a transaction, but it can only authorise a transaction which is made "in the management or administration" of the trust property. It will be seen that the court has power to give authority under this section:

(1) where the trustees propose to do an act not authorised by the general law or by the trust instrument;

(2) that act is in the management or administration of the trust property; and

(3) the court thinks it expedient to sanction it.

Section 57 is designed to secure that the property shall be administered as advantageously as possible in the interests of the beneficiaries, but the provision must be considered in conjunction with the general principle that the court will not rewrite a trust. The result is that the power will only be exercised to authorise specific dealings with trust property. In *Boardman* v. *Phipps*[45] the trustees held shares in a private company and had the opportunity to acquire further shares, although such acquisition was not authorised by the trust instrument. In subsequent litigation the court said that as the acquisition of these shares was so clearly in the interest of the beneficiaries, the proper course

---

[43] (1865) 2 Dr. & Sm. 340.
[44] *Post*, p. 394.
[45] [1967] 2 A.C. 46.

would have been for the trustees to have applied under section 57 for power to purchase the additional shares.

Section 57 does not itself authorise rearrangement of beneficial interests, but this may be effected particularly under the Variation of Trusts Act 1958, which is dealt with in Chapter 23.

VI. Administrative Powers Relating to Trust Property

Part II of the Trustee Act 1925 confers general powers on trustees, particularly with regard to the administration of property. Under these powers, trustees may where appropriate raise money by sale or mortgage, sell trust property at auction and insure the property. Although not mentioned by statute, trustees are bound to see that trust property does not fall into decay through want of repair.[46]

The provisions of the Trustee Act 1925 relating to insurance are somewhat curious. Section 19 gives the trustees power *if they so wish* to insure the property for an amount not exceeding three-quarters of the full value of the property. This section seems to envisage a standard considerably lower than that of the ordinary prudent man of business, who would at least in present times almost invariably insure, and for the full re-building cost of the property.[47]

Section 15 confers upon trustees the power to

"(a) accept any property, real or personal, before the time at which it is made transferable or payable; or
(b) ever and apportion any blended trust funds or property; or
(c) pay or allow any debt or claim on any evidence that he or they think sufficient; or
(d) accept any composition or any security, real or personal, for any debt or for any property, real or personal, claimed; or
(e) allow any time for payment of any debt; or
(f) compromise, compound, abandon, submit to arbitration, or otherwise settle any debt, account, claim, or thing whatever relating to the testator's or intestate's estate or to the trust."

A trustee will not be liable for any loss which occurs from the exercise of any of these powers, provided he has acted in good faith.[48] The consent of the beneficiaries is not necessary.[49] An example of the operation of the rule is *Re The Earl of Strafford*.[50] In that case, the settlor had settled valuable chattels, and his wife owned similar chattels. When the wife died, beneficiaries under her will took her chattels, but beneficiaries under the trust claimed that those chattels were trust property. A compromise was proposed under which,

---

[46] *Re Hotchkys, Freke* v. *Calmady* (1886) 32 Ch.D. 408.
[47] See, further, Kenny, "The Underinsured Beneficiary" (1982) 79 L.S.G. 755 (June 16). The Law Reform Committee recommend that trustees of new trusts should be placed under a duty to insure against such risks as against which an ordinary prudent man of business would insure.
[48] *Per* Eve J., *Re Greenwood* (1911) 105 L.T. 509.
[49] *Re Earl of Strafford* [1979] 1 All E.R. 513, C.A.
[50] [1979] 1 All E.R. 513, C.A.

broadly, the beneficiaries under the wife's will would take some chattels outright, take a life interest in others, and give up the remainder. The trustees were minded to accept the proposed compromise, but one of the beneficiaries under the trust objected. The Court of Appeal, held that it was for the trustees to decide whether they considered the compromise was in the interest of all beneficiaries taken together, and that, if they did, they had power to accept it despite the opposition of one of the beneficiaries.

Some powers over property can only be exercised on proof of legal ownership, and in respect of trust property these powers can only be exercised by the trustees. In *Schalit* v. *Nadler Ltd.*[51] the beneficiary solely entitled to trust property which was let levied distress for arrears of rent. It was held that only the trustee as legal owner could levy distress, so that the distress actually levied was wrongful. Similarly, only the legal owner can serve a notice to quit.

VII. MORTGAGING THE TRUST PROPERTY

Section 16 of the Trustee Act 1925 applies where trustees are authorised either by the general law or by the trust instrument "to pay or apply capital money subject to the trust for any purpose or in any manner." In these circumstances, section 16 gives the trustees power to raise the requisite money either by mortgaging or selling the trust assets. However, the section is construed narrowly, and is confined to the cases where money is required either to preserve assets or to advance capital. In *Re Suenson-Taylor's Settlement*[52] the trustees, who had very wide powers of investment, and who, in accordance with these powers, properly held a large area of land for investment purposes, wished to borrow upon the security of that land in order to buy further land. It was held that that would be outside the power conferred by section 16. The court observed, however, that there could be cases where it was necessary to purchase further land in order to protect existing investments. For example, if trustees own a house, it may be appropriate to buy land which the house overlooks, in order to prevent anyone else building upon it. The point was left open, but it seems that in these circumstances raising money by mortgage in order to effect the purchase might well be within the statutory power.[52a]

VIII. EXPENSES

It is shown later[53] that except in special cases a trustee is not entitled to be paid for his services. He is, however, entitled to be reimbursed all his expenses which have been properly incurred. This right of reimbursement is in respect both of money actually spent by the trustee, and of liabilities which he has incurred. Thus in *Benett* v. *Wyndham*[54] a trustee of an estate directed woodcutters, employed on the estate to fell some trees. The woodcutters were negligent, and allowed a bough to fall on a passer-by who was injured. The trustee, as legal

---

[51] [1933] 2 K.B. 79; and see *ante*, p. 8.
[52] *Re Suenson-Taylor's Settlement, Moores* v. *Moores* [1974] 3 All E.R. 397.
[52a] The Law Reform Committee recommend that trustees should have a general statutory power to purchase a residence for beneficiaries on mortgage.
[53] *Post*, p. 390.
[54] (1862) 4 De G.F. & J. 259.

owner of the estate, was sued, and he was allowed to reimburse himself the damages out of the trust fund. Normally the trustee is not entitled to interest on his expenses. It does not follow that a trustee will be allowed all his expenses: they must be reasonable and proper in all the circumstances. An ingenious trustee in *Malcolm* v. *O'Callaghan*[55] made journeys to Paris to be present at the hearing of a case in the French courts which concerned the trust, but which turned solely on a question of French law and for which the trustee's presence was in no way necessary. He was not allowed his expenses against the trust.

A trustee is entitled to be reimbursed the expenses of properly taking or defending legal proceedings on behalf of the trust in the same way as other expenses. But before taking or defending proceedings a trustee can apply to the court for its approval of his proposed action. It is not necessary for the trustee to obtain this approval, but if he does not do so, and he is unsuccessful, it will be up to him to prove that he had reasonable grounds for taking or defending proceedings. If he cannot prove this, he will be deprived of his costs.

The trustee's right of indemnity is generally against the trust property,[56] not against the beneficiaries. If, therefore, the trustee's right of indemnity exceeds the value of the trust property, he will not normally be able to claim the balance from the beneficiaries personally. The right of indemnity does, however, extend to the beneficiary personally:

(a) where the beneficiary was the creator of the trust[57];
(b) where the trustee is a bare trustee,[58] and
(c) where the trustee accepted the trust at the request of the beneficiary.[59]

IX. PAYMENT TO BENEFICIARIES

The general principle is that a trustee is absolutely responsible for ensuring that the right amount is paid to the right beneficiary. In *Eaves* v. *Hickson*[60] trustees paid trust money to the wrong person in reliance on a forged marriage certificate. They were held liable to make good to the rightful beneficiary so much as could not be recovered from the wrongful recipient. Similarly, where trustees paid trust money to a wrongful beneficiary, on an erroneous but bona fide construction of the trust instrument, they were held liable to make good the loss.[61] Where the trustees have in the particular circumstances acted honestly and reasonably, and ought fairly to be excused, the court has a discretion to grant them relief,[62] but this does not alter the trustees' primary obligation of ensuring payment to the rightful beneficiary.

---

[55] (1835) 3 Myl. & Cr. 52.
[56] Trustee Act 1925, s.30(2).
[57] *Matthews* v. *Ruggles-Brise* [1911] 1 Ch. 194.
[58] *Hardoon* v. *Belilios* [1901] A.C. 118.
[59] *Jervis* v. *Wolferstan* (1874) L.R. 18 Eq. 18, at p. 24.
[60] *Eaves* v. *Hickson* (1861) 30 Beav. 136.
[61] *Hilliard* v. *Fulford* (1876) 4 Ch.D. 389.
[62] Trustee Act 1925, s. 61, *post*, p. 460.

Where there is any doubt as to who is entitled to trust property, the trustees should apply to the court for directions, and will then be protected if those directions are complied with. If the beneficiary entitled cannot be traced, the trustees may pay the money into court, and so obtain a good discharge for it. And where one of several beneficiaries cannot be traced, the court may authorise the trustees to distribute the trust fund as if the beneficiary who cannot be traced were dead.[63] Nevertheless, the court will discourage trustees from making payment into court of trust money where there is no good reason for doing so, by making the trustees personally pay the costs of the application for payment in. The power of payment into court is one of the exceptional cases in which the wish of the majority of trustees binds them all.

The court discourages applications by trustees for protection where they incur no practical risk at all. Thus, in *Re Pettifor*[64] Pennycuick J. said that in normal circumstances the court would consider it an unnecessary waste of money for trustees to come to court and ask for liberty to distribute a trust fund on the basis that a woman of 70 would not have a further child.

In most cases of long-standing trusts, there cannot be any debts due from the trust of which the trustees are unaware. Where there is a possibility of outstanding debts, however, advantage should be taken of section 27 of the Trustee Act 1925. Under this section, the trustees may advertise in the *London Gazette*, and usually in another newspaper, their intention of distributing the trust fund, and requiring persons interested to send them notice of their claim. Claims must be sent in within the time fixed by the notice, which must not be less than two months after it is published. At the expiration of that time, the trustees are safe in distributing the trust fund after discharging only those claims of which they have notice. If subsequently a creditor comes forward, he may be able to follow the trust property into the hands of the beneficiary, but he has no remedy against the trustees themselves.

Trustees must, of course, remember that beneficial interests under the trust can be assigned or charged. Where an assignee makes a claim to trust property, the trustees will, before making payment, have to investigate his title to the interest assigned, and they will be obliged to give effect to effective assignments.

When a trusteeship is completed, the trustee is entitled to put himself into the position in which no further disputes can be raised about payments to the beneficiaries. To achieve this he is entitled to present his final accounts to the beneficiaries and to require them to give him a formal discharge from his trusteeship. If they refuse, he may have the accounts taken in court, that is, examined by an official of the Chancery Division, and in that way obtain confirmation that they are in order.

---

[63] The so-called "Benjamin Order": *Re Benjamin* [1902] 1 Ch. 723.
[64] [1966] Ch. 257.

CHAPTER 14

DELEGATION: THE EMPLOYMENT OF AGENTS

THE trustees may wish to engage others to assist them in the execution of the trust or the administration of trust property. This may be so, for example, where the trustees consider it appropriate for the trust accounts and records to be kept by a solicitor or accountant; or where particular action requires special skills, such as advising with regard to changes of investment; or where there are particular difficulties in administrations, as where trust property is situated abroad.

Where the trustees appoint any person to act on their behalf in the execution of the trust, he is known as their "agent."

Whenever an agent is appointed there are six questions to be asked:

1. What powers do trustees have for the appointment of agents?
2. Should the power be exercised?
3. In what manner is it to be exercised?
4. What is the extent of the agent's authority?
5. Can agents be paid from the trust fund.?
6. If an agent defaults, and loss is occasioned to the trust fund, to what extent are the trustees themselves liable for that loss?

(1) Powers to appoint agents

(a) **The trust instrument**. The trust instrument itself may confer an effective power for the appointment of agents.

(b) **Section 23(1) of the Trustee Act 1925.** This subsection gives the main power for the appointment of agents. It empowers trustees to appoint a solicitor, banker, stockbroker, or any other person to transact any business, or to do any act which is necessary in the execution of the trust, or the administration of the trust property.

It will be appreciated that what must be necessary is the doing of the act, or the transaction of the business, not the appointment of the agent. Accordingly, trustees have the power to appoint an agent to do an act even if they could have done it themselves.[1]

In practice, almost all agents are appointed under this power.

---

[1] See, however, p. 283, *post.*

(c) **Other powers.** Other, narrower, powers are:

(i)   Power to appoint agents to deal with property situated abroad[2];
(ii) Power to permit a solicitor to have a deed incorporating a receipt for money signed by the trustees.[3] This is required for an ordinary sale of trust property where a conveyance or transfer incorporating such a receipt will be handed over by the trustees' solicitor in exchange for the purchase money;
(iii) Power to permit a solicitor or banker to have a receipt for insurance monies signed by the trustees, so that the solicitor or banker can obtain the policy monies from the insurers.[4]
(iv) Power to employ a valuer in connection with a proposed loan of trust money which is to be secured by mortgage[5]; and
(v)   Power for trustees for the sale of land to delegate revocably their powers of management or leasing the land to the person who is entitled in possession to the net rents and profits.[6]

(2) Should the power be exercised?

The general rule is that trustees must consider the exercise of any power,[7] and, if they do decide to exercise it, that exercise is only good if the trustees consider that it is in the interest of the trust.[8] The power to appoint agents is subject to this general rule. There will usually be no difficulty where the agent is appointed to transact business which requires some special skill which the trustees do not themselves have. Even if an agent is appointed to do an act which the trustees could have done themselves, the appointment will be good if the trustees consider it to be in the interest of the trust.

(3) The manner in which the power is to be exercised.

Subject to any provision in the trust instrument to the contrary, all agents must be personally appointed by the trustees, and they must exercise reasonable care in deciding whether to make the appointment.

This is illustrated by *Fry* v. *Tapson*.[9] Trustees were prepared to lend trust money on mortgage, as they were entitled to do. The trustees did not exercise their own judgment as to the valuer to be appointed but relied on the advice of their solicitors. The surveyor chosen in fact was the agent of a mortgagor and had a financial interest in the transaction being completed. The money was lent, and when loss occurred, it was held that the trustees were bound to make good the loss. They would not have been made liable if they had made an independent choice of the agent themselves. This was an example of a decision which

---

[2] T.A. 1925, s.23(2).
[3] T.A. 1925, s.23(3)(*a*).
[4] T.A. 1925, s.23(3)(*c*).
[5] T.A. 1925, s.8.
[6] L.P.A. 1925, s.29.
[7] *Klug* v. *Klug* [1918] 2 Ch. 67.
[8] *Re Lofthouse* (1885) 29 Ch.D. 921. At p. 930.
[9] (1884) 28 Ch.D. 268.

the trustees ought themselves to have made, and not an act which could properly be delegated.

(4) The extent of the agent's authority.

The general principle is clear.

It is that trustees have to take the basic decisions themselves. For example, if there is a discretionary class of beneficiaries under the trust, the trustees must themselves decide the proportions in which the beneficiaries are to receive the trust property; or, if the trust has capital money, how it is to be invested. On the other hand they can employ agents to implement their decisions and to carry out most of the routine administration of the trust. Thus the trustees must make the decisions: they may employ agents to carry them out.[10] And they may employ agents whether or not they could have done the acts themselves.[11] This represents a marked change from the pre-1926 position, when a trustee could not properly appoint an agent unless it was reasonably necessary to do so, or the circumstances were such that a man of ordinry prudence would have appointed an agent had he been dealing with his own affairs.[12] If the trustees purported to delegate to an agent a function that they ought personally to have discharged, such as that relating to the distribution of a discretionary trust fund, the agent's decision would be ineffective.[13] Thus the money would have been distributed without a proper decision being made, and the trustees could be called upon to make good the money to the trust fund out of their own pockets.

There can often be difficulty in determining whether an agent is to be appointed to do a ministerial act, where the appointment is propery, or an act which requires the trustees' own decisions. This is particularly so with regard to investment. It is necessary for the trustees to take the decision on each sale and purchase, or, provided that they have laid down guidelines, can the trustees leave it to investment advisors to make the particular decisions? An actively-managed portfolio of stock exchange investments may require rapid decisions to be made, often within the day, and sometimes within the hour. Accordingly, private individuals may give stockbrokers or merchant bankers authority to deal with investments in whatever way they think fit. The interests of the trust fund may require such agents to have similar powers.

(5) Remuneration of agents.

An agent will have been properly appointed if:

---

[10] It follows that, in making the basic decisions, a trustee should not allow someone who is not a trustee to join in making those decisions: *Salway* v. *Salway* (1831) 2 Russ. & Myl. 215; *White* v. *Baugh* (1835) 3 Cl. & Fin. 44. But although the trustees must themselves make the decision, there is no objection to them *consulting* the beneficiaries: *Fraser* v. *Murdoch* (1881) 6 App.Cas. 855.

[11] *Re Vickery* [1931] 1 Ch. 572.

[12] *Re Weall* (1889) 42 Ch.D. 674; *Ex p. Belchier* (1754) Amb. 218; *Speight* v. *Gaunt* (1883) 22 Ch.D. 727.

[13] See, *e.g.*, *Wilson* v. *Turner* (1883) 22 Ch.D. 521; *post*, p. 356.

(a) the trustees had power to appoint him to carry out the particular matter for which he has been appointed;

(b) the trustees considered that the appointment was in the interest of the trust; and

(c) the trustees themselves decided to make the appointment.

Where these conditions are satisfied, the trustees are entitled to pay agents their proper remuneration from the trust fund.[14]

(6) Trustees' liability for agent's default

It might have been expected that if an agent is properly appointed,[15] trustees would not be liable for any loss which occurs if the agent defaults. However, because of inconsistency between two statutory provisions, there is some uncertainty as to the extent of the trustees' liability in such circumstances.

These provisions are:

(a) section 23(1), which gives the general power to appoint agents and which concludes by providing that trustees "shall not be responsible for the default of any such agent if employed in good faith"; and

(b) section 30, which provides that a trustee shall be answerable and accountable only for his own acts, receipts, neglects or defaults, and not for those of any other person with whom any trust money or securities may be deposited, or for any other loss "unless the same happens through his own wilful default."

Under the old law, it had been held in *Re Brier*[16] that where there was a provision exempting a trustee from liability for loss caused by an act of an agent unless the loss occurred through the "wilful default" of the trustee, the trustee was nevertheless liable for the loss because he failed to exercise reasonable supervision over the agent.

It would, therefore, appear at first sight that section 23(1) may be inconsistent with section 30. Suppose that an agent was appointed in good faith, but the trustee failed to exercise reasonable supervision over him, and loss occurred. If section 23(1) is applied, the trustee is not liable, because the test of liability is the *appointment* of the agent, and in this example the agent was appointed in good faith. But if section 30 applies, and the old law is followed, the trustee is liable, because he has been guilty of wilful default in not exercising adequate supervision.

It was against this background that *Re Vickery*[17] was decided in 1931. The executor of a will employed a solicitor to wind up the estate. At the time when he appointed him, he knew nothing about the solicitor which would suggest that he should not be appointed. Three months after his appointment, one of the beneficiaries under the will told the executor that the solicitor had previously

---

[14] T.A. 1925, s.23(1).
[15] *Supra.*
[16] (1884) 26 Ch.D. 238.
[17] [1931] 1 Ch. 572.

been suspended from practice, and although this was the case he had sub-sequently been allowed to practise again. The beneficiary asked the executor to employ another solicitor, and objected to the executor giving to the solicitor (in accordance with the usual practice) a signed authority so that he could obtain money on behalf of the estate from the Post Office Savings Department. The executor refused to take the matter away from that solicitor, who was then promising to settle it, but he did not do so, and ultimately absconded. The beneficiary sued the executor. Maugham J. observed: "It is hardly too much to say that [section 23] revolutionises the position of a trustee or an executor so far as regards the employment of agents. He is no longer required to do any actual work himself, but he may employ a solicitor or other agent to do it, whether there is any real necessity for the employment or not."[18] To this extent there is no quarrel with the decision, but the judge found that the solicitor was undoub-tedly appointed in good faith, and he also held that the executor was not himself guilty of "wilful default." As the agent was appointed in good faith, and the executor had not himself been guilty of wilful default, he was not liable for the money, either under section 23, or under section 30.

"Wilful default," the judge said, means either "a consciousness of negligence or breach of duty, or recklessness."[19] In coming to this conclusion, the judge purported to follow two decisions of the Court of Appeal: *Re Trusts of Leeds City Brewery Ltd.'s Deed*[20] and *Re City Equitable Fire Insurance Co.*[21] In doing so, Maugham J. appears to have altered the previous position as laid down in *Re Brier.*[22]

The decision has been criticised[23] in so far as it appears to decide that a trustee is no longer under an obligation to exercise supervision over his agent. It is possible to criticise the decision on several grounds. In the first place, the Trustee Act is generally a consolidating Act, and section 30 is a re-enactment of the substance of section 31 of the Law of Property Amendment Act 1859, under which *Re Brier* was decided. The decision in *Re Vickery* is therefore contrary to the presumption that a consolidating Act does not change the law. Secondly, the case of *Re City Equitable Fire Insurance Co.*, which contained the definition of wilful default which Maugham J. followed, was not a case on the law of trusts, and while for cases outside the law of trusts this may be adequate, it is alleged by some that this case ought not to apply to the employment of agents by trustees, because in connection with trusts "wilful default" has had the wider meaning, as in *Re Brier*, of including lack of reasonable care. Thirdly, it is difficult to reconcile this interpretation of section 23(1) with other parts of section 23. Subsections (2) and (3) of section 23, which deal with the power to appoint agents in specific circumstances, appear to be unnecessary. For example,

---

[18] [1931] 1 Ch. 572, at p. 581.

[19] And see *Wyman* v. *Paterson* [1900] A.C. 271; *Re Sheppard* [1911] 1 Ch. 50; *Robinson* v. *Harkin* [1896] 2 Ch. 415.

[20] [1925] Ch. 532.

[21] [1925] Ch. 407.

[22] (1884) 26 Ch.D. 238.

[23] See articles (1931) 47 L.Q.R. 330–332 (Potter); (1931) 47 L.Q.R. 463–465 (Holdsworth); (1959) 22 M.L.R. 381 (Jones).

section 23(3)(*a*) expressly empowers a trustee to appoint a solicitor to be his agent to receive trust money, yet in view of section 23(1), there would appear to be no need for this provision.

More important, *Re Vickery* does not resolve the apparent inconsistency between section 23(1) and section 30, and their tests of appointment in good faith and wilful default, respectively. Perhaps they are to be reconciled on the basis that a trustee will be liable for any loss which arises through the default of an agent who is *not* appointed in good faith, but that if he is appointed in good faith, the trustee will nevertheless be liable if he is guilty of wilful default in the sense mentioned.[24]

The force of the other criticisms remains. The present writers have no doubt that the decision in *Re Vickery* was technically incorrect on the legal principles previously established. They also believe that the result of the case is desirable. Due regard must indeed be paid to the fact that a trustee is looking after someone else's money, and must certainly not be flippant in so doing. But regard must also be had to the fact that the trustees may be acting without remuneration, and may derive no benefit whatever from their trusteeship, no matter how much time and trouble they devote to the trust. Surely Maugham J., while admittedly changing the law, introduced a measure of equity where little existed before. A trustee is still plainly liable if he is consciously negligent or reckless: why should he be liable for more?[25]

(7) Delegation of trusteeship

So far this chapter has been concerned with the delegation by a trustee of ministerial acts, while retaining his responsibility to take the fundamental decisions himself. In one case, however, a trustee may delegate the power to take the basic decisions. Under section 25 of the Trustee Act 1925[26] a trustee can by power of attorney delegate all or any of his trusts, powers and discretions. The delegation cannot be for a period exceeding one year, although there appears to be no restriction on the number of times on which a delegation can be made.

The delegation is made by power of attorney, and the donor must give written notice of the delegation to each of the other trustees, and to any other person who has a power of appointing new trustees.[27] This notice specifies the

---

[24] *Re Vickery* was distinguished by Cross J. in *Re Lucking's Will Trusts* [1968] 1 W.L.R. 866, on the basis that a person employed by a trustee as managing director of a business owned by the trust was not a person with whom trust money or securities were deposited within the meaning of s.30, and accordingly the test of "wilful default" was irrelevant. The trustee was held liable for the loss caused by the managing director's defalcations on the ground that he had failed in his duty to conduct the business of the trust with the same care that an ordinary prudent businessman would apply to his own affairs. See also *post*, p. 445.

[25] *Underwood* v. *Stevens*, discussed *post*, p. 446, is an example of the injustice of the pre-1926 position. The Law Reform Committee recommend that a trustee should be liable for the default of his agent unless:
    (i) it was reasonable for him to employ the agent;
    (ii) he took reasonable steps to ensure that the agent was competent; and
    (iii) he took reasonable steps to ensure that the agent did his work competently

[26] Substituted by Powers of Attorney Act 1971, s.9.

[27] Trustee Act 1925, s.25(4).

date when the power comes into operation, its duration, the donee, the reason why the power is given, and which of the trusts, powers and discretions are delegated. However, if this notice is not given, a person dealing with the donee of the power is not prejudiced.[28] The donee of the power stands in the same position as the donor, except that the donee cannot himself delegate.[29]

The delegation can in principle be to anyone but where there are only two trustees, one trustee cannot delegate to the other, except where that other is a trust corporation.[30]

The section is in practice rarely used. While it is useful in enabling a delegation of discretions, it has a disadvantage for the donor of the power in that the donor is liable for every act or default of the donee. Thus, even if the donee is only doing an act which could have been the subject of a section 23 delegation, the donor will nevertheless be fully liable. The section could work completely unjustly, particularly as the donor may have no control over the acts of the donee.

---

[28] *Ibid.*
[29] s.25(6).
[30] s.25(2).

CHAPTER 15

THE TAXATION OF A TRUST

In order to appreciate the contemporary significance of a trust, it is necessary to understand the basic principles of taxation which affect trusts. On the one hand, the prime motive for the creation of the trust may be the mitigation of the family's taxation liability.[1] On the other hand, when the trust is in being, taxation considerations will weigh heavily with the trustees. These considerations may influence the way in which the trust fund is invested,[2] how the trustees deal with income,[3] and the manner in which they exercise their discretion in favour of beneficiaries.[4] Trustees are concerned with four main taxes[5]:

1. stamp duty.
2. income tax;
3. capital gains tax; and
4. capital transfer tax

In particular circumstances they are also concerned with other types of taxation. For example, if they own land, they may be subject to development land tax and rates, but these other types of taxation are not considered in this chapter.

I. STAMP DUTY

Stamp duty is a once-and-for-all tax payable on a variety of different transactions. Where the transaction is one which gives rise to liability to stamp duty, the duty is paid at a stamping office of the Inland Revenue, and upon payment of the duty a stamp is impressed on the document showing the amount of the duty paid. It follows that if a transaction can be effected without any document, such as a purely oral declaration of trust,[6] no question of stamp duty can arise.

The main inducement to pay stamp duty is that a document which ought to be stamped but is not stamped cannot be admitted in evidence in any legal proceedings.[7] Further no registrar will register a stampable document which is

---

[1] *Ante*, p. 4.
[2] See, generally, Chap. 16.
[3] See *post*, p. 346.
[4] See *post*, p. 366.
[5] For charitable trusts see *ante*, p. 184. For a more detailed treatment of the problems raised in this chapter, see Mellows, *Taxation for Executors and Trustees* (5th ed., 1981).
[6] See, however, *ante*, p. 24 *et seq.*
[7] Stamp Act 1891, s.14(4). *Ram Rattam* v. *Parma Nand* (1945) L.R. 73 Ind.App. 28.

unstamped because if he does so, he renders himself liable to a fine.[8] Trustees will insist that a trust deed is properly stamped, because they may at any time have to justify their position, or their acts as trustees, by production in court of the trust deed.

A document must be stamped within 30 days of its execution.[9] Where it is not stamped within that period, the Revenue are entitled to charge as a condition for stamping the document out of time the amount of the duty, a penalty of up to £10, and interest on the unpaid duty.[10]

It is appropriate to consider liability to stamp duty on the inception of the trust; during the continuance of the trust; and upon its termination.

(1) Inception of trust

There is no general principle that every document by which every transaction is effected attracts stamp duty: a document is only stampable if it comes within one of the classes of documents specifically mentioned in the Stamp Act. One such class comprises conveyances or transfers which operate as voluntary dispositions.[11] This has been held to include a voluntary declaration of trust.[12] It also includes a declaration of trust which, while not voluntary, is not for full consideration,[13] but a declaration of trust upon marriage is exempt from the duty.[14]

The rate of duty is £1 for every £50 (or part of £50) of the value of the property.[15] It is payable only in respect of certain types of property, which, broadly, are those which can only be transferred by instrument, such as land, and stocks and shares. In other cases, such as a settlement of cash only, duty is payable at the fixed rate of 50p, irrespective of the size of the trust.[16] No stamp duty is payable in the case of conveyances, transfers or lettings to a charity.[17]

Many *inter vivos* settlements are created by means of two instruments, one the trust instrument which declares the terms of the trust, and the other the conveyance or transfer which transfers the legal title to the trustees. The instrument which transfers the beneficial interest is chargeable with *ad valorem* duty, and the other instrument is chargeable only with the fixed rate duty of 50p. If, therefore, a person who owns some B.P. shares wishes to create a settlement of them, he might execute a transfer of the shares to the proposed trustees, and then execute the trust instrument. The execution of the trust instrument causes the beneficial interest to pass, and that instrument will bear the *ad valorem* duty.

---

[8] S.A. 1891, s.17.
[9] S.A. 1891, s.15.
[10] S.A. 1891, s.15(1).
[11] Finance (1909–10) Act 1910, s.74(1).
[12] *Martin* v. *I.R.C.* (1930) 15 A.T.C. 631.
[13] Finance (1909–10) Act 1910, s.74(5).
[14] F.A. 1963, s.64.
[15] F.A. 1974, s.49(1). The rate is less where the value of the property does not exceed £40,000; F.A. 1982, s.128.
[16] Stamp Act 1891, s.62; Finance (1909–10) Act 1910, s.74, following the repeal of settlement duty by Finance Act 1962, s.30.
[17] F.A. 1982, s.129.

Where *ad valorem* duty, that is, duty which is assessed according to the value of the transaction, is payable, it can sometimes be avoided by creating the trust merely by an oral declaration. In a trust of any size, however, this is not convenient because a record of the exact terms of the trust is highly desirable. Accordingly, it became common for a settlor to make an oral declaration of trust in his solicitor's office, with one of the solicitor's secretaries taking a shorthand note of what was said. This would provide a permanent record. Although theoretically justifiable, the efficacy of this device is open to doubt, in view of *Cohen and Moore* v. *I.R.C.*[18] In that case settlors orally declared that they would hold certain securities upon the trusts declared by a draft deed. Five weeks later, the draft deed was executed. It was held that the verbal declaration and the later deed formed one transaction, so that duty was payable. The significance of *Grey* v. *I.R.C.*[19] in this connection was considered earlier.[20]

For a settlor who wishes to use a similar device, there would appear to be no objection to his making his declaration of trust by recording it with its complicated provisions on tape, and for the tape not to be transcribed for a considerable period. Almost certainly, a tape would not rank as a document, so that duty would not be exigible.

No stamp duty is payable on a will or on a grant of representation, so that no duty is payable on the creation of will trusts.

The obligation to pay stamp duty on the creation of a trust is that of the settlor, and it is not properly payable out of the trust fund unless the trust instrument contains an authority for the duty to be paid from the trust fund.

(2) **During administration of trust**

Where a conveyance or transfer is made without causing any change in the beneficial interests, that document attracts only the fixed duty of 50p.[21] Accordingly a deed of retirement or appointment of new trustees, or some other instrument executed in connection with such retirement or appointment, such as a transfer of shares from an old to a new trustee,[22] only attracts the fixed duty.[23]

If the trustees in the course of administration of the trust rearrange the investments, they will be liable to stamp duty on the purchase of assets at the same rate as a purchase by any individual. This is so notwithstanding that the value of the trust fund is not increased, for stamp duty is payable on each transaction, in this case, the purchase of shares. Stamp duty paid on such purchase documents ranks as part of the cost of the asset for capital gains tax purposes.[24]

---

[18] [1933] 2 K.B. 126.
[19] [1958] Ch. 375.
[20] See *ante*, p. 24.
[21] S.A. 1891, s.62; Finance (1909–10) Act 1910, s.74.
[22] Stock exchange securities are excluded from the automatic vesting provisions of Trustee Act 1925, s.40, see *ante*, p. 263.
[23] S.A. 1891, ss.23(1), 62.
[24] See *post*, p. 296.

(3) On termination of trust

In normal circumstances no *ad valorem* duty is paid on the termination of a trust, for by that time the beneficiary has become absolutely entitled beneficially, with the result that there is no change in the beneficial interests. If, however, the termination comes about by rearrangement of beneficial interests the rearrangement may constitute a voluntary disposition of a beneficial interest, and so be subject to *ad valorem* duty. Thus, in *Platt's Trustees* v. *I.R.C.*,[25] where a life tenant executed a deed releasing his life interest, thereby accelerating the interest in remainder and enabling distribution of the trust fund, *ad valorem* duty was held to be payable on the deed of release.

INCOME AND CAPITAL TAXATION GENERALLY

For the purposes of income tax, capital gains tax and capital transfer tax, trustees are treated as a separate and continuing body of persons.[26] Because trustees constitute a separate body, the liability of the trust to tax is computed without taking into account the trustees' personal tax position. Because trustees constitute a continuing body, the tax liability of the trust is unaffected by any changes in the persons who are from time to time the trustees. For most taxation purposes, therefore, a trust is treated almost as if it has its own separate legal personality.

III. INCOME TAX

The taxation of the income of trusts is in many ways more simple than the taxation of income of private individuals, because the various allowances and reliefs which affect the computation of an individual's liability do not apply.

The taxation of the income of a trust is based on these principles:

(a) The whole of the income of the trust is taxable, irrespective of its ultimate disposal.[27] Thus, the income of the trust is taxable whether it is paid to beneficiaries, absorbed in administration expenses, or accumulated.

(b) Trust income is generally taxable at the basic rate of income tax. This varies from time to time, but at present[28] it is 30 per cent.[29] In the case of a private individual, the effect of personal allowances is to exempt from income tax the first "slice" of his income. However, if his income is high—at present[29a] over £14,600—he is chargeable to income tax at a higher rate instead of at the basic rate.[30] In addition, where an

---

[25] (1953) 34 A.T.C. 292.

[26] The principle is assumed, but not expressly enacted, for the purposes of income tax and capital transfer tax. For other taxes see C.G.T.A. 1979, s.52(1) (capital gains tax), and Development Land Tax Act 1976, s.30(2) (development land tax).

[27] The rate at which income tax is paid will vary according to whether the trust is discretionary or not: *infra*.

[28] 1983/84.

[29] F.A. 1983, s.12(1)(*a*).

[29a] See n. 28.

[30] F.A. 1983, s.12(1)(*b*).

individual's investment income[31] exceeds £7,100, he is liable to an additional rate of 15 per cent. on that excess.[32] None of these complications generally applies to trust income. Whether the income is £1 per annum or £100,000 per annum that income is chargeable at the basic rate.

(c) There is one exception to the principle that all trust income is taxed at the basic rate. Accumulation and discretionary settlements have for long been used as devices to take income away from taxpayers who are liable to pay income tax at the higher rates. In an attempt to counteract this, it is provided that income which is to be accumulated, or which is payable under a discretion[33] is chargeable at the additional rate of 15 per cent. as well as the basic rate of 30 per cent.[34] This does not apply, however, to the extent that the income arises under a charitable trust, or is properly applied in the administration of the trust.[35] The beneficiary is in no worse position where the income is distributed to him as income,[36] for he can make a repayment claim if he is not liable to pay tax at the total rate of 45 per cent. on the top slice of his income.[37]

It follows from these principles that all payments of income from the trust to the beneficiaries are paid from a fund which has been taxed at the rate of 30 per cent. or at the rate of 45 per cent. Accordingly, with each payment of income, the trustees are bound to issue to the beneficiary a certificate of the tax notionally deducted from that payment.

The gross equivalent of the net payment made to the beneficiary is then regarded as part of the beneficiary's total income, and he may then obtain any repayment which is appropriate having regard to his total income.

An example may illustrate these principles. Suppose that a trust fund has an income of £1,200 per annum gross, and suppose also that the basic rate of income tax is 30 per cent. The administration expenses are £100, and the trustees are obliged by the trust instrument to accumulate one half of the income, and to distribute the other half to a beneficiary who has a fixed interest. The calculation then becomes:

Gross income	£1,200
Less: tax at basic rate on gross income	£360
	___
	£840
Less: administration expenses	£100[38]
	___
	£740

---

[31] This is any income which is not earned: F.A. 1971, s.32(4).

[32] F.A. 1983, s.12(1)(*b*).

[33] The discretion may be that of the trustees or of any other person.

[34] F.A. 1973, s.16.

[35] s.16(2)(*c*), (*d*).

[36] If the income is accumulated, and the beneficiary receives a sum from the accumulation, he receives a capital, and not an income, sum, and no repayment claim can be made.

[37] F.A. 1973, s.17.

[38] The expenses are paid from income taxed at the basic rate.

$\frac{1}{2}$ net income to be accumulated	£370	
Less: income tax at additional rate (15 per cent. × £528.50[39])	£79.28	
Net amount accumulated		£290.72
$\frac{1}{2}$ net income distributed	£370	

The beneficiary who receives £370 net is treated as having received £528.50 from which tax at the basic rate has been deducted. He has, therefore, suffered tax of £158.50. Suppose, however, that he has only a small income from other sources, and that this is sufficient only to absorb his personal reliefs and that with the trust income he will not be liable to income tax, even at the basic rate of 30 per cent. In these circumstances he can make a repayment claim, and recover from the Inland Revenue the tax which he has suffered. To do this, he will need to produce a certificate of deduction of tax issued by the trustees.

These principles lead to three general results which trustees will wish to bear in mind. First, as the whole income of the trust is taxable, liability to tax can only be avoided if non-income-producing assets are held by the trust. An example is for trusts to purchase pieces of silver or works of art.[40] A more prosaic example is the purchase of National Savings Certificates, which produce no income but are repayable on maturity with a capital bonus.[41] However, such increments will be of a capital nature for all purposes, so that a life tenant will not, in general, be entitled to any part of it.[42] While a trustee must keep tax considerations in mind, he must also keep in mind his general obligation to balance the interests of tenant for life and remainderman.

The second result of the basic principles is that where trustees have a discretion to accumulate income, they can only accumulate out of taxed income. Accordingly, accumulation is not a method of avoiding income tax completely, but, as is shown in a later chapter, in some circumstances it may be appropriate to accumulate income as capital, and then to make an advancement of capital.

The third result is that trustees will wish to consider the likely taxation result of a distribution of income upon the tax position of the beneficiary. If, as in the example given at page 293, the personal tax position of the beneficiary is such that he can make a repayment claim, a distribution of income to him will be clearly advantageous. If, however, the beneficiary is already paying income tax at a higher rate, the trustees will know that the beneficiary will also have to pay higher rate income tax on any income paid to him by the trust. Accordingly,

---

[39] The calculation is:
One half of gross income £600; less
one half of administration expenses (£50) grossed up at the basic rate to £71.50
= £528.50.

[40] Provided the pieces of silver are sold for a figure not in excess of £3,000, no capital gains tax is payable. Trustees hope, therefore, to dispose of the silver at a profit which will attract liability neither to income tax, because the profit is not of an income nature, nor to capital gains tax, because it is within the £3,000 limit.

[41] See *post*, p. 304.

[42] *Re Holder* [1953] Ch. 468. See, however, *post* p. 344.

where a gross payment of £500 is made to a beneficiary who is already paying
income tax on the top slice of his income at the rate of 50 per cent. his actual
position on current[43] figures would be:

Gross income from trust		£500
Less: income tax paid by trust at 30 per cent.		£150
		£350
Higher rate tax at 50 per cent. (on £500)	£250	
Less: income tax at basic rate paid by trustees	£150	
		£100
Net benefit to recipient		£250

Where they have a discretion as to the payment of income, in this situation
trustees will probably wish to pay the whole or most of the income to another
beneficiary with a lower personal rate of taxation; or to accumulate the income
and distribute as capital.[44]

IV. CAPITAL GAINS TAX

The object of capital gains tax is to make a charge on capital gains made
either by private individuals or by any body of persons, such as trustees.
Capital gains tax is generally[45] payable at the rate of 30 per cent. of the
difference between the value of the asset at the date of acquisition, and its
value at the date of disposal. The value of the asset at the date of
acquisition is adjusted to take account of inflation.[46] Where the value goes
down, the loss can be offset against future gains. Trustees are liable to pay
capital gains tax, on gains arising on trust assets in the same way as an
individual would on gains arising on his personal assets.

(1) **Bare trustees and other trustees**

For capital gains tax purposes it is necessary to draw a distinction between
bare trustees and other trustees. Where a beneficiary is absolutely entitled to an
asset as against the trustee, the asset is treated as if it were vested in the
beneficiary.[47] The position is the same where a beneficiary would be absolutely
entitled as against the trustee were he not an infant.[48] In *Tomlinson* v. *Glyns
Executor and Trustee Co. Ltd.*[49] trustees held property in trust for such of four
infant beneficiaries who should attain the age of 21 or marry under that age.
When the trustees disposed of certain investments at a profit, they claimed that
the infant beneficiaries were together absolutely entitled to the investments as

---

[43] 1983/84.
[44] See *post*, p. 366.
[45] Except where the total gains which would otherwise be chargeable do not exceed £5,600
in any year: F.A. 1982, s.80.
[46] F.A. 1982, s.5.
[47] C.G.T.A. 1979, s.46.
[48] *Ibid.*
[49] [1970] Ch. 112, C.A.

against the trustees, and that, therefore, this principle applied.[50] The Court of
Appeal held that infancy was not the only reason which, at the time of the
disposal of the investments, prevented the beneficiaries being absolutely entitled, because they only had a contingent interest until they reached the age of
21.

The trust provisions of the capital gains tax legislation only apply where
there are not one or more beneficiaries absolutely and concurrently
entitled to the whole of the trust property as against the trustees.

(2) Gains on the disposal of assets

When a trust is created *inter vivos* the trustees are deemed to acquire the
assets of the trust for a consideration equal to their market value at that time.[51]
Where an asset is purchased in an arm's-length transaction, the consideration,
together with expenses of purchase, constitutes the acquisition value.

Certain types of asset are exempt from capital gains tax,[52] but most of those
likely to be held by trustees are chargeable. When any asset which is not exempt
is disposed of for a consideration in excess of its acquisition value, that
difference is a chargeable gain. Where the trustees incur expense such as stamp
duty, legal costs and registration fees, in acquiring an asset, and in arranging for
its disposal, the total of those costs is added to the acquisition value and only the
difference is chargeable.

Thus, a simple transaction, without taking account of any adjustment to the
acquisition cost by virtue of inflation, would be:

Proceeds of sale of shares		£10,100
Deduct:		
purchase price	£8,000	
broker's commission on purchase	£100	
stamp duty on purchase	£80	
		£8,180
		£1,920
Deduct: expenses of sale		£120
Chargeable gain		£1,800

Capital gains tax payable: 30 per cent. of £1,800=£540.

Clearly, the most usual situation in which trustees will incur this type of
liability is where they switch assets in the course of the administration of the
trust. Equally clearly, the existence of capital gains tax will have an inhibiting
effect on changing assets.

---

[50] If the trustees had succeeded in their contention there would still have been a capital
gains tax liability. However, it would have been calculated according to a special basis which
was then in force and only open to individuals: F.A. 1965, s.21.

[51] C.G.T.A. 1979, s.29A; F.A. 1981, s.90.

[52] The main exemptions are assets having a predictable life not exceeding 50 years (other
than leases); proceeds of insurance policies in most circumstances; and in general private
dwelling-houses used for owner-occupation.

Capital gains tax only applies to gains which have accrued since 1965 and there are a number of transitional provisions which apply to assets which were acquired before but disposed of after that date.[53]

(3) Beneficiary becoming absolutely entitled

When a beneficiary becomes absolutely entitled to the whole or any part of the trust property, the trustees are deemed to have disposed of the assets to which he is entitled at that date, and the beneficiary is deemed to have acquired them at their then value. The beneficiary will become absolutely entitled either when some condition is fulfilled, such as attaining the age of majority, or when the trustees make a decision to pay or transfer the asset to him. In principle, a liability to capital gains tax will arise on the deemed disposal, but hold-over relief may be available.[54]

If after this time the trustees continue to hold the assets in their name, they do so as nominees for the beneficiary. In this case, the asset is deemed to be held by the beneficiary for capital gains tax purposes, so that no further liability can accrue to the trustees.[55]

In principle, one beneficiary can become absolutely entitled as against the trustees even though there are other benficiaries who do not. If, therefore, property is held upon trust for such of Adrian, Brendan and Clarendon who attain the age of 25, and if more than one of them in equal shares, upon reaching the age of 25 Adrian will in principle, become absolutely entitled even though Brendan and Clarendon are still under that age.[56] However, where the settled property consists of land, it seems that one beneficiary cannot become absolutely entitled if the other beneficiaries do not also do so.[57]

(4) Other persons becoming absolutely entitled

Section 54 of the Capital Gains Tax Act 1979 applies whenever a person becomes absolutely entitled as against the trustees, even if that entitlement is not beneficial. So, in *Messrs. Hoare Trustees* v. *Gardner*[58] the section was held to apply where trustees of one settlement took assets out of that settlement and made them subject to the trusts of a new settlement. The position is generally the same where, in exercise of a power of advancement, trustees of a settlement transfer settled property to themselves to be held on the trusts of a sub-settlement created ad hoc for the purpose of receiving that property.[59]

(5) Termination of life interest

When a life interest in possession comes to an end otherwise than on the death of the life tenant, there are no capital gains tax consequences if the

---

[53] C.G.T.A. 1979, Sched. 5.

[54] C.G.T.A. 1979, s.54. As to hold-over relief, see p. 372.

[55] C.G.T.A. 1979, s.46.

[56] *Stephenson* v. *Barclays Bank Trust Co. Ltd.* [1975] 1 All E.R. 625; *Pexton* v. *Bell* [1976] 2 All E.R. 914.

[57] *Crowe* v. *Appleby* [1976] 2 All E.R. 914 at p. 923.

[58] [1979] Ch. 1.

[59] *Ibid. Hart* v. *Briscoe* [1978] 1 All E.R. 791.

property continues to be settled property.[60] Thus, if trustees hold upon trust to pay the income to Edward until he reaches the age of 30, and thereafter to Frederick, there are no capital gains tax effects when Edward reaches that age. However, if a life interest in possession comes to an end otherwise than on the death of the life tenant, and the property then ceases to be settled, a person will have become absolutely entitled, and the position will be as stated in (3) or (4) above.

If a life interest in possession comes to an end on the death of the life tenant, the trustees are deemed to have disposed of the trust assets at their market value at that date, and to have re-acquired them at that value.[61] However, although the base cost of the assets is uplifted in this way, no capital gains tax is payable.[61] This is because on the death of the life tenant, capital transfer tax[62] will usually, but not always,[63] be payable.

V. CAPITAL TRANSFER TAX

Capital transfer tax was introduced by the Finance Act 1975. As it applies to trusts, the legislation draws a basic distinction between settled property in which there is an interest in possession and settled property in which there is no interest in possession.

(1) Interests in possession

There is no statutory definition of an interest in possession for the purposes of capital transfer tax. However, it may be said that a beneficiary has an interest in possession in settled property if he has a present right of present enjoyment of the net income, if any, of the settled property without any further decision of the trustees being required.[64]

The basic rule is that where a beneficiary has an interest in possession, he is treated for the purposes of capital transfer tax not as owning that interest, but as owning the settled property itself.[65] Suppose that property worth £100,000 is held upon trust for Douglas for life, with remainder to Edwin. The actuarial value of Douglas' life interest in possession may be only, say, £20,000, but he is treated as if he owned the property itself, worth £100,000. If a beneficiary disposes in his lifetime of an interest in possession, the same amount of tax will be payable as if he had given away property which he owned outright.[66] Accordingly, if Douglas assigns his interest in possession, the same amount of

---

[60] Exceptionally, if capital gains tax was not paid when assets were transferred *in specie* into trust, that gain which was "held-over" on that occasion will be chargeable on the death of the life tenant: F.A. 1982 s.84(3).

[61] C.G.T.A. 1979, s.55(1); F.A. 1982, s.84.

[62] *Ibid.*

[63] If some exemption applies. An example is where on the death of the life tenant, his spouse takes the next life interest.

[64] *Pearson* v. *I.R.C.* [1980] 2 All E.R. 479, H.L.

[65] F.A. 1975, Sched. 5, para. 3(1).

[66] para. 4(2).

tax would be payable as if he had made a lifetime gift of £100,000.[67] Likewise, if a beneficiary who has an interest in possession dies, the amount of capital transfer tax payable is the same as it would be if the beneficiary died owning the settled property outright.[68]

Although the amount of tax is calculated by reference to the personal circumstances of the beneficiary, the tax is payable out of the settled property, and the trustees are responsible for ensuring that payment is made.[69]

From the principle that a beneficiary who has an interest in possession is treated as owning the settled property itself, it follows that if the interest in possession comes to an end and, at the same time, the beneficiary becomes absolutely entitled to the settled property, there will be no liability to capital transfer tax.[70] Before the coming to an end of the interest he is treated as owning the settled property. He has not, therefore, made any transfer of value. It also follows that if a beneficiary sells his interest in possession for the actuarial value of that interest, he will be treated as making a transfer of value. Consider again the example given above of Douglas who has an interest in possession in settled property which is worth £100,000, but the value of the interest itself is only £20,000. If Douglas sells his interest in a commercial transaction at arm's length for the full value of £20,000, there will be a liability to tax as if he has made a gift of £80,000. Before the sale he is treated as owning property worth £100,000. After the sale he has cash of £20,000. He is, therefore, treated as if he had transferred value to the extent of £80,000.

There are certain exceptions from the charge to tax which would normally arise on the termination of an interest in possession.[71]

(2) Future interests

The corollary of the rule just considered, that a beneficiary with an interest in possession is treated as owning the settled property itself, is that, in general, there is no liability where a beneficiary disposes of a future interest in settled property. This is so whether the interest is disposed of in the beneficiary's lifetime[72] or on his death.[73]

(3) No interest in possession

Where there is no interest in possession, the legislature has, very broadly, attempted to impose the same charge to tax as if the property had not been settled. To this end, tax is chargeable at 30 per cent. of the ordinary lifetime rate on the capital value of the settled property at each tenth anniversary of the

---

[67] Upon the assumption that Douglas had made no chargeable transfers of value within the previous 10 years the tax would be £7,375: F.A. 1982, s.90.

[68] F.A. 1975, ss.22(1), 23(1), an Sched. 5, para. 3(1).

[69] s.25(3). The beneficiary has a concurrent personal liability.

[70] Sched. 5, para. 4(3).

[71] The main exceptions are where the beneficiary becomes entitled to a further interest in possession in the whole of the settled property (Sched. 5, para. 4(3)); where the settled property reverts to the settlor (para. 4(5)); and where the interest is disposed of for family maintenance (s.46).

[72] F.A. 1975, s.20(3).

[73] ss.22(1), 23(1).

creation of the trust.[74] This is equivalent to a charge at the full rate every 30 years or so. In addition, where property is taken out of trust, there is an "exit" charge in respect of the period for which it has remained in trust since the last decennial anniversary.[75]

Although trusts which have no interest in possession have the cash flow disadvantage that tax has to be paid every 10 years, they have the advantages that:

(a) tax is always payable at the lifetime rates, rather than the higher deathtime rates, even if a charge to tax occurs at about the time of the death of a beneficiary; and

(b) the trust is treated generally as if it were a separate legal person. Accordingly, tax is payable only according to the circumstances of the trust itself: the circumstances or asset value of the beneficiary is irrelevant, even if all the income has been paid to him.

(4) Accumulation and maintenance settlements

There are certain exceptions to the charge to tax on trusts where there is no interest in possession, the most important one relating to accumulation and maintenance settlements. An accumulation and maintenance settlement is generally one created by a person for his children or his grand-children.[76] The entitlements under the settlement can be kept discretionary until the child or grandchild reaches the age of 25, or the income can be accumulated until that time. Provided that it is certain that by the time he has reached the age of 25 the child or grandchild will obtain either the whole or a part of the settled property, or an interest in possession in the whole or a part of the settled property, the normal liability to capital transfer tax on trusts with no interest in possession does not arise.[77]

---

[74] F.A. 1982, ss.105, 109.
[75] F.A. 1982, ss.108, 112.
[76] F.A. 1982, s.114(2)(b).
[77] F.A. 1982, s.114(4).

CHAPTER 16

INVESTMENT

I. THE GENERAL STANDARD OF CARE

THE duty of a trustee in investing trust funds is to take such care as an ordinary prudent man would take if he were under a duty to make the investment for the benefit of other persons for whom he felt morally bound to provide.[1] Lord Watson in *Learoyd* v. *Whiteley*[2] specified the requirement as follows:

> "As a general rule the law requires of a trustee no higher degree of diligence in the execution of his office than a man of ordinary prudence would exercise in the management of his own private affairs. Yet he is not allowed the same discretion in investing the moneys of the trust as if he were a person *sui juris* dealing with his own estate. Business men of prudence may, and frequently do, select investments which are more or less of a speculative character but it is the duty of a trustee to confine himself to the class of investments which are permitted by the trust and likewise to avoid all investments of that class which are attended with hazard. So long as he acts in the honest observance of these limitations the general rule already stated will apply."

In addition to adhering to this general standard of care, a trustee is also bound to make his investments in such a way that those entitled in possession will obtain a reasonable income and yet the capital will be preserved for those entitled to it in remainder.[3] A balance must be secured so that all beneficiaries are treated equally and fairly.

It follows from the foregoing that even if the trustee invests in securities authorised by the Trustee Investments Act 1961,[4] or by the trust instrument itself,[5] he will not necessarily be protected from attack by the beneficiaries. Even an authorised investment may in the particular circumstances of the case be unjustified and amount to a breach of the trustees' general duties of care and impartiality. But in circumstances such as these the onus would be on the

---

[1] *Re Whiteley* (1886) 33 Ch. D. 347 at 355, *per* Lindley L.J.; affirmed *sub nom. Learoyd* v. *Whiteley* (1887) 12 App. Cas. 727.
[2] *Ibid.* at p. 733.
[3] *Re Whiteley, ante,* at p. 350, *per* Cotton L.J.
[4] *Post,* p. 310.
[5] See *post,* p. 314.

beneficiaries to establish that the investment was imprudent, and not for the
trustees to show the converse.[6] Moreover, in addition to these general duties,
certain positive duties in relation to investment are now expressly imposed by
the Trustee Investments Act 1961,[7] and these will apply to any power of
investment, whether it is exercised under or outside the Act.

Variation and continuation of investments. The trustees have, as one would
expect, the power to vary investments already made,[8] and also to continue these
investments even if they have since ceased to be authorised.[9] But these powers
are, of course, subject to the general and statutory[10] duties of care and impartiality incumbent on a trustee.

II. TYPES OF INVESTMENT

It has just been indicated that when any investment is contemplated, the trustee
will have to give due consideration to the interests of all the beneficiaries, and he
will have to hold the balance equally between them. Thus if trust money is held
upon trust for A for life, with remainder to B, it would prima facie be wrong to
invest all the money in an investment which produced a high rate of income, but
little or no capital appreciation, for to do so would be to benefit the tenant for
life at the expense of the remainderman. Further, as will be shown later in this
chapter, before deciding on an investment, a trustee must generally consider
advice—and consider is the operative word: he must not unthinkingly follow
such advice—on whether the contemplated investment will be satisfactory.
Again, he must diversify the trust investments, which means not merely that the
trust fund must be held in different investments but, so far as is appropriate to
the circumstances of the trust, that it must be held in different *types* of
investment.

Before he can adequately do any of these things, a trustee must have some
knowledge of the characteristics of different types of investment. (Investments
are colloquially termed "securities," but that term is somewhat dangerous: a
"security" in this sense is not necessarily "secure.") The points to consider with
any investment are, *inter alia*,

(a) whether or not that investment is a "fixed-interest" security;
(b) whether or not the capital value will fluctuate; and
(c) if the capital value will fluctuate, in what way such fluctuation is likely.

If a security is a "fixed-interest" security, the amount of interest or dividend
which is produced will never alter. The trustee who buys £1,000 Treasury 12 per
cent. Stock 1987 knows that, whatever happens to the economic state of the

---

[6] *Shaw* v. *Cates* [1909] 1 Ch. 389, at p. 395, *per* Parker J.
[7] s.6(1)(a)(b), discussed at *post*, p. 318.
[8] *Hume* v. *Lopes* [1892] A.C. 112.
[9] Trustee Act 1925, s.4, as modified by the Trustee Investments Act 1961, s.3(4), Sched. 3,
para. 2, and discussed *post*, p. 316.
[10] T.I.A. 1961, s.6(1)(a)(b), and see *post*, p. 318.

nation, he will receive £120 per annum income. On the other hand, if he invests in ordinary shares of commercial companies, known as "equities," he does not know what he will receive, for this will depend entirely on the amount of the dividend which the companies in each year decide to pay. In bad years they may pay nothing, but in other years they may pay a larger amount than any fixed-interest security.

As regards capital value, there are only a few types of security where there will be no fluctuation. This will only occur where such securities are purchasable only from the Government or other person issuing them, and are not bought and sold among private individuals. The best-known examples are National Savings Certificates, which may be bought over the counter of the Post Office or Trustee Savings Bank, and some bonds issued by local authorities.

By contrast, the capital value of all other securities, whether of the Government, local authorities, or commercial undertakings dealt with on a stock exchange, will fluctuate. To understand the terminology used in connection with this fluctuation, it is necessary to distinguish between the nominal price of an investment, and its market price. The nominal price is the value of the investment as named on its face, and at which, usually, it was originally issued. The market price is the price at which that security can for the time being be purchased. Suppose that the Government issued in 1950 a new stock which carries interest at £4 per cent. and that a person purchased from the Government a holding of £100 of the stock for £100 cash. Suppose also that in 1985 someone buys on the Stock Exchange that holding for £80 cash. The purchaser would be described as buying that holding of £100 nominal stock for a market price of £80. The interest, of course, is always calculated on the nominal value, and so however much the market price alters, the amount of interest will always be the same. When a security is bought for the same amount of cash as its nominal value—in the example just given, the purchase in 1950 of £100 nominal stock for £100—that security is said to be bought at "par."

The other term which is used in this context is "yield." This is the amount of income from a security expressed as a percentage of the market price paid for it, and not of its nominal price. So if £80 cash is paid for £100 nominal £4 per cent. stock, as the interest is fixed at £4 p.a., the yield is

$$£\frac{4}{80} \times 100 = £5 \text{ per cent.}$$

More precisely, the "yield" as just described is the "interest only" or "flat" yield. Where an investment is purchased at less than its nominal value, but will be redeemed at its nominal value there may also be calculated its "redemption yield." Very broadly, the redemption yield measures the gain to be expected on the redemption of the security together with the income which will be derived.[11]

[11] The redemption yield is, strictly, the amount by which the eventual capital sum which will be obtained on the redemption of the security, together with the income which will arise until redemption, has to be discounted to reduce the security to its present value.

It must be stressed that there are many factors which will govern fluctuations of market price, but in the case of Government securities, there are two in particular. First, there is the general level of interest rates obtainable elsewhere. If the normal yield at any time is £10 per cent. from investments which are considered "safe," the market price of Government securities is likely to be adjusted so that that security will produce a yield of about £10 per cent. If the market price were substantially higher, no one would buy it, because they could obtain a safe £10 per cent. yield elsewhere. The second factor is whether and at what pace inflation (and so, depreciation in the purchasing power of money) is likely to occur. If a period of rapid inflation is forecast, most investors will not favour fixed-interest securities, but will choose investments from which the return is likely to increase as inflation occurs; thus lack of demand will force down the market value of the fixed-interest securities. The most notorious example is $3\frac{1}{2}$ per cent. War Loan, which now[12] has a market value in the region of £36 for each £100 nominal of stock.

In the case of ordinary shares in commercial companies, the yield will also be important, and this may be expected to be rather higher than from Government securities, for a commercial undertaking cannot give the capital guarantee which the Government does and the yield is greater to compensate for this. Companies of national standing can become insolvent. But there are two other important factors which influence the capital value of ordinary shares. First, the anticipated ability of the company to pay dividends in the future at least at the rate which it has paid for them in the past. Secondly, the company's prospects for any increased profits and growth in the future.

With these principles in mind, the major types of investment can be considered as follows:

(1) Fixed-interest securities

(a) **National Savings Income Bonds.** The capital value of these securities issued by the Government never changes, and the investor is guaranteed that he will receive back the amount he invested. These bonds are not, strictly, fixed interest securities because the rate of interest paid is adjusted from time to time in line with general changes in sterling interest levels. The interest is paid monthly.

(b) **National Savings Certificates.** These are also Government securities, but differ from National Savings Income Bonds because the interest is not paid as it accrues, but is added to capital. When the certificates are repaid, the investor therefore receives back the exact amount of his investment, together with the accumulated interest in the form of an addition to capital.[13]

(c) **Building society investments.** Investments in building societies are of two main kinds: on deposit accounts and on share accounts. The difference is that, should the building society be wound up, the depositors are paid out in full

---

[12] June 1983.
[13] As to the entitlement to the increment, see *post*, p. 344.

before the shareholders. For this reason, the shareholders receive a slightly larger income, usually £¼ per cent. above the rate paid to the depositors, but in practice investments both in deposit accounts and in share accounts in building societies which are recognised as suitable for trustee investments[14] are regarded as absolutely safe, although only investments on deposit account are within the narrower range of "trustee investments."[15] The interest is usually payable twice yearly, or it can be added to capital.

Although dealt with here under the heading of fixed-interest securities, building society investments are not strictly fixed-interest ones because the rate of interest does fluctuate slightly, but not usually by a large amount. There is, however, no variation at all in the capital value of building society investments.

(d) **"Gilt-edged" securities.** This term, which is a hark-back to days when securities of the British Government were thought of more highly than today, denotes stocks issued or guaranteed by the Government, by the nationalised industries, and by some Commonwealth governments. They are fixed-interest securities, but as they are dealt with on the Stock Exchange[16] their capital value does fluctuate.

There are two categories of gilt-edged securities: dated and undated stock. Where stock is dated—for example 5½ per cent. Funding Stock, 1987–91—the investor knows that at some time between the stated dates the security will be redeemed at its nominal value. If, therefore, trustees buy £100 5¾ per cent. Funding Stock, 1987–91, in 1982 for £84, they know that by 1991 the Government will in effect buy back the stock from them for £100.

Undated stocks are often never redeemed, and the holders of them can never know how much their holdings will realise on the market at any future time.

Some British Government securities are "index-linked." These are considered later.[17]

(e) **Debentures.** A "debenture" is an acknowledgment of indebtedness by a company supported by a mortgage or charge created by the company over its assets, or a bond issued by a company unsupported by such a charge.[18] A private individual can only mortgage or charge property which he has at the time when that mortgage or charge is created, and a debenture may likewise be secured by a charge on a specific item of a company's property. But a company has an advantage over individuals in that it may create a "floating charge" which is a general charge over all its assets. Such a charge does not restrict the company from dealing with its assets, but should any liquidation occur, the charge which until then has been "floating" above the company's assets sud-

---

[14] Under the provisions of House Purchase and Housing Act 1959, s.1. See also T.I.A. 1961, Sched. 1, Pt. II, para. 12.

[15] *Post*, p. 311.

[16] Persons who have National Savings Bank accounts may purchase "gilts" through the Post Office, and at their option have the dividends credited to their National Savings Bank account. In this case the Post Office acts as intermediary, and it purchases the security on the Stock Exchange. Thus, although in this case the securities may be purchased through the Post Office, the principle is not altered.

[17] *Post*, p. 307.

[18] Companies Act 1948, s.455; T.I.A. 1961, Sched. 1, Pt. IV, para. 4.

denly "descends" upon them, and converts itself into a fixed charge over those assets. This is a convenient way for a company to support its borrowing with security without impeding its dealings with its assets. But there is no need for a debenture to be supported by any security. If it is not, it operates in the same way as an unsecured loan to a private individual. For investment purposes, debentures are frequently equated with preference shares, with which they will be considered further.

(f) **Preference shares.** Preference shares are shares issued by commercial companies carrying a fixed rate of interest, and in this respect they are similar to debentures. The rate of interest is usually but not necessarily indicated in the title, *e.g.* 6 per cent. Preference Shares. The 6 per cent. is the rate of interest, calculated by reference to the nominal value of the stock, and not to its market value. As long as the company makes a profit, or, usually, has reserves of profits from previous years, the holder is paid his dividend.

Debenture holders stand in the position of lenders to the company, and they are entitled to have their interest paid first. Preference shareholders are in the position of investors in the company, and they rank next after the debenture holders. It is only after the debenture and the preferense shareholders have been paid that the company can declare a dividend on its ordinary shares.

There is a risk, in some cases more theoretical than real, that the company will not have any money, and in this case, of course, the debenture holder or preference shareholder will receive nothing. To compensate for this risk, the yield on debentures and preference shares is usually higher than on gilt-edged. Frequently both debentures and preference shares are redeemeable at a given date in the same way as dated gilt-edged stocks, and sometimes the holder has the option to convert the shares into ordinary shares at a stated time. Both debentures and preference shares may be dealt with on the Stock Exchange,[19] so that their capital value fluctuates.

There are two special classes of preference shares. The first is the *cumulative preference share*. The significance of the word "cumulative" is that if in any year the company does not pay a dividend, the dividend for that year will be paid out of any profits for future years. The other special type of preference share is the *participating preference share*. This type of share combines the characteristics of preference and ordinary shares. The company first pays the shareholders a dividend up to the amount of their preference—say, 6 per cent.; it then pays the ordinary shareholders a dividend of the same amount, and if there is still any money available for distribution, it is divided equally between holders of the participating preference and ordinary shares. Participating preference shares are, therefore, preference shares which are capable, subject to certain conditions, of participating in profits normally reserved for ordinary shareholders. Preference shares which are non-participating do not carry this right.

---

[19] "May" be dealt with on the Stock Exchange, because private companies, whose securities are not handled by the Stock Exchange, may nevertheless issue debentures and shares. When these securities change hands, the price is a matter for direct negotiation between buyer and seller, unless some provision is made in the articles of association to govern the price.

(2) **Inflation-adjusted securities**

A recent development has been the issue of British Government securities which carry a low rate of interest, but the capital value of which is adjusted in accordance with increases in the Index of Retail Prices. Most of these securities are dealt in on the Stock Exchange,[20] but there are also index-linked National Savings Certificates.[21]

Index-linked stocks which are dealt in on the Stock Exchange have a base figure determined by the Retail Prices Index in force eight months[22] before the stock was issued. The amount of interest payable, and the amount payable on the redemption of the stock are then both adjusted for movements in the Retail Prices Index.

The amount payable on the redemption of index-linked National Savings Certificates is similarly calculated. In addition, certain bonuses are also payable.

(3) **Ordinary shares**

Ordinary shares, or "equities," are the basic type of share issued by commercial companies. In each year the company decides the amount available for distribution after paying its expenses and making provision for future requirements. The holders of debentures and preference shares are then paid out, and however much is left is distributed between the ordinary shareholders (with, sometimes, the participating preference shareholders also benefiting). The dividend on the ordinary share, therefore, fluctuates with the trading profits of the company. If the company is flourishing, as its trading profits go up so will its ordinary dividends, and as the dividend increases so people will be prepared to pay more for the shares, or, in other words, the capital value goes up as well. But the reverse is the case when the company does badly.

Equities have a distinct advantage in times of inflation, for as inflation goes on, so the price of the company's products will increase, and this will lead to more money being available for dividends. The purchasing power of these dividends may well be no more than before, but at least the investment stands the chance of keeping pace with inflation, and so preserving its purchasing power.

Speaking generally, equities are the least safe of the various types of investment. For this reason their capital value fluctuates more than that of the other types.

Some equity shares produce a fairly small income, because rather than distribute its profits the company may prefer to plough back much of its profit into its business. In this case, although the dividends are small, the value of the company itself may be growing, and this will lead to an increase in the value of the shares. On the other hand, some shares will pay a high dividend but the prospects of the company may be precarious, or the profitability of the company

---

[20] At present (June 1983) there are seven stocks with redemption dates varying from 1988 to 2011. Some of these stocks are available on the National Savings Stock Register.

[21] The 2nd Index-linked Issue National Savings Certificates. The first issue, the so-called "granny bonds" were available only to those who had reached retirement age.

[22] The eight-month lag is for administrative convenience in making the calculations.

may be unlikely to increase, in which case there is not likely to be much capital appreciation of the shares. And it must be remembered that capital appreciation is likely to benefit the remainderman more than the life-tenant.[23]

(4) Unit trusts

The managers of these trusts buy other Stock Exchange securities and invite the public to buy units in the fund. The managers then receive the dividends from the securities, pay the expenses, and themselves a salary, and distribute the remainder to the holders of the units. A holder of such a unit has, therefore, a minimal stake in numerous companies, and thus spreads the risk. But at the same time he receives less than he would have done had he invested directly in the most profitable companies in which the managers invest, and it must be remembered that the managers take out their remuneration before any money is available for the unit holders. One advantage of investing in unit trusts is that the managers are in a position to keep a day-to-day eye on the investments, and they have the ready opportunity for altering investments at the appropriate time.

Unit trusts are often organised to cope for special needs, *e.g.* low income and high capital appreciation, or high income and low capital appreciation, or something between the two.

(5) Non-income producing investments

The traditional meaning of the word "investment" is an asset which produces income[24] with the connotation that it is likely to produce a surplus on revenue account over the anticipated period of holding of the asset.[25] This is still the legal meaning of the word. However, as a result of fiscal legislation it has become more and more prudent in many situations to reduce or eliminate income, and to seek capital appreciation. Consequently in general and financial usage, the word now implies any asset which will produce a good return, even if that is entirely in the form of capital appreciation.

The fiscal legislation has produced the following results:

(a) income, when paid to a beneficiary, is taxable in his hands up to a maximum effective rate of 75 per cent.[26] Capital gains realised by trustees or a beneficiary are taxable at the maximum rate of 30 per cent.;

(b) where trustees receive income in the first instance, and accumulate it, that income is, broadly, subject to income tax at 45 per cent.[27] If they hold an asset which never produces income, their liability is to capital gains tax only, and this is payable only when the asset is disposed of.[28]

---

[23] Although, of course, if the capital appreciation occurs because the dividends are being increased, the tenant for life will benefit by virtue of this increase in the dividends.

[24] See *Re Power* [1947] Ch. 572; see *infra*.

[25] See the reasoning in *Cooke* v. *Haddock* (1960) 39 T.C. 64; *Johnston* v. *Heath* [1970] 3 All E.R. 915; [1970] 1 W.L.R. 1567.

[26] Including the investment income surcharge: see *ante*, p. 293. Finance Act 1974, s.5

[27] See *ante*. p. 293.

[28] See *ante*, p. 295

As a result, trustees have increasingly sought to lay out trust funds in the acquisition of non-income, or low-income, producing assets. It must be stressed that this can only be done where there is an express power in the trust instrument[29] but, given this power, the following are some of the possibilities which have recently found favour.

(a) **Split-level shares and units.** In principle these are either equity shares or units in unit trusts. The device depends on there being two classes of shares or units. One class carries the entitlement to all income, but no capital appreciation. The other class carries entitlement to all capital appreciation, but no income. Shares and units in the former class are usually taken up by bodies which are exempt from income tax, such as charities and pension funds. Shares and units in the latter class are usually taken up by private individuals and trustees. It will be appreciated that in normal circumstances shares and units in the latter class, although paying no dividends, will steadily increase in value, and that value will be realised on disposal.

(b) **Single-Premium Bonds.** The essence of this arrangement is that a policy of assurance is effected with an insurance company for the payment of one premium only, which is paid at the outset. The insurance company invests the funds in an agreed manner, such as in equities or in property. At an agreed date, often after the expiry of 10 years, or on the earlier death of the life assured, the policy matures, and the payee receives a sum equivalent to the original premium paid, together with a profit which depends on the success which the insurance company has had in the investment of its funds. In principle, the total proceeds of the policy are received as capital.[30]

(c) **Chattels.** A wide variety of chattels have been purchased by trustees as growth investments. Over the last few years trustees have invested in works of art, antique furniture, silver, silver bullion and oriental carpets. Almost invariably these are unsuitable as investments unless one has considerable freedom of choice as to the time of disposal: due to volatility of the various markets, a period of some years may have to elapse before it becomes a good time to sell.

(d) **Loans to beneficiaries.** In some circumstances, it may be thought desirable that capital appreciation should accrue to a beneficiary rather than to the trustees. In such circumstances, the trustees may wish to lend trust funds to the beneficiary, interest free, perhaps securing the laon by taking a charge over the assets which the beneficiary purchases with them. On the death of the beneficiary, the loan is repaid from his estate. However, where this is done, the whole of the capital appreciation accrues to the beneficiary, and not to the fund as a whole, so that this could only be proper where it is expressly authorised by the trust instrument, or all other beneficiaries affected agree.

---

[29] *Re Power* [1947] Ch. 572.
[30] Although, so far as the trustees are concerned, the total proceeds rank as a capital receipt, a charge to income tax may arise.

(6) **Foreign currency securities**

As well as considering the type of investment to be made, trustees will wish to consider the currency of the investment. For example, trustees may wish to invest part of the fund in the stocks of foreign governments or companies, such as United States Treasury Bills, denominated in United States dollars, or Australian equity shares. Most of the types of investment which have so far been described have their counterparts in other countries. In addition, it is possible to invest in "currency funds." In essence, these are shares in companies[31] who apply the whole of their funds in making deposits in the various leading currencies of the world. By this spread, some protection is obtained against a fall in the exchange rate of sterling and those other currencies.

III. TRUSTEE INVESTMENTS ACT 1961

Under the general law trustees are entitled to invest funds only in investments authorised *either* by express terms of their trust instrument *or* by statute. Until the Act was passed the investments authorised by statute were extremely limited. They were largely governed by section 1 of the Trustee Act 1925. Generally speaking, the statutory trustee list of investments (the "Statutory List" as it was usually called) was restricted to the following stock issued by the British Government and governments of Commonwealth countries and colonies; stock guaranteed by the British Government; stock and mortgages issued by British local authorities; mortgages of land in Great Britain, among others. The essential point—on which criticism tended to fasten—was the restricted nature of these investments. Practically all of them carry interest at a fixed rate and are repayable at par. And this took no account of the decline, over the years, in the value of the pound. In the first place, eventual *repayment* of invested capital at its nominal par value would involve a *capital* loss in real values. Secondly, the income received by a life-tenant might remain nominally the same but, again, over the years, it will have become progressively worth in real value less than at the date the trust was established. And these two difficulties would become more and more acute as the trust itself became older. We are, of course, pre-supposing here that investments were made in securities authorised by the Statutory List. But until recently there might be no alternative, because, unless a wider power of investment was conferred by the trust instrument, the trustees were restricted to the Statutory List. Indeed, many trusts over 40 years of age would be drawn so as to comprehend only these investments and the result has been that a large number of trusts have suffered income and capital losses on the lines already mentioned. One striking omission from the List—understandable no doubt in 1925—was that there was no power to invest in equities. From the short-term viewpoint this was fortunate, for in the economic depression from which Britain suffered in the decade after the Act was passed, gilt-edged securities were generally far better investments than equities. But from the longer viewpoint it appears to be the position that those

---

[31] For taxation reasons, the companies are incorporated outside the U.K., most frequently in Jersey.

trusts which contained an unrestricted power of investment—thus enabling investment to be made in equities—have fared a great deal better than those restricted to the Statutory List. Accordingly, in the past 25 years or so, settlors have been advised to give their trustees very much wider investment powers than those contained in the List. But this practice left untouched those many trusts which conferred only the statutory investment powers.

It is not surprising, therefore, that many voices were raised against the continuation of this state of affairs. Among others the Nathan Committee in 1952 advocated reform, and in 1955 a White Paper stated that the Government intended to introduce a reform of the law. During the period before the Act was passed some relaxations occurred. For example, charities have long had the power to go to the court for an extension of their investment powers, but it was only as a result of the decision in *Re Royal Society's Charitable Trusts*[32] that this was generally realised. Of more general importance, the power to apply to the court was extended to all trusts—non-charitable trusts as well as charitable trusts—by the Variation of Trusts Act 1958[33]; many applications have been made under the Act for an extension of investment powers as well as for a variation of beneficial interests.

An application to the court, however, costs time and money. What was required was a general reform of the law based on section 1 of the Trustee Act 1925, without any obligation on the trustees to apply to the court. The reform was at long last achieved, but in a linguistically complex form, by the Trustee Investments Act 1961, which came into force on August 3, 1961.[33a]

The basic point about this Act is that it replaces the old Statutory List. The new List is set out in the First Schedule to the Act. This is divided into three parts. Parts I and II are concerned with the "narrower-range investments" and Part III with the "wider-range investments" so called.

(1) Narrower-range investments

The investments specified in Part I include Defence Bonds, National Savings Certificates and National Savings Bank deposits and are conveniently described as "small savings" investments. In general terms, they are the type of investment which can be made over the counter at a Post Office or Trustee Savings Bank, and advice is not necessary because there is no fluctuation in capital value. They are placed in this separate category because it is unnecessary for a trustee to seek expert advice before investing in this class, whereas it is required for investment in Parts II and III securities.[34] The investments specified in Part

---

[32] [1956] Ch. 87.

[33] See *post*, p. 413.

[33a] The Law Reform Committee consider that the 1961 Act is out of date. They recommend that authorised investments should be divided into those which can be made without advice and those which can only be made with advice; and that the trustees should be free to invest in such proportions as they choose.

[34] s.6(2). The narrower-range investments specified in Pt. I also now include Ulster Development Bonds (Trustee Investments (Additional Powers)(No. 2) Order 1962 (S.I. 1962 No. 2611), which came into force on December 5, 1962); National Development Bonds (Trustee Investments (Additional Powers) Order 1964 (S.I. 1964 No. 703), which came into force on May 15, 1964); British Savings Bonds (Trustee Investment (Additional Powers) Order 1968 (S.I. 1968 No. 470), which came into force on April 1, 1968).

II approximate to those in the old Statutory List. But they also include certain securities which did not previously rank as trustee investments, *i.e.* (i) fixed-interest securities[35] registered in the United Kingdom issued by local or public authorities[36] in the Commonwealth or by the World Bank[37]; (ii) debentures[38] of United Kingdom companies which comply with certain prescribed conditions as to paid-up capital and dividend records[39]; and (iii) loans to most building societies.[40]

(2) **Wider-range investments**

The narrower range did not excite a great deal of attention; but the new wider range did. This, which is contained in Part III of the First Schedule, includes (i) shares, stock and debentures of certain United Kingdom companies[41] (ii) shares of certain designated building societies[42]; and (iii) units of authorised unit trusts.[43] It is to be noted in particular—and this is the striking feature—that equities and other securities of the United Kingdom companies are included. But such investments in United Kingdom companies are, as will now be seen, hedged round with restrictions.

(3) **Companies eligible for investment**

The rules now to be mentioned apply to investment in debentures (Part II securities) and in shares and stock (Part III securities).

In the first place, they will not constitute trustee investments unless they are quoted on a recognised stock exchange.[44] Secondly, shares and debenture stock must be fully paid up or issued on terms that they are to be fully paid up within nine months from the date of issue.[45] And, thirdly—and this is the most stringent test of all—the company must have a total issued or paid-up capital of at least £1 million[46] and also have paid in each of the immediately preceding five years a dividend on all its shares.[47] There is no statutory requirement as to the *amount* of the dividend which has to be paid. In order to ensure that its shares

---

[35] *i.e.* securities which under their terms of issue bear a fixed rate of interest: Sched. 1, Pt. IV, para. 4. "Securities" includes "shares, debentures, Treasury Bills and Tax Reserve Certificates": *ibid.* Variable-interest securities have been added by Trustee Investment (Additional Powers) Order 1977 (S.I. No. 831).

[36] Sched. 1, Pt. IV, para. 4.

[37] *Ibid.* para. 5. This paragraph now also includes fixed-interest securities issued in the U.K. by the Inter-American Bank (Trustee Investments (Additional Powers) (No. 2) Order 1964 (S.I. 1964 No. 1404). Bank of Ireland War Stock also added (Trustee Investments (Additional Powers) Order 1966 (S.I. 1966 No. 401)).

[38] "Debenture" includes for this purpose debenture stock and bonds whether containing a charge on the assets or not, and loan stock and notes (Sched. 1, Pt. IV, para. 4).

[39] Sched. 1 Pt. II, para. 4; *ibid.* Pt. IV, para. 3. These requirements are the same as for Pt. III investments, *infra.*

[40] Trustee Investments (Additional Powers) Order 1981 (S.I. 1981 No. 1547).

[41] Sched. 1, Pt. II, para 1; *ibid.* Pt. IV, para. 3.

[42] Sched. 1, Pt. III, para. 2.

[43] *Ibid.* para. 3.

[44] Sched. 1, Pt. IV, para. 2(*a*).

[45] Sched. 1, Pt. IV, para. 2(*b*).

[46] Sched. 1, Pt. IV, para. 3(*a*).

[47] Sched. 1, Pt. IV, para. 3(*b*).

will continue to be trustee investments, when a company experiences bad trading conditions, it will often pay a small dividend on its shares, even if it is as little as 0.01p a share.

(4) Division of the fund

The trustees cannot make or retain investments in the wider range unless the trust fund is divided into two parts, a narrower-range part and a wider-range part.[48] And only the wider-range part can be used for investment in the wider-range investments specified in Part III.[49] This division, which is perhaps the most important general feature of the Act, is to be made into two equal parts (the "50:50 rule")[50] and once made it is permanent and the two parts of the fund are kept separate.[51] It has the consequence that the wider-range part can be invested in wider-range investments, although there is nothing to prevent the trustee from investing it in the narrower-range investments if he chooses. On the other hand, the narrower-range part *must* be invested in narrower-range investments.

Moreover, in order to make sure that the division is permanent, provision is made for "compensating transfers" if property is transferred from the narrower range to the wider range.[52] Thus if property forming part of the narrower range is invested in a wider-range investment there must be a compensating transfer from the wider range in the opposite direction; or, alternatively, it must be sold and reinvested in narrower-range investments as soon as possible.[53]

(5) Accruals

Again, it may be that property accrues to the trust fund after the division. Some difficulties may arise here. For this purpose a distinction has been made between various classes of accrual. If property accrues to a trust fund in right of ownership of property that is already in their hands (*e.g.* on a bonus issue of shares or on the foreclosure of a mortgage) or was previously in their hands (*e.g.* where trustees have sold shares but retained their right to a bonus issue), then it will accrue to that part of the fund which contains or contained the investment that generated it.[54] But in any other case the trustees must ensure that the value of each part of the fund is increased proportionately by the same amount, and this may mean that a compensating transfer must be made from one part of the fund to the other.[55] This would prove to be necessary where, for example, dividends or income are received as capital, where an expectancy falls in or the proceeds of sale of an expectancy are received, or where a gift is made to trustees on the trusts of the settlement.

---

[48] s.2(1).

[49] s.2(1)(2).

[50] s.2(1). The Treasury may, by order, direct that on any division made during the continuance of the order, the wider-range part shall be such proportion of the whole, being greater than one-half but not more than three-quarters, as may be prescribed by the order, and any such order may be revoked by a subsequent order prescribing a greater proportion: s.13.

[51] *Ibid.*

[52] s.2(1).

[53] s.2(2). [54] s.2(3)(*a*). [55] s.2(3)(*b*).

(6) **Withdrawals**

Although, in general, compensating transfers may be necessary, special provision is made for one class of withdrawal. For it is provided that withdrawals from a trust fund in *the exercise of any power or duty*[56] of the trustees may be made from either part of the fund at their discretion.[57] In this case there is no need for compensating transfers. For example, if there is £1,000 in the narrower range and £1,000 in the wider range, and the trustees have to raise £500 for taxation or to pay it to a beneficiary absolutely entitled or to appropriate it to a separate trust fund or any other purpose, the £500 can be taken from either part of the fund at the trustees' discretion. This may well mean that the 50:50 rule will be partially abrogated unless, of course, £250 is taken from each part. This breach in the rule is presumably justified by the advantage of giving a certain latitude to trustees in the performance of their powers and duties in this respect.[58]

Moreover, there are certain ancillary provisions governing the trustees' power to appropriate part of the fund to form a separate trust fund. If at the time of appropriation the original fund was divided into a wider-range and a narrower-range part, it will be necessary to make a division of the new fund if it is intended to make use of the new investment powers as to that fund. But this division need not necessarily be 50:50. It is provided that the wider-range and narrower-range parts may be constituted:

(i) on the 50:50 basis; *or*
(ii) so as to bear the same proportion to each other as the two corresponding parts of the original fund bore at the date of appropriation; *or*
(iii) "in some intermediate proportion."[59]

This third alternative requires elucidation. It will presumably apply to a case where at the date of appropriation the 50:50 rule applies to the original fund, but in fact the wider-range part has increased beyond 50 per cent. (*e.g.* 60 per cent. of the whole) so that the proportions are 60:40 and not 50:50. In this case the wider-range and the narrower-range parts of the appropriated funds may be constituted in any proportion between 60:40 and 50:50. It could legitimately, for example, be in the proportion of 55 for the wider-range and 45 for the narrower.

It should also be noticed that no provision is made for compensating transfers between the two parts of the original fund which is not appropriated to form a separate trust fund. Thus if at the date of appropriation £10,000 is comprised in wider-range investments and £8,000 in narrower-range investments and £3,000 is appropriated out of the narrower-range funds, the proportion in which the original fund will now be constituted will be altered to 2:1.

(7) **Special range**

It is provided that the statutory powers of investment are additional to any

[56] See T.A. 1925, s.10(4).
[57] s.2(4).
[58] See 234 H. of L. Official Report 13, 14.
[59] s.4(3).

special powers, *e.g.* conferred by the will or settlement or by the court[60] or by Parliament.[61] As a result, provision also had to be made for cases where special powers of investment were contained in the trust instrument which the trustees wish to combine with the powers under the Act. Accordingly, it is enacted that any property (not including narrower-range investments but including wider-range investments) which trustees are entitled to hold pursuant to such special powers must be carried to a separate "special-range" part of the fund.[62] So it may well happen, if the Act is made use of in cases where the trust contains a special power of investment of some sort, that the fund will be divided into three parts—a special-range part, a wider-range part and a narrower-range part.

Difficulties of administration may, however, arise if "special-range" property is converted. If it is, the trustees must ensure that the value of *both* the narrower range and the wider range is increased by the same amount, if necessary by compensating transfers so that the 50:50 rule is maintained.[63] For example, the trust may confer a special power of investment in land, and the trustees may hold land pursuant to this power. Assume that they also hold gilt-edged securities but wish to take advantage of the Act and invest in equities. The land, if the trustees wish to retain it, is carried to a separate part of the fund, *viz.* the special range. The gilt-edged securities are divided into a narrower-range part and a wider-range part, and the trustees may then invest the wider-range part of these securities in equities. If further land accrues to the trust it will also have to be carried to the special range. But if some of the land is converted into securities authorised by the Act, the proceeds of the conversion will have to be dealt with in such a way that the wider-range part and the narrower range are each increased by the same amount.

There is no doubt that the wider-range part of investments can at any time be used to purchase more land under the special power. Whether the narrower-range part of the investments can be used for this purpose is not at all clear. If indeed it can be so used, it might have the surprising result that the narrower-range investments could be exhausted in exercising the special power so that the trust fund would be constituted of only wider-range investments and land acquired under the special power. This would seem to be contrary to the whole principle of equality as between gilt-edged and equities which in general underlies this legislation, but there does not appear to be anything in the Act to prevent it happening. If this is so an unexpected lacuna in the Act is revealed. However, it would be dangerous for trustees to take advantage of this, for it could perhaps be impugned as a breach of the trustees' general duties of care and of their statutory duties of ensuring diversification.[64]

---

[60] *e.g.* under the Variation of Trusts Act 1958; see *post*, p. 413. See also s.15, which preserves the power of the court to confer investment powers wider than those given by the 1961 Act; and see *Re Cooper's Settlement* [1962] Ch. 826; *Re Kolb's Will Trusts* [1962] Ch. 531; *Re Clarke's Will Trusts* [1961] 1 W.L.R. 1471; *Re University of London Charitable Trusts* [1964] Ch. 282; and see *post*, p. 424.
[61] s.3(1).
[62] s.3(3), Sched. 2.
[63] Sched. 2, para. 3.
[64] *Infra.*

These provisions relating to special-range property do not apply where the trustees' powers of investment were conferred or varied by an order of the court made within the period of 10 years ending on August 3, 1961, or by an enactment or statutory instrument made within the like period or by a local Act passed within the session 9 & 10 Eliz. 2.[65] If this has happened and the trustees now wish to make use of the Act, the normal rules as to division of the fund into a narrower range and a wider range apply, but the trustees cannot make use of the Act so as to make or hold wider-range investments whilst any wider-range investments are comprised in the narrower-range part of the fund.[66] The rule of general law that a trustee may retain an investment which has ceased to be authorised[67] is thereby overridden for this purpose.[68] To take an example, the trusts may have been varied within the prescribed period by the court to enable the trustees to invest 75 per cent. of the fund in what are now described as wider-range investments (*e.g.* the units of a unit trust scheme). The trust fund would, therefore, have to be divided in the usual way, but because certain wider-range investments would be comprised in the narrower-range part of the fund these would have to be sold for reinvestment in the narrower-range investments, and until this was done the trustees would not be able to make any investment in the units of a unit trust. They would be unable to make use of the statutory powers until a true division had been effected. Because this situation would arise, it is obviously much more likely that an application would be made to the court to seek the extension of investment powers required,[69] and not rely on the Act.

(8) Duties of trustees

Trustees naturally have, as a matter of general law, a duty of care and impartiality in making investments, and this is so whether these are made under the Act or under a special power of investment.[70] But the Act itself imposes certain positive statutory duties in addition. First, they must have regard to the need for securing diversification in so far as is appropriate to the circumstances of the trust.[71] No doubt circumstances legitimately to be taken into account would be the smallness of the fund or the life-tenant's paramount need of income. Secondly, they must have regard to the suitability to the trust of investments of the class proposed *and* of the *particular* investment as an investment of that class.[72] The sort of problem with which trustees will be faced here is whether, and to what extent, for instance, present income should be sacrificed to future growth, and much will depend on arriving at a decision on the actual needs of the beneficiaries, the expected duration of the trust and, most important today, the beneficiaries' tax position.

---

[65] s.3(4).
[66] Sched. 3, para. 1.
[67] T.A. 1925, s. 4; *ante*, p. 302.
[68] Sched. 3, para. 2.
[69] Under V. of T.A. 1958; and see *post*, p. 413.
[70] See *ante*, p. 301.
[71] s.6(1)(*a*).
[72] s.6(1)(*b*).

The way in which these factors have to be considered is shown by taking three examples:

(a) If trustees are holding money for an infant beneficiary when he attains 18 in, say 1988, they might invest not merely in any gilt, nor merely in any dated gilt, but in 3 per cent. Transport Stock 1978–88. This particular stock will be redeemed in 1988 at its highest value, just in time for the money to be paid to the beneficiary, and it has the added attraction that the increase in its capital value will be exempt from capital gains tax, whereas increases in the capital value of most other investments will be subject to that tax.

(b) If a very small sum is to be held for a fairly short period—say, between five and 10 years—but the beneficiary has adequate income from other sources, National Savings Certificates might be a suitable investment, for although the rate of interest is small, this interest is free of tax[74] and the certificates are also exempt from capital gains tax.[75]

(c) If the beneficiary currently entitled to the income of the trust has a small total income, the trustees might endeavour to invest at least part of the fund in a security which produces a high income so far as they consider this consistent with their duties to the remainderman. But this will not be *any* security which produces a high income, nor necessarily *any* security which produces a high income and is considered particularly safe. For where a beneficiary's total income is small, he is able to make an income tax repayment claim, but in so far as his income consists of dividends from securities, the repayment claim is limited to the "tax credit" in respect of the dividend. This does not apply, however, where the income is derived from abroad. Accordingly, where the beneficiary can make a repayment claim, the trustees will look for a company which has virtually the whole of its activities in England, so that a full tax credit will be available.

It is in the light of this type of consideration that there becomes apparent the full significance of the requirement for trustees to have regard to the suitability both of the class of investment proposed, and of the particular investment as an investment of that class.

Furthermore, with the exception of investments in the small savings investments listed in Part I, the trustee must, before deciding on an investment, obtain and consider proper written advice as to whether the investment is satisfactory, and here he must take into account the statutory requirements mentioned above. The operative words are "obtain and consider"; the trustee is not therefore bound to follow the advice. Different considerations apply to a mortgage investment. In this case the advice is not required to extend to the suitability of the loan in question: this is a matter that depends on the valuation required by section 8 of the Trustee Act 1925.[76]

---

[73] C.G.T.A. 1979, s.67(1).
[74] Income and Corporation Taxes Act 1970, s.95.
[75] C.G.T.A. 1979, s.71.
[76] See *post*, p. 319.

It is also enacted that a trustee retaining any investment which has been made must decide at what intervals the circumstances and particularly the true nature of the investment make it desirable to "obtain and consider" proper written advice as to whether it should be retained, and he must obtain and consider it.[77]

The question now is, what is "proper advice"? It is the advice of a person whom the trustee reasonably believes to be qualified to give it by reason of his financial ability and experience.[78] But these requirements will not apply where one of two or more trustees is himself so qualified: he may well be qualified as a stockbroker or solicitor to give advice and he may properly give it.[79] He is not under a duty to obtain and consider advice from another source. The position is the same where one of the trustees is a trust corporation, such as a bank. If an officer of the corporation gives advice, it will be unnecessary to take further advice.[80]

(9) The fifty-fifty rule

It has already been seen that this rule is not, though of general application, absolute. But, apart from this, provision is made for the new powers to be extended or varied by Order in Council, so the 50:50 rule could conceivably be changed in the future. It is enacted for this purpose that the Treasury may by order direct that the proportion of a trust fund which may be invested in equities shall be increased from one-half to a maximum of 75 per cent.: when such an order is operative trustees who wish to avail themselves of the Act will have to divide it in the proportions prescribed by the order, while trustees who have already made a division must make a further division if they wish to take advantage of the new proportion.[81] As yet no order has been made.

(10) Saving for powers of the court

It is expressly enacted that the extension of investment powers provided for in the Act is not to lessen the court's power to confer wider powers on trustees.[82] This will in particular refer to the Variation of Trusts Act 1958. The interaction between the latter statute and the 1961 Act will be dealt with when the subject of variation of trusts is considered.[83]

(11) Generally

What is the significance of this Act generally? Clearly its most important and controversial, feature is the division of the fund into two parts. There is no doubt a case for saying that only a limited and carefully prescribed proportion of the trust fund should be invested in wider-range investments, and the remainder in gilt-edged: at present this proportion is in general on a 50:50 basis. It was thought that the problem of administration in maintaining a division into two parts, or three if special-range property is added, would be a decisive factor in

---

[77] s.6(3)(5).
[78] s.6(4).
[79] s.6(6).
[80] s.6(4)(6).
[81] s.13.
[82] s.15.
[83] See n. 59 and see *post*, p. 424.

practice, particularly for the smaller private trusts, in deterring the trustees of such trusts from operating the statutory scheme. But despite these difficulties and the complexity of the language of the statute, it seems that many trustees are making use of the Act for old-established trusts. Nevertheless, it would seem that the practice in respect of newly established trusts will remain as it has been for the last 30 years. That is to say, trustees will be given an absolute discretion to invest trust funds as they think fit. There is then no need to rely on the Act or enter into its complicated computations. Admittedly an unrestricted power of investment has its dangers: if the trustees take advantage of it they may well benefit the trust, but they may make an unfortunate investment to the loss of all concerned. But it is likely that the present practice will continue.

IV. MORTGAGES OF LAND

(1) **General principles**
Investment in a mortgage of land will be an authorised investment within the meaning of the Trustee Investments Act 1961 falling within the narrower range requiring advice if made on a mortgage of property in the United Kingdom if it is freehold property or leasehold property where the unexpired term is not less than 60 years.[84] This kind of investment, whether within or outside the statutory limits, may also be expressly authorised by the trust instrument.

But a trustee is not always justified in investing the trust funds on mortgage. He must naturally act in good faith and with reasonable care and impartiality. He should not therefore make this sort of investment simply for the benefit of one of the beneficiaries and certainly not for the benefit of a person who is not even a beneficiary.[85] The rule that a trustee is not necessarily free from responsibility because he invests in an authorised security[86] applies with considerable force to investment on mortgage; and the limitations imposed by both general principles such as these and by statute on the trustee's powers show this clearly.

Certain general propositions have been established by the caselaw. Accordingly a trustee should, in the absence of express authority to do otherwise, invest only in *first legal* mortgages of freehold or leasehold land within the limits prescribed. It should be a first mortgage because it is desirable that the mortgage should enjoy priority. He should therefore avoid second mortgages since a first mortgagee may exercise the power of sale in such circumstances as to leave nothing for the second mortgagee.[87] He should obtain the legal estate and avoid equitable mortgages because otherwise he might be postponed to a prior incumbrancer of whom he

---

[84] Sched. 1, Pt. II, para. 13.

[85] See *Whitney* v. *Smith* (1869) L.R. 4 Ch. 513 at 521; *Re Walker* (1890) 62 L.T. 449.

[86] See *ante*, p. 310.

[87] *Norris* v. *Wright* (1851) 14 Beav. 291; *Lockhart* v. *Reilly* (1857) 1 De G. & J. 464. The Law Reform Committee recommend that trustees should have power to lend on second mortgage.

might not have notice.[88] He should also avoid what is called a contributory mortgage (*i.e.* a joint loan by the trustees and other persons) because in such a case the trustees would not possess complete control.[89] On the other hand, a sub-mortgage, if legal, may be quite proper, for here the mortgagee will mortgage to the trustee and the latter will obtain the legal estate.[90]

But the Trustee Investments Act 1961 may now have modified the necessity for a first legal mortgage because, having declared that mortgages of freehold property and certain leasehold property are narrower-range investments,[91] it gives "mortgage" the same definition as in the Trustee Act 1925.[92] And this definition includes "every estate and interest regarded in equity as merely a security for money,"[93] and this would include an equitable mortgage. Lewin suggests that the effect of the Act is to sweep away the old prohibitions on inferior types of mortgage.[94] But it is highly doubtful whether this was the legislative intention and it seems safer for trustees to assume that the old restrictions still apply.

(2) Statutory duties

A trustee should also observe the statutory rules relating to the value of the property.

Various conditions in relation to value which are expressly imposed by the Trustee Act 1925—and which are unaffected by the Act of 1961—should be fulfilled before investment is made in this class of security. It must be emphasised that the rule is that he "should," as a matter of prudence, fulfil these conditions: he is *not bound* to do so.[95] But he would be unwise in ignoring them because they provide cogent evidence of the exercise of care.[96] The material provisions are found in section 8 of the 1925 Act.

It is here enacted that a trustee lending money on the security of any such property will not be chargeable with breach of trust by reason only of the proportion borne by the amount of the loan to the value of the property at the time when the loan was made if it appears to the court:

(1) In making the loan the trustee was acting upon a report as to the value of the property made by a person whom he reasonably believed to be an able practical surveyor or valuer instructed and employed independently of any owner of the property, whether such surveyor or valuer carries on business in

---

[88] *Swaffield* v. *Nelson* [1876] W.N. 255. This is the reasoning but, of course, it antedates the statutory registration of land charges under the Land Charges Act 1972. If a trustee registered the charge a subsequent mortgagee could not take without notice of it, and the trustee would seem to be sufficiently protected.
[89] *Webb* v. *Jonas* (1888) 39 Ch.D. 660.
[90] *Smethurst* v. *Hastings* (1885) 30 Ch.D. 490.
[91] s.1(1); Sched. 1, Pt. II, para. 13.
[92] s.17(4).
[93] T.A. 1925, s.68(7).
[94] (16th ed.), pp. 370, 371.
[95] *Palmer* v. *Emerson* [1911] 1 Ch. 758.
[96] *Re Stuart* [1897] 2 Ch. 583 at p. 592; *Palmer* v. *Emerson* [1911] 1 Ch. 758 at p. 769. See also *Chapman* v. *Brown* [1902] 1 Ch. 785.

the locality where the property is situated or elsewhere.[97] In interpreting this provision Kekewich J. held in *Re Walker*[98] that the trustee need only believe the surveyor or valuer to be able; but he must in *fact* be employed independently of the owner of the property. The point about employment was doubted by Warrington J. in *Re Solomon*,[99] where he seemed to think that a *belief* of independent employment would be sufficient. But, according to the natural meaning of the words in the section, it seems that Kekewich J. was right.

In deciding whether the surveyor or valuer is an able practical man, it would appear that the trustee must still exercise his own judgment: he cannot, for example, trust blindly to the nomination of his solicitor, nor of course to that of the mortgagor's solicitor.[1] He need not, however, necessarily be a local man, nor have specialised local knowledge.[2]

(2) The amount of the loan does not exceed two-thirds of the value of the property as stated in the report.[3]

This is the utmost limit, and a trustee ought not to lend more even if the surveyor advises that a greater proportion may be advanced; indeed in many cases, in order to leave a margin for depreciation it will be advisable to lend less. Everything depends on the particular property. If it is liable to deteriorate or is specially subject to fluctuations in value then a prudent trustee will, assuming that the investment is itself a proper one, require a larger margin for protection.[4]

The question next arises, what is the position if the trustee lends more than two-thirds? Section 9 provides the answer. It is enacted that if a trustee makes such a loan but the security is otherwise a proper investment—the *amount only* being exceeded—then it will be deemed to be an authorised investment for the proper sum and the trustee will only be liable in respect of the excess with interest. Thus in *Shaw* v. *Cates*[5] the trustee had advanced £4,400 on real security. This was held to be a proper investment only for £3,400. The trustees were, therefore, liable only to make good the excess of £1,000 with interest.

(3) The loan is made under the advice of the surveyor or valuer expressed in the report.[6] This means, of course, that he must actually advise the trustee that the investment is a proper one.

(3) **Limitations to the statutory provisions**

It will be observed that section 8 of the Trustee Act 1925 provides relief from

---

[97] s.8(1)(*a*).

[98] (1890) 62 L.T. 449 at p. 452; and see also *Re Somerset* [1894] 1 Ch. 231 at p. 253, *per* Kekewich J.

[99] [1912] 1 Ch. 261 at p. 281. Compromised on appeal [1913] 1 Ch. 200. See also *Shaw* v. *Cates* [1909] 1 Ch. 389.

[1] *Shaw* v. *Cates* [1909] 1 Ch. 389 at p. 404, *per* Parker J.

[2] There is no such requirement in the Act. However the trustee should not ignore the importance of local knowledge in arriving at a correct valuation, see *Fry* v. *Tapson* (1884) 28 Ch.D. 268.

[3] s.8(1)(*b*).

[4] See *Shaw* v. *Cates* [1909] 1 Ch. 389 at pp. 398, 399 and also *Palmer* v. *Emerson* [1911] 1 Ch. 758 at pp. 765, 766.

[5] *Ibid.*

[6] s.8(1)(*c*).

liability "by reason *only of the proportion*[7] borne by the amount of the loan to the value of the property." It also refers to lendings on the security of property "on which he can properly lend." Section 9 refers to a security which is "otherwise proper," the amount only being exceeded. These words would appear clearly to provide protection only in matters of value and will not be of assistance where the nature of the security itself comes into question. The trustee must establish in the first instance the propriety of the investment independently of value.[8] It seems to follow that a trustee would be liable in any case for advancing money on speculative property and particularly on wasting property and his liability would be based on the fact that he should never have lent the money on such a security in any case, not because (even if such is the case) he has lent too much. Yet curiously enough, Warrington J. held in *Re Solomon*[9]—and Parker J's general approach in *Shaw* v. *Cates*[10] could also be considered as being to the same effect—that if the property is of a speculative character and the trustee acts on the valuer's report which has been made in the manner prescribed he will be entitled to protection. However, this approach, even though perhaps commendable as a matter of policy in enabling a trustee to rely on an expert's advice, seems contrary to principle.

(4) Purchase of land

If the trustees are only entitled to invest in trustee securities they are not entitled to *purchase* land. Moreover, even if the purchase of property is expressly authorised it will not necessarily authorise purchase for *residence* only. Thus in *Re Power*[11] the clause was to the effect that "all moneys required to be invested under this my will may be *invested* by the trustee in any manner in which he may in his absolute discretion think fit . . . including the purchase of freehold property in England and Wales." Jenkins J. held that the trustees were not entitled to purchase a dwelling-house with vacant possession for the occupation of a beneficiary: "investment" entails an income yield and the purchase of a home for occupation does not yield income.

Trustees can only purchase land in two cases:

(i) if they have an express power for this purpose under the trust instrument. A precedent investment clause commonly used in practice enables this to be done. There is also a model clause in use today which is designed to circumvent the decision in *Re Power*.[12] It gives an absolute discretion to the trustees to invest as they think fit

---

[7] Our italics.
[8] *Re Walker* (1890) 62 L.T. 449, *per* Kekewich J.; *Blyth* v. *Fladgate* [1891] 1 Ch. 337, *per* Stirling J.
[9] [1912] 1 Ch. 261.
[10] [1909] 1 Ch. 389.
[11] [1947] Ch. 572 distinguishing *Re Wragg* [1919] 2 Ch. 58 (where the property would yield income). The Law Reform Committee recommend that the rule should be reversed by statute.
[12] *Ibid.*

and also empowers them to purchase property for the residence of a beneficiary. But of course the same solution can be achieved by any provision which expressly confers the power to purchase for residence; or

(ii) if they can rely on a special statutory power appropriate to the circumstances of the case. Such a statutory power will arise, first, under section 73(1)(xi) of the Settled Land Act 1925, under which capital money can be used to purchase land. Secondly, under section 28(1) of the Law of Property Act 1925 trustees for sale of land can purchase land with the proceeds of sale provided that they have not ceased to be trustees for sale within the statutory definition contained in section 205; they will have ceased to be such if they have parted with all the land held on trust for sale.[13]

It has been seen[14] that in ordinary circumstances trustees have no statutory power to mortgage trust assets in order to purchase further assets,[15] although an express power to that effect can be validly contained in the trust instrument.

V. INVESTMENT CLAUSES

The general rule is conventionally stated to be that clauses in trust deeds enlarging the trustee's powers of investment beyond the scope authorised by law are construed strictly.[16] To what extent, however, this rule is in practice followed today is debatable. Indeed it is arguable that nowadays investment clauses are to be given a liberal interpretation. But this is, of course, a generalisation of which one cannot dogmatically say whether it is right or wrong. A number of illustrations from the caselaw on each side of the line—one from the late nineteenth century and the others from the present day—will be considered. A well-known case is *Bethell* v. *Abraham*,[17] where trustees were empowered to "continue or change securities from time to time as to the majority shall seem meet." This clause was strictly construed by Jessel M.R., who held that the words related merely to determining the time at which a change of securities was to be made: it did not authorise a substantive change of investment outside the authorised range. This case may be compared with the more recent decision in *Re Harari's Settlement Trusts*[18] where the clause empowered the trustees to invest in such investments as to them seemed fit. This was held by Jenkins J. to relate to any investments outside the authorised range. A similarly liberal result was arrived at in *Re Peczenic's Settlement*[19] by Buckley J.—with the exception only of investments on personal security which were

---

[13] See *Re Wakeman* [1945] Ch. 177; *Re Wellsted's Will Trusts* [1949] Ch. 296.
[14] *Ante*, p. 279.
[15] *Re Suenson-Taylor's Settlement, Moores* v. *Moores* [1974] 3 All E.R. 397.
[16] *Re Peczenic's Settlement Trusts* [1964] 1 W.L.R. 720 at p. 722, *per* Buckley J.
[17] (1873) L.R. 17 Eq. 24.
[18] [1949] 1 All E.R. 430.
[19] [1964] 1 W.L.R. 720.

clearly excluded by the trust instrument. These illustrations may be thought to manifest a difference in attitude to investment clauses in the modern law. But the true position would seem to be that it is entirely a question of construction of the particular investment clause before the court, and although previous cases may be helpful they will not necessarily be decisive.[20]

Use of one of the well-known model clauses which clearly give to the trustees unrestricted investment powers (including a power to purchase property for residence purposes,[21] and also invest on personal credit[22]) will, of course, avoid any difficulties of construction. The use of such a power is often advised today. At the same time it will be appreciated that even if the trustees have this power they must still act with reasonable care and impartiality in deciding on their investments.[23]

VI. ANCILLARY STATUTORY POWERS

(1) Redeemable stock

The trustees are entitled to invest in authorised securities[24] notwithstanding the fact that they are redeemable and even if the price paid exceeds the redemption value[25]; and the trustees are entitled to retain them until redemption.[26]

(2) Bearer securities

A trustee is entitled, unless expressly prohibited by the instrument creating the trust, to retain or invest in securities payable to bearer which, if they had not been made thus payable, would have been authorised investments.[27] But it is required that until sold the bearer securities should be deposited by the trustee with a bank for safe custody and collection of income.[28] If this deposit is made accordingly the trustee will not be liable for any loss incurred,[29] and, moreover, it is provided that any sum paid in respect of the deposit itself or collection of income is to be paid out of the income of the trust property.[30]

(3) Lending on mortgage

A supplementary power is conferred on trustees properly lending money on

---

[20] See also, in addition to the cases cited in text. *Re Maryon-Wilson's Estate* [1912] 1 Ch. 55; *Re McEacharn's Settlement Trusts* [1939] Ch. 858; *Re Hart's Will Trusts* [1943] 2 All E.R. 557; *Re Douglas' Will Trusts [1959] 1 W.L.R. 744 (affirmed on another point [1959] 1 W.L.R. 1212): Re Kolb's Will Trusts* [1962] Ch. 531 (interpretation of various investment clauses).

[21] See *Re Power* [1947] Ch. 572 and *ante*, p. 322.

[22] Only an express power to lend on personal security will enable such a loan to be made: see *Khoo Tek Kong* v. *Ching Joo Tuan Neoh* [1934] A.C. 529 (P.C.); *Re Peczenic* [1964] 1 W.L.R. 720; *cf. Re Laing's Settlement* [1899] 1 Ch. 593. See also *Tucker* v. *Tucker* [1894] 1 Ch. 724.

[23] See *ante*, p. 301.

[24] *i.e.* under the T.I.A. 1961.

[25] T.A. 1925, s.2(1).

[26] *Ibid.* s.2(2).

[27] *Ibid.* s.7(1).

[28] *Ibid.* s.7(1), proviso.

[29] *Ibid.* s.7(2).

[30] *Ibid.*

the security of trust property[31] to contract that the money will not be called in for a fixed period not exceeding seven years provided that interest is paid within a specified time not exceeding 30 days after it becomes due and provided also that the mortgagor is not in breach of any covenant contained in the mortgage for the maintenance and protection of the trust property.[32]

(4) Sale of land

If land is sold by trustees in fee simple or for a term having at least 500 years to run they may contract that the payment of any part of the purchase-money not exceeding two-thirds be left on mortgage.[28] But it is essential that the mortgage contains a covenant by the mortgagor to keep any buildings insured to their full value.[34] So far as this situation is concerned, it is not necessary for the trustees to obtain a report as to value, and they are not liable for loss by reason of the security being insufficient.[35]

(5) Capital reorganisations and bonus issues

(i) Where any securities[36] of a company are subject to a trust, the trustees may concur in any scheme or arrangement (a) for the reconstruction of the company; (b) for the sale of all or any part of its property or undertaking to another company; (c) for the acquisition of the securities of the company, or of control thereof, by another company[37] (d) for its amalgamation with another company; (e) for the release, modification or variation of any rights, privileges or liabilities attached to the securities. And they are entitled to take up any new securities in lieu of the old securities, and furthermore are not responsible for any loss if they act in good faith. They can also retain any new securities for any period for which they could properly have retained the original ones.[38]

(ii) If any conditional or preferential right to subscribe for any securities in a company is offered to trustees in respect of their holdings in the company, they may (a) exercise the right and apply capital money subject to the trust in payment of the consideration or (b) renounce such right or (c) sell it for the best consideration that can be reasonably obtained to any person including a beneficiary. And they are not liable for any loss, provided they act in good faith. If the right is sold the consideration will be capital money.[39] The power to subscribe for securities includes a power to retain them as if they were the original holding, but subject to any conditions which attach to that holding.[40]

---

[31] *Ante*, p. 320.
[32] T.A. 1925, s.10(1).
[33] *Ibid*. s.10(2).
[34] *Ibid*.
[35] *Ibid*.
[36] This term includes shares and stock: *ibid*. s.68(13).
[37] Para. (*c*) was added by T.I.A. 1961, s.9(1).
[38] s.10(3); T.I.A. 1961 s.9(1).
[39] T.A. 1925, s.10(4).
[40] T.I.A. 1961, s.9(2).

Consents. The supplementary powers of investment considered under heads (3), (4) and (5) above are exercisable subject to the consent of any person whose consent to a change of investment is required by law or by the trust instrument.[41]

(6) **Deposits and payment of calls**

Pending the negotiation and preparation of any mortgage or during any time when an investment is being sought, the trustees may deposit the trust money in a bank. Any interest payable is applicable as income.[42] They may also apply capital money subject to a trust in payment of the calls on any shares subject to the same trust.[43]

VII. Continuing Supervision

In addition to making investments, trustees are under a duty to keep them under review to the same extent as would a prudent businessman when dealing with his own affairs.[44] In the case of holdings in large quoted public companies, a periodic review will usually be sufficient. However, where the trustees have a majority holding or some other special position of influence, they will be expected to take advantage of it. If a reasonably prudent businessman would require information about the company's affairs which is not generally available, trustees will need to obtain it. If a reasonably prudent businessman would insist on board representation, or board control, trustees will themselves need to insist on it.

In *Bartlett* v. *Barclays Bank Trust Co. Ltd. (No.*1),[45] a person incorporated a company to manage his properties. He then settled almost the whole of the shares in the company upon trust for his wife and issue. Initially the board included members of the settlor's family, but that gradually changed. The trustees, however, while sending a representative to statutory meetings of the company, did not seek representation on the board. The company purchased a property opposite the Old Bailey, at a price well in excess of its investment value, in the hope that it would obtain planning permission for development. It did not do so, and later disposed of the property at a loss. Brightman J. held that the trustees were in breach of their duty to obtain the information which, as majority shareholders, was open to them.

Information is not, however, an end in itself,[46] and must be used to protect the interests of the beneficiaries. If necessary, a trustee must intervene to remove directors and procure the appointment of his own nominees.[47]

---

[41] T.A. 1925, s.10(5).
[42] s.11(1).
[43] s.11(2).
[44] [1980] Ch. 515.
[45] See, *e.g. Re Lucking's Will Trust* [1968] 1 W.L.R. 866; *ante*, p. 270 where trustees had information but did not use it.
[46] [1980] Ch. 515 at p. 530.
[47] Companies Act 1980, s.68.

Some professional trustees and trust corporations are reluctant to assume this responsibility, and look for a provision in a trust instrument which negatives what would otherwise be their duty to interfere in the management of companies in which they are shareholders.

VIII. INSIDER DEALING

A particular problem arises with regard to "insider dealing." The Companies Act 1980 imposes wide-ranging prohibitions on dealing in securities about which a person has price-sensitive information; on communicating that information to others; and procuring others to deal in securities when the person communicating the information is not himself free to deal.[48] If a person who is a director of a company, and thereby obtains price-sensitive information about the company, is also a trustee of a trust which holds shares in the company, he is immediately placed in a position of conflict of duty. On the one hand he must not contravene the Companies Act, which creates criminal offences. On the other hand, he must do the best that he can for the trust.

Section 68(11) of the 1980 Act provides that a trustee who, in that capacity, deals in securities is presumed to have done so otherwise than with a view to financial advantage[49] if he acted on the advice of a person who:

(a) appeared to him to be an appropriate person from whom to seek such advice; and
(b) did not appear to him to be prohibited by the legislation from dealing in the securities.

However, there is no corresponding presumption in relation to another offence created by the 1980 Act, namely that of communicating inside information to someone else in circumstances where the individual communicating it knows[50] that the recipient will make use of it for the purpose of dealing in securities.[51]

Accordingly, where a trustee has obtained inside information, it seems that he should obtain advice from the trust's investment advisers about that security, without arousing in them suspicion, and without disclosing his own information. If, then, he acts on that advice, or joins with his co-trustees in acting on that advice, he will not himself commit any offence.[52] However, in many cases where a trustee is known to be in a position in which he is likely to be able to obtain inside information, it will be impossible for a trustee to seek such advice without in so doing arousing suspicion. In these circumstances, the only prudent course might be for the trustee to resign his trusteeship.

---

[48] And so, not to have committed any offence: s.68(8).
[49] Or has reasonable cause to believe.
[50] s.68(7).
[51] s.68(11).

CHAPTER 17

APORTIONMENTS

IT will be seen[1] that a fundamental rule is that a trustee must not allow a conflict
of interest to arise between his own personal position and his duties to the
beneficiaries. The sister rule is that where there is a conflict between the
interests of different beneficiaries, a trustee must hold a balance between them.
This is not so much because this is what the settlor actually did intend, for he
may well never have given the matter any thought, but rather because equity
presumes that this is what the settlor would have intended had he directed his
mind to the point. One does not therefore have to find any actual evidence of
intention on the part of the settlor for this principle to apply, yet on the other
hand he is able to provide expressly or by implication that the principle shall not
operate. Avoidance of a conflict of interest is of particular importance in
relation to investments: it is also this principle which underlies the rules
governing apportionments.[1a]

I. APPORTIONMENTS BETWEEN CAPITAL AND INCOME

(1) The principle

Let us suppose that Basil settles property upon trust for Clare for life, with
remainder to Priscilla absolutely. Let us also suppose that the trust property
consists of

- (a) £5,000 3½ per cent. War Stock;
- (b) the cow Buttercup;
- (c) the right under his grandfather's will to receive £15,000 on the death of his
  father, Bert. (This right is called a reversionary interest.)

If these assets are retained in their present form the holding of War Stock will
produce a steady income, and a capital sum will be available to Priscilla on the
death of Clare. Buttercup, a fine milk-yielding cow, may produce at first a high
income, but as she grows old and her milk production decreases, she will
become less and less valuable. She may well die before Clare, and if this is the

---

[1] *Post*, p. 403.
[1a] The Law Reform Committee recommend that the rules of conversion and apportionment referred to in the first part of this chapter should be replaced by a new statutory duty to
hold a fair balance between beneficiaries with different interests.

case, Clare will have derived the whole of the benefit from her, and Priscilla will have had none. The opposite is the case with the reversionary interest. Until Bert dies, income is paid to neither Clare nor Priscilla, and if Clare dies before Bert, she will have received no benefit at all from this asset. Equity presumes that it was not Basil's intention that the beneficiaries should be treated so haphazardly and their fortunes left so much to chance. The basic solution is, therefore, that Buttercup and the reversionary interest should be sold and the proceeds invested in authorised securities, so that the income may be paid to Clare, and a capital sum preserved intact for Priscilla.

This basic solution is not, however, always easy to apply, and in working it out there are three questions to consider:

1. Is there a duty to convert a particular asset into an authorised investment?
2. If so, does the income have to be apportioned between the date when the duty arises, and the date when the conversion actually takes place?
3. If so, how is such apportionment calculated?

These questions are progressive, so that if the answer to any one is "no," there is no need to consider the questions which follow it.

(2) **Is there a duty to convert?**

The duty to convert the trust property into authorised investments may arise

(a) if the trust instrument so directs; or
(b) by operation of the rule in *Howe* v. *Lord Dartmouth*.[2]

The most frequent case of an express direction to convert occurs when there is a trust for sale, but any direction to convert is for this purpose equally adequate. The rule in *Howe* v. *Lord Dartmouth*[3] directs conversion of an asset to take place where there is no express direction in the trust instrument, but only where all the following conditions are satisfied:

(a) the trust was created by will;
(b) there are at least two beneficiaries, and they are entitled in succession;
(c) the property consists of residuary personalty;
(d) the asset is wasting, reversionary or of an unauthorised character; and
(e) there is no contrary intention in the will.

The rule does not apply to a settlement *inter vivos*, for here it is said that the terms of such settlements must be observed strictly, as the settlor knew exactly the state of the assets when the settlement was created.[4]

The only one of the foregoing conditions which is likely to cause difficulty is to decide whether there is a contrary intention. In *Re Sewell's Estate*[5] the

---

[2] (1802) 7 Ves. 137.
[3] For an up-to-date account of the rule, se L.A. Sheridan, "*Howe* v. *Lord Dartmouth* Re-examined" (1952) 16 Conv. (N.S.) 349.
[4] *Per* Cozens-Hardy J. in *Re Van Straubenzee* [1901] 2 Ch. 779; and see *Milford* v. *Peile* (1854) 2 W.N. 181; *Hope* v. *Hope* (1855) 1 Jur. (N.S.) 770.
[5] (1870) L.R. 11 Eq. 80; see also *Simpson* v. *Earles* (1847) 11 Jur. 921.

trustees were given a *discretion* as to what part of the testator's estate should be converted. This was held to have excluded the rule in *Howe* v. *Lord Dartmouth* because a discretion to convert was inconsistent with a *duty* to convert which *Howe* v. *Lord Dartmouth* would impose. However, in order to exclude the rule, the power must be consciously exercised.[6] In *Alcock* v. *Sloper*[7] property was left upon trust for A for life, and after A's death upon trust for it to be sold and the proceeds divided between various named beneficiaries. Here too it was held that the rule in *Howe* v. *Lord Dartmouth* was excluded, because the express duty to convert on the death of A was inconsistent with an implied duty to convert on the death of the testator, which would be implied under *Howe* v. *Lord Dartmouth*.

The decision in *Alcock* v. *Sloper*[8] must be contrasted with that in *Re Evans*,[9] where property was given to trustees upon trust for A for life, and after her death upon trust to be divided into three equal shares and distributed to three other members of the family. It was held here that *Howe* v. *Lord Dartmouth* did apply, because the division on the death of A could be of property in either its converted or unconverted form, so that the directions in the will were not inconsistent with a duty to convert implied by *Howe* v. *Lord Dartmouth*. Where the settlor shows an intention that the property should be enjoyed *in specie* this clearly negatives the rule.[10] Bennett J. took this a stage further in *Re Fisher*[11] by saying that where there is a trust for conversion with a power to postpone, the settlor thereby shows that he intends that the property may be enjoyed *in specie*, and that this also is inconsistent with a duty to convert which would be imposed by *Howe* v. *Lord Dartmouth*. However, in the later case of *Re Berry*,[12] Pennycuick J. refused to follow *Re Fisher*. Although the logical basis of *Re Fisher* is clear, Pennycuick J. commented that that decision was "contrary to the whole current of authority." It was an attempt to extend the scope of the exceptions from *Howe* v. *Lord Dartmouth* too far.

The cases turn on fine differences in wording, and while it may be very difficult to say on any particular set of facts whether *Howe* v. *Lord Dartmouth* is excluded, the rule itself is clear: has the testator made any provision which is expressly or impliedly inconsistent with a duty to convert at the date of death? If he has not done so, and the other conditions listed above are fulfilled, *Howe* v. *Lord Dartmouth* will apply.

(3) Whether there is a need to apportion income

If there is a duty to convert, it is explained below that conversion should take place either at the date of death, or as at one year from the date of death.[13] It will be obvious that in the former case it is impossible to effect actual conversion

---

[6] *Re Guinness* [1966] 1 W.L.R. 1355.
[7] (1833) 2 My. & K. 699; *Daniel* v. *Warren* (1843) 2 Y. & Coll.C.C. 290.
[8] (1833) 2 My. & K. 699.
[9] [1920] 2 Ch. 309.
[10] *Macdonald* v. *Irvine* (1878) 8 Ch.D. 101.
[11] [1943] Ch. 377.
[12] [1962] Ch. 97.
[13] *Post.*

at that date, and in the latter case actual conversion will often be delayed. The question therefore arises whether, in the event of conversion being delayed, the tenant for life is entitled to the actual income produced by the asset until it is converted, or whether he is entitled only to an apportioned part of it. The primary rule is that if the testator has provided, expressly or by implication, that the tenant for life is to enjoy the actual income which the property produces, then that intention prevails. Where it cannot be shown that the testator expressed any such intention, then the following rules apply.

First, where the trustees improperly postpone conversion, an apportionment will be ordered. Thus in *Wentworth* v. *Wentworth*[14] the trustees had a power to postpone conversion until a certain date. The trustees improperly postponed conversion beyond that date, and the Privy Council held that apportionment should be made as from that date.

Secondly, where the property is realty, the tenant for life is entitled to the actual income which the property produces. It will be remembered that *Howe* v. *Lord Dartmouth* never operates to impose a duty to convert realty, so that if such duty exists in respect of realty, it must be as a result of an express trust for conversion.

Thirdly, in the case of personalty, the tenant for life is entitled only to an apportioned part of the income, unless there is an intention that he shall enjoy the asset *in specie*.[15] Thus the presumption is in favour of the enjoyment of actual income in the case of realty, and of only an apportioned part of the income in the case of personalty.

(4) How is the apportionment calculated?

If there is a duty to convert, and if, because the property has not been converted by the due date, the income has to be apportioned until conversion takes place, how is such apportionment calculated? Where the asset concerned is a reversionary interest, the rule in *Re Earl of Chesterfield's Trusts*[16] applies. This is dealt with below. As regards other property which has to be converted, it is necessary first to ascertain the valuation date. At common law there was a presumption that the executor's functions in administering the estate ought to be completed within one year from the death of the testator. From this the rule evolved that where there is no power to postpone sale, conversion ought to be effected within one year from the date of death, and in this case, in order to calculate apportionments of income, the asset is valued as at one year from the date of death.[17] If, however, there is a power to postpone, this negatives the intention that the property should be valued as at one year from the date of death, and, because a better date could not be thought of, in this case the property is valued at the date of death.[18]

---

[14] [1900] A.C. 163.
[15] *Re Chaytor* [1905] 1 Ch. 233. Where there is a trust for conversion with a power to postpone, the beneficiary will only receive an apportioned part of the income: *Re Berry* [1962] Ch. 97.
[16] (1883) 24 Ch.D. 643.
[17] *Re Eaton, Daines* v. *Eaton* (1894) 70 L.T. 761.
[18] *Re Owen, Slater* v. *Owen* [1912] 1 Ch 519; *Re Parry, Brown* v. *Parry* [1947] Ch. 23.

Thus

(a) if there is no power to postpone, the valuation date is one year from the date of death, but

(b) if there is a power to postpone, the valuation date is the date of death.

Whichever is the valuation date, the tenant for life is entitled to interest on the value of the asset as at the valuation date from the date of death until the date of actual conversion. Traditionally, the rate of interest applied has been 4 per cent.,[19] but as this is unrealistically low, it may be that the court would now adopt the rate which is equivalent to the court's short-term investment account.[20] If the actual income is larger, the balance is added to capital. If the actual income is smaller than the appropriate rate, the tenant for life receives that actual income, and is entitled to have it made up from future surpluses of income, or, if there are none, from capital when the asset is sold. The deficiency cannot be made good from previous surpluses of income, because these have already been notionally added to capital.

An example may assist. Suppose that copyrights of a book are left upon trust for Angela for life, with remainder to Mary. Suppose also that the copyrights are worth £1,200 at the date of death, and £1,000 one year from the date of death. Suppose further that the copyrights are not sold until three years after the date of death, and that for these three years the royalties actually received are

Year 1 £70
Year 2 £32
Year 3 £48

It is necessary first to ascertain the valuation date. Where there is a power to postpone, this will be the date of death. At this date the copyrights are worth £1,200, so that, if the appropriate rate of interest is 4 per cent., Angela is entitled to 4 per cent. × £1,200 = £48 a year. In year 1 she will receive £48, the balance of £22 being added to capital. In year 2 she will receive £32, with the right to make good the deficiency of £16 in the future. In year 3 she will receive £48, and will be entitled to a further £16 from the sale of the copyrights to make good the deficiency in year 2. If, however, there is no power to postpone, the valuation date is one year from the date of death. Angela is therefore entitled to receive 4 per cent. × £1,000 = £40 p.a. In year 1 she will receive £40, with £30 being added to capital. In year 2 she will receive £32. In year 3 she will receive £40, plus £8 to make good the shortfall in year 2.

At this point it is again stressed that the questions posed at the beginning of this discussion—is there a duty to convert; if so, does the income have to be

---

[19] The actual rate of interest is in the discretion of the court, but 4 per cent. is usually taken as the appropriate figure: see *Re Lucas* [1947] Ch. 558: *Re Parry* [1947] Ch. 23; *Re Berry* [1962] Ch. 97.
[20] See *Bartlett* v. *Barclays Bank Trust Co. Ltd.* (*No.* 2) [1980] Ch. 515; *post,* p. 451. See also *Re Fawcett* [1940] Ch. 402; *Re Parry* [1947] Ch. 23.

apportioned; if so, how is such apportionment calculated—are progressive. Therefore it is only if there is a duty to convert that it is necessary to consider whether the income has to be apportioned, and it is only if there is a duty to convert and if the income does have to be apportioned that it is necessary to make the type of calculation just considered.

(5) Re Earl of Chesterfield's Trusts[21]

A special method is necessary for calculating apportionments of reversionary interests, because these do not actually produce any income until they fall into possession. At the outset it may be noted that reversionary interests are saleable. Thus, going back to the example on page 328 one of the assets which Basil left upon Clare for life, with remainder to Priscilla, was the right to receive £15,000 on the death of his father, Bert. At Basil's death the trustees could have sold that reversionary interest. The price which they would obtain would be largely governed by Bert's age at the date of Basil's death, but whatever they would have received could have been invested in authorised securities, the income paid to Clare for life, and the capital held for Priscilla. But it is usually economically better not to sell, but to retain the reversionary interest until it falls into possession. If this is done before the money that is eventually received is invested, it is clearly equitable to pay part of the amount received to Clare as compensation for the fact that she has had no income from the asset since the trust came into operation. The rule in *Re Earl of Chesterfield's Trusts* provides that where a reversionary interest which ought to be converted is retained until it falls into possession, part of it is to be treated as arrears of income and paid to the tenant for life, and only the balance is to be regarded as capital.

The rule itself says that the proportion of the amount actually received which is to be regarded as capital is that which if invested at 4 per cent. compound interest with yearly rests would, after allowing for the deduction of income tax at the basic rate for the time being in force, have produced the sum actually received. It remains to be decided whether 4 per cent. is still the appropriate rate of interest to be applied.[22] "Yearly rests" are the intervals at which the interest is compounded.[23]

---

[21] (1883) 24 Ch.D. 643.

[22] See *ante*, p. 332.

[23] The calculation can be complicated, but, for those who do not have super mathematical skills, the most straightforward method of making the calculation will be to follow these steps:

1. Determine the gross rate of interest to be applied. Traditionally this has been 4 per cent., but, as has been noted, a higher rate may be appropriate.

2. Deduct the basic rate of income tax, to give a net rate of interest.

3. Calculate the amount which £100 would produce if invested for the period between the date of death and the date when the reversionary interest falls in at the net rate of interest.

4. Apply to the amount received when the reversionary interest falls in the fraction. See p. 333.

$$\frac{£100}{\text{the compounded sum (at 3)}}$$

5. The product is the capital element.

6. The balance is the income element.

In this example, suppose that Bert lived for three-and-a-quarter years after the trust came into operation, and assuming that the basic rate of tax throughout that period was 30 per cent. the trustees would find that £13,711 invested when the trust came into operation at 4 per cent. compound interest with yearly rests would, after allowing for the deduction of tax at 30 per cent. have produced £15,000 at the date when this sum was actually received.[24] The £13,711 would therefore be invested by the trustees as capital, and the remaining £1,289 would be paid to Clare as income for the preceding three-and-a-quarter years.

The same rule applies to other property which does not produce any income. Thus it applied in *Re Duke of Cleveland's Estate*[25] to a debt which bore no interest and was not receivable immediately. And in *Re Chance*[26] compensation for the refusal of planning permission under Part I of the Town and Country Planning Act 1954[27] was held to be apportionable.

---

[24] Following the steps outlined in note 23, the calculation is:

1. Gross rate: taken as 4 per cent.
2. Basic rate of income tax: 30 per cent. The net rate is, therefore,

$$4 \text{ per cent.} \times \frac{70}{100} = 2.8 \text{ per cent.}$$

3. The compounded amount £109.40 is calculated as follows:

Period	Amount on which calculated	Rate	Interest for period	Total at end of period
Year 1	£100.00	2.8%	£2.80	£102.80
Year 2	£102.80	2.8%	£2.88	£105.68
Year 3	£105.68	2.8%	£2.96	£108.64
Last 3 months	£108.64	2.8% × ¼	£0.76	£109.40

4. The capital element of the amount received, £15,000 is:

$$£15,000 \times \frac{100}{109.40} = £13,711$$

5. The income element is (£15,000−£13,711) = £1,289.

[25] [1895] 2 Ch. 542.

[26] [1962] Ch. 593.

[27] The Town and Country Planning Act 1947 provided, in general terms, that an owner of land could not carry out any building or other works on his land without obtaining the permission of the local authority, and without paying a "development charge." The value of land was often less after the passing of this Act than before it, and in an effort to give to the landowner compensation, it was proposed that a £300 million fund would be established, on which landowners could make a claim for the depreciation in the value of their land. The fund was, in fact, never set up and the system was changed under the Town and Country Planning Act 1954, whereby the amount of the landowner's claim, plus one-seventh of it for interest (less payments for certain events made before the 1954 Act came into force), formed what is known as an "unexpended balance of established development value." Where such a balance exists, in certain cases compensation is payable up to the amount of that balance where an application for planning permission is refused. This was the situation in *Re Chance*. Part of the interest of the decision lies in the fact that an inexpended balance of established development value, and so of money paid under the system, represents interest and the amount of that interest could be determined. Wilberforce J., however, took the whole amount of the compensation received, and apportioned that.

(6) Leaseholds

In view of the decision in *Re Brooker*[28] it is necessary to give special consideration to apportionments involving leaseholds. Before 1926, a residuary gift of leaseholds was treated in the same way as any other gift of residuary personalty. However, in *Re Trollope*[29] Tomlin J. said that the effect of *Re Brooker* was that "so far as leaseholds are concerned, the rule of *Howe* v. *Lord Dartmouth* is gone."[30]

Section 28(2) of the Law of Property Act 1925 provides that where "land" is held upon trust for sale, then subject to any contrary direction in the trust instrument, the net rents and profits of the land until sale are to be paid in the same manner as if they were income from authorised investments made with the proceeds of sale of the land. Pending conversion of land, therefore, a tenant for life is entitled to the actual rents and profits so received. In *Re Brooker* there was an express trust for conversion of leaseholds and it was held that as the definition in the Law of Property Act of land included land of any tenure, the tenant for life was entitled by virtue of section 28(2) to the actual income from leasehold property as if it were the actual income from an authorised investment.

In the light of this decision, in general terms it seems desirable that the position should be the same where the duty to convert arises by virtue of the rule in *Howe* v. *Lord Dartmouth* and not, as in *Re Brooker*, where there was an express direction to convert. As has been shown, the rules previously discussed in this chapter equate the position when the duty to convert arises expressly with that where it is implied by *Howe* v. *Lord Dartmouth*, and *Re Brooker* has been followed in the case of a trust for sale imposed by statute.[31]

Nevertheless, it has been suggested[32] that where the duty to convert leaseholds arises only by virtue of *Howe* v. *Lord Dartmouth* the pre-1926 position still applies. The basis of this suggestion is that section 28 of the Law of Property Act refers to a "disposition on trust for sale" and that this does not apply where the duty to convert is only implied by *Howe* v. *Lord Dartmouth*, for then there is not a gift of property on trust for sale, but a gift of property upon which a trust for sale is imposed by operation of law. Further, it is said, *Howe* v. *Lord Dartmouth* only applies where there is no express duty to convert, and as there was an express duty in *Re Brooker,* *Howe* v. *Lord Dartmouth* was, strictly, irrelevant to *Re Brooker*.

Despite these objections however, *Re Brooker* has been generally accepted as establishing that in the case of leaseholds, the tenant for life is entitled to the actual income however the duty to convert arises, and it is now very doubtful whether this will be altered. It would surely be regrettable if it were.

---

[28] [1926] W.N. 93.
[29] [1927] 1 Ch. 596.
[30] [1927] 1 Ch. 596 at p. 601.
[31] *Re Berton* [1939] Ch. 200.
[32] Bailey (1930–32) 4 C.L.J. 357.

Leaseholds with over 60 years to run are authorised investments,[33] and so cannot be subject to *Howe* v. *Lord Dartmouth*.[34]

II. OTHER APPORTIONMENTS

(1) The rule in Allhusen v. Whittell[35]

There will always be an interval of time between the date of death and the date when an asset is realised. Where a person creates a trust by will in favour of persons in succession, and there are debts and liabilities to be paid, it would appear that the life-tenant will gain increasingly as that delay increases. Suppose, for example, that the gross assets of an estate amount to £20,000, and that debts amount to £5,000, and suppose that the estate is held upon trust for persons in succession. If the debts are paid forthwith, the life-tenant will have the income from the remaining £15,000. If, however, the debts are not paid for a year, the life-tenant will receive the income for that year of £20,000. The essence of the rule of apportionment laid down in *Allhusen* v. *Whittell* is to charge the tenant for life with interest on the amount subsequently used for the payment of debts, so that, broadly, the tenant for life is placed in the same position as if the debts had been paid on death.

In its modern form[36] the rule requires a calculation of the average income of the estate from the date of death to the date of payment, taken net after deduction of income tax at the basic rate.[37] The tenant for life is charged with interest at that rate, so that the debt once paid is regarded as being paid partly from income and partly from capital.

A simple example will show the operation of the rule. Suppose that a debt of £500 is paid one year from the date of death: that the average income of the estate taken throughout that period is £4 per cent.; and that the basic rate of income tax during that year is 30 per cent. The calculation is therefore:

Take a basic unit of		£100.00
Add		
Average income for one year at £4 per cent.	£4.00	
Less tax	£1.20	
		£2.80
		£102.80

---

[33] Settled Land Act 1925, s.73; Law of Property Act 1925, s.28. By contrast, sometimes houses held on a shorter lease may be a burden rather than an asset, for example, where the cost of repairs is high, and the rent obtainable is controlled. In these cases, the court may sanction a payment of capital to the lessor to induce him to accept a surrender of the lease: *Re Shee* [1934] Ch. 345. See also Trustee Investments Act 1961.

[34] *Re Gough* [1957] Ch. 323.

[35] (1867) L.R. 4 Eq. 295.

[36] *Re McEwen* [1913] 2 Ch. 704; *Re Wills* [1915] 1 Ch. 769; *Corbett* v. *C.I.R.* [1938] 1 K.B. 567.

[37] *Re Oldham* (1927) 71 S.J. 491.

Each debt paid one year from death is therefore regarded as being paid in the proportion:

$$\frac{100.00}{102.80} \text{ from capital; and}$$

$$\frac{2.80}{102.80} \text{ from income.}$$

Thus, the debt of £500 will be paid:

$$\frac{100.00}{102.80} \times £500 = £486.38 \text{ from capital; and}$$

$$\frac{2.80}{102.80} \times £500 = £13.62 \text{ from income.}$$

This £13.62 will be charged to the tenant for life.

It is easy to appreciate the theoretical justification for this rule, and it is also easy to see its practical defects. In particular, a separate calculation is necessary for each debt paid at a different time. Further, where payments are to be made a considerable time after death, as where the testator in his lifetime entered into a convenant to pay an annuity, and the annuity was charged on the residue of his estate, the proportion borne by income steadily increases.[38] Except where very large debts are involved or where a very long delay occurs in payment, the trouble of making the calculation does not justify the small adjustment between tenant for life and remainderman, so that it is now very common to exclude the operation of the rule.

(2) **The rule in Re Atkinson**[39]

Where an authorised mortgage forms part of the estate, and upon realisation of the security by sale, the proceeds of sale are insufficient to pay the outstanding principal and interest in full, the proceeds of sale are apportioned between the tenant for life and remainderman in the proportion which the amount due for arrears bears to the amount due in respect of principal. This is the rule in *Re Atkinson*[40] and it applies to any mortgage which was received from the testator or settlor, and any *authorised* mortgage taken by the trustee himself.

Suppose that during his lifetime the testator made a mortgage advance of £25,000 upon the security of a house at £12 per cent. interest. Suppose also that the mortgagor pays a total of £1,200 interest and that the property is

---

[38] *Re Dawson* [1906] 2 Ch. 211; *Re Perkins* [1907] 2 Ch. 596; *Re Poyser* [1910] 2 Ch. 444.
[39] [1904] 2 Ch. 160.
[40] *Ibid.*

sold for £23,000 three years after death, no part of the capital secured by the mortgage having been repaid. The apportionment of the £23,000 is as follows:

Capital outstanding		£25,000
Interest outstanding:		
3 years at £12 per cent. on £25,000	£9,000	
less: actually paid	£1,200	
		£ 7,800
Total capital and interest due		£32,800

Capital element of proceeds of sale $= \dfrac{£\ 25,000}{£\ 32,800} \times £23,000 = £17,530$

Income element of proceeds of sale $= \dfrac{£\ 7,800}{£\ 32,800} \times £23,000 = £5,470$

Total proceeds of sale	£23,000

The scope of the rule is in doubt. In principle it ought to apply whenever an asset carrying both capital and interest at a fixed rate is realised at a loss and it has been held to apply to an amount received in a liquidation on account of principal and arrears of interest due under a holding of debenture stock.[41] However, the rule is not applied where preference dividends are in arrears.[42]

The rule in *Re Atkinson* is applied only to a capital sum realised on the sale of a security, and not to income received from the asset. Thus, if under a power contained in a mortgage the trustees take possession of the property, and let it, the net rents are applied entirely in the discharge of arrears of interest, and only when they have been paid in full is the surplus applied as capital.[43] If there are arrears of interest outstanding at the date of death, those are paid in full before interest due to the estate for the period from the date of death to the date of extinction of the mortgage.[44]

Where the trustees foreclose under a mortgage, the mortgagor then loses all title to the property, and the property itself becomes an asset of the estate. Accordingly, from the date of foreclosure the tenant for life is entitled to the whole of the net rents and profits until sale[45] but if there are arrears of interest before foreclosure, it seems that a *Re Atkinson* apportionment will be made when the property is ultimately sold.[46]

---

[41] *Re Walker* [1936] Ch. 280; cf. *Re Taylor* [1905] 1 Ch. 734.
[42] *Re Sale* [1913] 2 Ch. 697; *Re Wakley* [1920] 2 Ch. 205.
[43] *Re Coaks* [1911] 1 Ch. 171.
[44] *Ibid*.
[45] L. of P.A. 1925, s.31; *Re Horn* [1924] 2 Ch. 222.
[46] *Re Horn* [1924] 2 Ch. 222 at p. 226.

There is no authority whether income tax should be deducted in making a calculation for the purposes of the rule in *Re Atkinson*. It is suggested that the appropriate method of applying the rule is first to ascertain the arrears of interest, and the proportion due to income without taking into account income tax. When that proportion has been calculated, the tenant for life's entitlement should be reduced by an amount equal to income tax at the basic rate on that sum.

III. APPORTIONMENTS RELATING TO STOCKS AND SHARES

Dividends

In contrast to the apportionments already considered, which apply to unauthorised investments, apportionments of a different type are sometimes necessary in the case of authorised investments.

The first case is of apportionment of dividends received for shares. Thus, if shares are left on trust for Peter for life, with remainder to Paul for life, it may be necessary, on the death of Peter, to apportion dividends between Peter's estate and Paul. The Apportionment Act 1870 applies to most types of periodical payment which are deemed to accrue from day to day. If, therefore, Peter dies on the fifty-ninth day of a year, and the company declares a dividend amounting to £150 for that calendar year, 59/365ths of £150 will belong to Peter's estate, and the balance will be payable to Paul. The period stated by the company in respect of that dividend will govern all beneficiaries. Suppose a company pays no dividend in 1982 and 1983, but pays a dividend in 1984, three times as large as normal, which is stated by the company to be for 1984. Suppose also that Peter dies on the fifty-ninth day of 1984, as the company has stated that the divdend is for 1984, Peter will only be entitled to 59/365ths. It may have been thought more equitable in some circumstances for Peter to have received 789/1096ths (being the fraction of days for the period 1982, 1983 and 1984 for which Peter has lived) but this is not the rule.[47]

It is necessary to make a time apportionment when there is alteration in the class of income beneficiaries. In *Re Joel*,[48] for example, a fund was held upon trust for the testator's grandchildren contingently on their attaining the age of 21. The gift carried the intermediate income, which could accordingly be used for the grandchildren.[49] Goff J. held that each time a member of the class died under 21, or a new grandchild was born, the income of the trust ought to be apportioned so that each member of the class enjoyed only that part of the income attributable to the period for which he was alive.

---

[47] *Re Wakley* [1920] 2 Ch. 205. The Law Reform Committee recommend that the statutory rule should not apply on the death of a testator by whose will a trust is created.
[48] [1967] Ch. 14. The Law Reform Committee recommend that the rule in this case should be abrogated.
[49] See *post*, p. 348.

The taxation rules, however, differ from those laid down by the Apportionment Act. For taxation purposes, the whole of the dividend is treated as the income of the person who, under the trust, is entitled to income on the day on which the income is payable.[50] Suppose, therefore, a fund is held upon trust for Roger for life, with remainder to Susan for life; that Roger dies on February 15, 1985; that one of the assets of the trust fund is a holding of shares in a company which pays dividends in respect of a year ending on March 31; and that in June 1985 the company declares a dividend for the year ended March 31, 1985. Roger's estate will be entitled to most of the dividend, although the whole of the dividend will form part of Susan's income for the year assessment 1985/86.

Purchases and Sales Cum and Ex Dividend

Apportionment may be thought to be appropriate where stocks and shares are bought and sold. There are several factors which affect the price of stock exchange investments, such as the yield which is obtained,[51] the stability of the company concerned, the general economic condition of the country as a whole, and the future prospects of the company, but one of the short-term factors is the date when the dividend is to be paid. This will clearly be an artificial example, but assuming all other factors remain constant, if a dividend of £500 is payable on January 1 and July 1 on a holding of stock worth £20,000, on January 2 the stock is worth £20,000 but its value on June 30, the day before the payment of the next dividend, will be £20,000, plus £500, *i.e.* £20,500.[52] Suppose therefore that trustees purchase stock on January 2 for £20,000 and sell it for £20,500 on June 30, does the whole of that £20,500 belong to capital, or is the sum apportioned, £20,000 being attributed to capital and £500 to income? After all, had the holding been kept for one day longer, the £500 would have been received as a dividend, and treated as income. Somewhat surprisingly, there is no apportionment, and the whole amount received is deemed to be capital. The explanation for this apparently inequitable rule is that there are in practice so many factors which affect the value of shares that it is thought too difficult to lay down any set rules to govern how the apportionment is to be calculated. It has, however, been said that if the rule of non-apportionment leads to a "glaring injustice" apportionment will be ordered.[53]

Bonus Shares

Considerable difficulty has been caused where a company issues bonus

---

[50] *I.R.C.* v. *Henderson's Executors* (1931) 16 T.C. 282; *Bryan* v. *Cassin* [1942] 2 All E.R. 262; *Wood* v. *Owen* [1941] 1 K.B. 92; *Potel* v. *I.R.C.* [1971] 2 All E.R. 504.

[51] *Ante*, p. 303.

[52] In fact the holder of the stock will pay income tax on the dividend, so that the additional worth is £500 less tax.

[53] *Per* Harman J. in *Re MacLaren's Settlement Trusts* [1951] 2 All E.R. 414 at p. 420.

shares. Suppose the capital of a company consists of 10,000 £1 ordinary shares, and suppose also that the company has prospered, and has made an accumulated profit, which has been retained, of £5,000. If the company distributes the £5,000 to its shareholders, this sum is clearly income. On the other hand the company may decide to retain that sum of £5,000 permanently by using it for the issue of 5,000 additional shares, and then the new shares are distributed free to the existing shareholders in the company on the basis of one new share for each two shares already held. Are these new shares to be treated as income? The general rule is that they are capital, and must be held by the trustees as such, although of course the tenant for life will obtain benefit from them by virtue of the fact that he will be entitled to the dividends which they produce.[54] Where, however, the company has no power under its articles of association to create new shares in this way, so that it ought to have distributed the profit in cash, it was decided in *Bouch* v. *Sproule*[55] that the shares distributed are regarded as income.

Bouch v. *Sproule* was considered in the Privy Council decision of *Hill* v. *Permanent Trustee Co. of New South Wales*,[56] where Lord Russell of Killowen laid down certain principles.[57]

1. Where a company makes a distribution of money among its shareholders, it is not concerned at all with the way in which the shareholders deal with that money. Thus, where the shareholder is a trustee, the company is not itself concernd with whether the money is treated as capital or income.

2. Unless a company is in liquidation, it can only make a payment by way of a return of capital under a scheme for the reduction of capital approved by the court.[58] (Restrictions are placed on a reduction of capital by a company so that creditors of the company shall not be prejudiced.) In any other case, apart from liquidation, it follows that if the company is able to distribute money it must be profit, so far as the company is concerned.

3. Generally, therefore, where the shareholder is a trustee, he will receive the money as income, and it will be payable to the tenant for life. This will not be the case, however, if there is some provision in the trust instrument to the contrary, or if the following principle applies.

4. Where the company has power under its articles of association to utilise its profits by adding them to capital, and issuing bonus shares

---

[54] *I.R.C.* v. *Blott* [1921] 2 A.C. 171.
[55] (1887) 12 App.Cas. 385.
[56] [1930] A.C. 720.
[57] [1930] A.C. 720 at pp. 730–732.
[58] See now, Companies Act 1948, s.67.

representing the amount of that additional capital to its shareholders, those shares are capital.

5. Where the company's capital is increased in this way, its assets are undiminished (for the cash never leaves its hands), whereas if a distribution of profits is made, the company's assets consequently are diminished.[59]

An additional principle was, in effect, added by Plowman J. in *Re Outen*,[60] to the effect that where under a power in its articles of association a company capitalises profits, not by using the profits to issue new shares, but by issuing some other investment in the company, that other investment is capital in the hands of the trustee-shareholder.

Re Outen is not without interest. In 1962 Imperial Chemical Industries Ltd. made a take-over bid for Courtaulds Ltd. by offering to acquire from members of Courtaulds their stock in that company. The bid was resisted by the directors of Courtaulds, who in order to persuade the stockholders not to sell stock procured the capitalisation of £40 million reserves, representing capital profits, and used this to make a free issue of a new loan stock to the stockholders. Before the take-over battle, a testatrix had left her holding of stock to the trustees upon trust, and in due course they, along with other stockholders in Courtaulds, were issued with a holding of the loan stock. The question arose whether this loan stock was to be treated as capital or as income. The capitalisation of the reserves was in accordance with the company's articles of association.

Plowman J. held that although Courtauld's decision did not involve the creation of new shares in Courtaulds, it effected a capitalisation under which any further character of divisible profits was taken away from the assets that were the subject of the capitalisation. The company's decision was binding on the shareholders, and the loan stock was therefore capital.

A further complication on the theme occurs where the company gives the shareholder the option either to have bonus shares, or cash. The test is whether the company intends to make a capital distribution, or whether it really intends to distribute income.[61]

Capital Profits Dividends

A series of cases were decided in about 1951 with regard to "capital profits dividends." A substantial part of the business of Thomas Tilling & Co. Ltd. consisted of operating buses and coaches. When this part of the company's business was nationalised, the company was compensated by an amount of British Transport stock, which in turn the company distributed among its shareholders as a capital profits dividend. The question arose whether the stock so distributed should be regarded as capital or as

---

[59] Though why this should be relevant to a trustee is difficult to understand.
[60] [1963] Ch. 291.
[61] *I.R.C.* v. *Fisher's Executors* [1926] A.C. 395.

income. In *Re Sechiari*[62] and *Re Kleinwort*[63] it was held that trustees received the stock as income, so that it belonged to the tenant for life. The position was not the same as in the case of the issue of bonus shares in the company making the distribution, in which case the increase in the number of shares entitles the holders to participate in future dividends, but an isolated payment, complete in itself, and from which no future benefit will accrue directly from the company. In *Re Kleinwort*, however, Vaisey J. considered that where special circumstances existed, the sum received was properly apportionable between capital and income. There would, in his opinion be special circumstances where the trustees had committed a breach of trust, particularly in not maintaining a balance between the conflicting interests of different beneficiaries. Thus if in such a case the trustees acting solely with the intention of benefiting the tenant for life at the expense of the remainderman invested in shares in a company in the expectation of a capital profits distribution, they would commit a breach of trust, and doubtless the court would apportion the dividend between income and capital. In *Re Rudd*,[64] however, it was held that merely because the trustees, who foresaw the capital dividend, and so could have sold the stock with a large profit for capital, did not do so, they did not thereby commit a breach of trust. The court thus refused to apportion the capital profit dividend received. The case seems to depend on the motive of the trustees: they did not intend to prejudice the remainderman.

Special circumstances existed, however, in *Re MacLaren*.[65] After it became known that Tillings intended to distribute the British Transport stock among its shareholders, the tenant for life consented to the purchase of Tilling stock as a capital investment. Here it was held that the tenant for life, knowing what would happen, must be regarded as having consented to the British Transport stock being regarded as capital, and that it was to be treated as capital.

Although it has been appropriate to illustrate the principle by reference to the Tilling cases, the principle applies to any case where the company makes a capital profit and distributes that profit either in cash or in some other valuable form.

Scrip Dividends

In the ordinary case, where a company issues bonus shares, the reserves or profits which are used within the company to back the bonus shares are retained by the company as long-term capital, and as has been seen,[66] in general the shares themselves are received by the trustees as capital. In the case of capital profits dividends, the company is passing on to its shareholders a profit which it has received, and the company does not itself

---

[62] [1950] 1 All E.R. 417.
[63] [1951] Ch. 860.
[64] [1952] 1 All E.R. 254.
[65] [1951] 2 All E.R. 414.
[66] *Ante*, p. 340.

retain any long-term benefit from the distribution. In the ordinary case, such dividends are received by the trustees as income.

Taxation

It is necessary to distinguish the treatment of these various types of scrip for general purposes of trust administration and for purposes of taxation. Where scrip dividends are issued, and where shares are held which carry with them the right to receive bonus shares,[67] then if the company is resident in the United Kingdom[68] the shares received are treated as income. Tax is payable as if a dividend had been paid of an amount which, after deducting income tax at the basic rate in force, equals the value of the scrip at the date of issue.[69] If the scrip is passed to an income beneficiary, the notional amount of the dividend is treated as part of his income for income tax purposes. If the scrip is retained by the trustees as an accretion to capital for a remainderman there will be no liability on them,[70] whereas if it is retained by the trustees of a discretionary or accumulation settlement there will be some further liability on them.[71]

If, however, the company which pays the dividend is resident outside the United Kingdom, the shares which are received are treated as capital for taxation purposes if they would be so treated for the purposes of trust administration.[72]

IV. APPORTIONMENTS IN RESPECT OF NATIONAL SAVINGS CERTIFICATES

It has been seen[73] that, by virtue of the Apportionment Act 1870, it may be necessary to apportion by time dividends or other income between the person entitled to the income before an event, such as death, and the person entitled after that event. It is, however, first necessary to establish that the amount in question is of an income nature. The problem arises in particular with the increment over the purchase price which is payable on the encashment of National Savings Certificates. In *Re Holder*[74] the testator in his lifetime purchased National Savings Certificates for £375, which were encashed after his death for £534. Roxburgh J. held that, by

---

[67] That is, the terms upon which the shares are issued gives the shareholders the right to call for bonus shares.

[68] F. (No. 2) A. 1975, s.34.

[69] If, therefore, the basic rate of income tax is 30 per cent. and an issue of scrip is made which is worth £100, the company will be treated as if it paid a dividend of £142.85 from which income tax had been deducted (£142.85 less £42.85 tax = £100.)

[70] Because, in general, income received by trustees subject to deduction of tax at source is not further taxable in their hands: see *ante*, p. 292.

[71] Trustees of this type of settlement are liable for income tax at the basic rate together with the additional rate of 15 per cent. See *ante*, p. 293. In the example given in note 69, therefore the trustees would be liable to pay in addition 15 per cent of £142.85 = £21.43.

[72] *I.R.C.* v. *Wright* (1926) 11 T.C. 181.

[73] *Ante*, p. 339.

[74] [1953] Ch. 468.

virtue of the terms on which the certificates were issued by the Government, the increment up to the date of death was capital. It was conceded that the increment which arose between the date of death and the date of encashment was to be treated as income, but the point was not argued. Although the basis for the concession does not appear from the report of the case, it would appear to be a correct concession, following the rule in *Re Earl of Chesterfield's Trusts*.[75]

V. APPORTIONMENT OF OUTGOINGS

Subject to contrary directions in the trust instrument, expenses which relate solely to the income of a trust, such as the cost of making an income tax return, are primarily payable out of income, and other expenses, such as the cost of appointing new trustees or of bringing legal proceedings, are payable out of capital.

Where an audit takes place, however, the trustees may apportion the cost of this between capital and income in such proportions as they think fit.[76]

VI. EXCLUDING APPORTIONMENTS

The apportionment rules are designed to achieve fairness and in most cases it is easy to see the logic behind them. Nevertheless, it is becoming increasingly common for them to be expressly excluded. Partly this is due to taxation considerations, but in the main it is because the calculations which have to be made under some of the rules are so complicated that it is far simpler from an administrative point of view for apportionments to be excluded. Ironically, then, the long-term effect of the rules has probably been the reverse of what equity intended.

---

[75] (1883) 24 Ch.D. 643; see *ante*, p. 333.
[76] T.A. 1925, s.22(4).

CHAPTER 18

INCOME FROM THE TRUST FUND

THERE are five questions to be asked about the income from the trust fund, namely:

1. What is the relationship between income received by the trustees from the assets which comprise the trust fund and the income to which the beneficiaries are entitled?
2. Which beneficial interests under the trust carry the right to income?
3. Are the trustees entitled to retain income?
4. How are the trustees to apply income where the beneficiary is an infant?
5. What are the taxation consequences of entitlement to income?

I. INCOME OF THE TRUST FUND

(1) The accounting period

One of the fundamental elements in the concept of income is that of time: it is only possible to speak of the income of trustees, or, indeed, of any person, if one knows the period of time which is to be considered. For taxation purposes, the period to be considered is, generally,[1] the year of assessment which ends on April 5. Where a trust is created otherwise than on April 6, the first accounting period for taxation purposes will be from the date of the creation of the trust until the following April 5; and the final accounting period is from April 6 to the date of termination of the trust.

There are, however, no corresponding statutory rules for the purposes of general trust administration. The legislature may have assumed that the basic period of account would be 12 months,[2] but the trustees can select any period which they wish.[3] In practice, most trustees adopt for the purposes of trust administration the same accounting period as is adopted for taxation.

(2) Gross and net income

The trustees may derive income from a number of sources during an accounting period. For example, they may receive dividends, bank deposit interest, and rent. From this gross income there will be deducted:

---

[1] The general rule applies for income tax and capital gains tax. For development land tax, the year ends on March 31.
[2] See, e.g. T.A. 1925, s.22(4) authorising trustees to have the trust accounts audited once in every three "years."
[3] Unless the trust instrument itself prescribes the accounting period.

346

(a) the expenses of the management of the trust so far as applicable to income; and

(b) any other payments which the trustees make in the exercise of administrative powers.

However, the net income will usually only be determined at some point of time after the end of an accounting period. This is because trustees have a reasonable time[4] within which to exercise powers and discretions, and they often wish to wait until the end of an accounting period so that they can see the amount of gross income received in that period.

(3) Trust management expenses

Expenses of a recurrent nature are generally payable out of income, unless the trust instrument otherwise provides. Thus, there is payable from income general rates in respect of real property owned by the trust[5]; rent payable in respect of leasehold property owned by the trust[6]; income tax[7]; and the cost of the preparation of annual accounts and income tax returns.[8]

The expenses which are payable from capital are discussed later.[9]

Although, in general, expenses are payable either from income or from capital according to their nature,

(a) the trust instrument can direct how the expenses are to be borne[10]; and

(b) in certain instances, the trustees are given a discretion.

Thus, where the trustees require the trust accounts to be audited under the statutory power,[11] they have an absolute discretion to pay the fees of the auditor from income or from capital, or partly from income and partly from capital.

(4) Administrative powers

In *Pearson* v. *I.R.C.*[12] the House of Lords drew a distinction between administrative powers and dispositive powers. Where payments are made by the trustees out of income in the exercise of administrative powers, these payments are treated in the same way as trust management expenses, that is, they are deducted from the gross receipts in determining the amount of the net trust income. Payments which are made in the exercise of a dispositive power are applications of net trust income.

In many respects, there is no clear authority as to what powers are to be regarded as administrative and what dispositive. However, in the absence of authority, the following classification is suggested:

---

[4] See, *e.g. Re Gulberkian's Settlement Trusts (No. 2), Stephens* v. *Maun* [1970] Ch. 408.

[5] *Fountaine* v. *Pellet* (1791) 1 Ves. Jun. 337, 342.

[6] *Re Gjers* [1899] 2 Ch. 54; *Re Betty* [1899] 1 Ch. 821.

[7] *Re Cain's Settlement* [1919] 2 Ch. 364.

[8] See *Shore* v. *Shore* (1859) 4 Drew 501.

[9] *Post,* p. 366.

[10] However, the court may override the direction in the trust instrument: *Re Tubbs* [1915] Ch. 137; *Re Hicklin* [1917] 2 Ch. 278.

[11] T.A. 1925, s.22(4).

[12] [1980] 2 All E.R. 479, H.L.

Administrative powers

    (i) power to charge for services;

    (ii) power to retain commission, brokerage, directors' fees;

    (iii) power to engage and pay agents and professional advisers;

    (iv) power to hold investments in nominee name, or by a custodian, and to pay the nominee or custodian;

    (v) power to insure trust assests, and to pay the premiums;

    (vi) power to insure the life of the settlor, and to pay the premiums;

    (vii) power to pay taxes and duties (as to which see *Pearson* v. *I.R. Comrs.* itself); and

    (viii) power to use income to improve land.

Dispositive powers

    (i) power to accumulate income;

    (ii) power to pay or apply income to or for the maintenance, education, or benefit of another beneficiary;

    (iii) power to allow another beneficiary to use trust assets (even if on the exercise of that power an interest in possession in the assets is not created);

    (iv) power to pay the premiums on a policy of assurance which is effected for the benefit of another beneficiary; and '

    (v) power to pay or apply income in securing the discharge of an obligation owing by another beneficiary, or in guaranteeing the performance of an obligation by another beneficiary.

Powers of advancement, although affecting beneficial entitlement, are treated as "similar to" administrative.[12a]

(5) Net trust income

The net trust income in respect of an accounting period may, therefore, be said to be:

    (a) the aggregate of the gross income received[13] in that period from all the trust assets; less

    (b) trust management expenses paid from income either by virtue of their nature or pursuant to a provision in the trust instrument; and less

    (c) other payments made from income in the exercise of an administrative power.

In the remainder of this chapter, the net trust income in this sense is referred to as the trust income.

II. GIFTS CARRYING INCOME

When the amount of the trust income has been ascertained, it is then necessary

---

[12a] *Lord Inglewood* v. *I.R.C.* (1982) *The Times*, 20 December.

[13] In many respects it is uncertain whether, to be taken into account, an amount must be received, or whether it can merely be receivable.

to determine whether any beneficiary is entitled to it. If a beneficiary is entitled, his interest is said to carry the intermediate income. The possibilities are:

(a) a beneficiary is entitled to the income without any further decision of the trustees being necessary. This will usually be the case where trustees hold a fund upon trust to pay the income to Adam for life, with remainder to Eve;
(b) no person is entitled, as where the trustees accumulate it;
(c) a beneficiary is entitled to the income, but only in the exercise of the trustees' discretion; and
(d) the income has not been effectively dealt with, and so is held on a resulting trust for the settlor, or, in the case of a will trust, for the testator's residuary beneficiaries or those entitled on intestacy.

With regard to vested gifts, a gift will carry the intermediate income unless:

(a) the trust instrument provides that it is to be paid to someone else; or
(b) the trust instrument provides that the income is to be accumulated, and added to capital.[14]

The position relating to contingent gifts is dealt with by section 175 of the Law of Property Act 1925.

This section which applies only to wills coming into operation on or after January 1, 1926, provides that except in so far as the testator has otherwise expressly disposed of his income, the following types of gift carry the intermediate income from the testator's death:

(a) contingent or future specific devises or bequests[15] of property, whether real or personal;
(b) contingent residuary devises of freehold land;
(c) specific or residuary devises of freehold land to trustees upon trust for persons whose interests are contingent or executory.

The effect so far as vested and contingent interests under trusts coming into force after 1925 is as follows:

(a) the directions of the settlor or testator always prevail. Accordingly, if the trust instrument directs that the income is to be accumulated, that direction will prevent the gift from carrying the income.[16] Likewise, even if the gift is vested, and there is a direction for the payment of the income to another, that direction will prevail. An example would be if property was held in trust for a minor absolutely, but with a provision that until he attained the age of majority, the income should be paid to his cousin. Again if payment is expressly deferred until a future date, the gift will not

---

[14] *Re Stapleton, Stapleton* v. *Stapleton* [1946] 1 All E.R. 323.
[15] A "devise" is a gift of realty by will; a "bequest" is a gift of personalty by will.
[16] *Re Turner's Will Trusts* [1937] Ch. 15; *Re Ransome* [1957] Ch. 348; *Re Reade-Revell* [1930] 1 Ch. 52.

carry the intermediate income.[17] If there is no such direction:

(b) in the following cases it is assumed that there is no provision in the trust instrument to bring the gift within the scope of para. (a);

(c) a vested interest will always carry the intermediate income;

(d) a contingent interest arising from a settlement carries the intermediate income provided the contingency is attaining the age of majority or the happening of some event before that age;

(e) a contingent gift by will carries the intermediate income if it is of
   (i) residuary personalty[18];
   (ii) residuary realty[19];
   (iii) a specific gift of personalty, other than a pecuniary legacy, or realty[20];

(f) in general a pecuniary legacy does not carry the intermediate income. To this general principle there are two exceptions, when the gift does carry the intermediate income, namely,
   (i) if the gift was by the father of the infant, or by some other person who stood *in loco parentis* to him, and
      (1) if the gift is contingent, the cotingency is not the attaining of an age greater than 18[21] and
      (2) there is no other fund set aside for the maintenance of the legatee.[22]
      This is the effect of the words in section 31(3) of the Trustee Act that the section "applies to a future or contingent legacy by the parent of . . . the legatee if and for such period as, under the general law, the legacy carries interest for the maintenance of the legatee";
   (ii) the testator directs the legacy to be set apart from the rest of his estate for the benefit of the legatee.[23]
      Of course, if the testator shows an intention that the gift shall carry the intermediate income, this will prevail under the first rule considered.

There is little logic in the distinction between contingent pecuniary legacies and other contingent gifts of personalty.

III. RETENTION OF INCOME

Where trustees do not pay out or apply the income they will have either

(a) accumulated it; or

(b) retained it in its character as income.

---

[17] *Re Geering, Gulliver* v. *Geering* [1964] Ch. 136.
[18] *Re Adams, Adams* v. *Adams* [1893] 1 Ch. 329; unaffected by the 1925 legislation.
[19] L.P.A. 1925, s.175.
[20] L.P.A. 1925, s.175.
[21] *Re Jones, Meacock* v. *Jones* [1932] 1 Ch. 642; F.L.R.A. 1969, s.1.
[22] *Re West* [1913] 2 Ch. 245.
[23] *Re Medlock* (1886) 55 L.J.Ch. 738.

(1) Accumulation

Accumulation is the conversion of what was income into capital. It occurs at the moment at which the trustees decide to accumulate the income and while no formality is required, the desirable practice is for the decision to accumulate to be recorded carefully in the trust's minutes.

Income will only be accumulated if:

(a) there is a trust or power to do so;
(b) the trust or power is not for an excessive period; and
(c) the trustees decide to give effect to the trust, or to exercise the power.

(2) Trust or power to accumulate

Trustees have no general power to accumulate income. In *Re Gourju's Will Trusts*[24] trustees held a fund upon protective trusts,[25] after the fixed interest of the principal beneficiary had come to an end.[26] They sought to accumulate the income, but Simonds J. said[27]: "I come to the conclusion that the obligation of the trustees is to apply the trust income as and when they receive it for the purposes indicated in the subsection. . . .

Putting it in a negative way, they are not entitled, regardless of the needs of the beneficiaries, to retain in their hands the income of the trust estate."

The trust or power to accumulate may arise:

(a) by statute[28] in the case of income which is held for the benefit of an infant beneficiary, to the extent that the income is not used for his maintenance[29]; or
(b) by provisions in the trust instrument.

(3) Excessive powers

Where the trust is subject to English law, a trust to accumulate can only be prescribed for a maximum of one of the following periods[30]:

(a) the life of the settlor;
(b) a period of 21 years from the death of the settlor;
(c) the duration of the minority or respective minorities of any person or persons living or *en ventre sa mère* at the death of the settlor;
(d) the duration of the minority or respective of minorities of infant beneficiaries who, if of full age, would be entitled to the income;
(e) a term of 21 years from the creation of the settlement; and
(f) the duration of the minority or respective minorities of any person or persons in being when the settlement is created, whether or not they are beneficiaries or have any other connection with the settlement.

---

[24] [1943] Ch. 24.
[25] Under T.A. 1925, s.33.
[26] See *ante*, p. 120.
[27] [1943] Ch. 24 at p. 34.
[28] T.A. 1925, s.31.
[29] See, *post*, p. 354.
[30] L.P.A. 1925, s.164; Perpetuities and Accumulations Act, 1964, s.13. These periods do not apply where the settlor is a body corporate: *Re Dodwell & Co. Ltd.'s Trust Deed* [1978] 3 All E.R. 738.

Usually the period of 21 years in (e) above is taken.

If, at the end of the prescribed period, the income is payable to a beneficiary who is an infant, the income can still be accumulated under the statutory trust to accumulate.[31]

If a trust or power prescribes accumulation for a period which is longer than that prescribed by statute, the provision is void only as to the excess.[32]

Where it is desired to accumulate for a period longer than the maximum permitted by statute, it is possible to establish the trust under a jurisdiction which recognises a longer period. Northern Ireland is popular for this purpose.[33]

(4) Exercise of power

Trustees must exercise any discretion within a reasonable time. What is reasonable depends on the facts of each case. In *Re Gulbenkian's Settlement Trusts (No. 2)*[34] trustees learned in April 1957 of a decision[35] which cast doubt on the validity of a provision in the trust instrument, and they then retained the income without accumulating it. The doubt was not resolved until the decision of the House of Lords in *Re Gulbenkian's Settlement Trusts (No. 1)*[36] in October 1968. Plowman J., held that their retention of the income was not unreasonable in the circumstances, and they could still exercise their discretion in respect of the income which had arisen since 1957. It follows that if they act reasonably, trustees can retain income as income for a considerable time and then accumulate it.

If the trustees are under a duty to accumulate, that duty is not extinguished by lapse of time. In this case, the trustees can give effect to that duty long after the income has arisen, and, if they do not do so, the court will direct them to do so.[37] If, however, the trustees merely have a power to accumulate, that is, a duty to consider whether to accumulate, but not a duty to exercise the power, the power is lost if they do not act within a reasonable time.[38]

(5) Taxation effects of accumulation

It is frequently found that instruments which impose trusts or confer powers to accumulate also provide that payments from capital can be made to beneficiaries. It may well be, then, that in a particular case the trustees have a power to distribute income as it arises to members of a discretionary class and a power to accumulate the income. There may also be a trust or power at some later date to distribute the accumulations as capital to the same persons. What is the difference to the beneficiary? The position is

---

[31] T.A. 1925, s.31(2).

[32] *Re Joel's Will Trusts* [1967] Ch.14.

[33] For an example of the use of trusts governed by the law of Northern Ireland for this purpose, see *Vestey* v. *I.R.C.* [1979] 3 All E.R. 976, H.L.

[34] [1970] Ch. 408.

[35] *Re Gresham's Settlement* [1956] 1 W.L.R. 573, subsequently overruled.

[36] [1970] A.C. 508.

[37] *Re Locker's Settlement Trusts* [1978] 1 All E.R. 216; see, *ante*, p. 274.

[38] *Re Gourju's Will Trusts* [1943] Ch. 24; *Re Wise* [1896] 1 Ch. 281; *Re Allen-Meyrick's Will Trusts* [1968] 1 W.L.R. 499.

often largely governed by tax considerations. Suppose that the trustees of a
fund receive a gross income of £1,000 p.a., and that they have a discretion
either to distribute it as income, or to accumulate it. Suppose that two of
the discretionary objects are George, whose top tax rate[39] is 30 per cent.[40]
and Harry, whose top tax rate is, with the investment income surcharge,[41]
75 per cent. The trustees are themelves liable for tax at a total of 45 per
cent. on income which may be accumulated.[42] Of the £1,000 received by
them, they will, therefore, be required to pay £450 in tax.[43] If they then
distribute it as income, before it is accumulated, the beneficiary is treated
as having received a gross payment of £1,000, from which tax at 45 per
cent. has been deducted. In the case of George, his top rate is 30 per cent.,
and he could recover by way of a repayment claim the difference between
the tax which he ought to have suffered on the £1,000, namely £300, and
the tax which he has actually suffered, namely £450. In the final result,
therefore, he receives £550 from the trustees, and £150 by way of tax
reclaim. On the other hand Harry, who is liable to tax at 75 per cent., will
be required to pay to the Revenue the difference between the tax which he
has suffered on the £1,000, and the tax which is appropriate to his top rate.
He will have received £550 from the trustees, but will have to pay £300 of
this to the Revenue. Suppose, however, that the trustees accumulate the
net income of £550, and then at some later stage distribute it as a capital
payment. In this case it is treated as capital for all income tax purposes, so
that no repayment claim can be made,[44] and no further liability can arise.
Thus, George will be worse off, because he will not be able to recover the
£150 from the Revenue, but Harry is better off, for he will not have to pay
the additional tax of £300.

A distribution from capital which has been derived from accumulated
income will, however, be treated in the same way as any other distribution of
capital. It may, therefore, give rise to a liability to capital transfer tax.[45]

(6) Retained income

As income can be converted into capital only by the decision of the trustees to
accumulate it, in strict theory the income will never be accumulated without that
decision. However, if the trustees are under a duty to accumulate, the longer a
period elapses the greater will be the willingness of the courts to hold that there
has been an accumulation. Likewise, the courts will infer that the decision to
accumulate has been taken if the trustees act in a manner which indicates that

---

[39] See *ante*, p. 292.
[40] These examples assume that the top tax rate will not be altered if the beneficiaries
receive another £1,000 gross income.
[41] At 15 per cent.
[42] The provision also applies to income subject to a discretion: F.A. 1973, s.16.
[43] In this example, the expenses of the trust are ignored. That part of the income which is
applicable to the expenses of the trust payable out of income is not subject to the additional
charge.
[44] Finance Act, 1973, s.17.
[45] Finance Act, 1982, ss.105 *et seq.* See, *ante*, p. 298.

income has been accumulated. This will be so, for example, where trustees complete an income tax return for the trust showing the income as having been accumulated.[46]

(7) Beneficial entitlement

Special rules apply where income has been accumulated during the minority of an infant beneficiary.[47] Apart from these, and subject to any provision in the trust instrument, income which has been accumulated will be added to capital, and the beneficiary entitled to capital will become entitled also to the accumulations. Income which is retained by the trustees without being accumulated will belong to the beneficiary, if any, who is entitled to income.

IV. Maintenance of Infant Beneficiaries

(1) Trust instrument prevails

Section 31 of the Trustee Act 1925 confers upon trustees a power to apply income in the maintenance of infant beneficiaries.[48] However, it was decided in *Re Turner*[49] that all the provisions of section 31, whether they are expressed as powers or as duties, are in fact only "powers conferred by this Act" for the purposes of section 69(2) of the Act. Section 69(2) provides that "the powers conferred by this Act on trustees" apply only in so far as there is no intention expressed in the trust instrument that they should not apply. Although, therefore, the general principle is that the statutory powers are additional to any powers in the trust instrument, any of the statutory powers, including the power of maintenance, may be expressly excluded under section 69(2).

The statutory power of maintenance will be excluded:

(a) if there is an express power of maintenance, to the extent that the express power is inconsistent with the statutory power;
(b) if there is any other inconsistent provision in the trust instrument, such as a direction to accumulate the whole of the income; or
(c) there is a provision expressly excluding the statutory power.

Re Erskine's Settlement Trusts[50] is an example of the second and third of these circumstances.

In that case the settlor created a settlement for the benefit of his grandson Richard, who became entitled to the capital of the fund upon attaining the age of 22. The question concerned the entitlement to income until Richard attained that age. The trust instrument provided that the income should be accumulated during the lifetime of the settlor and thereafter until Richard reached the age of 22. It also provided that the statutory powers of maintenance and advancement

---

[46] Under F.A. 1973, s.16.
[47] See *post*, p. 357.
[48] There is no statutory power to maintain adult beneficiaries.
[49] [1937] Ch. 15.
[50] [1971] 1 W.L.R. 162.

should not apply. The provision for accumulation was void,[51] and Stamp J., following *Re Turner*, held that the statutory power of maintenance was effectively excluded. In the result the income was undisposed of, and belonged to the settlor's estate.

While, however, it is possible to exclude the statutory power, it will only be excluded if there is a clear expression of intention to that effect. If the trust instrument is silent on the point, the statutory power will apply.

(2) The statutory power

The statutory power to maintain is contained in section 31 of the Trustee Act 1925. This provides[52] that where property is held upon trust for any infant, then during the infancy of that person the trustees may, if in their discretion they think fit, pay the whole or part of the income to the parent or guardian of the infant beneficiary, or otherwise apply it for or towards his maintenance, education, or benefit. The trustees are under a duty to accumulate the whole of the income which is not paid or applied in this way.[53]

It follows from what has been said earlier in this chapter that the trustees will have a power to maintain unless:

(a) the gift to the infant beneficiary does not carry the intermediate income[54]; or
(b) the power has been excluded.[55]

The statutory power has the following noteworthy features:

(a) it applies where the interest of the beneficiary is vested, and to this extent overrides the apparent provisions of the trust instrument. Suppose, for example, that trustees hold a fund upon trust for Cedric for life, with remainder to Edmund; that the statutory power applies; and that Cedric is under the age of 18. The terms of the trust instrument would suggest that Cedric is entitled to the whole of the income, yet section 31 has the effect that while Cedric is under the age of 18, he will be entitled only to that part, if any, of the income which the trustees decide to pay or apply for his maintenance;
(b) it also applies where the interest of the beneficiary is contingent. An example is where the trust fund is held upon trust for Fergus if he attains the age of 30[56];
(c) although section 31 refers to vested interests, it applies also to vested interests which are defeasible, as where a fund is held upon trust for Solly but if he dies under the age of 30, then for Holly;

---

[51] Because it was contrary to L.P.A. 1925, s.164.
[52] T.A. 1925, s.31(1).
[53] s.31(2).
[54] *Ante*, p. 348.
[55] *Supra*.
[56] Where the interest is contingent, it must also be shown that the gift carries the intermediate income: see p. 349, *ante*. If it does not do so, there will be no income available for the trustees to pay or apply.

(d) the power only applies while the beneficiary is under the age of 18[57];

(e) where section 31 is not excluded, the trustees are under a duty to consider whether to exercise their power, but they need not exercise it. In deciding whether, and, if so, to what extent, to exercise the power, the trustees are directed by section 31 *to have regard to*

the age of the infant;

what other income, if any, is available for his maintenance;

his requirements; and

"generally to the circumstances of the case."

If the trustees know that other income is available for the maintenance of the infant, and the total amount available exceeds the needs of the infant, then so far as is practicable a proportionate part only of each fund should be paid or applied for his maintenance.

The trustees may pay the money which they decide to use either to the infant's parent or guardian,[58] or they may directly apply it for his maintenance, education or benefit;

(f) the statutory power applies whatever the nature of the property[59]; and

(g) where the power is to be exercised, the trustees must exercise it positively and not merely pay out the money for the infant's maintenance without considering whether it is desirable to do so. In one case[60] where the trustees made automatic payments to the infant's father without exercising any discretion, the court ordered that money to be repaid to the trust fund. But as long as the trustees exercise their discretion in good faith the court will not interfere with their decision.[61]

(3) Accumulation of surplus income

All income which is not paid to the parent or guardian of the infant beneficiary, or applied by the trustees for his maintenance, education, or benefit is to be accumulated.[62]

Although, by being accumulated, the surplus income becomes capital, the trustees may use the income accumulated in previous years as if it were income of a later year, provided that the interest of the beneficiary continues in that later year.[63]

(4) Income arising after age 18

There is no statutory power to maintain an adult beneficiary. The general principle is that the beneficiary is thereafter entitled either to the whole of the

---

[57] Family Law Reform Act 1969, Sched. 3, para. 5. See *post* p. 357, as to the position when the beneficiary reaches the age of 18.

[58] *Sowarsby* v. *Lacy* (1819) 4 Madd. 142.

[59] *Stanley* v. *I.R.C.* [1944] K.B. 255; *Re Baron Vestey* [1951] Ch. 209.

[60] *Wilson* v. *Turner* (1883) 22 Ch.D. 521; and see p. 83.

[61] *Re Bryant* [1894] 1 Ch. 324; *Re Lofthouse* (1885) 29 Ch.D. 921.

[62] T.A. 1925, s.31(2). The manner in which the accumulations are dealt with is discussed at *post* p. 357.

[63] *Ibid.*

income[64] or none. It is, however, possible for the trust instrument to confer an express power to maintain.[65]

In *Re McGeorge*,[66] a testator devised land to his daughter, but declared that the devise should not take effect until the death of his wife. It was held that this was a future specific devise within section 175 of the Law of Property Act, and so prima facie carried the intermediate income. The daughter was over 18 and claimed the intermediate income, but her claim was defeated. Cross J. held that by deferring the enjoyment of the property until after the widow's death the testator expressed the intention that the daughter should not have the intermediate income. The income was, therefore, to be accumulated.

Where, on attaining the age of 18, the beneficiary has only a contingent interest in the trust property, he would, in the absence of any other provision, have no entitlement until he satisfied the contingency. However, section 31(1)(ii) has the effect of accelerating the beneficiary's interest. It provides that after attaining the age of 18, the trustees shall[67] thenceforth pay to the beneficiary the income from the trust fund, and the income from accumulations[68] until either the contingency is satisfied, or until the contingency fails.

(5) Accumulations at age 18

When the infant beneficiary attains the age of 18, the trustees will hold the accumulations, including income from the accumulated fund which has itself been accumulated:

(a) in accordance with any provision of the trust instrument; and, if there is no such provision
(b) either
  (i) for the beneficiary absolutely; or
  (ii) as an accretion to the capital of the trust property.[69]

A beneficiary will become entitled to the accumulations:

(a) in any circumstances in which the trust instrument so provides; or
(b) if:
  (i) during infancy, his interest was according to the settlement vested; *and*
  (ii) he attains the age of 18[70]; or
(c) if:
  (i) he attains the age of 18; *and*
  (ii) is then entitled to capital.[71]

---

[64] *Re Jones' Will Trusts* [1947] Ch. 48.
[65] *Re Turner* [1937] Ch. 15.
[66] [1963] Ch. 544.
[67] Despite this apparently mandatory provision, the section can be excluded: Re Turner [1937] Ch. 15.
[68] T.A. 1925, s.31(1)(ii).
[69] T.A. 1925, s.31(2).
[70] s.31(2)(i)(*a*). This also applies if he marries under the age of 18, and had a vested interest until marriage.
[71] s.31(2)(i)(*b*). This also applies if he marries under the age of 18.

For this purpose, he is entitled to capital if
- (a) the property is realty, and the beneficiary is entitled to:
    - (i) a fee simple absolute; or
    - (ii) a fee simple determinable; or
    - (iii) an entailed interest[72]; or
- (b) the property is personalty, and the beneficiary is entitled to the property:
    - (i) absolutely; or
    - (ii) for an entailed interest.[73]

In any other case, the accumulations are added to the capital of the property from which they arose.[74] Where they arose from a share of a fund, and that share continues to exist as a separate share, the accumulations are an accretion to that share, and not to the fund as a whole.[75] This is in contrast to the position where the beneficiary dies before attaining the age of 18 (or marrying under that age), in which case, subject to any provision in the trust instrument, the accumulations are an accretion to the fund as a whole.[76]

This point arose for consideration in *Re Sharp's Settlement Trusts*.[77] A settlement was created by which a power of appointment was conferred over a fund, and the children of the settlor were entitled equally in default of appointment. The settlor had three children, Penelope, who attained her majority in 1964; Russell, who attained his majority in 1967; and Joanne who was still an infant. Income had arisen under the settlement since 1966, and the trustees allocated it to the three children equally. Between 1966 and when Russell attained his majority in 1967 his share of accumulated income amounted to about £5,000. Since 1967, his share of income had been paid to him. Between 1966 and the date of the hearing, in May 1972, Joanne's share of accumulated income amounted to about £41,000 and the accumulation was continuing. The question was as to the entitlement to the accumulation which had arisen of Russell's share; and of the accumulation which was arising of Joanne's share. The fund was of personalty, and Pennycuick V.-C. held that the entitlement of Russell and Joanne was not absolute, because their shares were subject to the power of appointment which could still be exercised. There is an anomaly here[78] because if the property had been realty, and the interest of the beneficiaries was a determinable fee,[79] they would have been entitled to the accumulations. However, in this case, Russell and Joanne were not

---

[72] See *Re Sharp's Settlement Trusts* [1972] 3 W.L.R. 765, *per* Pennycuick V.-C. at 768.
[73] *Re Sharp's Settlement Trusts, ante.*
[74] s.32(2)(ii).
[75] *Re Sharp's Settlement Trusts, ante.*
[76] See *Re Joel* [1967] Ch. 14; *ante*, p. 339.
[77] *Re Sharp's Settlement Trusts, Ibbotson v. Bliss* [1972] 3 W.L.R. 765.
[78] See Pennycuick V.-C. at p. 156.
[79] Although not a fee simple on condition. As to the distinction, see Megarry and Wade, *The Law of Real Property* (3rd ed.), pp. 75 *et seq.*

entitled outright to the accumulations. Penelope said that the accumulations were accretions to their shares only, as those accumulations were derived from income which the trustees had allocated to their shares. Pennycuick V.-C. held in their favour, so that the accumulations from Russell's share were held, with that share itself, for Russell subject to any future exercise of the power of appointment, and Joanne's share was likewise to be held, contingently on her attaining her majority. So far as Russell was concerned, therefore, he would be entitled to the income from his share, as increased by the accumulations.

The manner in which trustees deal with accumulations when a beneficiary reaches the age of 18 is illustrated by the following table. For the purposes of the table:

(a) "Conditions A" means that the beneficiary had a vested interest during infancy and attains the age of 18; and
(b) "Conditions B" means that the beneficiary attains the age of 18 and becomes entitled to the capital.

The entitlement to accumulations on obtaining the age of 18 is illustrated by the following table:

Trust instrument provides for fund to be held for	Circumstances	Entitlement	Remarks
Andrew absolutely[80]	Andrew attains 18	Andrew	Conditions B
	Andrew dies under 18	Andrew's estate	The entitlement is by virtue of the original gift, not s.31
Brian for life	Brian attains 18	Brian	Conditions A
	Brian dies under 18	Added to capital	Neither Conditions satisfied
Charles for life if he attains 18	Charles attains 18	Added to capital	Charles' interest during infancy was contingent only; and he does not become entitled to the capital
	Charles dies under 18	Added to capital	Neither Conditions satisfied
Douglas if he attains 18	Douglas attains 18	Douglas	Conditions B
	Douglas dies under 18	Added to capital	Neither Conditions satisfied
Edward if he attains 30	Edward attains 18	Added to capital	Neither Conditions satisfied
	Edward dies under 18	Added to capital	Neither Conditions satisfied

---

[80] Andrew's infancy being the only reason why he could not call for the capital to be transferred to him.

Frank, but if he dies under 30, for George	Frank attains 18	Frank	Although Frank's interest was defeasible, it was vested, and Conditions A is satisfied
	Frank dies under 18	Added to capital	Neither Conditions satisfied
Henry, but if he dies under 18, for Ian	Henry attains 18	Henry	Conditions A
	Henry dies under 18	Added to capital	Neither Conditions satisfied

It will be seen from this table that:

(a) where the beneficiary dies under the age of 18, the accumulations will always be added to capital, except where the property was held for an infant beneficiary absolutely (the example of Andrew);

(b) where the beneficiary has a life interest which is contingent on his attaining the age of 18, or some later age, then, notwithstanding that he satisfies the contingency, the accumulations are added to capital (the examples of Charles and Edward); and

(c) the distinction between a contingent interest (the examples of Charles and Edward) and a vested interest which is defeasible (the example of Frank) is crucial.

V. TAXATION CONSEQUENCES

Section 31 and the action taken by trustees under it can have a material effect on the tax position of the beneficiary. In considering these taxation consequences it is necessary to keep in mind that:

(a) section 31 can be excluded; and

(b) where, according to the terms of the settlement, an infant beneficiary has a vested life interest, by section 31 that interest is converted into a life interest contingent on his attaining 18. This is because, notwithstanding the terms of the settlement,

    (i) during the minority of the beneficiary the trustees will have a power to maintain and a trust to accumulate the remaining income; and

    (ii) the beneficiary (or his estate) will only become entitled to the accumulations if he attains the age of 18.

The latter point can lead to confusion. In order to determine the destination of accumulations, whether or not a beneficiary had during his infancy a vested interest, regard is paid only to the terms of the trust instrument. For other purposes, however, the nature of the beneficiary's interest is determined by the terms of the trust instrument as modified by the section itself.

(1) **Income tax**

It has been seen[81] that the trustees are liable to income tax at the basic rate[82] on all income which they receive, regardless of whether it is used for the payment of trust management expenses, paid to a beneficiary, or accumulated; and if they have a discretion with regard to income, or are directed to accumulate it, there is a liability to an additional 15 per cent.[83]

If section 31 applies, then whether or not under the terms of the trust instrument the beneficiary's interest was vested or contingent, the trustees have a discretion, in that they have a power to maintain, so that there is a liability to the additional rate of 15 per cent. However, there is no further liability on the beneficiary unless the income was actually paid out to him, or applied for his benefit.

There is, however, a further rule, under which a beneficiary will be taxable on the whole of the net trust income if he has a vested interest in it. He is taxable according to the income tax rates which govern his own income, but he is entitled to credit for the income tax paid by the trustees in respect of the trust income paid to him. Suppose, therefore, that Harry has income apart from the trust of £36,000, of which £10,000 is unearned; that the income of the trust fund is £2,000, on which the trustees pay tax, at 30 per cent. of £600; that £250 is used for trust management expenses; and that £1,150 is paid to Harry. Harry's liability is as follows:

The trustees have received	£2,000
on which they have paid tax at 30% of	£ 600
leaving	£1,400
from which they have paid trust management expenses of	£ 250
leaving net income paid to Harry of	£1,150
This is treated as a gross sum of	£1,642.86
from which income tax[84] has been deducted of	£ 492.86
	£1,150.00

---

[81] *Ante*, p. 292.

[82] At present (1982/83) this is 30 per cent.: F.A. 1982, s.20.

[83] The additional rate is not payable in respect of that part of the gross income which was paid out in trust management expenses: F.A. 1973, s.16(2)(*d*).

[84] In effect, the £600 paid by the trustees is attributed: as to

$$\frac{250}{1400} \times 600 = 107 \cdot 14 \qquad \text{to trust management expenses}$$

$$\frac{1150}{1400} \times 600 = 492 \cdot 86 \qquad \text{to income paid to Harry}$$

So that Harry's trust income is:

the amount paid to him	£1,150.00	
and the tax deducted	£ 492.86	
		£ 1,642.86
which is added to his other income of		£36,000.00
		£37,642.86

On the "slice" of income between £36,000 and £37,642.86, the present rate of income tax[85] is 75% to give a liability of (75% × £1,642.86)   £ 1,232.15

Henry suffered by deductions   £ 492.86

and has a further liability of   £ 739.29

Using the figures of this example:

(a) if the whole of the income is accumulated, the total liability will be that of the trustees, as follows:

Gross income		£2,000
less: tax at the basic rate, as before	£600	
less: tax at the additional rate of 15% on that part of the gross income of the trust £2,000 as is not used in the payment of trust management expenses		£ 250
	£1,750	£1,750
that is: 15% × £1,750	£ 262.50	
so that the total tax paid is	£ 862.50	£ 862.50
and net amount accumulated is		£ 887.50

(b) if the whole of the income is treated as Harry's the total tax payable, as before is   £1,232.15

leaving the benefit[86]   £ 410.71

The income will be treated as that of Harry, during Harry's minority, if:

(a) he is absolutely entitled to both capital and income, so that his infancy is the sole reason why he cannot call for the capital to be

---

[85] For 1983/84, including the investment income surcharge.

[86] The net income paid to Harry, £1,150, less the further tax payable by him in respect of it, £739.29.

transferred to him, and either he, if he lives, or his estate, if he does not, will be entitled to the accumulations[87]; or

(b) according to the terms of the trust instrument, Harry is entitled to the whole of the income, and section 31 is excluded, so that the trustees do not have power to accumulate any part of it.

In all other circumstances, only that income which is actually paid to Harry, or applied for his benefit, is treated as his for income tax purposes.[88] The remainder of the income, which is accumulated, is taxable in the hands of the trustees at the effective rate of 45 per cent.

(2) Capital transfer tax

It was explained earlier[89] that the capital transfer tax legislation[90] divides settled property into two main categories, according to whether or not there is, at the time being considered, an interest in possession in it. A beneficiary has an interest in possession if he is entitled to the trust income without any further decision of the trustees being requisite,[91] or, probably, if the accumulations will be his in any event.[92] Subject to certain exceptions, a charge to tax arises whenever an interest in possession terminates.[93]

In general, if there is no interest in possession in settled property, and one arises, there is a charge to capital transfer tax at that time.[94]

However, special capital transfer tax privileges are given to "accumulation and maintenance settlements." These are governed by section 114 of the Finance Act 1982, which was drafted with section 31 of the Trustee Act in mind. Section 114 of the 1982 Act provides that a settlement is an accumulation and maintenance settlement at a given time if,[95] at that time:

(a) there is no interest in possession in it;

(b) the income is applied for the maintenance, education or benefit of a beneficiary, and to the extent that it is not so applied, it is to be accumulated; and

(c) it can be said that one or more beneficiaries will, on attaining a specified age not exceeding 25, become beneficially entitled either

(i) to the settled property itself; or

(ii) to an interest in possession in the settled property.

---

[87] *Roberts* v. *Hanks* (1926) 10 T.C. 351; *Edwardes Jones* v. *Down* (1936) 20 T.C. 279.

[88] *Stanley* v. *I.R.C.* [1944] K.B. 255.

[89] *Ante*, p. 298.

[90] F.A. 1975, Sched. 5.

[91] *Pearson* v. *I.R.C.* [1980] 2 All E.R. 479, H.L.; *ante* p. 347.

[92] See I.R. Press Notice, (1976) L.S.G. February 2. As property held absolutely for a person is not settled property for capital transfer tax (F.A. 1975, Sched. 5, para. 1(2)), this will only apply where the trust instrument directs accumulations to be dealt with in this way.

[93] F.A. 1975, Sched. 5, para. 4.

[94] F.A. 1982, s.108.

[95] Only the basic conditions are given in the text: certain further ancilliary conditions must also be satisfied: F.A. 1982, s.114(2).

Where the conditions for an accumulation and maintenance settlement are satisfied:

(a) the trust is not subject to what would otherwise be a charge to tax on every tenth anniversary of the date of its creation[96]; and

(b) there is no charge to tax when a beneficiary becomes entitled either to an interest in possession in the settled property or to the settled property itself.[97]

The following table[98] illustrates the interaction of section 31 of the Trustee Act and the capital transfer tax provisions.

---

[96] By virtue of F.A. 1982, s.102(1)(b).

[97] F.A. 1982, s.114(4).

[98] Do not try to learn this table. It is intended to show how it is necessary to consider (a) the terms of the trust instrument; (b) whether the gift carries the intermediate income and (c) whether s.31 is or is not excluded.

Inter-action of Trustee Act 1925, s.31 and Capital transfer tax provisions

Trust instrument provides for	Section 31 Applies			Section 31 Excluded		
	C.T.T. category during minority	Whether charge to tax on death under age 18	C.T.T. effect on attaining 18	C.T.T. category during minority	Whether charge to tax on death under age 18	C.T.T. effect on attaining 18
Andrew absolutely	Personal	Yes	Personal	Personal	Yes	Continues to be personal
Brian for life	Acc. & Mtce.[1]	No	Brian becomes entitled to I.I.P.	I.I.P.	Yes	I.I.P. continues
Charles for life if he attains 18	Acc. & Mtce.[2]	No	Charles becomes entitled to I.I.P.	(i) I.I.P. if gift carries intermediate income (ii) D.T. otherwise	Yes / No	(i) I.I.P. continues (ii) I.I.P. arises, if gift then carries intermediate income; and charge to tax
Douglas absolutely if he attains 18	Acc. & Mtce.[3]	No	Personal	Personal	Yes / No	Personal. No charge to tax / Personal. Charge to tax
Edward if he attains 30	(i) Acc. & Mtce.[4] if gift carries intermediate income (ii) D.T. otherwise	No	(i) I.I.P. if gift carries intermediate income (ii) D.T. otherwise	(i) I.I.P. if gift carries intermediate income. (ii) D.T. otherwise	(i) Yes (ii) No.	I.I.P. if gift continues to carry the intermediate income (i) I.I.P. arises if gift begins to carry intermediate income. Charge to tax (ii) Otherwise D.T. continues
Frank, but if he dies under 30, for George	Acc. & Mtce. if gift carries intermediate income	No	I.I.P. if gift carries intermediate income. No charge to tax	I.I.P. if gift carries intermediate income	Yes	If gift carries intermediate income, I.I.P. continues
Henry, but if he dies under 18, for Ian	Acc. & Mtce. if gift carries intermediate income	No	Personal. No charge to tax	I.I.P. if gift carries intermediate income D.T. if gift does not carry intermediate income	Yes / No	Personal. No charge to tax if gift has carried intermediate income Personal. Charge to tax

(1) The apparent interest in possession of Brian is removed by s.31.
(2) The conditions for an accumulation and maintenance settlement are prima facie satisfied because Charles will become entitled at an age not exceeding 25.
(3) Provided that the gift carries the intermediate income.
(4) The vested defeasible interest of Edward is converted by s.31.

CHAPTER 19

APPLICATIONS OF TRUST CAPITAL

IN general, entitlement to capital will depend on the terms of the trust instrument in the case of a fixed interest trust, or on the decision of the trustees in the
case of a discretionary trust. However:

(a) as in the case of entitlement to income, the quantum of capital which is
available for beneficiaries will be determined after the payment of those
costs and expenses which are attributable to capital[1]; and

(b) even in the case of a fixed interest trust, the trustees may take decisions
which will (i) alter the time at which a beneficiary will take capital; or (ii)
which will affect the quantum of his entitlement.

The main powers which will affect the quantum of entitlement are the three
"A"s, namely Advancement, Appointment, and Appropriation. Appointments have been dealt with previously. Accordingly, after dealing with expenses payable from capital, this chapter is concerned primarily with the powers
of advancement and appropriation.

I. EXPENSES FROM CAPITAL

It has been seen[2] that, in general, recurrent expenses are generally payable out
of the income of the trust fund. This is partly because of the recurrent nature of
these expenses, and partly because such expenses are generally for the benefit
primarily of the beneficiary who is entitled to income. The corollary is that, in
principle, there is payable out of the capital of the trust fund expenses which

(a) constitute capital expenditure on one or more assets of the trust; or

(b) apply to the trust as a whole, and can, therefore, be said to be for the
benefit of all beneficiaries.

Examples of expenses which are treated as capital expenditure on an
asset are calls on shares which are partly paid[3]; sums applied in discharging
mortgage debts[4]; and sums applied in improving land and buildings.[5]
Where a building is purchased by the trustees in a derelict state, the cost of

---

[1] As to net income, see *ante*, p. 347.
[2] *Ante*, p. 347.
[3] *Todd* v. *Moorhouse* (1874) L.R. 19 Eq. 69; Trustee Act 1925, s.11(2).
[4] *Whitbread* v. *Smith* (1854) 3 De G.M. & G. 727; *Marshall* v. *Crowther* (1874) 2 Ch.D.
199.
[5] *Earl of Cowley* v. *Wellesley* (1866) L.R. 1 Eq. 656 *Re Walker's Settled Estate* [1894] 1 Ch.
189.

putting it into good condition at the outset will be treated as if it were part of the purchase price, and so be chargeable to capital.[6] Ordinary repairs are, in principle, payable out of income, but where the repairs can be said to be for the benefit of all beneficiaries, the court may direct that the whole or part of the cost is to be borne by capital.[7]

The second category of expense which is borne by capital covers those items relating to the trust as a whole, and which can be said to be for the benefit of all beneficiaries. Examples are the costs of the appointment of new trustees[8]; of making changes in investment; of obtaining legal advice as to the extent of the trustees' powers[9]; and taking or defending court proceedings for the protection of trust assets.[10]

It has been mentioned[11] that in certain circumstances, either by statute or the trust instrument, trustees are given a discretion whether outgoings are to be paid from income or capital. This power must be exercised so that the particular outgoings will be borne equitably between the beneficiaries with different interests.[12]

II. ADVANCEMENT

(1) The concept

In essence, advancement consists of the payment or application of a capital sum in order to establish a person in life, or to make permanent provision for him.[13] An advancement is often of an amount which, in the light of the circumstances of the recipient, is large, and where a payment is large in this sense, there is a presumption that it is made by way of advancement.[14]

It is not now generally necessary to consider in the administration of trusts[15] whether a payment is, strictly, by way of advancement, because either under the statutory power, which is considered below, or under an express power in the trust instrument, the trustees will usually have a power to apply capital for the advancement or other benefit of a beneficiary.

(2) The statutory power

The statutory power is contained in section 32 of the Trustee Act 1925. This

---

[6] *Re Courtier* (1886) 34 Ch.D. 136.

[7] Under the Settled Land and Trustee Acts (Courts' General Powers) Act 1943 and Emergency Powers (Miscellaneous Provisions) Act 1953.

[8] *Re Fulham* (1850) 15 Jur. 69; *Re Fellows' Settlement* (1856) 2 Jur. (N.S.) 62.

[9] *Poole* v. *Pass* (1839) 1 Beav. 600.

[10] *Re Earl of Berkeley's Will Trusts* (1874) 10 Ch. App. 56; *Re Earl De La Warr's Estates* (1881) 16 Ch.D. 587; Stott v. *Milne* (1884) 25 Ch.D. 710.

[11] *Ante*, p. 279.

[12] *Re Lord De Tabley* (1896) 75 L.T. 328; *Re Earl of Stamford and Warrington* [1916] 1 Ch. 404.

[13] *Boyd* v. *Boyd* (1867) L.R. 4 Eq. 305; *Taylor* v. *Taylor* (1875) L.R. 20 Eq. 155; *Re Hayward, Kerrod* v. *Hayward* [1957] Ch. 528; *Hardy* v. *Shaw* [1975] 2 All E.R. 1052.

[14] *Per* Jessel M.R., *Taylor* v. *Taylor* (1875) L.R. 20 Eq. 155 at p. 157; *per* Goff J., *Hardy* v. *Shaw* [1975] 2 All E.R. 1052 at p. 1056.

[15] It is otherwise in the administration of estates: see Administration of Estates Act 1925, s.47(1).

section gives trustees a power to pay or apply capital for the benefit of any beneficiary who is interested in the capital of the trust fund, whether his interest is vested or contingent, and whether or not it is liable to be defeated by the exercise of a power. If the power is exercised, there is always one, and there may be two important effects:

1. The beneficiary who is advanced receives benefit from the capital earlier than he otherwise would. If, for example, trustees hold a fund upon trust for Gerald for life, with remainder to Harry, and if, during the lifetime of Gerald,[16] the trustees pay part of the fund to Harry, Harry takes the benefit of that part at that time, rather than having to wait until the death of Gerald; and

2. The beneficiary who is advanced receives benefit from the capital whereas otherwise he might not have received any benefit. Suppose that trustees hold a fund upon trust for Ian if he attains the age of 30, but, if he dies under that age, for John. Suppose also that the trustees pay part of the trust fund to Ian when he is aged 22, and that he dies when he is aged 25. Had that payment not been made, because Ian did not satisfy the condition he would have received no capital benefit.

There are four limitations on the statutory power, which are now to be considered.

(a) **Extent of power.** The trustees can make payments by way of advancement or benefit on more than one occasion, provided that the total which is paid or applied does not exceed one half of the presumptive or vested share of the beneficiary.[17] It was decided in *The Marquess of Abergavenny* v. *Ram*[18] that where, at the time of the advancement, the trustees pay out one half of the share, then the power is exhausted, and no further advancement can be made even if the value of the remaining trust assets appreciates.[19] Suppose that there have been no previous advancements; that the trustees made an advancement of £25,000 in 1980; that the value of the whole of the trust fund at that time was £50,000; and that in 1985 the value of the remainder of the trust fund is £80,000. The trustees fully exhausted their power in 1980, and can make no further advancement in 1985. If, however, they only advanced £24,000 in 1980, so that their power was not fully exhausted, in 1985 they could advance the further sum of £28,000.[20]

---

[16] As to the need for Gerald to give his consent, see *post* p. 369.

[17] T.A. 1925, s.32(1), proviso (*a*).

[18] [1981] 2 All E.R. 643.

[19] The decision was on a provision of the Marquess of Abergavenny's Estate Act 1946, but it is of equal application to s.32 of the Trustee Act 1925.

[20] The calculation is:

Value of fund in 1985	£ 80,000
Add: amount previously advanced	£ 24,000
	£104,000
One half thereof	£ 52,000
less: previously advanced	£ 24,000
Maximum further advance	£28,000

(b) **Bringing into account.** The second limitation is that if, after a beneficiary has been advanced, he is, or becomes, absolutely and indefeasibly entitled to the trust property, or a share in it, he must bring into account the amount of his advancement.[21] Suppose, therefore, that trustees hold a fund upon trust for James and John in equal shares if and when they attain the age of 30; that the trustees paid £20,000 by way of advancement to James when he was aged 26; and that when they attain the age of 30 the fund is worth £100,000. On the distribution of the trust fund, the amounts which James and John receive are:

Value of fund	£100,000
Amount advanced	£ 20,000
Total	£120,000

Entitlement

	James	John
$\frac{1}{2}$ × £120,000	£60,000	£60,000
Less: advancement	£20,000	—
Net entitlement	£40,000	£60,000

Where an advancement was not made in cash but *in specie*, the amount to be brought into account is the value of the asset at the time when the beneficiary becomes absolutely and indefeasibly entitled to his share.[22]

If the beneficiary had only a contingent or defeasible interest, and never becomes absolutely and indefeasibly entitled, there is no claw-back of the amount advanced to him. By making an advance to a contingent beneficiary, therefore, the trustees can partially defeat the interests of other beneficiaries.

(c) **Consent where prior interests.** If a beneficiary has a prior interest, he must be of full age and consent in writing to the advancement. This is because any advancement will prejudice his interest. Thus if £10,000 is settled upon trust for Mary for life, with remainder to Derek, the trustees have a power to advance £5,000 to Derek, but only if Mary consents. If Mary consents and the advancement is made, thereafter her income will be that produced by the remaining £5,000 and not, as previously, by £10,000. A person on whom property is settled on protective trusts will not normally forfeit his life interest by consenting to an advancement.[23]

(d) **Nature of trust property.** The fourth limitation on the statutory power is that it applies only to money or securities, or to land which is held on trust for sale, and is treated as being converted into money.[24]

---

[21] T.A. 1925, s.32(1), proviso (*b*). The Law Reform Committee recommend that the amount to be brought into account should be increased by reference to movements in the Index of Retail Prices.

[22] See, *e.g. Hardy* v. *Shaw* [1975] 2 All E.R. 1052.

[23] See *ante*, p. 125.

[24] T.A. 1925, s.32(2).

(3) **Extensions and exclusions of statutory power**

The statutory power will apply even where there is no mention of it in the trust instrument, but the power is one which falls within the scope of section 69(2)[25] and so may be excluded by the settlor or testator in the trust instrument. Thus, in *Re Evans's Settlement*[26] Stamp J. held that where the trust instrument provided that the trustees could advance up to £5,000, this by implication excluded the statutory power of advancing up to one-half of the prospective interest. Further, in *I.R.C.* v. *Bernstein*,[27] where there was a direction to accumulate income during the settlor's lifetime, the Court of Appeal held that this was a sufficient indication that the settlor did not intend the statutory power of advancement to apply.

It is more likely, however, that the statutory power will be extended. The most usual extensions give the trustees a power to advance up to the whole and not merely half of the beneficiary's share; extend the power to realty; and in some cases, do away with the need to obtain the consent of beneficiaries having prior interests.

(4) **Purpose of advancement**

It has been seen[28] that, originally, a power of advancement was held to relate to some substantial preferment in life. Examples were the purchasing of a commission in the Army[29]—the modern equivalent would be purchasing a partnership in a practice—purchasing or furnishing a house,[30] or even establishing a husband in business.[31] It has also been seen that this need for substantial setting up in life is now modified by the inclusion in the statutory power of "benefit," which is a word of wide import. But the trustees must still consider whether a particular gift is for the benefit of the beneficiary. In *Lowther* v. *Bentinck*[32] it was held that the payment of his debts was not for the benefit of a beneficiary, though in special circumstances a payment to a beneficiary to enable him to discharge his debts might be a benefit for this purpose. It is, however, quite clear that the trustees must not make an advancement to benefit themselves. In *Molyneux* v. *Fletcher*,[33] where the trustees made an advance to a daughter-beneficiary to enable her to pay her father's debts to one of the trustees, this was held to be an improper exercise of the power.[34]

In most cases the "benefit" for which an advancement is made is material benefit. In some circumstances, however, the court will authorise an advancement to be made for the moral, and not necessarily material, benefit of the beneficiary. In *Re Clore*[35] the beneficiary was entitled to an interest in a trust

---

[25] *Ante*, p. 354.
[26] [1967] 1 W.L.R. 1294.
[27] [1960] Ch. 444.
[28] *Ante*, p. 367.
[29] *Lawrie* v. *Bankes* (1857) 4 Kay & J. 142.
[30] *Perry* v. *Perry* (1870) 18 W.R. 482.
[31] *Re Kershaw's Trust* (1868) L.R. 6 Eq. 322.
[32] (1875) L.R. 19 Eq. 166.
[33] [1898] 1 Q.B. 648.
[34] And see *post*, p. 404.
[35] [1966] 1 W.L.R. 955.

fund of considerable value, and he felt a moral obligation to make payments to charity. Pennycuick J. authorised this on the basis, it seems, that as the beneficiary felt this obligation, payment by the trustees was only relieving him of a financial obligation which he would otherwise have sought to meet from his personal funds. The judge made it clear, however, that the beneficiary must feel the moral obligation, and that the trustees were not at liberty to make payments in satisfaction of what *they* considered to be the beneficiary's moral obligation if the beneficiary did not share their view. Except where, perhaps, small amounts are involved, it is prudent for trustees to seek the prior sanction of the court before making advancements of this nature.

Just as trustees cannot properly make an advancement to benefit themselves,[36] they cannot make an advancement with a view to benefiting some other person. In *Re Pauling's Settlement Trusts*[37] the bankers Messrs. Coutts & Co. were trustees of a fund which was held upon trust for a wife for her life, with remainder on her death to her children. The trust instrument contained an express power for the trustees to advance to the children up to one-half of their share with the consent of the wife. The husband of the life-tenant, who was the father of the children, lived beyond his means, and sought to obtain part of the trust moneys. A series of advancements were made, nominally to the children, but the money was used for the benefit of their father, or generally for the family. Thus the proceeds of one advancement were used to purchase a house for the father in the Isle of Man, and the proceeds of another advancement to discharge a loan incurred by the mother. The trustees had been advised by counsel that so far as the trustees were concerned they were paying the money to the children for their own absolute use, and that, in effect, what the children did with the money was not the trustees' concern. This view was unanimously rejected by the Court of Appeal (Willmer, Harman and Upjohn L.JJ.), who considered that "the power [of advancement] can be exercised only if it is for the benefit of the child or remoter issue to be advanced or, as was said during argument, it is thought to be 'a good thing' for the advanced person to have a share of capital before his or her due time. . . . [A] power of advancement [can] be exercised only if there is some good reason for it. That good reason must be beneficial to the person to be advanced; [the power] cannot be exercised capriciously or with some other benefit in view."[38]

In their consideration of the circumstances in which an advancement could properly be made, the Court of Appeal drew a distinction between the situation where the *beneficiary* applies for an advancement for a particular purpose and the situation where the trustees themselves stipulate the purpose to which the advancement is to be put. As Willmer L.J. said: "if the trustees make the advance for a particular purpose which they state, they can quite properly pay it over to the advancee if they reasonably think they can trust him or her to carry out the prescribed purpose. What they cannot do is to prescribe a particular

---

[36] *Molyneux* v. *Fletcher, supra.*
[37] [1964] Ch. 303.
[38] *Ibid.* at 333; [1963] 3 All E.R. 1 at p. 8.

purpose, and then raise and pay the money over to the advancee, leaving him or her entirely free, legally and morally, to apply it for that purpose or to spend it in any way he or she chooses . . . this much is plain, that if such misapplication [of the money advanced] came to [the trustees'] notice, they could not safely make further advances for particular purposes without making sure that the money was in fact applied to that purpose, since the advancee would have shown him or herself quite irresponsible."[39]

The court expressly left open the question whether, in the event of money which was advanced for a particular purpose being used for something different, that money could be recovered by the trustees. This possibility apart, once the trustees have paid over the money, they have no further legal control over it, and they must, therefore, ensure that the beneficiary is under a moral obligation to apply the money to the purpose intended.

(5) Adult beneficiaries

While, as has been seen,[40] the statutory power of maintenance applies only to infant beneficiaries, the statutory power of advancement can be exercised in favour of beneficiaries of any age.[41]

(6) Taxation

Where there is an advancement, there may be a liability both to capital gains tax and capital transfer tax. If the advancement is made in cash, there can be no liability to capital gains tax in respect of the advancement itself, although if the trustees disposed of chargeable assets in order to produce funds with which to make the advancement, a liability to capital gains tax may have arisen according to the general principles.[42] If, however, the advancement is made *in specie*, at the time when the trustees decide to make the advancement, they will be deemed to have disposed of the asset at its market value at that time, and then to have re-acquired it at that value as nominees for the beneficiary.[43] If the asset had risen in value since it was acquired, the same capital gains tax results will ensue as if the asset were actually sold for that value. However, provided that the beneficiary is resident in the United Kingdom, the trustees and the beneficiary can elect that "hold-over" relief[44] shall apply.[45]

With regard to capital transfer tax, if the advancement is to a beneficiary who immediately before the advancement had an interest in possession, there will be no liability to capital transfer tax by virtue of the advancement.[46] In any other case there will be a liability,[47] although in the case of small advancements, this

---

[39] [1964] Ch. 303 at pp. 334, 335.
[40] *Ante*, p. 355.
[41] In *Hardy* v. *Shaw* [1975] 2 All E.R. 1052 there was an advancement, in the strict sense, in favour of persons who were middle-aged.
[42] *Ante,* p. 296.
[43] Capital Gains Tax Act 1979, s.54.
[44] As to which, see *ante*, p. 297.
[45] Finance Act 1980, s.79; Finance Act 1982, s.82.
[46] Finance Act 1975, Sched. 5, para. 4(3).
[47] Para. 4(2).

liability may be reduced by the use of the annual exemption[48] of the beneficiary who has the interest in possession.[49]

III. SETTLED ADVANCES

(1) Generally

Originally, an advancement consisted of an outright payment of money or transfer of an asset to a beneficiary, but during this century[50] it has become established that a power of advancement can, in principle, be exercised so that the money or property is not transferred outright, but becomes held on new trusts for the benefit of the beneficiary to be advanced.[51] This is usually done in one of three ways:

(a) if the beneficiary is *sui juris,* the trustees might make an outright payment to him, thereby putting him in the position of creating a new settlement[52]; or

(b) the trustees might exercise a power given to them in the trust instrument by declaring that thenceforth they will hold a part of trust fund on separate trusts for the benefit of the beneficiary to be advanced[53]; or

(c) a new settlement might be created, either by the trustees or by some other person, usually with a nominal sum of money, so that a convenient "vehicle" is established. The trustees of the existing settlement then transfer the amount to be advanced to the trustees of the new settlement to be held on the trusts declared by it, as an addition to the funds of that settlement.[54]

It follows that the trustees of the original settlement may, but will not necessarily, be the trustees of the advanced fund.

Whichever method is used, whether by way of resettlement, appointment, or transfer to a new settlement, it will be convenient in this chapter to refer to funds passing from an existing settlement into a new settlement.

Where there is to be an advance into settlement in one of these ways, the questions which arise are:

(i) is the proposed advance for the benefit of the beneficiary to be advanced?

---

[48] For 1983/84 this is £3,000. There will be no tax payable if the taxpayer has not used his 10 year nil rate band.

[49] Finance Act 1981, s.94.

[50] Following certain decisions at the end of the last century.

[51] The principle has long been established. See *Re Halstead's Will Trusts* [1937] 2 All E.R. 570; *Re Moxon's Will Trusts* [1958] 1 W.L.R. 165; *Re Ropner's Settlement Trusts* [1956] 1 W.L.R. 902; *Re Wills' Will Trusts* [1959] Ch. 1; *Re Abraham's Will Trusts* [1969] 1 Ch. 463; *Re Hastings-Bass* [1975] Ch. 25; *Pilkington v. I.R.C.* [1964] A.C. 612.

[52] In *Roper-Curzon* v. *Roper-Curzon* (1871) L.R. 11 Eq. 452, where it was necessary for the court to give its sanction to an advancement, it refused to give that sanction unless the beneficiary did resettle the amount to be advanced.

[53] See, for example, *Hoare Trustees* v. *Gardner* [1978] 1 All E.R. 791.

[54] See, for example, *Hart* v. *Briscoe* [1978] 1 All E.R. 791; *Pilkington* v. *I.R.C.* [1964] A.C. 612.

(ii) can the proposed advance be also for the benefit of other beneficiaries?

(iii) to what extent can the new settlement confer an effective dispositive discretion on the trustees? and

(iv) what perpetuity period applies to the new settlement?

(2) Benefit of the advanced beneficiary

Any advancement, whether outright or into settlement, must be for the benefit of the beneficiary to be advanced. The cases establish the following principles:

(a) In general, "benefit" means direct financial benefit, so that it is likely that there will not be a valid exercise of the power of advancement if the quantum of the beneficiary's interest is reduced. The point is likely to arise where the trustees wish to advance into a protective trust for the benefit of the beneficiary to be advanced. In *Re Morris*[55] Jenkins L.J. laid down the principle that a "power of advancement is a purely ancillary power, enabling the trustee to anticipate by means of an advance under it the date of actual enjoyment by a beneficiary . . . and it can only affect the destination of the fund indirectly in the event of the person advanced failing to attain a vested interest." So he held that an advance into settlement upon protective trusts was not valid because it altered the beneficial interests.

As will be seen,[56] however, some advances into settlement upon protective trusts are valid. This requirement that the advancement is to be for the direct financial benefit of the beneficiary is, however, subject to the following points.

(b) An advance into settlement will be for the benefit of the beneficiary if the tax liability which would otherwise arise in respect of the funds held for the beneficiary is mitigated.[57] The position was summarised by Viscount Radcliffe in *Pilkington* v. *I.R.C.*[58] when he said[59] that ". . . if the advantage of preserving the funds of a beneficiary from the incidence of (tax)[60] is not an advantage personal to that beneficiary, I do not see what is."

(c) If, in order to effect the tax mitigation, it is necessary for the beneficiary not to take any, or any direct, financial interest in the advanced fund, the advancement may still be proper. The decision in *Re Clore's Settlement Trusts*[61] has been mentioned.[62] That case was concerned with the transfer of funds into a charitable settlement under which the beneficiary took no beneficial interest.[63]

(d) In determining whether an advancement into settlement is for the benefit of a beneficiary, there must be considered all the terms of the instrument which

---

[55] [1951] 2 All E.R. 528.
[56] *Post*, p. 376.
[57] *Re Ropner's Settlement Trusts* [1956] 3 All E.R. 332; Re Meux [1958] Ch. 154; *Re Wills' Will Trusts* [1959] Ch. 1
[58] [1964] A.C. 612.
[59] At p. 640.
[60] In this case, the tax was estate duty.
[61] [1966] 1 W.L.R. 955.
[62] *Ante*, p. 370.
[63] The decision may depend on its particular facts.

constitutes the new settlement, and not merely those under which the trustees are in practice likely to act. In *Re Hunter*[64] where a testator settled property upon trust for his sister for life, with remainder to her children with "such provision for their respective advancement maintenance and education" as the sister should appoint. One of the sister's sons was financially unstable, and became bankrupt shortly after she made her will. In an attempt to enable her son to enjoy the benefit of part of the trust property, she purported to appoint that property upon protective trusts for her son. Cross J. held the trust invalid, following the dictum of Jenkins L.J. in *Re Morris*[65] that protective trusts should not be regarded "merely as a device to enable a forfeiting life-tenant to enjoy the income notwithstanding purported alienation and so forth or the event of his or her bankruptcy, and that the discretionary trust should be regarded merely as machinery to that end and not as really designed to confer any beneficial interest on the issue nominally included in it. The validity or otherwise of the discretionary trust declared in the event of forfeiture must, in my view, be determined by reference to what the trustees are empowered to do under such a trust, and not by reference to what they would in fact be likely to do, or be expected to do, under it."

(e) A beneficiary may derive a benefit from knowing that financial provision is being made for his wife and children. So, in *Re Halsted's Will Trusts*,[66] Farwell J. held that trustees in exercising a power of advancement for a beneficiary could properly settle funds upon trust for the beneficiary, his wife and his children.

(f) There is no necessary connection between "benefit" and "need." Thus, the advancement of funds may be valid if the trustees consider that it is for the benefit of the beneficiary, irrespective of his need.[67]

(3) Other beneficiaries

Property will only be settled if at least one person other than the beneficiary to be advanced has some interest in it, whether vested or contingent. The fact that one or more other persons will or might benefit does not in itself make defective an advance into settlement. This is one of the several points which the House of Lords decided in *Pilkington* v. *I.R.C.*[68] In that case a testator set up a will trust under which the trustees were directed to hold the trust fund upon trust, broadly, for the benefit of testator's nephew Richard, for life, with remainder to such of his children as he should appoint, or, in default of appointment, for all of his children in equal shares. Richard had three children, all born after the death of the testator, of whom one was Richard's daughter Penelope. When Penelope

---

[64] [1963] Ch. 372.
[65] [1951] 2 All E.R. 528; *ante*, p. 374.
[66] [1937] 2 All E.R. 570.
[67] In *Re Pilkington's Will Trusts* [1961] Ch. 466 the Court of Appeal had held that there could only be a valid advancement into settlement where the benefit to be conferred was related to the real or personal needs of the beneficiary. This was rejected by the House of Lords in *Pilkington* v. *I.R.C.* [1964] A.C. 612.
[68] [1964] A.C. 612.

was still very young, the trustees wished to advance funds into a new settlement for her benefit. Accordingly, her grandfather proposed to create a settlement under which the income would be accumulated, or used for Penelope's maintenance until she reached the age of 21. Penelope was to be entitled to income on attaining that age, and to the capital on attaining the age of 30. Other members of the family were to benefit if Penelope died under the age of 30. The trustees of the original settlement proposed to transfer one half of Penelope's share under that settlement to the trustees of the proposed new settlement. The House of Lords held that, in principle,[69] this would be within the trustees' power of advancement, notwithstanding the fact that other members of the family might benefit.

(4) Dispositive discretions under new settlement

In *Re Wills Will Trusts*[70] Upjohn J. said[71] that "a settlement created in exercise of the power of advancement cannot in general delegate any powers or discretions, at any rate in relation to beneficial interests, to any trustees or other persons, and in so far as the settlement purports to do so, it is *pro tanto* invalid." This has led to the view that an advance into a discretionary settlement would be unauthorised. It has also led to the view that if there is an effective advancement into a settlement upon protective trusts, the discretionary trusts which would otherwise arise on the termination of the principal beneficiary's life interest would be ineffective. Both the dictum of Upjohn J. and the views developed from it follow the maxim *delegatus non potest delegare*.

The present writers think that the better view is that discretions can be conferred on the trustees of the new settlement. In the first place, in *Pilkington* v. *I.R.C.*[72] Viscount Radcliffe said[73]: "I am unconvinced by the argument that the trustees would be improperly delegating their trust by allowing the money raised to pass over to new trustees under a settlement conferring new powers on the latter. In fact I think the whole issue of delegation is here beside the mark. The law is not that trustees cannot delegate: it is that trustees cannot delegate unless they have authority to do so. If the power of advancement which they possess is so read as to allow them to raise money for the purpose of having it settled[74] then they do have the necessary authority to let the money pass out of the old settlement into the new trusts. No question of delegation of their powers or trust arises." The present writers interpret this as meaning that provided that the power in the original settlement is sufficiently wide, the advancement can properly be made into a new settlement which does confer dispositive powers on the trustees; and that the statutory power, or an express power to the like effect, will be construed as being sufficiently wide.

---

[69] The actual appointment was void as a contravention of the perpetuity rules.
[70] [1959] Ch. 1.
[71] At p. 13
[72] [1964] A.C. 612.
[73] At p. 639.
[74] Which was how the paper was read by the House of Lords.

Furthermore, where there is an advancement into settlement, the principle of *delegatus non potest delegare* will rarely be observed in its entirety. It is clear that the new settlement may itself include powers of advancement.[75] While in concept a power of advancement may be a power merely to bring forward the date at which a beneficiary would otherwise enjoy the trust property,[76] it has been seen[77] that the exercise of such a power may well alter the beneficial entitlement to the funds advanced.

Thirdly, if in appropriate circumstances,[78] there can be a valid advancement into a settlement under which the beneficiary to be advanced takes no beneficial interest, it is absurd if there cannot be a valid advance into a settlement under which he is a discretionary beneficiary.[79]

While it is thought, therefore, that there is no fundamental objection to the new settlement conferring upon the trustees dispositive powers, in any particular case it is still necessary to show that that is for the benefit of the beneficiary who is being advanced.

(5) The perpetuity period

Where the trustees of an existing settlement make an advance into a new settlement, for the purposes of the perpetuity rules they are treated as if they had exercised a special power of appointment. Accordingly, the interests limited by the new settlement, as read back into the original settlement, must comply with the perpetuity rule. It was on this ground that the House of Lords held that the proposed appointment in *Pilkington* v. *I.R.C.*[80] would have been void.

The Perpetuities and Accumulations Act 1964 will only apply to the advancement if the original settlement itself was made after July 15, 1964,[81] so that the old perpetuity rule will continue to govern many advancements. Where, however, the 1964 Act does apply, the interests under the new settlement will be treated as valid until, if at all, it becomes established that they will vest outside the perpetuity period.[82]

If all of the interests purportedly conferred by the new settlement will not vest within the perpetuity period, the result will depend on whether the effective provisions of the new settlement when taken by themselves, will be for the benefit of the beneficiary to be advanced, and will not be totally different in effect from what the trustees intended. This is shown by the decision in *Re Hastings-Bass (deceased)*.[83] In that case trustees transferred from an existing

---

[75] *Re Mewburn* [1934] Ch. 112; *Re Morris* [1951] 2 All E.R. 528; *Re Hunter's Will Trusts* [1963] Ch. 372.
[76] *Re Morris* [1951] 2 All E.R. 528; *ante*, p. 375.
[77] *Ante*, p. 375.
[78] As in *Re Clore's Settlement Trust* [1966] 1 W.L.R. 955; *ante*, p. 374.
[79] Although the issues of benefit and delegation are separate, much greater tax mitigation may be achieved by using discretionary, rather than fixed interest, trusts.
[80] [1964] A.C. 612; *ante*, p. 375.
[81] Section 15(4) will apply to exclude the Act in the case of original settlements made before that date.
[82] Section 3; *ante*, p. 184.
[83] [1975] Ch. 25.

settlement the sum of £50,000 to be held upon the trusts of a new settlement, intending that transfer to be an advancement for the primary benefit of a beneficiary, William. The trustees misunderstood the effect of the new settlement, under which William took a life interest, but all the remaining provisions of which were void because of contravention of the rule against perpetuities. The first question was whether the statutory power of advancement could be exercised where the effect was to give the advanced beneficiary, in this case William, only an interest in income, and no interest in capital. The court held that this was a sufficient "application" of the funds, and that the appointment was not necessarily defective on that ground.

The second question was one of more general application: was the purported exercise of the power effective when the trustees did not fully appreciate the effects of the new settlement, and so could not take into account all the relevant circumstances? The court held that where trustees purport to exercise a power in good faith, then even if the effect of that purported exercise is different from that intended by the trustees, the court would only interfere with the purported exercise in two circumstances. First, the court would interfere if the result actually achieved was not authorised by the trustees' power. Secondly, the court would interfere if it was clear that the trustees would not have acted as they did had they not taken into account considerations which they ought not to have taken into account, or if they had not failed to take into account considerations which they ought to have taken into account. In this case, the effect of conferring upon William an effective life interest was to achieve a substantial saving of estate duty.[84] It was likely, therefore, that the trustees would have acted, broadly, as they did if they had appreciated the true effect of the advancement, and the court held that the exercise of their power was valid.

If, however, had they appreciated the true effect of their action, the trustees would not have acted as they did, their purported exercise of the power would have been void.[85]

(6) Taxation

Just as a liability to capital gains tax may arise in the case of an ordinary advancement,[86] so it may arise in the case of a settled advance. The capital gains tax legislation treats most settlements as if they were a separate legal person, so that if an asset is transferred from one settlement to another settlement, the asset is deemed to be disposed of by the trustees of the transferring settlement and acquired by the trustees of the acquiring settlement. However, the capital gains tax legislation does not prescribe rules for determining what constitutes a separate settlement. For example, if the trustees of a settlement declare that they will thenceforth hold part of the trust fund on separate trusts for the benefit of a beneficiary to be

---

[84] The capital transfer tax rules are different, and no tax would be saved if the facts were repeated at the present time.

[85] e.g. Re Abraham's Will Trust [1969] 1 Ch. 463.

[86] Ante, p. 372.

advanced, does that part become subject to a new settlement, or does it remain within the original settlement. In *Roome* v. *Edwards*[87] Lord Wilberforce said[88] "Since 'settlement' and 'trusts' are legal terms, which are also used by businessmen or laymen in a business or practical sense, I think that the question whether a particular set of facts amounts to a settlement should be approached by asking what a person, with a knowledge of the legal context of the word under established doctrine and applying this knowledge in a practical and commonsense manner to the facts under examination, would conclude."

Presumably this new creature of the law, the man on the omnibus which sets out from Clapham but which goes up Chancery Lane, would consider whether there are separate provisions governing beneficial entitlement, separate trustees, separate trust property and separate administration.

If there is not a separate settlement, there is no deemed disposal and re-acquisition for capital gains tax purposes. If there is a separate settlement, then, in principle, the trustees of the original settlement are deemed to dispose of all the assets which become subject to the new settlement at their market value at the time, and to re-acquire them at that value.[89] However, if the acquiring settlement is resident in the United Kingdom, hold over relief can be claimed.[90]

There may also be a liability to capital transfer tax if there was an interest in possession under the original settlement, and the same beneficiary does not have an immediate interest in possession under the new settlement.[91] There will not usually be a liability if there was no interest in possession either under the original or the new settlement,[92] but in other cases there usually will be.[93]

IV. OTHER APPLICATIONS OF CAPITAL

In some cases, the power of maintenance and advancement contained in the trust instrument, or the statutory powers, will not be sufficient for a beneficiary's needs. Where this is so there are four other possibilties:

(a) maintenance from capital;
(b) application to the court under section 53 of the Trustee Act 1925;
(c) application to the court under its inherent jurisdiction;
(d) application to the court to vary the trust. This is considered at page 000.

(1) Maintenance out of capital

Although, in principle, income is to be used for the maintenance of a beneficiary,[94] it is just possible that trustees can use capital for this purpose.

---

[87] [1981] 1 All E.R. 736, H.L.
[88] At p. 739.
[89] *Roome* v. *Edwards* [1981] 1 All E.R. 736, H.L.
[90] Finance Act 1980, s.79; Finance Act 1982, s.82.
[91] Finance Act 1975, Sched. 5, para. 4(2).
[92] Finance Act 1982, s. 121.
[93] Finance Act 1982, s. 108.
[94] See *ante*, p. 354.

Section 31 of the Trustee Act 1925 clearly envisages that only income will be used for maintenance, and in a note to the old case of *Barlow* v. *Grant*[95] it was said that "the court will not permit executors and trustees to break in upon the capital of infants' legacies without the sanction of the court, and the court itself, though it will break in upon the capital for the purpose of advancement, will rarely do so for maintenance." But however rarely a court might exercise its power to use capital for an infant's maintenance, it does have such a power. Lord Alvanley said in *Lee* v. *Brown*[96] that: "The principle is now established that if an executor does without application what the court would have approved, he shall not be called to account, and forced to undo that merely because it was done without application." The extent of this dictum—the case was on advancement—is not clear, and it is just possible that a trustee who maintained out of capital would not be called upon to make good the capital if the court would itself have ordered maintenance out of capital.

Quite apart from its doubtful legality, however, there would be taxation disadvantages in doing so, for in respect of every £1 taken out of the capital for this purpose, the trustees would have to deduct income tax at the basic rate and pay it over to the Revenue.[97] Where, however, an advancement of capital is made, no income tax is payable, and by making an advancement, one can usually achieve the same result now as a purported maintenance out of capital.

(2) Section 53

Section 53 of the Trustee Act 1925 provides that where an infant is beneficially entitled to any property, the court may "with a view to the application of the capital or income thereof for the maintenance, education, or benefit of the infant" make an order appointing a person to convey the infant's interest on his behalf. This section is chiefly used where the infant's interest is small, and produces very little income, but where, if the interest were sold, the proceeds could be used for the infant's maintenance or benefit.[98] It was, however, pointed out in *Re Meux*[99] that this section does not give a power to dispose of the infant's interest whenever it is merely for the infant's benefit: there must be "a view to the application" of the capital or income for the maintenance, education or benefit of the infant. It seems that it must be intended to *apply* the capital or income in some way for the benefit of the infant. In *Re Heyworth's Contingent Reversionary Interest*[1] the court refused to give its consent under section 53 to a proposal merely to sell the infant's interest, and hand over a cash sum, without there being any clear idea as to what was to happen to that money thereafter. On the other hand, where it is proposed to resettle the money, and

[95] (1684) 1 Vern. 255.
[96] (1798) 4 Ves. 362.
[97] See *ante*, p. 293.
[98] *Ex p. Green* (1820) 1 Jac. & W. 253; *Ex p. Chambers* (1829) 1 Russ. & M. 577; *Ex p. Swift* (1828) 1 Russ. & M. 575.
[99] [1958] Ch. 154.
[1] [1956] Ch. 364.

the transaction as a whole is for the infant's benefit, the court has held that the fact of resettling was a sufficient "application" to come within section 53.[2]

An example of the use of this power is contained in *Re Bristol's Settled Estates*.[3] In that case there were two tenants in tail of settled land, the Marquess of Bath and his infant son Lord Jermyn. The estate was a large one and to save estate duty it was, in essence, intended that the existing settlement should be terminated, part of the property paid absolutely to the Marquess, and the remaining part resettled. Provided the Marquess lived for a period of five years (and an insurance policy was to be taken out to cover this) both he and the ultimate beneficiaries would gain by the arrangement, the only loser being the Revenue. Before the scheme could be put into operation, it was necessary for the entailed interest to be barred. The Marquess could bar his entail, and were he not a minor, Lord Jermyn could have barred his entail with the consent of the Marquess as the protector of the settlement. The court made an order under section 53 appointing a named person to execute with the consent of the protector of the settlement an assurance on behalf of Lord Jermyn barring his entailed interest in the property, so that the capital and income could, under the proposed scheme, be appointed for his benefit.[4]

Clearly within the terms of the provisions of section 53 are schemes for raising money for the education of an infant, or to provide a house or purchase a share in a partnership for him.[5]

(3) Inherent jurisdiction

In limited circumstances the court has an inherent jurisdiction (quite apart from the Variation of Trusts Act 1958) to modify the terms of the trust.[6] One of the occasions in which it will do so is where a settlor or testator has made some provision for a family, but has postponed the enjoyment, for example, by directing accumulation of the income for a set period. Where this is done, the trustees cannot themselves use the income to maintain an infant, but the court will assume from the fact that the settlor has made provision for the family that he did not intend to leave the children inadequately provided for. The court has, therefore, in some cases directed that the income or part of it is not to be accumulated, but is to be used for the maintenance of the infant.[7]

V. APPROPRIATION

Appropriation occurs when trustees effectively set aside part of the trust property and earmark it for a specific purpose. For the purposes of trust law

---

[2] *Re Meux, ante.*
[3] [1965] 1 W.L.R. 469; [1964] 3 All E.R. 939.
[4] See also *Re Lansdowne's Will Trusts* [1967] Ch. 603.
[5] *Re Baron Vestey's Settlement* [1951] Ch. 209.
[6] See further, as to the circumstances in which the court may vary beneficial interests in this and other cases, *post,* p. 409.
[7] *Havelock* v. *Havelock* (1881) 17 Ch.D. 807; *Re Collins* (1886) 32 Ch.D. 229; *Revel* v. *Watkinson* (1748) 1 Ves. Sen. 93; *Re Walker* [1901] 1 Ch. 879; *Greenwell* v. *Greenwell* (1800) 5 Ves. 194; *Cavendish* v. *Mercer* (1776) 5 Ves. 195; *Errat* v. *Barlow* (1807) 14 Ves. 202.

generally, the effect of appropriation is that beneficiaries who have an interest in the appropriated fund have no rights in respect of the non-appropriated property, and the beneficiaries of the non-appropriated property have no rights in respect of the appropriated fund.

The position is as follows:

(i) trustees do not have any general power to appropriate[7a];

(ii) the trust instrument may direct appropriation, or confer on the trustees a power to appropriate;

(iii) if the trust instrument directs different property to be held on different trusts, that will be treated as an implied direction to appropriate.[8] If, therefore, the trust instrument directs one-quarter of the property to be held on trust for Pinky for life, with remainder to her issue, and the other three quarters to be held on trust for Perky for life with remainder to her issue, then separate funds should be appropriated;

(iv) it seems that if property is held on trust for sale, the trustees have an implied power to appropriate, unless there is a direction to the contrary in the trust instrument[9];

(v) a mere power to appropriate, whether express or implied, will require the consent of adult beneficiaries affected, although not of infant or unborn beneficiaries. However, the power may go beyond one merely to appropriate, so that it is a power to appropriate without any consent being requisite. Consents are not requisite where the trust instrument directs appropriation;

(vi) personal respresentatives are given a statutory power of appropriation,[10] but this does not apply to trustees.

[7a] The Law Reform Committee recommend that trustees should be given a statutory power of appropriation.

[8] *Fraser* v. *Murdoch* (1881) 6 App. Cas. 855; *Re Walker* (1890) 62 L.T. 449; *Re Nicholson* [1936] 3 All E.R. 832.

[9] *Re Nickels* [1898] 1 Ch. 630; *Re Brooks* (1897) 76 L.T. 771.

[10] By s.41 of the Administration of Estates Act 1925.

CHAPTER 20

THE POSITION OF A BENEFICIARY UNDER A TRUST

IN general terms, as long as a trust is being properly administered and is continuing, a beneficiary has no right to interfere in its administration, but has passively to wait to receive the benefit appropriate to him under the trust. If, however, the trust is not being properly administered, the beneficiary can take steps to compel its proper administration, and in any case may take certain action to preserve his position. Ultimately, however, the destiny of the trust may lie in his hands, for if various conditions are fulfilled, he can bring the trust to an end even if this appears contrary to the wording of the trust instrument.

I. CONTROL OF TRUSTEES' DISCRETION

Two fundamental principles govern the control of trustees by beneficiaries:

(a) so long as the trust continues, decisions which have to be made in the administration of the trust are to be made by the trustees alone; and

(b) all the beneficiaries under the trust, if *sui juris* and between them absolutely entitled, may bring the trust to an end.[1]

The court is jealous to preserve the trustees' powers, largely because the main function of trustees is to control the trust as a whole, and the right to exercise all the decisions necessary goes to the root of trusteeship. Thus, even where it has power to do so under the Variation of Trusts Act 1958, the court will not approve an arrangement which could override the discretionary powers which the trustees intend to exercise.[2] The leading case on the subject is *Re Brockbank*.[3] It was mentioned in an earlier chapter[4] that where no person is named in a trust instrument as having a power to appoint new trustees, then the existing trustee or trustees are given that power by section 36 of the Trustee Act 1925. In *Re Brockbank* the beneficiaries, all *sui juris* and between them absolutely entitled to the whole of the beneficial interest under the trust, wished to appoint a person as a new trustee, against the wishes of the existing trustee. It was held that the appointment of new trustees was a power given to the existing trustees, and this power could not be exercised by the beneficiaries.

---

[1] See *post*, p. 387.
[2] *Re Steed's Will Trusts* [1960] Ch. 407, also discussed *post*, p. 420.
[3] [1948] Ch. 206.
[4] *Ante*, p. 252.

It has been suggested,[5] probably correctly, that while the beneficiaries cannot cut down the trustees' powers, they can add to them. This right, if it exists, is to add only to the trustees' powers, and not to their duties, so that their discretion is preserved intact, but is enlarged.

The main areas in which beneficiaries seek to control the trustees' discretion is with regard to investments, and in respect of the exercise of the discretion under discretionary trusts. In both respects the trustees' position is essentially the same. They must take note of any representation made to them, for these representations may properly affect the exercise of their discretion. Thus, if one of the beneficiaries passes to the trustees confidential information that shares in a particular company are likely to improve rapidly, the trustees will give that full consideration in deciding whether to buy. But the decision must be theirs, for they are the persons who can best judge the interests of all beneficiaries, and they are the persons who are answerable.

To the general rule that the trustees should listen, but must alone make the decisions, there are certain exceptions:

(a) the trustees' discretion may be limited by contract. Thus, where a person acts as nominee for another, the terms of the arrangement between them may require the trustee-nominee to act in accordance with the directions of the beneficiary;

(b) the trustees' discretion may be limited by the terms of the trust instrument itself. The usual form of this limitation is to require the consent of a beneficiary or other person to the sale of a particular asset, but there is no reason in principle why it should not be restricted in some other way;

(c) there is a third exception of uncertain extent, which arises from the decision of the Court of Appeal in *Butt* v. *Kelson*.[6]

In *Butt* v. *Kelson* the trustees of a trust held a large proportion of the shares in a private limited company, of which they were also directors by virtue of their trust shareholding. The question arose how far the beneficiaries could control the votes of the trustees both as directors and as shareholders. It was held that the trustees' votes as directors could not be controlled by the beneficiaries, while their votes as shareholders could be controlled. The apparent inconsistency of this curious result may be explained on the basis that under company law directors have duties to all the shareholders, and not only to those shareholders, if any, whom they represent, with the result that it would have been inconsistent with this obligation if the trustees were compelled to vote as directors solely in accordance with the wishes of the beneficiaries. But their votes as shareholders were not subject to this conflict of duty. Nevertheless, it would seem at first sight that the manner in which the voting power was to be exercised should be a matter for the trustees' discretion, free from interference by the beneficiaries. On this ground *Butt* v. *Kelson* was

[5] Underhill (12th ed.), p. 521.
[6] [1952] Ch. 197.

criticised by Upjohn J. in *Re Whichelow*[7] as being inconsistent with *Re Brockbank*. It is, however, possible to regard a right to vote in a company as a property right and for special considerations to apply to such votes, but *Butt* v. *Kelson* is probably incorrect in so far as it allows beneficiaries to control the votes of trustee-shareholders, and should not be extended.

II. RIGHT TO COMPEL DUE ADMINISTRATION

Whether or not a beneficiary suspects any improper conduct on the part of the trustees, he may insist that the accounts of the trust are audited by any solicitor or accountant who is acceptable to the trustees. If agreement cannot be reached on the auditor, the audit is carried out by the Public Trustee. Unless special circumstances exist, the audit cannot be carried out more than once in every three years, and if a beneficiary does require more frequent audits, he will be ordered personally to pay the costs.[8] Although it is convenient to consider this provision here, the position is the same where the trustee requires an audit to be carried out.

Where the beneficiary thinks that the trust is not being properly administered, or where there is some point of doubt relating to the administration of the trust, and in certain other circumstances, he may make an application to the court.[9] There are two types of application:

(a) an application on summons for the determination of a specific question or questions; and
(b) an action for general administration of the trust.

It is desirable for the former method to be used where possible, because it is cheaper, quicker and simpler than the latter.

The following are examples of the circumstances in which it may be appropriate to apply to the court on summons:

(a) for the approval of a specific transaction for which permission is not given by the general law, or by the trust instrument, but which is thought to be in the interests of the beneficiaries as a whole.[10] In most cases, of course, this type of application will be made by the trustees[11];
(b) to direct the trustees to do a particular act which they ought to do or to refrain from doing a particular act which they ought not to do. The act referred to must be one which the trustees are under a definite obligation to do or not to do: it is not appropriate for a beneficiary to question by this means an act which a trustee has a discretion to do[12];

[7] [1954] 1 W.L.R. 5.
[8] Trustee Act 1925, s.22(4); Public Trustee Act 1906, s.13(5). The Law Reform Committee recommend that s.13 of the 1906 Act should be repealed.
[9] For the comparable circumstances in which the trustee might wish to make an application to the court, see *ante*, p. 277.
[10] See *Boardman* v. *Phipps* [1967] 2 A.C. 46 (which was in fact an example of the circumstances where an application should have been made); and *ante*, p. 277.
[11] See *ante*, p. 277.
[12] *Suffolk* v. *Lawrence* (1884) 32 W.R. 899.

(c) to direct the payment of money in the hands of the trustees into court[13];

(d) as to the construction of the provisions of the trust instrument, or to ascertain the class of beneficiaries;

(e) to determine any other specific question which arises in the administration of a trust.

Generally it is not appropriate to use this method where the subject-matter of the proposed application will involve third parties, or in an action against trustees for breach of trust where the facts are in dispute.

It will be seen that almost all specific questions which arise in the administration of a trust can be dealt with by summons in this way. An action for the general administration of a trust, that is, where the court itself is to become responsible for the whole administration of the trust, will accordingly usually only be necessary where there is constant dispute between the trustees; where the circumstances of the trust give rise to recurring difficulties which would require frequent single applications to the court; and where prima facie doubt exists as to the bona fides of the trustees.

III. RIGHT TO ENFORCE CLAIMS

As part of his right to compel the due administration of the trust, a beneficiary can apply to the court if the trustees fail to take action to preserve the trust property.[14] A cause of action against a third party might itself be an item of trust property. The court might direct the trustees to enforce that claim, or it might allow the beneficiary to sue direct for the benefit of the trust, where necessary using the name of the trustee.[15] Alternatively, a beneficiary is able to sue the trustees, and make those who are alleged to be under obligations to the trust co-defendants.

In *Wills* v. *Cooke*[16] the trust property included a farm which was subject to a tenancy. The trustees retained solicitors to advise them with regard to the administration of the trust, but, it was alleged, the solicitors failed to advise the trustees to take action to increase the rent in accordance with the Agricultural Holdings Act 1948. One of the beneficiaries sued the solicitors direct, claiming that the trustees had a right of action against them, and that that right was an item of trust property. On an interlocutory application, Slade J. held that that right might be an item of trust property, and that the statement of claim should not be struck out. He also said, however, that the right would not have been an item of trust property if the trustees had entered into the contract with the solicitors solely for their own protection and benefit.

IV. RIGHT TO TERMINATE A TRUST

If there is only one beneficiary under a trust who is *sui juris*, or if there are two or

---

[13] As to the circumstances in which money is payable into court, see T.A. 1925, s.63.

[14] *Fletcher* v. *Fletcher* (1844) 4 Hare 67.

[15] As in *Foley* v. *Burnell* (1783) 1 Bro. C.C. 274, a case of trespass to trust land.

[16] (1979) L.S.G., July 11.

more beneficiaries, and they are all *sui juris* and they are all in agreement, he or they can bring the trust to an end irrespective of the wishes of the trustees or of the creator of the trust. This is the rule in *Saunders* v. *Vautier*.[17] There are two reasons for this rule. First, equity regards the trustees as primarily holding the balance between various beneficiaries with conflicting interests. Where all the beneficiaries are of the same mind, the basic reason for the trustees' existence has gone. But as has been seen, if the beneficiaries still want the trust to continue, they cannot generally control the trustees' discretion: either the trust must be terminated, or the trustees must be allowed to get on with their job. Secondly, the voluntary trust is in equity the equivalent of the gift at common law,[18] so that as a general principle once the trust is created the settlor has no longer any control over it, just as, if he had made an outright gift of property, he would have had no control over what was done with that property. Thus if all the beneficiaries are *sui juris* and between them entitled to the whole of the beneficial interest in the trust property, the settlor's provisions expressed in the trust instrument will not prevent them from bringing the trust to an end.

In *Saunders* v. *Vautier* itself, a trustee held a sum of money upon trust to accumulate the income until a specified date, and then to pay it to a beneficiary. The beneficiary reached the age of 21, and so became *sui juris*, before the date specified for distribution. He successfully claimed that the capital and accumulated income to date should be paid over to him.

If, however, the trust instrument had provided that the beneficiary did not obtain a vested interest until he survived to the specified date, then he would not have been able to invoke the rule without the concurrence of the person entitled in default of his attaining that age.[19]

If the beneficial interest is sold, the purchaser stands in the same position as the vendor, and if the vendor could have brought the trust to an end the purchaser will be able to do so if he is *sui juris*. If the beneficial interest is mortgaged, the mortgagee cannot bring the trust to an end as long as the beneficiary still has a right under the mortgage to have his beneficial interest redeemed upon payment of the amount secured.[20]

The rule also applies where beneficiaries are entitled in succession. So if property is held upon trust for A for life, with remainder to B for life, with remainder to C, if A, B and C are all alive and *sui juris* and they all join in, they can bring the trust to an end. Where a trust is brought to an end in this way, the beneficiaries can compel the trustees to convey the property to whomever they direct,[21] and if the trustees refuse, they will personally have to pay the cost of the beneficiaries' application to the court.

Use may also be made of the rule in *Saunders* v. *Vautier* to overcome the

---

[17] (1841) Cr. & Ph. 240. See also *Josselyn* v. *Josselyn* (1837) 9 Sim. 63; *Gosling* v. *Gosling* (1859) Johns. 265; *Wharton* v. *Masterman* [1895] A.C. 186; *Re Johnston* [1894] 3 Ch. 204; *Re Smith* [1928] Ch. 915; *Re Lord Nunburnholme* [1911] 2 Ch. 510; *Berry* v. *Geen* [1938] A.C. 575.

[18] *Re Bowden* [1936] Ch. 71.

[19] *Gosling* v. *Gosling* (1859) Johns. 265; *Re Lord Nunburnholme* [1912] 1 Ch. 489.

[20] This is the conclusion from *Re Bell, Jeffrey* v. *Sales* [1896] 1 Ch. 1.

[21] *Re Marshall* [1914] 1 Ch. 192; *Re Sandeman's Will Trusts* [1937] 1 All E.R. 368.

specific difficulty in *Re Brockbank*.[22] Thus, if beneficiaries dislike the existing trustees, or the existing trustees' choice of a new trustee, they may combine together, bring the existing trust to an end, set up a new trust on exactly the same terms, but with their nominees as trustees, and direct the old trustees to convey the trust property to the new trustees. This method is effective, but it may be expensive. *Ad valorem* stamp duty is sometimes payable on the formation of a trust *inter vivos*.[23] In certain circumstances, there can also be certain taxation disadvantages in the breaking of a trust.

On the termination of a trust there will often be a liability both to capital gains tax and to capital transfer tax. If a trust is terminated, and the trustees sell the investments comprising the trust fund, they will be liable to capital gains tax on any increase in value which has accrued while the investments have been subject to the trust. If, however, the trustees distribute the assets *in specie*, the beneficiaries will become absolutely entitled to the assets as against the trustees,[24] and, in principle, a liability to capital gains tax will arise as if the trustees had disposed of the assets on the open market for their full value at the time when the beneficiaries became entitled.[25] However, if the beneficiaries are resident in the United Kingdom, they may claim "hold-over" relief.[26] Under that relief, the beneficiaries are treated for capital gains tax purposes as acquiring the assets at their base cost to the trustees.[27] By claiming this relief, the liability for the payment of tax is deferred until the beneficiaries actually dispose of the assets.

The position with regard to capital transfer tax is more complicated. Suppose that a fund of £100,000 is held upon trust for Elizabeth for life with remainder to Angela, and that it is agreed to bring the trust to an end by paying £40,000 to Elizabeth and £60,000 to Angela. It has been seen[28] that where a beneficiary has an interest in possession in settled property he is treated for capital transfer tax purposes as if he was beneficially entitled to the settled property itself.[29] Accordingly, immediately before the termination Elizabeth would be treated for capital transfer tax purposes as being beneficially entitled to £100,000, whereas after the termination she would only be entitled to the actual sum of £40,000. There would, therefore, be a capital transfer tax liability as if Elizabeth had made a chargeable transfer of value of £60,000.[30]

So far as concerns Angela, she has given up a reversionary interest in a fund of £100,000 in order to obtain an immediate outright payment of £60,000. There

---

[22] [1948] Ch. 206; *ante*, p. 383.   [23] See *ante*, p. 290.

[24] This concept was considered at p. 297, *ante*.

[25] Capital Gains Tax Act 1979, s.54.

[26] Finance Act 1982, s.82.

[27] Finance Act 1980, s.79.

[28] *Ante*, p. 298.

[29] Finance Act 1975, Sched. 5, para. 3(1).

[30] The actual amount of the tax depends on the previous chargeable transfers of value which Elizabeth had made, or which she is treated as having made: F.A. 1975, s.37.

is no liability to capital transfer tax upon her, because usually[31] no tax is payable where a person disposes of a reversionary interest.[32]

---

[31] This rule does not apply where the person disposing of the reversionary interest acquired it for value, or was himself the settlor (F.A. 1975, s.24(3)(*a*); Finance Act 1976, s.120(1)).
[32] F.A. 1975, ss.20(3), 24(3).

CHAPTER 21

TRUSTEES' REMUNERATION AND BENEFITS

THE fundamental rule is that the office of trustee is gratuitous, that is, that the duties must be performed by the trustee without remuneration or profit. The development of this rule was due in part to the fact that trustees were often members of the family and persons of substance, who were prepared to act as trustees as part of the general obligations of kinship. In more recent years, however, it has come to be recognised that the management of money and assets is an activity which requires skill, aptitude, and often considerable technical support. Accordingly, it is now very common for trustees to be either professional advisers, such as solicitors and accountants, who do so as part of their ordinary professional practice; or banks and similar trust companies. Such trustees are generally prepared to act only if given adequate recompense.

I. MODERN COMMERCIAL REMUNERATION TERMS

Throughout this chapter, it will be helpful to keep in mind what a professional trustee or a commercial trust company may wish to obtain. The main items are:

1. Fees for acting as a trustee, including the administration of the trust.
2. Where the trust property includes shares in a company and the trustees act as directors of that company, fees for acting as a director of the company.
3. Commissions customarily paid by third parties in respect of business transacted on behalf of the trust. For example, where a person is appointed as an agent of an insurance company, it will usually pay to that agent commission in respect of business placed by him with that company. Likewise, stockbrokers pay commission to certain agents in respect of stock exchange business placed with them. Where a trustee carries on a professional practice or commercial business, he will wish to retain these commissions.
4. Profits made by the trustee from services performed for the trust as its customer. For example, if a bank acts as a trustee, but also acts as a banker to the trust, it will wish to retain for itself its ordinary commercial profit derived from acting as banker.

The remainder of this chapter considers the extent to which the trustee will achieve these objectives.

II. FEES: THE GENERAL RULE

The general rule has already been stated, namely that a trustee is not entitled to claim any salary or remuneration for carrying out the trusteeship.[1] This extends to the case where the trusteeship involves running a business belonging to the trust. In *Barrett* v. *Hartley*,[2] for example, a trustee had managed a business for six years, and had done so with such success that a large profit accrued to the beneficiaries. But when the trustee claimed remuneration he was unsuccessful, it being held that his efforts were merely part of the duties imposed upon him by accepting the trusteeship. It has even been held, in *Re Gates*,[3] that when a solicitor-trustee employs his firm to act as solicitors to the trust, if there is no charging clause in the trust instrument the firm is not entitled to charge for its services, and this was so despite the fact that the solicitor-trustee had agreed with his partner that he himself would receive no part of the fee. Where, however, there is a charging clause, the remuneration is not regarded for income tax purposes as mere bounty, with the result that the solicitor is entitled to treat it as earned income.[4]

In some cases the rule can operate inequitably, and sometimes even harshly. But it can also operate illogically. In Chapter 14 it was explained that even in the absence of any provision in the trust instrument, a trustee has wide powers under section 23 of the Trustee Act 1925 to appoint agents to do most of the work (although not to take the decisions) relating to the trust, and the trustee is entitled to pay the agent for so doing. The result is, therefore, that if there is no provision in the trust instrument for the payment of the trustee, the trustee can out of the trust funds pay an agent to do most of the work, but that if he does the work himself, as was presumably intended by the settlor, then he cannot be paid. The general rule that a trustee may not be paid for his services was firmly established in the eighteenth century, at which time an agent could only be employed in very limited circumstances. Having regard to the wide power that now exists of appointing agents, the rule may now require revision. Although a trustee cannot obtain remuneration, he is, of course, entitled to be reimbursed actual payments which he has properly made in connection with his trusteeship. This extends to the costs of taking or defending proceedings where he has acted reasonably in so doing. His right to reimbursement is contractual.[5]

III. FEES: EXCEPTIONS TO THE GENERAL RULE

There are the following exceptions[6] to the general rule:

---

[1] *Robinson* v. *Pett* (1734) 3 P. Wms. 249; *Re Thorpe* [1891] 2 Ch. 360; *Re Barker* (1886) 34 Ch.D. 77.

[2] (1866) L.R. 2 Eq. 789.

[3] [1933] Ch. 913; followed in *Re Hill* [1934] Ch. 623 and *Re French Protestant Hospital* [1951] Ch. 567. [4] *Dale* v. *I.R.C.* [1954] A.C. 11.

[5] *Re Spurling's Will Trusts* [1966] 1 W.L.R. 920.

[6] In *Tito* v. *Waddell* (*No. 2*) [1977] Ch. 106 (*ante*, p. 6) it may be thought that there was a clear conflict of interest, but the type of "trust" considered in that case is not dealt with in this book.

(1) **Power in trust instrument**

The creator of the trust can authorise the trustees to be paid for their services, and it is common for this to be done where a professional person is appointed a trustee. Provisions to this effect are, however, construed strictly, and against the trustee, so that a very wide clause is necessary if, for example, a solicitor-trustee is to be entitled to charge for work done by him in the administration of a trust which could have been done by someone not a solicitor.[7]

Accordingly, the usual form of charging clause is to the following effect:

> "Any trustee for the time being hereof being a solicitor accountant or other person engaged in any profession or business shall be entitled to charge and be paid all usual professional or other charges for business transacted time expended and acts done by him or any partner of his in connection with the trustes hereof including business and acts which a trustee not being engaged in a profession or business could have done personally."

Provided that the charging clause is wide enough, a trustee is entitled to engage a company which he controls to carry out work on behalf of the trust, and to pay that company for so doing. In *Re Orwell's Will Trusts*[8] George Orwell created a trust by his will, the will containing a clause authorising the trustee[9] to charge for services performed by him or his company.[10] Vinelott J. held that the company could be paid, and, further, that the trustee need not account for the remuneration which he himself received from the company.[11]

If there is a charging clause, the trustee cannot charge what he likes, but only what is reasonable. Where the trustee is a solicitor, the beneficiaries can insist on having his charges taxed, that is, assessed by an officer of the court. Whether or not the trustee is a solicitor, if the trustee takes from the trust fund an amount in excess of what the beneficiaries consider is reasonable, they may bring an action against the trustee for breach of trust.[12]

It is customary for commercial trust companies, as well as The Public Trustee, to make a charge on an *ad valorem* basis. As an illustration, the fees charged by the Public Trustee[13] for acting as the trustee of an ordinary trust are:

(a) *Acceptance fee*

On the first £50,000	$2\frac{3}{4}$ per cent.
On the excess over £50,000 up to £75,000	2 per cent.
On the excess over £75,000 up to £100,000	1 per cent.

---

[7] *Harbin* v. *Darby* (1860) 28 Beav. 325; *Re Chapple, Newton* v. *Chapple* (1884) 27 Ch.D. 584.   [8] [1982] 3 All E.R. 177.

[9] The case concerned the literary executor of the will, who, for the purposes of remuneration, was held to be in the same position as a trustee.

[10] The clause authorised the trustee to charge for work done by him "or his firm." Although, generally, the expression "firm" denotes an unincorporated partnership, the court held that in this clause it extended to a private company.

[11] *cf. Re Gee* [1948] 1 All E.R. 498; see *post*, p. 399.

[12] *Re Wells, Wells* v. *Wells* [1962] 1 W.L.R. 784.

[13] From April 1, 1983: Public Trustee (Fees) Order 1983.

On any excess over £100,000 $\frac{1}{2}$ per cent.
Minimum fee £550

(b) *Administration fee*
Due annually on April 1 on the net capital value of funds under administration.

On the first £25,000   2½ per cent.
On the excess over £25,000 up to £100,000   2 per cent.
On the excess over £100,000 up to £1m $1\frac{1}{2}$ per cent.
On any excess over £1m $\frac{1}{2}$ per cent.
Minimum fee £20

(c) *Activity fees*

(i) *Investment fee*
On the sale, purchase or repayment of any investment or land or on an advance on mortgage 0.65 per cent.
(ii) *Income collection fee*
On the gross income actually received by the Public Trustee 3½ per cent.
   (There is no fee on income paid direct from source to a beneficiary.)
(iii) *Additional work*
A reasonable additional fee may be charged according to work involved for various matters including:
(i) dealing with a business
(ii) dealing with assets outside the United Kingdom
(iii) dealing with freehold or leasehold property or a mortgage and for duties of an unusual, complex or exacting nature.

(d) *Withdrawal fee*
Three times the administration fee for the year previous to the withdrawal.

The position where the trustee has agreed a fixed level of remuneration and wishes to increase it is considered below.[14]

(2) **With authority of the court**
The second exception to the general rule is that under its inherent jurisdiction the court may:

(a) authorise a trustee to be remunerated where there is no charging clause[15];
(b) authorise a trustee to retain remuneration which he has already received[16]; and
(c) authorise a trustee to charge in excess of what the trustee agreed to receive when accepting appointment.[17]

---

[14] *Post*, p. 395.
[15] *Bainbridge* v. *Blair* (1845) 8 Beav. 558; *Re Freeman's Settlement Trusts* (1887) 37 Ch.D. 148; *Re Masters* [1953] 1 All E.R. 19; *Re Worthington (deceased)* [1954] 1 All E.R. 677.
[16] *Forster* v. *Ridley* (1864) 4 De G.J. & Sm. 452.
[17] *Re Duke of Norfolk's Settlement Trusts* [1981] 3 All E.R. 220, C.A.

In some of the older cases, the court was not averse to allowing the trustee reasonable remuneration. In the old case of *Brown* v. *Litton*,[18] for example, the captain of a merchant ship took with him on a voyage a sum of money to use in trade. During the voyage he died, and his mate, on assuming command of the vessel, took possession of the money and with it made considerable profits in trade. The mate was ordered to account for his profits, but Harcourt L.K. nevertheless held him entitled to a fair remuneration, which was to be fixed by the court, for his trouble.

More recently, the policy adopted by the court was that it would only authorise a trust to receive remuneration where his services were of exceptional benefit to the trust.[19] Such a case was *Boardman* v. *Phipps*.[20] Mr. Boardman was the solicitor to the trustees of a will, who held among other assets 8,000 out of an issued 30,000 shares in a private company. Mr. Boardman, thinking there was considerable scope for making a profit, considered with the trustees whether they should acquire the remaining shares in the company, but the trustees refused, partly because under the terms of the trust instrument they had no power to acquire additional shares in the company.[21] Mr. Boardman then, by using knowledge which he had gained as a solicitor to the trust, fought a takeover battle for control of the company. As Wilberforce J. observed at first instance, "it is interesting, and at times fascinating to watch, through the long correspondence that has been put in [evidence], the manner in which [Mr. Boardman] drives [the chairman of the company] from one prepared position to another until the fruit is ready to drop into his hand."[22] Eventually the fruit did indeed drop. Mr. Boardman acquired virtually all the shares in the company other than those held by the trust, some at a price of £3, and others at a price of £4.50. Having gained control of the company, he was able to dispose of some of the assets, and to reorganise the business, as a result of which the shares became worth over £8 each. He had therefore made a profit of over £75,000 on the shares which he had acquired, as well as substantially increasing the value of the shares held by the trust. The beneficiaries then claimed that profit. On the facts, it was held that Mr. Boardman would have been unable to have conducted negotiations without the knowledge gained as solicitor to the trust, and as such he became a constructive trustee and so was liable to account for his profit. The Court of Appeal and the House of Lords[23] considered, however, that Mr. Boardman was "a man of conspicuous ability, of great energy, clarity of mind and persistence . . . with a flair for negotiation," and although he was made to disgorge his profit, he was allowed by the court "generous remuneration." He was allowed remuneration because he had exceptional abilities in this

---

[18] (1711) 1 P.Wms. 140.

[19] See, *e.g. Protheroe* v. *Protheroe* [1968] 1 W.L.R. 519, where the trustee was only entitled to reimbursement of his actual expenses. See *post*, p. 402.

[20] [1967] 2 A.C. 46; see also *ante*, p. 277.

[21] The court said that application should have been made to the court for permission to purchase these shares. See *post*, p. 277.

[22] [1965] Ch. 922 at p. 1014.

[23] Upholding Wilberforce J.

respect, and had exercised them for the benefit of the trust. In other words, the average trustee, and even the average professional trustee, would not have been able to have achieved the results which Mr. Boardman achieved.

In *Re Duke of Norfolk's Settlement Trusts*[24] a trust company accepted the trusteeship of a discretionary trust on the basis that it would receive a low, fixed, annual fee. It became involved in an extensive re-development programme in the Strand and applied (a) for special remuneration in respect of the re-development, which was granted[25]; and (b) an increase in the ordinary standard of remuneration. The Court of Appeal held that it could authorise an increase in the agreed level of remuneration, but it would only do so if the experience and skill of the trustee made it in the interest of the beneficiaries to do so. The Court of Appeal also held that it was relevant to take into account remuneration charged by other trust companies, but it is not clear how much reliance is to be placed on that.

(3) Agreement with all beneficiaries

The third exception to the general rule is that if the beneficiaries are all *sui juris* and between them absolutely entitled to the whole of the beneficial interest under the trust, they can validly agree with the trustees that they shall be paid. Such agreements are construed strictly, in the same way as provisions for payment in the trust instrument.[26]

Where all the beneficiaries do not agree, or some are not *sui juris*, individual beneficiaries can agree with a trustee for his remuneration, but that agreement binds only the individual beneficiary, and not the trust property as such.

(4) Judicial trustees

A judicial trustee may always charge for his services.[27]

(5) Custodian trustees

A custodian trustee is entitled to charge fees equivalent to those which the Public Trustee could charge for acting as a custodian trustee.[28] However, this only enables the custodian trustee to charge for the services which he performs in that capacity. In *Forster* v. *Williams Deacon's Bank*[29] an attempt was made to use the device of custodian trusteeship to overcome the absence of a charging clause in the trust instrument. In that case Williams Deacon's Bank had been appointed both managing trustee and custodian trustee. It was appreciated that the bank could not charge *qua* managing trustee, but it was anticipated that it could derive its remuneration from its capacity as a custodian trustee. The Court

---

[24] [1981] 3 All E.R. 220, C.A.
[25] At first instance ([1978] 3 All E.R. 907), and not reversed by the Court of Appeal.
[26] It seems that the agreement has to be concluded with the beneficiaries before the trustee takes up his office: *Douglas* v. *Archbutt* (1858) 2 De G. & J. 148; *Re Sherwood* (1840) 3 Beav. 338. This appears to be contrary to principle.
[27] Judicial Trustees Act 1896, ss.1(5), 4(1).
[28] Public Trustee Act 1906, s.4.
[29] [1935] Ch. 359.

of Appeal rejected the device, however, holding that the deed merely constituted the bank the sole trustee so that the inability to charge remained. A similar attempt in a later case was held to be totally ineffective.[30]

Although when he has been validly appointed a custodian trustee may always charge for his services, he may only charge for his services in his capacity as custodian trustee. Thus in *Re Brooke Bond*[31] an insurance company was a custodian trustee under the trust deed securing the pension scheme of Brooke Bond & Co. Ltd. Under the terms of the trust deed the managing trustees were entitled to effect with any insurance company a policy assuring the payment of the pensions under the scheme. The managing trustees proposed to effect the policy with the custodian trustee. Cross J. held that the custodian trustee could not without the authority of the court contract with the managing trustee for its own benefit, but, application having been made to the court, the learned judge authorised the managing trustees to effect the policy with the custodian trustee on the basis that the latter need not account for its profit, on condition that the terms of the policy were approved by an independent actuary.

(6) **The Public Trustee**

The Public Trustee is always entitled to charge for his services.[32] Details of some of the fees which he currently charges have been given previously.[33]

(7) **Trust corporations**

As has been seen,[34] the court has a power to appoint a trustee, and will do so principally where one cannot be appointed without the assistance of the court. When the court does so, it has power to authorise the trustee to be paid, and where it appoints a trust corporation to be a trustee, it will almost invariably authorise that corporation to be paid. But in principle, as regards remuneration, a trust corporation is in exactly the same position as an individual trustee. While, in principle, it is not entitled to charge merely because it is a trust corporation,[35] it may well be that the court will approve the payment of fees according to the trust corporation's ordinary scale of fees, particularly where the beneficiaries do not object.[36]

Once a trustee has been appointed by the court, he generally has no further connection with the court, but the court may also, on the application of any person interested in the trust, appoint someone to be a judicial trustee. A judicial trustee, who is usually the Public Trustee, the Official Solicitor, or a trust corporation, becomes for the purpose an officer of the court, and as such he is able at any time to obtain the directions of the court without formality. Unless there has been mismanagement, the court will only in exceptional

---

[30] *Arning* v. *James* [1936] Ch. 158.

[31] [1963] Ch. 357.

[32] Public Trustee Act 1906, s.9. Administration of Justice Act 1965, s.2; Public Trustee (Fees) Act 1957.

[33] *Ante*, p. 392.

[34] *Ante*, p. 258.

[35] See also *Re Barbour's Settlement, ante.*

[36] *Re Codd* [1975] 2 All E.R. 1051.

circumstances appoint a judicial trustee where suitable private persons are willing to act as trustees.[37] A judicial trustee may always charge for his services.[38]

(8) The role in Cradock v. Piper

The rule known as the rule in *Cradock* v. *Piper*[39] is a curious exception to the principle that a solicitor-trustee, like any other trustee, may not charge for his services (in the absence of authorisation by the trust instrument or by the court). The effect of this rule is that where a solicitor-trustee acts as a solicitor for himself and his co-trustees in litigation relating to the trust, and the costs of acting for both of them do not exceed the expense which would have been incurred if he had been acting for the co-trustee alone, then he may be paid his usual costs.

The rule is firmly established[40] but it is quite illogical. If it is proper for a solicitor to be paid his usual fees for litigation, why is it not proper for him to be paid his usual fees for non-litigious work? In *Re Corsellis*[41] Cotton L.J. made a feeble attempt to justify the difference. "There may be this reason for it," he said, "that in an action, although costs are not always hostilely taxed, yet there may be a taxation where parties other than the trustee-solicitor may appear and test the propriety of the costs, and the court can disallow altogether the costs of any proceedings which may appear to be vexatious or improperly taken." There is, however, little merit in this explanation. In the first place, even where there is the usual charging clause, or remuneration for non-contentious business is authorised by the court, this will not authorise payment for acts which are not properly done. And again, where there is an express power for a solicitor-trustee to charge, a beneficiary can always insist that a solicitor-trustee's bill of costs be taxed,[42] and it has even been decided that where the beneficiaries are dissatisfied with a bill, it is the solicitor-trustee's duty to inform the beneficiaries of their right to have it taxed.[43] There remains, therefore, no logic in the distinction between court proceedings and other business for this purpose. But the rule is firm.

(9) Trust property abroad

Where the trust property is situated abroad, and the law of the country where the property is situated allows payment, the trustees appear to be entitled to retain their emoluments. In *Re Northcote*[44] English executors had to get in assets of the deceased in America. To do so they had to obtain a grant of probate in the State of New York, under the law of which they were entitled to a

---

[37] *Re Chisholm* (1898) 43 S.J. 43.
[38] Judicial Trustees Act 1896, s.1.
[39] (1850) 1 Mac. & G. 664.
[40] *Broughton* v. *Broughton* (1855) 5 De G.M. & G. 160; *Lincoln* v. *Windsor* (1851) 9 Hare 158; *Re Baker* (1886) 24 Ch.D. 77.
[41] (1887) 34 Ch.D. 675 at p. 682.
[42] *Re Fish* [1893] 2 Ch. 413.
[43] *Re Webb* [1894] 1 Ch. 73.
[44] [1949] 1 All E.R. 442.

commission on the value of the assets. They deducted this for themselves, and the English court held they need not account for it to the trust.

IV. DIRECTORS' FEES

The second type of remuneration which a trustee might seek to retain is fees paid to him as a director of a company in which the trust fund is invested. There are three questions:

1. Is the trustee-director in principle liable to account for his director's fees?
2. If so, are there any exceptions to the principle?
3. If he does account, how are the fees treated in the administration of trust?

(1) **Liability to account**

There are two preliminary points. First, in the case of private companies, the articles of association often endeavour to prevent the directors from acting contrary to the interests of shareholders by providing that any person who becomes a director must himself hold, or must within a short, specified time acquire, a number of shares in that company. In this way it is hoped that as the director will wish to advance the value of his own shares, he will also be acting in the interests of the other shareholders. Secondly, by section 117 of the Companies Act 1948[45] a company is not allowed to take notice of the fact that shares might be held upon trust, and as far as the company is concerned, it deals with trustees who are registered holders of shares in exactly the same way as shareholders who are beneficially entitled. It will therefore be apparent that directors can use shares which they hold as trustees as their share qualification: if they do so, will they be allowed to keep their directors' fees?

The first case was *Re Francis*.[46] Under the articles of association of a company, the holders of a certain number of shares were entitled to vote themselves directorships. Such shares were held by the trustees on behalf of the trust, and they procured their appointment as directors. Kekewich J., following the general principle that a trustee cannot profit from his trusteeship, held that they had to account to the trust for their fees. This case, however, was not even cited in *Dover Coalfield Extension Ltd.*,[47] which introduced new considerations. The Dover company held shares in the Consolidated Kent Collieries Corporation, with whom they did business. In order to protect the interests of the Dover company, a director of the Dover company was appointed a director of the Kent company. As a director, he had a contract with the Kent company which governed the services which he was to perform for the company, and it regulated his remuneration. The articles of association of the Kent company required directors to acquire 1,000 shares within one month from being appointed a director. So that he should be registered with the appropriate number of shares, the Dover company therefore transferred to the director this number of shares, which he held upon trust for the Dover company. It

---

[45] Replacing provisions of previous Acts.
[46] (1905) 74 L.J.Ch. 198.
[47] [1908] 1 Ch. 65.

was not disputed that he had to account to the Dover company for the dividends on those shares, and he did in fact to do so, but he claimed that he did not have to account for his directors' fees. The Court of Appeal held he could retain his directors' fees: although he could not have continued in office without the shares, he was appointed a director by an independent board of directors before he had acquired the shares, and his directorship did not therefore automatically flow from his trusteeship.

In *Re Macadam*,[48] following *Re Francis*,[49] trustees who by virtue of the trust shareholding were able to elect themselves directorships and in fact did so were held liable to account for their fees, but this was distinguished in *Re Gee*,[50] where Harman J. said that in some circumstances, even where a trustee is able through his voting rights to compel his appointment as a director, he is nevertheless entitled to retain his fees, if his appointment was in fact independent of his trust shareholding.

In his judgment in *Re Gee* Harman J. reviewed the previous cases. He concluded that the test was: Has the trustee used powers vested in him *qua* trustee to procure his appointment as a director? To be liable to account the trustee therefore

(a) must have powers *qua* trustee
(b) which he himself uses
(c) to procure his appointment as director.

If any of these elements is missing, he may retain his fees—as in *Re Dover Coalfield*—where he has his directorship first, and although he has powers *qua* trustee, he does not use those powers to procure his appointment as a director. Similarly, if he has a majority shareholding in a company beneficially, as well as a minority holding *qua* trustee, and votes himself a directorship, his directorship will be the result of his beneficial voting power, and not that *qua* trustee. Likewise, where others hold the majority shareholding, and the trustee has a minority shareholding, and he is appointed a director by the votes of the others, although he has powers *qua* trustee he does not use those powers to procure his appointment. The court will consider all the circumstances to see whether or not the appointment was truly independent of the voting powers held *qua* trustee.

In *Re Orwell's Will Trusts*,[51] the facts of which have already been given,[52] Vinelott J. distinguished *Re Gee*. He held that while the general rule is that a trustee must account for any benefit, such as remuneration, which a person obtains from a company as a result of his position as a trustee, this rule does not apply if the company was properly entitled to be paid from the trust fund, and there is no other nexus between the company with which the trustee is connected and the trust fund.

---

[48] [1946] Ch. 73.
[49] (1905) 74 L.J.Ch. 198.
[50] [1948] Ch. 284.
[51] [1982] 3 All E.R. 177.
[52] *Ante*, p. 392.

(2) **Exceptions**

Where a trustee-director is, in principle, not entitled to retain his director's fees, there are two circumstances in which, nevertheless, he may do so.

(a) *Power in trust instrument*

The settlor can include an effective power in the trust instrument authorising the retention of director's fees. This power may be express or implied. So, in *Re Llewellin*[53] where the testator had expressly provided that the trustees could use the trust shares to acquire directorships, it was held that he had also impliedly authorised them to retain their directors' fees.

(b) *With authority of the court*

The court can authorise a trustee-director to retain his director's fees. In deciding whether to exercise this power, it will consider the extent of the skill and effort which has been applied. The general rule is that a trustee is expected to exercise in the discharge of his trusteeship the effort and skill which a prudent man of business would in general undertake in the management of his own investments. A trustee-director is expected to exercise the same standard when acting as a director. So, in *Re Keeler's Settlement Trusts*[54] the court directed that an inquiry should be held as to the extent to which trustee-directors had exerted effort and skill above that standard, and held that they could retain their directors' fees, but to that extent only.

(3) **Application of fees**

Where a trustee-director is obliged to account for his director's fees, and does so, it seems that, notwithstanding the revenue character of those sums so far as the company is concerned, in the administration of the trust they are to be treated as an addition to the settled property, and added to capital.[55]

V. COMMISSIONS

The third category of payment which a trustee might seek to retain is commissions paid by third parties.

(1) **The general rule**

The general rule is that the trustee is accountable for commissions which he receives in respect of trust business.

The test is not whether the trust has suffered a loss, but whether the trustee has made a profit. Thus, in *Williams* v. *Barton*[56] the trustee was a stockbrokers' clerk who was paid commission earned on business introduced by him to his firm. He arranged for his firm to value the trust assets, and was duly paid his commission. It was held that he had to account for that commission. There was no suggestion that the valuation of the trust assets was improper or unnecessary,

---

[53] [1949] Ch. 225.
[54] [1981] 3 All E.R. 888.
[55] *Re Francis* (1905) 74 L.J. Ch. 198.
[56] [1927] 2 Ch. 9.

but nevertheless the trustee was not entitled to make a profit from it. The trustee might have been tempted to have the assets valued more frequently than was in fact necessary.

(2) Exceptions

The trust instrument can, and often does, empower trustees to retain commissions. The court, no doubt, also has power to authorise this, but there appears to be no reported case in which it has exercised this power.

Furthermore, the rule does not apply where the recipient of the commission is discharging a duty imposed by statute, and in so doing does not act harshly or oppresively. So in *Swain* v. *The Law Society*[57] the House of Lords held that the Law Society was entitled to retain the equivalent of commission paid in respect of the compulsory insurance against negligence which solicitors are obliged to maintain.[58] The Law Society was required to apply that commission for the benefit of the profession as a whole.

VI. COMMERCIAL PROFITS

The last category of benefit which, in ordinary circumstances, a trustee might seek to keep is profits derived by him in carrying on a business, where the trust is a customer of that business.

(1) The general rule

As in the case of commissions, it seems that the trustee is liable to account for the profit.[59]

(2) Exceptions

The trust instrument can empower trustees to retain their profit. So, in *Re Sykes*[60] two brothers who were wine merchants were appointed the trustees of a will under which one of the assets of the trust was a public house. Under the terms of the will, they were authorised to supply wine to the public house, and they were held entitled to their usual profit for doing so.

The court also has power to authorise trustees to retain a commercial profit.

VII. OTHER FINANCIAL BENEFITS

Finally, it should be noted that there is a general rule that a trustee is not to be entitled to profit in any way from his trusteeship unless he is authorised to do so by the trust instrument or by the court. An extreme, if unusual, example is *Sugden* v. *Crossland*[61] where a person was anxious to become a trustee of a will. He therefore paid the existing trustee £75 to retire and appoint him in his place. It was held that the retirement and appointment was ineffective, and also that the £75 belonged to the trust.

---

[57] [1982] 2 All E.R. 827, H.L. see *ante*, p. 10.
[58] The Solicitors Act 1974, s.37.
[59] *Re Sykes* [1909] 2 Ch. 241.
[60] [1909] 2 Ch. 241.
[61] (1856) 3 Sm. & G. 192.

place. It was held that the retirement and appointment were ineffective, and also that the £75 belonged to the trust.

A further example is *Webb* v. *Earl of Shaftesbury*,[62] where Lord Eldon held that trustees were not entitled to exercise sporting rights over land held by them as trustees. He held that either the rights should be let, for the benefit of the beneficiaries, or if they could not be let, should be held for the heirs of the settlor on a resulting trust. The trustees could not themselves derive any benefit.

In view of the foregoing, it need hardly be said that, quite apart from the rules relating to investments,[63] a trustee might not use trust moneys in his own trade or business. If he does so, he will be liable to account for the profit he makes, or, at the beneficiaries' option, compound interest.[64]

The rule applies not only to profits which are made at the expense of the trust, but also to profits which are made without any loss to the trust at all, but which are derived by virtue of the trusteeship. In *Protheroe* v. *Protheroe*[65] a husband and wife purchased a leasehold property, and although they owned the property in equity in equal shares, the property was in the husband's name alone. The wife took proceedings for divorce but the husband was able after protracted negotiations to purchase the freehold reversion in the property. If the leasehold interest were sold separately it would have had a value of £2,450, but if the unencumbered freehold were sold it would have a value of £3,950. Lord Denning M.R. held that as the lease was held by the husband, he had a special advantage in purchasing the freehold, and he could exercise that advantage only for the benefit of himself and his wife as trustees under the trust. He was, however, allowed reimbursement of the cost of the freehold.

The general rule applies automatically where the trustee derives a profit from a matter which is directly related to the trust.

Where the profit is indirect, in some circumstances the court will inquire whether there was in fact any conflict between duty as a trustee and personal interest. This may be relevant where trust money is lent on mortgage, and the borrower pays the lender's legal costs in connection with the mortgage. If, therefore, a solicitor is a trustee, and the trustees lend money on mortgage to one of the solicitor's clients, the client will be responsible for the costs of the mortgage.

It was held in *Whitney* v. *Smith*[66] that in such circumstances the solicitor could keep the fee paid by the borrower.

---

[62] (1802) 7 Ves. 480.
[63] *Ante*, pp. 301 *et seq.*
[64] *Post*, pp. 451 *et seq.*
[65] [1968] 1 W.L.R. 519.
[66] (1869) 4 Ch.App. 513.

CHAPTER 22

AVOIDING A CONFLICT OF INTEREST

I. GENERALLY

IT is a rule which goes to the foundation of English trust law that unless the trustee is authorised to do so by the trust instrument or by the court, he must not place himself in a position where his duty as a trustee might conflict with his personal interest.[1] This is because in accepting office as a trustee he has undertaken to do the best he can for the beneficiaries, and if there were a conflict of interest he might be tempted not to do so. As corollaries of this rule, it is clearly established as general principles that, as was shown in the previous chapter, a trustee may not receive any payment for his services; he may not purchase property belonging to the trust; and he may not derive any indirect benefit from his trusteeship. There are certain exceptions to these principles, which are mentioned in the text, but otherwise the rules are absolute. In particular, it is not a question of whether the trustee has been unfair, for the court will usually not inquire into the fairness of the transaction, but whether he has contravened the rule at all. Thus take the case of the purchase by a trustee of property belonging to a trust. In the event of a trustee purchasing trust property, even if he pays a full market value, and even if that full market value is ascertained by an independent valuer, the transaction can still be upset by the beneficiaries.[2]

There are more specific reasons why the rule should be as it is. In the case of a purchase or other dealing with the trust property, if the trustee were allowed to make a profit, he might be tempted to take advantage of peculiar knowledge of the trust property which he had gained as a trustee. Suppose, for instance, that a piece of land belongs to a trust, and that a trustee discovers that there is a valuable deposit of natural gas beneath it. There would be the danger that the trustee would conceal that fact, purport to purchase the land at what appeared to be a fair market value, and afterwards make his profit by selling the gas rights.[3] It is not that the court assumes that all trustees are crooks, but rather the impossibility in many cases of the court ascertaining whether an unfair advantage has been taken. Thus, in the illustration just given, if the trustee denied that he knew of the gas deposits, it might well be impossible to prove him wrong.

Apart from questions of remuneration, the issues generally arise:

(a) in the execution of the trust;

---

[1] See Marshall (1955) 8 C.L.P. 91.
[2] *Wright* v. *Morgan* [1926] A.C. 788.
[3] See *Ex p. Lacey* (1802) 6 Ves. 625.

(b) in dealings with the trust property; and

(c) in competing with the trust.

II. The Execution of the Trust

If a trustee takes a step in the execution of the trust which in other circumstances would be proper, but which is in fact taken with a view to his deriving some benefit, that step is a breach of trust. So, in *Molyneux* v. *Fletcher*,[4] where the advancement was made with the stipulation that the beneficiary should use it to repay a debt to the trustee, it was held that the advancement was a breach of trust, there being a conflict of interest between the trustee's interest and duty. Likewise, the trustee of a discretionary trust cannot in principle, accept repayment of a debt due to him by a beneficiary if the repayment comes from discretionary payments made to him by the trust.[5]

However, if there is no bargain between the trustee and the beneficiary, so that the beneficiary is free not only legally but morally to deal with the money as he wishes, it seems that there is no obligation to the trustee receiving sums by way of gift, or by way of loan repayment, from the beneficiary. More particularly is this so if the trustee was not the sole trustee. In *Butler* v. *Butler*[6] trustees made a mortgage advance on proper security.[7] The borrower was free to use the proceeds of that advance as he wished, but used part of it to discharge a debt owing to one of the trustees. It was held that the creditor-trustee could properly accept repayment.

III. Purchases of Trust Property

To prevent the possibility of fraud and abuse,[8] equity has evolved the rule that a trustee must not purchase trust property.[9] The only exceptions are if he is authorised to do so by the trust instrument or by the court; if all the beneficiaries being *sui juris* and between them absolutely entitled to the whole of the beneficial interest in the property, and being given full information as to the transaction, consent to it; or, in exceptional cases, if there was in fact no conflict between a trustee's interest and duty and the beneficiary did not look to the trustee to protect his interest. It is emphasised that the honesty of the trustees is irrelevant, and that where the foregoing conditions are not satisfied the trustees must not purchase trust property even at full market value.[10]

In *Wright* v. *Morgan*[11] a trustee acquired an option to purchase land held on the trusts of a will, although he was not himself authorised by the will to purchase the land. The option was to purchase at a market value to be fixed by

---

[4] [1898] 1 Q.B. 648.

[5] *Peyton* v. *Robinson* (1823) 1 L.J. (o.s.) Ch. 191   [6] (1877) 7 Ch.D. 116.

[7] As to the requirements for proper security, see p. 319, *ante*.

[8] *Per* Sir W. Grant, *Lister* v. *Lister* (1802) 6 Ves. 631.

[9] *Ex p. Lacey* (1820) 6 Ves. 625; *Whelpdale* v. *Cookson* (1747) 1 Ves.Sen. 9; *Fox* v. *Mackreth* (1788) 2 Bro.C.C. 400; *Aberdeen Ry.* v. *Blaikie Brothers* (1854) 1 Macq. 461 (H.L.).

[10] *Tito* v. *Waddell* (*No. 2*) [1977] 3 All E.R. 129, at p. 241.

[11] [1926] A.C. 788.

an independent valuation. This was done, but nevertheless the court set the sale aside. The fact that the price was to be fixed independently was not sufficient, for the trustees could themselves fix the *time* at which the property was to be sold, and this could clearly have a substantial effect on the price ultimately received. Similarly, it has been held in an old case[12] that a trustee must not purchase trust property which is put up for auction, as he is in a position to discourage bidders.

In principle, there seems no reason why a trustee should not purchase trust property if all the beneficiaries, being *sui juris* and between them absolutely entitled to the whole of the beneficial interest in the property, agree. It will be seen in due course that the remedy where there is an improper sale is the equitable one of applying to have the disposition set aside. Just as the court will not upset it where the beneficiaries are regarded through laches as having acquiesced, so the court will not do so where the beneficiaries have genuinely agreed to the sale. For such agreement to be effective, the trustees would have to disclose to the beneficiaries *all* the information which they have about the property. Nevertheless, although it is theoretically possible for an unimpeachable sale to take place in this way, there are two serious objections to it. First, the onus will lie on the trustee-purchaser to show that the beneficiaries were given full information, and that they all freely gave their consent. Secondly, the property may be virtually unmarketable. The liability to have a sale set aside effects subsequent purchasers with notice, so that in most cases it is almost impossible to sell land where the title shows that the vendor formerly held land as a trustee. Even if there is an agreement placed with the deeds that the beneficiaries have consented, a subsequent purchaser cannot be sure that the trustee gave to the beneficiaries all the information in his possession before they entered into the agreement. Only in highly exceptional circumstances, therefore, would a subsequent purchaser complete his purchase.

Where a trustee does purchase trust property, the transaction is not void, but voidable only, at the instance of a beneficiary. Only in most extraordinary circumstances will the court refuse to set aside a purchase, provided the trustee cannot successfully raise against the beneficiary a defence of delay, or laches. An example of a case where the court refused to upset a transaction is *Holder* v. *Holder*.[13] In that case a testator appointed his widow, a daughter, and a son. Victor, to be his executors and trustees. Victor at first took a few minor steps in connection with the administration of the estate, but then took no further part. One of the assets consisted of a farm of which Victor had a tenancy. The farm was offered for sale at an auction subject to Victor's tenancy, and Victor purchased it. Another son sought to set the transaction aside, but the Court of Appeal refused to do so, on the ground that there were the following special circumstances present in the case: Victor had played no real part in the administration of the estate; there was in fact no conflict of interest and duty,

---

[12] *Whelpdale* v. *Cookson* (1747) 1 Ves.Sen. 9.
[13] [1968] Ch. 353.

because the beneficiaries knew that Victor would bid for the property; and they did not look to him to protect their interests. Victor took no part in instructing the auctioneer or in arranging the sale, and he had no special knowledge of the property as a trustee. It is, however, only where there are extraordinary facts that the court will refuse to set aside the sale.

In some cases—*e.g.* where some of the beneficiaries are not *sui juris,* or are unborn or unascertained—it is necessary and, for the reasons just given, in almost all other cases highly prudent, to seek the approval of the court to the transaction. The court requires to be satisfied that the sale is in the interests of all the beneficiaries before it will grant its approval, and the evidence on this point must be very clear.[14]

Where the trustee was granted an option to purchase *before* he became a trustee, he may exercise that option after he becomes a trustee.[15]

(1) Circuitous devices

The rule has been strong enough to prevent evasion by various methods.[16] In the first place, although a sale to a relative is not necessarily bad,[17] a purchase taken in the name of the trustee's children will usually be upset[18] and it is very risky to take a purchase in the name of the trustee's wife.[19]

Nor can the rule be overcome by selling to a limited company of which the trustee is the majority shareholder[20] or, according to an American case, of which he has control.[21] It seems that a sale by a trustee to a company of which he is a member, but which he does not control, is not *ipso facto* voidable, but if the beneficiaries seek to upset it, the company may have to show that the trustee had taken all reasonable steps to find a purchaser, and that the price paid by the company was at the time adequate.[22]

It is equally offensive to the rule to sell the property to a third person, with an agreement or understanding for its repurchase.[23] However, in *Re Postlethwaite*[24] it was held that where there was no agreement or understanding for repurchase at the time of the sale to the third person, the fact that the trustee had sold the property to that person with the *hope* of being able to repurchase was not a sufficient ground for setting the sale aside.

Finally, a sale may be upset if a trustee retires with the intention that the property will be conveyed to him after his retirement. If, however, a sufficient length of time has elapsed between the retirement and the sale for the court to

---

[14] *Farmer* v. *Dean* (1863) 32 Beav. 327; *Campbell* v. *Walker* (1800) 5 Ves. 678.

[15] *Vyse* v. *Foster* (1874) L.R. 7 H.L. 318.

[16] *Whitcomb* v. *Minchin* (1820) 5 Madd. 91; *Re Bloye's Trust* (1849) 1 Mac. & G. 488.

[17] *Coles* v. *Trecothick* (1804) 9 Ves. 234.

[18] *Gregory* v. *Gregory* (1821) Jac. 631.

[19] *Ferraby* v. *Hobson* (1847) 2 Ph. 255; *Burrell* v. *Burrell's Trustees,* 1915 S.C. 333.

[20] *Silkstone and Haigh Moor Coal Co.* v. *Edey* [1900] 1 Ch. 167.

[21] *Eberhardt* v. *Christina Window Glass Co.* (1911) 9 Del.Ch. 284. It would be in line with thinking here to apply this principle in England.

[22] *Farrar* v. *Farrars Ltd.* (1888) 40 Ch.D. 395.

[23] *Williams* v. *Scott* [1900] A.C. 499.

[24] (1888) 37 W.R. 200; 60 L.T. 514.

be satisfied that the ex-trustee has not taken any advantage of knowledge about the property gained while he was a trustee, the sale will be upheld. Such a transaction was upheld in *Re Boles and the British Land Company's Contract,*[25] where there was an interval of 12 years between retirement and purchase.

(2) The beneficiaries' remedies

Where there has been an improper sale, it is voidable, not void. The legal title will therefore pass to a purchaser, and the transaction cannot be upset against a bona fide purchaser without notice that the vendor-trustee in fact sold to himself. With this qualification, the beneficiaries can apply to have the disposition set aside against whosoever has the legal estate. It will be recalled that the beneficiaries do not have to show they have suffered any loss. Where the beneficiaries require the land to be reconveyed to them, they can also require payment into the trust fund of all rent received from the land.[26] Alternatively, if the trustee has resold at a profit, the beneficiaries can claim that profit.[27] If the trustee sold to a purchaser without notice at less than the true value, the beneficiaries can require the trustees to account for the difference between the price paid and the true value with interest.[28]

As this is an equitable remedy, the beneficiaries will not be successful if they delay unreasonably before taking proceedings once they are aware of the circumstances. Further, if from their conduct the beneficiaries are taken to have acquiesced in the transaction, they cannot thereafter seek to have the sale set aside.

(3) Purchase of a beneficiary's interest

Slightly different rules apply where there is a purchase by a trustee not of the trust property but of a beneficiary's interest in the trust property. The rule here is that such a transaction is entirely valid if the trustee has given adequate consideration for it[29] *and* has given to the beneficiary all the information which he knows about that interest. Provided this is done, so that the beneficiary is able to exercise an independent judgment and the parties are at arm's length, there is no need for the relationship of trustee and beneficiary to be terminated.[30]

IV. COMPETITION

Where the trust property includes a business, or the trustees carry on any income earning activity, a trustee must not commence a business or activity on his own account which will compete with that of the trust. Thus, in *Re*

---

[25] [1902] 1 Ch. 244.
[26] *Silkstone and Haigh Moor Coal Co. v. Edey* [1900] 1 Ch. 167.
[27] *Baker v. Carter* (1835) 1 Y. & Coll.Ex. 250.
[28] *Lord Hardwicke v. Vernon* (1800) 4 Ves. 411.
[29] *Ex p. Lacey* (1802) 6 Ves. 625; *Coles v. Trecothick* (1804) 9 Ves. 234; *Luff v. Lord* (1864) 34. Beav. 220.
[30] *Randall v. Errington* (1805) 10 Ves. 423; 8 R.R. 18.

Thomson[31] one of the assets of a trust was a yachtbroker's business, which was being carried on by the trustees. One of them sought to set up on his own a similar business in the same town, which would have competed with the trust business, but the court granted an injunction restraining him from doing so.

The decision in *Re Thomson* appears to be at variance with that in the earlier Irish case of *Moore* v. *M'Glynn*.[32] There the court had refused an injunction, though it thought that the setting up of a competing business would be a good ground for removing the trustee from his trusteeship. It was said that a breach of trust would only be committed if in carrying on the new business the trustee practised deception, or solicited the customers from the old shop. It is sometimes suggested that this decision can be reconciled with that in *Re Thomson* on the basis that the yachtbroker's business was so specialised that any other yachtbroking business in the town was bound to compete with the trust business, even if the customers were not solicited. This is a possible solution, but it does not appear to have been the basis of the decision in *Re Thomson*. *Re Thomson* seems clearly right in principle, and it may well be that *Moore* v. *M'Glynn* would not now be followed. As has been shown, in other circumstances the court has been so astute to find a conflict of interest that it is doubtful if it would stop itself from finding a conflict where the same business was being carried on, at least if it were serving the same locality.

Where, however, a person who is carrying on a business is then appointed to be a trustee, the position seems to depend on whether the person making the appointment knew of that business. If he did, the trustee will be entitled to continue his business, but if it then appears that there is an actual conflict of interest, he may be required to resign, or be removed.[33]

---

[31] [1930] 1 Ch. 203.

[32] [1894] 1 Ir.R. 74.

[33] See, by analogy, *Peyton* v. *Robinson* (1823) 1 L.J. (o.s.) Ch. 191; *Moore* v. *M'Glynn* [1894] 1 Ir.R. 74.

CHAPTER 23

VARIATION OF TRUSTS

If the beneficiaries are *sui juris* and absolutely entitled they can, if they think fit, terminate the trust and if they so choose, set up new trusts in respect of the trust property.[1] But if the beneficiaries are not thus qualified it is necessary that an application be made to the court for a variation of the trusts. It is important to make a distinction for this purpose between two classes of variation by the court: (i) variation concerned with the *management or administration* of the trusts, and (ii) variation of the *beneficial interests* arising under the trusts.

I. MANAGEMENT AND ADMINISTRATION

(1) The inherent jurisdiction of the court

The court has always had an inherent jurisdiction to sanction a departure from the terms of a trust, but it is now clearly established that this applies only to the management or administration of the trust. It does not apply to any rearrangement of the rights of the beneficiaries to the beneficial interests themselves,[2] with the exception only of cases of "maintenance"[3] and "compromise,"[4] assuming that the latter amounts to a variation in the true sense of the word.[5] The jurisdiction, although still somewhat nebulous, was defined by Romer L.J. in *Re New*[6] to cover an "emergency" which has arisen in the administration of the trust, *i.e.* something for which no provision is made in the trust and which could not have been foreseen or anticipated by the author of the trust. The inherent jurisdiction is, therefore, of distinctly limited scope. In *Re New* itself the trustees of shares in a company were authorised by the court as a matter of emergency to concur in a scheme under which shares were exchanged for more realisable shares in a new company. The sanction of the court was required because the trustees had no power of investment in the new shares under the terms

---

[1] See *ante*, p. 387.
[2] *Chapman* v. *Chapman* [1954] A.C. 429 at pp. 454, 455.
[3] See *post*, p. 412.
[4] See *post*, p. 412.
[5] This is perhaps doubtful because it seems that the court's sanction to a compromise of disputed rights (which is what "compromise" in this context means) does not result in a variation of the beneficial trusts but only brings to an end any dispute about them. See *post*, p. 412. for further discussion of "compromise" in this sense.
[6] [1910] 2 Ch. 534.

of the trust instrument. This was in the circumstances a transaction in the nature of "salvage" of the trust property.[7]

(2) Trustee Act 1925, s. 57

The inherent jurisdiction has been largely superseded by section 57 of the Trustee Act 1925. This is based on a concept wider than that of emergency. The basis of the section is *expediency*. It provides in effect that the court may empower trustees (but not Settled Land Act trustees[8]) in the management or administration of the trust property to perform any act which is not authorised by the trust instrument if in the opinion of the court it is expedient. The ambit of the section was considered by the Court of Appeal in *Re Downshire's Settled Estates, Re Chapman's Settlement Trusts* and *Re Blackwell's Settlement Trusts*.[9] According to Lord Evershed and Romer L.J. in their joint judgment, "The object of section 57 was to secure that trust property should be managed as advantageously as possible in the interests of the beneficiaries, and, with that object in view, to authorise specific dealings with the property which the court might have felt itself unable to sanction under the inherent jurisdiction, either because there was no actual 'emergency' or because of inability to show that the position which called for intervention was one which the creator of the trust could not reasonably have foreseen; but it was no part of the legislative aim to disturb the rule that the court will not rewrite a trust."[10] Moreover, the court must be satisfied that the proposed transaction is for the benefit of the whole trust and not simply for a beneficiary.[11]

The section does not, therefore, confer on the court any general jurisdiction to vary beneficial interests. It is limited to the managerial supervision and control of trust property by the trustees and cannot be stretched further than that.

However, subject to this decisive limitation, it is an overriding provision to be read into every trust.[12] And it has been used for various purposes, for example, to authorise the partitioning of land where the necessary consent could not be obtained,[13] the sale of a reversionary interest which the trustees had no power to sell until it fell into possession,[14] or to blend two charitable funds into one.[15] Indeed the section has also been used to extend trustees' investment powers[16]

---

[7] The principle was applied in *Re Tollemache* [1903] 1 Ch. 955.

[8] T.A. 1925, s.57(4).

[9] [1953] Ch. 218; Denning L.J. dissented. On appeal to the House of Lords in *Re Chapman's Settlement Trusts*: affirmed *sub nom. Chapman* v. *Chapman* [1954] A.C. 429, it was conceded s. 57 did not apply. In the House of Lords, the statement of law in the C.A. regarding s. 57 was neither approved nor disapproved and, therefore, is still good law.

[10] *Ibid.* at p. 248.

[11] *Re Craven's Estate (No.2)* [1937] Ch. 431.

[12] *Re Mair* [1935] Ch. 562.

[13] *Re Thomas* [1930] 1 Ch. 194.

[14] *Re Cockerell's Settlement Trusts* [1956] Ch. 372; *cf. Re Heyworth's Contingent Reversionary Interest* [1956] Ch. 364.

[15] *Re Shipwrecked Fishermen and Mariners' Benevolent Fund* [1959] Ch. 220.

[16] *Re Brassey's Settlement* [1955] 1 W.L.R. 192; *Re Shipwrecked Fishermen and Mariners' Benevolent Fund, supra;* not following *Re Royal Society's Charitable Trusts* [1956] Ch. 87.

but an application for this purpose should now preferably be made under the Variation of Trusts Act 1958.[17]

II. VARIATION OF BENEFICIAL INTERESTS

It has been seen that the foregoing relates only to variations in pursuance of the management and administration of the trust. We are now concerned with the more drastic rewriting of a trust which is involved in the variation of the beneficial interests themselves. The cases in which the class of variation is permissible will now be considered.

(1) Settled Land Act 1925, s.64

This provides that the court may sanction any transaction *affecting or concerning the settled land or any part thereof or any other land* (not being a transaction otherwise authorised by the Act or by the settlement) which in the opinion of the court would be *for the benefit* of the settled land, or any part thereof, or the persons interested under the settlement.[18] Furthermore, the word "transaction" is widely defined to include (*inter alia*) a "compromise or other dealing or other arrangement."[19] And it is now clear that the section—as was held by the majority of the Court of Appeal in *Re Downshire*[20]—confers an ampler jurisdiction than that conferred by section 57 of the Trustee Act 1925.[21] Indeed it enables the beneficial interests under the settlement to be remoulded, and is not restricted to steps of an administrative character.

The section is applied not only to settled land but also to land held on trust for sale. In *Re Simmons*[22] Danckwerts J. reached this conclusion on the ground that section 28 of the Law of Property Act 1925 gave to trustees for sale the powers conferred by the Settled Land Act 1925, and these included in the power conferred by section 64.

(2) Matrimonial Causes Act 1973, s.24

Under this Act, replacing earlier legislation of longstanding, the Family Division of the High Court has a wide jurisdiction, after pronouncing a decree of divorce or nullity of marriage, to vary the trusts contained in any ante-nuptial or post-nuptial settlement which has been made for the benefit of the parties to the marriage or the children of that marriage.[23] It is clearly established that the jurisdiction extends to a rearrangement of beneficial interests: and the fact that a saving of capital transfer tax or other taxes will result will have no bearing on the exercise of this jurisdiction.[24]

---

[17] See *post*, p. 413, and see *Re Coates' Will Trusts* [1959] 2 All E.R. 51 at p. 54; *Re Byng's Will Trusts* [1959] 2 All E.R. 54 at p. 57.

[18] s. 64(1) (our italics). The powers have been extended by the Settled Land and Trustee Acts (Court's General Powers) Act 1943, s.1, as amended by the Emergency Laws (Miscellaneous Provisions) Act 1953, s.9.

[19] s. 64(2).

[20] [1953] Ch. 218.

[21] *Ante*, p. 277.

[22] [1956] Ch. 125.

[23] Matrimonial Causes Act 1973, s. 24.

[24] See *Thomson* v. *Thomson and Whitmee* [1956] P. 384.

(3) Maintenance

The position here is and has long been that where a testator or settlor has made his disposition in such a way—and this will especially occur in trusts for accumulation—that the immediate beneficiaries have no fund for their present maintenance the court will assume that the intention to provide sensibly for the family is so paramount that it will order maintenance in disregard of the trusts.[25] An order for maintenance will obviously result in a variation of the beneficial interests. Moreover, the jurisdiction is not restricted to cases of "emergency,"[26] nor is it dependent on the beneficiaries being infants.[27]

(4) Compromise

It was the decision of the House of Lords in *Chapman* v. *Chapman*[28] on the question of compromise which led directly to the passing of the Variation of Trusts Act 1958.[29] It has long been clearly established that the court may sanction a "compromise" on behalf of an infant or unborn person where proposed by persons beneficially interested in the trusts who are *sui juris* and protect the trustees accordingly. This is, like the power to award maintenance,[30] part of the inherent jurisdiction of the court, and also enables, where it applies, beneficial interests to be varied. But the important question is, what is meant by a "compromise"?

The Court of Appeal in *Re Downshire Settled Estates, Re Chapman's Settlement Trusts* and *Re Blackwell's Settlement Trusts,*[31] in the majority opinion of Evershed M.R. and Romer L.J., held that the word "compromise" should not be construed narrowly so as to be confined to a compromise of *disputed* rights, but covered any arrangement between tenant for life and remainderman. In *Re Downshire* and *Re Blackwell* the court held that the arrangement proposed was in the nature of a compromise in the wider sense of the word, and sanctioned it accordingly. But in *Re Chapman* they refused to do so because there was no compromise even in this extended sense: the court was merely being asked to destroy trusts which had been expressly declared. In *Re Chapman* Denning L.J. dissented on the broad principle that the court had the power to deal with the property and interests of infants or other persons under disability in a manner not authorised by the trust whenever the court was satisfied that what was proposed was most advantageous for them, provided that everyone of full age agreed to it. The learned Lord Justice was prepared to give a very wide meaning indeed to the inherent jurisdiction of the Court.

The majority of the Court of Appeal in *Re Chapman* had shown the jurisdic-

---

[25] *Re Downshire Settled Estates* [1953] Ch. 218 at p. 238, *per* Evershed M.R. and Romer L.J., considered in *Chapman* v. *Chapman* [1954] A.C. 429 at pp. 445, 455–457, 469, 471; see *ante*, p. 411. See also *Re Collins* (1886) 32 Ch.D. 229 at p. 232; *Havelock* v. *Havelock* (1881) 17 Ch.D. 807.

[26] See *ante*, p. 409, and see *Hayley* v. *Bannister* (1820) 4 Madd. 275.

[27] *Revel* v. *Watkinson* (1748) 1 Ves.Sen. 93.

[28] [1954] A.C. 429.

[29] *Post*, p. 413.

[30] *Supra.*

[31] *Supra.*

tion to be limited in some degree by holding that the word "compromise," however widely construed, would not cover every kind of arrangement. But it was the House of Lords in *Chapman* v. *Chapman*,[32] in affirming the decision of the Court of Appeal, which re-examined the meaning of the term for this purpose. Lords Simonds, Morton and Asquith were in no doubt that the power of the court to sanction a compromise in a suit to which a person was not a party, such as an infant or unborn person, did not extend to cases where there was no real dispute between the parties. Lord Cohen alone was prepared to hold that the jurisdiction of the court extended to compromise in the wide sense between tenant for life on the one hand and remainderman on the other. This decision establishes clearly that a compromise means a compromise of a disputed right and this is as far as the inherent jurisdiction of the court goes.[33]

Consequences of Chapman v. *Chapman*

It appeared from this decision that in *Re Downshire* and *Re Blackwell* the Court of Appeal had gone too far in giving the word "compromise" an unnatural meaning. But quite apart from this there had been a number of schemes approved in the Chancery Division shortly before the decision of the House of Lords, on the basis of what may perhaps be called the "quasi-compromise" principle which then held the field, and the orders there made had accordingly been made without jurisdiction.[34] Moreover, it now became fashionable to scrutinise settlements with a view to finding a provision of sufficient ambiguity or uncertainty in its effect on the beneficial interests to form a peg on which to hang a compromise of a "genuine" dispute.

This bizarre situation could not long continue, and the Law Reform Committee was invited in 1957 to consider the position. They reached the conclusion that the result produced by *Chapman* v. *Chapman* was most unsatisfactory. It was pointed out that on a decree of divorce or nullity the Divorce Court had the power to sanction variations in the marriage settlement even if these were designed to produce a saving in estate duty or tax. And the Committee asked: Why should an infant whose parents are happily married be in a worse position than an infant whose parents are divorced? The recommendations of the Committee were given legislative effect in the Variation of Trusts Act 1958.

(5) **Variation of Trusts Act 1958**[35]

The reason behind the anxiety to invoke the jurisdiction of the court to vary beneficial interests on the basis of a "compromise" was to minimise tax or estate duty liabilities which would be attracted with full force if the trust remained

---

[32] *Supra.*
[33] Not a compromise of a simulated dispute; *Re Powell-Cotton's Resettlement* [1956] 1 W.L.R. 23.
[34] See, *e.g. Re Leeds (Duke) and Re the Coal Acts* 1938 *to* 1943 [1947] Ch. 525. *Re Downshire Settled Estates, supra,* and *Blackwell's Settlement Trusts, supra,* may also be taken to be overruled on this point, but the decisions may still stand on the application of S.L.A. 1925, s.64; see *ante,* p. 411.
[35] For a detailed discussion of the relevant case law, see Harris (1969) 33 Conv.(N.S.) 113, 183.

unaltered. For example, the old-fashioned settlement with its succession of limited interests had, in particular, fallen out of favour, because on the death of each limited owner estate duty was leviable on the value of the whole settled funds. And a great deal of ingenuity was and is devoted to the formulation of schemes dividing up the trust funds between those interested in capital and income, respectively, in such a way that tax is saved.

Tax.[36] These schemes were formerly presented to the court for its sanction under the head of "compromise" and are now presented under the Variation of Trusts Act 1958. Although Lord Morton said in *Chapman* v. *Chapman*[37] that if the court had power to approve and did approve schemes for the purpose of avoiding taxation "the way would be open for a most undignified game of chess between the Chancery Division and the legislature," the plain fact remains that very many applications under the Act have been made successfully for this very purpose alone.[38]

Yet despite these realities, echoes of judicial repugnance towards tax avoidance can still occasionally be heard and it is arguable, if only faintly, as a result of the controversial decision in *Re Weston's Settlements*[39] that certain forms of tax avoidance may be regarded as illegitimate. In this case the applicants applied for an order for approval of an arrangment by which property settled on English trusts should be freed from those trusts and settled on a Jersey settlement. The purpose of the exercise was to avoid a heavy liability to capital gains tax and estate duty.[40] Stamp J. at first instance said: "I am not persuaded that this application represents more than a cheap exercise in tax avoidance which I ought not to sanction, as distinct from a legitimate avoidance of liability to taxation."[41] The Court of Appeal, however, tended to place emphasis on other factors, nor indeed did Stamp J. ignore them. As is shown in the next chapter,[42] the primary basis of the Court of Appeal decision appears to be that no administrative benefits would accrue in transferring the settlement to Jersey because the family had been living in Jersey for only a few months and probably they would not stay there. There was also doubt as to the competency of Jersey courts to administer trusts.[43] And finally the element of moral or social benefit was stressed. On this Lord Denning M.R. said:

> "There are many things in life more worthwhile than money. One of these things is to be brought up in this our England which is still 'the envy of less happier lands.' I do not believe that it is for the benefit of children to be

---

[36] See also *post*, p. 429.

[37] *Ante*, at p. 412.

[38] See, *e.g. Re Norfolk's Will Trusts, The Times* March 23, 1966 (purpose to reduce duty on estates worth £3m.).

[39] [1968] 2 W.L.R. 1154 (Stamp J.); [1969] 1 Ch. 223, C.A.; and see *post*, p. 439 for further discussions of this decision.

[40] Approximately £160,000.

[41] [1968] 2 W.L.R. 1154 at p. 1162.

[42] At p. 440.

[43] [1968] 2 W.L.R. 1154 at p. 1162 *per* Stamp J.; [1969] 1 Ch. 223 at p. 247, *per* Harman L.J.: a doubt which appears to be unfounded: see *post*, p. 441.

uprooted from England and transported to another country simply to avoid tax. . . . Children are like trees: they grow stronger with firm roots."[44]

The case can be legally justified on the grounds just mentioned. But to introduce notions of "legitimate" and "illegitimate" tax avoidance would seem to be uncontrollably vague and unworkable.[45]

The taxation results of the termination of a trust described at page 388 apply equally on the termination of a trust by order of the court.

The Act. The Variation of Trusts Act, which came into force on July 23, 1958, applies to trusts of real and personal property, whether the trusts arise before or after the passing of the Act, under any will, settlement or other disposition.[46] The court may, if it thinks fit, by order approve an arrangement varying or revoking all or any of the trusts, or enlarging the powers of the trustees of managing or administering any of the trust property, on behalf of four classes of beneficiaries or potential beneficiaries.[47] These are as follows:

(A) persons having, directly or indirectly, a vested or contingent interest who by reason of infancy or other incapacity are incapable of assenting;

(B) persons, whether ascertained or not, who may become, directly or indirectly, entitled to an interest at a future date or on the happening of a future event, if they then answer a specified description or qualify as members of a specified class, but not including such persons if the future event had happened at the date of application to the court[48];

(C) persons unborn;

(D) persons who will be interested as discretionary beneficiaries under protective trusts[49] if the interest of the principal beneficiary should fail or determine.[50]

---

[44] [1969] 1 Ch. 223 at p. 245, and see *post*, p. 439.

[45] We speak here of "tax avoidance," not "tax evasion." The latter amounts to a criminal offence and clearly a scheme which "evaded" tax could not be sanctioned. But to take advantage of the existing tax laws for one's own benefit and thereby "avoid" tax is generally regarded as being a legitimate exercise: see also Bretten [1968] 32 Conv.(N.S.) 194; Harris [1969] 33 Conv.(N.S.) 183 at 191 *et seq*.

[46] s.1(1).   [47] *Ibid.*

[48] For decisions on the meaning of this paragraph, see *Re Suffert's Settlement* [1961] Ch. 1; *Re Moncrieff's Settlement Trusts* [1962] 1 W.L.R. 1344. Briefly, however, if the class in question is, for example, the statutory next-of-kin of a living propositus, then the latter is treated as having died at the date of application to the court, and thereupon the next-of-kin become ascertainable. Since the "future event" (the death of the propositus) has notionally happened, a member of the class of next-of-kin who is in existence cannot be bound by an order for variation without his consent (see *Re Suffert's Settlement, supra.*)

[49] See *ante*, p. 120.

[50] s. 1 (1) and see also s. 1 (2), which defines "protective trusts" as the trusts specified in T.A. 1925, s. 33(1)(i) and (ii) or "any like trusts." For the meaning of this last expression, see *Re Wallace's Settlement* [1968] 1 W.L.R. 711 at 716, *per* Megarry J.: "The word 'like' requires not indentity but similarity; and similarity in substance suffices without the need for similarity in form or detail or wording."

In clases (A), (B) and (C) above the court will only approve the arrangement if it is for the benefit of the persons mentioned in those classes. But in class (D) the benefit of the persons there mentioned need not be considered.[51] And if a beneficiary falls within class (D) and also within one of the other classes so that different heads of jurisdiction may apply, it is only necessary to apply for approval under (D). The four paragraphs are alternative, so that if one can bring the case within (D) it is not necessary to establish a benefit.[52]

(i) *General effect of the Act*

The Act largely gives to the court the jurisdiction for which Denning L.J. contended in *Re Chapman's Settlement Trust*.[53] It has commendably done away with the hair-splitting technicalities involved in a "compromise," and it has attracted a great many applications to the court since it was passed. But it must be emphasised that, although the jurisdiction is wide in many respects, it is in particular limited in the sense that it only empowers the court to authorise arrangements on behalf of the persons designated in the Act, as if they were all ascertained and *sui juris*. It does not enable the court to override any objection—even if it is unreasonable—or dispense with the consent—even if it is unreasonably witheld—of any beneficiary who is in fact ascertained and *sui juris*: in such circumstances, the Act cannot be invoked.

(ii) *Trusts to which Act applies*

Section 1 (1) of the Act provides that the Act applies where "property, whether real or personal, is held on trusts arising . . . under any will, settlement or other disposition." It seems, however, that the Act does not apply to every type of trust. Proceedings had been commenced on behalf of children who were alleged to have been born with physical deformities as a result of their mothers having taken the drug thalidomide during pregnancy. These proceedings had been settled upon the basis that the manufacturers of the drug paid into court nearly £6m. on terms that there should be paid out or applied various sums "in such manner as the judge may direct to or for the benefit of each (deformed) child." In *Allen* v. *Distillers Co. (Biochemicals) Ltd.*[54] an application was made for the payment of money out of court to be held by trustees on the terms of a draft which was submitted to the court for approval. Under the terms of settlement of the original proceedings, each child was entitled to payment on attaining the age of majority, whereas under the proposed draft settlement deed, the trustees were to be empowered to defer the date upon which the child would be entitled. The court held that it had no jurisdiction under the Act to approve the "variation" of the terms upon which the

---

[51] s.1(1), proviso, and see also *post*, p. 419.

[52] *Re Turner's Will Trusts* [1960] Ch. 122.

[53] *Supra*. In *Re Chapman's Settlement Trusts (No. 2)* [1959] 1 W.L.R. 372 an application to vary substantially the same scheme was granted under the Variation of Trusts Act 1958.

[54] [1974] 2 All E.R. 365.

money had been paid into court. Eveleigh J.[55] said[56] that the terms upon which the money had been paid into court was not "a trust of the kind referred to in the 1958 Act. The Act contemplates a situation where a beneficial interest is created which did not previously exist and probably one which is related to at least one other beneficial interest."

(iii) *Specific considerations*

(a) **Benefit.** The only essential guidance specifically provided in the Act as to the principles on which the exercise of the jurisdiction is based is that, with the exception of Class (D) above (discretionary beneficiaries under protective trusts), the arrangement should be for the *benefit* of the persons designated in the Act[57] on whose behalf approval of the arrangement is sought. There must be a definite benefit, even if it is not purely financial, conferred on such persons. Thus in *Re Van Gruisen's Will Trusts*[58] it was shown that actuarially the provisions for infants and unborn persons were more beneficial to them under the proposed arrangement than under the trusts of the will, and the arrangement was approved. But Ungoed-Thomas J. sounded a warning note when he said: "The court is not merely concerned with the actuarial calculation . . . the court is also concerned whether the arrangement as a whole, in all the circumstances, is such that it is proper to approve it. The court's concern involves, *inter alia,* a practical and businesslike consideration of the arrangement, including the total amount of the advantages which the various parties obtain and their bargaining strength." The same reasoning was applied in the earlier decision of *Re Clitheroe's Settlement Trusts*,[59] where the arrangement was designed to exclude any future wife from the class of objects of an immediate discretionary trust,[60] but in compensation gave her the benefit of a covenant by the settlor to pay the trustees an annual sum for her benefit. Danckwerts J. sanctioned the arrangements in principle but required evidence to show that it was in fact for the benefit of a future wife.

The rule that a "benefit" is all-important has caused some, though very few, applications to fail. For example, the Court of Appeal in *Re Steed's Will Trusts*[61] refused to sanction a variation sought by the beneficiary enabling her to take the whole beneficial interest, because it did not take sufficient account of a "spectral spouse" for whom the trusts were also designed and whom the beneficiary

---

[55] As he says in the judgment, "a common lawyer with this problem" of what constitutes a trust.

[56] At p. 374.

[57] s.1(1), proviso.

[58] [1964] 1 W.L.R. 449.

[59] [1959] 1 W.L.R. 1159.

[60] It was not a protective trust, so the proviso to s. 1 (1) did not apply.

[61] [1960] Ch. 407. See also *Re Cohen's Settlement Trusts* [1965] 1 W.L.R. 1229. (Where it was proposed to substitute June 14, 1973, in lieu of the applicant's death as the date when the persons to take were to receive the capital of the settled funds. Stamp J. refused the application on behalf of unborn beneficiaries because it could happen (even if it was a remote eventuality) that the applicant might survive the proposed date, and under the arrangement such persons would have no interest in the fund, whereas they would under the original settlement.)

might conceivably marry. Again, in *Re Tinker's Settlement*,[62] Russell J. declined to accept the argument that it was for the benefit of unborn persons as members of a family viewed as a whole that something reasonable and fair, but to their financial detriment, should be done.

The test was applied once more in *Re T.'s Settlement Trusts*[63] though this was only one ground of the decision. In this case Wilberforce J. refused to approve a proposed arrangement to transfer an infant female's share of settled funds to trustees to hold on protective trusts for her life, with remainders over. The infant would otherwise have become absolutely entitled in possession to the funds on attaining 21, and the arrangement had been devised because she had shown herself to be irresponsible in matters of money. The judge based his refusal (*inter alia*) on the ground that the proposals were not confined simply to dealing in a beneficial way with the special requirements of the infant. Another proposal for variation was later approved: this was to the effect that the infant's right to capital should be deferred for a time, she being given a protected life interest in the meantime.

The principle adumbrated by Danckwerts J. in *Re Cohen's Will Trusts*[64] may arguably be something of an aberration to the trend of authority. It was submitted that in the unlikely event of one of the testator's children predeceasing his widow, then aged nearly 80, the proposed arrangement would not be advantageous to his grandchildren, some of whom were infants. But it was held that risk of some kind was inherent in every application under the Act and this risk being one which would be reasonable for an adult, the court would take it on behalf of the infant.

In practice it seems that with a variation which is, when viewed broadly, for the financial benefit of the beneficiaries, but involves risks (particularly if a beneficiary were to die within a short time after the variation is made), the court is inclined to require such risks to be covered by insurance, even if the premiums are paid for out of income, and so at the expense of an infant beneficiary.[65]

But in some cases it is unnecessary to apply to the court because the risks are non-existent. Thus it has been held[66] that trustees can properly and with complete safety deal with their funds on the basis that a woman of 70 will not have a further child and an application under the Act is inappropriate: "the Act is concerned to vary trusts applicable in events which will or may happen and not to cover impossible contingencies."[67]

Moral or social benefit. Practically all the cases have been concerned with *financial* benefit which is a mundane consideration admitting of reasonable

---

[62] [1960] 1 W.L.R. 1011.

[63] [1964] Ch. 158.

[64] [1959] 1 W.L.R. 865. *cf. Re Cohen's Settlement Trusts* [1965] 1 W.L.R. 1229 (*ante*, p. 417, n.61).

[65] For an example, see *Re Robinson's Settlement Trusts* [1976] 3 All E.R. 61.

[66] *Re Pettifor's Will Trusts* [1966] Ch. 257.

[67] *Ibid.* at pp. 260, 261, *per* Pennycuick J. See also *Re Westminster Bank Ltd.'s Declaration of Trust* [1963] 1 W.L.R. 820 where an order was made under V.T.A. 1958, in respect of a woman aged 50.

proof. But it is now established that this is not necessarily the only consideration to be taken into account by the court. Thus in *Re T.'s Settlement Trusts*[68] the judge approved the alternative scheme of variation because on the special facts of the case the evidence showed that the infant beneficiary was irresponsible and immature: "there appears to me to be a definite benefit for this infant for a period during which it is to be hoped that independence may bring her into maturity and responsibility to be protected against creditors."[69] This decision was followed by Megarry J. in *Re Holt's Settlement*[70] where he said (on a scheme postponing vesting of interests in children from 21 years to 30 years): "The word 'benefit' in the proviso to section 1 of the Act of 1958 is . . . plainly not confined to financial benefit, but may extend to moral or social benefit. . . ."[71] This rule was confirmed by the decision of the Court of Appeal in *Re Weston's Settlements*.[72] For this purpose it was decided that it was for the benefit of children to be educated in England rather than in Jersey.

Perhaps an even broader view of "benefit" in this context was taken in *Re Remnant's Settlement Trusts*,[73] where Pennycuick J. approved an arrangement deleting forfeiture clauses whereby the interests of certain children were subject to forfeiture if they practised Roman Catholicism or married a Roman Catholic. The basis of the case appears to be that such provisions might operate as a deterrent to them in the selection of a husband and also as a source of possible family dissension.

Benefit in administration. An arrangement which results in improvement in the general administration of the trust may also be a "benefit" within the meaning of the Act. As will be shown,[74] it is on this ground that the courts have approved applications for the export of trusts to countries abroad where the beneficiaries are resident.

(b) **Discretionary beneficiaries under protective trusts.** It has already been stated that it is unnecessary, by way of exception to the general rule, to show a benefit to the persons falling within class (D).[75] Nevertheless, it is clearly established that their interests cannot be simply ignored. As Wilberforce J. held in *Re Burney's Settlement Trusts*,[76] in approving an arrangement varying discretionary trusts, the discretionary power conferred on the court has still to be judicially exercised and it is incumbent on the applicant to make out a case for interfering with protective trusts. Indeed, the basic principle had been stated

---

[68] [1964] Ch. 158.

[69] *Ibid.* at 162.

[70] [1969] 1 Ch. 100.

[71] *Ibid.* at p. 121.

[72] [1969] 1 Ch. 223; for further discussion of this case, see *post*, p. 439 and *infra*. See also *Re C.L.* [1969] 1 Ch. 587 (mental patient surrendered his protected life interest and contingent interest in remainder. *Held* (Cross J.), that it was for the patient's benefit because in all probability it was what the patient would have done if of sound mind).

[73] [1970] Ch. 560, *cf. Re Tinker's Settlement* [1960] 1 W.L.R. 1011.

[74] *Post*, p. 438.

[75] s.1(1), proviso.

[76] [1961] 1 W.L.R. 545.

earlier, more generally, by Lord Evershed M.R. in *Re Steed's Will Trusts*,[77] where he said that "the court is bound to look at the scheme as a whole and when it does so, to consider, as surely it must, what really was the intention of the benefactor." The requirements were spelt out in *Re Baker's Settlement Trusts*,[78] where Ungoed-Thomas J. said that where property was held on protective trusts for the benefit of the applicant and an application was made to vary those trusts, evidence (including in this case that of the financial position of the applicant and her husband) should be laid before the court to show to what extent the protective trusts continued to serve any useful purpose.

(c) **Meaning of "arrangement."** There is no doubt that the term has been widely construed to cover many classes of variation. "It is," as Lord Evershed M.R. has said in *Re Steed's Will Trusts*,[79] "deliberately used in the widest possible sense to cover any proposal which any person may put forward for varying or revoking trusts." It need not, therefore, necessarily be *inter partes*. Views of the trustees are relevant but not conclusive and, if necessary, will be overridden.[80]

The wide meaning attached to an arrangement was, however, modified in *Re T.'s Settlement Trusts*.[81] Here Wilberforce J. refused, as the alternative and primary ground for his decision, to sanction the arrangement initially proposed because it amounted to a completely new settlement and that was beyond the jurisdiction conferred by the Act. If this represents the true position there are limits to the conception of an "arrangement," but it might be thought to be an unjustified abridgment of the court's jurisdiction.

Nevertheless subsequent case law seems to have accepted the distinction between "variation" and "resettlement." For example, in *Re Ball's Settlement*[82] Megarry J. laid down the following test to be applied: "If an arrangement changes the whole substratum of the trust, it may well be that it cannot be regarded as merely varying that trust. But if an arrangement, while leaving the substratum, effectuates the purpose . . . by other means, it may still be possible to regard that arrangement as merely varying the original trusts, even though the means employed are wholly different and even though the form is completely changed." In this case the judge held that although the arrangement sought rescinded all beneficial and administrative trusts of the settlement and substituted new provisions, he could approve it because it preserved the "general drift" of the old trusts.

The fact remains that a pedantic distinction has grown up between "variation" and "resettlement" for which there appears to be no sanction in the words of the Act, nor any practical justification.

---

[77] [1960] Ch. 407 at p. 421.
[78] [1964] 1 W.L.R. 336.
[79] [1960] Ch. 407 at p. 419.
[80] *Ibid.* at p. 420.
[81] [1964] Ch. 158; and *ante*, p. 418.
[82] [1968] 1 W.L.R. 899. See also *Re Holt's Settlement* [1969] 1 Ch. 100 at p. 117 (Megarry J.).

Court orders. It now seems to be established that it is the arrangement itself and not the order of the court which effects the variation.[83] But it is necessary (so it seems) to regard the order of the court and the arrangement as having been made at the same time.[84] The arrangement will, however, be embodied in, or referred to in, the order, and where this causes a disposition of beneficial interests, stamp duty is payable, usually at the rate of 2 per cent. of the value of the interest passing. In *Thorn* v. *I.R.C.*,[85] Walton J. had to consider the nature of the disposition affected. A trust fund was held upon protective trusts for the settlor's wife for life, with remainder to the settlor's daughter for life, and ultimately for the children and remoter issue of the daughter. An order, had been made under the Act approving a variation on behalf of the unborn and unascertained issue of the daughter. The trustees contended that in giving its approval, the court, in effect, dealt with the interest of each unborn or unascertained person. Each interest, looked at separately, would have had almost no value. However, Walton J. held that the order effected the disposition of the totality of the separate interests which therefore fell to be valued as a composite whole.

(d) **Fraud and public policy.** It is a statement of the obvious that if a variation is fraudulent or contrary to public policy it will not be sanctioned. A case of some interest on this point is *Re Robertson's Will Trusts*,[86] where the applicant had exercised a special power of appointment in favour of his children as a preliminary to the proposed arrangement. His purpose and intention in making the appointment was to benefit his children and not himself. Later he was advised that his financial position would in fact be improved if the appointment were made and the scheme approved. But Russell J. held that to suppose his original purpose and intention had been changed or added to was unjustified. It followed that there was no fraud on the power, though, if there had been, the court would not have been able to approve the scheme.

However, subsequent case law appears to indicate a certain conflict as to the precise principles to be applied. In *Re Wallace's Settlement*[87] Megarry J. said that the fact that protected life tenants had executed appointments in favour of their children in itself raised a case for inquiry because the life tenants benefited by the arrangment; but on the evidence he was satisfied that there was no fraud on the power because the benefit to the life tenants was not substantial and they had intended to make the appointment before the arrangement was approved.

---

[83] *Re Holt's Settlement* [1969] 1 Ch. 100. See also *Re Holmden's Settlement* [1968] A.C. 685 at pp. 701, 705, 713; *Spens* v. *I.R.C.* [1970] 1 W.L.R. 1173 at pp. 1183, 1184. Megarry J. in *Re Holt* followed *Re Joseph's Will Trusts* [1959] 1 W.L.R. 1019, not *Re Hambledon's Will Trusts* [1960] 1 W.L.R. 82, which held that the court order effected the variation.

[84] *Re Holt, supra* at p. 115. The main reason for this requirement seems to be that decisions made on the basis of *Re Hambleden (supra)* would have been made without jurisdiction.

[85] [1976] 2 All E.R. 622.

[86] [1960] 1 W.L.R. 1050.

[87] [1968] 1 W.L.R. 711.

However, in *Re Brook's Settlement*[88] Stamp J. adopted a rather different approach. He held that the exercise of a special power of appointment amounted to a fraud on the power and he was unable to approve the variation Here one of the purposes of the appointment (by a protected life tenant in favour of his children from which he would also benefit from a division of the capital) was to enable the life tenant to obtain what he could not otherwise get, namely capital rather than income. This was enough to invalidate the appointment.

The important feature of *Re Brook* is that the judge emphasised that the question is whether the *purpose* of the appointment amounted to a fraud, not, as was apparently suggested in *Re Wallace*, the *effect* of the appointment on the financial position of the appointor. It is thought that *Re Brook* applies the correct principle.

Release. The difficulties that may thus arise as a result of a fraud on the power, however inadvert, may in some circumstances be avoided by releasing the power. For no question of a fraud on a power can arise on a mere release. And it has been held that, provided that the power in question can be released,[89] the court will approve an arrangement varying a settlement even though the objects of the power are ignored.[90] There appears to be some doubt whether the release should be affected by deed, or whether it can be inferred from the facts. The latter would seem sufficient.[91]

Even if the power cannot be released (*e.g.* if it was given to the donee *qua* trustee)[92] it still seems possible to apply to the court for an arrangement extinguishing the power because this amounts to varying or revoking a trust within section 1 of the 1958 Act. But because the power is not of itself releasable the court is likely to impose conditions on the release. Thus Stamp J. in *Re Drewe's Settlement*,[93] in approving an arrangement, insisted that it could only be effected by deed and with the consent of the trustees.

Public policy. Considerations of public policy were neatly side-stepped by Buckley J. in *Re Michelham's Will Trusts*.[94] Approval was sought to an arrangement whereby trust property was transferred to the applicants absolutely. The efficacy of the scheme depended on their continuing to remain unmarried. Insurance policies were therefore to be effected which would ensure that if either did in fact marry, certain sums would become available to replace the funds thus transferred. The policies included a stipulation that the insurers should be indemnified by a Swiss bank if the policy moneys became payable. The bank proposed to give the indemnity on terms that it, in turn, should be

---

[88] [1968] 1 W.L.R. 1661.
[89] See *Re Will's Trust Deeds* [1964] Ch. 219, and *ante*, p. 90 and see Hawkins (1968) 84 L.Q.R. 64.
[90] *Re Christie-Miller's Settlement* [1961] 1 W.L.R. 462; *Re Courtland's Settlement* [1965] 1 W.L.R. 1385; *Re Ball's Settlement* [1968] 1 W.L.R. 899.
[91] In *Re Ball* Megarry J. insisted on a formal release, but in *Re Christie-Miller* and *Re Courtland* an inferred release was regarded as sufficient.
[92] See *ante*, p. 91.
[93] [1966] 1 W.L.R. 1518.   [94] [1964] Ch. 550.

indemnified by one or other of the applicants if the moneys became payable. The judge, in approving the arrangement, held that although the counter-indemnities given by the applicants to the bank ought to be regarded as tending to discourage the applicants from marrying, that would not affect its validity. This was so because if the counter-indemnities were unenforceable by the bank on grounds of public policy—and that was a question of Swiss law—that fact alone would not relieve the bank from its obligation to indemnify the insurers.

(e) **Form of application.** An application should normally be made by a life-tenant or other person entitled to the income of the trust funds. It should only be made by the trustees, as Russell J. said in *Re Druce's Settlement Trusts*,[95] where "they are satisfied that the proposals are beneficial to the persons interested and have a good prospect of being approved by the court, and further, that if they do not make the application no one else will." As these principles were satisfied in this case it was held to be a proper case for an application by the trustees. In the ordinary way the trustees will be respondents, as will be all the existing beneficiaries, adult and infant and the Attorney-General[96] if the existing settlement contains a charitable trust. It is, moreover, the duty of persons appointed guardians *ad litem* for an infant to take proper legal advice and apprise themselves fully of the nature of the application and the manner in which the beneficial interest of the infant is proposed to be affected.[97] At the same time it is recognised that there is a limit to the necessity for joinder of parties. So it seems unnecessary, for reasons of practicality and expense, to join persons who are merely potential members of a class. Thus, it has been held that it is unnecessary to join persons who are only interested as the objects of a power which may never be exercised.[98] And the same has been applied to persons interested under protective trusts which it is proposed to vary: as Wilberforce J. said in *Munro's Settlement Trusts*,[99] the court looks prima facie to the trustees as watchdogs to see that interested parties' interests are protected.

(f) **Extent of jurisdiction.** The Act does not extend to Scotland[1] or Northern Ireland.[2] Jurisdiction is accordingly witheld from the courts of these countries. But this does not oust the jurisdiction of the *English* courts to vary a Northern Ireland or Scottish or indeed any foreign settlement. And it has been held in *Re Ker's Settlement Trusts*[3] that the court has jurisdiction to vary a settlement of which the proper law was that of Northern Ireland and in *Re Paget's Settlement*[4] where the proper law was believed to be that of New York.

---

[95] [1962] 1 W.L.R. 363.
[96] See *Re Longman's Settlement Trusts* [1962] 1 W.L.R. 455.
[97] *Re Whittall* [1973] 1 W.L.R. 1027.
[98] *Re Christie-Miller's Marriage Settlement* [1961] 1 W.L.R. 462.
[99] [1963] 1 W.L.R. 145. *cf. Re Courtland's Settlement* [1965] 1 W.L.R. 1385.
[1] s.2(1).
[2] s.2(2).
[3] [1963] Ch. 553.
[4] [1965] 1 W.L.R. 1046.

(g) **Trustee Investments Act 1961.** The Trustee Investments Act 1961[5] expressly preserves the discretion of the court under the Variation of Trusts Act 1958 to extend the trustees' powers of investment. And many applications have been made under the Variation of Trusts Act 1958 to extend the trustees' investment powers as well as to vary the beneficial trusts. The question, however, is: Are the trustees entitled under the Act of 1958 to obtain investment powers greater than those conferred by the Act of 1961? The answer in most of the reported cases is, No. Thus, in *Re Cooper's Settlement*,[6] Buckley J. held that the court must be satisfied that there are "special circumstances" in which the trustees should be given wider powers than the "normally appropriate" powers indicated by the Act of 1961. The fact that the extension of investment powers proposed was part of an arrangement to vary beneficial interests was specifically rejected as amounting to a special circumstance justifying a departure from the scope of the statutory scheme. Likewise in *Re Kolb's Will Trusts*,[7] where the settlor clearly wished to invest the whole fund in equities and it was only because of the wording of the instrument that the trustees did not have the power to do so, Cross J. doubted whether this fact alone constituted such special circumstances as to justify an extension of the powers of investment conferred by the Act of 1961. An in *Re Clarke's Will Trusts*[8] Russell J. was only prepared to go so far as to substitute the requirements of the dividend history demanded of wider-range securities, in place of those provided for in the trust instrument.

Only in one reported case have "special circumstances" justifying an extension been found. This is *Re University of London Charitable Trusts*,[9] a case relating to charitable trusts. Wilberforce J. held (*inter alia*[10]) that he was entitled to extend the range of investment beyond that permitted by the Act of 1961 because, if he did not, the benefits of a proposed combined investment pool which would arise from the saving of administrative expenses, convenience of administration and the practicability of dividing the combined pool into parts would be frustrated. But apart from this case the possible meaning of "special circumstances" remains open. It is, however, difficult on the basis of the present case law to visualise these being present in a private trust.[11]

(h) **Law of Property Act 1925, s. 53(1)(c).** In *Holt's Settlement*[12] Megarry J. held that trusts are varied effectively by the arrangement (taking effect when the court order is made) even though it does not comply with section 53 (1) (c) of the Law of Property Act 1925. This requires that the disposition of an equitable interest should be in writing.[13] In coming to this

---

[5] s.15; and see *ante*, p. 318.
[6] [1962] Ch. 826.
[7] [1962] Ch. 531.
[8] [1961] 1 W.L.R. 1471.
[9] [1964] Ch. 282.
[10] See also *ante*, p. 239.
[11] See *ante*, p. 315.
[12] [1969] 1 Ch. 100.
[13] For further discussion of this section and the cases, see *ante*, p. 24.

conclusion the judge relied on *Oughtred* v. *I.R.C.*,[14] on the basis that the arrangement gave rise to a constructive trust and therefore the requirements of section 53(1)(c) could be ignored because of section 52(2) which exempts constructive trusts from these requirements. But in fact *Oughtred's* case went the other way: the House of Lords held that the fact that a contract is specially enforceable (as is an arrangement under the Variation of Trusts Act) and a constructive trust has come into being is irrelevant: section 53(2) did not provide an exception in this sort of case and writing is still required. As a further ground for his decision the judge held that Parliament in the 1958 Act had impliedly authorised an exception to section 53(1)(c), but here again this implication is difficult to deduce from the language of the statute. The decision on this point seems to be erroneous even though it has been the practice of the courts in many cases prior to *Re Holt* to ignore the statutory requirements.

(i) **Trustee Act 1925, s.53.**[15] Under this section the court has the poser to make vesting orders in relation to an infant's beneficial interest. In some cases it may prove necessary to combine an application under this section with one under the Variation of Trusts Act 1958. This happened in *Re Bristol's Settled Estates*[16]; where Buckley J. authorised the execution of a disentailing assurance on behalf of an infant tenant in tail in remainder so that the property could be dealt with for his benefit under a proposed "arrangement" which the judge also approved.

(j) **Perpetuity.** The Perpetuities and Accumulations Act 1964[17] applies only to instruments taking effect after the commencement of the Act.[18] The question is how far this provision affects variations made under the Act of 1958. In *Re Holt's Settlement*[19] Megarry J. held that an arrangement (taken with the court order[20]) was an "instrument" for this purpose, with the result that provisions deriving their validity from the 1964 Act might be included in the arrangement; and this would apply not only to trusts created since the commencement of the 1964 Act but also to those created before this date.[21]

But one difficulty does remain. The problem is whether the instrument must take effect as a "disposition." The 1964 Act tends to suggest that this is necessary.[22] The point did not arise in *Holt's* case because the applicant there surrendered a life interest and this amounted to a "'disposition." It seems,

---

[14] [1960] A.C. 206, See *ante*, p. 28.
[15] *Supra*.
[16] [1965] 1 W.L.R. 469; see also *Re Lansdowne's Will Trusts* [1967] Ch. 603.
[17] See *ante*, p. 98.
[18] s.15(5).
[19] [1969] 1 Ch. 100.
[20] See *ante*, p. 421.
[21] The same principle was applied but no reasons given in *Re Lloyd's Settlement* [1967] 2 W.L.R. 1078 in relation to s. 13 and the accumulation periods.
[22] See ss.1, 3(5).

however, that if the arrangement does not involve a disposition, then the benefits of the 1964 Act cannot be utilised in respect of subsequent variations of the original trusts.[23]

---

[23] See *Re Holmden's Settlement* [1968] A.C. 685 where it was suggested that a mere alteration of the period for which discretionary trusts should continue was not a "disposition."

CHAPTER 24

EXPORTING TRUSTS

I. MOTIVES

A PERSON may wish to create a new trust abroad, or to export an existing trust for a variety of reasons. Generally, these are one or more of the following:

1. The beneficiaries or a majority of them are resident abroad, or are intending to reside abroad, and it will be most convenient for the trust to be administered in the country in which they are resident.[1]
2. There is a widespread fear that future United Kingdom legislation might aim to achieve a more even distribution of wealth among members of the community, and that this can only be achieved by, in effect, confiscating part of the assets of those who are thought to be wealthy. A wealth tax is only one form which such legislation might take. It is not for us to comment here on the ethics or political wisdom of any such measures, but man is an essentially greedy animal, and having acquired assets, will usually go to great lengths to retain them. Some have thought that if assets are transferred abroad, and held by trustees, then they will be safe from the tax gatherer's preying hands, particularly if the present owner does not retain any legal entitlement to them.
3. From time to time, there is an associated fear that as a currency, sterling may not be stable, and that the value and security of wealth may be enhanced if it is held abroad.
4. Occasionally, it is desired to take advantage of foreign rules of law. Although it is not "foreign" in this sense, a particular example is Northern Ireland where it is possible to direct accumulation for a period of 60 years.
5. But in most cases there are two predominant motives. The first is to ensure so far as possible that funds are protected from any re-introduction of United Kingdom exchange control.
6. The second predominant motive is to save tax.

This chapter is concerned with the extent to which these two last objectives can effectively be achieved. It examines the main aspects of the law which apply

---

[1] This was the reason for the approval of the court given in *Re Seale's Marriage Settlement* [1961] Ch. 574; and in *Re Windeatt's Will Trusts* [1969] 1 W.L.R. 692; [1969] 2 All E.R. 324. See *post*, p. 438. See also *Re Whitehead's Will Trusts* [1971] 1 W.L.R. 833; *post*, p. 438.

when a person resident in the United Kingdom wishes to create a new trust abroad or when an existing United Kingdom trust is transferred abroad. Trusts which are administered abroad are commonly referred to as "off-shore"[2] trusts.

II. EXCHANGE CONTROL

United Kingdom exchange control legislation is currently[3] in suspense. It was intended, when enacted, to conserve the United Kingdom's gold and foreign currency resources, and to assist the balance of payments by restricting the outflow of funds from the United Kingdom. While the legislation was in operation, very broadly, a person resident in the United Kingdom[4] who wished to purchase an investment or other asset abroad[5] had to do so in one of three ways, namely:

(a) with currency purchased through the official foreign exchange market. This was controlled strictly by the Bank of England, acting as the exchange control authority. In principle, the Bank of England gave permission for the use of foreign currency purchased at the official rate of exchange only where the investment was likely directly to promote United Kingdom exports, or where it promised an early benefit to the balance of payments. Permission was not generally given for personal investment.

(b) With "investment currency." After the introduction of exchange control, persons who were resident in the United Kingdom and who had foreign currency securities[6] were obliged, when they sold them, to sell them through controlled channels for sterling. The proceeds of sale, known as investment currency, were available for sale to other United Kingdom residents, but because of the shortage of investment currency, this was at a premium often in excess of 40 per cent. This applied even where the resident investor wished to sell one foreign currency security, and to re-invest the proceeds in another such security.

(c) With the proceeds of foreign currency borrowings. These were sums borrowed abroad in a currency other than sterling. A foreign currency borrowing required the permission of the Bank of England. This was not generally available to private investors.

When foreign currency securities were purchased, irrespective of the source of the funds, the certificates for the securities had to be held by depositories designated by the Bank of England.

---

[2] The expression includes anywhere outside the U.K., and so includes the Channel Islands and the Isle of Man.

[3] Since October 24, 1979.

[4] Or in the other Scheduled Territories, namely the Channel Islands, the Isle of Man, the Republic of Ireland and Gibraltar.

[5] That is, outside the Scheduled Territories. A special relaxation applied in the case of investment in other EEC countries.

[6] *i.e.* securities denominated or payable in any currency other than sterling.

[7] Most banks and practising solicitors were so designated.

While the control was in force, an individual who wished to invest abroad was therefore subject to numerous restrictions; almost invariably substantial extra cost. Furthermore, there was always the risk, that in acute national financial circumstances the Government would take action to compel those securities to be realised. Furthermore, there was a general prohibition on maintaining foreign currency bank accounts.

In 1979 the legislation was suspended, but not repealed.[8] It can be brought into operation again by Order made by H.M. Treasury.[9] Since 1979, many individuals resident in the United Kingdom have created trusts with a view to enabling their funds to be free of any reintroduction of the control. The strategy is based on the premise that where the trustees are resident abroad, and the investments are situated abroad, the trustees will not themselves be subject to United Kingdom exchange control legislation; and the beneficiary, not having the power to control the trustees, will himself not be able to procure that the funds are brought within the scope of the control. In current jargon, such non-resident trustees are said to be "non-compellable."

The fear that exchange control might be re-introduced has, therefore, been a powerful stimulus to the formation of new off-shore trusts.

In the case of existing trusts, when the legislation was in force all trusts were classified as resident or non-resident. This depended on the residential status of the settlor, in the case of an *inter vivos* trust, or of the deceased at the date of his death in the case of a will trust. Where the trust was resident, there was no restriction on the appointment of non-resident trustees as such; but the assets could only be transferred to them with the consent of the Bank of England which was only sparingly given. In general, permission was always refused unless it could be shown that all possible beneficiaries were themselves non-resident. On the other hand, there were very few onerous restrictions on trusts which had throughout their existence been non-resident, or which had been made non-resident before the original introduction of exchange control.[10]

Accordingly, there is also a movement towards making existing trusts non-resident, and taking the assets abroad, while there is no restriction on so doing.

III. TAXATION

1. *Taxation generally*

In order to determine the taxation advantages of a trust which is for the time being non-resident[11] it is necessary to consider the taxation liability of:

---

[8] By the Exchange Control (General Exemption) Order 1979 (S.I. 1979 No.1660) and the Exchange Control (Revocation) (No. 2) Direction 1979 (S.I. 1979 No. 1162)

[9] Under the Exchange Control Act 1947.

[10] By the Defence (Finance) Regulations 1939, issued under the Emergency Powers (Defence) Acts.

[11] For the sake of simplicity, in this chapter the expression "non-resident" is used to mean both non-resident in the strict sense, and non-ordinarily resident.

(a) the trustees; and
(b) the beneficiaries.

2. *Income Tax*

(1) **The trustees**

An underlying principle of United Kingdom income tax law is that a person is liable to income tax

(a) if he is resident here, on his total world-wide income; but
(b) if he is not resident here, only on income which is derived from a source in the United Kingdom.

It follows that, in the case of non-resident trustees:

(a) they will not be liable in respect of income derived from sources outside the United Kingdom; but

(b) they will be liable in respect of income derived from sources within the United Kingdom to the same extent as trustees who are resident here. It has been seen[12] that, in principle, this liability will be
   (i) at 30 per cent. in the case of fixed interest limits; and
   (ii) at 45 per cent. in the case of discretionary or accumulating trusts.[13]

Accordingly, the trustees will be free of United Kingdom income tax if all the investments are made abroad.

(2) **The beneficiaries: actual income**

Where a beneficiary is entitled to income from a foreign trust, he is liable to income tax on that income[14] whether or not he actually receives it.[15] This is so irrespective of the territory in which the trust assets are situated. No income tax saving is effected, therefore, where the beneficiary is actually entitled to the income.

(3) **The beneficiaries: other benefits from income**

Were there no other provision, the beneficiaries would escape liability if income was accumulated abroad, and either retained abroad, or paid to them as capital. To counter this, there are two far-reaching anti-avoidance provisions.

(a) *Section 478, Taxes Act 1970*

Section 478 of the Income and Corporation Taxes Act 1970 applies where:

(i) an asset is transferred to a person abroad.[17] This requirement is satisfied even if the asset has not been transferred from the United

---

[12] *Ante*, p. 293.

[13] *Ante*, p. 293, *I.R.C.* v. *Regent Trust Co. Ltd., The Times* November 30, 1979.

[14] Under Case V of Schedule D : Taxes Act 1970, ss. 109, 122.

[15] Liability is deferred if it is impossible to remit the income to the United Kingdom: s. 418. If the person entitled to the income is resident but not domicled in the United Kingdom, foreign income is only liable to United Kingdom income tax if remitted to the United Kingdom.

[16] The expression includes money, and property or rights of any kind: s. 478(8)(*b*).

[17] *i.e.* out of the United Kingdom.

Kingdom. So, if Andrew, a resident of, say, South Africa, offers to make a gift of R2,000 to Bertram, who is a United Kingdom resident, but Bertram directs Andrew to pay that sum to trustees on his behalf in Guernsey,[18] the payment of that sum will constitute a transfer of an asset for this purpose;

(ii) the transfer was by the tax payer or his spouse[19];

(iii) by virtue of, or as a consequence of, that transfer, either directly or indirectly[20] the income is payable to a person or company resident abroad[24]; and

(iv) a United Kingdom resident enjoys, or has power to enjoy, that income. The definition of "power to enjoy" is very wide indeed.[22]

Where the section applies the income arising abroad is treated as the income of the United Kingdom resident for income tax purposes[23] to the extent to which it is not actually distributed to others. There are two exceptions to this provision:

(a) where the Board of Inland Revenue is satisfied that tax avoidance was not the purpose or one of the purposes for which the transfer was effected.[24] Even if the avoidance of tax was not the primary purpose of the transfer, it will almost invariably be one of the purposes, so that this exception is more apparent than real;

(b) where the transfer was part of a *bona fide* commercial transaction, and not designed for the purpose of avoiding tax.[25]

---

[18] Which is "abroad" for this purpose.

[19] *Vestey* v. *I.R.C.* [1979] 3 All E.R. 976, H.L.

[20] This follows from the application of the general principle to a transfer by "an associated operation." s.478(4) defines "associated operation" in relation to any transfer as "an operation of any kind effected by any person in relation to any of the assets transferred or any assets representing, whether directly or indirectly, any of the assets transferred, or to the income arising from any such assets, or to any assets representing, whether directly or indirectly, the accumulations of income arising from any such assets."

[21] For this purpose, "income" does not include director's remuneration.

[22] s. 478(5) provides that for the purposes of the section an individual is deemed to have power to enjoy the income of a person resident or domiciled out of the United Kingdom if

"(a) the income is in fact so dealt with by any person as to be calculated, at some point of time, and whether in the form of income or not, to ensure for the benefit of the individual, or

(b) the receipt or accrual of the income operates to increase the value to the individual of any assets held by him or for his benefit, or

(c) the individual receives or is entitled to receive, at any time, any benefit provided or to be provided out of that income or out of moneys which are or will be available for the purpose by reason of the effect or successive effects of the associated operations on that income and on any assets which directly or indirectly represent that income, or

(d) the individual has power, by means of the exercise of any power of appointment or power of revocation or otherwise, to obtain for himself, whether with or without the consent of any other person, the beneficial enjoyment of the income, or may, in the event of the exercise of any power vested in any other person, become entitled to the beneficial enjoyment of the income, or

(e) the individual is able in any manner whatsoever, and whether directly or indirectly, to control the application of the income."

Even this is extended by s.478(6).

[23] This does not apply to income which the foreign resident actually distributes to others.

[24] s. 478(3)(*a*).

[25] s. 478(3)(*b*).

In most cases, therefore, where a United Kingdom resident forms a trust abroad, and places money or other assets in that trust, under which he or his spouse is a beneficiary, section 478 will apply, and there will be no saving of income tax. Indeed, the liability can be greater than if the income arose within the United Kingdom. In *Lord Chetwode* v. *I.R.C.*,[26] Lord Chetwode created a settlement in the Bahamas, which owned the entire share capital of a Bahamian investment company. It was held that Lord Chetwode was assessable on the whole[27] of the income of the investment company, and that he could not even deduct the expenses of the management of that company in computing the amount of income to be brought into account for tax.

(b) *Finance Act 1982, s.45*

Section 478 of the 1970 Act applies only where, *inter alia*, the transfer of assets was made by the taxpayer or his spouse. Section 45 of the Finance Act 1981 applies where an individual who is resident in the United Kingdom can benefit under a foreign trust, but who was not a settlor in relation to it. If, therefore, Edward creates a non-resident discretionary settlement under which he and his son Frank are discretionary beneficiaries, during Edward's lifetime section 478 will apply. However, after Edward's death, provided Frank took no part in setting up the arrangments, he will only be liable, if at all, under section 45 in respect of income which he does not receive as income.[28]

Under section 45, it is necessary to calculate the income of the foreign trust which arose after March 9, 1981 directly or indirectly from a transfer of assets, and which can be used for providing a benefit for an individual who is ordinarily resident in the United Kingdom. Thus, in the example, income which is accumulated after the death of Edward is relevant income for this purpose, because it is capable of providing a benefit for Frank at some time in the future. A running notional record is then kept of this income, but no liability arises at that stage. When, however, the individual receives a benefit from the trust which is not taxable as ordinary income, the value of that benefit is treated as forming part of his income for the year in which he actually receives it.[29] Thus, if the trustees make a discretionary capital payment to Frank, he will be subject to income tax on it to the extent that it is covered by income which has arisen to the trustees.

In summary, therefore, the general position is that:

(a) a beneficiary resident in the United Kingdom will be liable to income tax on the actual income which he receives or to which he is entitled;
(b) the settlor will be liable to income tax on income retained within the trust unless it cannot be applied for his benefit, this liability being to tax when the income arises; but

---

[26] [1977] 1 All E.R. 638.
[27] In practice, the Revenue do allow a very limited deduction from the gross income in respect of the costs of collecting that income.
[28] Finance Act 1981, s. 45(2).
[29] s. 45(2)(a).

(c) other beneficiaries[30] will only be liable to income tax retained within the trust when they actually receive benefit from it.

Non-resident trusts are, therefore, a useful means by which the liability to income tax can be deferred.

3. *Capital Gains Tax*

(1) **Types of non-resident trust**

For capital gains tax purposes, a trust will, in principle, only be regarded as non-resident if

    (a) the general administration of the trust is ordinarily carried on outside the United Kingdom. There is no definition of this, but it probably means where the trustees meet, or, if it is large enough to have its own secretariat, where that secretariat is situated; and

    (b) the majority of the trustees are not resident or ordinarily resident in the United Kingdom.[31]

This is so even if the settlor was resident in the United Kingdom at the time when the trust was created.

However, a trust will also be regarded as non-resident if:

    (a) all the trust property is derived from a person who is not domiciled or resident in the United Kingdom;

    (b) Some or all of the trustees are individuals or companies whose business consists of or includes the management of trusts or of acting as trustees; and

    (c) a majority of the trustees are either such persons, or persons who are actually non-resident.[32]

These trusts are regarded as being non-resident even if their general administration is actually carried on in the United Kingdom.

Trusts which are treated as non-resident trusts for capital gains tax purposes are divided into two categories, which are known[33] as

    (a) section 80 trusts; and

    (b) fully foreign trusts.

A "section 80" trust, that is, a trust which is within section 80 of the Finance Act 1981, is one in which, during the year of assessment[34] being considered:

    (i) the trustees are non-resident;

    (ii) if the trust was created *inter vivos*, and the settlor is still alive, the settlor

---

[30] Apart from the settlor's widow.
[31] Capital Gains Tax Act 1979, s.52(1).
[32] C.G.T.A. 1979, s.52(2).
[33] Colloquially, not by statute.
[34] From April 6 to the following April 5.

(a) was domiciled and resident in the United Kingdom at the time when the settlement was created; or

(b) is domiciled and resident in the United Kingdom in the year of assessment being considered; or

(iii) if the settlement was created *inter vivos* and the settlor is dead, he was domiciled and resident in the United Kingdom when the settlement was created; or

(iv) if the settlement was created by will, the testator was domiciled and resident in the United Kingdom at the date of his death.

A "fully foreign trust" is one which is non-resident, and which is outside the scope of section 80.

(2) The trustees

In common with non-resident individuals, non-resident trustees are not chargeable to capital gains tax in respect of gains arising on the disposal of assets, even if the assets are situated in the United Kingdom.[35] This is so whether the trust is a section 80 trust, or a fully foreign trust.

(3) The beneficiaries: section 80 trusts

The provisions of section 80 of the Finance Act 1981 are similar to those of section 45.[36] A notional record is maintained of all gains which accrue to the trustees after March 9, 1981. These are known as "trust gains." When the trustees make a capital payment to a beneficiary[37] that payment is treated as representing a capital gain to the extent of the available trust gains. Suppose, therefore, that the trustees realise the following gains, and make the following capital payments:

Year of assessment	Gains	Capital Payment
1981/82	nil	£8,000 to Andrew
1982/83	£20,000	nil
1983/84	£20,000	£15,000 to Brian
1984/85	£20,000	£50,000 to Charles
1985/86	£20,000	nil

The trust gains for 1981/82 are nil. Of the gains realised in 1982/83, £8,000 are attributed to Andrew for 1982/83, and the balance of £12,000 is carried forward to 1983/84. The trust gains for 1983/84 are (a) the balance brought forward from 1982/83, £12,000, and (b) the gains arising in the year, £20,000, less (c) £15,000 which is attributed to Brian. The balance of £17,000 is carried forward. In 1984/85 the trust gains total £37,000[38], so that the £50,000 paid to Charles is treated as

---

[35] Capital Gains Tax Act 1979, s.2(1). There is, however, a liability if the non-resident carries on a trade in the United Kingdom and disposes of trading assets.

[36] *Ante* , p. 432.

[37] Whether resident or non-resident.

[38] *i.e.* £17,000 brought forward from 1983/84, and the £20,000 which arises in 1983/84.

£37,000 of capital gains, and £13,000 of other capital. That balance of £13,000 will be taxable as a capital gain for 1985/86.

The provisions seem complicated, but they have the effect that no liability can attach to a resident beneficiary until he actually receives a captial payment. Accordingly, even where the trust is within section 80, deferment of capital gains tax can be achieved merely by retaining all capital within the trust.

(4) The beneficiaries: fully foreign trusts

No liability attaches to beneficiaries, even if resident in the United Kingdom, in respect of gains realised by the trustees of a fully non-resident trust. This is so whether or not the trustees make capital payments to the beneficiaries.

Where a beneficiary becomes absolutely entitled to assets as against the trustees of a fully foreign trust, he will, in general, be treated as acquiring those assets at a nil base cost, so that he will be taxable on the whole of the proceeds of sale when he disposes of the asset.[39]
taxable on the whole of the proceeds of sale when he disposes of the asset.

It will be appreciated that where an existing resident trust is exported, it will usually become a section 80, and not a fully foreign, trust.[40]

4. *Capital Transfer Tax*

Where settled property is situated in the United Kingdom, capital transfer tax will be payable in any event according to the ordinary rules discussed earlier, which depend on whether or not there is an interest in possession in that property.[41]

Where settled property is situated outside the United Kingdom, that property is "excluded property" for capital transfer tax purposes if, but only if, the settlor was domiciled outside the United Kingdom at the time when the settlement was made.[42] If property is excluded property, there will be no liability upon the coming to an end of an interest in possession,[43] or upon the making of a capital distribution out of the settled property,[44] or upon the decennial anniversaries of the creation of the settlement.[45]

The settlor will be treated as being domiciled in some part of the United Kingdom at the time when the settlement was created if:

(a) he would be treated as so domiciled according to the general law; or
(b) he would be treated as being so domiciled according to the general law within three years prior to the creation of the settlement[46]; or

---

[39] C.G.T.A. 1979, s.54, as amended by F.A. 1983.
[40] Because of the domiciliary and residential status of the settlor: see p. 434, *ante.*
[41] See *ante,* pp. 298 and 299.
[42] F.A. 1975, Sched. 5, para. 2(1)(*a*).
[43] para. 4(11).
[44] F.A. 1982, s.102(1)(*i*).
[45] *ibid.*
[46] F.A. 1975, s. 45(1)(*a*).

(c) he was resident in the United Kingdom for at least 17 out of the 20
years ending with that in which the settlement was made.[47]

The last two categories only have full application where the property
became settled after December 9, 1974.[48]

Previously a special rule applied where the settlor was domiciled in the
Channel Islands or the Isle of Man.[49]

Where, at the time when a settlement was made, the settlor was domiciled in
some part of the United Kingdom, that settlement will, in principle, be permanently within the purview of capital transfer tax. Strictly, capital transfer tax will
be payable even if the settlor, trustees, and all possible beneficiaries are resident
outside the United Kingdom, and all the settled property is situated outside the
United Kingdom.

In some circumstances, where a settlement is being exported, the parties are
content to rely on the rule that one state will not enforce the tax laws of another.
In other words, although capital transfer tax may be payable, the parties will so
conduct themselves that the tax cannot be recovered.

In other circumstances it may be possible to rely on a specific exemption
which applies to Government securities. Most United Kingdom Government
securities are issued[50] on terms that they are exempt from all United Kingdom
taxation, including capital transfer tax,[51] while they are in the beneficial ownership of persons who are neither domiciled,[52] nor ordinarily resident in the
United Kingdom. This exemption applies to settled property where a person
who is neither domiciled nor ordinarily resident in the United Kingdom has an
interest in possession in the securities.[53] If there is no interest in possession in
the securities, the exemption only applies if it can be shown that all known
persons for whose benefit the settled property or income from it has been or
might be applied are neither domiciled nor ordinarily resident in the United
Kingdom.[54]

It follows that where, for example, a fund is held upon trust for Andrew for
life, with remainder to Hamish, capital transfer tax will be avoided if, at the
death of Andrew, the fund is invested in exempt Government securities.

However, with one minor exception,[55] the liability to capital transfer tax does
not depend on the residential status of the trust. If the settlement was created by
a non-domiciled settlor, and the property is situated abroad, the excluded
property rules apply whether the trust is resident or non-resident. If the trust
property consists of exempt British Government securities, and the beneficiaries are non-domiciled and non-ordinarily resident, the exemption will

---

[47] s. 45(1)(b).
[48] F.A. 1975, Sched. 5, para. 2(2).
[49] See F.A. 1975, s.45(1)(c) as amended by F.A. 1983.
[50] Under s. 47 of the F. (No. 2) A. 1915, or s. 22 of the F. (No. 2) A. 1931.
[51] But the requirements for the exemption in the capital transfer tax legislation must be
satisfied : *Van Ernst & Cie S.A.* v. *I.R.C.* [1980] 1 All E.R. 677, C.A.
[52] "Domiciled" here has its ordinary, and not extended, meaning: F.A. 1975, para. 3(3).
[53] F.A. 1975, Sched. 7, para. 3(1)(b).
[54] para. 3(2).
[55] Finance Act, 1982, s.122m.

also apply whether the trust is resident or non-resident. Exporting a trust will, therefore, neither mitigate nor exacerbate the liability to capital transfer tax.

5. *Taxation Summary*

The preceding parts of this chapter have attempted to describe the effect of highly complex legislation. It will have been that if a new non-resident trust is created, or if an existing resident trust is exported:

(a) there will be no income tax saving in respect of income received, or receivable by a resident beneficiary;
(b) liability to income tax on accumulated or withheld income may be deferred until the benefit of it is received;
(c) liability to capital gains tax will be eliminated, in the case of a fully foreign trust, or deferred until a capital payment is received in the case of a section 80 trust; and
(d) liability to capital transfer tax will be the same as if the trust had remained resident.

IV. WHEN EXPORTING IS PROPER

Trusts are a peculiar creation of English law, and for several centuries it would not have occurred to trustees or beneficiaries to seek to export the trust. However, since the middle of the last century, when the question first arose and more particularly during the last 25 years, certain principles have been developed by the courts on an ad hoc basis. The present position is as follows:

(1) The English court does have power to appoint non-resident trustees of an English settlement[56] and it also has power to approve an arrangement under the Variation of Trusts Act by which non-resident trustees are appointed, and the trust fund is exported.[57] The appointment of foreign trustees is not, therefore, *ipso facto* bad.

(2) Where the court would itself be prepared to appoint non-resident trustees, and there are adequate powers under the Trustee Act or the trust instrument, an effective appointment can be made without the intervention of the court. In *Re Whitehead's Will Trusts*[58], the main beneficiary had emigrated to Jersey in 1959, and was found to be permanently resident there.[59] In 1969 the trustees, who were resident in the United Kingdom, executed a deed under section 36 of the Trustee Act[60] appointing persons resident in Jersey as new trustees, and retiring from the trusts. The resident trustees wished to be fully

---

[56] *Meinertzhagen* v. *Davis* (1844) 1 Coll.N.C. 355; *Re Long's Settlement* (1869) 17 W.R. 218; *Re Seale's Marriage Settlement* [1961] Ch. 574; *Re Whitehead's Will Trusts* [1971] 1 W.L.R. 833.
[57] *Re Seale's Marriage Settlement, supra*; *Re Windeatt's Will Trusts* [1969] 1 W.L.R. 692; *Re Whitehead's Will Trusts, supra*.
[58] [1971] 1 W.L.R. 833.
[59] [1971] 1 W.L.R. 833 at p. 838.
[60] See *ante* p. 260.

protected, however, and the deed of retirement and appointment was made conditional upon the main beneficiary obtaining from the court a declaration that the resident trustees were effectively discharged. The court made the declaration. The decision shows that in a proper case[61] the appointment of a non-resident trustee without the intervention of the court is fully effective and valid.

(3) If the court would not itself make the appointment, but there is a purported retirement of resident trustees and the appointment of non-resident trustees without the intervention of the court, the appointment is not void, but is voidable. In *Re Whitehead's Will Trusts*[62] Pennycuick V.-C. said[63]: " . . . the law has been quite well established for upwards of a century that there is no absolute bar to the appointment of persons resident abroad as trustees of an English trust. I say 'no absolute bar,' in the sense that such an appointment would be prohibited by law and would consequently be invalid. On the other hand, apart from exceptional circumstances, it is not proper to make such an appointment, that is to say, the court would not, apart from exceptional circumstances, make such an appointment, nor would it be right for the donees of the power to make such an appointment out of court. If they did, presumably the court would be likely to interfere at the instance of the beneficiaries. There do, however, exist exceptional circumstances in which such an appointment can properly be made. The most obvious exceptional circumstances are those in which the beneficiaries have settled permanently in some country outside the United Kingdom and what is proposed to be done is to appoint new trustees in that country."

(4) It is therefore necessary to know in what circumstances the court will itself appoint non-resident trustees. The fundamental principle is that the court will do so if it is in the interest of the beneficiaries.

(5) Subject to the following points, it will usually be in the interest of the beneficiaries for the trust to be administered and for the trustees to be resident in the same territory as that in which the beneficiaries, or a majority of them, reside. Thus, *Re Seale's Marriage Settlement*[64] was concerned with a marriage settlement made in 1931 at a time when the husband and wife were domiciled in England. The husband and wife subsequently emigrated to Canada with their children, and at the date of the hearing in 1961 they had been living in Canada for some years, and were domiciled in Canada. Buckley J. found as a fact that they intended to continue to reside there. It was desired to export the trust to Quebec by two stages: the appointment of a Canadian trust corporation to be a trustee of the marriage settlement and for the discharge of the English trustees; and then for the property subject to the marriage settlement to be transferred to the Canadian corporation as trustee of a new Quebec settlement. The new

---

[61] *i.e.* where the court would itself make the appointment.
[62] [1971] 1 W.L.R. 833.
[63] At p. 837.
[64] [1961] Ch. 574.

settlement followed as closely as possible the terms of the English settlement, but without certain protective life interests which were not recognised by the law of Quebec. Buckley J. was satisfied that it was to the advantage of all beneficiaries for the settlement to be exported, and he approved the arrangements. This was followed by *Re Windeatt's Will Trusts*.[65] The testator who was domiciled in England, created a will trust for the benefit of, *inter alios*, his daughter, and her children. The daughter and her children had lived in Jersey for 19 years prior to the application, and were held to be permanently resident there. Pennycuick J. approved an arrangement for two Jersey residents to be appointed, and for the trust assets to be transferred to them.

(6) In certain circumstances it will be in the interest of the beneficiaries for non-resident trustees to be appointed even if they are resident in a territory different from that where the trustees are resident. For example, it may be in the interest of the beneficiaries for the trust to be exported from the United Kingdom, so that it may cease to be liable to United Kingdom taxation. However, if the beneficiaries are resident in a territory which does not recognise, or is not fully acquainted with, trusts, it may be appropriate for the trust to be exported to a territory which does. In *Re Chamberlain*[66] where some of the beneficiaries were resident in France and the others in Indonesia the court approved an arrangement to export an English trust by the appointment of trustees resident in Guernsey.

(7) There have been no reported decisions in which the court has approved the export of an English trust where the beneficiaries are resident in England, and the purpose is to mitigate the liability to tax. However, in view of the attitude which the court has taken in the case of applications to mitigate tax in other circumstances[67] there seems to be no insuperable objection to the export of a trust in these circumstances.

(8) All the circumstances must, however, be taken into account. If the proposed exportation is not clearly in the interest of the beneficiaries, a predominant tax avoidance motive may lead the court to refuse to make the appointment. In *Re Weston's Settlements*[68] two settlements were made in 1964 for the benefit of the two sons of the settlor. A total of 500,000 shares in The Stanley Weston Group Ltd. were transferred to the trustees of those settlements. However, the settlor could not know that by the Finance Act of the very next year a capital gains tax would be introduced. The shares rose in value and, by the time of the hearing at first instance in 1968, there was a prospective liability to capital gains tax of £163,000. The settlor lived in England until 1967, and in the first half of that year he made three visits of a few days each to Jersey. He then purchased a house, in which he lived from August 1967. The application to the court was commenced in November 1967. This sought the appoint-

[65] [1969] 1 W.L.R. 692; [1969] 2 All E.R. 324.
[66] (1976) N.L.J. 1934.
[67] See *e.g. Pilkington* v. *I.R.C.* [1964] A.C. 612, *ante*, p. 375; and decisions on the variation of trusts at p. 414 *et seq., ante*.
[68] [1969] 1 Ch. 223, C.A.; [1968] 3 All E.R. 338; and see also *ante*, p. 414.

ment of two professional men in Jersey of impeccable standing as trustees of the two English settlements and the approval of an arrangement under which the property subject to the English settlements could be transferred to Jersey settlements in identical terms. It was hoped that in doing this the property subject to the settlements would be free of capital gains tax, and would also be free of estate duty under section 28 of the Finance Act 1949.[69] Both Stamp J., at first instance, and the Court of Appeal refused to sanction the arrangement. The courts were influenced by two main facts:

(a) there was clearly some doubt whether the settlor and his children, the main beneficiaries, would live in Jersey permanently; particularly as they had only been there for a few months prior to the date of the hearing. That was insufficient to show a settled intention, and the court was worried at the possibility that shortly after the arrangement was approved, and the shares sold free of tax, the beneficiaries would return to England[70]; and

(b) as was mentioned in the previous chapter[71] this was, according to Stamp J. "a cheap exercise in tax avoidance" which ought not to be sanctioned.[72] In the Court of Appeal Harman L.J. also described it as "an essay in tax avoidance naked and unashamed."[73] This seems to have disturbed the court despite the fact that numerous applications under the Variation of Trusts Act have had tax minimisation as one of their main factors.[74] One cannot help wondering whether the court was influenced by the feeling that the settlor, who was the son of a Russian immigré, and who had built up his fortune in England during the 1939–45 war, should not escape his normal tax liability.

With the advantage of hindsight, it seems that the trustees were unfortunately advised, and that the arrangement would have been approved if it had been made a few years later, so that it could be shown that the beneficiaries were genuinely settled there. Although in *Re Windeatt's Will Trusts*[75] Pennycuick J. expressed himself[76] to be "in the most complete agreement" with the decision in *Re Weston's Settlement,*[77] it is highly likely that that decision will be confined to its own facts.

(9) The court will not approve the appointment of non-resident trustees if they are resident in a territory which may be reluctant to enforce the trust. If both the trustees are resident abroad, and the assets are situated abroad, the English court will be incapable of protecting the beneficiaries, and it will, therefore, wish to be satisfied that, in the case of any maladministration, the

[69] Now replaced by capital transfer tax.
[70] [1969] 1 Ch. at pp. 245, 246 (Lord Denning M.R.).
[71] *Ante*, p. 414.
[72] [1968] 2 W.L.R. 1154 at p. 1162.
[73] *Supra* at p. 246.
[74] See *ante*, p. 414.
[75] [1969] 1 W.L.R. 692; [1969] 2 All E.R. 324.
[76] [1969] 1 W.L.R. at p. 696; [1969] 2 All E.R. at p. 327.
[77] *Supra*.

beneficiaries will be given protection by the local law. A third factor which influenced the Court of Appeal in *Re Weston's Settlement*[78] was that there was no equivalent of the Trustee Act in Jersey,[79] and that the Jersey court had not had to enforce any *inter vivos* settlement. While the general principle is clear, the particular objection in *Re Weston's Settlement* to Jersey appears to have been misconceived. In both *Re Windeatt's Will Trusts*[80] and *Re Whitehead's Will Trusts*[81] the court approved the export of trusts to Jersey.

V. METHODS OF EXPORTING

A trust can be exported simply by the resident trustees[82] appointing non-resident new trustees, and then retiring. At the time, the assets will be transferred to the new trustees, or will automatically vest in them.[83] This method is only likely to be satisfactory, however, if the new trustees are resident in a territory which either has a trust law based closely on English law, or which will give effect to English trust law.

In other circumstances, it may be necessary to alter the form of the settlement to take account of differences between English trust law and the law of the country to which the settlement is to be exported. This alteration can sometimes be effected by using a power in the trust instrument to revoke existing trusts, and to declare new ones. However, the usual form of this power could only be used to declare new "trusts" in the sense in which that term is understood by English law. Wider powers which may become more common include a provision to declare new beneficial interests as nearly as possible equating to trusts under English law. If there is no power in the trust instrument, an application to the court will be necessary under the Variation of Trusts Act 1958.[84]

VI. EXPORTING PART OF THE TRUST

There may be circumstances in which it is desired to appoint non-resident trustees of part but not the whole of the trust fund. Assuming that the circumstances are those in which the court would appoint non-resident trustees, there is no fundamental objection to this. In particular, section 37(1)(*b*) of the Trustee Act 1925 provides that a separate set of trustees may be appointed for any part of the trust property held on trusts distinct from those relating to any other part of the trust property. Under this provision, separate trustees can be appointed even although there is no alteration to the trustees of the remainder of the trust fund.

But as the trustees in *Roome* v. *Edwards*[85] found out, there are major

---

[78] [1969] 1 Ch. 223, C.A., *supra*.
[79] As this edition of this book is being prepared, comprehensive trust legislation is about to be enacted in Jersey.
[80] [1969] 1 W.L.R. 692, *ante*, p. 440.
[81] [1971] 1 W.L.R. 833, *ante*, p. 437.
[82] Or such other person who has the power of appointing new trustees (see *ante* p. 250).
[83] Under T.A. 1925, s.40; *ante*, p. 263.
[84] See *ante*, p. 413.
[85] [1981] 1 All E.R. 736, H.L.

risks in so doing. In that case, the House of Lords was concerned with a marriage settlement created in 1944. In 1955, a power of appointment was exercised in respect of a comparatively small part of the trust fund, whereby that part was thenceforth to be held upon trusts, to accumulate the income until a daughter of the marriage reached the age of 25, and then to transfer the capital of that part to her. From 1955, the appointed fund was administered as if it were a trust separate from the main fund. One of the assets of the main trust appreciated very substantially in value, and steps were taken with a view to the saving of capital gains tax.[86] The main fund, but not the 1955 fund, was exported, by the retirement of the United Kingdom trustees, and the appointment of trustees resident in the Cayman Islands. Shortly thereafter, the gain was realised, and the Crown claimed the tax from the trustees of the 1955 appointed fund, who were still resident. The House of Lords held that the 1955 fund and the main fund together comprised one settlement for capital gains tax purposes; and that the claim of the Crown succeeded by virtue of section 52(3) of the Capital Gains Tax Act 1979.[87] This provides that where part of the property comprised in a settlement is vested in one set of trustees, and part in another, they shall be treated as together constituting and acting on behalf of a single body of trustees. The resident trustees (of the 1955 fund) were therefore liable to pay the tax on the gain realised by the non-resident trustees (of the main fund). Lord Roskill gave a clear warning[88] : "Persons, whether professional men or not, who accept appointment as trustees of settlements such as these are clearly at risk under the [1979] Act and have only themselves to blame if they accept the obligations of trustees in these circumstances without ensuring that they are sufficiently and effectively protected whether by their beneficiaries or otherwise for fiscal or other liabilities which may fall on them personally as a result of the obligations which they had felt able to assume." Not only are there particular risks in the export of part but not the whole of a trust, but the decision in *Roome* v. *Edwards* is taken to reinforce the view that where resident trustees retire in favour of non-resident trustees without the intervention of the court, they should always seek adequate indemnities.

---

[86] The provisions for hold over relief did not apply at that time.

[87] Section 52(3) of the 1979 Act is the re-enactment of section 25(11) of the Finance Act 1965.

[88] [1981] 1 All E.R. 736 at p. 744.

CHAPTER 25

BREACH OF TRUST

A BREACH of trust occurs if a trustee does any act which he ought not to do, or fails to do any act which he ought to do with regard to the administration of the trust, or with regard to the beneficial interests arising under the trust. It would be undesirable to attempt an exhaustive list of circumstances in which a breach of trust can be committed, but the following are examples:

(a) investment of trust moneys in unauthorised investments;
(b) taking a profit from the trust not authorised by the trust instrument or by the court;
(c) manipulating the investments to benefit one beneficiary at the expense of another;
(d) negligently allowing trust property to remain under the control of one trustee only;
(e) paying trust property to the wrong person;
(f) purchasing trust property without authority;
(g) failing to exercise a proper discretion with regard to trust decisions.

Where there is an allegation of breach of trust, it is desirable to pose the following questions:

1. Has a breach of trust been committed?
2. If so, is the proposed defendant liable?
3. If so, what is the prima facie measure of liability?
4. Is there any right to contribution or indemnity?
5. Is the proposed plaintiff in time to sue?
6. May the proposed defendant be relieved from liability by the court or otherwise?

If these questions are applied to the problem involving breach of trust, they should be adequate to ensure that no relevant point is overlooked when looking at the position from the point of view of the trustee. If one is looking at it from the point of view of the beneficiary, it is also necessary to ask whether the beneficiary can take any other action if sufficient redress cannot be obtained from the trustees. This aspect of the problem is the subject of the last part of this chapter.

I. Own Acts of the Trustee

There will usually be little difficulty in ascertaining whether a breach of trust has been committed by a trustee during his trusteeship. Complications sometimes arise, however, in respect of acts done at the beginning and end of a trusteeship.

On appointment, a trustee should take certain steps. He should inspect the trust instrument to ascertain the terms of the trust, and to see whether any notices are indorsed. He should ensure that all the trust property is transferred into his name jointly with the other trustees, for he may be liable if he allows the property to remain in the hands of another.[1] He may wish to go through the trust papers to familiarise himself with the circumstances of the trust. If in doing so, or in any other way, he learns that a breach of trust has been committed, he must obtain satisfaction from the person responsible. Should the new trustee not do so, he will himself be liable for breach of trust for his own omission. The only exception to this principle is if he is reasonably satisfied that it would be useless to institute proceedings because, for example, the former trustee cannot be found, or is destitute.[2]

On the other hand, unless he has knowledge that a breach of trust has been committed, or there are suspicious circumstances, a new trustee may assume that there has been no breach of trust.[3]

When a trustee retires from a trust, in principle he remains liable for breaches of trust committed during his trusteeship, and his estate will be liable if he is dead. He is only relieved from liability if and to such extent as he may have been released by the continuing trustees, or by the beneficiaries being in possession of the relevant facts at the time.

It may sometimes happen that a breach of trust may occur shortly after one trustee retires. The retiring trustee will be liable if he contemplated that a breach of trust would occur, and he retired with the intention of facilitating it, or believing that it would occur, he retired to avoid being involved in it. He is liable because his motive in retiring was to enable the breach of trust to occur. If he merely realised that his retirement would facilitate the breach of trust, he will not *ipso facto* be liable,[4] but he will be liable if in addition to realising that his retirement would facilitate the breach, he foresaw, or ought reasonably to have foreseen, that such breach would in fact take place. In this case he would be failing in his duty to prevent a breach of trust occurring. It follows that if the retiring trustee did not foresee what would happen, but that the remaining trustees took advantage of his absence to perpetrate the breach, the retiring trustee has not himself failed in any of his duties and he will not be liable.[5]

Apart from this, a trustee is not liable for breaches of trust which occur after his retirement.

---

[1] He will only be liable if loss is caused as a result of the property being left in the hands of others: *Re Miller's Deed Trusts*, L.S.G. May 3, 1978.
[2] *Re Forest of Dean Coal Co.* (1878) 10 Ch.D. 450.
[3] *Re Stratham, ex p. Geaves* (1856) 8 De G.M. & G. 291.
[4] *Head* v. *Gould* [1898] 2 Ch. 250.
[5] *Head* v. *Gould, supra.*

II. ACTS OF CO-TRUSTEES

A trustee can never be liable for the acts of his co-trustee as such, but in certain circumstances he will be liable where a breach of trust is committed by his co-trustee if he himself has been in some way at fault. The position is governed by section 30 of the Trustee Act 1925, which was discussed earlier,[6] as interpreted by *Re Vickery*[7] and *Re City Equitable Fire Insurance Company*.[8]

The general intention of section 30 is clear. It is that a person is responsible for his own acts, neglects and defaults, and not for loss caused through the acts, neglects or defaults of any other person, including co-trustees and agents, unless the loss occurs "through his own wilful default."

It will be recalled that the difficulty arises from the meaning of the words "wilful default."

It was explained previously[9] that the interpretation of "wilful default" given in *Re Vickery* and *Re City Equitable Fire Insurance Co.* have been criticised by several writers because they do not represent the pre-1926 position. Section 30 of the Trustee Act 1925 replaced the now repealed section 31 of the Law of Property Amendment Act 1859, which itself merely incorporated the indemnity clause which it was usual practice to insert in trust instruments.[10] Cases decided on that indemnity clause and on the 1859 Act show clearly that the form of words purporting to exclude liability for loss unless it occurred through the wilful default of the trustee did not exclude liability even for purely passive and innocent breaches of trust.[11] It was thus formerly the law that a trustee would be liable for a breach of trust arising through the act or default of his co-trustee if he merely left a matter in the hands of his co-trustee without inquiry. The majority of pre-1926 cases fall into the following categories:

(a) where the trustee leaves a matter in the hands of his co-trustee without inquiry[12];
(b) where he stands by while a breach of trust of which he is aware is being committed[13];

---

[6] *Ante*, p. 285.
[7] [1931] 1 Ch. 572.
[8] [1925] Ch. 407.
[9] *Ante*, p. 286.
[10] See *Re Brier* (1884) 26 Ch.D. 238 at p. 243 (Lord Selborne).
[11] *Chambers* v. *Minchin* (1802) 7 Ves. 186; *Shipbrook* v. *Hinchinbrook* (1810) 16 Ves. 477; *Hanbury* v. *Kirkland* (1829) 3 Sim. 265; *Broadhurst* v. *Balguy* (1841) 1 Y. & C.C.C. 16; *Thompson* v. *Finch* (1856) 8 De G.M. & G. 560; *Mendes* v. *Guedalla* (1862) 8 Jur. 878; *Hale* v. *Adams* (1873) 21 W.R. 400; *Wynee* v. *Tempest* (1897) 13 T.L.R. 360; *Re Second East Dulwich Building Society* (1899) 68 L.J.Ch. 196.
[12] See the authorities quoted in note 11.
[13] In *Styles* v. *Guy* (1849) 1 Mac. & G. 422 at 433, Lord Cottenham stated that it is the duty of executors and trustees "to watch over, and if necessary, to correct, the conduct of each other." See also *Booth* v. *Booth* (1838) 1 Beav. 125; *Gough* v. *Smith* [1872] W.N. 18.

(c) where he allows trust funds to remain in the sole control of his co-trustee[14];

(d) where, on becoming aware of a breach of trust committed or contemplated by his co-trustee, he takes no steps to obtain redress.[15]

These rules sometimes operated inequitably in the case of passive breaches of trust. Thus, in *Underwood* v. *Stevens*[16] a trustee in good faith allowed trust funds to remain in the hands of his co-trustee, and when he made inquiries of his co-trustee as to certain transactions with those funds, the co-trustee gave false information. The trustee was held liable, however, notwithstanding that the trust instrument provided that trustees should not be liable for loss unless it occurred through their wilful default. The effect of the indemnity clause was, therefore, markedly different from the prima facie meaning of the words used. The effect of the decision in *Re Vickery*[17] has, in effect, been to modify the third of the rules stated above, in interpreting "wilful default" as a consciousness of negligence or a recklessness in the performance of a duty.

Section 30 (1) of the Trustee Act 1925 specifically exempts trustees from liability for signing receipts for the sake of conformity, unless they have actually received the trust money or securities. As all trustees have, as a general principle, to sign receipts, it will be appreciated that these documents frequently circulate among trustees prior to a transaction so that all necessary signatures are obtained by the time that the transaction is to be completed. A trustee is not liable if any breach of trust occurs merely as a result of his having signed such a receipt, though of course if, for example, having signed it he allows his co-trustee to obtain money with the document, and to retain that money for an unreasonable time, he will thereby have acted recklessly and will accordingly make himself liable.

The circumstances in which a trustee is liable for the acts of his agents have been considered in Chapter 14.

III. MEASURE OF LIABILITY

If the trustee has committed a breach of trust, what is the extent of his liability? The basic principles are:

(a) a remedy for breach of trust is to compensate the trust fund for the loss sustained, or to obtain for the trust fund any profit made by the trustee without authority; it is not to punish the trustee; but

(b) if the trustee has been fraudulent, or otherwise behaved particularly

---

[14] *English* v. *Willats* (1831) 1 L.J.Ch. 84; *Ex p. Booth* (1831) Mont. 248; *Child* v. *Giblett* (1834) 3 L.J.Ch. 124; *Hewitt* v. *Foster* (1843) 6 Beav. 259; *Wiglesworth* v. *Wiglesworth* (1852) 16 Beav. 269; *Byass* v. *Gates* (1854) 2 W.R. 487; *Trutch* v. *Lamprell* (1855) 20 Beav. 116; *Cowell* v. *Gatcombe* (1859) 27 Beav. 568; *William* v. *Higgins* (1868) 17 L.T. 525; *Rodbard* v. *Cooke* (1877) 25 W.R. 555; *Lewis* v. *Nobbs* (1878) 8 Ch.D. 591.
[15] *Boadman* v. *Mosman* (1779) 1 Bro.C.C. 68; *Wilkins* v. *Hogg* (1861) 8 Jur.(N.S.) 25 at 26 (Lord Westbury).
[16] (1816) 1 Mer. 712.
[17] [1931] 1 Ch. 572. *cf.,* however, *Re Lucking's Will Trusts* [1968] 1 W.L.R. 866.

badly, the court will reflect its displeasure by increasing the amount of interest payable by the defendant trustee above that which he otherwise would have been ordered to pay.

The following examples will illustrate these principles. All are concerned with the prima facie liability of the trustee, and do not take into account the possibility of some protection or relief being given to the trustee as discussed below.

(1) Payment to wrong person

Where the trustees pay trust money to the wrong person, their liability is to make good to the trust fund that amount, so that the correct beneficiary can be paid out the capital sum wrongly paid, together with interest.[18]

(2) Improper sale of authorised investments

If trustees improperly sell an authorised investment, and reinvest the proceeds in unauthorised investments, which are then sold at a loss, the beneficiaries have a choice. They can compel the trustees either to make good the difference between the sale price of the authorised investment and the proceeds of sale of the unauthorised investment, or to repurchase for the trust the authorised security, taking credit for the proceeds of sale of the unauthorised security. Suppose, therefore, that the trustees hold 400 I.C.I. shares (authorised by the Trustee Investments Act) which they sell for £1,000. That £1,000 is reinvested in the purchase of shares in the Uranium Exploration Co., which are not authorised. A year later these shares are sold for £200. The beneficiaries can compel the trustees to pay to the trust fund £1,000, the proceeds of the I.C.I. shares, less the £200 which they have paid in from the sale of the uranium shares. Alternatively, they can compel the trustees to purchase for the trust 400 I.C.I. shares, however much they might cost. If I.C.I. shares have doubled in price, the trustees will have to pay £2,000 for them, less the £200 received from the sale of the unauthorised investments.

This principle was taken a stage further in *Re Massingberd*.[19] In that case the trustees sold Consols and reinvested in an unauthorised security. The unauthorised security was in due course sold without loss, but by this time the price of Consols had risen. The court held that the trustees should place the beneficiaries in the same position as they would have been had no sale taken place, with the result that they had themselves to pay the increase in the price of the Consols.

In ascertaining their liability, trustees are not entitled to take into account any loss which would have been sustained if they had strictly performed the trust.[20] Suppose, therefore, trustees are directed to invest in investment A. They improperly sell that investment for £1,000 and invest that sum in investment B.

---

[18] See, *post*, p. 451, as to the rate of interest.
[19] (1890) 63 L.T. 296.
[20] *Shepherd* v. *Mouls* (1845) 4 Hare 500 at p. 504; *Watts* v. *Girdlestone* (1843) 6 Beav. 188; *Byrchall* v. *Bradford* (1822) 6 Madd. 235.

Investment B declines in value and is sold for £800, but investment A has also declined and its market price is £700. The trustees are liable to make good, at the option of the beneficiaries, the difference between £800 and £1,000, and they are not excused from liability by virtue of the fact that if investment A had been retained, the holding would have been worth only £700.

(3) Unauthorised investments

It is clear that trustees who invest in unauthorised investments may be called upon to sell those investments, and make good the loss.[21] On the other hand, if a profit is made, that profit accrues to the trust; similarly, with interest. If the trustees make an improper investment in a security which yields a very high income, the income beneficiary is entitled to interest at the ordinary rate, and the balance is then added to capital.[22] Once added to capital, it cannot then be set off against future deficiencies, either of capital on realisation of the investment, or of income.

If all the beneficiaries are ascertained and *sui juris* they may decide to accept an improper investment. In *Thornton* v. *Stokill*[23] it was held that if the beneficiaries did so, they could not in addition claim the difference between the value of the improper investment and the value which authorised investments would have if retained. But in the case of *Re Lake*[24] it was held that they could do so.

(4) Non-investment

Section 11(1) of the Trustee Act 1925 gives trustees the power to pay trust money into a bank while an investment is being sought. It seems, however, that this does not affect cases decided before the Act to the effect that moneys must not be left uninvested for an unreasonable time.[25] On the basis that the old rules still apply:

(a) if the trustees ought to have invested in a *range* of investments, as will usually be the case, their liability is limited to making good the difference between any interest actually received and the rate of interest fixed by the court.[26] The trustees are not liable for any capital loss, because it is impossible to ascertain it.[27]

(b) if the trustees ought to have invested in one specified security only, but did not do so, in the event of the price rising they can be compelled to purchase such an amount of that specified security as they could have purchased with the trust fund at the proper time.

(5) Use for personal purposes

If the trustees use the trust money for their personal purposes, they are liable

---

[21] *Re Salmon* (1889) 42 Ch.D. 351.
[22] *Re Emmets's Estate* (1881) 17 Ch.D. 142. As to the "ordinary" rate of interest, see *post*, p. 451.
[23] (1855) 1 Jur. 151.
[24] [1903] 1 K.B. 439.
[25] *Cann* v. *Cann* (1884) 33 W.R. 40.
[26] As to which, see *post*. p. 451.
[27] *Per* Wigram V.-C., *Shepherd* v. *Mouls* (1845) 4 Hare 500 at p. 504.

to pay back the amount used, or the value[28] of property improperly sold to provide the funds which the trustees use.

Special rules apply as to interest.[29] However, instead of receiving interest, the beneficiaries can require the trustees to pay over the actual profit received.[30] If the trustee has mixed the trust money with his own money, the beneficiaries may claim a proportionate share of the profits.[31]

(6) **Profit to trust fund**

It follows from the principle that the measure of liability is to compensate the trust fund for loss, that if there is a loss neither of income nor of capital, although the trustees may have committed a breach of trust, they will not be held liable. In *Vyse* v. *Foster*,[32] for example, trustees held land and money upon a common trust. Without authority they erected a bungalow on the land for £1,600 and this benefited the trust fund to a greater degree than £1,600. An attempt was made to say that the trustees were liable to pay £1,600 because this expenditure was unauthorised, but at the same time to say that the beneficiaries were entitled to the benefit of the bungalow which was trust property. The Court of Appeal and House of Lords rejected this argument, and it is only surprising that it was accepted at first instance.

(7) **Date at which loss to be assessed**

Where a trustee improperly deals with an asset which thereby ceases to be under his control, it is necessary to determine the date at which the loss to the trust fund is to be measured. Previously, when the values of many assets were more stable than at the present time, the loss was ascertained at the date when proceedings were commenced. Thus, in *Re Massingberd*,[33] where trustees improperly sold Consols, the Court of Appeal ordered them to pay the cost of replacing the Consols as at the date of the writ. However, in *Re Bell's Indenture*,[34] Vinelott J. said[35] that this was incorrect, and that the general principle was that the loss should be ascertained at the date of judgment.

If, however, the trustees improperly dispose of an asset but, had that disposal not taken place, they would at a later date properly have disposed of it, the loss is to be ascertained at that later date, and not at the date of the commencement or conclusion of proceedings. In *Re Bell's Indenture*[36] the court was concerned with a marriage settlement made in 1907 and a voluntary settlement made in

---

[28] Ascertained as at the date of judgment: *infra.*
[29] *Post*, p. 451.
[30] *Newman* v. *Bennett* (1784) 1 Bro.C.C. 359; *Ex p. Watson* (1814) 2 V. & B. 414; *Walker* v. *Woodward* (1826) 1 Russ. 107 at p. 111; *Att-Gen.* v. *Solly* (1829) 2 Sim 518; *Wedderburn* v. *Wedderburn* (1838) 4 My. & Cr. 41 at p. 46; *Jones* v. *Foxall* (1852) 15 Beav. 388; *Williams* v. *Powell* (1852) 15 Beav 388; *Macdonald* v. *Richardson* (1858) 1 Giff. 81; *Townend* v. *Townend* (1859) 1 Giff. 201; *Re Davis, Davis* v. *Davis* [1902] 2 Ch. 314.
[31] *Docker* v. *Somes* (1834) 2 My. & K. 655; *Edinburgh Town Council* v. *Lord Advocate* (1879) 4 App.Cas. 823.
[32] (1872) L.R. 8 Ch. 309; affirmed (1874) L.R. 7 H.L. 318.
[33] (1890) 63 L.T. 296, C.A.
[34] [1980] 3 All E.R. 425.
[35] At p. 439.
[36] [1980] 3 All E.R. 425.

1930. One person, Alexander, was a trustee of both settlements, and was a beneficiary under both settlements. In 1947, the trustees of the marriage settlement improperly sold a farm for £8,200, the purchasers being the trustees of the voluntary settlement. In 1949 the trustees of the voluntary settlement property sold the farm to a third party for £12,400. If the trustees of the marriage settlement had not sold the farm in 1947, they would have done so when the trustees of the voluntary settlement did so in 1949. Vinelott J. held that the liability of the trustees of the marriage settlement was to be limited to the value of the farm in 1949. He also held that no account should be taken of the fact that, if the trustees of the marriage settlement had sold in 1949, they would probably have reinvested the proceeds of sale in another farm, because it was impossible to determine how any such other farm would have appreciated or depreciated.

Where in other circumstances a defaulting trustee is liable to make a payment by way of restitution, that liability continues until restitution is actually made, and this is so even if the settlement has in the meantime come to an end. In *Bartlett* v. *Barclays Bank Trust Co. Ltd.* (*No.* 1)[37] trustees were held liable for permitting a company in which they had a controlling interest to engage in hazardous property speculation, and for the loss which ensued from the reduction in the value of the shares in the company. Three of the beneficiaries became absolutely entitled to their shares in 1974, but the trust company continued to hold the shares as nominees of the beneficiaries until September 1978 when the company disposed of all its speculative investments, and all the shares were sold. In *Bartlett* v. *Barclays Bank Trust Co Ltd.* (*No.* 2)[38] it was held that the loss suffered by the beneficiaries was to be assessed as at September 1978.

(8) No allowance for tax

Where a trustee takes trust moneys and applies them for his own purposes, he is liable to restore the moneys which he has taken, and he is not allowed to benefit from any reduction in the liability to tax which ensues from the misapplication.[39] A further point which arose in *Re Bell's Indenture*[40] was that if the trustees of the marriage settlement had not improperly sold the farm in 1947, but had retained it until 1949, sold it then, and reinvested the proceeds of sale, the value of the trust fund would have been much larger, than it in fact was. This would have given rise to greater liabilities to estate duty[41] on the deaths of successive beneficiaries. It was held, however, that the defaulting trustee was not entitled to reduce the amount which he had to pay to make good the breach of trust by the

---

[37] [1980] 1 All E.R. 139.

[38] [1980] 2 All E.R. 92.

[39] Thus, the rule in *British Transport Commission* v. *Gourley* [1956] A.C. 185, H.L. does not apply.

[40] [1980] 3 All E.R. 425; *ante*, p. 449.

[41] The forerunner of capital transfer tax.

amount of that saving in duty. This was followed[42] in *Bartlett* v. *Barclays Bank Trust Co Ltd. (No.* 2).[43] If the trustees in that case had not permitted the company to engage in loss-making speculative property investments, the company would have made larger dividend payments. This would have increased the income, and so the income tax liability of the beneficiaries. Likewise, if the company had not sustained losses, the shares could have been sold for a higher price, which would probably have increased the liability to capital gains tax. Brightman, L.J held, however, that the trustees were liable to make good the gross loss, and could not take into account the tax savings which has occured, even though this produced "a somewhat unjust bias"[44] against the trustees.

(9) Interest

Where a trustee has misapplied trust funds, he is liable not only to replace those funds, but also to pay interest. Likewise, a trustee is liable to pay interest where, by neglecting to make an investment, income is lost.[45]

There are two questions:

(a) at what rate is the interest to be calculated? and
(b) is the interest to be simple or compounded, and, if compounded, at what frequency?[46]

The approach of the courts, particularly with regard to the rate of interest, has changed in recent years, but the present position appears to be as follows:

(i) Although in the nineteenth century the ordinary rate was 4 per cent.[47] this is totally out of line with modern rates, and the general rule is now to be, broadly, a current commercial rate.
(ii) A current commercial rate has been taken as 1 per cent. above the minimum lending rate,[48] but the most recent authority[49] takes the rate allowed from time to time on the court's short term investment amount.[50] This rate, which is generally in line with that offered by the National Savings Bank, is varied from time to time by statutory instrument. The changes are usually made towards the beginning of a calendar year, and because the changes are made much less

---

[42] Although the report of *Re Bell's Indenture* at [1980] 3 All E.R. 425 is later than that of *Bartlett* v. *Barclays Bank Trust Co. Ltd. (No.* 2) at [1980] 2 All E.R. 92, an earlier report of *Re Bell's Indenture* had appeared at (1979) 123 S.J. 327.
[43] [1980] 2 All E.R. 92.
[44] At p. 96.
[45] *Stafford* v. *Fiddon* (1857) 23 Beav. 386.
[46] The differences are striking. On £10,000, 10 per cent. simple interest for 10 years will amount to £10,000; 10 per cent. interest compounded yearly will amount to £15,937; and 10 per cent. interest compounded half-yearly will amount to £16,533.
[47] *A.G.* v. *Alford* (1855) 4 De G.M. & G. 843; *Fletcher* v. *Green* (1864) 33 Beav. 426.
[48] *Wallersteiner* v. *Moir (No.* 2) [1975] Q.B. 373; *Belmont Finance Corporation* v. *Williams Furniture Ltd (No.* 2) [1980] 1 All E.R. 393.
[49] *Bartlett* v. *Barclays Bank Trust Co Ltd (No.* 2) [1980] 2 All E.R. 92.
[50] Established under s.6(1) of the Administration of Justice Act 1965.

frequently than those of the lending rate, the calculation is more straightforward.[51]

(iii) If a trustee uses trust money for his own purposes, he will be ordered to pay a higher rate if it is a reasonable conclusion that he would have realised a higher rate.[52] This is so without proof that the trustee did in fact derive a higher rate.

(iv) In the absence of special circumstances, the general obligation of the trustee is to pay simple interest,[53] but the court has a discretion to order interest to be compounded.

(v) The trustee will be ordered to pay interest compounded annually if there is an obligation to accumulate.[54] If, however, the trustee should have invested the fund in a specified investment, and there was an obligation to accumulate, the interest must be compounded at the intervals at which interest or dividends would have been received on that investment. So if the trustees would have received interest on the investment half-yearly, the compounding is half-yearly.[55]

(vi) The trustee will also be ordered to pay interest compounded annually if he has used trust money in his own business[56] or for commercial purposes, but probably not if he has used it in his professional practice.[57]

(vii) Although the purpose of ordering a trustee to pay compound rather than simple interest has been stated[58] to be not to punish the trustees, compounding does appear to be used for this purpose in certain cases of active and deliberate fraud or misconduct.[59]

Where a trustee pays interest, it remains to be decided whether the income beneficiaries are entitled to the whole of that interest. In *Bartlett* v. *Barclays Bank Trust Co Ltd. (No. 2)*[60] Brightman, L.J. said[61]: "To some

---

[51] The rates for recent years are

Date of change	Rate
March 1, 1974	9 per cent.
February 1, 1977	10 per cent.
March 3, 1979	12.5 per cent.
January 1, 1980	15 per cent.
January 1, 1981	12.5 per cent.
December 1, 1981	15 per cent.
March 1, 1982	14 per cent.
July 1, 1982	13 per cent.

[52] *A.G.* v. *Alford* (1855) De G.M. & G. 852.
[53] *Stafford* v. *Fiddon* (1857) 23 Beav. 386; *Burdilk* v. *Garrick* (1870) 5 Ch. App. 233; *Vyse* v. *Foster* (1874) L.R. 7 H.L. 318; *Belmont Finance Corporation* v. *Williams Furniture Ltd. (No. 2)* [1970] 1 All E.R. 393.
[54] *Raphael* v. *Boehm* (1805) 11 Ves. 92; *Re Barclay* [1899] 1 Ch. 674.
[55] *Re Emmet's Estate* (1881) 17 Ch.D. 142; *Gilroy* v. *Stephens* (1882) 30 W.R. 745.
[56] *Wallersteiner* v. *Moir (No. 2)* [1975] Q.B. 373.
[57] *Burdick* v. *Garrick* (1870) 5 Ch.App. 233; *Hale Sheldrake* (1889) 60 L.T. 292.
[58] By Lord Hatherley in *Burdick* v. *Garrick* (1870) 5 Ch. App. 233.
[59] e.g. *Jones* v. *Foxall* (1852) 15 Beav. 388; *Gordon* v. *Gonda* [1955] 1 W.L.R. 885.
[60] [1980]
[61] At p. 98.

extent the high interest rates payable on money lent reflect and compensate for the continual erosion in the value of money by reason of galloping inflation. It seems to me arguable, therefore, that if a high rate of interest is payable in such circumstances, a proportion of that interest should be added to capital in order to help maintain the value of the corpus of the trust estate. It may be, therefore, that there will have to be some adjustment as between life tenant and remainderman."

Although no decision was made on this point, the approach reflects that adopted where there is an unauthorised investment in a high income producing security.

(10) Losses on mortgage

Where an unauthorised investment is made which results in loss, the trustees are generally liable for the whole of that loss. But in the case of mortgages section 9 of the Trustee Act 1925 provides that where trust moneys are invested on "mortgage security which would at the time of the investment be a proper investment in all respects for a smaller sum" the trustee will only be liable for the excess over that smaller sum, although that may not represent the loss to the estate. A trustee is not, however, protected by this section where he ought not to have invested on the security of such property at all.[62]

(11) Set-off

If a trustee commits more than one breach of trust, he cannot set off a gain made in one transaction against a loss in another. But each transaction is considered as a whole. In *Fletcher* v. *Green*[63] trustees made an unauthorised investment on mortgage. The property was in due course sold at a loss, and the proceeds were paid into court. The court authorities invested the money in Consols, which rose in price. It was held that the trustees could offset the gain in the Consols against the loss on the mortgage, as these were two incidents in the same transaction. On the other hand, in *Dimes* v. *Scott*[64] trustees committed a breach of trust by failing to realise an unauthorised investment, which they ought to have sold and invested in Consols. Much later, some of the property was sold and invested in Consols. By that time, however, the market price had fallen considerably below the price at which they were standing when the investment should have been made. The trustees sought to offset the gain made in the Consols against the loss on the sale of the unauthorised investment. It was held that they could not do so, for there were here two transactions, not one. The breach of trust was in not realising the unauthorised investment. The gain arose from the authorised investment being at an unusually low figure. The decision is a hard one, and were similar facts to be put before the court today, the court might well strive to reach a different result. *Dimes* v. *Scott* was followed by *Wiles* v.

---

[62] *Re Walker* (1809) 59 L.J. Ch. 386, and see *ante*, p. 322.
[63] (1864) 33 Beav. 426.
[64] (1828) 4 Russ. 195.

Gresham.[65] Where trustees of a marriage settlement committed a breach of trust by negligently failing to recover from the husband the sum of £2,000 which he had covenanted to pay to them. They committed a further breach of trust by investing some of the other trust funds in the purchase of land without authority. The husband, however, with his own money, improved the land considerably, so that it became worth considerably more than when the trustees purchased it. When a claim was made against them for failure to recover the £2,000, the trustees sought to set off the profit made on the investment in the land, but were unable to do so because the transactions were distinct.

The cases show that while the rule is clear—that a gain can only be set off against a loss in the *same* transaction—it may well be difficult to decide whether two or more events are stages in the same transaction, or are separate transactions. The test seems to be that all individual steps taken in pursuance of a common policy can be treated as one "transaction" for this purpose. Thus, in *Bartlett* v. *Barclays Bank Trust Co Ltd.* (*No.* 1),[66] where the trustee allowed the company to embark on two speculative property developments as part of the company's policy of seeking to increase the cash funds available to it, the trustee was allowed to offset the profit from one development against the loss arising from the other.

IV. POSITION OF TRUSTEES INTER SE

Trustees are under a duty to act jointly, and unless the trust instrument provides to the contrary, they do not have authority to act individually. Decisions of trustees usually must be unanimous[67] and there is no question of a vote of the majority binding them all. Also, they may and should ensure that all the trust property and investments are placed in the names of them all. In principle, then, each trustee takes an equal part in the administration of the trust, and has an equal say in what happens to the trust property. Thus, if a breach of trust has been committed, each trustee should be equally liable. But the wronged beneficiary need not sue each trustee: he may sue them all, or on the other hand he may sue only one or two of them. For this reason the liability of trustees is joint and several.

If an action is successfully brought against only one trustee, the general rule is that he has a right of contribution against his co-trustees, so that in the result each trustee contributes equally to the plaintiff's damages. Despite the principle of contribution, a trustee who is sued may sometimes be in a very difficult position. If there are three trustees, Timothy, Titus and Tom, who commit a breach of trust involving the loss of £30,000, the beneficiary, Bruce, may choose to sue Timothy alone: Bruce has a right to recover £30,000 from Timothy, and he is not concerned with Timothy's right of contribution. Timothy can of course claim £10,000 each from Titus and Tom, but if Titus has now disappeared and

---

[65] (1854) 2 Drew. 258; 24 L.J.Ch. 264.
[66] [1980] 1 All E.R. 139. See also *ante*, p. 326.
[67] See *ante*, p. 271.

Tom has gone bankrupt, Timothy's claim will be unsatisfied. In the result, Timothy will have paid out £30,000 and will not have received anything. In order to achieve a greater degree of flexibility and a more equitable result, the operation of the rules of contribution between trustees for breach of trust was somewhat relaxed by the Civil Liability (Contribution) Act 1978. Under this Act, where the loss occasioned by the breach of trust occurs after 1978[68] the court has power to award, in favour of one trustee against another, contribution of such amount as is found to be just and equitable, having regard to the extent of the responsibility of the other trustee for the loss.[69]

The right of contribution does not exist where the trustee have been guilty of fraud.[70]

Under the old rules of equity which are now affected by the Civil Liability (Contribution) Act 1978,[71] there were three cases in which the defendant trustee might claim a complete indemnity from one of his co-trustees. These were:

(1) Breach of trust committee on advice of solicitor-trustee

Where one of the trustees was a solicitor, and the breach of trust was committed solely in reliance on his advice, then the solicitor-trustee must indemnify his co-trustees.[72] It was not sufficient to show merely that one of the trustees at the time of the breach was a solicitor: it must be shown that the other trustees were relying entirely on his advice. Thus in *Head* v. *Gould*[73] Miss Head and a solicitor, Mr. Gould, were the trustees of a settlement. They sold a house forming part of the trust property and instead of reinvesting the proceeds, in breach of trust paid the proceeds to the life-tenant, Miss Head's mother. Following an action by the remainderman against the two trustees, Miss Head sought to be indemnified by the solicitor, but she was unsuccessful. Kekewich J. found that she did not rely on Mr. Gould, but actively urged Mr. Gould to commit the breach. Where the breach of trust was committed principally on the advice of the solicitor-trustee, in order to resist successfully a claim by his co-trustee for indemnity it was for the solicitor-trustee to show that his co-trustee was in full possession of all relevant facts, and made an independent judgment. *Re Partington*[74] was a case involving improper investments. There, Stirling J. said: "I have got to consider the question, has [the solicitor] communicated what he did to Mrs. Partington [the co-trustee] in such a way as to enable her to exercise her judgment upon the investments, and to make them, really and in truth, her acts as well as his own?" The judge found in favour of Mrs. Partington, who was entitled to the indemnity.

(2) One trustee alone benefiting from breach

In *Bahin* v. *Hughes*[75] Cotton L.J. refused to limit the circumstances in which

---

[68] ss. 7(1), 10(1).
[69] ss. 1(1), 2(1).
[70] *Bahin* v. *Hughes* (1886) 31 Ch.D. 390.
[71] s.2(2): see *post*, p. 456.
[72] *Lockhart* v. *Reilly* (1856) 25 L.J.Ch. 697.
[73] *Head* v. *Gould* [1898] 2 Ch. 250.
[74] (1887) 57 L.T. 654.   [75] (1886) 31 Ch.D. 390.

an indemnity would be ordered. "I think it wrong," he said, "to lay down any limitation of the circumstances under which one trustee would be held liable to the others for indemnity, both having been held liable to the *cestui que trust*; but so far as cases have gone at present, relief has only been granted against a trustee who has himself got the benefit of the breach of trust, or between whom and his co-trustees there has existed a relation which will justify the court in treating him as solely liable for the breach of trust . . . ." In *Bahin* v. *Hughes* there were two trustees, one of whom was content to leave the administration of the trust to the other trustee. The other trustee acted honestly, but made an improper investment which caused loss. The passive trustee claimed an indemnity, but was unsuccessful. It is by no means clear how far Cotton L.J.'s dictum goes.

(3) Where trustee also a beneficiary

It was held in *Chillingworth* v. *Chambers*[76] that a trustee who was also a beneficiary and who had participated in a breach of trust must indemnify his co-trustee to the extent of his beneficial interest. This only applied if the trustee-beneficiary had, as between himself and his co-trustees, exclusively benefited from the breach of trust. Suppose therefore that Abraham and Ambrose were trustees of a trust, in which Ambrose had a beneficial interest worth £2,000, but in which Abraham had no interest. Suppose also a breach of trust was committed from which Ambrose derived some benefit, but Abraham did not—*e.g.* investment in unauthorised securities to bring in a higher income—causing a loss of £4,000. Ambrose would be liable to indemnify Abraham to the extent of £2,000, leaving the remaining liability of £2,000 to be shared by them equally. It is not clear whether for the rule in *Chillingworth* v. *Chambers* to apply it is necessary for the trustee-beneficiary actually to receive a benefit from the breach, or whether it is sufficient if the breach was committed with the intention to give him a benefit, but the latter view seems preferable.

Civil Liability (Contribution) Act 1978

Such questions of indemnity are now regulated by the Civil Liability (Contribution) Act 1978. It is provided[77] that in proceedings where contribution is claimed, the court has power to exempt any person from liability to contribute, or to direct that the contribution to be recovered shall amount to a complete indemnity. It appears to be unlikely that this provision will add materially to the cases in which indemnity was available under the old law.

V. Limitation of Actions

Assuming a breach of trust has been committed, and that some loss has occurred, the question then arises whether the beneficiaries are in time to sue. The history of limitation of actions in respect of breaches of trust has been highly complicated, but the position is now governed by the Limitation Act 1980, coupled with the application in certain respects of the equitable doctrine of

---

[76] [1896] 1 Ch. 685.
[77] s.2(1).

laches. "Laches" is delay in bringing action for so long that by his conduct the person wronged is deemed to have waived his claim.

There are two distinct situations, which are now considered.

(1) No statutory period of limitation

Section 21(1) of the Limitation Act 1980, provides that there shall be no statutory period of limitation in respect of an action by a beneficiary under a trust if the action is one:

"(a) in respect of any fraud or fraudulent breach of trust to which the trustee was a party or privy, or

(b) to recover from the trustee trust property or the proceeds thereof in the possession of the trustee, or previously received by the trustee and converted to his use."

It follows that whenever trustees have committed fraud or retained any of the capital of the trust, there is no question of any defence under the statute. Thus, in *Re Howlett*[78] where a trustee occupied property belonging to the trust, he was held to be outside the scope of the Act. Likewise, in *Wassell* v. *Leggatt*,[79] where a husband forcibly took property belonging to his wife, thereby becoming a trustee of it for her, and kept it until his death, his executors were unable to plead the statute.

Where the statute does not apply, the defence of laches may be raised. To establish this defence, it is necessary to show that the beneficiary has known of the breach of trust for a substantial period of time and has acquiesced in it. There are no fixed rules as to the period of time which must elapse: it must in the particular case be sufficiently long to enable the court to impute acquiescence. Likewise, if the beneficiaries clearly acquiesce after only a fairly short time, that will be a sufficient defence. It will be seen, therefore, that the essence of the defence is acquiescence on the part of the beneficiary when in full knowledge of the facts. Accordingly, it is generally considered that delay in taking action is merely evidence of acquiescence[80] although it has been suggested that mere delay may in itself constitute a separate defence apart from acquiescence.[81]

(2) Defence under the statute

(a) **Generally.** In other cases, the Limitation Act 1980 applies. Section 21(3) of that Act, which applies both to express trustees, and to implied or construc-

---

[78] [1949] Ch. 767.

[79] [1896] 1 Ch. 554; see also *Re Tufnell* (1902) 18 T.L.R. 705; *Re Eyre-Williams* [1923] 2 Ch.533.

[80] *Morse* v. *Royal* (1806) 12 Ves. 355; *Life Association of Scotland* v. *Siddal* (1861) 3 De G.F. & J. 58.

[81] *Per* Lindley L.J. in *Re Sharpe* [1892] 1 Ch. 154 at p. 168. See also *Smith* v. *Clay* (1767) 3 Bro.C.C. 639n.

tive[82] trustees, provides that actions to recover trust property or in respect of breach of trust are to be brought within six years from the date on which the right of action accrued. In the case of breach of trust, this is the date on which the breach occurred, and not when the loss was sustained.[83] Suppose, therefore, that a beneficiary knows that the trustees invest in unauthorised investments. At first the investments do well, but later lead to loss. Even though the loss may not be sustained for several years, the limitation period runs from when the unauthorised investment was made. Accordingly, in *Re Swain*[84] trustees were under an obligation to convert the deceased's assets into authorised investments. In breach of trust, they continued to carry on the deceased's business until the youngest beneficiary attained the age of 21. Eight years later, one of the other beneficiaries sought to make the trustees liable for the loss caused through carrying on the business, but they were held entitled to plead the statute.

Although in general no statutory period runs where the trustee has received trust property, a special rule applies where the trustee is also a beneficiary. If the trustee distributed the trust fund honestly and reasonably, but made an over-distribution to himself, the statutory period applies to the extent of his own share, and the excess is subject only to the doctrine of laches.[85]

Section 21(3) also provides that where a beneficiary has a future interest, for the purposes of the Limitation Act the right of action is deemed not to have accrued until his interest falls into possession. The effect of this is that a remainderman can take action in respect of breach of trust at any time during the subsistence of a prior life interest, or within six years from becoming entitled. The operation of section 21(3) is shown by *Re Pauling's Settlement Trusts*.[86] In that case improper advancements were made to beneficiaries, and the trustees pleaded, among other defences, that the period of limitation ran in their favour from the time when the advancements were made. In rejecting this, the Court of Appeal said that the interests of the children to whom the advancements were made were future interests, within the terms of the proviso to section 21(3), and that if an improper advancement was made, that did not start the limitation period running. As the advancement was improper, it did not bind the children at all. They could therefore, sue at the time when they ought to have received the whole of their share.

[82] s.19(2) only applies where the action is against a "trustee," and not where the action is against someone who, although in a fiduciary capacity, is not a trustee. In *Tito* v. *Waddell* (*No. 2*) [1977] Ch. 106 (*ante*, p. 6) the Crown was held not to be in a fiduciary position. However, Megarry V.-C. said (at p. 249) that even if the Crown had been in a fiduciary position, it would not have been a trustee, so that the claim would not have been barred by s.19(2) of the Limitation Act 1939, which is now re-enacted as s.21(3) of the 1980 Act. Further, the doctrine of laches applied, but was no bar in this case because it had not been pleaded.
[83] *Re Somerset* [1894] 1 Ch. 231.
[84] [1891] 3 Ch. 233.
[85] Limitation Act, 1980, s. 21(2).
[86] [1964] Ch. 303.

Section 21(3), however, must be read in conjunction with section 21(4), which provides that where the statute can be pleaded against a beneficiary, he cannot benefit from an action brought by a beneficiary against whom the statute cannot be pleaded.[87] Suppose, therefore, that trustees hold investments upon trust for Daphne for life, with remainder to Chloe. Suppose also that they sell one of those investments and improperly hand over the proceeds to Daphne's daughter. In the absence of fraudulent concealment Daphne will be debarred from suing after six years. Chloe may wait until Daphne's death before suing, but she may sue before then. If she sues before then, she can compel the trustees to make good the capital loss, but during the lifetime of Daphne the trustees can themselves retain the income from that property.

(b) **Fraud.** As has been stated, there is no statutory period of limitation for action in respect of a fraudulent breach of trust, but it will be appreciated that a non-fraudulent breach of trust may have been committed, and subsequently concealed by fraud. Special provision is made, therefore, for actions based on fraud, or actions concealed by fraud. Section 32, which is of general application and is not confined to actions for breach of trust, provides that where an action is based upon the fraud of the defendant or his agent, or where a right of action is concealed by fraud, "the period of limitation shall not begin to run until the plaintiff has discovered the fraud . . . or could with reasonable diligence have discovered it." For the purposes of this section, "fraud" is wider than the type of conduct which would give rise to an independent action, and in *Beaman* v. *A.R.T.S. Ltd.*[88] Lord Greene M.R. pointed out that the fraudulent conduct "may acquire its character as such from the very manner in which that act is performed."

The scope of section 32[89] was recently illustrated by *Eddis* v. *Chichester Constable.*[90] One of the assets of the trust in that case was a painting of St. John the Baptist by Caravaggio. The painting used to hang in a stately home where the life tenant lived, and in 1950 he lent it for an exhibition at Burlington House. During that exhibition he sold it to a consortium of art dealers, who subsequently sold it to an art gallery in Kansas City. The life tenant had no title to the painting, and when the trustees discovered the loss of the painting in 1963 they brought an action against, *inter alios*, the estate of the life tenant, who was by then dead, for damages for breach of trust. In the course of his judgment, Lord Denning M.R. said[91] . . . "one thing is quite clear: the right of action was 'concealed by the fraud' of the [life tenant]. I do not know that he did anything actively to deceive the trustees, but that does not matter. His wrongful sale of the heirloom was enough. It was a fraud; and by saying nothing about it, he concealed the fraud."

---

[87] *Re Somerset* [1894] 1 Ch. 231.
[88] [1949] 1 K.B. 550.
[89] The decision was on s.26 of the 1939 Act, which corresponded with s.32 of the 1980 Act.
[90] [1969] 2 Ch. 345.
[91] At p. 356.

VI. IF TRUSTEE PRIMA FACIE LIABLE, OBTAINING RELIEF OR EXEMPTION FROM LIABILITY

Even if an action can prima facie be brought against a trustee, it may nevertheless be possible for him to claim total or partial relief. The possibilities are:

(a) by a provision in the trust instrument;
(b) by an application to the court;
(c) by act of the beneficiaries, whether concurrence in or waiver of the breach;

and in addition the trustees may benefit
(d) by indemnity from the beneficiaries.

1. *Provision in the Trust Instrument*

It was stated above that the trust instrument can authorise a large number of acts which would not otherwise be open to the trustee. If the trustee takes advantage of that provision, he is, of course, not guilty of a breach of trust. But even if he is guilty of a breach, he can still be relieved from liability. Thus one clause in use is:

> "In the professioned execution of the trusts hereof no trustee shall be liable for any loss to the trust property arising by reason of any improper investment made in good faith or by reason of any mistake or omission made in good faith by any trustee hereof or by reason of any other matter of thing except wilful and individual fraud or wrongdoing on the part of the trustee who is sought to be made liable."

The golden rule is, therefore, always have a look at the trust instrument.

2. *Application to Court*

The court has power over a wide field before an act is done to sanction acts even if they would otherwise be a breach of trust.[92] Where no such application is made, however, by virtue of section 61 of the Trustee Act 1925 the court has a discretion to grant relief. The section provides that if it appears to the court that a trustee is or may be personally liable for any breach of trust but has acted honestly and reasonably, and ought fairly to be excused for the breach of trust or for omitting to obtain the directions of the court in the matter in which he committed such breach, then the court may relieve him either wholly or partly from personal liability.

Thus the trustee must

(a) have acted honestly;
(b) have acted reasonably; and
(c) ought fairly to be excused.

---

[92] For example, see *Boardman* v. *Phipps* [1967] 2 A.C. 46, discussed *ante*, p. 394.

"Honestly," here, means in good faith. "Reasonably" is a question of fact which depends on the circumstances of each case. The courts have consistently refused to lay down any rules[93] but there have been numerous applications under the section, and under the provisions which it replaced. In *Re Kay*[94] the applicant was an executor and trustee of a will of a testator who left over £22,000 with apparent liabilities of only about £100. Before advertising for claims, the executor paid to the widow a legacy of £300, and only afterwards learned of liabilities which exceeded the value of the estate. It was held that it was reasonable for the executor to assume that with an estate of this size liabilities would not approach the value of the estate, so that he could safely pay the legacy. The court therefore granted him relief.

Difficulties sometimes arise when a trustee has taken legal advice, but such advice was wrong. Although it is hard on the trustee, the fact that he has taken and has followed legal advice does not automatically excuse him from liability. In *National Trustee Co. of Australasia* v. *General Finance Co. of Australasia*,[95] for example, trustees followed the advice of their solicitors, but this advice was wrong. It was held in the special circumstances that they should not be granted relief. One of the factors to be taken into account is the size of the trust property. If the property is of low value, trustees would probably be reasonable in taking the advice of a solicitor, whereas if the trust fund were very large, the advice of Q.C. might well be warranted.

Two aspects of the section were considered by Plowman J. in *Re Rosenthal*.[96] The testator devised his house to his sister and left the remainder of his estate to his widow. The estate duty payable in respect of the house, amounting to £1,700, should have been paid by the sister, but the executors, who for this purpose were treated as trustees,[97] transferred the house to the sister without making any arrangements with her to secure the payment of the duty.[98] They paid £270 on account of the duty liability and were left to pay £1,500. One of the trustees, who was a solicitor and who was acting in connection with the administration of the estate, claimed to be entitled to rely on section 61. Plowman J. rejected this contention on two grounds. First, in respect of the £270 which had been paid, improperly, from residue, although he had acted honestly, he had not acted reasonably and had not shown that he ought fairly to be excused. On this ground Plowman J. took account of the fact that he was a professional trustee[99] and appears to have adopted a more stringent approach. Secondly, the question was whether section 61 could apply to an *anticipated*

---

[93] *Per* Byrne J. in *Re Turner* [1897] 1 Ch. 536; *per* Romer J. in *Re Kay* [1897] 2 Ch., at p. 524.

[94] [1897] 2 Ch. 518.

[95] [1905] A.C. 373.

[96] *Re Rosenthal, Schwarz* v. *Bernstein* [1972] 1 W.L.R. 1273.

[97] One of the persons appointed executors had purported to resign from his office through appointment of new trustees. This was probably invalid, but the so-called new trustees were treated by the judge as trustees for the purposes of the case.

[98] The liability of the sister arose under the Finance Act 1894, s.9(1). See *Re the Countess of Orford* [1896] 1 Ch. 257.

[99] [1972] 1 W.L.R., at p. 1278.

breach of trust. The remaining £1,500 which was still to be paid had not been paid from residue, and so no breach of trust had actually occurred in respect of it. The solicitor was in effect seeking a declaration that he was entitled to take this sum from residue. Plowman J. held that the section was incapable of giving relief in respect of a breach of trust which had not yet occurred.

It does not follow when it is shown that a trustee has acted honestly and reasonably that he will automatically be excused: it is only when these conditions are fulfilled that the court has a *discretion* to grant relief. It has been suggested that where a trustee takes the wrong advice of his solicitor, he ought to sue his solicitor. Where he does not seek to recover the loss from the solicitor (assuming the solicitor to be liable for negligence) the court would probably not excuse the trustee.

It is clear that it is far more difficult for a paid trustee to obtain relief than it is for an unpaid trustee to do so. In the *National Trustee Co. of Australasia* case the court had in mind the fact that the trustees were paid. But in *Re Pauling*[1] the Court of Appeal said that relief under section 61 can be granted to a paid trustee if the circumstances are appropriate, and a degree of relief was granted in that case to paid trustees who were bankers. But in its judgment the Court of Appeal held that "Where a banker undertakes to act as a paid trustee of a settlement created by a customer, and so deliberately places itself in a position where its duty as trustee conflicts with its interest as a banker, we think that the court should be very slow to relieve such a trustee under the provisions of the section."[2]

If the court does decide to grant relief, it has a discretion to grant partial or total relief.

3. By Act of Beneficiaries

A beneficiary who has once agreed to, or concurred in, a breach of trust cannot afterwards sue the trustees in respect of it. This applies only if three conditions are satisfied:

(a) that the beneficiary was of full age and sound mind at the time when he agreed or concurred;
(b) that he had full knowledge of all relevant facts, and the legal effect of his agreement or concurrence; and
(c) that he was an entirely free agent, and was not under any undue influence.

A good example of the working of this rule is *Nail* v. *Punter*[3] In that case

---

[1] [1964] Ch. 303.

[2] See also *Re Windsor Steam Coal Company (1901) Ltd.* [1929] 1 Ch. 151, and *Re Waterman's Will Trusts* [1952] 2 All E.R. 1054. In *Re Cooper (No. 2)* (1978) 21 O.R. (2d) 579 (Ontario) the two trustees were the senior partner in a trustee law firm, and one of his junior partners. The whole of the conduct of the administration was left in the hands of the senior partner, who stole Can. $180,000 and was sentenced to seven and a half years imprisonment. The court found that the junior partner had no reason to suspect the fraud of his senior partner, and that he had acted honestly and reasonably. It therefore granted him relief under the Ontario equivalent of s.61.

[3] (1832) 5 Sim. 555.

trustees held stock upon trust for a married woman for life, with remainder to such person as she should by will appoint. During her lifetime, the woman's husband persuaded the trustees to sell the stock and pay him the proceeds. The wife then brought an action against the trustees but, before it was concluded, died, having by her will appointed the stock to her husband. The husband endeavoured to claim the same remedy as his wife had sought. But the husband, having become a beneficiary by virtue of the exercise of the power of appointment, could not succeed because he had been a party to the breach.

A trustee is also protected from action if the beneficiaries subsequently learn of the breach, and acquiesce in it, or give the trustee a release. Again, the beneficiaries must be *sui juris*, have full knowledge of the relevant facts, and act as free agents. Often releases are granted formally under seal, but an informal release, if supported by consideration, will be effective. In *Ghost* v. *Waller*,[4] for example, part of the trust property was lost through a breach of trust. The beneficiary agreed through her solicitors by letter that in consideration of the trustees undertaking to assist in recovering part of the loss she would "give up all claims if she has any against her trustees for negligence." It was held that this was an effective release.

Neither a formal nor an informal release will be effective if the beneficiary was not in full possession of the facts. In *Thompson* v. *Eastwood*[5] the beneficiary was entitled to a legacy under a will. The trustee denied the beneficiary's right to that legacy by virtue of alleged illegality, and the dispute was settled on the payment by the trustee of a smaller sum than that to which the beneficiary was entitled. A formal deed of release was executed, but when the beneficiary discovered the true position, he was held entitled to claim the full legacy, despite the deed of release, and despite an interval of over 25 years from the breach.

In *Re Pauling*,[6] one of the defences put forward by the trustees was that the beneficiaries, when over 21, had consented to the improper advances being made. It is clear that had those consents been effective, the beneficiaries could not afterwards have succeeded in an action against the trustees. It has, however, long been clearly established that where an infant makes a gift in favour of his parent, there will be a presumption of undue influence on the part of the parent[7] and that this presumption will continue for a short time—the exact period is undefined and depends on the circumstances of each case—after the infant attains his majority.[8] As far as the trustees are concerned, what is the effect on an advancement to favour a parent and not a child of a consent given by that child which may be the result of undue influence? The Court of Appeal in *Re Pauling* said: "Without expressing a final opinion, we think that the true view may be that a trustee carrying out a transaction in breach of trust may be liable if

[4] (1846) 9 Beav. 497.
[5] (1877) 2 App.Cas. 215; and see *Re Freeston's Charity* [1978] 1 W.L.R. 741, C.A. (no acquiescence in a breach of a charitable trust).
[6] [1964] Ch. 303, and see *ante*, p. 371.
[7] *Huguenin* v. *Baseley* (1807) 14 Ves. 273.
[8] See *Lancashire Loans Ltd.* v. *Black* [1934] 1 K.B. 380.

he knew, or ought to have known, that the beneficiary was acting under the undue influence of another, or may be presumed to have done so, but will not be liable if it cannot be established that he so knew or ought to have known." A trustee who is asked to commit a breach of trust for the benefit of a parent on the basis of consent by a beneficiary just turned 18 ought, therefore, to be reasonably sure that the child is emancipated from the parent.

4. *Indemnification by Beneficiary of Trustee*

It has already been shown that, subject to the conditions just mentioned, a beneficiary who with full knowledge concurs in a breach of trust cannot afterwards sue his trustees. This would not, however, affect the right of other beneficiaries to take action, and if such action is taken the trustee may be able to claim an indemnity out of the beneficial interest of the beneficiary who is concerned in the breach. There are two rules which overlap:

(i)   under the inherent jurisdiction, the court has power to order a beneficiary to give the trustee an indemnity

   (a)   if he instigated[9] or requested[10] a breach of trust with the intention of obtaining a personal benefit (whether or not such personal benefit was in fact received) or

   (b)   if he concurred in a breach of trust and actually derived a personal benefit from it[11]

(ii) under section 62 of the Trustee Act 1925 the court may impound the interest of a beneficiary in the trust fund if he instigates or requests or consents in writing to a breach of trust by the trustee. Where the section applies, the court has a discretion whether to impound, and, if so, whether to impound the whole or only part of the beneficiary's interest.

It will be seen that section 62 applies irrespectively of personal benefit, or of a motive for personal benefit. On the other hand, section 62 only applies in the case of mere consent to a breach of trust if such consent was in writing, whereas the general jurisdiction of the court operates whether or not the consent is in writing. The court will not exercise its power to impound the beneficiary's interest unless the trustee can show that the beneficiary fully appreciated that the proposed action would constitute a breach of trust.

By a fairly robust construction, it was held in *Re Pauling* (*No.* 2)[12] that the power under section 62 can be exercised in favour of a person who is not a trustee at the time when the breach of trust occurred. In coming to this decision, Wilberforce J. was clearly influenced by the consideration that if the section only applied to persons who were trustees at the time of the application, the court might be loth to remove trustees before such application has been made, even if from the other circumstances of the case their removal was desirable.

---

[9] *Trafford* v. *Boehm* (1746) 3 Atk. 440.
[10] *Fuller* v. *Knight* (1843) 6 Beav. 205.
[11] *Montford* v. *Cadogan* (1816) 19 Ves. 635.
[12] [1963] Ch. 576.

Where a beneficiary unsuccessfully brings proceedings against a trustee alleging breach of trust, the trustee will be entitled to take his costs out of the trust fund and only if that is insufficient will an order be made against the beneficiary personally.[13]

VII. Personal and Real Basis of Remedies for Breach of Trust

So far this chapter has been concerned with the actions against trustees *personally* for breach of trust. So far as a beneficiary is concerned, this may be inadequate, and clearly will be if the trustees are insolvent. In these circumstances the beneficiaries may seek either a *personal* remedy against persons who have wrongly received the trust property or a *real* remedy operating against the trust property itself. Such circumstances involve considering the legal basis of remedies for breach of trust. In the leading case of *Re Diplock*,[14] Caleb Diplock by his will directed his executors to apply his residuary estate "for such charitable institution or institutions or other charitable or benevolent object or objects" as they should in their absolute discretion think fit. His executors distributed the residue amounting to over £200,000 among 139 charities. This was in fact done before the testator's next-of-kin challenged the validity of the bequest. The House of Lords, in the litigation that followed, held in *Chichester Diocesan Fund and Board of Finance (Ince.)* v. *Simpson*[15] that the bequest was invalid. *Re Diplock* was concerned with the next-of-kin's claims to recover the money from the executors and the charities which had received it.

The claims of the next-of-kin against the executors were eventually compromised, with the approval of the court. But actions continued for the considerable balance against the institutions which had participated in the distribution. The money had been devoted by the institutions to diverse purposes. In the majority of cases, the cheques sent to them had been paid into their general accounts at the bank. Some of such accounts were in credit: some were overdrawn, and some of the latter secured and some unsecured. In a few cases payment had been made into a special account. In others it had been earmarked for some designated purpose. In yet others the money had been spent on altering or enlarging existing buildings owned by the charity. The next-of-kin were concerned with recovering the money from the recipients. They based their claim under two heads. These were: (i) *in personam* and (ii) *in rem*. By the claim *in personam* was meant that they claimed against the charities personally by reason of the "equity" they had to recover the money. This "equity," according to their contentions, an unpaid creditor, legatee or next-of-kin possessed against an overpaid beneficiary or stranger to the estate. By the claim *in rem* was meant their alleged ability to trace assets which are identifiable—whether they are unmixed or have become part of a mixed fund—into the hands of volunteers, as were the charities in question in this case, which had wrongly received them.

---

[13] *Re Spurling's Will Trusts* [1966] 1 W.L.R. 920.
[14] [1948] Ch. 465; affirmed by H.L. *sub nom. Ministry of Health* v. *Simpson* [1951] A.C. 251.
[15] [1944] A.C. 341; and see *ante*, p. 218.

It should be noted that although *Re Diplock* was concerned with claims against innocent volunteers who had received property from the personal representatives, similar general principles apply where (indeed this is what usually happens) the claim is directly against trustees or persons in a fiduciary position. Furthermore, the proprietary remedy *in rem* is of more significance in the law of trusts than the claim *in personam* because, if it lies, it enables the beneficiaries to trace the trust money into the property acquired with it, in priority to the general creditors of the trustee, if he is insolvent, for the reason that a trust or fiduciary obligation attaches to it. But it is useful to discuss the basis of the claim *in personam* as well, as it was considered at length in *Re Diplock*.

1. *The Claim in Personam*

(1) **The moral claim of the charities**
It was argued for the charities that, notwithstanding the formal invalidity of the bequest, it should at any rate be taken that Caleb Diplock intended the institutions to enjoy the residuary estate in preference to his blood-relations and, therefore, it did not lie in the mouths of the next-of-kin to allege any "unconscientiousness" on the part of those whose claim was in accordance with the wishes of the testator, however ineffectually those wishes had been expressed. But this argument, based as it was on the postulate that the conscience of the recipients should be in some degree affected by their retention of the moneys, was rejected by the court as wholly untenable: "it is impossible to contend that a disposition which according to the general law of the land is held to be entirely invalid can yet confer upon those who, *ex hypothesi*, have improperly participated under the disposition some moral or equitable right to retain what they have received against those whom the law declares to be properly entitled."[16]

(2) **Recipient's notice of the invalidity of the gift**
It was argued for the next-of-kin that by the terms of the letter which accompanied all the executor's payments, and which though not entirely accurately set out the terms of the gift, the charities were given notice of the invalidity of the trusts, or at least were put on inquiry as regards their validity. And (so the argument ran) they were subjected to a constructive trust of the moneys they received in favour of the next-of-kin. But this argument, although admittedly it had some attraction, was rejected. "Persons in the position of the respondents, themselves unversed in the law, are entitled in such circumstances as these to assume that the executors are properly administering the estate."[17]

(3) **The next-of-kin's equitable right of recovery**
This argument, which the Court of Appeal subjected to an exhaustive analysis, was to the effect, as the court put it: "Apart from any notice which the respondents may have had of the true effect of the testator's will,

---

[16] [1948] Ch. 465, at p. 476.
[17] *Ibid.* at pp. 478–479.

they had in truth no right to receive any of the moneys paid to them and that . . . the unpaid next-of-kin had a direct claim, recognised and established by the courts of equity, to recovery from the respondents of the sums improperly paid to the respondents and properly belonging to the next-of-kin."

(a) **Mistake of law.** It was on this question that the judge in the court below[18] (Wynn-Parry J.) came to the conclusion that an unpaid beneficiary could only sue the wrongly paid recipient in equity when the payment had been made under a mistake of fact; and here there was a mistake of law.

It was acknowledged by the Court of Appeal that the mistake was one of law and, moreover, as Wynn-Parry J. had held, that as regards *common law* claims for money had and received the action would not lie where money had been paid under a mistake of law. But the fundamental point on which the court differed from the judge was that the common law claim was in no sense derived from equity but had a lineage altogether independent of it.[19] The court, taking the view that there was no "necessity in logic for the claim as being clothed, as it were, with all the attributes or limitations appropriate to the common law action for money had and received,"[20] went on to consider the relevant cases dating back as far as the days of Lord Keeper Bridgman and Lord Keeper Finch (afterwards Lord Nottingham L.C.) to see what principles had been established by them.[21] And having done so, the court rejected the contention that in equity the mistake under which the payment is made must be one of fact. As Lord Simonds said[22] in the House of Lords, where the decision was affirmed:

> "It would be a strange thing if the Court of Chancery having taken upon itself to see that the assets of a deceased person were duly administered was deterred from doing justice to the creditor, legatee or next-of-kin because the executor had done him wrong under a mistake of law. If in truth this were so, I think that the father of Equity would not recognise his own child."

It will also be appreciated that the unpaid creditor, legatee or next-of-kin would not himself be a party to the wrongful payment: the executor would be responsible for that. It is, therefore, difficult to see, as Lord Simonds said,

---

[18] [1947] Ch. 716.

[19] [1948] Ch. 465, at p. 480.

[20] *Ibid.* at p. 481.

[21] *Supra*, at p. 482. The cases cited and discussed at length included *Nelthrop* v. *Hill* (1669) 1 Ch.Cas. 135; *Grove* v. *Banson, ibid.* at p. 148; *Chamberlain* v. *Chamberlain* (1675) 1 Ch.Cas. 256; *Noel* v. *Robinson* (1682) 1 Vern. 90; *Anonymous* (1682) 1 Vern. 162; *Newman* v. *Barton* (1690) 2 Vern. 205; *Anonymous* (1718) 1 P.Wms. 495; *Orr* v. *Kaines* (1750) 2 Ves.Sen. 194; *Walcot* v. *Hall* (1788) 2 Bro.C.C. 304; *Gillespie* v. *Alexander* (1827) 3 Russ. 130; *Greig* v. *Somerville* (1830) 1 Russ. & My. 338; *David* v. *Frowd* (1833) 1 My. & K. 200; *Sawyer* v. *Birchmore* (1836) 1 Keen 391; *Thomas* v. *Griffith* (1860) 2 Giff. 504; *Fenwick* v. *Clarke* (1862) 4 De G.F. & J. 240; *Peterson* v. *Peterson* (1866) L.R. 3 Eq. 111; *Rogers* v. *Ingham* (1876) 3 Ch.D. 351; *Re Robinson* [1911] 1 Ch. 502; *Re Hatch* [1919] 1 Ch. 351; *Re Rivers* [1920] 1 Ch. 320; *Re Mason* [1928] Ch. 385; [1929] 1 Ch. 1,C.A.; *Re Blake* [1932] 1 Ch. 54.

[22] *Ministry of Health* v. *Simpson* [1951] A.C. 251, at p. 270.

what relevance the distinction between mistake of fact and law can have to such a situation.[23]

(b) **Administration of the estate by the court.** Wynn-Parry J. had also held that it was necessary that there must be or have been administration by the court before the equitable remedy *in personam* would lie. But the Court of Appeal, after analysing the cases,[24] came to the conclusion that they wholly negatived any such requirement[25]: if the court had administered the estate there would be every reason why equity should come to the rescue of an underpaid legatee if a wrong payment were made, but there seemed no reason why such administration should be essential.

(c) **Stranger to the estate.** The cases mentioned above[26] also established that it is irrelevant to the applicability of the remedy that the original recipient had no title at all and was a stranger to the estate.[27] No doubt many of the cases are concerned with providing equality between the original recipient and other persons having a like title to that of the recipient—*e.g.* next-of-kin—but there is no reason why the remedy should not be applied as against a stranger even though the effect of the refund will be actually to dispossess him rather than to produce equality.

(d) **The "conscience" of the recipient.** It had been argued that the conscience of the recipient, on which equity must fasten, was not affected in circumstances such as these. But the Court of Appeal decided that it is prima facie at least a sufficient circumstance that the charities had received some share of the estate to which they were not entitled.[28] As Sir John Leach said long before in *David v. Frowd*,[29] "a party claiming under such circumstances has no great reason to complain that he is called upon to replace what he has received against his right."

(e) **Conditions for the application of the equitable remedy.** The foregoing has shown that *Re Diplock* established (a) than an equitable remedy is available equally to an unpaid or underpaid creditor, legatee or next-of-kin, and (b) that a claim by the next-of-kin will not be liable to be defeated merely (i) in the absence of administration by the court; or (ii) because the mistake under which the original payment was made was one of law rather than fact; or (iii) because the original recipient had no title at all and was a stranger to the estate.[30]

But there is one important qualification that must be fulfilled before a claim by an unpaid beneficiary can succeed. This was stated by the Court of Appeal in *Re Diplock* as follows.[31]

---

[23] *Ibid.*
[24] See cases cited in note 21, *supra*.
[25] [1948] Ch. 465, at p. 489.
[26] See cases cited in note 21, *supra*.
[27] [1948] Ch. 465, at p. 502.
[28] *Ibid.* at p. 503.
[29] (1883) 1 My. & K 200, at p. 211.
[30] [1948] Ch. 465, at p. 502.
[31] *Ibid.* at p. 503.

"Since the original wrong payment was attributable to the blunder of the personal representatives, the right of the unpaid beneficiary is in the first instance against the wrongdoing executor or administrator: and the beneficiary's direct claim in equity against those overpaid or wrongly paid should be limited to the amount which he cannot recover from the party responsible. In some cases the amount will be the whole amount of the payment wrongly made, *e.g.* where the executor or administrator is shown to be wholly without assets or is protected from attack by having acted under an order of the court."[32]

In the actual case the claims of the next-of-kin against the executors or their estates were compromised. Accordingly it was held that the amount recovered from the executors should be apportioned among the charities in proportion to the money the latter had wrongly received. This meant that the maximum recoverable from an individual charity by the next-of-kin should be rateably reduced.[33]

(f) **No liability for interest**. The Court of Appeal established that the recipients were only liable for the principle claimed and not for any interest.[24]

(4) **Possible limitations of the remedy in personam**

Re Diplock was concerned with any claim in respect of the administration of an estate and was dealt with by the Court of Appeal and by the House of Lords[35] strictly on that basis. It is not, therefore, so clearly established that the principles laid down will apply with equal force between beneficiaries under a trust pure and simple, although there seems no cogent reason why they should not. But whether or not the case extends to the law of trusts, one problem has arisen and one day will require solution. Assume that an innocent volunteer uses money which he has wrongly received and expends it in a fashion which is not for his personal benefit. Will the claim *in personam* still lie against him to the extent of the moneys received? It has been suggested[36] with some force that the claimant should be left to his remedy *in rem* which, as will be seen, will entitle him to rank simply *pari passu* with the innocent volunteer. For otherwise the rule that the conscience of the recipient is affected by reason of the fact of overpayment, and accordingly that he is bound to disgorge whatever he has received, might work injustice.[37] The position of the innocent volunteer—and this is so whether he is a beneficiary under a trust or whether he is a stranger who has received part of the deceased's assets—may well require further consideration from a superior court.

---

[32] For early authority for this proposition, see *Orr* v. *Kaines* (1750) 2 Ves.Sen. 194; *Hodges* v. *Waddington* (1684) 2 Vent. 360.

[33] [1948] Ch. 465 at p. 506.

[34] The authority is *Gittins* v. *Steele* (1818) 1 Swanst. 200.

[35] *Sub nom. Ministry of Health* v. *Simpson* [1951] A.C. 251.

[36] See Nathan & Marshall, p. 462. See also Denning (1949) 65 L.Q.R. 37 at pp. 49–50; Jones (1957) 73 L.Q.R. 48.

[37] See *post*, p. 471.

2. *The Claim in Rem*

The Court of Appeal in *Re Diplock* also subjected the question of the next-of-kin's rights *in rem* to an exhaustive analysis. They did so primarily in case their decision on the basis of the remedy *in personam* was reversed by the House of Lords. But in *Ministry of Health* v. *Simpson* the House, in affirming the decision of the Court of Appeal, did not find it necessary to consider the question of rights *in rem*.

A right *in rem* in this context is concerned with actually "tracing" the money into the hands of the person who has wrongly received it, in this case into the hands of the charities themselves.

(1) Common law and equity

The Court of Appeal first pinpointed the basic distinction between the respective attitudes of common law and equity to claims *in rem* by formulating the following general propositions[38]:

(1) The common law approached the matter in a strictly materialistic way. It could only appreciate the "physical" identity of one thing with another. It could only treat a person's money as identifiable so long as it had not become mixed with other money. It could treat as identifiable with the money other kinds of property acquired by means of it, provided that there was no admixture of other money. This approach was based on the principle that the unauthorised act of purchasing was capable of ratification by the owner of the money,[39] and not to any known theory of tracing as was adopted in equity.

(2) "The common law did not recognise equitable claims to property, whether money or any other form of property. Sovereigns in A's pocket either belonged in law to A or they belonged in law to B. The idea that they could belong in law to A and they could nevertheless be treated as belonging to B was entirely foreign to the common law."[40]

(3) The remedies open to the common law were also extremely limited. Specific relief as distinct from damages (the normal remedy at common law) was confined to a very limited range of remedies as compared with the extensive uses of specific relief developed by equity. In particular the device of the declaration of charge was unknown to the common law and it was the availability of this device which enabled equity to give effect to its wide conception of equitable rights.[41]

(4) "It was the materialistic approach of the common law coupled with and encouraged by the limited range of remedies available to it that prevented the common law from identifying money in a mixed fund. Once the money of B had become mixed with the money of A its identification in a physical sense became impossible; owing to the fact of mixture there could be no question of ratification of an unauthorised act; and the only remedy of B, if any, lay in an action for damages."[41]

---

[38] [1948] Ch. 518 *et seq.*
[39] *Sinclair* v. *Brougham* [1914] A.C. 398, at p. 441, *per* Lord Parker.
[40] [1948] Ch. 465, at p. 519.   [41] *Ibid.* at p. 520.

The attitude of equity was quite different. As the Court of Appeal put it, it "adopted a more metaphysical approach. It found no difficulty in regarding a composite fund as an amalgam constituted by the mixture of two or more funds each of which could be regarded as having, for certain purposes, a continued separate existence. Putting it another way, equity regarded the amalgam as capable, in proper circumstances, of being resolved into component parts."[42] And, most important, this "metaphysical' approach, coupled with the remedy of a declaration of charge, enabled equity to identify money in a mixed fund.

(2) Purchase for value without notice

It must be emphasised at the outset of any discussion of the scope of the equitable remedy *in rem* that a transferee who is a *purchaser for value without notice* is immune from the remedy. The claim of the true owner of the money is extinguished just as all other equitable estates or interests are extinguished by a purchase for value without notice.[43] And what follows must be read subject to this overriding consideration.

(3) Extent of the equitable remedy in rem

It is clearly established that property or money—whether it is kept in a hole in the ground or paid into a separate bank account—is traceable into the hands of a recipient who has wrongly taken possession of it. The same applies where the money is used for the purchase of specific property. Indeed in these cases the common law, as well as equity, will provide a remedy for the purpose. In such case the beneficial owner is entitled at his election to take the property purchased with the trust money or have a charge on the property for the amount of the trust money. But, as already indicated, common law will not furnish a remedy where the property has been mixed with the recipient's own assets. It is here that equity takes the field. The principle was laid down by Sir George Jessel M.R. in *Re Hallett's Estate*[44] when he stated that where a trustee has mixed the trust money with his own and then purchased property with the mixture the beneficial owner can no longer elect to take the property because it is no longer bought with trust money simply and purely but with a mixed fund. But he is still entitled to a charge on the property purchased in respect of the amount of trust money laid out in the purchase.

The charge on the property would seem, therefore, to apply only to the extent of the actual trust money wrongly mixed, together with interest: it would take no account of any increase in value of the property purchased with its assistance. This has been justly criticised[45] on the ground that if there is *no* mixing, *i.e.* the trust money alone is used for the purchase of property, the beneficiary can elect to take the property (even if it has increased in value) if he chooses, and it is illogical to make a distinction where there *has* been a mixing.

---

[42] *Ibid.*
[43] *Ibid* at p. 539.
[44] (1880) 13 Ch.D. 696; applied in *Aluminium Industrie Vaassen BV* v. *Romalpa Aluminium Ltd.* [1976] 1 W.L.R. 676; and see *Re Bond Worth Ltd.* [1980] Ch. 228; *Borden U.K. Ltd.* v. *Scottish Timber Products Ltd.* [1981] Ch. 25; and see *post*, p. 474.
[45] Maudsley (1959) 75 L.Q.R. 234; Hanbury and Maudsley (11th ed.), p. 671.

Further, if a profit on the property is made, it would enable the trustee to profit from his own breach of trust contrary to the general rule.[46] In *Re Tilley's Will Trusts*[47] Ungoed-Thomas J. expressed the view *obiter* that a beneficiary could in these circumstances require the asset to be treated as trust property with regard to that proportion of it which the trust money contributed to its purchase, but this view does not appear to represent the law as laid down in *Re Hallett's Estate*, and it seems that one is left, until the House of Lords decides otherwise, with a charge for trust money with interest alone.

In *Re Hallett's Estate* the equitable right was asserted against the original "mixer" who was in a *fiduciary relationship* to the plaintiff. One of the important questions raised in *Re Diplock*, however, was whether a fiduciary relationship on these lines was essential or whether it extended to fasten liability on an *innocent volunteer* in the situation in which the charities found themselves. Wynn-Parry J. had held at first instance that the principle could not be thus extended. But the Court of Appeal overruled the judge and held that the true position was as follows:

> "Where an innocent volunteer (as distinct from a purchaser for value without notice) mixes 'money' of his with 'money' which in equity belongs to another person, or is found in possession of such a mixture, although that other person cannot claim a charge on the mass superior to the claim of the volunteer he is entitled to a charge ranking *pari passu* with the claim of the volunteer."[48]

The court came to this conclusion because, essentially, the decision of the House of Lords in *Sinclair* v. *Brougham*[49] dictated this result. This complex case was analysed with an acute sophistication, but the court was careful to point out that "we find the opinions in *Sinclair* v. *Brougham* in many respects not only difficult to follow, but difficult to reconcile with one another."[50] The essential facts of the case were that this was a contest between shareholders and depositors with regard to a miscellaneous mass of assets distributable by a liquidator in the winding-up of a building society. The deposits had been made, and the assets used, in connection with a banking business carried on in the name of the society but actually beyond its legal powers. Each of the two classes claimed priority over the other. The House of Lords held, on the principle on which *Re Hallett's Estate*[51] was decided, that the two classes should share rateably. Although this decision was not expressed to be an extension of the principle in *Hallett's* case, in fact it amounted to one. For as the Court of Appeal said, the decision in *Sinclair* v. *Brougham* showed that *Hallett's* case was an illustration of the wider principle that one whose money has been mixed with another's may trace his money into the mixed fund (or assets acquired with it) although the

[46] See *ante*, p. 403.
[47] [1967] Ch. 1179 at p. 1189.
[48] [1948] Ch. 518 at p. 522.
[49] [1914] A.C. 398.
[50] [1948] Ch. 465 at p. 518.
[51] (1880) 13 Ch.D. 696.

fund (or assets) is held by an innocent volunteer and even if the mixing has been done by him.[52]

It is now necessary to consider the conditions which must be fulfilled before an effective "tracing" can be made:

(a) **"Identifiable" property.** The claimant's money must be fairly "identifiable." "The equitable remedies presuppose the continued existence of the money either as a separate fund or as part of a mixed fund or as latent in property acquired by means of such a fund. If, on the facts of any individual case, such continued existence is not establishd, equity is as helpless as the common law itself."[53] Accordingly, if the fund, whether it is mixed or unmixed, is spent on a dinner, equity can do nothing. Damages might be available for breach of contract at common law, but there is no remedy in equity.[53] The same result will follow where the recipient has used the money to discharge loans, whether these are secured or unsecured: the plaintiffs cannot claim to be subrogated because the repayment extinguishes the debt.[54] Again, the position is the same if the moneys have been spent on the alteration and improvement of assets already owned by the recipient.[55] To underline this last point the Court of Appeal pointed out that the assets may not have increased (or may even have depreciated) in value through an alteration having been made.[56] The court also posed this hypothetical question: If the money had been spent on a new building, what would be the value of a building in the middle of Guy's Hospital (one of the recipients) without any means of access through other parts of the hospital property? If the charge was to be only on that new building it might have, taken in isolation, little or no value. And if you took the charge on the *whole* of the charity land "it might well be thought to be an extravagant result if the Diplock estate, because Diplock money had been used to reconstruct a corner of it, were to be entitled to a charge on the entirety."[56]

(b) Necessity for a "fiduciary" relationship. It is not enough, and the equitable remedy will not be available, if some person has, without legal title, acquired some benefit by the use of the money of another.[57] Putting it differently, if the facts amount to a case of "unjust enrichment" *simpliciter*, this will not be sufficient. It is essential to establish at the start "the existence of a fiduciary or quasi-fiduciary relationship or of a continuing right of property recognised by equity."[58]

It has already been seen that a fiduciary relationship may arise in various situations even in the absence of an express trust.[59] For example, it was held that it arose and, specifically, that the tracing remedy was available, in some-

---

[52] [1948] Ch. 465 at pp. 518 and 520; *cf.* Maudsley (1959) 75 L.Q.R. 234.
[53] *Ibid.* at p. 521.
[54] *Ibid.* at pp. 538–540.
[55] *Ibid.* at pp. 546–548.
[56] *Ibid.* at p. 547.
[57] *Ibid.*
[58] *Ibid.*
[59] See *ante*, p. 162.

what novel circumstances, in *Aluminium Industrie Vaassen BV* v. *Romalpa Aluminium Ltd.*[60] The plaintiffs, a Dutch company, sold to the defendants, an English company, aluminium foil, some of which the defendants sold to third parties. The plaintiffs' selling terms and conditions provided that ownership of the material to be delivered would only be transferred to the purchaser when he had paid for it. The English company went into liquidation owing money to the plaintiffs, but the receiver certified that £35,000 was held in an account in his name representing the proceeds of sale of aluminium foil. The plaintiffs argued that they were entitled to a charge on the money held in the receiver's account and to trace the proceeds of the sub-sales of their property in that account. This argument was upheld by the Court of Appeal which held that a fiduciary relationship has been created between the parties and accordingly that they were entitled to the tracing remedy.[61]

The question as to the time at which the fiduciary relationship should arise was considered in *Chase Manhattan Bank N.A.* v. *Israel-British Bank (London) Ltd.*[62] An American bank had mistakenly paid a sum of money twice over because of a clerical error to another American bank which had paid it into the defendant's bank in England. The defendant's bank became insolvent and the question was whether the American bank which had made the mistaken payment could trace that payment into its assets. It was held that it was entitled to do so. Goulding J. held that a person who paid money to another under a mistake of fact retained an equitable interest and the conscience of the payee was subjected to a fiduciary duty to respect that interest. It follows that the fund to be traced need not have been the subject of fiduciary obligations before it got into the wrong hands. It is sufficient if the payment into the wrong hands itself gave rise to a fiduciary relationship.

(c) **"Inequitable" consequences.** Tracing will not be permissible if the result will be *inequitable*. It would be inequitable, quite apart from the fact that the property cannot be identified,[63] to compel an innocent volunteer to disgorge moneys which have been spent on altering or improving its own property, for this would entail a sale of the property.[64] The same principle of equity applies where moneys have been used to pay off a loan, whether secured or unsecured, or indeed if it has been used for living expenses.[65]

(4) **Application of the equitable remedy in rem in a "mixed" fund**

It is now necessary to state the specific applications of the equitable remedy *in rem*, which will take effect subject to the conditions already mentioned, in relation to a *mixed fund*. It operates in different ways just as circumstances are

---

[60] [1976] 1 W.L.R. 676.

[61] See also in a commercial context, *Re Bond Work Ltd* [1980] Ch. 228; *Borden U.K. Ltd* v. *Scottish Timber Products Ltd.* [1981] Ch. 25; and generally, in relation to tracing in commercial transactions, Goode (1976) 92 L.Q.R. 360, 528.

[62] [1981] Ch.105.

[63] See *ante*, p. 473.

[64] [1948] Ch. 465 at pp. 546–550.

[65] *Ibid.* at pp. 548–550.

different: in some cases it results in priority to one or other claimants; in others, the claimants rank *pari passu*[66]:

   (i) Where a person is in a fiduciary relationship to another and has mixed moneys of another with moneys of his own, then the other takes priority.

  (ii) The same as in (i) follows where the person takes the money *with notice* that it is money held in a fiduciary capacity and proceeds to mix it with money of his own.

 (iii) Where the contest is between two claimants to a mixed fund made up of moneys held on their behalf and it is mixed together by a fiduciary agent, they will share *pari passu* because each of them is innocent.

 (iv) If a *volunteer* takes without notice (*e.g.* as a gift from a fiduciary agent such as the personal representatives in *Re Diplock*) he is compelled to admit the claim of the true owner (the next-of-kin in that case), and if there is no mixing he will hold on behalf of the true owner.

  (v) If the volunteer receives the money in the manner indicated in (iv) above, but he does mix the money with money of his own, he still has to admit the claim of the true owner. But—and here lies the vital difference—he can set up his own claim in respect of the moneys of his own which have been contributed to the mixed fund. The result is that they share *pari passu*. "It would be inequitable for the volunteer to claim priority for the reason that he is innocent. It would be equally inequitable for the true owner of the money to claim priority over the volunteer for the volunteer is innocent and cannot be said to act unconscionably if he claims equal treatment for himself. The mutual recognition of one another's right is what equity insists upon as a condition of giving relief."[67]

(5) Payment into banking account

It is useful to consider separately the common situation of trust moneys being paid into a banking account and the application of the remedy *in rem*.[68] It is here that the rule in *Clayton's Case*[69] requires discussion. The rule, supposedly one of convenience, attributes drawings out of a bank account to the order in which the moneys were paid in. The question is whether the rule applies to a case where trust funds are mixed with the trustee's own money by being paid into a bank account. It was decided by the Court of Appeal in *Re Hallett's Estate*[70] that the trustees in such

---

[66] The propositions in the text are set out in *Re Diplock* [1948] Ch. 465, at p. 539.

[67] *Ibid.* at p. 539.

[68] The court is entitled, for the purpose of giving effect to a defrauded plaintiff's equitable right to trace his money to order a bank to disclose the state of the account and the documents and correspondence relating to the account of a customer who was prima facie guilty of fraud: *Bankers Trust Co.* v. *Shapira* [1980] 1 W.L.R. 1274, C.A. and see *Banque Belge Pour L' Etranger* v. *Hambrouk* [1921] 1 K.B. 321, at p. 355: the plaintiff is entitled to lift the latch of the banker's door.

[69] (1816) 1 Mer. 572.   [70] (1830) 13 Ch.D. 696.

circumstances is deemed to exhaust his own money: the beneficiary in effect gets a first charge on the mixed fund. There is a presumption against a breach of trust in such a case,[71] and the rule in *Clayton's Case* does not apply.

But there is no such presumption with regard to remedying a withdrawal of trust funds in admitted breach of trust: accordingly subsequent payments by a trustee into the account will not be assumed to represent earlier withdrawals.[72] It has also been held, somewhat surprisingly, that if trust money is paid into an overdrawn account with the intention of reducing the overdraft and property is bought with money in the account, the breach halts at the date of payment in: the result is that a beneficiary is not entitled to any of the property purchased, the payment in of trust money merely going to reduction of the overdraft.[73]

However, it is established that the rule in *Clayton's Case* will apply to a situation where the trustee has mixed the moneys belonging to *two separate* trusts in a single banking account. This is apparently due to the difficulty involved in any attempt to attribute withdrawals rateably to the two funds.[74] The same consequence will follow where an *innocent volunteer* has mixed the trust money with his own.[75] But it must be emphasised that, although the rule will generally apply in these cases, it will *not* apply when the trustee or volunteer has earmarked a specific withdrawal of designated trust moneys. In this situation the beneficiary will be entitled to "trace" the moneys withdrawn into the asset which is purchased with them.[76]

It will be realised that this rule in any case will only come into play where the trustee is insolvent.

---

[71] *Roscoe* v. *Winder* [1915] 1 Ch. 62. See also *Re Oatway* [1903] 2 Ch. 356.

[72] *Roscoe* v. *Winder, supra.*

[73] *Re Tilley's Will Trusts* [1967] Ch. 1179.

[74] *Re Stenning* [1895] 2 Ch. 433; *Hancock* v. *Smith* (1889) 41 Ch. D. 456; *Re Hallett's Estate supra.*

[75] *Re Diplock* [1948] Ch. 465, at pp. 524, 539, 546.

[76] *Ibid.* at p. 552. (This part of the judgment was later rescinded, *ibid.* at p. 559 *et seq.*, because, the facts had been stated incorrectly, but the principle remains intact.) See also *Re Tilley's Will Trusts* [1976] Ch. 1179.

INDEX